THE INCOMPLETE, YEAR-BY-YEAR,
SELECTIVELY QUIRKY, PRIME FACTS
EDITION OF THE HISTORY OF

The
NEW ORLEANS
JAZZ & HERITAGE
FESTIVAL

e/PRIME PUBLICATIONS

Published by e/Prime Publications
913 Magazine Street
New Orleans, Louisiana 70130

First Edition
Published in 2005

Copyright © 2005 e/Prime Publications
Clifford, Jan and Smith, Leslie Blackshear, principal writers; McCaffrey, Kevin, editor

The Incomplete Year-by-Year Selectively Quirky Prime Facts Edition of
the History of the New Orleans Jazz & Heritage Festival

ISBN 0-9766154-0-1
Library of Congress control number 2001012345

Front Cover Photo by Philip Gould
Back Cover Photos by Michael P. Smith
Printed in Canada

e/Prime Publications' Collaborators for this book

PRINCIPAL WRITERS
Jan Clifford
Leslie Blackshear Smith

CONTRIBUTING WRITERS
Jerry Brock
Laura Westbrook
Dan Etheridge
Bud Brimberg
Lisa Boe
Kevin McCaffrey

CONTRIBUTING PHOTOGRAPHERS
Neil Alexander
Harold Baquet
Syndey Byrd
Jules Cahn
Keith Calhoun
Jan Gilbert
Philip Gould
Jackson Hill
Pat Jolly
Chandra McCormick
Owen Murphy
Scott Saltzman
Michael P. Smith
Zack Smith

EDITOR
Kevin McCaffrey

DESIGN AND LAYOUT
Tana Coman
Gensler Studio 585, Washington DC

COPY EDITOR
Jan Gilbert

ACKNOWLEDGEMENTS

This book is nothing less than a collaboration, and many people should be acknowledged and thanked:

We'd like to thank Don Marshall for his enthusiasm, trust and support as well as the board of the New Orleans Jazz & Heritage Foundation. Archivist Rachel Lyons was a deeply knowledgeable and indispensable guide in finding information, objects, and in helping us understand the material. Thank goodness the archive exists! Thanks to Quint Davis and his staff, particularly Louis Edwards and Matthew Goldman. Special thanks to George Wein and Arthur Davis, Doratha "Dodie" Smith-Simmons, Parker Dinkins, Pat Jolly, Vivian Cahn, Kalamu Ya Salaam, David Freedman, Ellis Marsalis, John and Paula Sidwell, Kathy Schorr, John Magill and Jude Solomon, Russell and Benjamin Jaffe, Sheila Ferran. Robert Markel, Rob Schauffler, Bea Shipp and staff at art4now, Angele Seiley, Mignon Faget, Studio Inferno, Allen Eskew, Paul Nakazawa, Reed Kroloff, and Jenifer Navard.

Thanks to all the musicians and others who gave us information and quotes.

Beyond the New Orleans Jazz & Heritage Foundation Archive, we consulted: the Hogan Jazz Archive, Tulane University Library, New Orleans Public Library, main branch Louisiana Collection, and Historic New Orleans Collection.

Thanks to Chance King and Leslie Elizabeth Doyle for their love and support during this project. I love you guys. I'd also like to thank Debbie Vidacovich, Christina Sperling – Munding, and Bobby Economou for the many boring hours on the phone they endured. Thanks to Chris Severin, Bob French, Herman Ernest and Keith Williams for being just a phone call away. Cheryl, thank you. Thanks to Fred Laredo for introducing me to so many astounding artists when I was just starting out. To all of the musicians in New Orleans – I wish I could have written about you and your lives and how much it means that you do what you do– moving hearts and connecting people to each other through your creativity. Thank you for everything you've given me. You are my family. I'd also like to thank my father for showing me Jazz Fest through his eyes. LESLIE BLACKSHEAR SMITH

Andrew Bascle, Philip Bascle, Eluard Burt, Cynthia Cashman, Claudia Dumestre, Jeanne Dumestre, Linda Floyd, Martha Little, Rhys McClure, Phillip Neal, Susan Otero, Judy Palmer, St. Expedite, Jonathan Scott at F & F Botanica, Keith Twitchell, Jack Varuso (the watermelon man) JAN CLIFFORD

Finally, thanks to the thousands of staff and volunteers who over the years have participated in the great multicultural success that is Jazz Festival. We've had a great time!

"A festival has to be a success in its home town before the world will realize it's something great."

GEORGE WEIN

This book is dedicated to all the musicians of Louisiana, living, deceased and aspiring, who so eloquently speak the language of our varied and unique living culture.

"Festivals are eternal. Festivals are ritual gatherings, fueled by music. They're where people come together for an annual ritual that's important in their lives. In today's society, things have gotten separate: you have locks on door and locks on cars, and cubicles at work. I think the Festival has always been a place where when people come together, they feel part of the community and they have a positive, shared human existence. The audience, the musicians and everyone remember that they're a community and that's the feeling that the Festival conveys. That's what the Festival is. The sum is greater than the parts. And it's that feeling where you remember what it's like to have a shared existence with a lot of people — strangers — and have it feel safe and empowering and loving and driven by music and that's what keeps you coming back for more. So I think that the feeling of family gathering that the Festival had; it has more than ever, because people need it more in their lives now."

QUINT DAVIS

Here's a music festival where over the years people have often gotten married at the event. What is it about the New Orleans Jazz & Heritage Festival that sets it apart from any other music festival in the world? The culture of community, the mystique of New Orleans, the talent pool from which to draw? New Orleans didn't always know how to put on a festival. It had to be invented, it had to be developed, and Quint Davis, who knows better than anybody by intent and execution, points out that Jazz Fest is a prismatic mirror of the many communities and cultures coming together to create it.

Thousands of people have contributed to its success each year. New Orleanians and Louisianans themselves are hardly conscious of their own genius for hospitality, but it is a kind of social contract that we welcome everyone who comes with legendary graciousness. The Festival is a gigantic showcase for that special set of skills, our philosophy of living, our pride in our culture, and our hope to preserve it while appreciating it as a living organism. This is why locals want to be there. We want to volunteer, work in the booths, and rub elbows with each other, share tips and recipes, and sometimes just stand in the rain together. We know how hard the staff works behind the scenes, and we want to enhance the experience for everyone's sake. This is our yard party, and the one place once a year that people from the myriad internal cultures get it on together and strut our stuff.

Preparing this book was not as easy as we envisioned. We thought the written record would be easy to find and plumb. Not so. We thought it would be easy to find all the ephemera and shirts and memorabilia we needed to chronicle the history. What we found was the record keeping was sometimes spotty and the Jazz Fest lives in personal collections of long-term fans as well as in their memories. Particularly rhapsodic moments live in thousands of oral histories yet to be recorded. We drew from an eyedropper's worth, we think. Across the board, we were struck by the sense of public ownership. No matter what the age of the informant, people feel personally connected to the New Orleans Jazz & Heritage Festival.

That sense of ownership, inclusion, and exchange motivates this book. It's time to bring the 35 years together in a kind of yearbook of the Festival. The deeper stories will be told later, but we wanted to chronicle this incredible city within a city, of hundreds of thousands of attendees each year, with its restaurants (food booths), its church (Gospel Tent), its museum (Heritage areas), its hospital, its transportation, its media center and its industry (the music stages). We wanted to remind fans of what went on in particular years, who was here, what silly things we did, and, primarily, what great music we experienced. We wanted to remember people who contributed and passed on. We wanted to remember how some of the best moments in our lives have happened and as we've moved forward, they have often been road marked by this event. As we said, the spirit, the vibe, the aura and synergy of this Festival have boosted many personal stories. This book tries to touch at least on most of these.

A generation–35 years–has passed. We never found out if there were any births on site, but we know people have brought week-old babies, three month olds, six month olds and their whole families. Some are now bringing their grandchildren. We wanted to establish what the Festival means to so many of us, the families within the families within the communities within the cultures. We should note that this event brought our music out of the smoky clubs, the supper venues, even the churches, and into the air and sunshine and exposure to more people than ever could have gotten to experience it.

The many communities within the Festival begin with the musicians. The whole thing wouldn't exist without them and without their history, their talent, their ideas or their taste. They stand among the best in the world; to be a musician from New Orleans (and Louisiana) is to be instantly respected. One of the small pleasures at the Fest is to notice the musicians meeting and greeting behind the stages, in the kind of warm familiarity that only confidence can allow. Notice who's playing with whom, on stage, and around town. This is a hometown jam playground and it's no coincidence musicians are knocking themselves out to try new combinations and licks. An extraordinary, at times historic, music convention we all get to witness. That's why we focus the book on the musicians. A musician in fact researched and wrote part of it, and we edited the photos to include the lion's share percentage of local musicians.

Furthermore, Executive Producer George Wein is a musician. Quint Davis was one himself, loves musicians and, to look at these yearly music schedules that is their record, they have consistently included more and more local musicians as they expanded the Festival. If you live here, you'll find the staff out at clubs and music events every time you go. They live and breathe the music. Festival Productions' staff represents hundreds of years of experience, which says a lot about its longevity and the group as a family. They all like attending shows and knowing the musicians, the culture of the city, the food. They love to promote it, too.

There are plenty of subcommunities within the Festival: the crafts people, Congo Square vendors, security, stage crews and especially the food vendors. There's a lot of camaraderie, and just plain trading goes on. Then there are the fans. We've tried to touch on their experiences as well. We've tried to show their adaptability, their creativity, and their willingness to extend and personalize their crowd experience. They own the show too, at the least by their example of peaceful coexistence, general lack of exploitation and their interest in relaxing, having a good time, and leaving their cares at the gate. We left their sense of fashion to the photos, rather than the text.

The photographs. We were blessed in our state to have many talented documentary photographers who have tirelessly made the scene and gotten great shots. Their work is the bulwark of this book. Their interest has been not only focused on the musicians, but the crowd, the moments, the feeling. To their credit, we ran a lot, but wished we could have shown more. As it stands, we selected shots for narrative and historic as well as aesthetic value. Through them, some legendary performers still live on these pages.

This history of the Festival shows the value of the ticket. Arena shows are expensive these days and feature a couple of acts. The incredibly multi-layered scheme of the Fair Grounds site, so carefully developed over the years, allows a fan to see full sets of a particular headlining act, or a top flight roster of particular kinds of music, or little tastes of all different kinds of music for one price. The ticket has always been cheaper than dinner downtown, too.

The history of the Festival shows its unparalleled success. More people know and appreciate our culture than ever before. More people have gotten to have a live experience with our musicians than ever would have happened. We've seen not only more major acts than we would have been willing to pay for, but importantly, more music from around the world. Several New Orleanians have actually eaten alligator and frog's legs when they might never have. And, we should note, that Gospel music, that ecstatic celebration within the African-American community, and once only the purview of Sunday morning radio for the white faithful, needs to be witnessed live and in person. The Jazz Festival, no matter what early skepticism there may have been, has succeeded in introducing this bedrock genre to a vast, appreciative audience.

The history of the Festival reveals also its successes in nurturing the community. This is the work of the Foundation, yes, but also the historical legacy of Koindu/Congo Square. Money from the Festival began to flow more freely into the neighborhoods because of a change in focus when this area was instituted. Something Kalamu ya Salaam, an early instigator, told us in an interview caused us not to break out a section on Congo Square, as might be expected. He explained that the thrust of the effort that resulted in Koindu was to create more of a share for the African American community. This financial sharing developed not only for black vendors, but also more deeply, in the neighborhoods. So the real meaning of Koindu/Congo Square is found in mentions of Foundation and Festival Productions outreach, like mentions of Kidd Jordan's youth workshops or the underwriting for security for second lines and street paraders. Koindu/Congo Square's success as more than a stage is integral within the Festival and we treated it as such.

Compiling this history of Jazz Fest taught us that we could claim we have passed our test of tolerance; we've celebrated life's riches in the best way, not alone. And we glimpsed what we thought we knew: that life indeed can be reduced for a moment to the simplicity of the important things—food (sustenance), music (spirit) and community (love). We expect everyone to tell us the particular moments, the characters, the anecdotes we missed putting in the book. We never put in the story of the stage crew that reformed the barricades to protect some nesting ducks, for instance. Here's an email address to send us those stories for the next edition: jazzfestbook@eprimeresearch.com. Or you can contact the Jazz & Heritage Foundation Archive to donate ephemera. Like we said, the history of Jazz Fest, until now, lives in the minds and hearts of those of us who just *had* to be there.

Raise a
MIGHTY
DUST

**THE YEAR-BY-YEAR HISTORY OF THE
NEW ORLEANS JAZZ & HERITAGE FESTIVAL**

1970

Bois Sec Ardoin and Sady Courville

The New Orleans Jazz & Heritage Festival – Jazz Fest – took nearly a decade of planning and maneuvering for the originators to hit upon the right formula. But when they got it right, it was really right, and Jazz Fest has fascinated music lovers from around the globe for 35 years. The 1970 "New Orleans Jazz Festival and Louisiana Heritage Fair" was the official beginning of the annual Festival we now know as the New Orleans Jazz & Heritage Festival.

In the early 1960s, a small circle of city officials and jazz patrons had discussed plans for a music event that would attract tour-

ists, with the express intention of capitalizing on New Orleans' reputation as the birthplace of jazz. Efforts to present a springtime outdoor music event were stymied by city segregation laws. While it was widely acknowledged that New Orleans music was integrated, neither audiences nor bands of different races were allowed to congregate in the same public space at the same time. After the passage of the 1964 Civil Rights Act, some city government officials still clung to the tenets of segregation and racism. Despite that fact, New Orleans had another heritage intertwined with the evolution of jazz: an historically continuous interchange of race and culture. Even when lawmakers and bigots had attempted to enforce segregation along color lines, musicians had always, regardless of race, played and traded ideas among themselves. Indeed, that spirit of interchange is directly responsible for the genre "New Orleans Jazz" and has led to the music now recognized as America's unique musical contribution to world culture. It was only New Orleans' governing authorities that needed to catch up to the times. Festivals with music and food were held in New Orleans in 1968 and 1969, chiefly supported and driven by New Orleans businessman Durel Black. One even began with a jazz mass for deceased musicians in St. Louis Cathedral. But personality conflicts and infighting dogged both festivals. Organizers agreed that a top-flight producer, preferably not someone from New Orleans with the requisite turf baggage, would be necessary to manage a successful festival. Eyes were on jazz pianist George Wein, who, along with Albert Grossman in 1954, had co-produced the Newport Jazz Festival. Before that, in 1959 Wein jumped on the folk

music bandwagon and produced the Newport Folk Festival, where Bob Dylan's career got a boost when Joan Baez asked him to sing with her. The energy generated at Newport among the fans and musicians began a groundswell of increasingly diverse festivals, most notably Monterrey in 1968 and Woodstock, in 1969. In George Wein's 2004 autobiography, *Myself Among Others,* Wein recalled an occasion in 1968, after nearly a decade of on and off conversations with New Orleans organizers, when he was approached to produce a jazz festival in New Orleans. That offer was quickly rescinded when then Mayor Vic Schiro learned that Wein's wife, Joyce, was African-American. The mayor and his advisors feared political embarrassment. By 1969, the political climate in New Orleans had evolved to a sufficiently tolerant degree that an offer was made to Wein. He accepted, and dubbed the new event (the world's longest title for a festival, he said), "The New Orleans Jazz Festival and Louisiana Heritage Fair." Wein modeled his ideas for the Festival on Tanglewood in

Kid Ory and Punch Miller

Boston. It was to be held on the last weekend in April 1970. The term "New Orleans Jazz Festival" referenced the night concerts on the riverboat *S.S. President* and in the Municipal Auditorium; while "Louisiana Heritage Fair" designated the music, food, culture and craft displays, like a street fair in Wein's words, to take place in Beauregard Square from noon until 6:00 p.m. It was the first outdoor festival to feature multiple stages.

Beauregard Square was the park adjacent to the Municipal Auditorium, and its history reached back to the days of slavery in New Orleans. African-Americans were denied the practice of dancing, drumming, and their native customs. Only on Sunday, and only in this designated part of the city, was it sanctioned that African-Americans could assemble to celebrate their own culture. They called it Congo Square. There was a multiplicity of reasons why this area was a fitting location for the birth of the Jazz & Heritage Festival. It was once the western border of Storyville, New Orleans' notorious red light district, where many jazz musicians plied their trade around the turn of the twentieth century. In fact, "Papa" Albert French rendered one of the first performances in the new Festival, when he played "The World is Waiting for the Sunrise," a favorite song of one of Storyville's most famous madams: Lulu White. Beauregard Square was bordered on one side by the French Quarter, on an adjacent side by what was once Storyville, and on another side by Faubourg Tremé, one of the most historically significant neighborhoods in the U.S. Many of the community's teachers, writers, and doctors emerged from among the Haitian Creole population, while the majority of politicians of color had made their homes there. Tremé's residents were some of the city's most renowned families of craftsmen, artisans, and musicians.. As such it was also birthplace of many well-schooled musicians who contributed to the development of jazz. Tremé was a thriving business zone that fell victim, like so many African-American neighborhoods, to "urban planning" when the state of Louisiana made the colossally wrong-headed decision to plow an interstate highway through Claiborne Avenue's neutral ground of beautiful live oaks and neighborhood meeting places. The neighborhood never regained its economic vitality.

Finally, the relational geography of Beauregard Square included Basin Street. So, when Punch Miller blew "Basin St. Blues" in his hot, sweet way, it was a pentimento of New Orleans history. As more African-Americans claimed their rightful heritage, Beauregard would be renamed Congo Square; and in a few years, the name Congo Square would also denote a specific portion of the Jazz Fest, with a stage designated for African-American diaspora music and goods.

Wein knew that he needed local people to make connections with local musicians. The tone for the Festival was set and remained strong for many years when Wein brought on Allison Miner and Quint Davis as Co-Directors. They were students working for Dick Allen in the Hogan Jazz Archive at Tulane University, and Allen recommended that Wein bring both aboard. Miner and Davis were possessed with high energy and an utter disregard for limitations. They brought a genuine love for

Olympia Brass Band and Friend at Buster Holmes' Restaurant

3:00 *Ragtime to Jelly Roll*
The New Orleans Ragtime Orchestra with Lars Edegran, Bill Russell, Orange Kellin, Lionel Ferbos, Paul Crawford, Frank Amacker, Chester Zardis, Irwin LeClere, Don Ewell, Cie Frazier and Louis Cottrell with Bill Russell and Dick Allen, M.C.s

SATURDAY, APRIL 25
12:00 The Eureka Brass Band Street Parade
12:30 *The Roots of Soul*
Rev. Fred Kirkpatrick, Rev. J.L. Kirkpatrick, Robert Kirkpatrick; Mount Calvary Gospel Singers
3:30 *Soul Now*
The Meters
Oliver and The Rockettes
The Joe Fox Trio
Larry McKinley, M.C.

SUNDAY, APRIL 26
NOON TO 6
Heritage Fair with Blues, Cajun, Gospel and Street Music and food of New Orleans and Southern Louisiana in Beauregard Square

NIGHT CONCERTS

WEDNESDAY, APRIL 22, 8:00 P.M.
Mississippi River Jazz Cruise on the Steamer President
Pete Fountain and His Orchestra
Clyde Kerr and His Orchestra

THURSDAY, APRIL 23, 8 P.M.
The Young Tuxedo Brass Band
Pete Fountain and His Orchestra
Sharkey and His Kings of Rhythm
Papa Albert French and The Original Tuxedo Jazz Band
The Dukes of Dixieland with Frank Assunto
Municipal Auditorium

FRIDAY, APRIL 24, 8 P.M.
Captain John Handy with Handy's Louisiana Shakers
The New Orleans Modern Jazz All Stars Ellis Marsalis, Mike Olsheski, Earl Turbinton, Joe Morton, John Brunious, Rudy Aikels, John Vidacovich and guest Edie Aikels
Mahalia Jackson
The Crescent City Community Choir: Director – Prof. Elliott Beal
Municipal Auditorium

SATURDAY, APRIL 25, 8 P.M.
The Onward Brass Band
James Rivers
Germaine Bazzle
Al Hirt & His Orchestra
Al Belletto Quartet
Duke Ellington and His Orchestra

SUNDAY, APRIL 26, 2:30 P.M.
Duke Ellington and His Orchestra
The Concert Choir of New Orleans, John Kuypers, Musical Director
City-wide College Dance Corp Directed by Kelly-Marie Berry

"I also sold hats — white hats, straw — with flowers or you could choose your decoration with ribbon. I can't tell you how sweet it was. You were a participant, not a spectator. Wandering around, you're producing the Fest. That participation is so difficult to achieve in modern society. With movies, or even CDs, you're a spectator. You were producing the as Jazz Fest."

Just by following your nose aura of what we know

JOANNE CLEVENGER

the music and a profound respect for the men and women who made it. Their approach guiding the Festival made it solid at the core.

Recognizing the possible economic advantage, the city of New Orleans became a sponsor. Miller, "The Champagne of Beers," donated $20,000 through a connection with native son Al Hirt. This would be Hirt's first Jazz Fest appearance, and he performed for less than half his usual fee. While Hirt was nationally famous and ungrudging about the money, the notion of paying locals less than national musicians would become a point of contention throughout the entire history of the Festival. Beauregard Square was the site of Louisiana Heritage activities.

Admission cost $3, and included music from at least 300 talented musicians, foodstuffs from local kitchens, handmade crafts, and other items. There were sudden, spontaneous entertainments like the impromptu performance of hippie dancers in short shorts with flower garland headpieces. People could "pass a good time" in an uncrowded, joyful atmosphere.

Thursday's events opened with host Dick Allen, also known as "Daddy Dick," or "Sweet Papa Allen." On a barebones stage, under the spreading live oak branches, Allen introduced Clifton Chenier. This was a landmark occasion, one of the very few times country musicians (as zydeco and Cajun players were then regarded) had been invited into the city to perform. Recordings available to the public were scarce, and both zydeco and Cajun musicians tended to stick with "the crawfish circuit": the dance halls and

bars that stretched from the south Louisiana bayous north and west into prairie country. These cultures were geographically isolated, socially localized, and largely ignored as economic entities. But when those fiddles jittered and accordions sang out in Beauregard Square, women in sundresses and men in city straw hats picked up the dance. Although it would be more than a decade before zydeco and Cajun music became widely known and appreciated outside of Louisiana, that moment was the beginning of a major shift in musical possibilities for dozens of families and bands.

There had been a few rumblings of appreciation for Louisiana music outside the state, fueled by young people's

Noel Rockmore

interest in folk music. Back in 1964, Cajun guitarist Dewey Balfa became a last-minute replacement at the Newport Folk Festival, playing guitar to accompany Gladys Thibodeaux and fiddler Louis LeJeune. Critics had predicted a poor reception for Cajun music, which at that time was losing its younger generation to rock and roll. Balfa has since recalled how touched he was at the enthusiastic applause of 17,000 fans that were begging for more, and how gratified he was that people outside of Louisiana could finally appreciate his native culture. That moment was one of the unexpected, but well-deserved, first sparks of widespread appreciation of Cajun music. Later, Dr. John and the Neville Brothers would set the world funkin' to a New Orleans beat and Paul Prudhomme would have chefs all over the place blackening everything in the kitchen, as the world got to know and love Louisiana's joie de vivre culture.

The Heritage Fair showcased Cajun, zydeco, brass band, gospel and blues, and the evening concerts were a riot of Dixieland and New Orleans Jazz. It was appropriate that the Heritage Festival featured a musical form indigenous to New Orleans. Some visitors may view brass bands and second lines as quaint theatrical performances, but African-American Louisiana natives know their intrinsically valuable place in local culture. Some of the oldest bands were organized in the 1800s and generations of musicians such as the Barbarin and Celestin families still keep the tradition, while spin offs such as the rambunctious Dirty Dozen Brass Band and Soul Rebels continue to reinterpret the music. It must have been an amazing sight for a visitor to see Mardi Gras Indians like the

Booker T. Glass

George Davis, Earl Turbinton, David Lee, Wilson Turbinton

Black Eagles, Wild Magnolias, and the Golden Eagles parading across the square. Miner and Davis had called Chief Bo Dollis, and agreed to meet him in a bar on Washington Avenue to ask if he would appear at Jazz Fest. To their amazement, Dollis and the 30 Indians who came with him agreed, and one of New Orleans' most original and beloved cultural art forms became a permanent part of Jazz Fest. There was an awning for the Gospel Tent, four rickety music stages (metal Mardi Gras stages donated by the city), and minimal sound equipment and…at first…no one else. Allison Miner, Joyce Wein and others raced around giving tickets away to passing school children and others sold tickets on a buy-one-get-four-free basis. According to an account in *Jazz Fest Memories*, written by Miner with photographs by Michael P. Smith, there was a thin canvas fence around Beauregard Square meant to encourage folks to enter and buy a ticket at the gate. New Orleanians have never been much for following the rules, and as soon as the music

started, neighbors within earshot took pocketknives to the fence and slipped into the celebration. Only 200 to 300 people attended, but they were the matches to a bonfire. Next year, thousands would show up. The 20 food

booths, some housed under fringed umbrellas, were a curious mélange of favorites such as red beans and rice, ham hocks and greens, grillades and grits, Creole succotash, jambalaya, shrimp and oyster gumbo, crawfish etouffeé, shrimp Creole, and more generic offerings such as popcorn, "natural foods," and ice cream.

The musicians and fans enthusiastically embraced Jazz Fest. Right from the start, the Festival offered a full-bodied immersion into Louisiana music, culture, and cuisine. It was a four-day celebration. Concerts in the Municipal Auditorium carried the celebration onward into the night, pairing local and national musicians in thematically staged performances. That night's concert brought the Young Tuxedo Brass Band onstage with Sweet Emma Barrett, Fats Domino, and others. The Young Tuxedo Band traced its lineage back into Storyville music halls and bordello parlors. Inexplicably, it took the National

"When our festival started in 1970, it was just the beginning of an opportunity for people to party together, to hear each other. The Civil Rights laws, the festival, and just the nature of the changing scene in America during the Sixties — people didn't want to hurt someone of another race; you didn't want to continue the bitter agony that had been prolonged for hundreds of years in this country. So celebrating their culture with everyone there, black and white, became an opportunity for people to say, "Hey, this is spectacular! I've never heard anything like this because my parents didn't allow me to go out and hear it, but now I'm really gonna party, and I'm really gonna enjoy it, and I'm going to forget all of my prejudices from childhood and I'm gonna see things differently. And I think that's what our Festival did." ALLISON MINER

Foundation for the Performing Arts until 1970 to pronounce jazz music a legitimate art form and classify it as "folklore." While that decree would later allow grant dollars to flow toward Jazz Fest, New Orleans didn't need a proclamation. The city had once again claimed her stature in jazz history. Although ticket sales were only $47,779, and expenses totaled $84,455, there was no talk of going back.

The Olympia Brass Band kicked off Friday's events, led by Grand Marshal Anderson Minor. Then young filmmaker and New Orleans music aficionado Woody Allen got the treat of a lifetime, playing clarinet in the second line. Allen was in town visiting friends but was compelled to climb onstage with Punch

Miller's Band at the Municipal Auditorium. Later that evening he would join a raucous jam with the Eureka Brass Band inside

Buster Holmes's restaurant. This would only be the first of legendary jams associated with clubs during the Festival. One

New Orleans poet and musician remembers walking near Beauregard Square and hearing the sound of a brass band with a powerful vocal accompaniment. As he came closer, he saw that the source of the unmistakable tremolo was gospel singer and New Orleans native Mahalia Jackson. Scheduled to sing in a musical at the Municipal Auditorium, Jackson had noticed the commotion in the square and come over to thrill onlookers with a spontaneous, full-throated "Just a Closer Walk with Thee" in a second line with the Eureka Brass Band. Quint Davis observed that moment as a defining one: a New Orleans gospel singer making a bridge between gospel music and traditional New Orleans jazz, singing a hymn with a marching brass band.

In the Heritage portion of events, Reverend Fred Kirkpatrick led a free heritage

Roosevelt Sykes

presentation on "the Roots of Soul" about how field songs, blues, gospel, and jubilee songs all contributed to the evolution of soul music. Shouting out, "Where are the black people?" Kirkpatrick urged African-Americans to hold fast to their heritage, and pass the knowledge along. One particularly poignant segment of his delivery explained how the song "Couldn't Hear Nobody Pray" came into being. African people brought to America as slaves were forbidden to speak in their native languages. They secretly shared those languages with their children in the evenings after work, under the guise of prayer.

Saturday night, Duke Ellington's Sacred Music concert at Municipal Auditorium drew raves from music critic Dave Cuthbert. Writing in the *Times-Picayune*, Cuthbert called Cootie Williams's trumpet playing "wild and beautiful like you wouldn't believe," and marveled, "How he can get such shadings and impressions from his music is a secret between Williams and his Maker." That night was also Al Hirt's first Jazz Fest performance. Moonlight concerts on the river-

boat *S.S. President* echoed New Orleans' history of riverboat bands performing along the Mississippi. Leaving at 8:30 p.m. the *S.S. President* chugged upriver under the Greater Mississippi River Bridge, turning at the Huey P. Long Bridge, and returning to dock around midnight. With no air conditioning and during one of New Orleans' famously muggy nights, the Pete Fountain and the Clyde Kerr orchestras performed for a sweat-soaked but enthusiastic inaugural audience of 2,200. These concerts aboard the *S.S. President* would delight music lovers for many years, until the steamboat relo-

cated to St. Louis in 1989.

The word "music" delineates from the Greek "from the muses." It is only fitting that in the city known as the birthplace of jazz, with streets named for muses such as Thalia, Terpsicore, and Polymnia, that the most good-natured, peaceful, playful, diverse music Festival in the U.S. would take root here. And it was pure inspiration that one of the first musicians booked for the new Festival was a blind, African-American blues man: Snooks Eaglin. Eaglin was pure music, the real deal, and a workingman's artist. That sums up music in New Orleans.

Percy Randolph. Babe Stovall and Willie Thomas

1971

Dizzy Gillespie

Louis Armstrong, jazz master and New Orleans' beloved native son, lay in a hospital bed in New York City during the 1971 Jazz Fest. Hopefully, it was a balm to his spirit to know that in the city of his birth, where his happiest moment came as King of Zulu during Mardi Gras, the Saturday night concert at the Municipal Auditorium was a "Tribute to Satchmo." The lineup included New Orleans' venerable jazz lions such as Wallace Davenport, Andy Moses, blind clarinetist Alvin Alcorn, and Punch Miller. Trumpet great Dizzy Gillespie served in that group, as did young Johnny Vidacovich, a drummer who would come to represent the new generation of New Orleans jazz musicians. To top it off, trumpet virtuoso Joseph "Sharkey" Bonano and his Kings romped through traditional jazz standards such as "Sister Kate" and "You Can Depend on Me" in a manner that would have made Satchmo smile.

But the climax of that bold and sentimental evening came when Kid Ory took the stage for his first New Orleans performance since leaving for California in 1919. Ory, in his 80s and then living in Hawaii, was known for having one of the best bands in New Orleans during the 1910s, and for his hiring Armstrong to perform. Although his voice was weakened from a recent bout of ill health, and the tailgate glissandos of earlier years were missing, Ory delivered his signature "Muskrat Ramble," a souvenir from an era that is the heart of New Orleans jazz. Hitting on a novelty note, the crowd was treated to a surprise in the form

what's going on?

GLOBALLY

Mainland China joins the UN.

Major-General Idi Amin establishes power in Uganda.

Violence worsens in Northern Ireland after Britain institutes policies of preventive detention and internment without trial.

NATIONALLY

26th Amendment to the U.S. Constitution is ratified, lowering the voting age from 21 to 18.

The first installments of "Pentagon Papers" appear in The New York Times.

The Supreme Court upholds a measure to bus children in order to enforce integration in schools.

LOCALLY

Dorothy Mae Taylor becomes the first African-American woman to hold state office in Louisiana.

Crude oil prices skyrocket, producing tremendous revenues called an "oil boom" in Louisiana.

Bagatelle, a plantation home, is moved up river by barge from its site near the Sunshine Bridge to its present location on the East bank.

Archie Manning is drafted by the Saints.

CULTURALLY

Popular films are: "A Clockwork Orange;" "Claire's Knee;" "The French Connection;" "The Conformist."

Duke Ellington records New Orleans Suite.

The "Jesus Movement" becomes a much-publicized element of American Christianity, giving rise to the term, "Jesus freak."

Bill Graham closes Fillmores East and West.

of eight-year-old Enrico Tomasso, whom producer George Wein had imported from Leeds, England. Tomasso took the stage and belted out a Louis Armstrong imitation with a voice as big as the auditorium. The crowd roared its enjoyment. Armstrong had performed in New Orleans during a 1968 Festival that was a precursor to the New Orleans Jazz & Heritage Festival. During that year, Armstrong's version of Bob Theile's and George David Weiss's "What a Wonderful World" became a hit in Britain, but had yet to receive wide airplay in the U.S. That was to be the last time Satchmo played New Orleans. He died on July 6, 1971, in New York.

The first Jazz Festival night concert was held in the Roosevelt Hotel on Baronne Street, now known as the Fairmont. In the famous Blue Room, where major vaudeville and later movie stars had performed, the band with Bobby Hackett and Armand Hug swung into "Bourbon Street Parade," prompting a gaggle of African-American kids to jump up and parade along with the music. One was wearing an Indian Chief suit and another twirled an umbrella. The surprise was a delightful one. The kids were from the fourth, fifth, and sixth grade class at Chester Elementary and were supposed to wait for "Didn't He Ramble" but instead took off

early. No matter. The children had infused Jazz Fest with a second line and an authentic bit of New Orleans culture.

There was no question that Jazz Fest should try a second year. Finally, under Wein's experienced direction, and with the firm support of Durel Black and Allen Jaffe, New Orleans had a music event that could be marketed as a tourist destination and that would also funnel income into local businesses. It just needed time to grow. Quint Davis's father, Arthur Davis, played a major role in keeping the Festival alive financially. Davis was a nationally recognized architect, and in those first few years contributed personal notes on loans to keep the Festival financially viable. Through his generous support, the Festival survived.

Although 1971 ticket sales brought in $31,094 and expenses ran $45,239, the Jazz & Heritage Foundation Board believed time was on their side. The Foundation was set up as a nonprofit organization to preserve and celebrate the music of New Orleans, with its chief responsibility being to oversee production of the New Orleans Jazz & Heritage Festival. Made up of jazz lovers, powerful local

WEDNESDAY, APRIL 21
Pete Fountain with Eddie Miller & Backup Band
Municipal Auditorium

THURSDAY, APRIL 22
Albert "Papa" French & The Original Tuxedo Jazz Band
Bobby Hackett
Armand Hug
Punch Miller New Orleans Jazz Band
Porgy Jones Plus Three
And Many Others
Main Ballroom – Roosevelt Hotel

FRIDAY, APRIL 23
Dizzy Gillespie
Ronnie Kole
Al Belletto Quartet
Murphy Campo
Kid Thomas Valentine & The Preservation Hall Jazz Band
New Orleans Ragtime Orchestra
Creole Fiesta Dancers
Municipal Auditorium

SATURDAY, APRIL 24
Dizzy Gillespie
Bobby Hackett
Tyree Glenn
Sharkey Bonano & The Kings of Dixieland
Dukes of Dixieland
New Orleans Trumpet Choir featuring Alvin Alcorn, Dave Bartholomew, Wallace Davenport, Thomas Jefferson & Punch Miller
Municipal Auditorium

THE LOUISIANA HERITAGE FAIR
THURSDAY, FRIDAY & SATURDAY
12 NOON TO 5 P.M.
in Beauregard (Congo) Square

Zion Harmonizers

businessmen, city officials, and artists, the Board drove all major decisions related to *Jazz Fest* and was in charge of George Wein and his staff. The mission included routing profits, if there were any, back into the music community. The Foundation Board, more than any other in the city, was diverse in race and culture. With no central office for planning, and what was then known as an "ad budget" of $3,000, out-of-town marketing was also out of the question. But word of mouth worked just

fine, and what began as a sweet street fair turned into a burgeoning crowd problem. Beauregard Square seemed suddenly too small for the wealth of musicians and heritage exhibitors.

Tickets were $3, and there were 20 food booths serving local favorites such as grillades and grits, Buster Holmes's red beans and rice (Satchmo used to sign his letters ("Red beans and ricely yours"), Sonny Vaucresson's sausages, and ham hocks and greens. Craftspeople displayed baskets, corn shuck dolls and jewelry. Musicians performed on the four stages and the occasional folding chair according to a kind of schedule, but there were no printed programs or official advance schedules. Meanwhile, musicians such as Dizzy Gillespie leaned against a fence, munched really good food, and passed time with fans. The day was punctuated by the joyful soaring sounds of parading bands such as the Olympia Brass Band.

Allen Fontenot and the Country Cajuns were back from last year. Fontenot would be invited back year after year for the life of the Festival. He was a tireless promoter of Cajun culture, and impervious to the notion that young people wanted nothing to do with their heritage. History has proven him right. Also on stage was Creole musician Alphonse "Bois Sec" (dry wood) Ardoin, one of the fathers of zydeco music. The Heritage Fair showcased Cajun, zydeco, gospel, and brass band music, while the Jazz Festival (night concerts) presented a combination of the best of New Orleans jazz musicians paired with major touring performers. Planners recognized that although the virtuosity of Louisiana indigenous musicians was superior quality, few were well known enough to lure visitors from out of town to a new music Festival. From the beginning, the plan was to pair local talent with "name" performers in order to bring tourists into New Orleans while appealing to local crowds at the same time.

In Beauregard Square, Roosevelt Sykes "The Honeydipper" delivered his bluesy ballads claiming he was a dangerous man who "just killed a chicken," James Rivers displayed early warning signs of the major talent he embodied, and the New Orleans Ragtime Orchestra revived rags recently uncovered in an archive. Ragtime devotees generally split ranks between those who preferred the Scott Joplin style (also known as the

Anderson Minor and Barbara Pyle

St. Louis style) with structured, measured tempo; and New Orleans Ragtime, which sometimes sounded like a high-flying confabulation of instruments hurling themselves in wild pursuit of good times. Sadly, during these times, venues for Dixieland jazz had decreased to a few clubs in the French Quarter. First supplanted by swing in the 1930s, and then bebop and modern jazz in the 40s and 50s, and nearly shoved aside altogether by the cerebral meanderings of jazz fusion in the 60s and 70s, traditional jazz had seemingly lost its footing on the stairway of popular music. It could be argued that the New Orleans Jazz & Heritage Festival was a power-

Snooks Eaglin

"My first Jazz Fest was actually my first professional gig as a musician in 1971 with the Fairview Baptist Church Christian Marching Band. We paraded in Congo Square. The guy that most impressed me was Bongo Joe; the way he could captivate an audience with a fifty gallon drum, two hammers wrapped in tin cans, beating that drum and singing his song "Little Doggie." I was 13 years old and I was thrilled to be there performing. I had no idea of the significance of the Louisiana Heritage Fair. That's what they called it then." LEROY JONES

Dizzy Gillespie and George Wein

ful player in reuniting traditional jazz with audiences and introducing a new generation to the men and women who quite literally built jazz out of the triumphs and sorrows of living in a city where deceased souls never really left they just hung around in the ethers and whispered new chords into the ears of musicians below.

Just as Miner and Davis had gone into a Washington Avenue bar to meet with Mardi Gras Indians and invite them into the Festival, so they went to Central City to meet with Sherman Washington, a stalwart in the gospel community. Washington brought the Zion Harmonizers into the Heritage Fair. The Zion Harmonizers and other gospel groups naturally brought a spiritual element into the mix, but they also served as a benchmark for showmanship. From the early days of matching somber suits and limited instrumentation, gospel performances at Jazz Fest have evolved into high-energy singing, dancing, shouting, and all-out exaltation, with choral attire ranging from the colorful plumage on hats and matching shoes to robes of vermilion, chartreuse, and royal purple. But some religious leaders felt that it was a sacrilege to allow beer drinkers in close proximity with gospel music. The Heritage Fair sold beer, and in New Orleans, laws permit the consumption of alcoholic beverages on any street in the city. However, Washington and choir director Lois Dejean made a decision that stood: if even one soul is touched by the word of the Gospel, then it is worthy to allow Festivalgoers their beverage freedom. Beer drinkers may get an occasional frown from one of the faithful, but that's as tough as it gets at Jazz Fest. And Washington's instinct must be credited: there can be no doubt that many souls have joined the spiritual celebration anew in these 35 years. Although hard to fathom today, the Gospel Tent was a red-and-white-striped awning with a simple piano sitting

Fairview Baptist Church

music scene

Duke Ellington records "New Orleans Suite."

Fess re-created the Four Hairs Combo for an appearance at the New Orleans Jazz & Heritage Festival.

The Sonny and Cher Comedy Hour debuts and features hits such as "I Got You Babe," music produced by Harold Batiste.

IN MEMORIAM

Louis Armstrong, Punch Miller, Harrie Shields, Jim Morrison, Duane Allman

on bare grass. (In 1970, there wasn't even a tent.) A few folding chairs, a growing audience, and some of the loudest, most glorious, heartfelt praise sanctified that patch of ground. The Gospel Tent has grown without ceasing into a hallowed tradition for some and a refuge for others.

Some performers didn't even have a tent or need one. Musicians like Babe Stovall just sat in a chair and played guitar. Percy Humphrey joined him on harmonica and David Salero, playing washboard with silver thimbles, pulled up a chair and the good times were on. A veteran street performer in Jackson Square, Stovall would become, in the odd democracy of New Orleans, a regular at the Festival destined to be world class. Some musicians melded a message with their music. Sister Gertrude Morgan was just such a formidable personality. She had been at the first Fest, and would visit her evangelical brand of folk art and "preachifying" upon audiences for years. In the way that folk art sometimes does, Sister Morgan's artwork traveled from

"Where it came from was George and Pete Seeger. I mean if George Wein is the father of Jazz Fest, Pete Seeger is the Grandfather of Jazz Fest, 'cause in 1954 George started the Newport Jazz Festival, which was the first big outdoor — before Woodstock — music festival with speakers and chairs and it wasn't in a concert hall. Then in 1959, they started — Pete Seeger's idea — the Newport Folk Festival and it was really the Newport Folk Festival that was the progenitor of Jazz Fest. Newport Folk Festival gathered together all the great — there are still people playing at Jazz Fest now that played that festival — they had Gospel, they had Blues, they had Cajun, they had Zydeco." QUINT DAVIS

its humble beginnings to be displayed, in 2004, in a major exhibition of her artwork at the New Orleans Museum of Art and the Museum of American Folk Art in New York City.

Although the Festival and accompanying night concerts were becoming popular, there was still a bright innocence about the event and the times. People brought their dogs and paraded them, and others flew kites, or batted volleyballs around. And there was

dancing. Always dancing.

There is simply never a shortage of food at any festival in Louisiana. There never has been, and it will never happen. But the 1971 Jazz Fest had a candy crisis. Jeanne Dumestre, who would later become a force in the forming of the venerable music club Tipitina's, suggested Quint seek out the old Roman Candy man who had roamed St. Charles Avenue in his mule-drawn cart for years. But Quint wanted pralines. Someone suggested Jeanne's sister Claudia, who said "Yes." So in typical New Orleans style, the Dumestres made theatre. They drove to Hattiesburg, Mississippi, to buy fresh pecans from Forest County Co-op, and ran them through Forests's gigantic shelling and cracking machines. Jeanne and Claudia strolled the Fest, dressed in long calico dresses and sunbonnets, with lovely baskets of pralines on their arms. And that's how they earned the title "pralinéres." They have each never missed a Jazz Fest since.

Quint Davis

THE NEW ORLEANS JAZZ & HERITAGE FESTIVAL FOUNDATION, INC.

For many people the New Orleans Jazz & Heritage Festival is the quintessential springtime event that delights the senses with sounds, tastes, food and music, arts and crafts; a fine-tuned combination of entertainment and education that displays the best of New Orleans and Louisiana culture. For the New Orleans Jazz & Heritage Festival Foundation, Inc. who presents the event and Festival Productions, Inc. (FPI) who produces it, the Festival is a year long, year after year responsibility.

The Foundation was incorporated on February 17, 1970 and the first Festival was held April 22 – 25 the same year. The Articles of Incorporation stated that the purposes of the corporation are: "To promote, conduct and operate in the city of New Orleans a Jazz Festival annually or more frequently as may be deemed desirable; to promote, preserve, encourage and advertise New Orleans jazz, folklore, blues – gospel music, Cajun music and soul music primarily and also all the ramifications and forms thereof; to utilize as

artists to the greatest extent possible jazz musicians of the city of New Orleans and State of Louisiana; to assist in the development of the city of New Orleans as a tourist center of the country; to favorably advertise the city of New Orleans and its institutions; to promote the general business of the greater New Orleans area; to cooperate with other business and civic organizations; to promote the cultural advancement and economic betterment of the metropolitan area of New Orleans and the state of Louisiana."

Comprehensively lofty ideals at the time in a parochial southern American city mired in a history of social and economic hardships; the responsible, forward looking people apparently knew that one of the greatest assets of this city was the people and their culture. Guided by the collaborative vision of George Wein, Allen Jaffe, Quint Davis, Allison Miner, Richard B. Allen, Dodie Smith Simmons and numerous others, early board members included Earl Duffey, Durell Black, Dr. Harry Souchon, Lester E.

Kabacoff, George Rhodes III, Larry McKinley, Dooky Chase, Winston Lil and Mayor Victor Schiro. Quint's father, Arthur Q. Davis, a respected and successful architect in New Orleans stepped up to the plate and co-signed a bank note to help cover expenses the first year. He later succeeded Earl Duffey as the second President of the Foundation.

Dodie Smith Simmons was instrumental in shaping the character of the Foundation and the Festival. Employed at the Southern Regional Office of C.O.R.E. (The Congress of Racial Equality) she soon found herself attracted to the sounds emanating from Preservation Hall. This led to her friendship with Mike Stark, Allen Jaffe and a job at the Hall. Dodie said, "When George Wein first came to town he would visit his friend Allen Jaffe at Preservation Hall. At the time I was working at the Hall and living upstairs. Allen and I would spend evenings together in the patio or at Johnny White's and discuss the local musicians and bands; who was active and where they were playing.

"The only night I didn't work

at the Hall was Thursday nights because that was college night at Joy's Tavern in Gert Town. Admission was fifty cents and my girlfriends and I would go hear Deacon John, Tammy Lynn and artists like that. I was mostly into rhythm & blues and jazz. Sometimes we would go to Gloria's Living Room in the lower 9th Ward."

Dodie owns the honor of being the first person to be employed by both the Festival and the Foundation. In 1974 she went to work for the Festival as the office manager. The first office was located on Barracks Street above what is now the Louisiana Pizza Kitchen. "It was just one large room," she said "they called me the Office Manager and that meant I did everything. In 1976 the office moved to 1205 N. Rampart Street and that is when Arthur Q. Davis asked me to work full time for the Foundation. He decided since they were paying rent that someone should be in the office. I was the office manager for the Foundation and I also booked the traditional jazz bands for the Festival."

From the mid to late 1970s the Festival grew by leaps and bounds as did the Foundation. In 1972 there were twelve board members and in 1979 there were 29. In his autobiography, George Wein describes a meeting with representatives from the African American community who demanded a roll in the Foundation and in turn the Festival. Kalamu ya Salaam was the most vocal at this meeting and he would later make an impact on the Foundation as a board member and then as Executive Director of the Foundation. This activity led to the creation of Koindu which later became Congo Square.

Muhammad Yungai, the first

Crafts Coordinator for the Koindu Marketplace explained, "In 1978 we formed the African American Jazz Fest Coalition. Our main rationale was that white promoters were making money off of our black culture and black vendors had essentially been locked out of the Jazz Fest. Sekou Fela was the first director of Koindu. In 1979 it became the first African Marketplace at a major Festival in the United States; a grand display of black artifacts and culture. Koindu means 'Place of Exchange' but I still haven't figured out exactly what language it is. A man from Sierra Leone suggested it."

George Wein invited a more diverse group of people into the fold of both the Foundation and Festival; yet he has publicly bemoaned that the Foundation was maintained after the Festival became a financial success. He blamed Allison Miner for that because she defended the Foundation and believed that it had an important role to play in the city.

The Community Grants program began in 1979 as a result of lobbying by the new African American participators. That year the Foundation gave awards totaling $75,000. The next grants program was in 1984; they awarded $106,702 to 64 local cultural agencies and individual artists. To date the Foundation's Community Grants Program has redistributed over $1 million to individuals and groups as diverse as painters, multi-media artists, writers, Mardi Gras Indians, parade clubs, painters, sculptors, lectures, documentarians, videographers, actors and others. Many people who receive these grants would not otherwise qualify for traditional non-profit funding sources.

On January 1, 1987, through the leadership of Kalamu ya Salaam, the Foundation purchased the license of WWOZ 90.7 FM for $150,000 that contributed to the station's operations for a three-year period. What appeared a perfect match proved a difficult task and the first years were tumultuous due to a series of poor management hires and various interim managers. It was during this time that David Freedman showed up at the station and requested to see the Public File. Acknowledging his experience, he was hired later and has now managed the station for thirteen years and has overseen its development and growth into the premiere roots music station in America. With the advent of Internet broadcasting the station's listeners reach the far corners of the globe.

On March 1, 1990 the Foundation created the Heritage School of Jazz. It is directed by musician and educator Edward "Kidd" Jordan. Kidd said, "The School is a year around after school program where we teach the basics of music. The students are elementary school age so we mainly deal with the fundamental aspects of music." The other instructors are Kent Jordan, Elton Heron and Jonathon Bloom. The classes are held weekdays from 4 to 6 p.m. at Southern University of New Orleans. Kidd Jordan estimates that 200 to 300 children have benefited from the program.

The Foundation Archive is located in an 1811 building constructed for use as a guesthouse at the corner of Toulouse and Dauphine. The archive is the direct result of the initial work of Allison Miner. Rachel Lyons is the archivist and she explained, "The cornerstone of the collection is over 2000 recordings from the African, Folk, Food and Allison Miner Music Heritage Stage. The second is the WWOZ tapes which are still unprocessed.

"The Archive is a public resource and also maintains internal records of the Foundation. We have visitors as diverse as professional anthropologists to high school kids. The Archive is open to the public by appointment."

The Foundation initiated support for many community programs over the years, benefiting the preservation particularly of music culture. Other initiatives include: the Tom Dent/Congo Square Lecture Series that presents local and national known artists, lecturers and entertainers presenting their talents and knowledge; the Neighborhood Street Festivals that presented free mini Festivals in the Tremé, Carrollton and Lower Ninth Ward neighborhoods; S.E.E.D. (Supporting Enfranchising Economic Development), a micro-lending program for the start-up of small, economically disadvantaged businesses; the Jazz Journey Concert Series that presents renowned jazz artists in concerts and educational workshops; the Workshop Series that brings musicians into local schools and universities to perform and interact with the students; support of the Musicians' Clinic that provides health care to local musicians and music professionals in conjunction with the LSU Healthcare Network and the Daughters of Charity; Raisin' The Roof, a homeownership program for musicians and artists in partnership with area banks and city agencies; Community Outreach that offers free tickets to the Festival to non-profit and com-

munity groups; and JazzNet, with the Contemporary Art Center through an endowment from the Doris Duke Charitable Foundation with support from the National Endowment for the Arts, presenting jazz concerts, artist residencies and new works.

During the tenure of the late board member Don "Moose" Jamison , he organized benefit concerts to raise money to buy instruments for inner-city children. He also acted as the official historian of the Foundation.

In 2004, the Foundation announced that it was putting out to bid the production of the 2005 Festival. In addition, the Foundation has put on hold their community programs due to a lack of funds, the result of a rained out day and financially unsuccessful nighttime concerts in 2004. Employees were laid off and some agreed to work at a reduced salary. Ultimately this threatened the business relationship between the Foundation and FPI and signaled a change at the Foundation.

This created shock waves throughout the cultural community. The Festival as produced by FPI is the financial engine that propels the Foundation. George Wein pointed out in an interview that he's been on boards of entities like the Lincoln Center in New York, and "the one thing the board has been responsible for is raising funds. This is something the Foundation here has never understood."

Nevertheless, the Foundation's positive impact on local music and culture is unquestionable and one can argue that they have fulfilled much of their original mission statement.

During its thirty-four year history the Foundation and the Festival has employed many fine people including writers, producers, technicians, caterers, photographers, stage crews and staff members, not to mention thousands of musicians. It would be negligent not to mention John Murphy and Nancy Oschenshlager as Directors of the Heritage Fair; Marsha Boudy the current Chief Administrative Officer; Charlie Bering, who booked contemporary jazz at the Festival and produced nighttime concerts; and each of the past Executive Directors who are John Murphey (Acting Director), Wallace Young, Kalamu ya Salaam, Tom Dent and Wali Abdel-Ra'oof. These and many more have made an indelible stamp on the organization.

Don Marshall, the new Executive Director, is taking a proactive stance to reshape the Foundation. He has prioritized at last hiring a Development Director to coordinate Foundation programs' needs with raising funds outside the Festival profits. Don said, "There is a new day for the Foundation and FPI and we are working together unlike ever before to program the Festival. The Foundation is looking forward to expand its role in local music education and economic development. As the Festival continues to grow and evolve it is critical that we remain true to our mission." Clearly the Foundation must look to new resources for additional funding to achieve these goals and refocus and reenergize the Foundation. Marsha Boudy believes that new blood at the Foundation plus the benefit of the Past Presidents' Senate creates the best scenario for the Foundation to move positively into the future.

1972

"We can't emphasize enough what an extraordinary event the Heritage Fair is. It is the only time when New Orleans' incredibly varied, rich and vital music comes together in one place. It should be a front page banner headline in The New York Times," raved New Orleans' weekly entertainment magazine Figaro. Jazz Fest had quickly come to embody what some might say were New Orleans' best qualities: deep-rooted musical talent, the celebration of a diverse and historically significant heritage, and a contagious joie de vivre. With its three evening concerts on Wednesday, Thursday and Friday, and the Heritage Fair on Friday, Saturday and Sunday, everyone loved the new Festival and the staff was dizzy with possibilities for adding more musicians into the mix.

After only two years, Jazz Fest lovers had grown to test the limits of Beauregard Square's capacity. Lines at the gate were already horrendous and people were urged to buy advance tickets at Werlein's for Music, Dooky Chase Restaurant, The Mushroom, Mason's Motel on Claiborne Avenue, and Bayou Records Uptown. Advance tickets were once again $2.50 and $3.00 at the gate. Children were welcome for $1. The variety of ticket outlets in some way represented the wide mix of Festivalgoers. Werlein's, housed in the ornate cream-colored building on the French Quarter side of Canal Street, was the oldest continuously operating music store in the U.S. Musicians inevitably ended up there for sheet music, instruments and equipment. Bayou Records was a destination on St. Charles Avenue, one of the grandest avenues in the nation. Dooky Chase was a landmark African-American owned fine dining restaurant near Tremé (its founder was on the Foundation Board), Mason's Motel was an African-American entertainment and lodging complex, and The Mushroom was an Uptown haunt frequented by Tulane and Loyola students.

The Louisiana Heritage Fair (the name for the daytime Festival) simply needed more space. Venues such as City Park were suggested, but the decision came down on the side of the Fair Grounds racetrack. George Rhodes, catering manager at the track, was a fan of jazz and a fan of the Festival from day one. He offered a swap for rental fees: the Fair Grounds Catering Service reaped all proceeds from concessions such as beer, soft drinks, peanuts, popcorn, and cotton candy in exchange for hosting the Festival on its site. With an attendance of 50,000 over four days, ringing cash registers told the tale. The Fair Grounds was a horseracing track with a grandstand, but 1972 was not the first time a fair had taken place there. The first Louisiana Agricultural and Mechanical Exposition was held on the same land in 1815, thus establishing

it as "The Fair Grounds." The Fair Grounds has been a racetrack since 1872, making it the oldest continuously operating horse racing track in the U.S.

Approximately 30 musical groups performed on five stages daily. Music acts were grouped into categories: soul, jazz, blues, gospel, country/Cajun, blues, and Afro-American. The aluminum stages, rickety Mardi Gras stands on loan from the city, were tiny by today's standards. There were no police barricades, so fans got up close and personal with favorite groups, even going so far as leaning on the stage during performances. Chairs were provided in front for those who wanted to sit, like many European Festivals do today. One unique hazard resulted from pairing of metal and electricity: although stage managers put down linoleum to protect against electric shock, there were still some stimulating moments. And on stages 14 feet by 14 feet, it was a challenge to squeeze in a drum set or a group of Mardi Gras Indians crowding the stage with no room for even one more feather on those voluminous "new suits."

HERITAGE FAIR SCHEDULE OF EVENTS

JAZZ
Olympia, Eureka, & Tuxedo Brass Bands, Lou Sino & The Bengals, James Rivers, Porgy Jones, Kid Sheik, Fairview Christian Marching Band, Santo Pecora, Tony Fougerat, Al Belletto Quartet, Southern University (B.R) Jazz Band

BLUES
Roosevelt Sykes, Fred McDowell, Robert Pete Williams, Clifton Chenier, Babe Stovall, Percy Randolph, Silas Hogan's Baton Rouge Blues Band featuring Guitar Kelly, Big Joe Williams

SOUL
Willie Tee and The Gaturs, Professor Longhair, Snooks Eaglin, Margie Joseph, Deacon John

COUNTRY/CAJUN
Meyers Bros. Bluegrass Boys, Allen Fontenot & The Country Cajuns, Hubert Davis and The Season Travelers, The All-Star Mamou Cajun Band

GOSPEL
Zion Harmonizers, Gospel Inspirations, Annie Pavageau and choir, Ott Singers, Youth Inspirational Choir, Sister Gertrude Morgan, New Orleans Spiritualettes, Macedonia Male Choir

OTHER
Mardi Gras Indians, Bongo Joe, Othar Turner & The Rising Stars

SPECIAL GUEST APPEARANCES
Friday: Jimmy Smith
Saturday: B.B. King
Sunday: Giants of Jazz

NIGHT CONCERTS

WEDNESDAY, APRIL 26, 8 P.M.
Jazz On The River
The World's Greatest Jazz Band
Papa French & The Original Tuxedo Orchestra
Steamer President

THURSDAY, APRIL 27, 8 P.M.
International Jazz Cabaret
Preservation Hall Jazz Band
Roosevelt Sykes
George Finola Sextet
Armand Hug, Raymond Burke
Wallace Davenport
Storyville Jazz Band
International Room, Fairmont Roosevelt Hotel

FRIDAY, APRIL 28, 80 P.M.
Jazz At The Ballroom
Ronnie Kole
Wild Bill Davidson, Barney Bigard
Sweet Emma
Percy Humphrey Sextet
Murphy Campo Sextet
New Orleans Ragtime Orchestra
The Louis Cottrell Orchestra
Bob Greene – Tribute To Jelly Roll

SATURDAY, APRIL 29, 8 P.M.
Night Of Stars
Nina Simone
B.B. King
Giants of Jazz – Art Blakey, Dizzy Gillespie, Al McKibbon, Thelonious Monk, Sonny Stitt, Kai Winding
Jam Session Featuring Jimmy Smith, Kenny Burrell & Others
Tuxedo Brass Band
Mardi Gras Indians

Fairview Brass Band

As a matter of fact, the flamboyant Ernie K-Doe, famous for recording the Allen Toussaint song "Mother-In-Law" tumbled off his stage, and in true K-Doe fashion leaped back up and kept on twirling. There were many other amazing moments during what was fast becoming a world phenomenon Festival. Abner Jay, a one-man-band from Georgia played "Dixie" (something that might not happen today) accompanied by a Cuban lady who performed a classic buck and wing dance in which her arms and legs threatened to take flight in a whir around a stock-still torso. And the Como Fife and Drum Corps from Mississippi demonstrated one of the first musical forms developed by African Americans in the U.S.

Their basic drumbeat was the forerunner for jazz drumming.

The Gospel Tent, a rudimentary arrangement of striped awning and folding chairs, was to become an economic catapult for New Orleans choirs, choruses, quartets, and multiple combinations thereof. Fantastic performances, heretofore seen and heard only behind church doors were now out in the open and more than one non-believer found salvation during a pulse-pounding, escalating chorus of "Praise His Ho-ly... Praise His Holy Name!" One writer marveled in *Figaro*, "The Mount Moriah Choir nearly ignited the tent with their high-octane performance. It's a wonder the Almighty didn't swoop them up

music scene

Dr. John's Gumbo released by Dr. John.

New Orleans Piano released by Professor Longhair.

In 1972, Gary Edwards begins Sound Of New Orleans Record Company by recording the Storyville Jazz Band at Montel Recording Studio in Baton Rouge, LA.

Pete Fountain publishes his autobiography: *A Closer Walk: The Pete Fountain Story*

Earl King records "Street Parade."

IN MEMORIAM

Mahalia Jackson, Sharkey Bonano, Frank Painia, Melvin Lastie, Billy Murcia, Berry Oakley

lish a Jazz Fest pullout supplement; it ran 68 pages and was the equivalent of a program.

Clifton Chenier, "King of Zydeco," with strong, veined hands and his gold teeth shining in the hot daylight, wailed away on the accordion while his brother Cleveland frailed the *frattoir* (washboard) with bottle openers. In earlier times, rub board, or washboard players used literal washboards and had to balance these "instruments" by sitting in chairs. That practice added little to the visual romance of the band. The Chenier brothers are credited with being the inventors of straps for the frattoir, freeing players to move with the music as God surely intended. The Chenier brothers delivered a show as

well as music, and inspired writer Jon Newlin to comment, "(they)...took Ellington's 'Don't Get Around Much Anymore' back in the alley."

Harking back to the roots of jazz, the 1972 Jazz Fest program, the first such guide printed for the Fest, featured a 1925 archival photograph, courtesy of the New Orleans Jazz Museum, of Ridgley's Original Tuxedo Jazz Band, which was formed from members of the Celestin Tuxedo Orchestra when it split in two groups in 1925. Albert "Papa" French would later assume leadership of the other half. Lingering on the reverence for musicians who gave New Orleans a worldwide reputation as a jazz touchstone, Jazz Fest staff tried to keep a balance between booking

Louisiana talent and bringing in outside bands. This practice had its roots in practicality. For example, music fans could easily catch local performers in clubs around New Orleans without paying a cover fee. Come Festival time, many locals wanted to hear musicians from out of town. Conversely, New Orleans was

George Wein, Barney Bigard, Wild Bill Davidson

famous for its musical talent, and visitors coming into the city wanted to hear the real thing. At least during those first two years in Beauregard Square, staff reasoned that big name acts were needed to draw an out-of-town audience (and pay for the Festival), and Louisiana musicians who played during the daytime Heritage Festival or on the same bill at the night concerts would also benefit. In fact, that truth has been borne

was dedicated to the memory of Sharkey Bonano, the famously egotistical bandleader and hot jazz trumpeter who had, only last year, performed a Jazz Fest tribute to Louis Armstrong, who passed away soon afterward. Bonano's death on March 27, just a month before Jazz Fest, was a poignant reminder that a

ably, the foremost gospel singer in the world, had passed away in Chicago in January. "Jazz at the Ballroom" was held in the beautiful ballroom of the then Jung Hotel, which was at that time the largest hotel in New Orleans. Performers included Ronnie Kole, Wild Bill Davidson, Barney Bigard, Sweet Emma

out over time that numerous local bands and gospel choirs have received attention from agents and talent scouts and have been booked to tour in the U.S. and Europe, gaining audiences far from their hometown roots.

There were three evening concerts. The Friday night concert

generation of virtuoso musicians who came of age in the early twentieth century was slipping away. Echoing that sadness, Allen Toussaint's father died unexpectedly just before Jazz Fest. Mahalia Jackson, who grew up in "the Black Pearl" section of New Orleans to become, argu-

Barrett, Percy Humphrey Sextet, the Murphy Campo Sextet, the New Orleans Ragtime Orchestra, The Louis Cottrell Orchestra, and Bob Greene's Tribute to Jelly Roll Morton. (Morton, born Ferdinand Lamothe, grew up in the Faubourg Marigny section of New Orleans, and adopted

"Mouton," his stepfather's name, later changing it to "Morton".) Kid Ory, another New Orleans great, had played with Jelly Roll Morton and the Red Hot Peppers in the 1910s and 20s, first in the Storyville District and later in other venues. Louis Cottrell, Jr., was also descended from jazz royalty. His father, Louis Cottrell, Sr., played alongside Ory, Morton, Bigard and others in the 1910s; and Cottrell, Jr., was to perform many nights for rapt audiences in that bare-bones shrine of authentic New Orleans Jazz: Preservation Hall.

The early 1970s were the heyday of soul and rhythm and blues music and Jazz Fest staff needed to look no further than around town to represent this genre. Professor Longhair; blind singer and guitar player Snooks Eaglin; Willie Tee and the Gaturs; and Deacon John and Duckbutter filled the bill. Professor Longhair developed a style of piano playing that predated rock and roll by a solid 25 years, and he was

Thelonius Monk   *Louis Cottrell, Jr.*

"The arrival of George Wein as festival producer was a bit of a culture shock for some of the New Orleans musicians. Some of us were accustomed to playing loose with the performance time and making it up at the end of the evening. George Wein had an assistant, Bob Jones, who introduced us to "New York" time instead of "New Orleans" time. Each set was 45 minutes with 15 minutes setup time for the next performance. Some of the performers attempted to stretch their time, but at the end of the 45 minutes, Bob Jones had the curtain closed before some of them finished. That reality was the beginning of a professional experience for many local musicians." ELLIS MARSALIS

already a certifiable legend around town and at Jazz Fest. He would return to close out Jazz Fest from Stage 2 until his passing in 1980. But in 1972, 'Fess was as-yet-unrecognized in the larger world of popular music, except for a small cadre of New Orleans musicians and fans. It became Quint Davis's and Allison Miner's mission to garner recognition for Professor Longhair. Along with others such as the Dumestre sisters, they threw parties and passed the hat to pay for the music.

With the move to the Fair Grounds, and the easing of cultural conventions in response to the revolutions of the 60s, fashions began to change. Under the trees downtown at Beauregard Square, young women just leaving work, presumably, still wore dresses and even head scarves and many men could be found wandering in with a jacket and long pants. But to attend you had to take the day off and actually go with purpose. Everybody seemed in on Kid Thomas's motto: "Let joy be unrefined!"

Some women went braless, some wore hot pants, and long straight hair on men and women signaled "hippie" status. "Pants are out! Sundresses are in!" proclaimed a fashion advertisement still selling convention. That being said, most people wore shorts and T-shirts, dressed as usual for the hot, humid days and nights. Mostly Festgoers dressed simply and carried only a camera or recorder. They wore suntan lotion, instead of sun block. In a few years, bikini tops would emerge in a crowd blissfully unaware of the phenomenon of "sun damage."

Sister Gertrude Morgan

1973

John Lee Hooker

It was the most crowd-pleasing Festival in the short history of Jazz Fest. As crowds numbering 10,000 came streaming through the gates on Thursday, one thing was clear: Jazz Fest had come of age. The *New Orleans States Item* called it a "four-day happening," and George Wein smelled a first-time profit. New Orleans Jazz & Heritage Festival was no longer a hometown event. A five-man television crew arrived from Japan to make a half hour documentary on jazz, and freelance journalists came on their own dime from France, hoping to hustle stories. The buzz was tangible. Talent scouts were starting to swarm the Fair Grounds and music clubs, and in their wake sprang impromptu performers and artists who played and sang for any audience around.

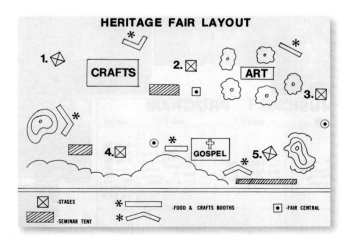

One of the most noticeable was Sister Gertrude Morgan, who, with the help of Larry Borenstein, erected a booth, ecumenically festooned with a Star of David and a crucifix, in order to display her paintings. Dressed all in white, and waving a homemade poster board megaphone, she warned all within earshot, "He knows your name and when you're coming." The Meters: Leo Nocentelli, Zigaboo Modeliste, George Porter and Art Neville, played to a huge crowd under a cloudless sky – that crowd swaying even harder when superstar Stevie Wonder climbed the stairs to stir up the funk. Wonder, known to be a Modeliste fan, played borrowed drums and organ on "Superstitious" as Neville and Modeliste graciously stepped aside. George Porter tells a story about Allen Toussaint: "Toussaint said that he thought he had heard all the music that could be played, until Stevie sat in on drums with us. Then Toussaint said- 'Hey *that's* all the music that can be played.' And then Zigaboo came back onstage and Allen said then *another* door opened." In 1973, after the Meters grooved and Stevie Wonder sat in they had to jump through more than doors to break down their stuff and run, because they were backing up Professor Longhair on another stage.

On the expanse of grass at the Heritage Fair, both reigning grand marshals Matthew "Fats" Houston and Anderson Minor were dressed in crimson red suits, matching top hats and white gloves of the Olympia Brass

Band. These two men had led brass band parades all over the city and in all weather conditions. They looked venerable, and Jazz Fest was honored by their presence. Parading brass bands were a uniquely New Orleans tradition. These were not the military band models that one sees at football games and municipal parades, although it is said that in 1830s New Orleans a black band from Boston performed

JAZZ AND HERITAGE FESTIVAL

APRIL 10–15, 1973

PRESENTED BY
NEW ORLEANS JAZZ & HERITAGE FOUNDATION, INC.
In Co-operation With
GEORGE WEIN
With The Assistance of A Grant From
JOS. SCHLITZ BREWING CO.

during military ceremonies with brass instruments, possibly setting the precedent. Many were born of the social aid and pleasure clubs and harkened back to the African tradition of personal adornment and tribal ritual as a form of meaningful entertainment. Danny Barker, massive plastic cigar clamped in his teeth,

THURS, APRIL 12

STAGE 1
Gary & Nada
Al Belletto
Cabaret
Phil Zito

STAGE 2
Mardi Gras Indians
Adolescence
Betty Casey

STAGE 3
Camelia Stompers
Bob Greene Trio
Sage
Gospel Tent
Ott Family
Spiritualettes
Zion Harmonizers
Rocks of Harmony

STAGE 4
True Bluegrass Boys
Allen Fontenot Country Cajuns

STAGE 5
Babe Stovall
Percy Randolph
Abner Jay
Drum & Fife Corps
Bukka White

SEMINAR
1:30 & 4:30
Jazz Recording – George Kay, Bill Russell, McRee, Jr.

FRIDAY, APRIL 13

STAGE 1
Abner Jay
Professor Longhair
Mardi Gras Indians
Kid Sheik Ramblers

STAGE 2
Wallace Davenport
Deacon John & Duckbutter
New Orleans Joy Makers
Drum & Fife Corps

STAGE 3
Robbie Lee
Ars Nova
Ellis Marsalis Sextet
Southern University Jaguar Lab Jazz Ensemble

GOSPEL TENT
Youth Inspirational Choir
Zion Harmonizers
Southern Bells
Rev. Clay Choir

STAGE 4
Babe Stovall
Percy Randolph
Halleluja Ramblers
Roosevelt Sykes
Bukka White

STAGE 5
Cappy's Hat Band
Mamou Band
Hubert Davis
Season Travelers
Les Moore
Russ Russell & Stingrays

SEMINARS
Afro-American Secular Music – Ellis Marsalis
Jelly Roll Morton – Bob Greene

SATURDAY, APRIL 14

STAGE 1
Murphy Campo
Drum & Fife Corps
Abner Ray

Professor Longhair

led the Fairview Baptist Church Christian Boys Band around the grounds in a parade filled with the descendants of famous jazz players such as Walden Williams, William Smith, Steve Catton, Donald Polk, Larry Davis, Jere Mims, Ernest Toussaint, Harry Sterling, Deborah White, Dwight Perria, Byron Washington, Gerry Anderson, Darrell Brock, and Diana Washington. In the Gospel Tent, irrepressible personalities Dr. Daddy-O and Vernon Winslow led a regular old-style gospel revival. On another plot of ground, the Holy Trucking Family led onlookers in a round robin of "Row, Row, Row Your Boat" while simultaneously sell-ing jewelry and other wares. One photograph from 1973 captures a lone Port-O-Let positioned by some trees. Little kids ran around naked and were safe in doing so.

Under the auspices of the Tulane Graduate School Students Association and the University Center Programming Board, two spin-off events took the Festival to Tulane University. Featured at Tulane's McAlister Auditorium were Abner Jay, the One Man Georgia Band; Professor Longhair; blues inter-preter Bukka White; Willie T and the Souls; Earl Turbinton; and the David Lee and George Davis Bands on April 8-10. Other bands performed at the

music scene

New Orleans Heritage Hall Jazz Band releases album on GNP Crescendo Records.

Dr. John releases "In the Right Place."

Professor Longhair tours Europe, headlining the 1973 Montreux Jazz Festival.

The Jamaican film *The Harder They Come*, starring Jimmy Cliff, is shown in America.

The Wild Magnolias release the self-titled LP on Polydor Records

Olympia Brass Band appear in the James Bond movie "Live and Let Die."

IN MEMORIAM

Anderson Minor, Gram Parsons, Gene Krupa, Bobby Darrin, Willie "The Lion" Smith

to bring international bands that played Louisiana music to perform at Jazz Fest. It was a trend that would bring many a magical musical moment to audiences who thought New Orleans musicians were the only purveyors of jazz. It was clear that the love of music and the joy of learning from the older generation were impervious to national borders.

In cooperation with the National Tea Council, a Jazz Fest talent search was conducted, under the direction of New Orleans musician and poet Eluard Burt. He staged competitions uptown, Community College in order to provide accessibility for kids from all neighborhoods. He chose independent judges that "understood the New Orleans sound, because both judges and the kids growing up in music, especially, had to understand that as a value." Burt's greatest pride was putting street musicians together with schooled musicians, and getting high school and university students together with "kids on the corner." "No black, no white — just New Orleans. Our music is the most powerful force on the planet. Like the administration or not, the Jazz Fest has been so successful in bringing people together," Burt said. Drawing on connec-

"The first time I played Jazz Fest was in 1973. I wasn't living in New Orleans at the time and was in town to perform at the Marriott Hotel. I just went out to the Fair Grounds to check it out and have some fun. Well, I was standing in the potty line and I remember I had a big afro, a yellow halter top and bell bottoms on because they were still fashionable. Anyway, I'm standing in the potty line and there are three ladies behind me and I can overhear them say, 'I wonder if Irma's singing this year?' and another woman says, 'Nah, she's down in Florida probably having another baby.' About a half hour later, Tommy Ridgley invited me on stage to sing as a guest. I walked up there and lo and behold those three women are standing right in front. I looked right at them and said, "Do I look like I'm in Florida having another baby?" IRMA THOMAS

James Rivers
Kid Thomas

STAGE 2
Earl King
Al Belletto
Bukka White
The Meters
Lee Dorsey

STAGE 3
Robert Pete Williams
Bayou Stompers
Mardi Gras Indians
Gentlemen of Jazz
Gospel Tent
Bro. Davenport & Choir
Gospel Soul Children
Samuel Burfect
Wilson Family
Geraldine Wright & Ebenezer BC Choir

STAGE 4
Kustbandet
Walter Washington
Professor Longhair
Jim Kweskin
Ernie K-Doe

STAGE 5
Hubert Davis & Season Travelers
Vin Bruce
Mamou Group
Clifton Chenier

SEMINAR
Danny Barker – Roots of Jazz

SUNDAY, APRIL 15

STAGE 1
New Iberia Stompers
Ragtime Orchestra
Bayou Stompers
Don Albert
Kid Thomas
Santo Pecora

STAGE 2
Roosevelt Sykes
Willie Tee & Gaturs
Mardi Gras Indians
The Souls

STAGE 3
Papa French
Drum & Fife Corps
Robert Pete Williams
Abner Jay
Bukka White
Porgy Jones
Gospel Tent
John Lee & L.B. Choir Ensemble
Samuel Burfect
Rocks of Harmony
Zion Harmonizers
1st Church of God & Christ Choir
New Hope BC Mass Choir

STAGE 4
Storyville Jazz Band
Doug Kershaw
Allen Toussaint
Professor Longhair

STAGE 5
Allen Fontenot & Country Cajuns
Hubert Davis & Season Travelers
Mamou Band
Clifton Chenier

SEMINARS
Armand Hug – New Orleans Piano
John Joyce – Jazz History

fest facts

Wielding a pirogue paddle, Upton Diez cooked jambalaya in a huge cast iron kettle over a wood fire, selling 5,000 portions over the course of that weekend; twice as many as last year.

New Orleans was the only city in the world presenting a living jazz heritage exposition.

Booker T. Glass, at 92, had been playing bass drum for the Olympia Brass Band for 72 years.

Stevie Wonder and George Porter

Festival, judges selected tapes to send to a Newport jury. Winners were offered a chance to perform at the New Orleans Jazz & Heritage Festival, and again at Newport in May. Winners were Bonnie Casey, a singer in local night clubs; The Cavaliers, LSU students from Louisiana State University of New Orleans; and Adolescence, a jazz group of Orleans Parish high schoolers under direction of Alvin Batiste.

Wein and Davis spoke about their intention to take the Jazz Fest to the Superdome next year, when its construction was completed. "Once we move indoors to the Superdome the New Orleans event will take its natural place as one of the great Jazz Festivals of the world," said Wein. *The New Orleans States Item* reported, "Completion of the Superdome will catapult the New Orleans Jazz & Heritage Festival to instant, world-wide stardom." It referred to Wein as "the world's greatest promoter of Jazz Festivals." Wein said that a domed stadium would "create a feeling of intimacy, allowing the people to interact with musicians and with each other in a sense of togetherness." "The New Orleans image is necessary to the Festival here since New Orleans has the greatest musical heritage of any city in the nation," reported *The Times-Picayune*. At Festivals in other cities, about half of the total attendance came from locals. Here in New Orleans, 90% came from the metropolitan area.

The music stages may have been small, but they were easy to load in. Musicians recount driving trucks full of "girls and beer" right up to the stage for set up. Fans could stand right next to the stage, and there was plenty of room to dance. Equipment was somewhat informal in these early years. For example, Alfred "Uganda" Roberts was hired for his signature percussion jams that attracted dozens of fellow drummers and onlookers. Centered on the infield, the jams went on for hours. They became so popular that finally Roberts was given a stage and amplification.

Although folks brought tents and blankets, there was none of the territory staking that came later, along with the overcrowding. For a five-stage, all-day music celebration, an introduction to handmade Louisiana crafts, a bounty of temptation in the form of heritage cuisine, good times with friend's and unrivaled original music, the admission price of $2 was the best bargain around.

Concerts on the riverboat jammed, but the *S.S. President* didn't sail. A tanker had collided earlier with 31 barges near the Percy St. Wharf on the west bank of the Mississippi River, setting them adrift and sinking one. But the shows went on in the cloying spring humidity. Pete Fountain played with the riverboat's house band, the Crawford Ferguson Night Owls. How hot was it? It was so hot that Fountain shed his toupee in favor of circulation. The "Salute to the King of Swing" honored one of world's greatest clarinet players, Benny Goodman, who had been playing since the 1920s. To achieve his sweet style he had studied the recordings of New Orleans jazzmen Leon Roppolo and

NIGHT CONCERTS

TUESDAY, APRIL 10, 8 P.M.
River Boat Cruise
Pete Fountain
Crawford-Ferguson Nightowls
S.S. President

WEDNESDAY, APRIL 11, 8:30 P.M.
Salute To The King of Swing
Benny Goodman Sextet
Preservation Hall Jazz Band w/ Billie
  & De De Pierce
Municipal Auditorium

THURSDAY, APRIL 12, 8:30 P.M.
Blues & Roots
Taj Mahal
Howlin' Wolf
Albert King
Mardi Gras Indians
Como Drum & Fife Corps
Municipal Auditorium

FRIDAY, APRIL 13, 8 P.M.
The Soul of Jazz
The Staple Singers
B.B. King
Dave Brubeck w/ Gerry Mulligan
Joe Newman
Margie Joseph
Municipal Auditorium

Johnny Dodds. Goodman was swinging suave in a dark suit and appeared unruffled in spite of the high humidity and frenzy of the crowd. Unfortunately, the microphones picked up every scrape and slide of the band's instruments, and the popping flashbulbs were blinding. Nonetheless, Goodman was a gracious bandleader, and even sat aside while his sidemen took solos.

Two cultural icons shared the bill with two generations of bluesmen in the Municipal Auditorium. The Como Fife and Drum Corps and the Mardi Gras Indians personified some of the oldest and most original music traditions in the U.S. Howlin' Wolf had built a career on the Delta blues, and Taj Mahal was coming up in the blues/jazz idiom. Stevie Wonder made his first Jazz Fest appearance during the "Night of Stars." The Olympia Brass Band with special guest star Kim Weston got a second line started and led the chant "We Need Love." The Ramsey

Claudia the "Praline Lady" Dumestre

Lewis Trio trilled and thrilled with "Slippin Into Darkness" and "Wade in the Water." Eddie "Fathead" Newman had spent six years with the Ray Charles Band and was making his first appearance in New Orleans since the early 1940s. He had also played lead trumpet with Count Basie, and was now added to Herbie Mann's group. Traditional jazz fans on the riverboat showed all the enthusiasm of arena rock

concerts, with shouts at the band, wild dancing, sneaking off to the upper deck to smoke reefer, and the most daring even found a dark corner of the upper deck to conjure the beast with two backs. In the first few years, fans were divided between "trad" jazz fanatics (many of whom were white) and fans of the evening concerts in the Municipal Auditorium, which came to hear concerts by African-Americans.

Howlin' Wolf

"I've played at every Jazz Fest since the beginning. Even in the days at Congo Square. I used to go to the little apartment that Quint and Allison had and go over the details. I had performed at a few festivals and I think they wanted my ideas. I never dreamed that it would grow as big as it has especially after that first year when it was such a small affair. I especially liked the time Governor Jimmie Davis sat in with my band and I remember he carried his own little amplifier up to the stage. I broke my bow that day and I will never forget that." ALLEN FONTENOT

1974

Puffy white clouds sailed over the Fair Grounds. With temperatures between 65° and 75°, the weather was perfect for grooving and the crowd was in that groove. Young men and women wearing perfectly circular shaped Afro hairdos, hippie girls in long Indian print skirts, older men in straw hats and short sleeved shirts, and ladies in checked cotton sleeveless shifts were all part of the good-natured mix. Babies in strollers, dogs with or without leashes, old folks moving slow – Jazz Fest was getting to be the place to people-watch. And over the three days of the Heritage Fair, there were more than 50,000 to watch. In only two more years, attendance would double.

It was said that in planning the move to the Fair Grounds, Wein had expressed doubts that African-Americans, "hillbillies," people from the country and the city could share the same outdoor space in a peaceful manner, without conflicts born of clashing cultures. Maybe it was New Orleans' long history (spoken or unspoken) of interconnected cultures. Or maybe it was the spirit of mutual respect that Miner, Davis, and their staff had woven into the soul of the Festival. Whatever benevolent force ruled the Jazz

Fest, that force decreed from the beginning that love would rule, and the music would rock.

The Fair Grounds infield seemed like an ocean of grass compared to Beauregard Square, and Festgoers took to the new location. They were beginning to count on seeing all their friends out there, and many made it a family outing. Young parents or musicians' families watched their children run free (no leashes, few strollers) while they picnicked in the grass. Some folks napped under the big oaks or grabbed a hunk of fifty-cent watermelon. It was after the summer of love and before Reaganomics. Some might say it was the nation's last few years of hope despite assassinations and the Vietnam War, before gas prices transferred focus to the pursuit of money as the currency of not just commerce, but social stature as well. "Cynical" was the dirty word, not "liberal." Cameras, tape recorders, and even videotape machines were all over the Fair Grounds. These were the days before attorneys outnumbered musicians. Robert Pete Williams, in a white straw hat and pin-striped jacket, was being taped and filmed by at least five people. From Rosedale, Louisiana, Williams had been touring since his release from Angola State Penitentiary in 1964. The crowd that gathered to hear Williams's jailhouse blues stretched from what is now the Fais Do-Do Stage nearly to the trees.

Babe Stovall showed up playing a borrowed guitar, because his own battered one had been stolen on Mardi Gras night. One of the many talented musicians who inhabited Jackson Square in the French Quarter and scrapped together a living playing for tips, Stovall held onto his comprehensively duct-taped guitar case. His family had been sharecroppers in Louisiana and Mississippi, and although being a street musician was no easy ride, it had to beat the hardscrabble farm life. Plus, the guitar music he'd been playing Delta-style for the past 50 years was a gift to all who were fortunate enough to get within earshot. Stovall's trick of playing the guitar behind his head was always a crowd pleaser. During those first stage-scarce years in Beauregard Square, Stovall didn't have — or need — a stage. He simply played from a metal folding chair.

Propelled by a booming economy, the U.S. manufacturing sector blazed away in the 1970s, cranking out consumer goods and sparking a seemingly insatiable market for them. But folding chairs, water bottles and all the accoutrements of Festival going were not yet in evidence— that would take advertising and branding geniuses and perhaps

SCHLITZ SALUTES
NEW ORLEANS JAZZ & HERITAGE FESTIVAL

Thursday–April 18
Opening Night Dance
on S.S. President
8:00 PM
Tickets–$6

Friday–April 19
Concert
Municipal Auditorium
8:00 PM
Tickets–$5, $6, $7

Saturday–April 20
Concert
Municipal Auditorium
8:00 PM
Tickets–$5, $6, $7

Louisiana
Heritage Fair
Friday–Saturday
Sunday–April 19, 20, 21
11:30 AM to 6:30 PM
Tickets–$2
Children under 12–$1

JAZZ AND HERITAGE FESTIVAL
"PRESENTED IN COOPERATION WITH
THE JOS. SCHLITZ BREWING COMPANY"

85907 © 1974 JOS. SCHLITZ BREWING CO., MILWAUKEE, WIS. AND OTHER GREAT CITIES

STAGE 1
11:00 Adolescence
11:40 The Jazz-Stronauts
2:00 Adolescence
3:00 University of Wisconsin Milwaukee Band
5:00 Chocolate Milk

STAGE 2
12:00 Your Father's Mustache Band
1:30 Babe Stovall
3:00 The Fairview Baptist Church Christian Marching Band
4:00 Sady Courville

STAGE 3
12:00 Patton's Pride
1:00 The Camelia Band
2:00 Patton's Pride
3:30 Babe Stovall
4:30 White Eagle New Orleans Band
5:30 The Jazz-Stronauts

STAGE 4
12:00 Percy Randolph
1:00 Guy Richards
2:00 Como, Miss. Drum and Fife Corps
3:30 Jeanette Carter
4:00 R.L. Burnside
4:30 The Onward Brass Band

STAGE 5
12:30 Texas Southern
1:30 The Don Albert Band
2:30 The Legends of Jazz
3:30 Texas Southern
5:30 Dave Williams

STAGE 6
3:00 Robert Pete Williams
4:30 The Mardi Gras Indians
5:30 Latin Chiefs

PARADE
3:00 Onward Brass Band

GOSPEL TENT
12:00 The Sunset Travelers
12:45 The Macedonia Male Chorus
2:15 The Russ Specials
3:00 The Ott Family
4:00 The Christians Harp
4:45 The Chosen Few
5:30 McDonogh #35 Choir and Cornile Hardy

SATURDAY, APRIL 20

STAGE 1
12:00 University of Wisconsin Milwaukee Band
12:30 Tommy Ridgley
2:30 Benny Spellman and Robert Parker
3:30 The Meters
4:30 Ernie K-Doe

STAGE 2
11:30 Babe Stovall
1:00 Snooks Eaglin
2:00 Como, Miss. Drum and Fife Corps
3:00 Hubert Davis and the Season Travelers
4:00 Russ Russell and the Stingrays
5:00 The Balfa Brothers

STAGE 3
12:00 The Stans Band
1:00 The Jazzola Six
2:00 Johnny Wiggs and his Bayou Stompers
3:30 Louis Cottrell and Blanche Thomas
4:40 Roosevelt Sykes

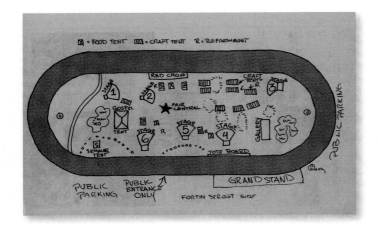

Map legend: X = FOOD TENT, ▥ = CRAFT TENT, R = REFRESHMENT

RED CROSS

CRAFT TENT

STAGE 1
GOSPEL TENT
STAGE 2
FAIR CENTRAL
STAGE 3
STAGE 5
STAGE 4
GALLERY
STAGE 6
SEMINAR TENT
TOTE BOARD

PUBLIC PARKING

PUBLIC PARKING
PUBLIC ENTRANCE ONLY
FORTIN STREET SIDE
GRAND STAND

Clifton Chenier

particularly the explosive success of Nike. No phalanxes of folding chairs claimed anyone's territory. Just good-times loving people in shorts and dresses and pants and sneakers and sandals. And the music, and good vibes. The Festival and a blanket at most were enough — the equipment to "enjoy" it came later. But sponsorships were not unknown; they just meant little more than posting a sign on a beer booth. Parker Dinkins, fresh out of Tulane Law School, came onto the Jazz Fest staff in 1974 as site manager and staff legal counsel, and contributed a structure that included legal necessities such as licensing, copyrights, and business contracts. Dinkins' expertise informed the growing enterprise and solidified good business practices so the Festival could begin to consider creating collectibles and mementos like silkscreen posters.

music scene

Frank Demond begins playing at Preservation Hall.

Sweet Emma Barrett begins fronting the Humphrey Brothers Band at Preservation Hall.

"Dr. John: New Orleans Swamp" is produced and aired on Soundstage from Chicago with Professor Longhair, The Meters and Earl King.

The Maple Leaf Bar opens its doors.

The Meters release "Rejuvenation" on Reprise Records.

"Nightbirds" is released by Patti Labelle, produced by Allen Toussaint.

IN MEMORIAM

Duke Ellington, Kid Ory, Jim Croce, George Brunies

Professor Longhair

European journalists were now traveling regularly to Jazz Fest, reporting back on the smoothly run outdoor Festival in the hot and humid lower coast of the U.S. The remarkable lack of problems and anarchy the Festival has always maintained has always been a magical testament to its production staff and patrons. New Orleans has often been referred to as the nation's most European city, making it a hospitable environment for tourists willing to cross the pond. And New Orleanians have felt the responsibility to be hospitable. Two chartered planes flew in from Europe for Jazz Fest, and four bands traveled from

"Anyway — we're all there and we're on the stage and all of the sudden Hector's having trouble starting his car, so he throws the hood up and he's tinkering with it and somebody says 'Oh my God — it's on fire.' It started small and people started panicking as it got out of hand and everybody was getting back and getting behind stuff, expecting it to blow. I ran over and got a bunch of towels, dipped them in the ice chest, ran over to the carburetor and just smothered the fire and put it out. Well, next year, all the stages had to have a fire extinguisher on 'em. It wasn't that anybody in the organization was so brilliant that they'd think all this shit up at once. It was a process (developing the Festival site details)." KEITH WILLIAMS

fest facts

Mother McGregor Jones broadcast her "Prayer Tower" show live from the Fair.

This was Chris Severin's first performance at Jazz Fest, and he made $90 playing with Henry Butler.

Wallace Davenport performed in a white suit with red buttons, red tie and red shoes fronting a band in somber brown suits.

Toronto. Journalist Max Harris wrote in *The Australian*, "The Fairview Baptist Dixieland Street Marching Band produces a blood-stirring and irresistible authenticity. The tatty uniforms are worn by grandfathers, fathers, and grandchildren.

There's a 12 year-old blowing cornet with the same confident zeal as a young Louis."

On the steamboat S. S. President, 2,000 mostly-white passengers paid $5.50 to dance to traditional jazz. Johnny Wiggs's cornet got the dancing started in

Babe Stovall

SATURDAY, APRIL 26

earnest. His rendition of "Frankie and Johnny" tore up the house—or the boat— according to local reports. With Jeff Riddick on piano, Leslie Muscutt on banjo, Butz Massicot on drums, Dr. Ray Benitz on bass, Clive Wilson on second cornet, Tom Elbert on trombone and Johnson "Fat Cat" McCree singing vocals, and the great clarinetist Raymond Burke (born in 1904), it was an evening worthy of reverence tickled with gaiety. These men were the real deal, having played authentic jazz alongside others who gave birth to the genre. Don Albert did a tolerable job of warming up the audience, which was waiting for Preservation Hall Jazz Band to get the dancing going. He played "Sleepy Time Down South" without giving in to slick imitation. It was by all accounts a beautiful spring night. Many impromptu jazz paraders pranced around the bandstand when Don "Kid" Albert launched into "Bill Bailey" and played it for a rollicking 15 minutes. Umbrellas were whirling. Kid Thomas Valentine and

the Algiers Stompers rounded out the concert, which lasted well after the boat docked at 11 p.m. The Algiers Stompers literally had the boat rocking.

Concerts at the Municipal Auditorium were sold out for the first time in the history of the Fest, which was good news after last year's money-losing streak. More than 9,000 sharply dressed fans turned out over the three performances, and the many late arrivals spawned traffic jams all around the auditorium. Sequins, lamé, synthetics and spandex slid and sparkled as disco fashions were applied to jazz fans. Friday, at the Municipal Auditorium, the evening concert started smoothly with the Jimmy Smith Trio. Smith's impromptu song and dance got the audience going, and then Joe Newman took it a notch further, opening up a groove for Stanley Turrentine's tenor sax. Herbie Hancock further elevated the frenzied crowd. Gladys Knight and her Pips danced up to and back from the microphone, but

Jeanette Carter

the sound was mixed so badly that Knight's voice drowned out the band. Even so, the audience screamed approval for the hits "If I Were Your Woman," "Midnight Train to Georgia," and the recently released

Benny Spellman

"Neither One of Us Wants to be the First to Say Goodbye."

On Saturday night, the audience was again exceptionally dressed and coiffed. Before the rest of the nation was gripped by *Saturday Night Fever,* funkadelic dance club style was driving late night fashion. Women and men teetered in platform shoes, long cuffed bell-bottomed slacks, and heavy eyeliner. Not being restricted to seats in the auditorium, people could range about and eat, drink, show off, and flirt, as they liked. Some found the movement and noise distracting from the music, while others reveled in the constant parade. The Staple Singers, with their gospel roots, immediately created a rapport with New Orleans' audiences. The line between gospel

and popular music had always been a thin one in the Crescent City, and many rock and roll performers had come up in the gospel tradition. Sometimes crossing over into rock and roll or blues became a hard choice, and people such as Aretha Franklin and B.B. King sometimes had to risk disapproval from religious family members to make their own music in their own way. But the Staples Singers, propped up by the solid Pops, took the audience "there" and back, reaching over the police barricade to touch hands with the beautiful people and heal the spirit.

Some audience members came as much to partake in the party as to listen to jazz. Top liners such as Earl "Fatha" Hines, Louis Jordan, and Yusef Lateef

were barely acknowledged. Lateef in particular, with his many bamboo instruments and modern jazz sax mixed with poetry in a similar vein, suffered from an aesthetic misbooking with the popular songs of Hines and Louis Jordan. "Knock Me A Kiss" was more in the evening's groove than the contemplative Lateef. But the hit of the evening was a last minute substitution. Bill Withers replacing Donny Hathaway was a welcomed one. Withers walked onstage and commanded the love of the audience as he sang to simple guitar accompaniment. He was a quiet counterpoint to an adoring audience that stood on chairs, danced, blew whistles, and sang along with "Ain't No Sunshine When She's Gone."

Maybe the electric performance transcendence on which Jazz Fest built its reputation was just in the air. Sunday's Heritage Fair culminated a weekend of stellar singing, shouting, and come-to-Jesus moments in the Gospel Tent. Mother McGregor Jones and Prayer Tower Choir, The Spiritualettes, and the Mount Moriah Choir delivered particularly spirited performances. As the day's heat finally began a slow fade, and southerly breezes shoved the humid air around, the Desire Community Choir closed out the Gospel Tent. On Stage 4, Earl King glared heavenward at the threatening blue-black clouds and bowed to a higher power by cutting his set short. Stiff winds that often signal a soon-to-follow downpour wreaked havoc with the New Orleans Ragtime Orchestra music stands. Fess coaxed supernatural rhythms

out of his ivories to close out Stage 2, Alphonse "Bois Sec" Ardoin wielded his accordion as he had a thousand times before, and the Olympia Brass Band hoped the rain would hold off a half hour longer as they ceremonially paraded toward the grandstands. Their silk umbrellas would be slight defense against a Louisiana downpour. Craftspeople were packing up, too. Voodoo dolls, positioned next to the nun dolls, went back into the box. Food vendors fended off latecomers and gave away already-cooked food to Festival staffers, who had learned to show up just as they were closing down. It was a race against the rain, but life was good.

NIGHT CONCERTS

THURSDAY, APRIL 18, 8 P.M.
Steamboat Stomp
Kid Thomas and The Preservation Hall Band
The Don Albert Band
The Johnny Wiggs Band
The Legends of Jazz
Steamer President

FRIDAY, APRIL 19, 8 P.M.
Gladys Knight and The Pips
Herbie Hancock
Jimmy Smith Trio
Stanley Turrentine
Joe Newman
Municipal Auditorium

SATURDAY, APRIL 20, 8 P.M.
The Staple Singers
Donny Hathaway
Yusef Lateef Quartet
Earl "Fatha" Hines
Louis Jordan

NEW ORLEANS JAZZ & HERITAGE FESTIVAL
April 18-21, 1974
STEAMER PRESIDENT / MUNICIPAL AUDITORIUM / FAIR GROUNDS RACE TRACK

Presented by
THE NEW ORLEANS JAZZ & HERITAGE FOUNDATION, INC.
In cooperation with the JOS. SCHLITZ BREWING COMPANY

© New Orleans Jazz & Heritage Foundation, Inc. 1974

B.B. King

1975

From the zillions of personal recollections in the world of Jazz Fest, most musicians who were on the scene in the 1970s make one point clear: George Wein, Allison Miner and Quint Davis were dedicated to bringing attention to Louisiana musicians, particularly the older generation, in whatever ways they could. One staff member in the early days said of Allison, "Allison was a hammer. She got things done. She took care of older black musicians. If not for her and Quint, we wouldn't know about Fess today."

Pianist James Booker was another such diamond-in-the-rough who only needed a sufficient audience to be seen for the genius he was. Booker debuted on Friday, April 22, on Stage 2, at 2:00 p.m. Although he had played on Ringo Starr's last album, only other musical luminaries largely knew Booker's talent. He was a musician's musician, sometimes enigmatic, sometimes unreliable. A fixture later at the Maple Leaf Bar and Toulouse Theater, Booker was one of the many whose career would receive a boost from the Jazz Fest appearance, just as Miner and Davis hoped. Booker himself described his style: "Human nature is the reason why I play the piano the way I do. But not just ordinary human nature; some people say I'm a freak of nature." With slicked down hair

what's going on?

GLOBALLY

South Vietnamese President Nguyen Van Thieu resigns as Communists overtake S. Vietnam, seize Saigon

Margaret Thatcher becomes leader of the British Conservative Party.

NATIONALLY

Two assassination attempts are made on the life of President Ford in California.

In the first international manned space flight, U.S. Apollo and Soviet Soyuz 19 spacecrafts link up and astronauts and cosmonauts share meals; U.S. Viking unmanned craft sets off to seek signs of life on Mars.

James R. Hoffa, former president of the International Brotherhood of Teamsters, disappears.

LOCALLY

Taylor v. Louisiana (419 U.S. 522) denies states the right to exclude women from juries.

St. Augustine High School celebrates as the first school in the state to win a state football championship with a 15-0 record.

The Superdome, the world's largest indoor stadium, is completed at a final cost of $163,313,315 for the building and grounds, leading to the building of several hotels and motels in the downtown area.

CULTURALLY

Unemployment rate in the U.S. reaches 9.2%, the highest since 1941.

In Seattle, Washington, Microsoft computer software company is founded by 19 year old Harvard dropout Bill Gates and 22 year old Paul Allen.

and in a velvet robe, Booker played "Junco Partner," "Eleanor Rigby," and even a flourish of a Chopin sonata. He dedicated "Make a Better World" to "all my friends at the Euterpe Center."

The aroma of Coppertone suntan lotion permeated the air in front of Stage 3 as Polka Dot Slim breezed through his harmonica set with the easy patter of a born raconteur. It was hot, humid, and sticky, and how those Mardi Gras Indians survived their full-feathered performances was a mystery. On Stage 4, the Yellow Jackets were parading their feathered finery. The Indians' rituals and customs were directly derivative of West African traditions, with basic instruments such as tambourine, drums, and rhythmic vocal patterns and chants, and subject to tribal hierarchy. Behind Stage 1, in the Gospel Tent, The Gospel Soul Children's syncopated chorus was enough to bring salvation raining down on the entire Jazz Fest. And when Bessie Griffin sang "How I Got Over," it was easy to see why the great Mahalia Jackson

brought Griffin with her to perform in Chicago, another city know for its great gospel talent.

Stage managers knew musicians would show up with their own gear (before the Fest grew into contracts with music equipment providers) and might need help with making everything work. Musicians often were missing a piece here and there: broken plugs and so on. One stage manager felt some musicians knew they could get their gear fixed if they were playing the Jazz Festival and waited until then to do so. In the early years, there wasn't a backline organized like today — artists brought their own gear and the effectiveness of running a Festival boiled down to transitioning the bands and their sometimes legendarily well-worn instruments on and off the stage.

Even so, punctuality has always been a religion at Jazz Fest and crews and bands seem to pretty much stick with the schedule. Over the years, this has cut into the continuance of encores for particularly masterful shows, but it's a small price to pay as smoothly as the Festival's

Irma Thomas

FRIDAY, APRIL 25

STAGE 1
1:30 Deacon John
2:30 M.G. Funk
5:00 Omega 2+5

STAGE 2
12:30 Murphy Campo
2:00 James Booker
3:00 The New Orleans Ragpickers
4:00 The Black Eagle Mardi Gras Indian Tribe
5:00 Dave Williams

STAGE 3
12:00 USL Jazz Ensemble
2:30 Sammy Burfect
4:00 The New Porgy Jones Experience
5:30 Raymond Burke and The Storyville Ramblers

STAGE 4
2:00 St. Marks Community Center Dance Troop
3:00 The Copas Brothers
4:00 Como Miss. Fife and Drum Corps
5:00 R.L. Burnside
5:30 Imani

STAGE 5
1:00 Brother Percy Randolph
2:00 Adolescence
3:00 SUBR Jazz Ensemble
4:00 The New Dukes of Dixieland
5:00 Sady Courville & Dennis McGhee

STAGE 6
1:00 Chris Burke & His New Orleans Music
2:00 Soren Houlind Copenhagen Ragtime Band
3:00 Chris Kenner
4:00 Marc Savoy
5:30 Robert Pete Williams

GOSPEL TENT
12:30 The Humble Travelers
1:00 The Mighty Chariots
1:30 The Friendly Travelers
2:00 Daneel No. 2 Youth Choir
2:30 The Gospel Inspirations
3:00 The Spiritualettes
3:30 Sister Elizabeth Eustis
4:00 The McDermit Singers and Christine Myles
4:30 The Southern Gospel Singers
5:00 Greater St. Andrew Choir (Camille Hardy, emcee)

SATURDAY, APRIL 26

STAGE 1
1:00 Chocolate Milk
2:00 Earl King & Lee Dorsey
3:00 Robert Parker & Tommy Ridgley
3:30 Benny Spellman & Ernie K-Doe
4:00 The Meters

STAGE 2
2:00 Cornbread
3:30 Bois Sec Ardoin
5:00 Ellis Marsalis & ELM '75

STAGE 3
1:00 Loyola University Jazz Band
1:30 Xavier University Jazz Band
2:30 Polka Dot Slim
3:30 The Society Jazz Band
5:00 Robert Pete Williams
5:30 The Jazzstronauts

STAGE 4
2:00 James Rivers
3:00 The Yellow Jackets Mardi Gras Indian Tribe

Ironing Board Sam

get a crack at the action. Just under the bandstand, a dozen or more photographers squatted before the microphones, hoping to capture the music and the sweat and the fervor for their readership back home. The stylish Admiral was a nod to the changing times. And the swirling currents of the Mississippi River carried them all: the boats, the music, and the dreams of the men and women who stepped out onto the dance floor.

The "Steamboat Stomp" on the *S.S. Admiral* was a traditional jazz lover's dream, featuring New Orleans jazz bluebloods such as Kid Thomas and his Preservation Hall Jazz Band, Blue Lu Barker with the prolific Danny Barker's Jazz Hounds, Santo Pecora and his Tailgate Ramblers, and Louis Cottrell and the Heritage Hall Band. Last year, Pecora and the Algiers Stompers had the boat literally rocking with trombone wah wahs on "On the Sunny Side of the Street." Then in his twenties, Pecora had played trombone as a stand-in for George Brunies with the New Orleans Rhythm Kings when they made one of the first jazz recordings in the 1920s for RCA Victor. Another example of the passing of talent and love for the music through generations was Louis Cottrell, Jr. The senior Louis Cottrell had played drums in A.J. Piron's Orchestra, one of the finest dance bands in New Orleans in the 1910s and 1920s. They performed at society dances in the city and on summer evenings at Tranchina's Restaurant on the pier at Lake Pontchartrain. Their signature song was "Dreamy Blues," later published as "Mood

music scene

New Orleans Rock and Roll band, Zebra is born in February.

Allen Toussaint releases "Southern Nights" on Reprise Records.

Paul McCartney flies Professor Longhair to California to play an exclusive private party on the Queen Mary.

Paul McCartney & Wings come to New Orleans to record "Venus and Mars" with producer Allen Toussaint.

Clifton Chenier records "Bogalusa Boogie" for Arhoolie Records.

IN MEMORIAM

William Brown, Arthur "Zutty" Singleton

on Wednesday, Thursday and Friday. With its streamlined body and long linear windows, the Admiral exemplified the Art Deco style. This was a departure from the quaint riverboat side-paddlewheel of the S.S. President. On the *S.S. President,* one felt transported back in time through the 1800s-period décor and the traditional jazz by the house band, Crawford Ferguson's Night Owls. The Admiral's capacity of 3,500 meant that those disappointed by earlier sold-out riverboat concerts might

> *"After three or four years, Quint's creativity became very evident. I created the whole concept but Quint kept adding to it new things and they kept doing things and I said 'You've got it, so run with it now.'"* GEORGE WEIN

Cyril Neville

4:00 The Meyers Brothers
5:00 Los Monarcas

STAGE 5
1:00 The Traditional Jazz Band of Sao Paulo
2:30 James Booker
3:30 R.L. Burnside
5:00 Allen Fontenot and His Country Cajuns
5:30 Roosevelt Sykes

STAGE 6
1:00 Brother Percy Randolph
2:00 Como Miss. Fife & Drum Corps
3:00 The Tuxedo Brass Band
4:00 Tuts Washington
5:00 Storyville Band

GOSPEL TENT
12:00 The Friendly Five
12:30 Prayer Tower Choir
1:00 Greater St. Stephen Youth Choir
1:30 St. Matthew Chapel Choir
2:00 Fifth African Youth Choir of St. Rose
2:30 The Stronger Hope Ensemble
3:00 The Zion Harmonizers
3:30 Brother Wallace Davenport
4:00 The Gospel Soul Children
4:30 Sister Bessie Griffin
5:00 The Gospel Choralettes
5:30 The Youth Inspirational Choir (Reverend Herman Brown, emcee)

SUNDAY, APRIL 27

STAGE 1
1:30 Sagitarios
2:30 Music Factory
4:00 Willie Tee
5:00 The Wild Magnolias

STAGE 2
12:30 SUNO Jazz Ensemble
2:00 The Crescent City Joymakers
3:00 The New Quartet
4:00 Al Belletto
5:00 Robert Pete Williams

STAGE 3
1:30 Brother Percy Randolph & Little Freddie King
2:30 Roosevelt Sykes
3:30 Clifton Chenier
4:30 The New Orleans Ragtime Orchestra
5:30 Professor Longhair

STAGE 4
1:00 Dr. Bill C. Malone & The Hill Country Ramblers
2:30 The Louisiana Aces
3:30 The Olympia Brass Band
5:00 Los Catrachos

STAGE 5
12:00 UNO Stage Band
1:00 Imani
2:00 Russ Russell & The Stingrays with Patty Dupree
3:00 Carlos Sanchez
4:00 Papa Albert French and The Tuxedo Orchestra
5:00 The Gentlemen of Jazz with Germaine Bazzle

STAGE 6
1:30 Como Miss. Fife and Drum Corps
2:00 R.L. Burnside
2:30 Ironin' Board Sam
3:30 Irma Thomas
4:30 Rockin' Dopsie & The Twisters
5:30 The Meyers Brothers

GOSPEL TENT
12:00 The Macedonia Male Chorus
12:30 The Masonic Kings

fest facts

The first commemorative Jazz Fest poster, designed by Sharon Dinkins and printed by Fred & Maria Laredo.

Ticket prices crept up to $8.

Ironing Board Sam debuted at Jazz Fest.

The U.S. Navy donated the steel drum band.

Wein and his crew toyed with celebrating next year's bicentennial with Jazz Fest in the Superdome, marketing the event as "the Hemisphere Music Fest."

Indigo," listing composers Duke Ellington and Barney Bigard. Piron disputed that credit. It was known among band members that clarinetist Lorenzo Tio, Jr. had originated the melody.

The scene on the Admiral brought the passing of one culture and the coming of another together in a contretemps. Some complained that the dancers were obstructing the view of the band for those in seats. The dancers countered that if music wasn't for dancing, then it was a dead art form. This argument had been kicked around for years, and indeed had always been a part of New Orleans history. Most

historical records agree that jazz was born in dance halls all over New Orleans. Additionally, the bars and bordellos of Storyville made proving grounds for some musicians, including the great Louis Armstrong. Jazz was dance music, pure and simple. And in a city such as New Orleans, with her French, Italian, African-American and Caribbean denizens, dance was a form of social interaction that bridged the difference of languages. Orchestras, which could consist of five, seven or more players, knew they had to pitch their repertoire with danceable songs. With the rise of free form improvisations of

the more cerebral be-bop and modern forms, jazz dancing faded from popularity. Critics claimed that jazz had become too removed from its true nature, and likened it to visual art that could only be seen in museums. Music lovers even split off into camps, with traditional jazz lovers labeled "mouldy figgs" and differentiated from modern jazz advocates. Fortunately, this disagreement at the "Steamboat Stomp" didn't come to blows, and it's probable that no one regretted their investment of $6.50 admission. Many did complain about debarking over the mounds of dirt at the as-yet-unfinished Spanish Plaza, however.

Another impressive debut took place in the food booths. New Yorker Joe Brennan unveiled "shrimp ya ya." It was enthusiastically embraced and became a sensation, possibly due in part to the sweet brown shrimp caught in waters bordering Louisiana. They have none of the iodine aftertaste as do shrimp from other waters. A

"It was like a family thing you know? You just come there and park your car, and all the musicians were so cool. They had their family, their kids running around and you know I'd supply a huge ice chest — just an ice chest — and everybody would come and make a deposit. The van was a dressing room, more or less. But I never was in it. I'd just be looking at the van and say 'now who is that in my van?'" HERMAN ERNEST

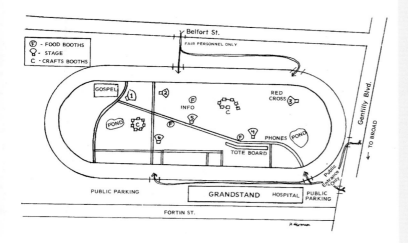

Legend:
- (F) - FOOD BOOTHS
- (stage) - STAGE
- C - CRAFTS BOOTHS

Belfort St.
FAIR PERSONNEL ONLY

GOSPEL

INFO

RED CROSS

POND

POND

PHONES

TOTE BOARD

Gentilly Blvd.
TO BROAD

PUBLIC PARKING

GRANDSTAND   HOSPITAL   PUBLIC PARKING

Public Entrance Only

FORTIN ST.

NIGHT CONCERTS

better adjusting of food booth placement (closer to the path, more room for Stage 6) pleased Festgoers, as did the chitlins and potato bread stuffed with green peppers, a favorite dish returning from last year.

From a four-poster waterbed frame to "the tiniest toy trombone in the world" to flower

James Booker

headpieces, craftspeople were enjoying a good year. Here again, booth placement had changed to two locations: from last year's block of booths was adjusted to a paisley shape on one side of the infield and another near the pond on the other side. Jazz Fest had now become the largest crafts exhibition in Louisiana. Craftsmen from 15 states were there, as was local float maker John Landry. Landry used his 20 years of collecting Mardi Gras throws to fashion miniature floats for sale. According to the 1975 official program, craftspeople also competed for a $500 prize donated by the Festival and local arts patrons.

The eccentric Bongo Joe still returned. Quint had heard about Bongo Joe from Chris Strachwitz at Arhoolie Records, and tracked him down in San Antonio.

"Everybody knows Katrina (George Porter's daughter). They've known her since she was Sierra's age (George's granddaughter) walking around Jazz Fest with a patch on her shirt saying 'I am the property of George Porter Jr.' We never had to worry about her because she would go to the Gospel Tent and spend all day; and about 6 o'clock when everything was starting to shut down, somebody from the Gospel Tent would just walk her back over to Stage 1." ARALEAN PORTER

Invited to the 1971 Festival, when he jammed with Dizzy Gillespie in Beauregard Square, he had become a fixture since then. Anyone who has experienced the phenomenon of Bongo Joe (George Coleman) will easily recall his booming chant over the solid pounding of the 55-gallon Texaco Firechief oil drums with drumsticks made of oilcans filled with BB shot, pebbles and rubber chair legs. The long-suffering oil drums had been not so lovingly shaped with a hand ax, bestowing a textural lumped, bumped,

and dented surface. He could get timpani sounds, rim shot sounds-hitting his pipe on the edge-keeping a rhythm going at the same time and then whistling and singing. In paratrooper boots, Bermuda shorts, a paisley shirt and a large fez, he was a pretty imposing fellow. Primarily a street performer, Bongo Joe took a break from his daily performances in front of the Alamo to come to the Fest. He fit right in.

As in other years, journalists and music critics from all over the world were on hand to record moments of magic and mayhem. On being informed about the arrival of an eminent jazz critic from France, local musician and wild card Eddie Condon said, "Who needs 'em coming here telling us about jazz. We don't tell them how to jump on a grape."

Professor Longhair

MUSIC TO THE EYES: A BRIEF HISTORY OF THE JAZZ FESTIVAL POSTER

The New Orleans Jazz Festival Poster was created by ProCreations Publishing Company in 1975 as a fifth anniversary fundraiser for the non-profit New Orleans Jazz & Heritage Foundation. But it took some detours and a bit of convincing before this now-legendary art print series got off the ground.

Bud Brimberg, ProCreations' founder, was in his last year of law school at Tulane University and, casting about for something else to study, cross-registered at the Tulane Business School in the only course offered to students with no business school background: Entrepreneurship. While others in the class built computer models of non-existent businesses, Brimberg asked if he could start a real business. "That's highly unorthodox," the professor replied, relenting when he was reminded that the course was about starting a business.

Brimberg's original idea was to record the gospel tent and release an album of music that, at that time, had little popular exposure. He approached George Wein, Executive Producer of the Festival, and asked what it would take. Wein gave Brimberg a dose of reality saying, "Unless you can track down, sign and pay hundreds of group managers, dozens of record companies, and hundreds more singers and musicians in these groups and their agents...you won't be recording anyone."

Brimberg was deterred by the monumental task of coordinating all the people who had to sign on and figuring out how much to pay each, let alone where the money would come from. But he still had to submit a project for school, so he tried to conceive another business around the then small, four year-old Festival. In what was a seemingly unrelated personal endeavor, he was also converting his living room back from its use a photo studio and searching for pictures for these walls.

"In those days, the choice was between a cheap offset poster of a fleur-de-lis with photos of Jackson Square, the Superdome and other tourist images or a $2,000 Picasso etching," Brimberg recalls. Why wasn't there something affordable yet artistically valid and printed to an art standard? The answer became obvious as Brimberg investigated: art was rare; good art even rarer. Wealthy people paid up for art they valued, promoted by a network of dealers who explained this esoteric business to them. For the rest of the market, there were tourist posters and "decorator" art, mostly without artistic interest. There had to be a middle ground, Brimberg thought—affordable valid art, produced to museum standards. He set about trying to create a product that fit these criteria.

Posters were a poor man's art in the 60s, used to entice people to concerts – sort of like one-page comic books, but young people had

adopted them as art in their homes. Few, other than works by Henri Toulouse-Lautrec and a handful of others, were taken seriously as art. Brimberg's vision was different. Afraid of another George Wein reality check, he approached Quint Davis, the Festival's other producer.

"We already have a poster," said Davis, pointing to a black and pink offset print stapled to telephone poles and listing the acts appearing at the Festival. Brimberg explained that his would be a numbered, limited-edition silk-screen and showed Davis pictures of classic posters produced almost a hundred years before. Davis was unmoved until Brimberg said, "I'll pay you a percentage of gross from the first dollar I take in. You have no risk and will make money even if I fail." The two shook hands.

Brimberg engaged a Tulane architecture student to format the Festival's logo into a poster in the art nouveau style. He hired a local printer to hand-pull the edition of 1,000 prints on rice paper Brimberg bought at Dixie Art Supply. The printer, the printer's girlfriend, the designer and Brimberg worked nights and weekends for a month mixing inks and pulling prints.

Brimberg took the first precious posters to the Festival and explained to anyone who would listen what a silk-screen print was and why it was such a good deal at $3.95. He manned the booth himself with a friend. When Brimberg took a stack of 300 posters onto the riverboat for

a night concert, a drunken patron baptized them with warm beer. Brimberg rushed back to printer to print their replacements.

No art gallery wanted to handle a poster. Frame shops weren't used to carrying art inventory, and didn't want to take the risk. Souvenir shops thought the prints too pricey. Brimberg made them a risk-free consignment offer. To his surprise, when he returned after the Festival to collect prints or money, some stores reordered. Brimberg's four-month effort yielded a profit of less than $500 but an "A" in the course. Collectors now pay almost $2,000 for a copy of this first poster – when they can find one. Brimberg doesn't even have one.

The poster was never meant to be a series, but innovation and luck propelled this modest project into the most collected poster in the world and a major source of funding for the Foundation. In 1976, Brimberg, who had by then moved to San Francisco to take the California bar exam, was asked by Davis to come back and make another one. The chance to return to New Orleans and postpone getting a real job appealed to him.

To try to get revenues up and justify the risk and time involved, an artist-signed edition of numbered posters was added that year to the unsigned, numbered edition. In 1977, the unsigned edition was expanded to meet demand. By 1980, the poster had become so famous the Library

of Congress chose it as the cover of their Quarterly Journal.

Over the years the poster became a cherished part of the Festival, picturing its many aspects. For the 20th anniversary of the Festival in 1989, ProCreations honored the contributions of Antoine "Fats" Domino with the first of its Performer series. In addition to the signed and unsigned editions, 500 numbered prints were signed by Fats and the artist, Richard Thomas. In subsequent years, this evolved into some artists "remarquing" a select few prints with individually done drawings.

The 1994 edition for the 25th anniversary marked the first commission given to an internationally renowned artist, resulting in Peter Max's diptych of past and present Jazz Festival greats. Appearing on the poster since then have been Louis Armstrong, Pete Fountain, the Neville Brothers, Dr. John, Professor Longhair, Al Hirt, Wynton Marsalis, Mahalia Jackson, Harry Connick, Jr. and the inventor of New Orleans Jazz, Buddy Bolden by artists including Rodrigue, Michalopoulos, Dureau, Pavy, Rogers and Hemmerling, among others. That year also saw the Congo Square poster, which had previously been published by others, brought into the same tent. Since then, the Congo Square poster has grown into a distinguished and sought-after series in its own right; showcasing affordable, hand-crafted silk-screen editions by primarily African-American masters, whose prints usually cost thousands of dollars. Both poster series have thrived through continued innovation that engages collectors' imaginations.

Opening day of each year's Festival sees throngs of collectors sprinting for the poster tent and the poster usually selling out before the Festival's end. The editions have grown in an attempt to meet demand and to maintain the original promise of providing affordable, collectible art. Despite this, collectors quickly bid up the price of each year's poster. Within a few years of release, most posters command several

times their publication price in the secondary market. Additional collectibles have been added over the years: in 1980, PosterCards™ – 4" x 6" color postcard reproductions; in 1981, Festival-inspired Hawaiian-style HowAhYa™ Shirts; in 1998, ceramic PosterTiles™; an expanded BayouWear™ clothing line in 1999, including aprons, shorts, vests, skirts, sundresses, second line umbrellas and body wraps; and, in 2004 ceramic FabTiles™ engineered so when installed on a wall they provide a seamless expanse of the New Orleans-themed BayouWear fabric motifs. In 1998 availability of Festival collectibles went global with the introduction of art4now.com which helped reduce the opening day frenzy for those in the know.

The poster was published by ProCreations from 1975 through 1990, when the Festival Foundation experimented with other approaches. In 1994, Brimberg was asked back and created IconoGraphx, later replaced in 1998 by art4now, the current publisher. With ProCreations consulting, these companies have maintained the vision of commissioning acclaimed artists and producing museum-quality posters, ceramics and clothing. By elevating the poster to a serious art form, they made New Orleans a globally recognized center of poster art and created unique collectibles, reflecting and extending the Jazz Fest experience beyond sound, time and geography.

1976

A wave of national pride swept the U.S. during this bicentennial year. Tall ships sailed in New York harbor; and from coast to coast, regions touted their contribution to the world's best democracy. Down here on the Third Coast, as usual, New Orleans was in its own time capsule. In the City That Care Forgot, natives wove history into the everyday, and the every day was about to make its own history. The Jazz & Heritage Festival expanded to two weekends and seven evening concerts.

Jazz Fest had now become so event-packed that planning and ruthless decision-making was required on the part of listeners to choose among so many diverse musical styles. Many eagerly awaited the Jazz Fest schedules in pullout sections from Figaro or the Times-Picayune, anguishing over whether to hear The New Leviathan Oriental Foxtrot Orchestra or Southern University of New Orleans Jazz Project, or choosing between R&B legends Johnny Adams or Lee Dorsey. Friends cajoled, argued, and made deals with each other about which stages to cover. Some struck out alone. Others gave in and tagged along. After all, musical tastes might differ, but there were hardly ever any bad options.

"Meet me at the flagpole," in the center of the infield, was a popular way to reconnect, and a sure thing, just like, "Meet me under the clock" at the downtown D.H. Holmes department store. Hippies spread out selling macramé ankle bracelets, taking advantage of the common meeting place to earn a little extra money. Seasoned Festgoers now knew if you waited at the flagpole long enough, you'd run into everyone you knew, and some people you saw only once a year during Jazz Fest. But who'd want to wait around? You still generally could pick out your friends from the growing, constantly moving throng.

The Heritage Fair design breathed out. Stage 1, in acknowledgement of the ever expanding attendance, was moved to just inside the perimeter of the south end of the infield. Finally, the gospel celebrations could be heard without sound bleed. Stage 5 moved into the space of last year's Stage 6, and Stage 6 became "the Jazz Tent" and was moved back near Stage 3. Food booths dotted more area of the infield, crafts were sprinkled in a wider distribution, and the map insert in Figaro indicated a broad expanse designated for "dancing room."

The weekend concerts pulled in 20,000 music lovers. On the first weekend, fans jammed on the side-wheel riverboat the S.S. President. The Friday concert was a study in regionally homegrown genius that couldn't have happened in the 60s. Allen Toussaint, Professor Longhair, and Clarence "Gatemouth" Brown was as good a line up as

one could experience, as evidenced that while at $6.50 per ticket, the cruise sold out, scalpers were selling (and getting) $25 or more. Henry Roeland Byrd, or "Professor Longhair" had been brought back from retirement, by a coterie of young people who recognized his genius. He had all but given up music, and was working as a custodian at the One Stop Record Shop on South Rampart Street. 'Fess was invited to play the second Jazz Fest in 71, and showed up with only

Bongo Joe

one sideman: drummer Edmund Kimbro. Allison Miner recalls racing over to another stage where Snooks Eaglin was to perform, and snatching him up to go onstage with Fess. According to Miner, "When the three of them started to play, the entire Festival stopped and everyone came over to see and hear these great musicians." It was the beginning of yet another incarnation of Professor Longhair's music career.

Allen Toussaint, an avowed disciple of Professor Longhair, is one of the world's great treasures of popular music. Although

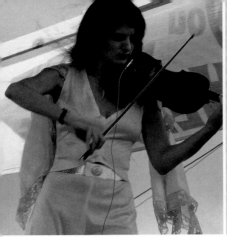

Scarlet Rivera

Toussaint never sought the limelight for himself, his genius has proved a veritable industry unto itself. Toussaint's early instrumental hits "Java" and "Whipped Cream," made famous by Al Hirt and Herb Alpert, respectively, were just the beginning. Toussaint had written hit records in every decade since the 1950s and his record producing and arrangements, especially funky with a balanced underlay of horns kept him constantly busy and paying for a signature gold Rolls Royce one could pick out on the infield from time to time. Known as the "innovator of swing guitar," Gatemouth Brown was playing violin and moving on to viola, mandolin, banjo and drums at the age of ten. He debuted in 1945 playing drums with the 18-piece Hoyt Huge Orchestra in San Antonio. After replacing an ailing T-Bone Walker at a club in Houston, Brown was discovered by Don Robey and signed to an exclusive recording contract. Although he became a major force as a jazz and jump guitar player, Brown secluded himself in the 1960s in Aztec, New Mexico, becoming a deputy sheriff, but emerging in the early 1970s to tour again zinging his newer fans with his upbeat fiddle work along with his sweet-as-barbecue guitar playing.

The Warehouse at 1820 Tchoupitoulas Street was one of the most popular rock and roll venues in the city. Fortunate indeed was the music lover who bought tickets for both Friday and Saturday's concerts. Billed as the "New Blues" concert, Albert King, Muddy Waters, Lightnin' Hopkins, Johnny Shines made a stellar line up. No other place on earth could

Charles Mingus

fest facts

Festival attendance swelled to 100,000.

The Festival offices moved from Barracks Street to 1205 Rampart Street, formerly the Old Loyalty Bar, which was once a brothel in Storyville. There were washbasins in each room, 12 towel racks in the bathroom, a hidden stairway, and an alarm.

Musician Peg Leg Sam had been making his own wooden legs for the past 40 years. He kept his harmonica in a bucket of ice water, fishing it out to embellish a tune.

Professor Longhair was now a traditional closer of the Fest.

Monk Boudreaux

boast being the summit of blues than this venue a stone's throw from the mighty Mississippi, and the evenings were classically filled with blues classics.

On Tuesday, April 13th, at the ballroom of the Royal Sonesta Hotel, Albert "Papa" French & the Original Tuxedo Jazz Band, The Preservation Hall Jazz Band, the New Orleans Ragtime Orchestra, and the Reverend Roosevelt Sykes sent hot jazz notes swirling around the chandeliers and raining back down on the dancers below. Sweet Emma was ill, and Phamous Lambert subbed for her with The Preservation Hall Jazz Band. At the Municipal

Auditorium, Harold Melvin and the Blue Notes, Bobby Blue Bland, the Max Roach Quintet, the Charlie Mingus Quintet provided an evening of smooth and popular entertainment. Harold Melvin, looking suave in full tails, performed the favorite songs "Wake Up Everybody" and "You Know How to Make Me Feel So Good." It's a mystery why this concert was not better attended, but those in the house gave Charlie Mingus a rousing standing ovation. And Bobby Blue Bland had the crowd in the palm of his hand with "I Pity the Fool" and "I'll Take Care of You." Jerry Lee Lewis was booked to play, but had to cancel due to an

Willie Tee and the Gaturs

music scene

Art, Aaron, Charles & Cyril Neville first perform together as backing group for George "Uncle Jolly" Landry and the album "Wild Tchoupitlouas."

The Meters tour as opening act for the Rolling Stones.

Beausoleil is formed by Michael Doucet.

IN MEMORIAM

Bobby Hackett, Freddie King, Howlin' Wolf, Chris Kenner, Jim Robinson, Leonard Lee, Victoria Spivey, Phil Ochs

impending surgery. A local newspaper ran Lewis' hospital room address so fans could send get-well cards. Imagine that today!

The blazing Louisiana sun beat down on the Fair Grounds, turning tourists lobster red. A spry Eubie Blake tickled his trademark tunes, raising the temperature of his adoring fans, exhorting, "You people are gonna kill me if you keep making me play that ragtime." As lagniappe he then played "Just Wild About Harry" and "Memories of You" and the 93-year old Blake was helped off the stage to a standing ovation. Rising star James Rivers pulled a cool surprise by warming up his bagpipes with a highland tune; and just as ears fell into the groove, Rivers turned to jazz, pulling notes that popped from a place only he could hear. It was an amazing trick and a terrific show. Percy Randolph, blues harmonica player, rode home after circling the Fest on his bike playing the blues on his harmonica rigged with amplifiers run off D batteries.

James Black was late for his "James Black Realization" set

when fans saw his car tearing across the field. He drove in, across the track, up on the infield to the stage 15 minutes into the set, with two police cars chasing him and sirens blaring. He had driven through a roadblock because he was late. He was arrested on the spot for speeding and outrunning the officers. Quint Davis saw the ruckus and sprung Black also on the spot, who promptly mounted his drum set and the James Black Realization was realized.

Violinist Scarlet Rivera was riding a wave of fame since her performance on *Desire*, Bob Dylan's latest album from his Rolling Thunder Revue era, still gathering critical and popular raves. Her performance on the last Sunday stole the rockers away from Gatemouth Brown

Chester Calhoun

and Asleep at the Wheel, but it's interesting to note all three featured hot violin work. Dylan's lifelong experimentation with orchestration and original musical pairings resulted in career visibility for many other musicians, and Rivera was one. During the set, Rivera's great backing band and the otherworldly rising and falling of the high wild violin sound was a perfect synch with New Orleans own dark and mysterious side.

It was the year of dueling flutes in the crafts area. Tulane faculty member Halsey Matteson, of "Termite Flutes" displayed his metallic instruments crafted from table legs and pipes, bamboo flutes, and dulcimers made from a variety of woods. Paul and Crow Johnson, from Austin, Texas, sold two-inch flutes of wood or sterling silver, made by hand, and backed up with a songbook. Bill and Rose Anne Bivens from Covington also made flutes and tambourines. All that an erstwhile Pied Piper needed was one of Miss Anne B. Lane's "Second-Line Jazz Umbrellas." She made

Max Roach
Henry Butler
Tuts Washington
Eubie Blake
New Orleans Ragtime orchestra
Jim Robinson Band
Doc Paulin Brass Band
Bill Malone & Hill Country Ramblers
Hurricane Brass Band
Los Catrachos
Lonnie Pitchford
Robert Pete Williams
Lonnie Pitchford
Peg Leg Sam
Uptown Rulers, DT & Aaron Neville
James Black NO Drum Suite
Henry Butler Group
Key West Junkanoos

NEW ORLEANS JAZZ & HERITAGE FESTIVAL
APRIL 9-18, 1976
Presented by
THE NEW ORLEANS JAZZ & HERITAGE FOUNDATION, INC.
in cooperation with the
JOS. SCHLITZ BREWING COMPANY
© New Orleans Jazz & Heritage Foundation, Inc. 1976

them for local brass bands, so they were the real deal. And at Jazz Fest, there were second lines all over the place. Even the country band Cornbread sparked a second line. One of the high-ticket items sold at the crafts tent was Marcel Anderson's jazz fountain, made from a bass horn, trumpet, clarinet, sax and two slide trombones. Adorned by copper leaves and tree trunk, the sculpture cost $5,000.

In later years, ubiquitous marketers and economic analysts would swarm all over events like Jazz Fest, with its enormous visibility and economic potential. In the early 1970s, the Festival lumbered along year-to-year, bailed out financially by Quint's father, Arthur Davis, and Festival producer George Wein if receipts were in the red. But when the sun went down on the 1976 Jazz Fest, the New Orleans Jazz & Heritage Foundation's figurative pockets were bulging. This Jazz Fest cleared a substantial profit. Festival popularity was clearly on the upswing. With the Festival profits looking like a sure thing, the Foundation Board began to talk about fixed dates for Jazz Fest. Such a plan would allow hotels, airlines and other tourist-oriented entities to more efficiently deliver audiences and swell gate receipts. In other business, the Foundation would soon begin to employ its good fortune toward local musicians, in the form of grants and awards.

James Booker

Earl King and the Rhapsodizers

1977

As The New Orleans Jazz & Heritage Festival rolled into its 8th year, it continued to grow and expand. As a matter of fact, it had expanded so much that the Festival production staff decided to add a second weekend. This decision would also spread the risk of loss of revenues due to rain. The Festival had rain insurance and its coverage guaranteed a payoff for rain cancellation as long as there was a specific minimum of moisture. A weatherman had to be stationed on hand to corroborate amounts of rain at the Fair Grounds. The cost of the policy was the same for one or two weekends. Three more days could only be better, right? Now Festival fans would have 6 days of music and food to enjoy.

New Orleanians love a good party and are famous the world over for the variety and quality of their local music and culinary expertise. Locals also love to eat. Alfred "Uganda" Roberts said that he thought the food might have something to do with the music in New Orleans.

" It makes the music better if you eat the right foods. In New Orleans, you can walk around the corner and get a nice po-boy or a good plate of red beans- maybe that's why so many of our musicians have to come back." Devotees of Professor Longhair should know that he made a point of eating grits and gravy four mornings out of five. He asked for this "old school" New Orleans breakfast all over the world and Uganda recalled that he'd just sigh when they didn't have this classic New Orleans Power Breakfast. "Well, just fry me an egg then" he'd say.

The last thing New Orleanians do before we leave New Orleans and the first thing we do when we get back is have a good meal, much like the growing throng of Jazz Fest "regulars" who were coming to eat breakfast at the Fair Grounds because they didn't want to miss a thing. By 1977, the Jazz Fest had begun to offer the New Orleans version of Lo Mein – "Yak-a-Mein" – noodles with vegetables, ground beef, salty brown broth and a hardboiled egg, halved. This was described in the newspaper as "a peculiar local night cap said to ward off hangovers after a night of hard drinking." The Yak- a Mein food booth probably did a roaring business, as the night music program offered such tasty stuff that the best Festival goers could hope for at the end of a long day was a short nap, or maybe just a shower and a change of clothes before heading back out for the start of the night concerts.

The seven night concerts, held in four locations around the city, featured some of the greatest names in jazz. Starting at 8:00 pm, the opening night evening concert on Friday April 15th presented the sublimely wonderful Ella Fitzgerald and the Tommy Flannigan Trio with Roy Eldridge. The Al Belletto Septet was featured on this bill,

Doc Watson

continuing the tradition of paring national acts with local legends, exposing artists to each other and expanding the sonic spectrum for visitors. Al Belleto, a native New Orleanian would recreate the big band sound of the excellent albums Stan Kenton produced for him. His customary rhythm section, comprised of Frank Pazzullo on piano, Vic Zepeto on drums and Rusty Gelder on bass soared beneath an exulted horn section; Chuck Easterling on the trumpet, Al Herman, trombone and Lee Hoppel on baritone sax and flute.

Tommy Flannigan had been Ms. Fitzgerald's pianist for the last twelve years or so and was joined by a wonderful backing line-up; drummer Ed Thigpen, formerly with the Oscar Peterson Trio, and by bassist Frank De La Rosa. Roy Eldridge who was an innovator of jazz trumpet in the 30's, and toured with Ella extensively in Europe in the 50's, joined her once again in New Orleans for this first night concert.

> *"In 1977, I had knee surgery and I couldn't dance around like I normally do during my show. Right before I went on the rain started coming down really hard. I was amazed, nobody moved, the people stood there in that rain. I normally sing from a set list but when I saw that I walked out on that stage and sang 'It's Raining.'"* IRMA THOMAS

The packed house had no idea that Stevie Wonder was in town until he showed up to surprise Ella at her show. Stevie was recording at Studio in the Country in Bogalusa and decided to take a ride into town. While she was out on stage singing "You Are The Sunshine Of My Life," he walked out unannounced, singing the bridge. With their arms around each other they finished the song as a duet and then received such a long, thunderous standing ovation that it felt like the roof would cave in. We've been told this was the first time these two

had performed live together. This has been cited as the best Jazz Fest memory ever by countless longtime Festival fans.

One of the all time Festival favorites, Bonnie Raitt, debuted on Saturday, April 23rd closing Stage 4. This was long before she crossed over to the huge, popular, commercial acceptance she garnered in the late Eighties and Nineties. Ms. Raitt charmed everyone with her ballsy blues guitar and her sweet soprano voice and the crowd went wild when Allen Toussaint came to sit in and play piano for a few songs. Allen and Bonnie

Olympia Brass Band

STAGE 4
2:00 Lee Dorsey
3:30 Chocolate Milk
5:00 The Meters

STAGE 5
1:30 Uganda's Drum Troupe
2:30 Balfa Freres
4:00 Robert Pete Williams
4:30 Coteau

JAZZ TENT
12:00 Royal Garden Jazz Band
1:00 The New Leviathan Oriental Foxtrot Orchestra
2:00 Ronnie Kole
2:30 Bob Greene
3:00 Ed Blackwell Group
4:00 Germaine Bazzle and The Gentlemen of Jazz
5:00 Louis Cottrell

GAZEBO A
1:30 Leigh, Joelle and Wanda
3:00 Percy Randolph & Little Freddie King
4:30 Uganda's Drum Troupe

GAZEBO B
12:30 Balfa Freres
2:00 Carl Sauceman & The Green Valley Boys
3:30 Bongo Joe

GAZEBO C
1:00 Robert Pete Williams
3:30 Gatemouth Brown
4:30 Big Joe Williams

GOSPEL
12:00 Good Hope B.C. Choir of Gretna
12:30 Voices of Revelation
1:00 Aline White
1:30 Fifth African B.C. Choir of St. Rose
2:00 Prayer Tower Church of God in Christ
2:30 Fairview B.C. Choir
3:00 Hope Ensemble
4:00 Gospel Choralettes of Kenner, La.
4:30 Gospel Inspirations, Lois Dejean
5:00 The Religious Five
5:30 New Orleans Westside Chapter Gospel Workshop Choir

SUNDAY, APRIL 17

STAGE 1
12:00 Kennedy High Band
1:00 U.S. Navy Steel Band
2:00 Percy Mayfield
3:30 Bobby Blue Bland
5:00 Jessie Hill
5:30 Professor Longhair

STAGE 2
12:00 Percy Randolph & Little Freddie King
1:30 Ironing Board Sam
3:00 Bill Malone and The Hill Country Ramblers
4:00 Hurricane Brass Band

STAGE 3
1:00 Uganda's Drum Troupe
2:30 Al Belletto
3:00 Henry Butler
4:30 Big Joe Williams

STAGE 4
1:00 U.N.O. Jazz Band
2:00 Sweet Poison with Willie West
2:30 Aaron Neville
3:00 Johnny Adams
3:30 The Wild Tchoupitoulas
4:30 Los Catrochos

were already well acquainted. Bonnie had recorded some of Toussaint's material back in 1974 when she cut "What is Success?" In 1977, New Orleans and the Jazz Fest embraced Bonnie. The weather was beautiful for her debut. With clear skies and a light breeze to keep everyone refreshed, it was a perfect ending to a lovely day. In addition to longtime musical compadre', Freebo, Bonnie was accompanied at the Festival by Will McFarland on guitar, Marty Grebb on keyboards and Dennis Whitted on drums.

Milton Batiste

Also debuting at the Jazz Festival in 1977 was child protégé Harry Connick Jr. At 9 years old this young man was already showing the talent that would later bring him major stardom, but when he hit the stage at Jazz Fest he was just one of many talented young New Orleans men and woman who had parents, uncles or cousins who played. Harry's father, District Attorney Harry Connick

Sr., was also a musician. Harry started playing when he was three years old and progressed so quickly that Connick, Sr., recognizing Harry's talent, put him under the tutelage of the legendary James Carroll Booker, the "Piano Prince" of New Orleans who joined Harry onstage.

The "Prince" came and sat next to Harry at the piano during his show and they played a tune together. There is a time honored tradition of mentoring young musicians of promise and New Orleans has gotten some really good results. Harry

Connick Jr., like so many others, is living proof. Harry's backing band on his debut was the legendary Walter Payton on bass, Andy Moses on clarinet and Freddie Kohlman on drums.

On Sunday, April 17th Eubie Blake, spry and timeless at age 94, boarded the S.S. President to offer an evening of music with the Wallace Davenport All Stars, the Zion Harmonizers, Louis Cottrell

and the Heritage Jazz band. The white-suited Blake radiated under the stage lights at the grand piano. The Zion Harmonizers are one of the longest standing and respected gospel groups in a city where there is a very strong tradition and variety of Gospel. Founded back in 1939 by the Rev. Benjamin Maxon, in 1977 the only original member was their director Sherman Washington, also the driving force behind the Gospel Tent at the Fair Grounds. Louis Cottrell, a New Orleans native brought the best of traditional jazz clarinet to the show with his six piece all star band; Waldren "Frog" Joseph on trombone, Walter Lewis on piano, Freddie Kohlman on drums, Placide Adams on bass, an Teddy Riley on trumpet.

Wallace Davenport, another native, who was gigging professionally with the Young Tuxedo Brass Band at age 13, went on to play first trumpet with the Count Basie and Lionel Hampton bands and spent eight years as the musical director of the Ray Charles band. He came home to stay in 1970 and New Orleans was thrilled to receive him. Mr. Davenport really "threw down" with the Harmonizers that night, having in recent years played a lot in church and having said in an earlier interview that he loved "to join the spirit of the choir"

Wednesday April 20th, the S.S. President featured Sonny Rollins, Charles Mingus and the Henry Butler group. Henry's group consisted of brother's Herman Jackson on drums and Randy Jackson on bass. On Friday, Natalie Cole and Willie Tee (Turbinton) were paired at

Lightnin' Hopkins

the Theatre of Performing Arts. Willie's brother Earl, who was living in New York, flew in to work with his brother's band.

The Theatre of Performing Arts treated the cognoscenti to a midnight show with the Crusaders and the James Rivers movement on Friday the 22nd. The James Rivers Movement represented the hometown trends of progressive jazz and

made a wonderful pairing with the funk-be-bop-rock of the Crusaders. Rivers started out playing clarinet at Booker T. Washington High School but had to switch to saxophone for the marching band. He ended up embracing all of the reed instruments and progressing on to flute, after hearing Rashaan Roland Kirk's interpretive style with the instrument. After seeing

James Rivers

someone playing the bagpipes on television he had to acquire that instrument too. Bagpipes were a bit tougher to master but the results of his labor were fantastic. People attending the show that night couldn't believe it when James and his band went into his jazz tinged, bagpipe rendition of "Amazing Grace".

Out at the Fair Grounds site, over 200 musical groups played over the six days of Jazz Fest.

The Festival layout was still confined within the infield, but the Fest now had ten stages presenting music, and one hundred and fifty crafts people presenting their work. Personal tents were being erected around the infield to accommodate families and friends who wanted to stay for the whole day in shady comfort like a big family picnic. Although the crowds were starting to get fairly large, folks could still move

freely around the grounds from stage to stage and even when it was "packed" in front of one of the main stages, there was still plenty of room to dance.

People brought Frisbees and a few even brought kites. Maybe it felt a little more like a family reunion than a commercial music Festival. The New Orleans Jazz & Heritage Festival was a success, but it still had that hometown feel.

"The year that Ella Fitzgerald and Stevie Wonder performed at the festival was an amazing experience. When my kids were young we'd go early in the morning and the first thing we'd do is get our soft shell crab poboy and lemonade. We would hang out with other families at the barricade behind the Fess Stage. Back then in the mornings everyone playing was local. You could go to the Fais Do-Do stage and hear a great local Cajun band and on another stage some great New Orleans blues." CHARMAINE NEVILLE

Balfa Freres

music scene

Tipitina's is opened by the SUMA24U Corporation.

Irma Thomas releases the album "Soul Queen of New Orleans."

Mardi Gras Records is started by Warren Hildebrand.

Stevie Wonder wins a Grammy for Best Album, "Songs in the Key of Life."

IN MEMORIAM

Blanche Thomas, Albert "Papa" French, Johnny Wiggs, Rahsaan Roland Kirk, Elvis Presley, Ronnie Van Vant

Alan Jaffe

GAZEBO A
12:30 Clancy "Blues Boy" Lewis
2:00 Brooklyn Boy Weiner & John Mooney
4:00 Butch Mudbone

GAZEBO B
1:00 Victor Sirker
2:00 Little Punch the Clown
3:00 Irving McLean

GAZEBO C
1:00 Louisiana Red
2:00 Deshotels Brothers
4:00 Dixie Blue

GOSPEL
1:30 Jefferson Elementary School Choir
2:15 Brother Billy Bow, The Gospel Blind Boy
3:00 God's Chosen Few
3:45 The Sensational Travelers
4:30 Gospel Seals
5:15 Second Morning Star B.C. Church Choir

SATURDAY, APRIL 23

STAGE 1
12:30 S.U.N.O. Big Band
1:30 University of Las Vegas Jazz Band
3:00 Sammy Burfect and The Polished Gentlemen
4:00 Ernie K-Doe
5:00 Los Manarchas

STAGE 2
1:30 Doc Paulin Brass Band
2:30 The Meyers Brothers
3:30 Carlos Sanchez
4:30 Bois Sec Ardoin

STAGE 3
1:00 Butch Mudbone
2:00 Walter Washington and The A.F.B.'s
3:00 James Rivers Movement
4:00 James Booker
5:30 Odetta

STAGE 4
12:00 Xavier Jazz Band
2:00 Willie Tee
3:00 The Wild Magnolias
3:30 Snooks Eaglin
4:30 Bonnie Raitt
5:30 Roosevelt Sykes

STAGE 5
12:30 Uganda's Drum Troupe
2:00 Aldus Mouton and The Wandering Aces
3:00 Key West Junkanoos
4:00 Phil Meeks and The Sundowners
5:00 Henry Gray and His Cats

JAZZ TENT
12:30 The Hall Brothers Jazz Band
1:30 Traditional Jazz Studio of Prague
2:30 Odetta Sings the Blues
3:30 Tuts Washington
4:00 The New Orleans Ragtime Orchestra
5:00 Kid Thomas and His Algiers Stompers

GAZEBO A
1:00 Andrew Jackson
2:00 Emile Guess
4:00 Victor Sirker Duo

GAZEBO B
12:00 The Meyers Brothers
2:00 Little Punch the Clown
3:30 Butch Mudbone

GAZEBO C
1:00 Guy Richards
3:00 Uganda's Drum Troupe
4:00 Irving McLean

GOSPEL
12:00 St. Luke Methodist Church
12:30 Southern Bells
1:00 True Vine Courageous Male Choir
1:30 Friendly Five
2:00 Singing Assembly of Houston, Texas
2:30 Wallace Davenport
3:00 Sister Bessie Griffin
3:30 First Church of God in Christ
4:00 Gospel Inspirations of Donaldsonville, La.
4:30 Gospel Soul Children
5:00 Mighty Chariots
5:30 St. Francis DeSales Choir

SUNDAY, APRIL 24

STAGE 1
1:00 Frogman Henry
2:00 Lightnin' Hopkins
3:00 Barbara Lynn and Heavy Traffic
4:00 Clifton Chenier
6:00 Fats Domino

STAGE 2
2:00 S.D. Courville and The Mamou Band
3:00 Olympia Brass Band
4:00 Meyers Brothers

STAGE 3
2:00 Kid Jordan
3:00 Mark Naftalan
3:30 Mike Bloomfield
4:00 Ellis Marsalis
5:00 Ruben Gonzalez – Mr. Salsa

STAGE 4
1:30 Tommy Ridgley
2:00 Irma Thomas
3:00 King Floyd
4:00 Larry Coryell
4:30 Butch Mudbone
5:00 Mike Bloomfield Blues Stars

STAGE 5
12:00 Uganda's Drum Troupe
1:00 Key West Junkanoos
2:00 Muchos Plus
3:00 Allen Fontenot and The Country Cajuns
4:30 Roosevelt Sykes

JAZZ TENT
12:30 Harry Connick, Jr.
1:30 Giorgio Gaslini
2:00 Willie Metcalf
3:00 Albert Walters & His Preservation Hall Band
4:00 James Black Concerto for Drums and Bass
4:30 Pat Fisher and Earl Turbinton
5:00 Papa French

GAZEBO A
12:30 Butch Mudbone
2:00 Louisiana Kid
3:00 Brooklyn Bob Weiner and John Mooney

GAZEBO B
12:30 Meyers Brothers
2:00 Little Punch the Clown
4:00 Emile Guess

GAZEBO C
4:00 Afro-Caribbean Jam with Irving McLean, Uganda, Muchos Plus & The Junkanoos

GOSPEL
12:00 Mt. Carmel B.C. Youth Choir

12:30 Humble Travelers
1:00 Othello Baptiste
1:30 Heavenly Stars
2:00 Greater St. Andrew B.C.
2:30 Calvacade of Gospel Stars
3:00 Zion Harmonizers
3:30 Mt. Moriah Choir No. 2
4:00 Spring Assembly, Houston, Tex.
4:30 Bessie Griffin (Special Guest)
5:00 McDonogh No. 35 High School Choir
5:30 Desire Community Chorus

NIGHT CONCERTS

FRIDAY, APRIL 15, 8 P.M.
Ella Fitzgerald and The Tommy Flanagan Trio, Roy Eldridge, Al Belleto Septet.
Municipal Auditorium

SUNDAY, APRIL 17, 8 P.M.
Eubie Blake, Wallace Davenport All Stars with The Zion Harmonizers, Louis Cottrell and The Heritage Hall Jazz Band.
S.S. President

TUESDAY, APRIL 19, 8 P.M.
Ronnie Kole, Alvin Alcorn Trio, Kid Thomas and The Preservation Hall Jazz Band.
Royal Sonesta Hotel Grand Ballroom

WEDNESDAY, APRIL 20, 8 P.M.
Sonny Rollins, Charles Mingus, Henry Butler Group.
S.S. President

THURSDAY, APRIL 21, 8 P.M.
Allen Toussaint, Irma Thomas, Clifton Chenier.
S.S. President

FRIDAY, APRIL 22, 8 P.M.
Natalie Cole, Willie Tee.
Theatre of the Performing Arts

FRIDAY, APRIL 22, 12 MIDNIGHT
The Crusaders, James Rivers Movement.
Theatre of the Performing Arts

1978

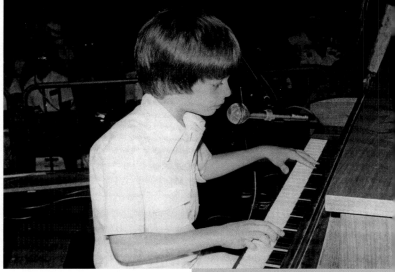

Harry Connick, Jr.

At the Fair Grounds, it looked like Jazz Fest was there to stay — at least for a while. The Fair Grounds administration continued to swap concessions revenue for rental fees in another new three-year contract, with an option for renewal in 1982-83. The Fest was surely in the money now. And the largest growth came from local attendees. The Jazz Fest grossed more than $837,000 ($133,000 at the gate) by the last Sunday. Income flowed in from food ($51,000), T-shirts ($18,605), and crafts ($21,500). The National Endowment for the Arts (before it was crippled by the right-wing culture wars in the 1990s) granted $15.000. Producing the Heritage Fair cost $301,775. The night talent had been paid $64,700 and Heritage Fair talent $111,291.

When the last snowball was slurped down and the last truckload of lumber carted away, the New Orleans Jazz & Heritage Foundation had a cash surplus of $350,000. That included $100,000 from last year. Naturally, opinions differed on how best to employ the largesse. Some board members wanted to expand the Festival. Wein, particularly influenced by Allison Miner, who had talked him into maintaining

Pinetop Perkins

the non-profit Foundation, wanted to give money back to the Louisiana community. The Foundation finally decided to make community grants totaling $25,000 to music endeavors, $25,000 in general grants, and $25,000 for African-American initiated projectsThe focus on grants to African-Americans as an ethnic exclusivity was just a warm-up. A much bigger power play was on the horizon. Most of the musicians and some craftspeople involved with Jazz Fest were African-Americans;

but still, some activist community members felt that white participants held too much decision-making power. Of the 20 Board members, only three were African-American.

The Board was challenged by a group of activists calling themselves The Afrikan American Jazz Festival Coalition. Spearheaded by Sekou Fela (aka George LaBeaud) Michael Williams, Mohammad Youngai, and Kalamu ya Salaam, and employing tactics from the early 1970s college protests, they inter-

Eubie Blake

Gatemouth Brown and Professor Longhair

rupted a Board meeting and threatened to not only boycott the Festival but also to "disrupt" it. That led to a meeting at the St. Bernard Community Center, with George Wein, Quint Davis, and Neal Koy of Miller Beer working to arrange a compromise.

The Coalition poured Miller beer on the ground to symbolically demonstrate their efficacy.

One of the sticking points for the Coalition was the perceived inequity of the crafts structure and resulting income. They accused Crafts Coordinator Patrice McMurray of discriminating against African-Americans and demanded her ouster, despite black artist Clifton Webb's involvement assisting her. The situation became so confrontational, according to accounts from the time, that Davis advised McMurray to stay in a hotel room for her own safety for a few days until things cooled off. It was an emotionally charged confrontation; but Wein was adamant that the Foundation wanted to forge an equitable relationship with the Coalition. "I kept repeating 'You can't force us do something we want to do in the first place,'" Wein said. "I've been a fighter all my life for integration." Then, as today and throughout Jazz Fest's history, an agreement was struck and the show went on. McMurray retained her position and oversaw the Contemporary Crafts area for years to come.

Consequently, the board hammered out a new crafts structure: twenty percent of the best of local crafts entries from this year would return next year, plus 20 folk craftspeople. The idea was to create a "bazaar" area with no emphasis on race, or the quality of goods sold. It was called "Crafts City." The rationale was to make available goods that were less expensive than the handcrafted items juried into the crafts area. This compromise would be considered a more equitable solution according to some, but others complained that now mass-manufactured crafts with no actual connection to African-Americans were cluttering up the Fest. That argument would circulate without resolution for the life of the Festival.

In Foundation Board meetings, there were other problems and solutions, too. One member asked for more "quality real jazz musicians" and less emphasis on popular music. Marian Kelly came up with the idea to stage a parking area at the Superdome, and shuttle people to the fest.

If one were fortunate enough to attend the entire schedule of the seven night concerts in 1978, one would be possessed of a listening spectrum of the

Robert "Pete" Williams

4:00 Les Vagabonds
5:00 Caledonia Society (Scottish Dancing)

STAGE 3
12:30 Red Beans & Rice Revue
1:30 Key West Junkanoos
2:30 Bois Sec Ardoin
3:30 Earl King
4:30 Tabby Thomas & the Mighty House Rockers

STAGE 4
1:00 Xavier University Jazz Band
2:00 Scooter Lee
3:00 Lee Dorsey
4:30 Doug Kershaw

PERFORMANCE TENT
1:00 Doc Watson
2:00 Scooter Lee
2:50 N.O. Square and Round Dance Association
3:30 Mardi Gras Indians
4:15 Tuxedo Brass Band
5:00 U.S. Navy Steel Drum Band

JAZZ TENT
12:30 Bob French & the Original Tuxedo Brass Band
1:30 Don Ewell
2:30 Al Belletto Quartet
3:30 Alvin Alcorn
4:30 Kid Jordan
5:30 Ernie Cagnolatti

GAZEBO A
12:30 Michael Eisele, Mr. Concertina
2:00 Butch Mudbone
3:00 Dixie Blue
4:00 Percy Randolph & Little Freddie King

GAZEBO B
2:00 Guy Richards
3:00 Kissko-Pop Mime Troupe
4:30 Michael Eisele, Mr. Concertina

GAZEBO C
12:00 Percy Randolph & Little Freddie King
1:00 Kissko-Pop Mime Troupe
3:00 Uganda
4:00 Butch Mudbone
5:00 Clancy "Blues Boy" Lewis

GOSPEL TENT
12:00 Good Hope Baptist Church Choir of Gretna
12:30 Voices of Revelation
1:00 Mighty Gospel Entertainers
1:30 Prayer Tower Church of God in Christ
2:00 Zion Harmonizers
2:30 Greater St. Stephen Baptist Church Choir
3:00 Hope Ensemble
3:30 Macedonia Church of God in Christ
4:00 Gospel Choralettes of Metairie
4:30 Mt. Kingdom Baptist Church Choir
5:00 Religious Five
5:30 Gospel Inspirations

SUNDAY, APRIL 9

STAGE 1
1:00 Barbara Lynn
2:30 Chocolate Milk
4:00 Roomful of Blues
5:00 Rockin' Dopsie & The Twisters

STAGE 2
12:00 June Gardner
1:00 Meyers Brothers
2:30 Troy I. De. And the Country Kings

evolution of jazz. As presumptuous as that may sound, just think about this lineup: The Steamboat Stomp on the S.S. Admiral brought together the Grammy-nominated singer/songwriter Allen Toussaint with New Orleans' favorite girl group the Dixi-Kups (the first year with that "K") and the newly formed Neville Brothers Band. Toussaint had reeled off a string of hit songs for such popular singers as Lee Dorsey, Aaron Neville, Dr. John, and the Meters. Furthermore, does anyone believe that Ernie K-Doe could become the titular "Emperor of the Universe" without the hit song, "Mother-in-Law"? The Dixi Kups had hit big with their 1964 "Chapel of Love," beating out a Beatles song on the charts; and their follow up "Iko-Iko" is still standard airplay on WWOZ radio in New Orleans. The Neville Brothers had come together

sound, accented by his signature piano coloratura style, has wowed audiences and provided top-flight backup for vocalists such as Frank Sinatra and Ella Fitzgerald. The Basie Band's latest album, "Prime Time," snared a Grammy for Best Jazz Performance by a Big Band in this same year. Joe "Every Day I Have to Tell the Blues" Williams was on the Basie ticket. They reunited to make the magic conjured earlier on their "Count Basie Swings, Joe Williams Sings" record, which became Basie's best selling album. Also on that bill was New Orleans favorite Germaine Bazzle with her Gentlemen of Jazz, who were Alvin Tyler, Eddie Collins, Herb Taylor, and Clyde Toval. Revisiting the salad days of ragtime and jazz in "Raggin' and Jazzin'", audiences could listen back over half a century to hear Eubie Blake, still spry at 96, play ragtime. Blake had actually retired in

he delighted audiences whether it was in the sweltering heat on Stage 2 or in the posh Mardi Gras Ballroom at the Marriott. On the bill with Blake were Kid Thomas Valentine and his Preservation Hall Jazz Band, the New Orleans Ragtime Orchestra, and the New Leviathan

"Robert Pete Williams saw me watching his hands and he slowed down so I could see how he did it. We could get close enough to the stage then: drive in a truck full of friends and beer. Musicians were willing to share and a lot of teaching went on." GEORGE DORKO

from each of their various other bands, and would, in a few years, become ambassadors for New Orleans funk and rock and roll, and carry their message the world over.

Bill "Count" Basie introduced the "jump rhythm" in "One O'Clock Jump" at the Roseland Ballroom in New York in the 1930s. His big band

1946, after playing vaudeville and bringing some of the first African-American performances to Broadway with hits such as "I'm Just Wild About Harry" and "Memories of You." Blake had dropped out of school at 16 to play music, so after retiring; he reconsidered and went back to school to learn composition. This was his third Jazz Fest and

Oriental Foxtrot Orchestra.

Different interpretations of ragtime music often divide along lines of the more structured St. Louis style; and the hell-bent-for-glory exuberance of New Orleans players. The New Orleans Ragtime Orchestra came together in 1967 when pianist Lars Edegran discovered a number of forgotten rags in the Hogan Jazz

Jimmy's Club on Willow Street opens it doors.

The Neville Brothers release their first album self-titled "The Neville Brothers."

Dr. John releases "City Lights."

Mahalia Jackson is inducted into the Gospel Hall of Fame

The Radiators and Astral Project form.

"Always For Pleasure," a film by Les Blank with Professor Longhair, Wild Tchoupitoulas, Black Eagles Mardi Gras Indians and more.

IN MEMORIAM

Louis Cottrell, Jr., Louis Prima, Maybelle Carter

Archive at Tulane University, and put together a band with the expertise to perform these songs. The band expanded its repertoire and brought seemingly lost pieces to Jazz Fest aficionados. On that same evening, the New Leviathan Oriental Foxtrot Orchestra contributed a unique slice of musical history to jazz lovers. Concentrating on music and arrangements that predate swing, the New Leviathan evolved from the concept of vaudeville pit bands or orchestras. Last year, their quirky novelty material and authentic renderings of historic "oriental fox-trots" won the band an appearance on "Saturday Night Live." The New Leviathan was a favorite for dancers.

Traditional jazz opened up the following week on Tuesday, when the "Tribute to Louis Armstrong" brought together The New York Jazz Repertory Company, plus Wallace Davenport and his All Star New Orleans Jazz Band. Jon Newlin, one of the most elocutionary music writers in New Orleans, said this of Louis Armstrong in the 1978 New Orleans Jazz & Heritage Festival Official Program: "Trumpet virtuoso and innovator, good-will ambassador, jester whose mockery (like that of Fats Waller) reduced to a shambles and simultaneously elevated the sentimental songwriting conventions of his golden period, self proclaimed inventor of scat singing, dapper displayer of sartorial syncopation, champion ballroom dancer, big band and small combo leader nonpareil, fountainhead of American jazz – Louis Armstrong is, like a handful of

Muddy Waters

3:30 James Black Ensemble
4:30 Oliver Morgan, Jessie Hill, Jean Knight

STAGE 3
12:30 Key West Junkanoos
1:30 Black Eagles
2:30 Lightnin' Hopkins
3:30 Louisiana Aces
4:30 Los Catrachos

STAGE 4
12:00 U.S. Navy Steel Drum Band
1:30 Dixi-Kups
3:00 Bobby Blue Bland
4:00 Olympia Brass Band
5:00 Professor Longhair

PERFORMANCE TENT
12:00 Majestic Brass Band
1:00 Furry Lewis
2:00 Roosevelt Sykes
3:00 Valarian's Voices
4:00 Wild Magnolias
5:00 Whispering Smith & The Jukehouse Raiders

JAZZ TENT
12:00 Sam Alcorn
1:00 Bob Greene
2:00 Wolverine Orchestra
3:00 Don Albert
4:00 Ronnie Kole
5:00 All Belletto Big Band

GAZEBO A
1:30 Emile Guess
3:00 Butch Mudbone
4:00 Meyers Brothers
5:00 Clancy "Blues Boy" Lewis

GAZEBO B
1:00 Percy Randolph & Little Freddie King
1:00 The Remoulade Quartet
3:30 Emile Guess

GAZEBO C
1:00 Kissko-Pop Mime Troupe
2:00 Uganda
3:30 Furry Lewis

GOSPEL TENT
12:00 Sensational Travelers
12:30 Mt. Carmel Baptist Church Choir
1:00 Gospel Tones
1:30 Friendly Five
2:00 Pentecost Youth Choir
2:30 Notes of Harmony
3:00 Ott Family
3:30 McDermott Singers
4:00 True Vine Male Chorus
4:30 St. Francis DeSales Church Choir
5:00 Gospel Cavaliers
5:30 Mt. Moriah Baptist Church

SATURDAY APRIL 15

STAGE 1
12:30 Copas Brothers
1:30 Exuma
3:00 The New Dave Brubeck Quartet
4:00 Odetta
5:00 Henry Gray & His Cats

STAGE 2
12:00 The Bluegrass All-Stars
1:00 Arthur Bleiken's Jazz Band with Beryl Bryden
2:00 Aldus Mouton & The Wandering Aces
3:00 Tommy Yetta
4:00 Louisiana Red
5:00 Irving McLean

other great artists, all things to all people." That evening's concert was a treasure trove of Satchmo souvenirs, including film clips, recordings such as the Hot Five's "Heebie Jeebies" and Armstrong classics performed by the New York Repertory Jazz Company. Lending his own sweet notes to the tribute was Wallace Davenport (who also played with the Zion Harmonizers and the Mount Moriah Youth Choir). Davenport was a prodigy who as a young man played with the Tuxedo Brass Band.

By Thursday night, the music had evolved into the 1950s and 1960s, and the S.S. Admiral sailed with a cargo of jazz hounds eager to hear newer influences. They got what they came for with the New Dave Brubeck Quartet, MyCoy Tyner, Patrice Fisher and Jimmy Robinson. Brubeck had actually appeared at one of the forerunners of the first Jazz Fest in the late 1960s, and was back this time in a new configuration with his sons Chris, Dan, and Darius. New Orleanians Patrice Fisher and Jimmy Robinson (on loan from Woodenhead)

contributed their own innovations to an evening with older jazz stars. Unusually, Fisher had adapted the harp as a jazz instrument, and Robinson performed on acoustic and electric guitar.

When the S.S. Admiral left port on Friday night, she was holding a boat full of blues. On board were B.B. King, Muddy Waters, Roosevelt Sykes and 2000 fans. A packed riverboat audience thrilled to "The Thrill is Gone," "Got My Mojo Working" and "Hootchie Cootchie Man." Two local jazz greats went stage to stage with the popular

Grover Washington, Jr. and Hubert Laws. The James Black Ensemble and Alvin Batiste. Backing Black were Jim Singleton on bass, David Torkanowsky on keyboards, Roger Lewis on baritone sax, Earl Turbinton on alto reeds, Tony Dagradi on tenor, and singer Mary Bonnette. "We're just trying to give people a little altitude," Black said. Batiste was soon to become one of the shaping forces in the University of New Orleans Jazz Studies program, along with Ellis Marsalis. But that was still a few years away.

"It was raining, and I wanted to leave and go out with my friends but Quint said 'Just try setting up.' So we set up and started playing "I Can See Clearly Now the Rain is Gone" and the clouds parted, the sun shone, and people were jumping up and down in the mud cheering. Both Channel 6 and 4 television stations opened the 6 o'clock news with that scene." ELUARD BURT

Johnny Adams

Lee Dorsey

STAGE 3
12:00 New Orleans Contemporary Dance Company
1:00 The Electric All Girl Band (AGB's)
2:00 Willie Tee
3:00 James Booker
4:00 Golden Eagles
5:00 Little Sonny & The Lastie Brothers

STAGE 4
12:30 SUNO Big Band
1:30 Queen Ida & Her Bon Ton Band
2:30 Sammy Berfect & Johnny Adams with The Polished Gentlemen
4:00 B.B. King
5:00 Ruben "Mr. Salsa" Gonzalez

PERFORMANCE TENT
12:30 Tuts Washington
1:30 Odetta
2:30 Sunnyland Slim
3:30 Balfa Freres
4:30 Musicians for Music

JAZZ TENT
12:00 Louis Nelson Big Four
1:00 Johnny Vidacovich Trio
2:00 Germaine Bazzle & The Gentlemen of Jazz
3:00 Ellis Marsalis
4:00 New Orleans Ragtime Orchestra
5:00 Onward Brass Band

GAZEBO A
1:00 Balfa Freres
2:00 Robert Pete Williams
4:00 Bluegrass All Stars

GAZEBO B
1:30 Louisiana Red
3:00 Jokers Wild
5:00 Robert Pete Williams

GAZEBO C
1:00 Bongo Joe
3:00 Irving McLean
4:00 Exuma

GOSPEL TENT
12:00 Masonic Kings
12:30 Gospel Chords
1:00 St. Luke Methodist Church Choir
1:30 Macedonia Male Chorus
2:00 Gospel Inspirations of Donaldsonville
2:30 Wallace Davenport
3:00 First Baptist Church Choir of Paradis
3:30 The Chapman Singers
4:00 Julia Doyle Bass
4:30 First Church of God in Christ
5:00 Thibodeaux Female Community Chorus
5:30 Gospel Soul Children

SUNDAY APRIL 16

STAGE 1
1:00 Frogman Henry
2:00 James Rivers
3:00 Irma Thomas
4:00 Ironing Board Sam
4:30 The Neville Brothers
5:30 The Wild Tchoupitoulas

STAGE 2
12:30 Robert Pete Williams
2:00 Exuma
3:00 Marc Naftalin
3:30 Irving McLean
4:00 Tim Williams & The Good Time Country Band
5:00 Snookum Russell

STAGE 3
12:30 Doc Paulin Brass Band
1:30 Henry Butler & Lady BJ
2:30 Russ Russell & The Rustlers
3:30 Louisiana Red
4:00 Allen Fontenot & The Country Cajuns
5:00 Odetta

STAGE 4
1:00 Clarence Gatemouth Brown
2:00 Roosevelt Sykes
3:00 Muchos Plus

4:00 Muddy Waters
5:00 Clifton Chenier & His Red Hot Louisiana Band

PERFORMANCE TENT
1:00 Odetta
2:00 Dennis McGee & Sady Courville
3:00 Sunnyland Slim
4:00 Shree Sun Rays
5:00 Hurricane Brass Band

JAZZ TENT
12:30 Louis Cottrell's Heritage Hall Jazz Band
1:30 Harry Connick, Jr.
2:00 Southern University at Baton Rouge Jazz Band
3:00 Alvin Batiste
4:00 Wallace Davenport
5:00 Kid Thomas & His Preservation Hall Jazz Band

GAZEBO A
12:00 Art Ryder's Electric Brass Band
1:30 Golden Sioux
3:00 Robert Pete Williams
4:30 Dennis McGee & Sady Courville

GAZEBO B
1:00 Louisiana Red
3:00 Young, Gifted & Black

GAZEBO C
1:00 Bongo Joe
2:00 George Dorko
3:00 Irving McLean
4:30 Exuma

GOSPEL TENT
12:00 Golden Chains Jubilee
12:30 Charles Singleton
1:00 Heavenly Stars
1:30 Southern Bells
2:00 Clementine Emery
2:30 Singing Assemblies of Houston
3:00 Gospel Inspirations
3:30 Calvacade of Gospel Stars
4:00 Greater St. Andrew Baptist Church
4:30 Desire Community Chorus
5:00 Gospellettes of Houston
5:30 Gospel Soul Children

NIGHT CONCERTS

FRIDAY, APRIL 7, 8 P.M.
Steamboat Stomp
Allen Toussaint, Dixi-Kups & The Neville Brothers
S.S. Admiral

SUNDAY, APRIL 9, 8 P.M.
Count Basie & His Orchestra with Joe Williams
Germaine Bazzle & The Gentlemen of Jazz
S.S. Admiral

TUESDAY, APRIL 11, 9 P.M.
A Tribute to Louis Armstrong
New York Repertory Company
Wallace Davenport & His All Star New Orleans Jazz Band
Mardi Gras Ballroom – Marriott Hotel

WEDNESDAY, APRIL 12, 8 P.M.
Raggin' & Jazzin'
Eubie Blake
Kid Thomas & His Preservation Hall Jazz Band
The New Orleans Ragtime Orchestra
New Leviathan Oriental Foxtrot Orchestra
Mardi Gras Ballroom – Marriott Hotel

THURSDAY, APRIL 13, 9 P.M.
The New Dave Brubeck Quartet
McCoy Tyner Patrice Fisher & Jimmy Robinson
S.S. Admiral

FRIDAY, APRIL 14, 8 P.M.
Blues On the River
B.B. King, Muddy Waters, Roosevelt Sykes
S.S. Admiral

SATURDAY, APRIL 15, 9 P.M.
Grover Washington
James Black Ensemble
Alvin Batiste
Municipal Auditorium

Joseph Adams and Olympia Brass Band

1979

The 10th Anniversary of the New Orleans Jazz & Heritage Festival saw "the world's biggest block party" grow one thousand fold from its beginnings in Congo Square. The official 1979 Jazz Fest program boasted that the Fest "had the potential to become the largest American music Festival in history," estimating attendance of 300,000. Producers George Wein and Quint Davis had ambitious plans: adding a third weekend of music to the usual two, and evening concerts by luminaries such as Ella Fitzgerald, Eubie Blake, Lionel Hampton, and The Dizzy Gillespie Quintet. The budget was $1million in a year when leisure suits cost $7 and McKenzie's Bakery lemon meringue pies were a mere $1.54.

In a move that would seem surprising today but seemed to make sense in light of the extended fair schedule, Jazz Fest producers limited the number of tickets for sale. "We have become concerned that crowds of the last Sunday of each year's Fair have become too large for people to really enjoy themselves," said Anna Zimmerman, Public Relations Manager for Jazz Fest. She also gave local reporters priority for press passes.

what's going on?

GLOBALLY

Shah of Iran is forced into exile and is replaced as Iranian leader by Ayatollah Khomeini, who heads Islamic fundamentalist government.

Earl Mountbatten of Burma, cousin of Queen Elizabeth II of England; is murdered in continuing I.R.A. bombing campaign.

NATIONALLY

Nuclear disaster is narrowly averted at Three Mile Island, Pennsylvania; reactor building is badly contaminated and 100,000 people are evacuated.

Department of Energy sues nine large U.S. oil companies for allegedly overcharging customers nearly $1 billion since 1973.

U.S. suspends Iranian oil imports and Iranian assets in the U.S. in retaliation for the holding of 50 U.S. hostages in Teheran.

First gay rights march in Washington, DC

LOCALLY

Local personality Jerry Falwell establishes national religious conservative organization the "Moral Majority."

A police strike by the New Orleans Policemen forces the cancellation of 13 Mardi Gras parades.

Crescent City Classic is run for the first time with 912 participants.

CULTURALLY

Gasoline sales on odd-or-even days are instituted in many states, including Louisiana.

Ku Klux Klan stages a 50-mile "white rights" march from Selma to Montgomery, Alabama.

Karen Silkwood is posthumously awarded $10,500,000 damages for negligent exposure to atomic contamination.

If disco's glittery fashion and Saturday Night Fever battled with punk energy and new wave intellectualism up north, Festivalgoers in halter tops and hot pants, dashikis and denim strolled, ate, report "The music was covered by a tent, so there wasn't a single guitarist electrocuted during intermittent rain at Saturday's Jazz & Heritage Festival." But it rained down in sluicing tor-

> *"I finished playing with (James) Booker and John Lee Hooker's drummer wasn't there for some reason and someone came and asked me, 'Look, do you want to stay and play another gig?' I'm like sure; I'm nineteen years old, of course! So I played with Hooker after that."*
>
> BUNCHY JOHNSON

danced and sang along to music for seven hours a day on eleven stages scattered over the infield of the New Orleans Fair Grounds. They danced to the wild zydeco beat and the lilting Cajun waltz, hopped and gyrated to mambo, samba, and Caribbean rhythms, head-bobbed to blues and folk, raised their hands high in praise of gospel voices, and danced the dance that defies description – so natural in New Orleans – to the honk and squawk of traditional jazz.

Rain on the first weekend prompted the Times-Picayune to

rents that swelled puddles and soaked tents and food booths, and when it was over, nearly 100 shoes were found buried in the muck. The first Sunday's activities were rained out entirely, and that combined with uncharacteristically low turnout for the evening performances resulted in lost revenues of $75,000. The windfall from 1978 covered the debt, but that must have been a wake-up call to Board members planning to use last year's surplus to expand the fest. Of the 300,000 projected fest-goers over three weekends, only half

Sun Ra

Tuxedo Brass Band and Nicholas Payton

that number showed. That figure equaled the 1978 attendance over the usual two weekends.

Four Main Stages, a Jazz Tent, Performance Tent, and two smaller stages (Gazebo A and Gazebo B) showcased an astonishing variety of traditional and progressive music including jazz, brass bands and marching clubs and societies, Afro and Caribbean, blues, folk, rhythm and blues, Cajun, Latin, zydeco, college and high school bands, and gospel. The Fair Grounds setup shifted to set aside and highlight the "diversity" that the organizers believed was already there.

Ellyna Tatum

After last year's struggle between African-American activists and the administration, a new program was created. Koindu (coin-doo), a West African word meaning "a place of sharing" was a designated area of five tents with banners in a horseshoe configuration, creating twenty 10 ft. X 10 ft. crafts booth spaces renting for $100 each, plus four booths of African diaspora derivative orientation given free at the discretion of the Koindu coordinator. Last year's "Crafts City" came under these auspices. Koindu was incorporated as a tax-exempt nonprofit organization, organized for educational purposes and copyrighted. The staff and legal counsel had a budget of $4,000. Koindu (later renamed the Congo Square Stage) reinforced the meaning of the African experience in the world as much as in the evolution of American music. Thus it became a "Festival inside of

a Festival," with its own music stage and African-American stage manager and crafts/heritage presentations. Marian Kelly Murphy around this time became the first African-American Board president, and several African-American community leaders were welcomed onto the Foundation board, which mission it was to insure the future of the Festival and doled out its profits to the neighborhoods and creative community. Bill Rouselle, Tom Dent, Emilio "Monk" Dupree and Reverend Herman Brown joined the board and contributed to the Koindu concept. But while it was a perceptual success, and contributed to scores of hippies appreciating the wisdom of the design of the African sun hat, it did little to energize the African-American community into greater attendance.

With attendance limited, the Festival was a pleasure to enjoy when it wasn't wet. Spread the length of the Fair Grounds infield, it was a leisurely stroll of music stages, a children's area, a first aid area, concessions booths

selling T-shirts, posters, programs and albums, and the crafts tents. Festgoers dragged ice chests in little red wagons to their favorite shady spot, or just wandered among the stages and tents, frequently dropping heads together to consult a program and pick the next band to see. There was enough room to stake out sun tents, lay on blankets, and slather suntan lotion. These rituals would later be believed to get out of hand and be controlled by one limitation after another. The racetrack grandstands provided a welcome respite from the hot sun, and fest goers who retreated to their shade a bit too much could still catch music from the Fest by purchasing the Festival Album for $6. Flying Fish Records produced

The Neville Brothers

3:30 Jerry Lee Lewis
5:00 L'il Queenie and The Percolators

STAGE 2
1:30 NOCCA Jazz Ensemble
2:15 Scooter Lee Show with Midnight Express
2:45 Barroom Buzzards
3:45 Tony Bazley
4:45 Little Sonny and Lastie Bros

STAGE 3
12:00 Oliver "Who Shot the La La" Morgan
12:30 Jean Knight
1:00 Jessie Hill
2:00 Electric AGB
3:15 Lawtell Playboys
4:15 Whispering Smith & The Jukehouse Rockers
5:15 Archer Dunn Sextet

STAGE 4
12:00 Deacon John
1:00 The Radiators
2:00 Pearls
3:00 Earl King
4:00 Dixi Kups
5:15 Fabulous Thunderbirds

JAZZ TENT
11:45 Tulane University Jazz Band
1:15 Murphy Campo
2:15 Snookum Russell
3:15 Willie Metcalf Quintet
4:15 John Vidakovich Trio
5:15 Kent Jordan Ensemble

GOSPEL TENT
12:00 Holy Faith Youth Choir
12:30 Prayer Tower Church of God in Christ
1:00 Rocks of Harmony
1:30 Macedonia Church of God in Christ
2:00 Hope Ensemble
2:30 Greater St. Stephen
3:00 Holy Ghost Gospeleers
3:30 Gospel Choralettes of Kenner
4:00 Present Truth
4:30 Good hope Baptist church, Gretna
5:00 Zion Harmonizers
5:30 The Youth Inspirationals

PERFORMANCE TENT
11:45 Immaculata Guitar Group
12:45 U.S. Navy Steel Drum Band
2:00 New Orleans Round & Square Dance Association
3:15 Billy Gregory

KOINDU STAGE
12:15 Ethiopian Poets
12:30 Key West Junkanoos
1:15 Freeman Fontenot
2:15 Mandingo Griot Society
3:45 Big Joe Williams
4:30 Mandingo Griot Society
5:15 Brian C. Parris and Progressive Steel Co.

GAZEBO A
12:30 Majestic Brass Band
1:45 Voodoo Macumba
2:45 Golden Sioux
4:30 Meyers Brothers

GAZEBO B
11:45 Percy Randolph & Little Freddie King
1:30 Big Joe Williams
3:00 Flora Molton
4:30 Freeman Fontenot

CHILDREN'S AREA
12:00 McDonough 15 Elementary School Band
1:00 Evelia Boudreaux, storyteller

10th ANNIVERSARY

NEW ORLEANS JAZZ AND HERITAGE FESTIVAL

APRIL 20-MAY 6, 1979

Schlitz

Guide/Schedule
photo by Michael P. Smith

6,000 albums for $1 apiece.

Jazz Fest meant warm weather – hot weather really, but under the oak tree near the entrance crowds still gathered round Danny Kimball's horseshoeing (the smell of his charcoal brazier often the welcoming first smell of Jazz Fest for repeat attendees) and to marvel at Monk Boudreaux's beading demonstrations of his next year's Mardi Gras Indian costume. Louisiana craftspeople embodied the art of the practical, such as Clence Ancelet, who fashioned rope from twisted cow tails,

and Abner Ortego, who crafted his first violin as a boy with mahogany from a wrecked ship.

Belying the huge popularity among all faiths and races of the Gospel Tent, Sunday's evening sun set on the "First Annual Gospel Boatride" on the S.S. President with the Dixie Hummingbirds, Dorothy Love Coates and her Singers, The Violinaires, the Zion Harmonizers, and the Youth Inspirational Choir. Dorothy Love Coates treated the audience to her signature "shamanistic high stepping, running, skipping, and twirling."

One music lover/reporter recalls Pete Seeger's first appearance at the Fest: "I wangled an interview and took him to Chez Helene for lunch, where he wolfed down three helpings of beet salad." In another year, Seeger's gig was on his birthday. The stage announcer told some of the audience beforehand, and when Seeger walked out, he led us in singing 'Happy Birthday.' We all cried." The Jazz Fest brought together traditional jazz

musicians reared on fish fries and speakeasies with newcomers exploring contemporary sounds with international musicians in a part-party, part-music swap fest. Musicians played at the Fair Grounds by day and moved into the clubs all night long, surprising locals and tourists with guest appearances. They dropped in on each other's sets and traded sidemen in the elusive search for a new sound with an old sound: a sound that came from somewhere that had never been heard before.

The next evening, as if it were possible, brought an equally energy-charged "Blues Boat Boogie" to the *S.S. President.* Bobby "Blue" Bland, Etta James

Etta James

and the EJ Foundation, Professor Longhair, and the Buddy Guy Blues Band with Junior Wells. That riverboat rocked with "Stormy Monday," "Turn On Your Love Light", and "Tell Mama." It was the height of Fess's popularity, as he held his own with everybody and his fans were treated to some of the best virtuoso double-handed piano playing he had ever done. The blues fans wandered all over the boat, catching a breeze off the river on the upper deck, or gaining respite from the stifling inside heat – was that from Buddy's guitar? – gazing from the stern at the lights of New Orleans on the surface of the Mississippi or stealing a kiss in the dark on the stairs.

Ella Fitzgerald's concert at the Theatre for the Performing Arts was to be broadcast live over National Public Radio, a first for the Jazz Fest. According to reports, the Foundation came up financially short for Ella's $19,000 fee, not including the $9,000 for the 85-piece orchestra to rehearse and perform. They had already distributed $75,000 in grants to the community. The Foundation staged a fundraiser, selling box seats for $75, orchestra seats for $50, seats on the parquet $25, and balcony seats for $15, hoping to make $30,000.

The ballroom presented a true legends night, "Raggin' and Jazzin'" with Eubie Blake, Earl "Fatha" Hines, Danny Barker and his Jazz Hounds with Blue Lu Barker in a program of "Cat House Music," and "An Evening at the Lyric Theatre" with the cast of "One Mo Time." Joanne Clevenger, now proprietress of Upperline restaurant, was the costume designer for "One Mo Time," and had traveled all over the globe with the show, designing costumes for as many as five companies at once. The S.S. President sailed under the stars in The Lionel Hampton All Star Big Band, and Ellis Marsalis Quartet Plus 2 on Thursday. The Dizzy Gillespie Quartet, Sun Ra and the Myth-Science Arkestra, Olatunji and His World African Orchestra delivered an otherworldly experience on Friday on the S.S. President. Olatunji's powerful shamanic drumming called forth the spirit of his ancestors and probably made them dance, too. Sun Ra left no doubt that he was

Pete Seeger

3:00 Theatre New Orleans "So Dis is New Orleans! Think It'll Float?"

SUNDAY, APRIL 22

STAGE 1
11:45 Southeastern Univ. Jazz Ensemble
12:45 Cache, with Ruben Gonzales
1:45 Lightnin' Hopkins
2:45 Marcia Ball
4:00 Flying Burrito Brothers

STAGE 2
12:00 Ngoma
1:15 Sady Courville & The Mamou Hour Band
2:15 Grassfire with Pat Flory
3:30 Ironing Board Sam
4:45 Tommy Yetta New Orleans Jazz Band

STAGE 3
12:00 Dillard Univ. Jazz Ensemble
1:30 Mucho Plus
2:45 Cornbread
4:00 Henry Grey and His Cats Tornado Brass Band

STAGE 4
12:00 Sammy Burfect and Johnny Adams
1:15 Tommy Ridgeley & The Untouchables with Bobby Mitchell
2:00 Robert Parker and Ernie K-Doe
3:00 Luther Kent and Trick Bag
4:14 Chocolate Milk Professor Longhair

JAZZ TENT
12:00 Southern Univ. at Baton Rouge Jazz Ensemble
1:30 Christiana Jazz Band
2:30 Andy Moses
3:45 Hurricane Brass Band
4:30 Mandingo Griots
5:30 Improvisational Arts Quartet with Kidd Jordan

GOSPEL TENT
12:00 Golden Chain Jubilees
12:30 Free Mission Baptist Church Choir
1:00 Southern Bells
1:30 Heavenly Stars
2:00 Christine Myles
2:30 Modern Gospel Quartet
3:00 The Heralds of Christ
3:30 The Ott Family
4:00 The Humble Travelers
4:30 New Genesis Baptist Church
5:00 Greater St. Andrew Church Choir
5:30 Desire Community Chorus

PERFORMANCE TENT
12:15 Andrew Hall's Society Jazz Band
1:30 U.S. Navy Steel Drum Band
2:30 Big Joe Williams
3:30 Edward Frank

KOINDU STAGE
12:15 Mandingo Griot Society
1:15 Voodoo Macumba
2:15 Key West Junkanoos
3:30 Nongowa African Dance Troupe
4:45 Golden Eagles

GAZEBO A
12:00 Evelia Boudreaux, Storyteller
12:30 Big Joe Williams
1:45 Percy Randolph & Little Freddie King
3:30 Sady Courville & The Mamou Hour Band
4:45 Flora Molton

an interplanetary emissary sent to deliver tonal cacophonous razzle-dazzle to Earthlings. Mission accomplished – the audience was spinning in orbit.

The international visitors were serious and educated jazz lovers, and many had listened with fanatical devotion to Louisiana musicians' recordings. Many

wonderful friendships, some of them to be lifelong, were formed at Jazz Fest. One such meeting took place on the Esplanade bus on the way to the Fest. Sascha Borenstein and Leslie Blackshear Smith were asked for directions by two young men from Germany. Of course, they didn't really need directions

– they were on the bus headed directly to Jazz Fest. But the young men were blues enthusiasts and all were soon engaged in lively conversation. One of the visitors has returned every year for Jazz Fest, and Sascha has visited him in Germany. They have become friends for life.

Although Jazz Fest had

Lionel Hampton

GAZEBO B
12:00 Flora Molton
1:45 Guy Richards
4:30 George Dorko

CHILDREN'S AREA
1:00 Youth Ensemble for Christ
2:00 Evilia Boudreaux
3:00 Calliope Puppet Theatre
**Victor Sirker and The Circuit
     Breakers,
     Rocking Dopsie and The
     Twisters

SATURDAY, APRIL 28

STAGE 1
11:45 University of New Orleans Jazz
     Band
1:30 Gatemouth Brown
2:45 Buddy Guy Blues Band with
     Junior Wells
4:00 Etta James
5:15 Clifton Chenier & His Red Hot
     Louisiana Band

STAGE 2
11:30 Kennedy High School Jazz Band
12:30 The Adolescents
1:45 Canal Street Jazz Band
3:00 Tim Williams and The Band of
     Gold

4:30 Mark Naftalin
5:15 Teddy Riley

STAGE 3
12:00 Sources
1:00 Louis Cottrell's New Orleans
     Jazz Band
1:45 Mark Naftalin
2:30 D.L. Menard and The Louisiana
     Aces
3:45 Exuma
4:45 Tuxedo Brass Band

STAGE 4
12:00 Xavier University Jazz Lab Band
1:30 Bobby McLaughlin, The King of
     Freak Revue
3:15 Wild Magnolias
4:00 James Rivers Movement
5:15 Swiss Movement

JAZZ TENT
12:00 Harry Connick, Jr.
1:00 New Leviathan Oriental Fox Trot
     Orchestra
2:00 New Orleans Joymakers with
     Jabbo Smith
3:00 Hot Strings
4:00 Bai Konte
5:00 Ellis Marsalis Quartet Plus Two

GOSPEL TENT
12:00 2nd Morning Star Combined
     Choir
12:30 Gospel Tones
1:00 Fairview Baptist Church Radio
     Choir
1:30 Macedonia Male Chorus
2:00 Russ specials
2:30 Friendly Five
3:00 Fantastic Violinaires
3:30 Notes of Harmony
4:00 1st Church of God in Christ
4:30 The Youth Inspirationals
5:00 the DL & M Ensemble
5:30 The Gospel Soul Children

PERFORMANCE TENT
12:00 New Orleans Square & Round
     Dance Ass'n.
1:00 Carlos Sanchez
2:00 Giorgio Gaslini
3:15 Ramsey McLean and The Lifers
4:00 Jazz Poetry
5:15 Sunnyland Slim

KOINDU
12:15 Bai Konte
1:15 Louis Celestin
2:45 New Orleans Contemporary
     Dance Company
4:30 Last Poet and Griots

GAZEBO A
12:45 Nelson Camp

2:15 Hazel Schleuter and The Delta
     Ramblers
4:00 Nelson Camp
5:00 Will Soto

GAZEBO B
1:15 Jack Cook
2:45 Will Soto
3:45 Louis Celestin
5:15 Chester Calhoun,
     ventriloquist.

CHILDREN'S
12:00 McDonough #15 Elementary
     School Band
1:00 Limited Unlimited
2:00 Free School Folk Dance
3:00 Theatre New Orleans

SUNDAY, APRIL 29

STAGE 1
11:50 Loyola University Jazz Band
12:45 Salt Creek
2:00 Troy L. De & The Country
     Kings
     plus Jana Jae
3:45 Russ Russell and The Rustlers
5:00 Wilfred La Tour and The Travel
     Aces
6:15 Clarence "Frogman" Henry

STAGE 2
12:30 Bob French
2:00 Alvin Young
3:30 Four Play
5:15 Wild Tchoupitoulas
6:15 Doc Paulin

STAGE 3
12:00 Snooks Eaglin
1:30 Odetta
2:15 Afromusicology
3:15 Les Vagabonds
4:15 Louis Celestin
5:00 Magnolia Brass Band
6:00 Exuma

STAGE 4
12:00 Eddie Bo and Take III
1:15 King Floyd
2:30 The Meters
3:45 Bobby Blue Bland
5:00 New Orleans Blues Giants
6:15 Southern Univ. at Baton Rouge
     Marching Band

JAZZ TENT
12:00 University Of New Orleans
     Jazz Ensemble
1:00 Walter Payton
2:00 New Orleans Ragtime
     Orchestra
4:00 Wallace Davenport

5:15 Alvin Batiste
6:15 Sam Rivers

GOSPEL TENT
12:00 2nd Mt. Carmel Youth Choir
12:30 Masonic Knights
1:00 Gospel Chords
1:30 Sensational Travelers
2:00 The Chapman Singers
2:30 The Young Adult Choir
3:00 New Orleans Spiritualettes
3:30 The Youth Inspirationals
4:00 God Renewed Gospel Ensemble
4:30 All God's Children
5:00 The Ott Family
5:30 The Christ Elite Chorale

PERFORMANCE TENT
12:15 Mardi Gras Chorus
1:15 Tuts Washington
2:15 Sunnyland Slim
3:00 Al Belleto
4:15 Odetta
5:15 Roosevelt Sykes

KOINDU
12:30 Bai Konte
1:30 Louis Celestin
2:30 Exuma
4:45 Last Poet and Griots
6:00 The Academy of Black Arts
     Performing Company

GAZEBO A
12:30 Will Soto
2:00 Emile Guess
6:30 Clancy "Blues Boy" Lewis

GAZEBO B
1:00 Clancy "Blues Boy" Lewis
2:45 Chester Calhoun
4:00 Joelle
5:30 Will Soto

CHILDREN'S AREA
12:00 Limited Unlimited
1:00 Gospel Israelites
2:00 Limited Unlimited
3:00 Calliope Puppet Theatre

SATURDAY, MAY 5

STAGE 1
12:15 Trac 1
1:30 Batiste Family Band
2:45 Dizzy Gillespie
4:15 Sun Ra
5:45 Como Fife and Drum Corps
6:15 Olatunji & His World African
     Orchestra

STAGE 2
11:45 Elleyna Tatum
1:00 DDT Jazzband
2:00 Flatland String Band

become a destination for music lovers all over the world, the Faubourg St. John residents bordering the Fair Grounds became increasingly agitated over the accumulation of litter, parked cars, and crowding that they feared could block response crews in an emergency. Finally, city officials worked out parking regulations. Wily residents looking to make some cash promptly figured out ways to move their own cars to other locations, and sold their parking passes. Perhaps in response, the first parking and shuttle service began in 1979. Fest goers could park at the Superdome ($1) and catch a $5 shuttle that included the price of admission. Tickets to Jazz Fest cost $3 in advance and $4 at the gate, and were sold at D.H. Holmes, Tulane University, University of New Orleans, Dooky Chase restaurant, Mason's Motel, the Superdome, the Mushroom, Leisure Landing, Werlein's for Music, and Raccoon Records in Lafayette.

3:15 Caledonian Society
4:30 Irving McLean
5:45 Yellow Jackets, Flaming Arrows

STAGE 3
12:00 June Gardner and Sam Alcorn
1:30 James Black Ensemble
2:45 Bois Sec Ardoin and Ardoin Family
4:00 Tabby Thomas & The Mighty Houserockers
5:15 Allen Fontenot & The Country Cajuns
6:30 Onward Brass Band

STAGE 4
12:30 Lastie Brothers with Huey "Piano" Smith and Al Johnson
2:15 Skor
2:45 Lee Dorsey
4:00 Doug Kershaw
5:15 Pete Seeger
6:15 Irma Thomas

JAZZ TENT
12:00 Ernie Cagnolotti
1:15 Southern Univ. in New Orleans Lab Band Charlie Parker Suite
2:45 Danny and Blue Lu Barker
3:45 Ronnie Kole
4:45 Germaine Bazzle and The Gentlemen of Jazz
5:45 James Black Solo
6:30 Randy Jackson

GOSPEL TENT
12:00 Mt. Arrat Baptist Church
12:30 St. Mark 4th Jr. Choir
1:00 Marine Baptist Church Youth Choir
1:30 St. Luke AME Church
2:00 St. Frances DeSalles Choir
2:30 Wallace Davenport
3:00 Gospel Inspirations of Donaldsonville
3:30 Zion Harmonizers
4:00 Morning Star Baptist Church of Thibodaux
4:30 New Comers of Christ
5:00 Thibodaux Female Community Chorus
5:30 Parish Prison Male & Female Choir

PERFORMANCE TENT
12:00 New Orleans Square and Round Dance Assn
1:00 Larry Sieberth
2:00 Pete Seeger
3:15 Irving MacLean
4:15 Coon Elder and Johnny Woods
5:15 Bai Konte
6:15 Pat Fisher and Jim Robinson Quartet

KOINDU
12:00 Phyllis Wheatley Drill Team
1:30 Robert Pete Williams
2:30 Olatunji
4:30 Southern Univ. African Ensemble
5:45 Shree Sun Rays

GAZEBO A
12:00 Como Fife and Drum Corps
1:45 Coon Elder and Johnny Woods
3:00 Bai Konte
4:30 R. L. Burnside
6:00 Flatland String Band

GAZEBO B
12:00 Robert Pete Williams
1:30 Bongo Joe
4:00 Butch Mudbone
6:30 R.L. Burnside

CHILDREN'S AREA
12:00 McDonough School Band
1:00 Nelson Camp
3:00 Theatre New Orleans

SUNDAY, MAY 6

STAGE 1
12:00 St. Augustine Jazz Band
1:30 Coon Elder and Johnny Woods
2:45 Dewey Balfa and Friends
3:45 Doc Watson
5:00 Vassar Clements
6:30 Olympia Brass Band

STAGE 2
12:00 Dewey Balfa and Friends
1:45 The Associates
2:45 Svare Forsland
4:00 John Mooney Blues Band
5:00 Robert Pete Williams
6:00 Ironing Board Sam

STAGE 3
1:00 Sam Brothers Five
2:30 Davis Torkanowsky Quintet
3:45 Lonesome Sunday
5:00 Barbara Lynn
6:15 Walter Washington

STAGE 4
11:30 Southern Univ. Big Band
1:15 Los Catrochos
2:30 Olatunji
3:45 World Famous Calypso Revue featuring Johnny Holt and Calypso Rose
5:15 The Neville Brothers
6:30 Professor Longhair

JAZZ TENT
12:15 Louis Nelson
1:15 Ed Blackwell
2:15 Henry Butler
3:15 Sun Ra

4:15 New Orleans Piano Masters
5:15 Percy Humphrey and His Preservation Hall Band
6:15 Kid Thomas and His Preservation Hall Band

GOSPEL TENT
12:00 Sister Imogene Haynes
12:30 Divine Grace Gospel Chorus
1:00 Truetones Gospel Singers
1:30 Ott Family
2:00 Mighty Chariots
2:30 Zion Harmonizers
3:00 St. Joseph Helping Hand
3:30 McDonough 35 High School
4:00 McDermott Gospel Choir
4:30 Pentecost Youth Choir
5:00 The Cavalcade of Gospel Stars
5:30 The Gospel Soul Children

PERFORMANCE TENT
12:00 Syd Selvidge
1:00 James Booker
2:00 Roosevelt Sykes
3:15 Irving McLean
4:30 Shree Sun Rays
5:45 Bai Konte
6:15 Earl Turbinton Jr.

KOINDU
12:30 Caribbean Folklore Dance Troupe
1:45 Irving McLean
3:45 Como Fife and Drum Corps
4:45 Olatunji
6:00 White Eagles

GAZEBO A
12:00 Robert Pete Williams
1:15 Bai Konte
2:30 Como Fife and Drum Corps
4:00 Syd Selvidge
5:30 Svare Forsland

GAZEBO B
2:00 Bongo Joe
4:30 R.L. Burnside
5:45 Coon Elder and Johnny Woods

CHILDREN'S AREA
12:00 Robert Pete Williams
1:00 Youth Ensemble for Christ and The Landrums
2:00 Nelson Camp
3:00 Calliope Puppet Theatre

NIGHT CONCERTS

FRIDAY, APRIL 20, 9 P.M.
Ella Fitzgerald & The New Orleans Philharmonic Symphony Orchestra – Leonard Slatkin Conducting
Theatre of the Performing Arts

WEDNESDAY, APRIL 25, 9 P.M.
Teddy Wilson, Alberta Hunter, Percy Humphrey & His Preservation Hall Jazz Band with Sweet Emma Barrett
Alvin Alcorn Jazz Band
Theatre of the Performing Arts

THURSDAY, APRIL 26, 7 P.M. & MIDNIGHT
Fire On the Bayou
Allen Toussaint
The Meters
Clifton Chenier
S.S. President

FRIDAY, APRIL 27, 8 P.M.
Blues Boat Boogie
Bobby "Blue" Bland
Etta James
Professor Longhair
Buddy Guy Blues Band with Jr. Wells
S.S. President

SUNDAY, APRIL 29, 8 P.M.
1st Annual Gospel Boat Ride
Dixie Hummingbirds, Dorothy Love Coates,
The Violinaires, Zion Harmonizers,
The Youth Inspirational Choir
S.S. President

WEDNESDAY, MAY 2, 9 P.M.
Raggin' & Jazzin'
Eubie Blake, Earl "Fatha" Hines, Danny Barker & His Jazz Hounds with Blue Lu Barker
Lyric Theatre – Cast of One Mo' Time
New Orleans Grand Ballroom – Hyatt Regency

THURSDAY, MAY 3, 9 P.M.
The Lionel Hampton All Star Big Band
Ellis Marsalis Quartet Plus Two
S.S. President

FRIDAY, MAY 4, 8 P.M.
Dizzy Gillespie
Myth-Science Arkestra
Olatunji & His World African Orchestra
S.S. President

SATURDAY, MAY 5, 9 P.M.
The Staples
Roy Ayres
Chocolate Milk
Municipal Auditorium

1980

Lil' Walter Cook and Creole Wild West

The city was mourning the death of one of the greatest innovators of the New Orleans sound, Professor Longhair. This Festival was dedicated to his memory, and everyone was offering up profound tributes. His sudden death on January 30, 1980 silenced the New Orleans music community and saddened music lovers the world over. Professor Longhair had been a major musical influence to virtually every New Orleans artist, regardless of style or background. Pianists like Mac Rebbenack, aka Dr. John, Eddie Volker of the Radiators, Harry Connick Jr., David Torkanowsky, and Allen Toussaint have dipped into the well of the great master and found inspiration and innovation in his playing.

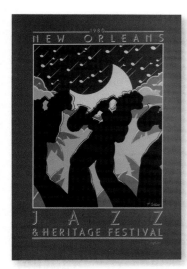

He had just finished a new album shortly before his death, entitled *Crawfish Fiesta*, for Alligator records featuring an all local line-up of the top musicians of the day including Dr. John on guitar, Johnny Vidacovich on drums, Jim Moore on baritone, Andy Kaslow and Tony Dagaradi on tenor sax, Alfred "Uganda" Roberts on percussion, and David Watson on bass. As Kaslow so aptly put it in the 1980 Festival program:

"Professor Longhair, left behind a tremendous musical

legacy which will be remembered for generations to come. Born Henry Roeland Byrd, "Fess" as he was widely known to the public, was a synthesizer of a variety of styles, which have been interwoven into the musical fabric of the Crescent City. A musician's musician, Byrd developed a concept which he sometimes called "Tockin' Rhythm", a blend of elements from such diverse idioms as blues, jazz, gospel, swing, barrelhouse, calypso, rhumba, pop, rock, and funk..."

R.L. Burnside

Henry Roeland Byrd's music had been embraced by the world and brought to a new generation of music lovers through the Jazz Festival and the music club Tipitina's, named after one of his signature songs. In the March 20th issue of Rolling Stone, Timothy White was quoted: " Friends, neighbors and fellow musicians had watched him struggle in impoverished obscurity for nearly half a century. In death, Longhair will be thought of as an 'innovator', in Wexler's words 'who may be remembered with Louis Armstrong and Sidney Bechet and Jelly Roll Morton as yet another gift from New Orleans to American blues and jazz'.

A local company named Sweet Molasses Inc., owned by graphic designer and artist Mischa Phillipoff and photographer Michael P. Smith had just designed a silkscreen poster featuring Fess entitled TIPITINA'S. Professor Longhair passed away before he had an opportunity to sign this limited addition silkscreen print, so his signature was lifted from his last contract performance at Tipitina's music club and incorporated into the poster. A special tent was set up for the sale of the poster and all proceeds went to Henry Byrd's widow, Alison, who sat in the tent for much of the Festival, signing prints and receiving the condolences of countless "Fess" fans. The advertisement for the sale of the Tipitina's poster reads; 'There would be no Tipitina's without Professor Longhair. The club was inspired by a heartfelt desire to provide a forum for the musical genius of this fine and friendly man.

Many performances that year were dedicated to his memory. Long time Jazz Fest fixture, the painter and folk artist Bruce Brice, a New Orleanian, who was already garnering national and international recognition, also created a commemorative poster expressing the "Professor's"

FRIDAY, APRIL 18

STAGE 1
11:45 McDonogh #15 Band
1:30 Sex Dog
2:45 Lastie Brothers, Miss B & Lil' Sonny Jones
4:00 Ron Cuccia & The Jazz Poetry Group
5:00 Oliver Morgan & Jessie Hill

STAGE 2
12:30 N.O.C.C.A. Jazz Group
1:45 Eluard Burt
2:45 Freeman Fontenot
4:00 Flatlands String Band
5:15 Willie Cole

STAGE 3
1:00 New Jazz Quintet
2:15 Woodenhead
3:30 Irving McLean
4:00 Touchstone
5:15 Muchos Plus

STAGE 4
11:45 U.N.O. Lab Band
1:00 S.U.B.R. Jazz Ensemble
2:15 George Porter's Joyride
3:15 Porgy Jones
4:15 Walter Washington
5:15 Charles Neville & House Band

JAZZ TENT
12:00 Dillard University Jazz Band
1:15 Hal Kelley
2:15 Tommy Yetta
3:30 One Mo' Time
5:00 Tuxedo Jazz Band

KOINDU
11:45 Phyllis Wheatley Drill Team
12:45 Fairview Brass Band
1:45 Congo Square Poets
2:45 S.U.N.O. African Ensemble
3:45 Dashiki Theatre
4:45 Alfred Roberts & Afro Cuban Jazz Ensemble

GAZEBO A
12:30 Percy Randolph & Alton Allen
1:00 Lil' Freddie King
2:30 George Dorko
3:45 Equinox
5:00 Freeman Fontenot

GAZEBO B
12:00 Art Ryder
1:45 Flatlands String Band
2:45 Percy Randolph & Alton Allen
3:15 Lil' Freddie King
4:00 Yellow Jackets

GOSPEL
12:00 Kennedy High School
12:30 Joseph Davis
12:45 Brother Billy Bower Gospel Blind Singer
1:00 Fortier High School
1:30 C & B Ensemble
2:00 True Vine Baptist Choir
2:15 The Smooth Family
2:45 New Orleans Echoes
3:00 Sister Alberta Harris Lewis
3:30 The Holy Angel Choir
4:00 The Melody Clouds
4:30 Leviticus Gospel Singers
5:00 New Orleans Comforters
5:30 Soul Searchers

KID'S TENT
1:00 Unlimited, Ltd.
2:00 McDonogh #15 Band

PARADE
3:00 Fairview Brass Band

Roosevelt Sykes and Big Joe Williams

life and accomplishments. In later years "Fess's" image would grace the sign above Stage 3 – a guiding, soulful inspiration musicians playing that stage would always feel.

Another sad loss to the Festival was the traffic death of nighttime stage crew manager Charles "Chuck" McMarron. Robert "Rock" Jones, Concert Production Manager, wrote in a dedication: "When a loss like this occurs you discover that you are not missing the person for the work that they did; you can always find another body to fill in.

"One particular year in the early 80's when punk rock was just starting to come on, there was a band from Baton Rouge and it was raining, and there was an ocean in front of the stage. I mean, there was more water than there was dry land and even less people, and they were all kind of standing outside the edge of the ocean and about 30 people were along the railing. Then the finale comes and the lead singer rips his shirt off and is just dancing crazy to this song called "Lather" and he had a can of shaving cream that he sprayed all over the place. Then he did something amazing: he cleared the barricades, dove head first off the stage into the ocean — a belly flop — and you knew this had to knock the wind out right. And he started stroking and swam across in the mud. All of a sudden, everybody dives in behind him and swims along. It was amazing. So he's a big rock star, he's got grass caked all over him, in his hair and he's looking disgusting. He comes back here and everybody wants his signature." KEITH WILLIAMS

What you miss is that relationship known as 'Friendship.' You miss those late conversations and meals at Mama Mia's, those laughs and sad tales at the Dream Palace at 3:00 a.m. 'God, don't you remember those Bill Hanley Black Boxes we dragged onto the boat, man I thought the boat might sink.' I can still hear him 'Come on, another beer!' Chuck you ole rascal, you were just a plain good ole boy- you took off and left us holding the bag, trying our damndest to get the show on the road. Missing you this year."

In perhaps the most remembered performance that year, Ironing Board Sam, self-titled "9th Wonder of the World," proved the validity of his moniker once again by wowing hundreds of excited onlookers during his show. Announcing that he would be playing "underwater" he kept the crowd in suspense for the first few numbers, giving them time to gaze and conjecture about what he was going to do exactly. Finally, he

climbed into the large tank full of water on the stage, put a smaller aquarium with a microphone suspended inside the top of it over his head and submerged himself. With only minor problems, including his first keyboard shorting out and the ladder breaking when he was coming back up, the show was flawless. Ironing Board Sam became the first underwater blues man, which was his goal for the 1977 Jazz Fest.

When Mr. Eddie Lambert, the site's electrical master, went to set up the power for Ironing Board Sam's show there was some mild confusion: " Everyone thought that I was Ironing Board Sam and everyone was taking my picture". He chuckled. " He said he was going to play his piano underwater and we got it ready for him. Well, he got into the tank, and got underwater and just stuck his hands out of the water and played and boy, that audience screamed. It was great."

With the attendance for the Festival reaching 188,000, the effects of this event were also having an impact on the club scene. The "cool jams"

music scene

WWOZ 90.7fm goes on the air December 4th.

Professor Longhair dies January 30th, the same day his album "Crawfish Fiesta" ships from the manufacturer.

Fats Domino appears in the Clint Eastwood movie "Any Which Way You Can."

Gambit Weekly begins publication.

IN MEMORIAM

Professor Longhair, Walter Lastie, George "Big Chief Jolly" Landry, Barney Bigard, John Lennon

SATURDAY, APRIL 19

STAGE 1
11:45 U.N.O. Jazz Band
1:00 Lil' Queenie & The Percolators
2:15 Tommy Ridgley, Bobby Parker, Bobby Mitchell & Ernie K-Doe
4:15 Lightnin' Hopkins
5:15 Pete Seeger

STAGE 2
12:30 Teddy Riley
1:30 Bois Sec
2:30 Roosevelt Sykes
3:30 Society Jazz Band
4:30 Grandma Dixie Davis
5:00 Sunbelt Bluegrass Band

STAGE 3
12:00 John Creel & The N.O. Square & Round Dance Association
1:00 Victor Sirker & The Circuit
2:00 Tim Williams
3:00 Louisiana Aces & Dewey Balfa
4:00 Zydeco Machine
5:00 Fiebre

STAGE 4
11:30 Southern Jazz Ensemble
12:30 Willie Tee
1:15 Wild Magnolias
2:15 Chocolate Milk
3:30 B.B. King
4:45 Greg Stafford Traditional Jazz Band

JAZZ TENT
12:15 Lady Charlotte & Her Men of Jazz
1:15 Joe Simon
2:15 Clyde Kerr, Jr. & Univision
3:15 Walter Payton's Jazzy Jazz Band
4:15 Kid Thomas Valentine's Preservation Hall Jazz Band
5:15 Kidd Jordan Improvisational Art Quintet

KOINDU
12:30 Ethiopian Theatre Poets
1:45 Michael Pierce & Divertimento
3:00 Exuma
4:15 Bai Konte
5:15 Nongowa Dance Troupe

GAZEBO A
12:30 Chris Smither
1:30 Bai Konte
3:00 Will Soto
4:00 Svare

GAZEBO B
12:00 Sunbelt Bluegrass Band
1:15 Grandma Dixie Davis
2:15 Carlos Sanchez
3:45 Chris Smither
5:15 Whispering Smith & The Jukehouse Rockers

GOSPEL TENT
12:00 Young Adult Choir
12:30 Voices of Faith Youth Choir
1:00 Macedonia COGIC
1:30 Hope Ensemble
2:00 Pentecost Baptist Church
2:30 Raymond Myles & The McDermott Singers
3:00 Good Hope Baptist Church
3:30 Gospel Choralettes of Kenner
4:00 The Russ Specials
4:30 Mt. Kingdom Baptist Church Choir
5:00 The Rocks of Harmony
5:30 Rev. Paul Morton & The Chorale of Greater St. Stephen

KID'S TENT
12:00 Robert M. Lusher School Chorus
1:00 Unlimited, Ltd.
2:00 Joker's Wild

were happening at every little club and bar in town, not just out at the Fair Grounds and at the main night events.

Even though the Jazz Fest hadn't crossed the boundaries of the dirt track that bordered the infield, it had certainly spread out into the city and the surrounding areas. Rosy's Jazz Hall on Tchopitoulas Street put together breathtaking shows pairing national acts with local musicians and all of the clubs began to take advantage of having access to artists they wouldn't otherwise be able to afford who were in New Orleans for the Festival.

Odetta

> *"We wanted to hurry up and get there early and get our (stage) set up done and then break out and go touch base with vendors that would come back here every year that we'd developed relationships with that went beyond actually Jazz Fest."* KEITH WILLIAMS

Clubs like Tyler's Beer Garden on 5224 Magazine Street uptown specialized in myriad amazing jazz jams, with musicians wandering in and either sitting intimately in the audience or sitting in on stage as they wished, to the delight of patrons soaking up beer, and the 10 cent oysters. One musician still remembers Tyler's was the only bar in town featuring fresh squeezed orange juice for your screwdriver (delivered by the cutest waitress to become a music writer).

The Blues Saloon in the French Quarter on the corner of Conti and Dauphine street had the late night blues jams, sometimes sliding well past sunrise with house regular Charlie Brent's' big band Trick Bag

featuring blues legend Luther Kent. On April 18th 1980 Etta James performed at the Blues Saloon with Charlie Brent's big band and Luther Kent. "That was a great show. As a matter of fact, that was the first time that I'd ever met her," remembered Luther. "I'd always loved her music, I mean, I was a tremendous fan of hers, but that was the first time I ever met her. She wasn't really part of the show that night. She had played earlier. She was upstairs in the dressing room when the band kicked off and she came running down the stairs. By the time she got there I was on the bandstand and she came and sat with me on my lap in my stool - till eight o'clock in the

Quint Davis

3:00   Unlimited, Ltd.
PARADES
2:30   Scene Highlighters, Money Wasters & Greg Stafford Traditional Jazz Band

SUNDAY, APRIL 20
STAGE 1
11:30 Kennedy High Jazz Band
12:45 Scooter Lee
1:45   Gatemouth Brown
2:45   Dave Brubeck
4:00   Jerry Lee Lewis
5:15   Olympia Brass Band

STAGE 2
12:30 Henry Gray
1:30   Germaine Bazzle & The Gentlemen of Jazz
2:30   Snooks Eaglin
3:45   Walter Mouton & The Scott Playboys
4:45   Troy Deramus & The Country Kings w/ The State Fiddle Champs

STAGE 3
11:45 Tulane Jazz Combo
1:00   Clark Vreeland & Friends
2:00   Dixi-Kups
3:00   Rockin' Dopsie & The Twisters
4:00   Earl King
5:15   Los Catrochos

STAGE 4
12:00 S.U.N.O. Big Band
1:15   Family Players
2:15   Luther Kent & Trick Bag
3:15   Etta James
4:30   Neville Brothers & Friends

JAZZ TENT
12:15 June Gardner
1:15   New Leviathan Oriental Foxtrot Orchestra
2:15   Danny Barker's Jazz Hounds with Blue Lu Barker
3:15   Onward Brass Band
4:15   Don Cherry, Charlie Haden & Ed Blackwell
5:15   Alvin Batiste Group

KOINDU
12:00 George Pack African Ensemble
1:00   Bai Konte
1:45   Don Cherry, Charlie Haden & Ed Blackwell
2:45   Los de Palacaguina, Otto De la Rocha, El Guadalupano
3:45   Odetta
4:30   James Black Group

GAZEBO A
1:00   Chakula & Chink
2:30   Mamou Hour Band
3:45   Irving McLean
4:45   Clancy "Blues Boy" Lewis

GAZEBO B
12:15 Guy Richards
1:30   Cousin Joe
2:30   Patrice Fisher & Jimmy Robinson
3:15   Bai Konte
4:15   Black Eagles
5:15   Christiana Jazz Band

GOSPEL
12:00 Jones Sisters
12:30 Southern Gospel
1:00   Southern Bells
1:30   Greater Macedonia Radio Choir
2:00   Sister Christine Myles
2:30   The Modern Quartet
3:00   The Heralds of Christ
3:30   The Humble Travelers
4:00   The Ott Family

Ironing Board Sam

"I like the fact that you can run into anybody; people like John Fogerty or David Hidalgo of Los Lobos will be hanging out in the midst of the crowds. I remember listening to Thelonious Monk and then walking to a small stage to hear Dennis McGee & Sady Courville playing to about five people and the contrast was awesome. In 1980, the year it really rained hard and people were walking around wearing garbage bags, Canray Fontenot got busted for DWI and I got to fill in for him and play with Freeman Fontenot on accordion and Bois Sec Ardoin on triangle. Those people were from a different time and Freeman almost never played with other people." MICHAEL DOUCET

morning. It was an incredible evening – it really was- she was real moved by the music. "

Brian Lee and the Jump Street 5 were at the Absinthe Bar on Bourbon Street, as well as a group of young men just out of music school who created a progressive band called "Astral Project" which would become one of the mainstays of the New Orleans Jazz scene. The Nexus on Elysian Fields was the Dew Drop Inn for many visiting national black artists, and the show "One Mo' Time" was running on Toulouse Street where James Booker could be found playing in the lobby on breaks. The music scene was already very vibrant, but during the Festival it kicked up another notch.

There was a lot of top-level jazz from many eras themed through in the New Orleans Jazz & Heritage Festival in 1980. Eubie Blake, at 97 returned for his fifth consecutive Jazz Festival performance, appearing in the

Dave Bartholomew and Lee Allen

Grand Ballroom of the New Orleans Hilton with Kid Sheik and the Storyville Ramblers along with The World's Greatest Jazz Band featuring Bob Haggart and Yank Lawson. Count Basie and his orchestra performed a night concert at the Theatre of Performing Arts with the Dave Brubeck quartet, and Lionel Hampton and his All Star Big Band kicked off the first riverboat concert, playing against the New Orleans Jazz & Heritage Festival All-Star Brass Band. Chick Corea, Flora Purim, and Larry Coryell performed at the Saenger on Canal Street, at the top of their jazz-fusion game. The last riverboat concert of the 11th annual Jazz & Heritage Festival featured a "strong program of contemporary jazz" with Sonny Rollins, Mc Coy Tyner, and local pianist Edward Frank leading an All-Star bebop Orchestra.

Locally, the jazz musicians were a large presence at the Festival Fair Grounds, much more so than in later years when more mainstream music began to be predominate. In 1980, jazz got the main stage.

In classic New Orleans style, the last night concert of the Festival this year was just like New Orleans cooking; a lot of crazy ingredients, pretty damn spicy, and you just couldn't tell by looking at it, but it smelled great, and tasted even better. Chic, "Freaked Out" while Patrice Rushen with her band offered another facet of modern soul music, and the Southern University Marching Band, under the direction of Isaac Griggs stomped everything that got in their way. Locals of discerning taste and humor could only have booked a combination like that. Robert Leslie Jones, Charles R. Bering, and Klondike Koehler handled the night concert production and would through many years of its heyday.

The Meters

4:30 New Genesis
5:00 Greater St. Andrew B.C.
5:30 Desire Community Chorus

KID'S TENT
12:00 Gospel Isrealites
1:00 Unlimited, Ltd.
2:00 Calliope Puppet Theatre
3:00 Unlimited, Ltd.

PARADES
2:30 Scene Booster, Fun Lovers & Olympia Brass Band

SATURDAY, APRIL 26

STAGE 1
11:30 Slidell Senior High Jazz Band
12:45 Tulane Big Band
2:00 Allen Fontenot & The Country Cajuns
3:15 Jimmie Davis and The Jimmie Davis Singers including Chuck Wagon Anna
4:15 Irma Thomas
5:15 Russ Russell & The Rustlers

STAGE 2
12:15 Robert Pete Williams
1:15 Athenian Room Band
2:15 Ironing Board Sam
3:15 Harmonica Williams & The Mighty Hawks
4:15 Ramsey McLean & The Lifers
5:15 Tornado Brass Band

STAGE 3
12:00 Jazz Dance Theatre
1:00 Mardi Gras Chorus
2:00 Salt Creek
3:00 Frog Island Jazz Band
4:00 Preston Franks & Soileau Playboys
5:00 Cache & Ruben "Mr. Salsa" Gonzalez

STAGE 4
12:00 Tavasco
1:00 Edward Frank Group
2:00 Sammy Berfect & Tony Owens
3:00 James Booker
4:00 Muddy Waters
5:15 Fats Domino

JAZZ TENT
12:00 Andy Moses
1:00 Louis Nelson Big Six
2:00 Ellis Marsalis & New Generation
3:00 Earl Turbinton, Jr. & The Afrikan Cowboy Revue
4:00 Louis Cottrell's New Orleans Jazz Band
5:00 Thomas Jefferson

KOINDU
12:00 St. Augustine Jazz Band
1:00 Voodoo Macumba
2:00 Theron Lewis Group
3:00 Mandingo Griot Society
4:00 Gil Scott-Heron (a solo performance)
5:15 Golden Eagles

GAZEBO A
12:15 Chester Calhoun
1:00 Bongo Joe
2:30 Como Drum & Fife Corp
3:15 Robert Pete Williams
4:30 R.L. Burnside

GAZEBO B
12:00 Napoleon Strickland
12:30 Jessie Mae Hemphill
1:15 R.L. Burnside
2:30 Silas Hogan & Guitar Kelly
4:15 Hot Strings
5:15 Mandingo Griot Society

GOSPEL
12:00 Second Mt. Carmel Choir
12:30 Sensational Travelers
1:00 Divine Grace
1:30 Macedonia Male Chorus
2:00 Mighty Chariots
2:30 St. Luke A.M.E. Church
3:00 Ambassadors for Christ
3:25 Fairview Baptist Church
3:50 St. Francis DeSales
4:20 God's Renewed Gospel Ensemble
4:50 Gospel Inspirations of Donaldsonville
5:15 Greater Ebenezer Chorus
5:40 Second New Guide Gospel Chorus

KID'S TENT
12:00 St. Francis DeSales Junior Choir
1:00 Jimmie Brown
2:00 New Orleans Free School Village Kids
3:00 Calliope Puppet Theatre

PARADES
2:30 Tornado Brass Band, Gentlemen Of Leisure, Calendar Girls

SUNDAY, APRIL 27

STAGE 1
12:00 Xavier Jazz Lab Band
1:15 Johnny Adams
2:15 Roosevelt Sykes
3:15 Percy Mayfield
4:30 Muddy Waters
5:45 Clifton Chenier

STAGE 2
12:00 Doc Paulin
1:00 Caledonian Society of New Orleans
2:00 Robert Pete Williams
3:00 New Orleans Rascals
4:15 Nathan Abshire Band

5:15 Meyers Brothers Bluegrass Band

STAGE 3
12:45 Maurice Barzas
2:00 The Radiators
3:00 The Latin American Band
4:00 Marcia Ball
5:00 Deacon John

STAGE 4
12:15 Loyola Big Band
1:30 James Rivers
2:30 Clarence "Frogman" Henry
3:30 Lee Dorsey
4:30 Dave Bartholomew
5:45 Allen Toussaint

JAZZ TENT
12:30 Ed Perkins
1:30 Dutch Andrus
2:30 Al Belletto Sextet
3:45 Mandingo Griot Society
4:30 Astral Project
5:30 Percy Humphrey
6:30 Young Tuxedo Brass Band

KOINDU
12:00 New Orleans Contemporary Dance
1:00 Como Drum & Fife Corps
2:00 Bryan Parris
3:00 White Eagle Indian Nation
4:15 Willie Metcalf & The Academy of Black Arts
6:00 Mandingo Griot Society

GAZEBO A
12:30 Bongo Joe
2:15 Butch Mudbone
3:15 Napoleon Strickland Fife & Drum Band
3:30 Jessie Mae Hemphill
4:00 R.L. Burnside
5:00 Robert Pete Williams
5:45 Bongo Joe

GAZEBO B
1:00 Hazel Schleuter

2:30 Chief Jolly
3:30 Tuts Washington
4:30 Sid Selvidge
5:30 Elmo Mendoza & Senior Citizen Serenaders

GOSPEL
12:00 Second Morning Star Combined Choir
12:25 Masonic Kings
12:50 Friendly Five
1:15 New Orleans Spiritualettes
1:40 McDonogh #35 Gospel Choir
2:05 Second Baptist Church 6th District
2:30 Heavenly Stars
2:55 First Baptist Church, Paradis, La.
3:20 DLM & W Singers
3:45 Community Correctional Center
4:10 Zion Harmonizers
4:35 First Church of God in Christ
5:00 Youth Inspirational Choir
5:30 Gospel Soul Children

KID'S TENT
12:00 Peyote Company
1:00 Jimmie Brown
2:00 Gospel Israelites
3:00 Calliope Puppet Theatre

PARADES
2:30 Young Tuxedo Brass Band, Olympian Aid, Burgundy Ladies, Doc Paulin Brass Band

NIGHT CONCERTS

TUESDAY APRIL 15, 8 P.M.
Count Basie and His Orchestra, Dave Brubeck Quartet
Theatre of Performing Arts

WEDNESDAY APRIL 16, 8 P.M.
Lionel Hampton All Star Big Band, All Star Brass Band
S.S. President

THURSDAY APRIL 17, 7 P.M. AND MIDNIGHT
Allen Toussaint, Lee Dorsey, Tommy Ridgley, Rhythm and Blues Superstars
S.S. President

FRIDAY APRIL 18, 7 P.M. AND MIDNIGHT
B.B. King, Taj Mahal, Earl King
S.S. President

SATURDAY APRIL 19, 8 P.M.
Mighty Clouds of Joy, Sensational Williams Brothers, Gospel Soul Children
Municipal Auditorium

MONDAY APRIL 21, 8 P.M.
Great Performances on Film
New Orleans Hilton

TUESDAY APRIL 22, 8 P.M.
World's Greatest Jazz Band, Eubie Blake, Kid Sheik and Storyville Ramblers
New Orleans Hilton

WEDNESDAY APRIL 23, 8 P.M.
Chick Corea, Flora Purim, Larry Coryell
Saenger Performing Arts Theatre

THURSDAY APRIL 24, 7 P.M. AND MIDNIGHT
Fats Domino, Dr John, The Neville Brothers
S.S. President

FRIDAY APRIL 25, 8 P.M.
Sonny Rollins, McCoy Tyner, Edward Frank All Star BeBop Orchestra
S.S. President

SATURDAY APRIL 26, 8 P.M.
Chic, Gil Scott-Heron, Patrice Rushen, Southern University Marching Band
Municipal Auditorium

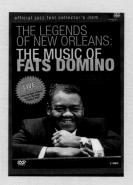

In 1979, Flying Fish Records produced 6,000 double albums that featured Allen Toussaint, Irma Thomas, Professor Longhair; Earl King; and Lee Dorsey on the riverboat S.S. President, that cost $6 each.

In 1988, Mardi Gras Records produced the album "The Best of Jazz Fest 1988."

In 1989 Ken Ehrlich produced a VHS video, "Best Of The Fest," featuring mainly national acts along with the Neville Brothers and Irma Thomas.

A live recording session at Snug Harbor Jazz Club in 1989 featured Ellis Marsalis, Earl Turbinton, Jr., Tony Dagradi and others. David Torkanowsky produced the record for Blue Note /Japan.

In 1990, the PBS network paid $40,000 for rights to two 90-minute programs. Public radio stations in 29 cities including Boston, Los Angeles, Washington, and Detroit broadcast six hours of the Jazz Fest live. Another 36 stations aired a delayed version. Some musicians covered were The Neville Brothers, Etta James, B.B. King, Gary Burton Reunion, Linda Ronstadt, Walter Hawkins, Zachary Richard and Flaco Jiminez. The broadcast was produced by WGBH radio in Boston with WWNO-FM and WWOZ-FM in New Orleans, WPFW-FM in Washington, DC and Murray Street Enterprises in New York City.

In 1991, Island Visual, a subsidiary of Island Records, released a two-hour special and a series of special interest shows and multiple home videos. Headlining were Wynton Marsalis; Harry Connick, Jr.; Miles Davis; B.B. King; the Neville Brothers; Dr. John; Leon Russell; the Indigo Girls; Koko Taylor; and Ruben Blades. Island Visual created three home videos for release in Japan that sold for around $100 each in American currency. On audio, WGBH radio produced "The 1991 New Orleans Jazz & Heritage Festival."

Michael Murphy Productions also created the "1993 New Orleans Jazz & Heritage Festival," with five hour-long specials and one 90-minute highlight show for NHK Productions in Japan.

"In 1994, Michael Murphy Productions also made the "1994 New Orleans Jazz & Heritage Festival," six one-hour and one 90-minute specials for NHK High Definition.

Arhoolie Records has produced "Clifton Chenier at the Jazz Fest" DVD and home video "J'ai Été Au Bal," narrated by Barry Jean Ancelet and Michael Doucet.

Jazz Fest masters' series CDs were released on the Scotti Brothers label under
- Traditionalist
- Trumpeters
- Bourbon St. Swing

In 2000, Michael Murphy Productions (MMP) produced "The N. O. Jazz & Heritage Festival 30th Anniversary Special," a two-hour program for the Japanese NHK Productions.

Also in 2000, Michael Murphy Productions created 48 hours of Internet programming entitled: "The 2000 New Orleans Jazz & Heritage Festival" with Sting, Erykah Badu, John Hiatt, Lyle Lovett, The Neville Brothers, Allen Toussaint and Bonnie Raitt, along with two television programs, a VH1 "Jazz Fest" Special, and "Legends of New Orleans: The Music of Allen Toussaint, Dr. John & The Neville Brothers" for PBS. On the internet, MMP's "2000 Jazz Fest Special" aired as a 10-day, 48 hours of total streaming-only broadcast with 50 acts.

In 2001, MMP produced a ten-hour marathon Jazz Fest Special with 34 acts on USA's Trio Digital Network: "Trio Goes To Jazz Fest 2001."

In 2002, MMP produced a second multi-hour special from the New Orleans Jazz & Heritage Festival for USA's Trio Digital Network, and on the internet, produced the "2002 Wonder Juke Service Jazz Fest Special," with 10 acts for streaming only broadcast, on Sony's internet radio division, SoNet.

In 2003, MMP produced a two-hour music-based documentary, "Dancing To New Orleans" on the culture and music of Louisiana for the Bravo Network; a PBS pledge program "Legends of New Orleans" featuring Fats Domino; and a 3.5 hour special from the 2003 New Orleans Jazz & Heritage Festival for SoNet.

1981

Betty Carter

On opening day, May 1, 1981, people and cars were already lining up at 9 a.m. on Gentilly Boulevard to get one of the 4,000 free parking spots within the Fair Grounds racetrack or to be first in line for the official poster, which had become a collectible item. By 11 o'clock when the gates opened, the temperature had already climbed to 78 degrees, the sun was shining, and everything was on track for a nice, sweaty day of music and food.

A tremendous amount of rain the previous year had turned the infield into a sloppy mess with calf-deep mud in certain spots and some dangerous slipping and sliding going on for visitors trying to eat, walk, and hold onto their posters at the same time. "The infield was built like a dish," Quint Davis said. "It's originally set up to drain the track." Fortunately, prior to the opening of the Fair in 1981 a new drainage system was installed and an asphalt walkway was constructed that wove its way about the infield. This was christened "The Main Thoroughfare" and allowed easier navigation over the length of the Fair Grounds infield in any kind of weather.

what's going on?

GLOBALLY

After 444 days in captivity, American hostages in Iran are released by the Iranian Ayatollah Khomeini.

Pope John Paul II is wounded in assassination attempt.

Israel annexes the disputed Golan Heights territory.

NATIONALLY

Sandra Day O'Connor becomes the first woman on the U.S. Supreme Court.

John Hinckley shoots President Ronald Reagan, Whitehouse Press Secretary Jim Brady and two others outside the Washington Hilton.

The 1st launch of a space shuttle (Columbia).

More than 12,000 US air traffic controllers go on strike and are dismissed.

LOCALLY

John Kennedy Toole is posthumously awarded the Pulitzer Prize for fiction for "A Confederacy of Dunces."

New Orleans International Airport expands, adding 1,500 acres with 26 airlines and 49 gates.

Plaisance holds its first Zydeco Festival.

CULTURALLY

Prince Charles of England marries Lady Diana Spencer.

IBM sells its first personal computer. The operating system, MS-DOS, was developed by Bill Gates's Microsoft.

Walter Cronkite retires from his anchorman position, to be succeeded by Dan Rather.

Pac-Man is introduced in the US and sparks a huge craze.

Of course, some locals were once again angry, hating change or innovation of any kind and some said that it "ruined everything."

However, most of the folks who had attended past Jazz Fests were delighted, and it also made it easier for people who got confused about where they were to find their way. If there was any doubt about the wisdom of this new addition, it was laid to rest quickly. Festival spokesperson Anna Zimmerman said the crowds were about the same as last year, but it may have felt heavier because most people were sticking to the asphalt.

Opening day was lovely. The Randolph Brothers got things started off in the Gospel Tent at noon and Koindu countered with the SUNO African Ensemble at 12:45. After Lady Charlotte opened the Jazz Tent at 12:30, Kid Sheik and his Storyville Ramblers got everybody tapping their toes to some good ole' traditional jazz. Steve Masakowsky brought a more progressive flavor to the Jazz Tent after Kid Sheik with Mars, featuring Larry Seiberth, James

Singleton, James Black and David Liebman. Victor Sirker and the Circuit Breakers entertained on Stage 5 at 4:15, right after the J Monque'd Blues band wrapped up their show. Victor's band was comprised of some of New Orleans finest musicians: Larry Sieberth once again on piano; Rickie Sebastian, drums; Dave Watson on bass; and Koko York presiding on vocals. It's a shame there weren't any parades or marching bands on opening day because the weather was so fine, but Saturday, May 2nd would bring them out in full force to christen the new asphalt.

Friday night, two great shows were offered on the S.S. President: The Caribbean Highlife Jamboree at 7 p.m. with Jimmie Cliff and Hugh Masekela Quintet followed by "The Midnight Blues

B.B. King

FRIDAY, MAY 1

STAGE 1
1:00 The Nightriders
2:00 Willie West & Southbound Transit with Gerry Hall
3:30 Ivan Neville & The Uptown
4:45 Ron Cuccia & The Big Tomato Band

STAGE 2
12:30 The Michael White Trio
2:00 John Wright Trio
3:30 George Slim Heard & The Bluff
5:00 Harmonica Williams & The Mighty Hawks

STAGE 3
1:00 Linda Albert
2:00 Joe Simon's Original Crescent City Jazz Band
3:15 Bourré
4:30 New Jazz Quintet

STAGE 4
12:15 East St. John High Dixieland Band
1:15 Fredrik Norén Band
2:30 Cathy Lucas & The Loose Band
3:45 BeauSoleil
5:00 Jazz Dance Theatre

STAGE 5
12:30 SUNO Big Band
2:00 Muchos Plus
3:15 J. Monque'D Blues Band
4:15 Victor Sirker & The Circuit Breakers
5:30 Dé Sire

JAZZ TENT
12:30 Lady Charlotte & The Men of Jazz
1:45 Kid Sheik's Storyville Ramblers
3:00 Steve Masakowski & Mars
4:15 Jasmine
5:15 Majestic Brass Band with Ellyna Tatum

KOINDU
12:45 SUNO African Ensemble
2:00 Contemporary Dance Co.
3:15 NOCCA Jazz Ensemble
4:30 Theron Lewis Group

GAZEBO
1:00 Nat Krasnoff
2:30 John Rankin
3:45 Cousin Joe

GOSPEL TENT
12:00 The Randolph Brothers
12:40 Brother Joseph Davis
1:00 Kennedy High School Gospel Choir
2:00 Fortier High School Gospel Choir
2:30 Aline White
3:00 Bunny & Bessie
4:00 God's Renewed Gospel Ensemble
4:30 The Melody Clouds
5:00 The Smooth Family of Slidell
5:30 Leviticus Gospel Singers

KID'S TENT
12:00 McDonogh #15 School Band
1:00 Floating Eagle Feather
2:00 Unlimited, Ltd.
3:00 Human Unity Council of New Orleans

SATURDAY, MAY 2

STAGE 1
12:15 Full Oo-Poo-Pa-Doo Revue with Jessie Hill, Reggie Hall, Bobby Lacour & The Young Little Rascals
2:15 The Cold
3:15 James Booker
4:15 Coteau Reunion
5:15 Ramblin' Jack Elliot
6:15 The James Cotton Band

STAGE 2
12:15 Fredrik Norén Band
1:15 Chris Smither
2:15 Dewey Balfa & Friends
3:15 Caledonia Society Pipers
4:15 Sunbelt Bluegrass Band

Jam" that brought together the Muddy Waters Blues Band, Little Milton Orchestra, James Cotton Band, and Walter "Wolfman" Washington & the Solar System Band. Local papers reported the first show to be sold out, and by the time the boat left the shore, the Blues Jam was packed.

On Saturday May 2nd during the day on Stage 1, The Full Oo-Poo-Pa-Do Review featuring Jessie Hill, Reggie Hall, Bobby

Lacour, and the Young Little Rascals got the ball rolling at 12:15, followed by The Cold at 2:15 and James Booker shortly after 3:00. The Cold was one of a handful of bands in New Orleans at the time playing New Wave Rock. New Orleanians rarely pay attention to things like "national trends" but the Cold hit it just right and were hugely popular locally with many big record deals discussed which sadly, fell through.

The Gospel Tent had an inspired day of booking starting with Macedonia B.C. Youth Choir and continuing on throughout the day. By the time The Raymond Myles Singers took the stage with his choir from Macedonia Baptist Church, the Holy Ghost was already strongly

present and accounted for. Mr. Myles brought out nine women, dressed to save souls, five suited tenors and basses, with a drummer and bass player to hold down the groove, and "church was out" as they say. At 4:30 when Raymond started his set, a standing room only crowd had already done a lot of soul searching and whooping for Jesus, and they may have been a little tired, what with the heat and all; but he quickly inspired the seated to stand and the silent to make some noise. The Williams Brothers finished out a perfect day "in the spirit" under the blue-and-white-striped tent top.

Sun Ra and his Solar Arkestra took his fans on a different kind of spiritual journey at Koindu with a hypnotic chant between

Alligator was served for the first time at Jazz Fest and sold out within hours of opening.

Teachers were hired to staff the Kids Tent.

The Heritage Fair was now financially supporting the night concerts.

Kid Thomas Valentine

James Brown and Rap: "Space Is The Place," and that's somewhere in and ahead of his time. Exuma followed, strumming guitar under his colorfully feathered Bahamas broadbill chapeau. George Porter's Joy Ride closed out Stage 5 after The Batiste Brothers Band, Lee Dorsey and Hugh Masekela had gotten everybody musically "right" by delivering great shows throughout the afternoon. On an international note: The New Orleans Rag Pickers of Tokyo came from Japan to perform in the Jazz Tent and did an excellent job of representing the sounds we know and love. Jazz Fest has always been a deep connection for the Japanese.

Saturday night it was back to the boat for a second helping of music on the river. Sometimes people eat too much and their tummies ache, sometimes they drink too much and get tipsy; but it doesn't seem possible to have too much good music. The worst thing that could happen would probably be an excess of happiness, and you might find yourself randomly screaming out some James Brown lyrics on a boat in the middle of the Mississippi River like "I Feel Good!" and dancing like the soul King himself which is what happened to thousands of Fest Fans who attended the triple threat of James Brown, Jr. Walker, and Deacon John.

On Sunday, May 3rd, Sun Ra and His Solar Arkestra played again, then handed the reins over

Radiators

STAGE 3
12:00 Slidell Sr. High Jazz Ensemble
1:00 Irving McLean
2:00 Billy Gregory
3:00 Les Moore
4:15 Woodenhead
5:30 Herman Jackson Group

STAGE 4
12:15 Loyola Big Band
1:15 N.O. Square & Round Dance Association with Johnny Creel
2:15 Clinton Broussard & Zydeco Machine
3:15 Salt Creek
4:30 The Scooter Lee Show
5:45 Banda Fiebre

STAGE 5
12:00 UNO Jazz Band
1:15 Buck Whet Zydeco Ils Sont Partis
2:30 Batiste Brothers Band
3:30 Lee Dorsey
4:45 Hugh Masekela
6:15 George Porter's Joyride

JAZZ TENT
12:15 Dillard University Jazz Ensemble
1:15 New Orleans Rag Pickers of Tokyo
2:30 Earl Turbinton, Jr.
3:30 Louisiana Repertory Jazz Ensemble
4:30 New Orleans Ragtime Orchestra
5:45 Edward "Kidd" Jordan Improvisational Arts Co.

KOINDU
12:15 Frank Parker Group
1:30 Carl LeBlanc & Nature
2:30 John Chipman "King of the Goat Skin Drum"
3:00 Blind Blake
3:45 The Black Eagles
4:45 Sun Ra & His Solar Arkestra

GAZEBO
12:30 Chester Calhoun
1:45 Percy "Brother" Randolph & Little Freddie King
3:00 The Wild Tchoupitoulas
4:00 Silas Hogan & Guitar Kelly
5:00 John Chipman "King of the Goat Skin Drum"
5:30 Blind Blake

GOSPEL TENT
12:00 Macedonia B.C. Youth Choir
12:30 New Orleans Comforters
1:00 The Modern Gospel Quartet
1:30 The Friendly Five
2:00 The Hope Ensemble
2:30 The Rocks of Harmony
3:00 Marine Baptist Church Youth Choir
3:30 The Crown Seekers
4:00 Mt. Kingdom Baptist Church Choir
4:30 Raymond Myles Singers
5:00 Avondale Community Chorus
5:30 The Gospel Choralettes of Kenner
6:00 The Williams Brother

KID'S TENT
12:00 Robert M. Lusher School Choir
1:00 New Games
2:00 New Orleans Free School Village Kids
3:00 Floating Eagle Feather
4:00 Calliope Puppet Theatre
5:00 Unlimited, Ltd.

PARADES
2:30 Men's Moneywasters, Ladies' Moneywasters & Gentlemen of Leisure SA&PCs with Onward Brass Band

"We had the Solar Arkestra and they did the "Space is the Place" jam, but I'd also booked him (Sun Ra) to play a piano solo in the Jazz Tent — and he came to do a solo and people started showing up — guys from the train station — guys from the bus station — taxi cabs — at that time you could drive on the field and they just kept on showing up — so by the time he got on stage, he had about a nine piece piano solo." QUINT DAVIS

music scene

The Neville Brothers release "Fiyo on the Bayou."

Black Top Records is started in New Orleans.

IN MEMORIAM

"Polo" Barnes, Booker T. Glass, Matthew "Fats" Houston, Tony Schiro, Martin "Chink" Abraham, John Hawkins, Stanley John, Joseph "Cornbread" Thomas, Albert Fernandez Walters, Robert Pete Williams, Hoagy Carmichael

to funky Lil' Queenie and the Percolators who then passed it on to the most magical Odetta to close the first weekend of music on Stage 4. While all of this was occurring, thousands of sweaty, tired, sunburned, happy people danced their way to the close of lovely weekend to parades and second lines that wove their way along the new asphalt track.

That night at the Fairmont Imperial Ballroom, The History of New Orleans Style Jazz on Film was offered at 8 p.m. In 1980, this event was so well attended that it was moved to

the Ballroom to provide more space for music history buffs to view the vintage, pre-video, footage collected by jazz film expert David Chertok. This musical education aspect of the Festival helped to give a deeper appreciation of where the music came from and how it was evolving.

Monday the 4th brought a night of Dixieland at the Fairmont Imperial Ballroom once again with Bob Crosby (brother of Bing) and the Bob Cats; Chris Barber Jazz and Blues Band from across the "big pond" as many local musicians say, in England;

and the George Finola Jazz Band and Placide Adams Original Dixieland Hall Jazz Band. Mr. Crosby would bring in three of his original sidemen for this show, bassist Bobby Haggart, trumpeter Yank Lawson, and guitarist Nappy Lamare. This band was voted "Best All-American Jazz Band" in 1938 by "Downbeat" magazine and was a must see for traditional jazz fans.

Tuesday, May 5th, also in the Imperial Room, Cab Calloway, the original "hip talk" master brought his silver tongue and his killer band back to entertain at the Festival, along with drum master Panama Francis and the Savoy Sultans and pianist extraordinaire Dorothy Donegan.

Luther Kent and Trick Bag decided to kick their presentation up a notch on the riverboat President on Wednesday, May 6th when they shared a bill with our own musical Midas Allen Toussaint, who brought Ernie "Mother in Law" K-Doe along as his guest vocalist. Tommy Ridgley and the Untouchables opened this show with a soulful set and got it started out right. But when Luther and his

Big Band took the stage, under the direction of Charlie Brent, dressed in white tuxedos with tails for their first scorching, hard rocking, Big Band Blues arrangement and Luther's gigantic voice blasted out over the crowd, the packed boat went nuts. When Luther was asked about the tuxedo anomaly, he replied that he always knew they'd clean up well and he just wanted to do something extra special for the show.

Thursday May 7th on the *S.S. President*, the evening show du jour was the Dexter Gordon Quartet, Betty Carter and her trio, and Jimmy Smith. This Jazz Cruise was billed as a "Be-Bop Boatride" and brought together three truly fine masters of the art form. Locals Steve Masakowski and James Black backed Jimmy Smith's jazz organ in the opening slot on this show.

The Jazz Jam Session at Prout's Alhambra Nightclub was filled to capacity with an enthusiastic crowd of avid jazz lovers on Thursday night, following the Be-Bop Boatride starting at 1:00 am and featuring a huge line-up of contemporary jazz musicians that played well into the morning.

Friday, May 8th at the Theatre of Performing Arts, Ms. Nancy Wilson shared the bill with the Ramsey Lewis Quartet, and local contemporary jazz group, Tony Dagradi and Astral Project. These young local players were making their mark as the hottest jazz group in town, in addition to one of the hardest working rhythm sections in New Orleans.

With all of the "must see" late night shows going on, it was a good thing the music at the Fair Grounds didn't start 'til after noon. Out there the next day the ladies' marching clubs helped to wake everybody up and get the sweat flowing freely backed by the Young Tuxedo and Fairview Brass Bands.

The closing acts on Saturday, May 9th kept the folks at the Fair Grounds on their feet–no matter how tired they were from the plethora of night shows offered this year. But after a shower and a short nap they were ready that night for James Rivers Movement that shared the bill with the Crusaders and Mongo Santamaria in the Municipal Auditorium.

Some rain earlier in the day on Sunday put the new "Main Thoroughfare" to the test; and it passed with flying colors, leaving only a few muddy patches and no shoes lost in the quagmire. Some people may not have liked the look of it, but it worked like a charm.

Jules Cahn

"Jimmy Page came and sat in with us four nights in a row — he was just blown away. He loved the blues, man — he was just blown away. Mick Fleetwood came in one night and says 'Man I wanna play. I love playing with a big horn section.' So I said 'Man come on up and play drums, you know?' And he came up and played until 5:00 in the morning. I turned around and his hands looked like raw meat. They were blistered everywhere, but he wouldn't quit playing." LUTHER KENT

GOSPEL TENT
12:00 C & B Ensemble
12:30 The Jones Sisters
1:00 2nd Mt. Carmel Choir
1:30 Gaza B.C. Youth Choir
2:00 True Tone Singers
2:30 The Masonic Kings
3:00 Divine Grace Choir
3:30 Chosen Soul Searchers for Christ
4:00 Voices of Faith Youth Choir
4:30 St. John Radio Choir
5:00 Heralds of Christ
5:30 The Desire Community Chorus
6:00 The Williams Brother

KID'S TENT
12:00 Tom Foote
1:00 New Games
2:00 Gospel Isrealites
3:00 Floating Eagle Feather
4:00 Carrollton Youth Chorus
5:00 Unlimited, Ltd.

PARADES
4:00 Olympia Aid Society, The Jumpers & Beautiful Ladies Marching Club SA&PCs with The Olympia Brass Band and Doc Paulin Brass Band

SATURDAY, MAY 9

STAGE 1
12:30 The Music of Shangri-la
1:45 A Taste of N.O. with Al Johnson, Huey Smith, Little Sonny & David Lastie
3:00 Tommy Ridgley, Bobby Mitchell, Ernie K-Doe
4:45 Roy Brown & Kid Johnson
6:00 Dr. John

STAGE 2
12:00 Mardi Gras Chorus
1:00 Svare
2:00 Hot Strings
3:00 Washboard Leo & Poulet Brulé
4:00 Hazel Schleuter & The Delta Ramblers with The Komenka Ethnic Dance Ensemble
5:15 Raful Neal & The Neal Brothers Band
6:15 Frank Trapani's Jazz Band

STAGE 3
12:00 SUBR Jazz Band
1:15 Small Sand Trad Band of Norway
2:15 Enigma Force
3:15 Valerian's Voices
4:15 Dave Williams

STAGE 4
12:15 Arion with Philip Manuel
1:30 Bobby Powell
2:45 Astral Project
3:45 Paky Saavedra & Los Bandidos
5:00 Deacon John & The N.O. Blues Revue with Earl King & Butch Mudbone
6:15 Zachary Richard

STAGE 5
12:00 Holy Cross High School Jazz Band
1:15 Allen Fontenot & The Country Cajuns
2:30 Marcia Ball
3:45 Doug Kershaw
5:00 Preston Franks & The Soileau Playboys
6:00 Tim Williams Band

JAZZ TENT
12:00 Xavier Jazz Ensemble
1:00 James Black Group
2:00 Louis Nelson Big Six

3:00 New Leviathan Oriental Foxtrot Orchestra with The Pfister Sisters
4:15 Thomas Jefferson Jazz Band
5:15 Cecil Taylor
6:15 Ramsey McLean & The Lifers

KOINDU
12:30 Vietnamese Art Ensemble
1:45 Shango Rising
2:45 Teddy Riley & His N.O. Jazz Masters
3:45 The Wild Magnolias
4:45 Neptune Jazz Band of Zimbabwe
6:00 Willie Metcalf

GAZEBO
12:30 Randy East
1:30 Butch Mudbone
2:30 David & Roselyn
3:30 Mozart on 5th
4:30 Will Soto
5:30 Bongo Joe

GOSPEL TENT
12:00 Second Morning Star Baptist Church Choir
12:30 Antioch Baptist Church Youth Choir
1:00 The Religious Five
1:30 Fairview B.C. Youth Choir
2:00 St. Luke A.M.E. Choir
2:30 Southern Bells
3:00 Morning Star B.C. Choir of Thibodeaux, LA
3:30 The Herman Finley Singers
4:00 Gospel Inspirations of Donaldsonville
4:30 St. Francis DeSales Gospel Choir
5:00 The Nationally Known Gospel Cavaliers
5:30 Greater St. Stephen Baptist Church Choir
6:00 Dorothy Love Coates Singers

KID'S TENT
12:00 New Games
1:00 Nelson Camp
3:00 Calliope Puppet Theatre
5:00 Tom Foote

PARADES
4:30 Ladies' Zulu, Calendar Girls & Burgundy Ladies SA&PCs with Young Tuxedo Brass Band and Fairview Brass Band

SUNDAY, MAY 10

STAGE 1
12:15 St. Augustine Jazz Band
1:15 The Dixie Kups
2:15 The Dave Bartholomew Band with Lloyd Washington
3:45 The Meters
4:45 Clifton Chenier
6:00 Allen Toussaint

STAGE 2
12:00 Hollis Carmouche Jazz Band
1:00 Sady Courville & The Mamou Hour Band
2:15 Elmo Mendoza & The Senior Citizen Serenaders
3:15 The Golden Stars Mardi Gras Indians
4:30 The Amazing Ironing Board Sam
5:45 The Ardoin Family Band

STAGE 3
12:15 Southeastern University Jazz Ensemble
1:15 Walter Payton
2:15 Rick Kriska Crescent
3:30 Russ Russell & The Rustlers with Rufus Thibodeaux

5:00 Walter Mouton & The Scott Playboys

STAGE 4
12:00 Clyde Kerr, Jr. & Univision
1:15 Mark Naftalin
2:15 Sonora Latina
3:15 James Booker
4:15 The Radiators
5:30 Clarence "Frogman" Henry

STAGE 5
12:15 Ruben "Salsa" Gonzalez
1:15 Willie Tee
2:30 Clarence "Gatemouth" Brown
3:45 Mongo Santamaria
5:15 Margie Joseph
6:15 The James Rivers Movement

JAZZ TENT
12:30 Neptune Jazz Band of Zimbabwe
1:30 Tuts Washington
2:30 Urban Spaces
3:30 Alvin Batiste
4:30 Danny Barker's Jazz Hounds with Blue Lu Barker
5:30 Kid Thomas Valentine & His Algiers Stompers

KOINDU
12:30 Ngoma
2:00 SUNO Jazz Ensemble
3:15 White Eagles Mardi Gras Indians
4:15 The Fred Kemp Group
5:30 Solar

GAZEBO
12:30 Will Soto
1:45 Bongo Joe
3:45 Spencer Bohren
5:00 Flatland String Band
6:00 Clancy "Blues Boy" Lewis

GOSPEL TENT
12:00 New Orleans Spiritualettes
12:30 The Mighty Chariots
1:00 Christine Myles with Johnny B. Keller
1:30 The Ott Family
2:00 St. Joseph Helping Hand Church Choir
2:30 Dimensions of Faith
3:00 McDonogh #35 Gospel Choir
3:30 Plymouth Rock B.C. Chorus of Reserve, La.
4:00 Gospel Chords
4:30 Zion Harmonizers
5:00 Pentecost B.C. Youth Choir
5:30 Church of God in Christ Choir
6:00 The Gospel Soul Children
6:30 Dorothy Love Coates Singers

KID'S TENT
12:00 Jimmie Brown
1:00 New Games
2:00 Gospel Isrealites
3:00 Calliope Puppet Theatre
4:00 Fairview B.C. Band
5:00 Tom Foote

PARADES
3:00 Scene Boosters & Fun Lovers SA&PCs with Pinstripe Brass Band & Dirty Dozen Brass Band

NIGHT CONCERTS

FRIDAY, MAY 1, 7 P.M.
Caribbean Highlife Jamboree
Jimmy Cliff
Hugh Masekela Quintet
Riverboat S. S. President
FRIDAY, MAY 1, 12 MIDNIGHT
Midnight Blues Jam
Muddy Waters Blues Band
Little Milton Orchestra
James Cotton Band

Walter Washington & The Solar System Band
Riverboat S. S. President
SATURDAY, MAY 2, 7 P.M. & MIDNIGHT
The James Brown Show & Orchestra
Jr. Walker & The Allstars
Deacon John
Riverboat S. S. President
SUNDAY, MAY 3, 8 P.M.
The History of New Orleans Style on Film
Louis Armstrong, Armand Hug, Sweet Emma ...
Imperial Ballroom – Fairmont Hotel
MONDAY, MAY 4, 8 P.M.
Bob Crosby & The Bob Cats
Chris Barber Jazz & Blues Band
The George Finola Jazz Band
Placide Adams Original Hall Jazz Band
Imperial Ballroom – Fairmont Hotel
TUESDAY, MAY 5, 8 P.M.
Cab Calloway
Panama Francis & The Savoy Sultans
Dorothy Donegan
Imperial Ballroom – Fairmont Hotel
WEDNESDAY, MAY 6, 8 P.M.
New Orleans Rhythm & Blues
Allen Toussaint
Ernie K-Doe
Luther Kent & Trick Bag
Tommy Ridgley & The Untouchables
Riverboat S. S. President
WEDNESDAY, MAY 6, 8 P.M.
New Orleans Jazz & Heritage Festival Jam Session – Part I
Louis Nelson, Preston Jackson, Jack Willis, Kid Sheik, Teddy Riley, Kid Thomas, Raymond Burke, Michael White, Pud Brown, Emanuel Sayles, Chester Jones, Jeanette Kimball, Olivia C. Cook, Herman Sherman, Anthony Lacen, Walter Payton, Harold Dejan, Harry Connick, Jr., Freddie Lonzo, Stewart Davis, Allen Jaffe, Bob Greene, Sherwood Mangiapane, Wendell Eugene, Frank Parker, Frank Fields, John Brunious, Frank Parker, Stanley Stevens, Les Muscutt, Emanuel Paul, Manny Crusto, ...
Imperial Ballroom – Fairmont Hotel

THURSDAY, MAY 7, 8 P.M.
Jazz Cruise
Dexter Gordon Quartet
Betty Carter & Her Trio
Jimmy Smith
Riverboat S. S. President
THURSDAY, MAY 7, 1 A.M.
New Orleans Jazz & Heritage Festival Jam Session – Part II
Ellis Marsalis, Willie Tee, Willie Metcalf, Rusty Gilder, Bill Huntington, James Black, Tony Bazley, Smokey Johnson, Clyde Kerr, Jr., Emery Thompson, Chuck Easterling, Freddie Lonzo, Earl Turbinton, Edward Kidd Jordan, James Rivers, Erving Charles, Edward Frank, Fred Kemp, Rick Kriska, Michael Pierce, Alvin Batiste, Kent Jordan, Steve Masakowski, Elton Herron, Dooky Chase, Chuck Berlin, Clarence Ford, Alvin Fielder, Lloyd Lambert, Charles Neville, Richard Payne, Charlie Burbank, Ralph Johnson, Johnny Horn, Duke Barker, Don Suhor, Jud Berger, Roger Lewis, Harry Nance, Miles Wright, Kirk Ford, Carl LeBlanc, Vic Zipeto, Wendell Brunious, Willie Cole & Eddie Collins
Prout's Club Alhambra
FRIDAY, MAY 8, 8 P.M.
Nancy Wilson
Ramsey Lewis Quartet
Tony Dagradi & Astral Project
Theatre of the Performing Arts
FRIDAY, MAY 8, 12:30 A.M.
Great Black Music: Ancient to the Future
Art Ensemble of Chicago
Cecil Taylor
Edward "Kidd" Jordan & The Improvisational Arts Company
Municipal Auditorium
SATURDAY, MAY 9, 9 P.M.
The Crusaders
Mongo Santamaria
James Rivers Movement
Municipal Auditorium

Marc and Ann Savoy with Clifton Chenier (in background)

1982

This Jazz & Heritage Festival was a hot one musically and environmentally. Although cloud cover cooled things off and kept it from being brutal on opening day, Friday April 30th, the sun and heat increased over the weekend. Many people were thanking God for the shade of the Gospel and Jazz Tents by closing time on Sunday. *The Times Picayune* newspaper reported that nearly 95,000 people attended on the first Sunday. Long lines of people gathered where water was flowing freely from two upright pipes near the poster booth, waiting for their opportunity to douse their heads, necks, and handkerchiefs before jumping back into the musical and gastronomic fray.

Festival officials said more than 8,000 people came out on opening day and many headed straight for the posters. Early in the day lines were 30 and 40 people deep and Festival attendees waited for as much as an hour for their signed, or unsigned limited edition prints.

The official poster had become so popular and collectible that the Jazz & Heritage Festival put a cap on how many could be sold each day. Each person was only allowed to buy one poster at a time, but you could make your purchase, get back in line, and buy another one for as long as you liked, or until the poster sold out for the day. They did this in the hopes that true Jazz Festival fans would have a better shot at getting the poster for a reasonable price, instead of having galleries come in to purchase them in bulk and then resell them at inflated prices. The 1982 edition was 12,500 prints with limits sold on each day. It took just shy of an hour to sell 800 signed, numbered posters on opening day. The price for the signed edition was $80.25 each. Two thousand prints of the unsigned version were made available on opening day for $26.75 each – a little easier for the Festival lover who was looking for a memory. One pleasant and memorable occurrence was a large increase in Port-O-Lets at the Fair Grounds, and also a division of male and female. The girls could no longer blame the boys for being messy, but the boys were "pissed" that they ostensibly lost half their options

for relief. The gender designation provided no extra solution for the problem of knocking toilet paper into the effluvia, and so women to this day who plan ahead and carry extra toilet paper in their purses make the most new friends at Jazz Festival.

As the heat continued to rise and the rain refused to come, the limited space under the trees and shady sides of the tents became the premium real estate at the Fair Grounds. Over the weekend, people even climbed up into the racetrack stands to escape the masses on the infield and to find a little additional shade. A sun block booth, later a staple, would have been as popular as the official poster booth with lines at least as long. Several newspaper articles comment on the "bright red necks and faces" that became a common site on this hot, sweaty year.

The heat may have had something to do with a little "moment" that occurred during a show on the second Sunday, May 9th. Irma Thomas, queen of New Orleans Rhythm and

King Nino & His Slave Girls

"In 1982 we finally got to film footage of Clifton Chenier performing at Jazz Fest. On Saturday night he played on the riverboat and he was really great and the next day he was at the Fair Grounds and he wanted to show up Fats Domino and prove that he was the king. So when it was a special show for him he would drag out his PA system and set it up. As a result the sound was awful. There were all sort of whizzing and whirling and odd sounds coming from those speakers. It's amazing that we got anything to use. We put that footage in the documentary 'Jai Ete Tu Bal.'" CHRIS STRACHWITZ

Blues was in the middle of her show when she started waving her handkerchief in the air during "I Done Got Over It." All of her fans followed suit in this New Orleans second line dancing tradition, waving napkins and handkerchiefs while they joined in the chorus. But there was one girl that didn't have a hankie. Sitting on her boyfriend's shoulders to get a better view of the show, she ripped off her halter-top and started waving that. Irma said it was a sight to behold with her generously endowed chest slapping her boyfriend "up side the head" as she bounced up and down on his shoulders. " I almost lost my whole band." Irma laughingly remembered.

Every traditional jazz lover was excited about a new addition for the 1983 Jazz & Heritage Festival. The "Hot Jazz Classic" was a cooperative venture between Festival management and Tulane University's William Ransom Hogan Jazz Archive. Jazz Archive curator, Curtis D. Jerde, touted the Hot Jazz Classic as the "first international music celebration devoted exclusively to vintage New Orleans Jazz." This series encompassed a variety of media including concerts, films, symposia on the art form, a "jazz picnic" at the Fair Grounds, and a "reunion" honoring pre-1940 musicians.

The highpoint of the Tulane Hot Jazz Classic was "Jazz Picnic", from noon to six on May 7th out at the fair site which included an abundance of performers executing the living history of classic New Orleans Jazz. This "jazz picnic" would be remembered as a "Festival within a Festival" and would have an effect on programming, creating some wonderful changes in the Festival layout the following year. It would be some time before the Jazz & Heritage Festival added a permanent second Friday, but this charming day of musical history is still remembered by those who were lucky enough to know about it.

On picnic day at the Fair Grounds, the New Eclipse Band started it all off in the Jazz Tent at high noon, with the Michael White Quartet beginning at 12:15 on the Stage 1 bandstand. White continues to this day exploring the creative possibilities of traditional jazz, even acquiring new fans with his critically acclaimed 2004 CD, Dancing In The Sky, which breathed fresh air into the old genre. The music continued throughout the day with this staggered start time; New Reliance Orchestra-1:00, Kid Thomas Valentine and the Algiers Stompers- 1:15, New Orleans Creole Orchestra at 2:00, Kid Sheik- 2:15. Louisiana Repertory Jazz Ensemble kept it moving at 3:00, and fifteen minutes later the Original Camelia Jazz Band was introduced on Stage 1. New Orleans Ragtime Orchestra kicked it in at 4:00, and at 4:15 One Mo' Time began. The Kids weren't getting younger, just better.

The film series offerings for the Hot Jazz Classic were truly the highlight for some. Amazing, rare, live footage of original jazz innovators shot in pre-video days captured the magic and the fire of the earliest jazz artists. Some of the features in this Three-hour program were Louis Armstrong, Wingy Manone, Kid Ory, Sidney Bechet, and many others. This film presentation was brought to New Orleans by one of the preeminent collectors of jazz films, David Chertok.

Another new item of note in 1983 were venue changes

Pete Fountain

STAGE 2
12:00 East St. John High School Jazz Band
1:00 Square Dance Association with Johnny Creel
2:15 Black Eagles Mardi Gras Indians
3:15 Carlos Sanchez
4:30 James Booker
5:30 Champion Jack Dupree

STAGE 3
12:30 Bobby Breaux Quartet
1:45 Allen Fontenot & The Country Cajuns
3:00 Tabby Thomas & The Mighty House Rockers
4:30 Irving McLean
5:45 Mars

STAGE 4
12:15 UNO Jazz Band
1:15 Sonora Latina
2:30 Buckwheat Zydeco
3:30 Onward Brass Band
4:45 Fats Domino
5:45 At Taste of New Orleans with Little Sonny

JAZZ TENT
12:00 Holy Cross High School Jazz Ensemble
1:15 Lady Charlotte's Jazz Band
2:30 Jasmine
3:45 Astral Project
5:00 Wynton Marsalis
6:00 Louis Nelson Big Six

KOINDU
12:15 Xavier Jazz Lab Band
1:30 Edward Perkins Group
2:30 Voodoo Macumba
3:30 Golden Stars Mardi Gras Indians
4:30 The Doug Carn Group
5:45 George Pack African Ensemble

GAZEBO A
1:45 Jim Turner
3:00 Butch Mudbone
4:15 David & Roselyn

GAZEBO B
1:15 Scott Goudeau
2:30 Snooks Eaglin
3:45 Hazel Schleuter & The Delta Ramblers
4:45 BeauSoleil

GOSPEL TENT
12:00 Greater Asia B.C. Choir
12:40 The Religious Five
1:20 The Spiritual Wonders
2:00 Union Bethel A.M.E. Cathedral Choir
2:40 The Pure Hearts Community Choir
3:20 The Friendly Travelers
4:00 The Southern Bells
4:40 The Ott Family
5:20 Pentecost Youth Choir
6:00 Desire Community Chorus

PARADES
4:00 Mellow Fellows, Gentlemen of Leisure & Burgundy Ladies SA&PCs with Doc Paulin Brass Band

for the nighttime events. There were no hotel ballroom concerts on the bill, although the Riverboat *S.S. President* hosted more nighttime functions than ever. The riverboat shows are legendary in the memories of all longtime Jazz Festival devotees and this particular year focused

on a more eclectic mix for a more far-reaching audience.

Friday, April 30th started the series with "Louisiana Gumbo." In Louisiana, no two gumbos are alike- the only thing they have in common is that they taste great, as long as the chef knows how to cook. In this case, the chef was

night concert producer Charlie Bering, with Robert Leslie Jones as production manager and John "Klondike" Koehler working as technical liaison. Charlie was a master "chef" when it came to music, and the ingredients he used in his "Louisiana Gumbo" left nothing to be desired: Fats Domino, Wynton Marsalis, and the Dirty Dozen Brass Band.

Fats Domino and the Dave Bartholomew Band had worked together for the last forty-five years or so in 1983 and you just couldn't get any tighter. Wynton Marsalis was a mere twenty years old and was already reaching an exalted status with his forays into every kind of jazz. A student of Juilliard, The Berkshire Center at Tanglewood, and most recently a stint with Art Blakey's Jazz Messengers had added even more flavor to his musi-

music scene

Lucille (BB King's guitar) is stolen backstage at Ole Man River.

Stevenson Palfi releases his documentary "Piano Players Rarely Ever Play Together" featuring Professor Longhair, Tuts Washington and Allen Toussaint.

Ernie K-Doe begins to host a show on WWOZ.

The Neville Brothers release "Nevillization."

Ellis Marsalis releases "Father and Sons."

IN MEMORIAM

Dave "Fat Man" Williams, Nathan Abshire, Roy Brown, Henry "Booker T." Glass, "Lightnin'" Hopkins, Joe Lambert, Amos Landry, August Lanoix, Furry Lewis, Chief Percy "Pete" Lewis, Thelonious S. Monk, Red Weaver, Robert Coqville, Thelonious Monk, Wingy Manone

James Black

cal "Gumbo." The Dirty Dozen Brass Band, one of the youngest Brass Bands in the Crescent City, was already achieving huge popularity with their tight, funky, fresh arrangements. They "rolled the boat" and the sweat flowed freely. "Louisiana Gumbo" was good to the last drop.

On Friday, May 7th, the combination of Rita "Give Me Some Of Your Sen-sey" Marley who brought the spirit of the "Kings Music" from Jamaica, and the Neville Brother's "Fiyou on The Bayou" created so much smoke on the boat that this night concert transcended mere music and became a spiritual experience for everyone who attended. Exuma the Obeah man, born in the Bahamas added a little calypso along with his strong and diverse Caribbean rhythms. Resplendent in a huge hat with

feathers and playing his syncopated guitar beat, Exuma was a Fest favorite for a few years in the eighties. This lineup cruised under the banner "Caribbean meets New Orleans," and was sold out well in advance.

"The Blues Boat" on Sunday May 8th featured B.B. King, Etta James, and New Orleans own Lil' Queenie and the Percolators whose core was Leigh Harris (Lil' Queenie) and John Magnie, later of the subdudes. They had become one of the most popular bands in the city and had been together for almost five years at the time of this performance. They would do their last show at Tipitina's around three months later to a packed house saying goodbye. As often happens to great original groups, they got into legal difficulties and confusions over

SUNDAY, MAY 2

STAGE 1
12:45 Tommy Ridgley with Jessie Hill, Bobby Mitchell & Ernie K-Doe
2:45 Clarence "Gatemouth" Brown
4:00 Clarence "Frogman" Henry
5:00 Percy Mayfield
6:15 Dr. John

STAGE 2
12:15 Southeastern Jazz Ensemble
1:15 Caledonia Society
2:30 Sady Courville & The Mamou Hour Cajun Band
3:30 Night Breeze
4:30 Sybil Kein's Gumbo People
5:45 Odetta

STAGE 3
12:30 Bobby Marchan & Higher Ground
1:30 Russ Russell & The Rustlers
2:45 Los Catrachos
3:45 Clinton Broussard & Zydeco Machine
4:45 Blind Sam Myers & Nu Ash Band
6:00 New Jazz Quintet

STAGE 4
12:15 Tulane Big Band
1:15 Troy L. Deramus & LA State Fiddle Champions
2:45 Radiators
3:45 Lee Dorsey
4:45 Chuck Berry
6:00 Clifton Chenier & His Red Hot Louisiana Band

JAZZ TENT
1:00 N.O. All-Star Women's Jazz Ensemble
2:00 Frank Trapani Jazz Band
3:00 James Drew
4:15 Ellis Marsalis Quintet
5:30 Kid Thomas & His Algiers Stompers

KOINDU
12:00 Dillard University Jazz Band
1:15 Muchos Plus
2:30 Ngoma
3:30 Antonio York
4:45 David "Fathead" Newman & Hank Crawford
5:45 Willie Metcalf with Laverne Butler

GAZEBO A
2:00 Lucinda Williams
3:15 Brother Percy Randolph
4:15 Spencer Bohren

GAZEBO B
1:15 Scaniazz Jazz Band
2:15 Golden Eagles Mardi Gras Indians
3:15 Teddy Riley & His N.O. Jazz Masters
4:30 Johnny Vidacovich
5:30 Hot Strings

GOSPEL TENT
12:00 The Gospel Marionetts
12:40 The Famous True Tones
1:20 The Masonic Kings
2:00 True Believers of Christ
2:40 St. Monica Kings
3:20 The Friendly Five
4:00 Voices of Faith
4:40 Avondale Community Choir
5:20 The Sensational Williams Brother

"In 1982 on the Riverboat President the Festival presented Dewey Balfa and Friends, Clifton Chenier and Doug Kershaw. When Clifton came on he played his heart out. Every person on the boat danced to this exceptional performance. Clifton churned out the rhythm on his accordion so strong that it could have made a dead man dance. In the Baptist Church there is a saying when a gospel group sings so fantastically that the church would empty after their performance because no one wants to hear anything else. They call that 'turning the house out.' That night Clifton turned the house out. After several encores by Clifton, Doug Kershaw came on and the boat began to empty. Quint realized there was a problem and as people headed for the exits he had Clifton's band come up on the back of the stage. People started to turn around and walk towards the stage. Doug Kershaw thought he had finally caught our attention and sawed on that fiddle like a mad man. Then he turned around and saw Clifton's band standing there and in an outrage he smashed his fiddle onto the stage and walked off. At that point Clifton walked back on with his crown and the King made the crowd go wild." JERRY BROCK

Alvin Batiste

The "Jazz Jam Session" at Prout's Alhambra Nightclub, was back by popular demand on Thursday May 6th starting at 11:45 pm. Featured pianists: Ellis Marsalis and David Torkanowsky. Featured saxophonists: Earl Turbinton, Kidd Jordan, Tony Dagradi, and Red Tyler. Featured drummers: Alvin Fielder, Smoky Johnson, and John Vidacovich. Alvin Batiste on clarinet and Clyde Kerr on trumpet in addition to a non-stop "Dew Drop Inn" of heavy hitters made this one of the hottest tickets for serious jazz lovers. The hot out of town players who were in town rallied to the beacon of these high caliber local players and everyone in town knew there'd be the once in a lifetime exchanges that only happened at Jazz Festival.

Tyler's Beer Garden was also hosting a jam this year. On Sunday May 9th "Jazz at Tyler's" had a wonderful lineup backed by one of the great New Orleans

Rhythm sections: Ellis Marsalis, Jim Singleton, and the legendary James Black on drums. Sonny Stitt and Eddie "Lockjaw" Davis were featured on this bill and a standing room only house consumed this offering of jazz with zeal. In 1982, Tyler's was being credited with bringing together New Orleans most accomplished jazz artists in combinations that hadn't been seen in New Orleans for a number of years.

Noah's Jazz Club on Esplanade and N. Robertson was another "Dew Drop Inn" for top local jazz artists and featured Laverne Butler with Harry Connick Jr., on piano, Lady BJ. Phillip Manuel, Germaine Bazzle, Lillian Boutté, and others backed by top local sidemen all through the Festival. To read this list, years later, is to understand how people could spend all day at the Fair Grounds and stay up all night in the clubs.

an unclear management deal (unclear meaning that every one had a different very clear idea); and in the end, the only people who got paid were the lawyers.

Earl Turbinton

GOSPEL TENT

12:05 The Mighty Chariots
12:40 The Heavenly Stars
1:15 N.O. Spiritualettes
1:50 Second B.C. Choir – Sixth District
2:25 Community Correctional Choir
3:00 The Heralds of Christ
3:35 The Greater Macedonia B.C. Choir
4:10 The Zion Harmonizers
4:45 Sister Bessie Griffin
5:20 Christine Myles with The Raymond Myles Singers
5:55 Gospel Soul Children

PARADES

2:45 Big Jumpers, Olympia Aide & Ladies Zulu SA&PCs with Majestic Brass Band & Dirty Dozen Brass Band

NIGHT CONCERTS

SATURDAY, MAY 1, 8 P.M.
Swamp Jam
Dr. John
David "Fathead" Newman
Hank Crawford
Clifton Chenier
Riverboat President
SUNDAY, MAY 2, 8 P.M.
Big Band Dance
Woody Herman & The Thundering Herd
Dave Bartholomew's Big Band
Chuck Easterling's Big Band
Riverboat President
TUESDAY, MAY 4
Spyro Gyra
Gato Barbieri
Saenger Performing Arts Center
WEDNESDAY, MAY 5, 8 P.M.
New Orleans Rhythm & Blues
Allen Toussaint
Irma Thomas & Aaron Neville
James Booker
Riverboat President
THURSDAY, MAY 6, 8 P.M.
Hubert Laws
Freddie Hubbard
Stanley Turrentine
Riverboat President
THURSDAY, MAY 6, 11:45 P.M.
Jazz Jam Session
Ellis Marsalis, David Torkanowsky, Clyde Kerr, Jr., Earl Turbinton, Kidd Jordan, Tony Dagradi, Red Tyler, Alvin Fielder, Smokey Johnson, John Vidacovich, Alvin Batiste and many more
Prout's Alhambra Nightclub
FRIDAY, MAY 7, 8 P.M.
Caribbean Meets New Orleans
Rita Marley, Neville Brothers, Exuma
Riverboat President
SATURDAY, MAY 8, 8 P.M.
B.B. King, Etta James, Lil' Queenie & The Percolators
Riverboat President
SUNDAY, MAY 9, 8 P.M.
Sonny Stitt, Eddie "Lockjaw" Davis, Ellis Marsalis, James Black & Jim Singleton
Tyler's Beer Garden
SUNDAY, MAY 9, 11:45 P.M.
Cedar Walton, Buster Williams, Billy Higgins, Earl Turbinton, Clyde Kerr, Jr., and Tony Dagradi
Faubourg Restaurant

PARADES

2:15 Scene Booster & Fun Lovers SA&PCs with Olympia Brass Band and Charlie Barbarin Memorial Brass Band

SATURDAY, MAY 8

STAGE 1
1:00 St. Augustine Jazz Band
2:15 Ruben "Mr. Salsa" Gonzalez
3:30 Earl King with The Deacon John Blues Revue
5:00 Pete Fountain
6:15 Neville Brothers

STAGE 2
12:15 Mardi Gras Chorus
1:15 White Eagles Mardi Gras Indians
2:15 Ronnie Kole Trio Plus One
3:15 Dewey Balfa & Friends
4:15 Roosevelt Sykes
5:15 Rusty Mayne Trio

STAGE 3
12:45 Rock-A-Byes
2:00 Tim Williams Band
3:15 Sonny Landreth Blues Band
4:30 Zachary Richard
5:45 Woodenhead with Angelle Trosclair

STAGE 4
12:15 Loyola Faculty Jazz Ensemble
1:15 Dixie Kups
2:30 James Rivers Movement
3:45 Rita Marley
5:00 Batiste Brothers
6:00 Dave Bartholomew

JAZZ TENT
12:30 Fred Kemp Quintet
1:30 Placide Adams Original Dixieland Jazz Band
2:30 Al Belletto Quartet
3:30 Ramsey McLean & The Lifers
4:45 Sonny Stitt, Eddie "Lockjaw" Davis, Cedar Walter, Buster Williams & Billy Higgins
5:45 Danny Barker

KOINDU
12:00 SUNO African Ensemble
1:00 Caleb-El
2:00 Academy of Black Arts Jazz Ensemble
3:00 Preston Frank & The Soileau Playboys
4:15 Ayocuan
5:30 Richie Havens

GAZEBO A
1:30 Bongo Joe
3:30 George Dorko
4:45 Will Soto

GAZEBO B
1:00 John Mooney
2:00 Sunbelt Bluegrass Band
3:00 Frog Island Jazz Band
4:00 Leroy Jones Jazz Band
5:00 Svare & Vernon Pleasant

GOSPEL TENT
12:00 The Jones Sisters
12:40 Macedonia B.C. Youth Choir
1:20 Star Lights Gospels Singers
2:00 St. Luke A.M.E. Choir
2:40 Fisher Home Project Choir
3:20 Moses B.C. Youth Choir
4:00 Morning Star B.C. Gospel Choir
4:40 Gospel Inspirations
5:20 Greater St. Stephens B.C. Choir
6:00 St. Francis DeSales Choir

PARADES
4:00 Tremé Sports & Third Division Rollers SA&PCs with Young Tuxedo Brass Band

SUNDAY, MAY 9

STAGE 1
12:15 Bell Jr. High School Band
1:15 Henry Gray Review
2:45 Caliente
4:00 Irma Thomas
5:00 Etta James
6:15 Allen Toussaint

STAGE 2
12:45 NOCCA
2:00 Walter Payton's Ballet Filé
3:15 Tuts Washington
4:15 James Booker
5:30 Ayocuan

STAGE 3
12:30 George "Slim" Heard
1:45 Belton Richard & The Musical Aces
2:45 Johnny Adams with Walter Washington
4:00 Edward "Kidd" Jordan Improvisational Arts Ensemble
5:15 Blues Rockers

STAGE 4
12:45 Los Bandidos
1:45 Scooter Lee
3:00 Lil' Queenie & The Percolators
4:15 B.B. King
5:30 Rockin' Dopsie & The Twisters

JAZZ TENT
12:30 New Leviathan Oriental Foxtrot Orchestra
1:30 Red Tyler & The Gentlemen of Jazz with Germaine Bazzle
2:30 Thomas Jefferson
3:45 James Black
5:00 Earl Turbinton
6:00 Percy Humphrey & The Crescent City Joymakers

KOINDU
12:15 Wild Magnolias Mardi Gras Indians
1:30 Khadija's Afro-Ethnic Dance Ensemble
2:45 Theron Lewis Group
4:00 Exuma
5:15 Lady B.J. & Company

GAZEBO A
1:00 Bongo Joe
2:45 Will Soto
3:45 Lillian Bennett

GAZEBO B
1:15 A.J. Loria
2:30 Buddy Ellis Group
3:45 Ardoin Family Band
5:00 Cousin Joe

1983

By now, locals in the City of New Orleans were starting to divide into two categories where the New Orleans Jazz & Heritage Festival was concerned: those who thought it was wonderful and wanted the whole world to come to town to share the joy and the festivities, and those who looked back nostalgically to the glorious days of poorly attended shows with more than ample room to dance and no lines for the bathrooms. Bunny Matthews, a local writer, humorist and artist, also the creator of New Orleans' two most famous "Yats," Vic and Nat'ly, was of the latter group.

On April 29,[th] 1983 in the *Times Picayune* Lagniappe section, Bunny expressed his opinion very eloquently with a short piece entitled *A Modest Proposal.* Jonathan Swift wrote another piece of the same title in 1729, addressing the Irish importuning the citizens of Great Britain. However the circumstances were considerably different in the dilemma of how to solve the influx of starving Irish, versus a major influx of New Orleans tourists who spent a lot of money. Most New Orleanians were only too happy to provide

what's going on?

GLOBALLY

US invades Grenada after coup on the island; more medals are handed out during the invasion than during the entire Vietnam war.

A two-year drought in Ethiopia brings famine to millions, and Ethiopia appeals for aid for 4 million victims.

Pioneer 10 becomes the first manmade object to leave the solar system.

NATIONALLY

Sally Ride becomes first American woman in space.

Hackers invade sensitive military computers such as Los Alamos National Laboratory.

President Ronald Reagan signs a bill creating a federal holiday to honor American civil rights leader Martin Luther King, Jr.

LOCALLY

Edwin W. Edwards becomes the first three-term governor of Louisiana.

New Orleans' Pontchartrain Beach Amusement Park closes its gates permanently.

Ernest Johnson and Germaine Curley became the first black and first woman to win seats on Plaquemines Parish Council, ending the sixty-year Perez family dynasty.

CULTURALLY

The CD is introduced to the general public.

Final episode of "M*A*S*H" (1972) airs, viewed by 125,000,000 people.

Cellular phones make their first U.S. appearance in Chicago.

"Just Say No" is the new tool to combat growing drug use in the US.

food and lodging to our international visitors. But reflective of what would continue to be an ongoing complaint among some locals, Bunny had a few interesting notes of social commentary in his proposal:

"This is not my favorite time of the year. My favorite time of the year is when the Jazz Festival is over and all the visitors from California, Tokyo and spots in-between are gone. New

Orleans, in my estimation, is not big enough for all of us.

"The Jazz Festival is certainly not big enough for all of us. It's a dilemma, but no one can do much about it. I can't think of anything that would work; if ticket prices were raised in an effort to exclude all but the most sincere devotees, the sincere devotees would probably turn out to be the visitors from California, Tokyo and spots in-between. Tokyo-ites I'm not so sure of, but Californians will pay anything if they think it will make them hipper than their next-door neighbor. Orleanians, on the other hand would prefer getting in free. If they have to pay, anything over a $1.50 is too much."

Mr. Matthews went on to suggest the possibility of two Jazz

Festivals; one that would be free for locals which would require presentation of a valid Louisiana drivers license or birth certificate, and another on the following weekend for everybody else. The expensive "outsider" Festival on the second weekend would pay for the locals "Free Fest" the first week. He states that the Californians would gladly pay a dollar a piece for crawfish.

The close of Bunny's "modest proposal" is very clever- " This all sounds at bit unAmerican you say? Why of course- what do you expect? This isn't America. This is New Orleans!" Many, in 1983, shared Bunny's position. Some New Orleanians were resentful of the crowds, but at the same time, extremely proud of being from a town that could create a Jazz Festival that the whole world wanted to come to.

Meanwhile, the traditional jazz nighttime concert series on the *S.S. President* had been discontinued due to poor attendance. The series used to attract families and older jazz buffs that brought picnic baskets of home-cooked treats and held annual family outings listening to old school New Orleans music. But when hampers were banned from the boat

---

Ernie K-Doe

and ticket prices were raised to cover the rising costs of staging concerts, attendance dropped off and consequently traditional jazz series was cancelled.

Dodie Smith-Simmons, one of the associate producers of the 1983 Jazz & Heritage Festival lamented this loss; "traditional jazz just doesn't bring in the money- it only reaches a certain crowd, mainly older people and foreigners, but very few young people. Living here, you take it for granted. When it's an everyday event, you don't pay much attention to it."

Danny Barker also felt that traditional jazz on its own wouldn't be able to garner the type of attendance required to carry an extended music Festival in New Orleans because of access to this music every day of the week, but still, the Jazz &

Heritage Festival was designed to highlight local music and culture. The Festival wanted to make sure that this important music, integral to our history and culture in New Orleans, would continue to be properly represented. This year around 30 traditional jazz ensembles were booked to play at one of the Festival's new features: the Economy Hall Jazz Tent.

The new Economy Hall also featured seating in the round and a hard floor for spectators who might feel the urge to get up and dance, and they did. On opening day, April 29th 1983, the Razzberrie Ragtimers officially opened Economy Hall at 11:00 followed by the West End Jazz Band, Michael White Quartet, Hot Strings of New Orleans, and Kid Sheik's Storyville Jammers, who closed out the day. The dancing was spirited, encom-

passed all races and ages, and appropriately couldn't stay within the confines of the floor, with spontaneous second lines happening more than once a day. Anyone who thinks traditional jazz is irrelevant should visit the tent today. Classic jazz is alive

fest facts

Ten radio stations were broadcasting live reports from the Fair Grounds.

The Radio Flyer red wagons caused traffic jams on the blacktop walkway. Anna Zimmerman, head of public relations, asked people to leave them at home.

Deep fried soft shell crawfish debuted in the food booth at $3.50 for 5 crawfish.

The Fest took 6-8 months to prepare. 20 office personnel started in October, then 2-3 weeks out, the staff hired 200 + to set up booths and stages.

and appreciated in Economy Hall, and often the crowd is now too large for the tent.

Charlie Bering was night concert producer once again, giving weight to the old saying- "if it ain't broke, don't fix it" It was another inspired year of evening concerts. Reggie Houston, a local musician often to be found accompanying Charmaine Neville, was assistant to Charlie Bering for the night concerts and to Joanne Schmidt during the day. No doubt he was gigging around town and at the Festival too, but no one in the music industry really sleeps during Jazz

Festival; so you might as well put both feet in. Just ask George Porter, Johnny Vidacovich, David Torkanowsky, Chris Severin, Herman Ernest, and a slew of other great New Orleans musicians who pretty

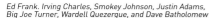
Ed Frank. Irving Charles, Smokey Johnson, Justin Adams, Big Joe Turner, Wardell Quezergue, and Dave Batholomew

4:15 Rockin' Tabby Thomas & His Mighty House Rockers w/ Henry Gray & Whispering Smith
5:45 Lil' Queenie & Backtalk

STAGE 3
11:45 East St. John H.S. Jazz Band
1:15 Ernie K-Doe & The K-Doe Naugahyde w/ Jean Knight
2:45 The Sheiks
4:15 Zachary Richard
5:30 Los Banditos

STAGE 4
11:30 Tulane Jazz Ensemble
12:45 James Rivers Movement
1:45 Tommy Ridgley & The Untouchables w/ Robert Parker, Jessie Hill, Bobby Mitchell & Frankie Ford
3:45 Roy Orbison
5:15 Windjammer

FESTIVAL TENT
12:15 Mike Pellera Quartet
1:45 Red Tyler & The Gentlemen of Jazz w/ Germaine Bazzle
3:00 Cousin Joe
4:00 James Black Ensemble
5:30 Archie Shepp

ECONOMY HALL
12:15 Caledonia Jazz Band of Norway
1:30 Widespread Jazz Orchestra
2:45 New Orleans Ragtime Orchestra
4:00 Danny Barker's Jazz Hounds w/ Blue Lu Barker
5:15 Solar

KOINDU
11:30 Xavier Jazz Lab Band
12:45 Kush
1:45 John Delafose
2:45 Theron Lewis Group
3:45 Kidd Jordan & The Improvisational Arts Quintet
4:30 Saxon Superstars of Nassau, Bahamas
5:15 Solar

GAZEBO
12:30 Professor Gizmo
1:15 Son Ford Thomas
2:15 Professor Gizmo
3:00 Rising Star Drum & Fife Corps
4:15 Bongo Joe

GOSPEL TENT
12:00 The Jones Sisters
12:40 Mt. Kingdom B.C. Choir
1:20 Praising His Name Gospel Chorus
2:00 Fisher Home Project Choir
2:40 Pure Heart Community Choir
3:20 The Crown Seekers
4:00 Phase 1 Gospel Singers
4:40 The Southern Bells
5:20 Avondale Community Chorus

PARADES
1:15 Third Division Rollers & 6th Ward High Rollers SA&PCs with Young Tuxedo Brass Band
4:30 Koindu Parade with Saxon Superstars of Nassau, Bahamas

SUNDAY, MAY 1

STAGE 1
12:15 ELS
1:45 Caliente
3:15 Rufus & Carla Thomas
4:30 Dirty Dozen Brass Band
6:00 Al Green

Cleveland Chenier, Dewey Balfa, Marc Savoy, Doug Kershaw, Clifton Chenier

"When the Neville Brothers first started playing at the Festival Professor Longhair would close out the Fest. After he passed away in 1980 the Festival gave that spot to us and that was the highest honor that we could receive. The people start gathering before we go on and by the time we hit the stage there is a sea of people stretching to the edge of the race track." CHARLES NEVILLE

much don't sleep during the Festival. In 1983, James Black was playing everywhere, as was James Booker, Earl King, and the great Danny Barker.

The opening night concerts on April 29th featured an Allen Toussaint produced evening on the Riverboat *President* with Lee Dorsey, Ernie K-Doe, Tommy Ridgely, and two new finds of Mr. Toussaint's: Carla Baker and Cinnamon. Lee Dorsey, ex-prizefighter and auto repairman whose first hit "Ya Ya" in 1961 brought him onto the national

scene, turned in a stunning performance. He opened with "Holy Cow" and when he performed his version of "Ride Your Pony" it was as fresh as his recording of it that flew up the charts in 1965. "Working in the Coal Mine," like "Ride Your Pony" was a wonderful sing along for all of the fans stuffed into the Riverboat. K- Doe opened and closed with "Mother-In-Law" to the crowds delight and Allen Toussaint shared some of his other hits-not being sung by his friends on the stage. Tommy Ridgely did

his own version of "Ooh- Poo-Pa-Do" and also featured his brother Sammy on some vocals.

The Theatre of Performing Arts offered *"A Tribute to Mahalia Jackson"* written by Ted Gilliam. This stirring tribute to "The Worlds Greatest Gospel Singer" was a compilation of words and songs immortalized by New Orleans own Mahalia and re-expressed on this inspirational evening by Naomi Washington with the New Birth Missionary B.C. Choir, the Gospel Soul Children, Zion Harmonizers,

and Dr. Daddy O, the city's premier gospel disc jockey.

Saturday April 30th was a really tough day to choose your music. The Caledonia Jazz Band of Norway kicked it off at 12:15 in Economy Hall as Mike Pellera's Quartet started in the Festival Tent. Red Tyler and the Gentlemen of Jazz came on after Michael at 1:45, the same time Tommy Ridgely and the Untouchables with Robert Parker, Jessie Hill, Bobby Mitchell's and Frankie Ford began on Stage

4. The James Black Ensemble followed by Archie Shepp closed the Festival Tent.

Roy Orbison followed by Windjammer closed Stage 4. Bucky Barrett, guitarist for Roy for 17 years or so, remembered the Jazz Festival very fondly and loved the stage crew and sound. Steve Eggerton and George Porter were making that stage go in 1983 with the further assistance of Rick Arnstein, Rene Crusto, and Steve Sullivan.

Windjammer was a New Orleans group which included

Al Hirt closes club on Bourbon Street.

The Rebirth Brass Band forms.

Wynton Marsalis is the first to win a Grammy Award simultaneously in jazz and classical categories

WWOZ presents the New Orleans R&B Revue at Municipal Auditorium.

The Dirty Dozen Brass Band record first album, Feet Don't Fail Me Now.

IN MEMORIAM

James Booker, Eubie Blake, Roosevelt Sykes, Lee Dorsey, Benny Goodman, Sippie Wallace, Eddie "Lockjaw" Davis, Sonny Terry, Thadeus Jones, Francine Fleming, Alton Pernell, Albert Sabi, Dino Santangelo, Emmanuel Sayles, W. Alonzo Stewart, Gerald Tillman, Thomas Jefferson, Sal Grisaffi, Clarence Garlow, Moses Asch, Preston Jackson, Walter Nelson, Lawrence Trotter, Tyrone Maupin, MacKinley "Muddy Waters" Morganfield

Big Joe Turner

Karl Dennis singing lead, Chris Severin on bass, and Anatole Domino (son of Fats) on piano. Windjammer had gotten a major label deal and garnered national attention. Their new vinyl album included a song "Live without Your Love" written by Angelle Trosclair and Mike Pellera, which charted nationally.

Saturday night, April 30th on the *S.S. President* was one out of control night of R&B funk. Charlie Bering and his team really outdid themselves again this year with this triple threat. We can't believe the boat didn't sink from so much hard dancing. Rufus "Walking the Dog" "The Funky Penguin" Thomas, his daughter Carla "Gee Wiz B-A-B-Y" Thomas,

Junior "Shotgun" "Roadrunner" "What Does it Take" Walker funked it up in grand fashion.

Big Joe Turner turned it out with Luther Kent and Trick Bag- a perfect pairing arranged by Quint Davis. A group called "The Metrics" with George Porter and Zigaboo Modeliste followed Luther and Big Joe's blues extravaganza. One of our bright stars, Lady B.J. Thomas, closed Koindu with her group Spectrum.

Second lines and parades during the day provided non-stop excitement for Festivalgoers as they walked from stage to stage or went to grab some of the wonderful food available in the food areas- Young Tuxedo Brass Band, 3rd Division High rollers, 6th Ward High Rollers,

majestic Brass Band, Olympia Aide Club, Ladies Zulu, Big Jumpers, Doc Paulin Brass Band, Calendar Girls, Tremé Sports, The original 6th Ward Dirty Dozen Kazoo Band, Olympia Brass Band, Charles Barbarin Brass Band, Scene Boosters, Fun Lovers and the Avenue Steppers kept it all lively on the infield.

The New Orleans Jazz And Heritage Festival offered five days of music at the Fair Grounds in 1983 and the newest addition was hugely successful. The newly christened Economy Hall Tent was packed both weekends and was as full as it could hold on Sunday May 8th, when Percy Humphrey and the Crescent City Joymakers took the people home to close another year.

3:00 John Fred & The Playboys
4:30 Vassar Clements
6:00 The Radiators

STAGE 2
12:45 Russ Russell & The Rustlers
2:15 Dewey Balfa & Friends
3:45 Alvin Batiste
5:15 Marcia Ball

STAGE 3
11:30 Dillard University Jazz Band
12:45 Bobby Marchan & Higher
Ground w/ Oliver Morgan & The
Dixi-Kups
2:45 Deacon John Blues Review w/
Earl King
4:15 Marcel Dugas
5:45 Lonnie Brooks

STAGE 4
11:45 Southern Univ. Baton Rouge
Jazz Ensemble
1:00 Ruben "Mr. Salsa" Gonzalez
2:15 Roy Ayers
3:45 Batiste Brothers Band
5:15 Burning Spear

FESTIVAL TENT
12:30 New Jazz Quintet
1:30 A.J. Loria
2:30 Kent Jordan Quintet
3:30 Bobby McFerrin & Trio w/
Johnny Adams
4:30 Beausoleil
5:30 Astral Project

ECONOMY HALL
12:30 One Mo' Time Band & Singers
1:45 Roosevelt Sykes
2:45 New Leviathan Oriental Foxtrot
Orchestra
4:00 Louis Nelson Big Six
5:15 Placide Adams Original
Dixieland Hall Jazz Band

KOINDU
12:00 Edward Perkins Group
1:00 George Pack African Ensemble
2:00 Antonio York
3:00 Fred Kemp Quintet
4:15 Les Ballets Bacoulou D'Haiti
5:30 Pharoah Sanders

GAZEBO
1:00 The Country Three
2:00 David & Roselyn
3:00 Mt. Pontchartrain String Band
4:00 Yellow Jackets
5:00 Billy Gregory

GOSPEL TENT
11:30 Brother James Chapman
12:10 Macedonia B.C. Youth Choir
12:50 Greater N.O. St. Luke B.C.
Youth Choir
1:30 St. Luke A.M.E. Choir
2:10 Second Morning Star B.C.
Combined Choir
2:50 Morning Star B.C. Choir
3:30 First Church of God in Christ
4:10 St. Francis DeSales Golden
Voice Choir
4:50 Wallace Davenport Gospel
Singers
5:30 Youth Inspirational Choir

PARADES
2:30 Calendar Girls & Tremé Sports
SA&PCs with Doc Paulin Brass
Band

SUNDAY, MAY 8

STAGE 1
12:15 Los Catrachos
1:45 Willie Tee
3:00 Buddy Guy & Jr. Wells

4:30 Clarence "Gatemouth" Brown
6:00 The Neville Brothers

STAGE 2
11:45 Loyola Faculty Ensemble
1:00 Sady Courville & Mamou Hour
Cajun Band
2:30 Al Belletto Quartet
4:00 Wild Magnolias Mardi
Gras Indians
5:30 Scooter Lee

STAGE 3
12:00 St. Augustine Jazz Band
1:15 John Mooney & The
Bluesiana Band
2:45 Eddie Bo with David Lastie Band
4:15 Taj Mahal
5:30 Clifton Chenier & His Red Hot
Louisiana Band

STAGE 4
11:45 Southeastern Univ. Jazz
Ensemble
12:45 Lowell Fulsom with Kid
Johnson Band
2:15 Irma Thomas
3:30 Al Hirt
5:00 Allen Toussaint

FESTIVAL TENT
12:30 Earl Turbinton
1:45 Jasmine
3:00 Walter Mouton & The Scott
Playboys
4:15 N.O. Saxophone Ensemble
5:30 Ellis Marsalis Quartet

ECONOMY HALL
12:00 All Star Band
1:15 New Eclipse Brass Band
2:30 Linda Hopkins
4:00 Tuts Washington
5:00 Kid Thomas & His Algiers
Stompers

KOINDU
11:30 Kumbuka African Drum &
Dance Collective
12:30 The Calebel Experience
1:30 Ngoma
2:30 Eddie Harris
4:00 Turtle Band of Belize
5:15 Lady B.J. & Spectrum

GAZEBO
1:30 George Dorko
3:00 Brother Percy Randolph w/
Spencer Bohren
4:30 Miss Lillian Bennett

GOSPEL TENT
11:30 Singing Voices of Christ
12:10 C&B Ensemble
12:50 Voices of Hope
1:30 Voices of Faith
2:10 Divine Grace Gospel Choir
2:50 The Heralds of Christ
3:30 The Zion Harmonizers w/
Christine Myles
4:10 Greater Macedonia B.C. Choir
4:50 Helen Brock New Gospellettes
5:30 Gospel Soul Children

PARADES
1:00 The Original 6th Ward Dirty
Dozen Kazoo Band
3:30 Olympia Brass Band & Charles
Barbarin Brass Band with Scene
Boosters, Fun Lovers
& Avenue Steppers SA&PCs

NIGHT CONCERTS

FRIDAY, APRIL 29, 7:30 P.M.
A Tribute to Mahalia Jackson
Naomi Washington with The New
Birth Missionary B. C. Choir
Gospel Soul Children
Zion Harmonizers
Dr. Daddy-O
Theater of Performing Arts
FRIDAY, APRIL 29, 8 P.M.
A Southern Night
Allen Toussaint, Lee Dorsey, Tommy
Ridgley, Ernie K-Doe, Carla Baker,
Cinnamon
Riverboat President
**SATURDAY, APRIL 30, 7 P.M. &
MIDNIGHT**
Rhythm & Blues on the River
Tina Turner, Rufus & Carla Thomas,
Junior Walker & The Allstars
Riverboat President

SUNDAY, MAY 1, 9:30 P.M.
Inside & Out
The Archie Shepp Quartet
Contemporary Arts Center
MONDAY, MAY 2, 8 P.M.
A Night of Song
Carmen McRae
Jon Hendricks & Company
Bobby McFerrin with Astral Project
Theater of Performing Arts
TUESDAY, MAY 3, 8 P.M.
The Beauty of the Piano
Oscar Peterson
Herbie Hancock
Theater of Performing Arts
WEDNESDAY, MAY 4, 8 P.M.
*Three Generations of New Orleans
Singers*
Blue Lu Barker, Germaine Bazzle,
Lady B.J.
Prout's Club Alhambra
WEDNESDAY, MAY 4, 8:00 P.M.
A Fais Do-Do
Doug Kershaw & The Kershaw Family
Clifton Chenier & His Red Hot
Louisiana Band
Dewey Balfa & Mark Savoy with The
Cajun All-Stars
Riverboat President
THURSDAY, MAY 5, 8 P.M.
Bebop & All That Jazz
Elvin Jones & The Jazz Machine
Chico Freeman Quintet
Jazz All Stars w/ Jimmy Smith,
Stanley Turrentine, Kenny Burrell
and James Black
Riverboat President
FRIDAY, MAY 6, 7 P.M. & MIDNIGHT
Caribbean on the Mississippi
Third World, Toots & The Maytals, Les
Ballets Bacoulou d'Haiti
Riverboat President
SATURDAY, MAY 7, 8 P.M.
The Blues Cruise
Taj Mahal, Albert Collins, Willie Dixon
& The Chicago Blues All Stars
Riverboat President
SUNDAY, MAY 8, 9:30 P.M.
Pharoah's Music
Pharoah Sanders
SUNO Jazz Ensemble
SUNO Science Lecture Hall

1984

Jim Jenkins

Finally, Cajun, zydeco, Louisiana bluegrass, swamp-pop and all the eclectic in-betweens would have an official home at the New Orleans Jazz & Heritage Festival with the dedication of Stage 2. Like the Economy Hall Tent for traditional jazz lovers, the Fais Do-Do stage would be a beacon for every two stepping, waltzing, accordion loving Louisiana music fan who loved to "Laissez les bon temps rouler." Fais Do-Do means literally to "make sleep," but its Cajun idiomatic meaning is that once the children have gone to bed, the adults are free to play, and they would on opening day, April 27th at the 1984 New Orleans Jazz & Heritage Festival.

The stage had unofficially been the home of country and Cajun bands, but now newcomers would know exactly where to go to get a dose of Bayou Boogie. Filé from Lafayette, Louisiana, offered up accordion based dance and traditional Cajun music and were the first group to christen the new designation. Throughout the day, families spread blankets, children ran around and got nice sunburns and the dancing in front of Fais Do-Do was dusty and sublime. A new Jazz Fest tradition was born

what's going on?

GLOBALLY

The European Space Agency launches the world's largest communications satellite.

Half a million people in Manila demonstrate against the regime of Ferdinand Marcos.

NATIONALLY

Geraldine Ferraro is the first woman to run for vice-president from a major political party.

The United States and the Vatican establish full diplomatic relations.

A US pilot shot down over Lebanon is released by Syria after Jesse Jackson intervenes.

A 15-day-old baby, "Baby Fae," has a baboon's heart transplanted into her but dies 20 days later.

LOCALLY

The 1984 Louisiana World Exposition, a world's fair, is hosted in New Orleans. The theme is "The World of Rivers: Fresh Water as a source of Life."

First "A Tribute to the Christmas Tree" event held. It is later renamed "Celebration in the Oaks."

The newly-renovated Jax Brewery opens, a six-story arrangement of shops, restaurants and businesses.

For eight weeks, 550 St. John the Baptist Parish school employees staged the largest strike in Louisiana history, resulting in a 5% raise for teachers.

CULTURALLY

Apple Computer, founded by Stephen Wozniak and Steven Jobs, releases the Macintosh personal computer.

"This Is Spinal Tap" - Spinal Tap, the world's loudest band, is chronicled by hack documentarian Marti DeBergi on what proves to be a fateful tour.

Deacon John

for some who would be back year after year to meet friends from all over the world in front of the Fais Do-Do to dance and show their love for this music.

John Delafose cranked it up for the people after File' finished their set; old school traditional Cajun was served by Canray Fontenot & Bois-Sec Ardoin; and closing out the first day of Fais Do-Do, was Bourré, one of the only Cajun bands from New Orleans in 1984. At this writing, a visitor to New Orleans might think that the music originated here, but it is only in recent years that Cajun and Zydeco have begun to permeate the French Quarter and Mid City Bowling Lanes. Perhaps the New Orleans Jazz & Heritage Festival can take some credit for bringing this music to a wider audience, and George Wein's connection to the Newport Jazz

Festival had to have helped also.

To many locals' chagrin, ticket prices were raised again and New Orleanians howled at paying six bucks for a full day of music, notwithstanding the quality and quantity. In spite of these complaints, attendance was great and the bumper to bumper traffic and lines at the main entrance on Gentilly Boulevard must have made Heritage Fair Director Nancy Ochsenschlager smile at the end of the day, once they were all in.

Bo Diddley made his Jazz Festival debut on opening day. This high intensity, founding father of rhythm and blues tore it up from 5:00 to 6:00 p.m. and would be back to play future Festivals. A living legend, he strummed his rectangular guitar over many of the songs that laid the foundation of rock and roll. New Orleanians can say what they want about the

Ray Charles

big acts that have come to Jazz Fest. Look back on the opportunities of having seen legends like Bo Diddley, Jerry Lee Lewis, Chuck Berry, James Brown, Odetta, and Van Morrison and you can appreciate Quint Davis's broad-reaching tastes, knowledge, and programming skills.

That programming skill was coupled with Quint's deeply plugging into the local music scene and tracking new trends. Lil' Queenie and the Skin Twins, comprised of John Magnie and Bruce McDonald with Michell

Seguin from Quebec playing percussion, entertained the first weekend, but we were graced twice in 84' with Leigh "Lil' Queenie" Harris. The following week saw her back again for the Percolators reunion. The Tim Green Quintet was on Koindu and Lillian Boutte' gave it her all in Economy Hall. The Head Start Singing Angels in the Gospel Tent and the Aubry Twins with their group Fresh Air, which was really hot in 1984, were also performing. But there are always hard musical choices to

be made at Jazz Fest. Saturday April 28th brought us James Rivers for the jazzy soul, the Metrics, (one half of The Meters) with Joseph "Zigaboo" Modeliste and George Porter representing New Orleans funk, and Tony award winning home girl Linda Hopkins, in Economy Hall.

One band we are all curious about is the Now Band, which closed Stage 4 on opening day.

Throughout the first weekend at the Fair Grounds, the weather was hot and the music was hotter. There was a little

Linda Hopkins

Cosimo Matassa

intermittent rain to cool folks off, but for the most part, the best strategy was to give yourself up to the groove, dance, and eat a lot of food and drink as much as possible. The *Times Picayune* reported that Joyce West from Charity Hospital brought 35 of her psychiatric patients out on opening day to enjoy the music and food as she had for the last fifteen years. "Music is one of the best therapies," she told reporter Gayle Ashton.

Fats Domino, eternal crowd pleaser and consummate performer, was scheduled to close Stage 4 on Saturday, but was unable to sing because he had given so much at the show the night before. The Riverboat *President* show sold out quickly and people were so enthusiastic that Fats just kept going through timeless hit after hit. "The audiences wanted him to keep performing" Anna Zimmerman, Festival spokesperson said. "The next day he was too hoarse to sing at the Fair Grounds." The

show in question was billed as the "Jazz Fest Anniversary Party" sponsored by Liberty Bank. It featured the triple threat of the Neville Brothers, Dr. John, and Antoine "Fats" Domino in that order.

On the riverboat that night, some complained about the sound not being up to the task of overcoming 2,500 or so loud, ardent Festival partiers, but the Nevilles kicked it off with as much juice as could be mustered, and with the solid Willie Green laying down the funk on drums. However, Aaron Neville's poignant ballad "Ariane" was unable to cut through the noise of the crowd and Dr. John, performing solo, also had some difficulties rising above the din. It's a shame, because people missed some beautiful moments, especially Mac's tribute to the late James Carol Booker who had passed away on November 8th 1983. Fats, when he took stage, pounded the crowd into submission with "Hello Josephine,"

STAGE 2
11:30 The Sundown Playboys
1:00 Frankie Ford's Swamp Pop Jam with Johnny Allen, Warren Storm, Van & Grace Broussard, Rod Bernard & Jivin' Gene
2:45 Sam Brothers Five
3:45 Don Montoucet & The Wandering Aces
5:00 Clifton Chenier & His Red Hot Louisiana Band

STAGE 3
11:45 Edu & The Sound of Brazil
12:45 Kent Jordan Quintet
2:00 Marcia Ball
3:30 Bobby Marchan & Higher Ground
4:45 John Mooney & The Bluesiana Band

STAGE 4
11:45 Tulane University Jazz Band
1:15 The Metrics
2:45 Tommy Ridgley & The Untouchables with Bobby Mitchell & The Dixie Kups & Benny Spellman
4:30 Fats Domino

FESTIVAL TENT
11:30 NOCCA Jazz Ensemble
12:30 Carlos Sanchez Flamenco Troupe
1:30 Lloyd Glenn
2:30 Improvisational Arts Quintet
3:45 A.J. Loria
5:00 Al Belletto Quartet

ECONOMY HALL
11:30 Frank Federico Jazz Band
12:30 Small Sand Trad Band
1:30 Kid Thomas Valentine & The Algiers Stompers
2:30 Neptune Jazz Band of Zimbabwe
3:30 Linda Hopkins
4:45 Onward Brass Band

KOINDU
11:45 Theron Lewis & Unit 7
12:45 Golden Star Hunters Mardi Gras Indians
2:00 Gary Brown & Feelings
3:30 Porgy Jones Band
4:30 Daniel Ponce

GAZEBO
1:00 Professor Gizmo
2:15 Van Williams
3:30 Bill & Bobbie Malone's Country Band
4:45 Roy Bookbinder

GOSPEL TENT
12:05 The Famous Jones Sisters
12:40 The Melody Clouds
1:20 Sensational Gospel Tones
2:00 The New Orleans Spiritualettes
2:40 The New Orleans Comforters
3:20 New Zion Trio Plus One
4:00 The Dynamic Smooth Family
4:40 Sammy Berfect & The Dimensions of Faith

PARADES
3:00 The Swingers & The Golden Trumpets SA&PCs with Charles Barbarin Brass Band

SUNDAY, APRIL 29
STAGE 1
11:30 S.U.N.O. Jazz Ensemble
12:45 Los Banditos
1:45 Tim Williams Band
3:00 Bobby "Blue" Bland
4:30 The Batiste Brothers Band
6:00 Al Green

Denise Moore recalls her first performance with her uncle Deacon John Moore at the New Orleans Jazz & Heritage Festival: "I thought they'd throw tomatoes at me because I wasn't singing the blues. Deacon wanted me to sing more contemporary selections, and I was really nervous. I remember singing "Dancing in the Streets" and "My Guy" and the people really getting into it. When we got to "Take Me With You" by Prince it really got the crowd moving. There was a whole group of guys from the Tulane University fraternity house that stood at the front of the stage screaming, 'We love you!' That really made me feel at home."

Kelly Sullivan

music scene

Tipitina's closes.

Tuts Washington dies August 5th following a performance at the World's Fair.

Cyril Neville forms the band Endangered Species

Allison Miner manages Louisiana Folklife Pavilion at World's Fair presenting D.L. Menard almost daily.

Rebirth Brass Band releases debut record "Here To Stay" on Arhoolie Records

James Rivers contributes to soundtrack of Eastwood movie "Tightrope."

IN MEMORIAM

Percy Mayfield, Alberta Hunter, Sadie Goodson, Isidore "Tuts" Washington, William "Count" Basie

"Red Sails in The Sunset," "Let the Four Winds Blow," "Blueberry Hill," "I'm Gonna Be a Wheel Someday" and he would not be denied. Fats and his fans left the boat "wore out."

Al Green closed Stage 1 on Sunday, April 29th with a classic high-energy performance, leaving all the women at the Fair Grounds swooning to the ground and gasping for breath. Rita Coolidge closed Stage 4 after hanging around the Festival most

of the day and walking around with her sister and Charmaine Neville wearing funny sunglasses and having a good time.

Although the traditional jazz nighttime concerts had consistently drawn smaller audiences, it returned with a stellar program on April 29th aboard the *S.S. President.* The "*Salute to New Orleans Jazz*" would pull out all the stops to make sure the evening was successful. Pete Fountain would headline on an

evening concert that included Linda Hopkins with the New Orleans Storyville Jazz Band, and Percy and Willie Humphrey's Preservation Hall Jazz Band.

Fountain turned in a stunning performance, and New Orleans' own Linda Hopkins, with her old school "I came up in church and you're gonna hear me in the back row" voice, pulled out all the stops on her set, from "Give Me a Pigsfoot and A Bottle of Beer" to "Ain't Nobody's Business if I

Jordan Family, Clyde Kerr, Alvin Fielder, and Elton Herron

Do." The first female from New Orleans to win a Tony, Linda was powerful and gracious. At one point in her show she invited friend and local vocalist Lillian Boutté up on stage to sing "Nobody Knows You When You're Down and Out." They delighted the crowd with "Everyday I Have the Blues." The pair went on to tell the sad story "A Good Man Is Hard To Find." These two divas shone like jewels in a setting of superb accompaniment.

Percy and Willie Humphrey's Preservation Hall Jazz Band, opened, showing the youngsters how it's 'sposed to be done, flawlessly executing the music they've known and loved for decades. At the close of the concert program a jam session had been arranged.

"International New Orleans Jazz Jamboree" featuring groups from three continents; The Neptune Jazz Band from Zimbabwe, Africa; The New Orleans Rascals of Osaka, Japan; and the Sensation Jazz Band of Canada. The hearts of traditional jazz purists were encouraged—the sun will never set on traditional New Orleans Jazz.

On May 5th, when Mason Ruffner and the Blues Rockers opened Stage 4 at 11:45, everyone was afraid that rain would come to stop the music. It never did. The final two days at the Fair Grounds felt like rain, looked like rain and it was forecast to rain, but Jazz Festival staff must have done some serious no-rain dances to keep the storms away. The

Dr. John played a tribute to James Booker, and in Gambit, Gary Esolen wrote a poignant story about listening to that tribute when it washed over him for the first time, and in the middle of 2,000 happy, foot stomping people, that he would never hear Booker again. He was "standing arm in arm with a woman I had met scarcely two hours before, and I cried because James Booker is dead."

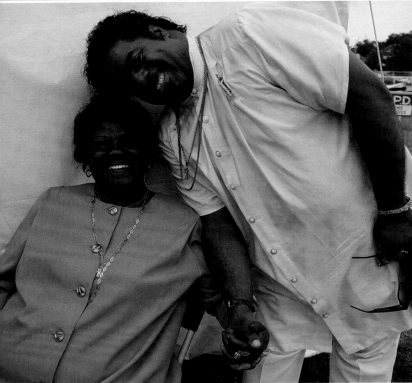

Christine and Raymond Myles

Red Tyler and Germaine Bazzle

sky did not fall and turn the last weekend of the Fair into a mud fest. It was very overcast, with the occasional breeze to make you think you weren't as hot as you actually were, and there were a couple of rolls of thunder to test the commitment of Festival fans; but the people kept coming. Some folks weren't familiar with the fact that you can indeed get horrible sunburn from overcast weather, so those who forgot to wear their sun block or a really big hat got a little toasty, but no one seemed to mind, much.

The 1984 World's Fair came and went to New Orleans amidst much hoopla and high expectations for huge returns, Many locals were disappointed with the World's Fair and its huge financial debacle. To its credit, it borrowed a lot of attitude from Jazz Fest, particularly the music and most importantly the long-term display of indigenous culture.

Ironically, with this year being the permanent honoring of Cajun music at the Fair Grounds, scholars look back on this event as a watershed of new interest in Louisiana's Cajuns. Was it ticket prices that failed to bring in locals again and again? Or just too much hype and too little substance? After all, New Orleans had already had the Jazz Festival for fifteen years running and we knew how to do it. The World's Fair didn't stand a chance.

SATURDAY, MAY 5

STAGE 1
12:00 Southern University Baton Rouge Jazz Band
1:30 Troy Deramus & The Country King Show
3:00 The Dirty Dozen Brass Band
4:30 Grandmaster Flash
6:00 Irma Thomas & The Professionals

STAGE 2
12:00 The Dusenberry Family Singers
1:30 Sampy & The Bad Habits
2:45 Dewey Balfa & His Musical Brothers
4:00 BeauSoleil
5:30 Fernest Arceneaux & The Thunders

STAGE 3
11:45 Mason Ruffner & The Blues Rockers
1:00 Lucinda Williams
2:15 Ruben "Mr. Salsa" Gonzalez
3:45 A-Train
5:15 The Sheiks

STAGE 4
12:30 Quicksilver featuring Afro
2:00 Saxon Superstars of Nassau, Bahamas
3:00 John Lee Hooker
5:00 Jerry Lee Lewis

FESTIVAL TENT
11:30 East St. John Dixieland Band
12:30 Jasmine
1:45 Ellis Marsalis Quartet
3:00 Alvin Batiste
4:15 Willie Metcalf
5:30 Ed Blackwell, George Adams, Don Pullen & Reggie Workman

ECONOMY HALL
11:30 Jimmy Mazzy Trio
12:30 Teddy Riley Jazz Band
1:45 Placide Adams Original Dixieland Hall Jazz Band
3:00 Louis Nelson Big Six
4:15 Cousin Joe
5:15 Danny Barker & His Jazz Hounds with Blue Lu Barker

KOINDU
11:30 Koindu Allstars
12:30 Oliver Morgan with Jean Knight & Jessie Hill
1:45 Yellow Jackets Parade
2:30 Kidd Jordan's Elektrik Band
4:00 James Black Ensemble
5:15 Odetta

GAZEBO
12:45 Hazel & The Delta Ramblers
2:00 John Rankin
3:30 Rising Star Drum & Fife Corps
5:00 R.L. Burnside

GOSPEL TENT
11:30 Daneel Pre-Vocational School Choir
12:10 St. Luke A.M.E. Choir
12:50 Franklin Ave. B.C. Choir
1:30 Aline White & Christine Myles
2:10 The Rocks of Harmony
2:50 Morning Star B.C. Combined Choir
3:30 Gospel Inspirations
4:10 Pure Light B.C. Mass Choir
4:50 Regular B.C. Combined Choir
5:30 The Chorale of Greater St. Stephen

PARADES
3:00 Third Division Rollers & Avenue Steppers SA&PCs with Majestic Brass Band

SUNDAY, MAY 6

STAGE 1
12:00 Satisfaction
1:30 Charles Brown
3:00 Louisiana Purchase
4:30 The Manhattans
6:00 The Neville Brothers

STAGE 2
12:15 Clark & The Dixie Ramblers
1:45 Walter Mouton & The Scott Playboys
3:00 Maurice Barzas & The Mamou Playboys
4:30 Queen Ida & The Bon Temps Zydeco Band
5:45 Ardoin Family Band

STAGE 3
11:45 Creole Wild West Mardi Gras Indians
12:45 Rockin' Tabby Thomas & His Mighty House Rockers with Henry Gray
2:30 Caliente
4:00 Deacon John Blues Revue
5:30 Bill Monroe & The Bluegrass Boys

STAGE 4
11:30 U.N.O. Jazz Band
12:30 Banda Fiebre
2:00 Lil' Queenie & The Percolators Reunion
3:30 Steel Pulse
5:00 Lee Dorsey

FESTIVAL TENT
11:30 Snooks Eaglin
12:30 Earl Turbinton Quintet
1:45 The Survivors
3:00 Odetta
4:15 Mose Allison
5:30 Woody Shaw

ECONOMY HALL
11:30 Pud Brown Jazz Band
12:30 Tommy Yetta Jazz Band
1:45 Percy Humphrey & His Crescent City Joymakers
3:00 Tuts Washington
4:00 Joe Newman
5:15 Olympia Brass Band

KOINDU
11:30 Xavier University Jazz Ensemble
12:45 Rising Star Drum & Fife Corps
2:15 Johnny Adams & Walter Washington & Solar System Band
3:30 Ngoma
4:30 Saxon Superstars of Nassau, Bahamas
5:15 Exuma

GAZEBO
1:00 Will Soto & Four Play
2:15 Mt. Pontchartrain String Band
3:30 R.L. Burnside
4:45 Miss Lillian Bennett

GOSPEL TENT
11:15 James Family
11:50 The Heavenly Stars
12:30 The Gospel Chords
1:10 Famous Zion Harmonizers
1:45 Lois DeJean & The Youth Inspirationals
2:20 Raymond Myles Singers
3:00 Desire Community Chorus
3:35 Famous Corinthian Gospel Singers
4:50 Greater Macedonia B.C. Choir
5:30 The Gospel Soul Children

PARADES
1:30 Scene Booster SA&PC with Young Tuxedo Brass Band
5:15 Economy Hall Parade with Fun Lovers SA&PC

NIGHT CONCERTS

FRIDAY, APRIL 27, 7 P.M.
Jazz Fest Anniversary Party
Fats Domino
Dr. John
The Neville Brothers
Riverboat President

SATURDAY, APRIL 28, 7 P.M.
Soul at the Saenger
Ray Charles, the Raelettes & The Ray Charles Orchestra
Al Green
The Dave Bartholomew Big Band w/ Guest Johnny Adams
The Saenger Theater

SUNDAY, APRIL 29, 8 P.M.
Salute to New Orleans Jazz
Pete Fountain
Linda Hopkins
Percy & Willie Humphries Preservation Hall Jazz Band
Riverboat President

TUESDAY, MAY 1
Stanley Clarke & George Duke
Gato Barbieri
Steve Masakowski & Mars
Theater of Performing Arts

WEDNESDAY, MAY 2, 7 P.M.
Tribute to Muddy Waters
The James Cotton Band
Taj Mahal
The Fabulous Thunderbirds
Etta James
Pinetop Perkins
Bob Margolin
Special Film Segment
The Riverboat President

THURSDAY, MAY 3, 9 P.M.
Jazz Cruise
Sonny Rollins
Herbie Mann & The Family of Mann
Ellis Marsalis Tribute to Duke Ellington w/ Guest Vocalists Germaine Bazzle & Laverne Butler
The Riverboat President

THURSDAY, MAY 3, 12 MIDNIGHT
Prout's Jazz Jam I
George Adams, Don Pullen, Reggie Workman, Ed Blackwell
Prout's Club Alhambra

FRIDAY, MAY 4, 7 P.M.
The Golden Age of Rock & Roll
Roy Orbison
Johnny Rivers
Irma Thomas & The Professionals
The Riverboat President

FRIDAY, MAY 4, 12 MIDNIGHT
Prout's Jazz Jam II
Woody Shaw
Joe Newman
Prout's Club Alhambra

Jazz Fest is an annual explosion of music. The air is literally filled with melodies blown through clarinets and horns, strummed through guitars, played on pianos, and rhythms beaten on drums of all sizes and materials. During the day this music emanates from the Fair Grounds location, while at night the clubs fill with those whose insatiable appetites for live music has drawn them out for one of many all night sets going on throughout New Orleans. For these two or three weekends a year it would be hard to dispute the claim that New Orleans is the most musically prolific place on earth. The spirit of Jazz Fest does however maintain a year round presence in the city — 90.7 on your FM dial.

WWOZ — your jazz and heritage station — broadcasts from the non-commercial end of the FM frequencies, surrounded by college and public stations unified by their non-profit motives for exploiting radio technology. It has done so since December 4th 1980 and has grown from the most grass roots of

beginnings into an internationally celebrated outlet for one of the world's most musical cities. No other station in New Orleans, or the world, exists solely to promote our local musicians and their music, and all in a non-commercial, community owned, volunteer run setting. WWOZ is also synonymous with the Jazz & Heritage Festival, having conducted live broadcasts from the festival for 22 of the station's 24-year history. The story of this incredible radio station is one that must be told in conjunction with the history of Jazz Fest.

The WWOZ story starts in the mid 1970's with the Brock brothers, Jerry and Walter, who were heavily involved in the running of the non-commercial radio station KCHU ("Kay-CHOO — the wet spot on your radio dial") in Dallas. KCHU was established under the tutelage of Lorenzo Milam, the self-financed founder of non-commercial radio in the U.S.A., and the author of the community radio bible, 'Sex and Broadcasting.' Milam had been devoting much of his time and financial resources to keep some

spaces on the FM frequency available to groups with motives other than profit and religion. Jerry Brock said of Milam: "He is the founder of non-commercial radio in America. He founded or co-founded the first twelve non-commercial radio stations in the country. This is before NPR."

One of Milam's extensive (and expensive) frequency availability searches identified the 90.7 slot in New Orleans. The Brock brothers relocated to the Crescent City with the sole purpose of attaining the requisite FCC construction permit, and opening a public radio station devoted to the musical arts of New Orleans and Louisiana.

To this end the Nora Blatch Educational Communications Foundation, Inc. was established. Named for a pioneering radio technology engineer and active feminist from the 1920's, the Nora Blatch Foundation was established in 1976. Jerry Brock reflected "it was the history and the tradition of Lorenzo Milam to name the founding organization after an early pioneer in radio who had never gotten their due". As it was also the intention of Jerry and Walter to honor the legacy and history of women in broadcasting, all of the original board members of the Nora Blatch Foundation were women.

The FCC permit was approved within the year (which was unusually fast) and the Brocks faced the mountainous challenge of getting WWOZ off the ground and onto the airwaves. The next four years however were dominated by courtroom drama as opposed to radio broadcasts as this nascent community radio endeavor was forced to take on some of New Orleans' most powerful institutions that opposed 90.7 FM being home to a community run radio station such as WWOZ. In 1976, conservative power brokers nationwide, particularly the religious right, had identified Lorenzo Milam as an enemy, which by association made Jerry and Walter and the concept of WWOZ very unpopular in certain circles in New Orleans. Between 1976 and 1980, the Brocks had to respond to multiple counter-petitions to the FCC regarding various perceived 'problems' with the WWOZ construction permit. Many of these counter petitions were concerned with the potential for such a station to erode the moral fiber of the city and other such absurdities.

The Brocks also had some substantial local supporters however, and on December 3rd 1980 an FCC commissioner called Jerry and informed him that WWOZ could go on the air with one condition — that they do so within 24 hours. The Brocks responded to this request and set up a tape loop using an excerpt from 'Stay Cool Babylon' by Ras Michael and the Sons and Daughters of Negus. The loop repeated the lyrics 'Stay cool Babylon, you don't know what you're doin'' over and over for the entire first broadcast day. With this request for calm, WWOZ was on the air, the date was December 4th 1980.

To get to this stage, the Brocks had relied on the generosity of many New Orleanians who shared their vision for a local community radio station. The workload however

moved up a notch once the on-air commitment needed to be maintained. What followed was a six-year period consisting of various part-time jobs, many 60 hour plus working weeks at the station and a steady diet of ramen noodles.

Six months after WWOZ made its debut on the FM airwaves, Jerry and Walter begun broadcasting from the station's first official home, the upstairs of the world famous live music venue Tipitina's in Uptown New Orleans. Prior to this, Jerry and Walter stayed up all night making tapes of shows and then spending the requisite 10 broadcast hours the next day at the transmitter located in a shack in Bridge City, LA. At Tipitina's WWOZ aired taped shows and took live calls from listeners, and, for another six months until they could afford a remote control for the transmitter, one of the brothers had to drive across the Huey P. Long Bridge every morning to turn the transmitter on and then again at 10.30 every night to turn it off again.

The early days in Tipitina's were, according to volunteer programmer of 22 years, Mike "Mr. Jazz" Gourrier, "primitive." The "cramped quarters" Mike Gourrier talked about were however the location where WWOZ established the feel — or 'vibe' — that it has maintained throughout the years. According to Gourrier some of the highlights of these early years were moments when New Orleans musicians came by the studio and shared their stories live to air. "The first live interview I conducted on WWOZ was with Donald Harrison. This was his first ever interview on radio also and he took the time to join to join me in the studio above Tips when he was on a break from working with Art Blakey's Jazz Messengers."

Tipitina's was also the place where Jerry Brock instituted the programming structure that has remained largely unchanged to this day. WWOZ's devotion to the music and culture of New Orleans and Louisiana has not come about by accident, as Jerry explained, "When Walter and I arrived in New Orleans our initial plan was for a much more eclectic broadcast schedule. But

once we got our feet on the ground in New Orleans and began to discover the city we realized that what was greatly lacking locally was that they didn't have any New Orleans and Louisiana music on the radio. It hit us like a brick between the eyes that we needed to devote this station to New Orleans and Louisiana culture and music."

This deliberate policy to promote and celebrate local music has remained unchanged. On WWOZ today, each programmer brings a wealth of selective good taste to the "blues, jazz, Cajun, zydeco, gospel, Brazilian, Caribbean and a whole lot more" that WWOZ broadcasts.

Listening to 'Gentilly Jr.' on a Monday night is a blues history lesson via the scenic back roads (who is in a hurry with this rich subject matter after all?), and tuning in to Bob French on Friday mornings is an authentic New Orleans Jazz experience rivaled only by Sunday second-line parades. The combined musical knowledge and personal record collections of these and other on-air programmers are essential ingredients in the WWOZ recipe.

During the summer of 1984, WWOZ moved to its current location in Armstrong Park. The Brocks and many other WWOZ volunteers had been working on the new studio for months prior to the move, and although the new space was far from luxurious, it was an entire building dedicated solely to WWOZ's mission.

And, it did contain brand new top quality broadcast equipment. In true New Orleans style this relocation was celebrated with a parade from Tipitina's to the new site. This move also placed WWOZ at the geographical center of New Orleans music heritage, surrounded by the remains of the Treme neighborhood

(home to many of the city's musical pioneers past and present), Congo Square, the French Quarter, and nearby to the site where the famed Storyville once stood (now occupied by the Iberville Public Housing complex).

It was also around this time that the notion of selling WWOZ's broadcast license and operational responsibilities to the New Orleans Jazz & Heritage Foundation (the same Foundation responsible for Jazz Fest) was first being considered. At the end of 1986 the sale of WWOZ took place. The NOJ&HF purchased the station for $150 000, approved by the FCC. This pivotal moment in WWOZ's history was approved by a vote of three core WWOZ staff, the Brocks and engineer Ken Devine. The

result was 2 to 1 with the younger and more energetic Jerry Brock the only dissenter. At the NOJ&HF end of the deal, then board Director Kalamu Ya-Salaam was solely responsible for attaining the support and resources necessary for the purchase.

Kalamu Ya Salaam had been a supporter of WWOZ's community radio mission, as well as a volunteer programmer, since the station's early days at Tips. He was well aware of the competitive atmosphere regarding access to the extremely limited broadcast licenses in New Orleans, and that WWOZ need only falter slightly for a well financed and well organized takeover of their FCC permit to manifest. With this in mind, Ya Salaam felt the move to relocate the WWOZ license under the auspices of the Jazz & Heritage Foundation would "help preserve the fiscal stability and cultural stamina of the mission," and by extension, the likelihood that WWOZ could meet its broadcast requirements.

According to Jerry Brock, the NOJ&HF got a very good deal. "They agreed to pay $150 000 over a five year period of time...though it was easily worth over a million dollars. We realized it was a good deal for them but who else was there who would maintain the type of programming we had established. We felt OZ was

the 24-hour, 365-day-a-year jazz and heritage festival. We couldn't imagine a better pairing."

The transfer of ownership from the original WWOZ board to the NOJ&HF was an at times messy road. After various problems with new management and a threatened volunteer walk out, the NOJ&HF successfully petitioned the Brocks to return and steer the station back on its path. The Brocks did so for a short while before eventually leaving for good — "What had been a smooth ship from day one with all sorts of positive community input, good will; it became chaos."

After a series of failed attempts at hiring a competent station manager to replace the Brocks, David Freedman was eventually appointed. Coming from a background in Community Radio, he had the required skills to utilize the committed volunteer team and their vast array of talents and ideas, and, ensure that they all work together to make WWOZ great. Under David Freedman's leadership, WWOZ has maintained a large and committed volunteer base that is crucial to the day to day running of this, and every other public radio station. At the time of the 2005 Jazz Fest, the station maintains a volunteer roster that includes 112 'on-air' volunteers who either preside over a regular weekly time-slot, or who function as stand in personnel for the regular dj's, and, 170 extra volunteers who take care of the station's other administrative and promotional needs.

David Freedman, and the staff and volunteers, have also guided WWOZ through significant improvements in its technical broadcasting capabilities, including, perhaps most importantly, the process of broadcasting on the Internet. It was 1993 when the station responded to the potential of the then recent phenomenon of the World Wide Web. By establishing the capabilities to make the broadcast available over the Internet, WWOZ's New Orleans music broadcasts became immediately accessible to any person in the world with Internet access. Dwayne Breshears, WWOZ programming manager, pointed out that the trends in membership characteristics since this time confirm the global appeal of New Orleans music.

"The WWOZ membership base is truly global. We have members in Australia, New Zealand, Sweden, we even get them from the South Pole!"

The exact extent to which the Internet has expanded the WWOZ listener base is impossible to quantify, an examination of the traffic on the website does however give some indication as to the scale of global exposure. With 4 million 'hits' to the site in February 2004 being referred to as an average month, this exposure is most definitely significant.

The membership base is the most important constituency of the vast majority of public radio stations. WWOZ is no different, relying heavily on membership dues for revenue to run a station with a dedicated not-for-profit motive. At the end of 2004, WWOZ had 3,577 members. Many of these members are locals who recognize the importance of the role of the station in the cultural life of the city, and more importantly, are prepared to make a financial contribution to make sure WWOZ's work can continue. It is also important to note however that the fastest growing component of the station's membership base represents citizens of other countries. Is it fair to say these people recognize the significance of New Orleans music on a global cultural scale? One can only assume so.

The global diversity of the station's current membership base, as well as the continual growth of the gross number of members, indicates a healthy future for WWOZ. With the demonstrated ability of the station's management and volunteer staff to continue to deliver a radio product with the same 'flavor' that has fuelled the growth already witnessed, the future looks even brighter. As Dwayne Breshears puts it;

"At WWOZ we have welcomed growth, and we have made sure that we are growing but not changing so we lose our identity in the process. It is incredible to see how we have grown, but in many ways we are the same as we always were."

In 2000 the U.S. Congress voted to create the National Registry of Recordings. In 2001 the WWOZ tape library, produced prior to the Foundation's ownership, was selected as one of the first fifty selections into this registry. It is titled "The Crescent City Connection." Approximately 1,200 reel-to-reel tapes including documentaries and programs featuring Art Neville, James Booker, Preston Jackson, Danny Barker, Bobbie Mitchell and Ernie K-Doe and hundreds of others were ranked along side Thomas Edison's first recording,

Louis Armstrong, Bessie Smith, Billie Holiday and Franklin Roosevelt's fireside chats. They are now housed in the Foundation archive at 901 Toulouse Street.

WWOZ AT JAZZ FEST

WWOZ is in most people's minds the official Jazz Fest radio station. It has earned this reputation by providing live broadcasts from the Fair Groundsgrounds for what will be 23 consecutive years in 2005. For those unable to attend Jazz Fest, WWOZ provides a fantastic opportunity to participate in one of the greatest cultural events in the world.

Jazz Fest made its radio debut in 1982. In this year, Jerry and Walter Brock, and some WWOZ volunteers set up camp — literally, according to Jerry Brock who described their

Jazz Fest presence that year as a "lean-to"—and interviewed musicians live to air. Within their "lean-to" they had managed to establish a phone connection back to the studio and in this way Jerry at Jazz Fest communicated with Walter at the console back in Tipitina's to coordinate the show.

"It was me at the Jazz Fest and my brother Walter at the station. I'd say 'OK Walter, we've got Dr. John coming up for an interview' and Walter would go and pull Dr. John recordings." There were no broadcasts of the music until 1984 when WWOZ broadcast the Dirty Dozen Brass Band and Harry Connick, Jr.

In keeping with the trajectory of WWOZ, the now streamlined, hi-tech, online audio product delivered from the Fair Groundsgrounds by WWOZ had simple grass roots beginnings with the Brock brothers holding the microphones. These days WWOZ holds court in its own far more spacious and well-equipped tent, complete with fresh fruit and water for those lucky enough to hold the WWOZ membership Jazz Fest Brass Pass. Broadcasts of exceptional audio quality are provided by a complete onsite production team, and jazz fans stuck in the south pole drilling ice cores for climate change research can log on to Aaron Neville singing "Amazing Grace" live in New Orleans.

1985

In 1984, the Festival stopped allowing people to bring in coolers, another annoyance for locals who felt that the Fair Grounds should be an extension of their own backyards. Locals, and a small handful of out of towners had been erecting small "pavilions" some in the same location for the several years running and would "set up house" each day and just "go visit" the music and food. For the most part, like the fine art of "stoop sitting" they would hang out and greet friends and strangers throughout the day. The loss of the coolers was a sad blow to all these small encampments.

However, some people still brought coolers in 1985 anyway, although the numbers were greatly reduced. The cooler ban's only enforcer seemed to be pre-Festival publicity. The guards didn't stop the few who carried in coolers, but the majority of the Jazz & Heritage Festival regulars weren't willing to risk the delays of testing the ban by hauling in an ice chest. To the old guard still sneaking in coolers and beer, this was a pyrrhic victory. For many locals resentful of the new rules that had developed over the years, acceptance was the word of the day because this tradition was another casualty of

STAGE 1
12:15 J. Monque'D Blues Band
1:30 The Up Towners
2:30 Retsam D'nim
3:45 Fernest & The Thunders
5:15 The Batiste Brothers

STAGE 2
12:00 Nieve
1:30 Wayne Toups & Creole
Cajun Band
3:00 Java
4:30 Mighty Sam McClain & The
Wayne Bennett Blues Band

STAGE 3
12:00 Tulane University Jazz
Ensemble
1:15 J.D. & The Jammers
2:45 Uncle Stan & Auntie Vera
4:15 The Cold

WWL-TV STAGE 4
12:00 Ray Bonneville
1:15 Hazel & The Delta Ramblers
2:30 Golden Star Hunters
3:30 John Rankin
4:45 Filé

FESTIVAL TENT
12:00 N.O. Jazz Couriers
1:15 Sally Townes
2:30 Spencer Bohren
3:30 Jasmine
4:45 Mars

ECONOMY HALL
12:15 Jazz Cats
1:30 Banu Gibson
2:45 Lloyd Lambert Jazz Band
4:15 Pud Brown

KOINDU
12:00 Calvin Durand Quartet
1:15 Los Cometas
2:15 High Quality
3:30 Ed Perkins & The Leroy Jones
Quartet
4:30 Lady BJ Spectrum

WDSU / PIZZA HUT KID'S TENT
12:00 McDonogh #15 Elementary
School Band
1:00 Evangeline Armstrong
2:00 American Gypsy Theatre
3:00 Floating Eagle Feather
4:00 Kumbuka Dance & Drum
Collective

RHODES / WYLD GOSPEL TENT
12:00 Humbler Travelers
12:45 N.O. Headstart Singing Angels
1:30 Happy Action Family Singers
2:15 Fortier H.S. Gospel Choir
3:00 Leviticus Gospel Singers
3:45 Kennedy H.S. Gospel Choir
4:30 Orleans Parish Prison Choir

PARADES
4:00 Sixth Ward Swingers & Rebirth
Brass Band

STAGE 1
12:30 Walter Payton & Ballet Filé
2:00 Gary Brown & Feelings
3:30 Bar-Kays
5:00 Irma Thomas
& The Professionals

progress. Frankly, many felt the "lightness of unbeerable being" not having to lug or drag coolers around. People were able to work their way deeper into the crowds without having these roadblocks and see the acts better without some guy adding two feet to his height by standing on a cooler in front of them. Cleanup Krewe has not recorded estimates on the reduction of broken or crushed Styrofoam or plastic coolers they had to pick up and add to landfills.

This change occurred because the owners of the Fair Grounds received the revenues from the beer and soft drink concession instead of rent for Jazz Fest, and they had refused to sign the new lease agreement without the cooler ban. There would be a stricter crack down in later years, but the ban by honor system was relatively successful the first year, cutting down an estimated sixty percent of outside refreshments carried on site. No matter. Attendance was excellent on opening day.

The big news was about the opening night concert on Friday, April 26th showcasing two innovators, one whose career had already spanned four decades and another whose star was on the rise. Both Wynton Marsalis and Miles Davis attended Julliard and by a very young age were expanding musical boundaries and testing their own limits. Like Miles, Wynton also arrived at Julliard at age 18, and started gigging shortly after, first in the pit of the Broadway musical, "Sweeney Todd" and then as a member of Art Blakey's Jazz Messenger's group. In 1985, at age 24, Wynton had already garnered Grammy Awards in both the jazz and classical categories. Nationally known and

based primarily in New York, he had been lionized as the next Miles Davis and the best player to come from the city in a long time. He was also responsible for a new intellectualism and respect for the history of jazz and its cultural place in American society. A whole new generation of jazz players came to the fore, dressed for success and improvising new phrases in the old language.

At the Theatre for Performing Arts, these two masters of the trumpet headlined one of the most anticipated shows of 1985, which sold out right away. But

when they came together, on the same bill for two shows, they didn't jam together as everyone had hoped. Fans were treated to some moments of transcendent playing from both virtuosos; indeed Wynton's band was especially tight that night. Miles characteristically turned his back on the audience and musically took them into his own private space with the help of his band. To their credit, both made the night about the music, and the rapturous talk by attendees filing out was about this solo or that piece, not a comparative

study on style and execution.

Echoing this theme, Prout's Club Alhambra hosted an equally interesting jazz and film summit entitled *The New Generation*" which showcased a new crop of "youngsters" making their mark in the New Orleans scene. Terrence Blanchard, who in 1985 was director of Art Blakey's Jazz Messengers, Donald Harrison, Victor Goines, and Marlon Jordan joined with veterans Ellis Marsalis, Earl Turbinton Jr., Jim Singleton, Johnny Vidacovich, and others allowing the more established experts of the medium to listen to and share with the new crop emerging. Producers Joanne Schmidt and Charlie Bering had to be pleased anticipating the musical fireworks.

David Chertok was back on the scene with his wonderful vintage film segments of some of the masters of jazz: John Coltrane, Art Blakey, Sonny Rollins, Miles Davis, Charlie Parker, Billie Holliday, Dizzy Gillespie and Lester Young. These clips gave the young men featured on Friday the 26th inspiration and helped the packed house to appreciate what they were listening to. Many of the artists shown in film on this evening had played the Jazz Fest in its infancy. How cool is that? The Prout's Jazz Jams had been growing steadily over the last few years, and had turned into "must sees" for all jazz aficionados. On Saturday April 27th Prout's brought us another official Jazz Fest offering with a similar format combining of music and film.

Miles Davis

STAGE 2
12:15 Hector Gallardo & His Songo Allstars
1:30 Troy L. Deramus & His Country King Show
3:00 Clifton Chenier & His Red Hot Louisiana Band
4:30 A-Train

STAGE 3
12:00 Bryan Lee & The Jumpstreet Five
1:15 Willie Tee
2:30 Martha Reeves
4:00 Benny Spellman, Lee Allen w/ Red Tyler & Smokey Johnson Band

WWL-TV STAGE 4
12:00 Boogie Bill Webb
1:15 Ironin' Board Sam
2:30 Bourre
3:45 Van Williams
4:45 Dewey Balfa

FESTIVAL TENT
12:00 Dillard University Jazz Ensemble
1:00 Woodenhead
2:15 Ramsey McLean & The Survivors
3:30 Larry Coryell & Emily Remler
4:45 Leo Kotke

ECONOMY HALL
12:00 Kid Sheik & His Storyville Ramblers
1:15 Cousin Joe
2:15 Pfister Sisters
3:15 Tribute to Sidney Bechet w/ Bob Wilber & Joanne Horton
430 Onward Brass Band

KOINDU
12:15 Tim Green / Dave Goodman Quartet
1:30 Rising Star Drum & Fife Corps
2:15 White Cloud Hunters
3:15 Delfeayo Marsalis Quintet
4:30 Terence Blanchard & Donald Harrison Quintet

WDSU / PIZZA HUT KID'S TENT
12:00 Lusher Elementary School Chorus
1:00 James "Mr. Magic" Williams
2:00 Evangeline Armstrong
3:00 Khadija's Ethnic Dance Ensemble
4:00 New Orleans Free School Village Kids

RHODES / WYLD GOSPEL TENT
12:00 The Wimberly Family
12:45 Macedonia B.C. Youth Choir
1:30 St. Luke A.M.E. Gospel Choir
2:15 Franklin Avenue B.C. Choir
3:00 N.O. Spiritualettes
3:45 Dimensions of Faith
4:30 Regular B.C. Choir

PARADES
3:00 Ladies Zulu & The Jammers SA&PCs with Tuba Fats and The Chosen Few

SUNDAY, APRIL 28

STAGE 1
12:30 S.U.N.O. Jazz Ensemble
1:30 Rocking Sidney
3:00 Louisiana Purchase
4:30 The Staple Singers
6:00 The Neville Brothers

music scene

Ellis Marsalis released *Homecoming* with Eddie Harris.

Irma Thomas signs to Rounder Records

Rockin' Sidney wins Grammy Award for Best Ethnic or Traditional Folk Recording for "My Toot Toot."

IN MEMORIAM

Josiah "Cie" Frazier, Oscar "Chicken" Henry, Ralph Chester Jones, Frank Moliere, Herman Sherman, Stanley Williams

"Jazz Fest provided something very special for me. I had been living in Los Angeles for many years. My body was out there but my soul had never managed to escape New Orleans. In the early 80's I came back for Jazz Fest and I decided then that I had to find some way to come home. The year before they started the Jazz Studies program at U.N.O. I had decided that I would come back and start a jazz education program. When the U.N.O. program started in 1989 that provided me with the means to return and Jazz Fest was a catalyst for that." HAROLD BATISTE

"*The New Direction*" featured David Murray, Oliver Lake, Kidd Jordan, Alvin Batiste, Tony Dagradi, Clyde Kerr, Ramsey McLean, Al Fielder, Elton Herron, Hurley Blanchard and Darrell Lavigne, and was billed as contemporary jazz. The film segment of this evening had live performances captured on film of Thelonious Monk, McCoy Tyner, John Coltrane, Cecil Taylor, Cannonball Adderly and others.

The New Storyville Jazz Hall (later Margaritaville), next to the French Market, was also hosting some new players getting a chance to play with old timers. Traditional jazz would be the focus of these two shows entitled

"*Jazz at Storyville.*" The first night would feature Kid Sheik, Freddie Lonzo, Michael White, Buddy Charles, Sadie Peterson, Stanley Stephens and Stuart Davis. They would be joined by European imports The Caldona Jazzband of Oslo, Norway, and the Riverboat Stompers, of Italy. The following night brought Dick Wellstood, John Simmons, Frank Naundorf, Chris Burke, Ron Simpson, Maggie Kinson, Andrew Hall and Allen Jaffe. The European Classic Jazz Band of Holland joined them. The ubiquitous David Chertok was also showing films of classic performances of top local and national artists both nights.

Out on the infield the Bar-Kays, one of the originators of the "Memphis Soul Sound" showed the people how they funk in their home town wearing striped tights and white boots and driving the people wild, right before our lady of soul Irma Thomas came on to close Stage 1 for the day. Many of Irma's hardcore fans were sporting "We love you Irma" shirts and buttons, which she appreciated.

Sippie Wallace and the Staple Singers were two highlights on Sunday, April 28th. Sippie was one of those powerful women innovators, playing and singing the blues and writing her own saucy material like the song

"You Got To Know How" that Bonnie Raitt recorded back in 1972. She was known for her straight no chaser approach and she was also cute and gracious. Ms. Wallace mesmerized the standing room only Economy Hall Tent with her adorable smile and her saucy lyrics. She handled her band like the pro she was, controlling them with a simple hand gesture. Sippie would stop occasionally and ask the crowd "How am I doing?" The crowd roared their approval.

Guitar lovers were not forgotten. Thursday, May 2nd, once again on the *President*, "Guitar Explosion" featured Stevie Ray Vaughn and Double Trouble with Albert King and Clarence "Gatemouth" Brown. Just typing the lineup is all one needs to say. Saturday, May 4th on boat, Bobby "Blue" Bland was joined

by Ry Cooder and Bonnie Raitt. These two young musicians had embraced the blues and helped to open this style of music to a broader audience. Ry Cooder had already made waves as a writer and composer and as a session player with the likes of the Rolling Stones, Taj Mahal, and Captain Beefheart. Bonnie Raitt, a west coast girl, fell in love with old style Delta Blues and never looked back. Her recordings back in 1985 showed her strong affinity to Son House, Mississippi John Hurt and Fred McDowell. Her ballsy slide guitar work and her sweet soprano voice had been breaking hearts nationwide; and since her first performance at the New Orleans Jazz & Heritage Festival in 1977, she had been adored by the Crescent City. Bobby Bland, a living legend, had fun playing with "the chil-

Benny Spellman

Wynton Marsalis, Miles Davis, George Wein, and Joyce Wein

dren." Both Ry Cooder and Bonnie Raitt had shows the following day at the Festival.

King Nino and His Slave Girls was another quirky offering. This group was the brainchild of local composer/performer A.J. Loria. Many local white girls used to vie for the honor of being one of his "slave girls." Estella Denson, a wonderful vocalist who went on to sing with Cyndi Lauper may have been the only black "slave girl" to have a tenure in this fun group.

Run DMC performed on Stage 3 at 3:45 p.m. Interestingly, no explanation of their musical style exists in the program book. Most of the artists performing are explained in a short paragraph. This group would be the first rap act to reach the top ten in

1986 with the hit song "Raisin' Hell." They would also go on to be the first rap artists to win a Grammy with their song "King of Rock." Run DMC was comprised of Jam Master Jay, Joseph Simmons, and Darryl McDaniels. Festival Producers were prescient to get them when they did.

Throughout the entire Festival, on every day, both weekends, as was customary, second lines, brass bands, Indians, and Social Aid and Pleasure Clubs marched, played, danced, challenged and made a lot of noise pulling multitudes of people out of food and beer lines to dance along. This has always been one of the best ways to get from one side of the infield to another – like catching the bus, but different. Rebirth Brass

Band and the Six Ward Swingers marched on opening day at 4:00 p.m. from their respective start points across the Fair Grounds. Chosen Few and Zulu Ladies on Saturday at 3:00 pm and Doc Paulin Brass Band along with the Scene Boosters closed out the first weekend of this beautiful New Orleans tradition. Saturday, May 4th brought out the Young Tuxedo Brass Band, the Avenue Steppers and Tremé Sports Social Aide and Pleasure Club. Sunday, May 5th, The Olympia Brass Band and Olympia Social Aid and Pleasure Club closed out the celebration on the infield.

For anyone who hadn't had enough, the music and dancing would continue on late into the night at clubs and "After Fest" parties all over town.

STAGE 2
12:15 Lil' Queenie & The Boys of Joy
1:30 Johnnie Allan & The Memories
2:45 The Dusenbery Family Singers
4:00 Doc Watson
5:30 Deacon John Blues Revue

STAGE 3
12:45 John Mooney
2:15 Johnny Adams & Walter
Washington Solar System Band
3:45 Run DMC
5:15 Third World

WWL-TV STAGE 4
12:30 Klaus Weiland
1:45 Svare Forsland
3:00 The Whitstein Brothers
4:15 Mt. Pontchartrain String Band
5:30 Allen Fontenot &
the Country Cajuns

FESTIVAL TENT
12:15 NOCCA Jazz Ensemble
1:30 Debria Brown & Moses Hogan
2:30 James Black Ensemble
3:45 Kent Jordan Quintet
5:15 Arnett Cobb w/ Red Tyler, Fred
Kemp & Edward Frank Trio

ECONOMY HALL
12:00 Tennessee Tech Tuba Ensemble
1:00 Michael White Quartet
2:00 Frank Federico Jazz Band
3:00 Dick Wellstood
4:00 Widespread Jazz Orchestra
5:15 Kid Thomas Valentine & His
Algiers Stompers

KOINDU
12:15 Family
1:30 Hezekiah & The House Rockers
2:45 A Taste of New Orleans w/
Robert Parker
3:45 Barbados Tuck Band Parade
4:15 Creole Wild West
5:00 Barbados Tuck Band Parade
5:30 Uptown Affair & 21st Century

WDSU / PIZZA HUT KID'S TENT
1:00 Hynes Elementary
School Chorus
2:00 Colleen Salley
3:00 Taifa
4:00 Sax Machine
5:00 The Outreach Dancers

RHODES / WYLD GOSPEL TENT
12:00 Holy Name Gospel Singers
12:50 The Famous Rocks of Harmony
1:40 Macedonia B.C. choir of Rayville,
La.
2:30 Morning Star B.C. Choir
3:20 The Mighty Chariots
4:10 Gospel Inspirations
5:00 Mildred Clark & The
Melodyaires of Columbus, Ohio
5:50 St. Monica Catholic Church
Choir

PARADES
3:45 Avenue Steppers & Treme
Sports SA&PCs with Young
Tuxedo Brass Band

SUNDAY, MAY 5

STAGE 1
12:00 U.N.O. Jazz Band
1:00 Tommy Ridgley & The
Untouchables w/ The Dixi-Kups,
Frankie Ford & Bobby Mitchell
3:00 The Radiators
4:30 Ry Cooder
6:00 Allen Toussaint

STAGE 2
12:00 Pop Combo w/ Lenny Zenith
1:30 Clarence "Frogman" Henry
2:45 Caliente
4:00 Tania Maria
5:30 Roy Ayers

STAGE 3
12:00 Jr.'s Ultimate Blues Experience
1:15 Snooks Eaglin w George Porter,
Jr. & Zigaboo Modeliste
2:15 Bonnie Raitt
3:45 Clarence "Gatemouth" Brown
5:15 Doug Kershaw

WWL-TV STAGE 4
12:00 Ardoin Family Band
1:15 Bois Sec Ardoin & Canray
Fontenot
2:15 Beasoleil
3:30 Dave Van Ronk
4:45 Mason Ruffner & The Blues
Rockers
6:00 Russ Russell & The Rustlers

FESTIVAL TENT
12:30 Al Farrell
1:45 Chris Owens
3:00 Dirty Dozen Brass Band
4:00 Ellis Marsalis w/ special guests
Ron Carter, Smitty Smith &
Germaine Bazzle
5:30 Improvisational Arts Quintet

ECONOMY HALL
12:00 Brian White's Magna Jazz Band
1:00 Miss Lillian Bennett
2:00 Tennessee Tech Tuba Ensemble
3:00 New Leviathan Oriental Foxtrot
Orchestra
4:15 Wallace Davenport N.O. Jazz
Band
5:30 Percy Humphrey & His Crescent
City Joymakers

KOINDU
12:15 Theron Lewis & Unit 7
1:30 White Eagles Mardi Gras Indians
2:30 Rockin' Dopsie & His
Cajun Twisters
3:45 Bobby Marchan & Higher
Ground w/ Ernie K-Doe and
Gerri Hall
5:30 Exuma

WDSU / PIZZA HUT KID'S TENT
1:00 McDonogh #42 Children's Choir
2:00 David & Roselyn
3:00 American Gypsy Theatre
4:00 Floating Eagle Feather
5:00 Kumbuka Dance & Drum
Collective

RHODES / WYLD GOSPEL TENT
12:00 Rev. Donald Watkins
12:45 The Famous Smooth Family
1:35 Avondale Community Chorus
2:25 Sherman Washington & The
Zion Harmonizers
3:15 Helen Brock & The Famous
Gospellettes of Houston
4:05 Greater Macedonia B.C.
Senior Choir
4:55 Gospel Choralettes
5:45 Gospel Soul Children

PARADES
5:15 Olympia Aid SA&PC with
Olympia Brass Band

NIGHT CONCERTS

**FRIDAY, APRIL 26, 7:30 P.M. &
MIDNIGHT**
Miles Davis
Wynton Marsalis
Theatre of Performing Arts

FRIDAY, APRIL 26, MIDNIGHT
Jazz & Film presented by David
Chertok
The New Generation
Prout's Club Alhambara

**SATURDAY, APRIL 27, 7:30 P.M. &
MIDNIGHT**
The Staple Singers
Allen Toussaint
The Dirty Dozen Brass Band
Riverboat President

SATURDAY, APRIL 27, MIDNIGHT
Jazz & Film presented by David
Chertok
The New Direction
Prout's Club Alhambara

TUESDAY, APRIL 30, 8 P.M.
Sarah Vaughn and Trio
Ellis Marsalis — solo piano
Theatre of Performing Arts

WEDNESDAY, MAY 1, 9 P.M.
Spyro Gyra
The James Rivers Movement
Riverboat President

WEDNESDAY, MAY 1, 8:30 P.M.
Jazz & Film presented by David
Chertok
Traditional New Orleans Jazz
The New Storyville Jazz Hall

THURSDAY, MAY 2, 8 P.M.
Guitar Explosion
Stevie Ray Vaughan & Double Trouble
Albert King
Clarence "Gatemouth" Brown
Riverboat President

THURSDAY, MAY 2, 8:30 P.M.
Jazz & Film Presented By David
Chertok
Traditional New Orleans Jazz
The New Storyville Jazz Hall

FRIDAY, MAY 3, 7 P.M. & MIDNIGHT
Ry Cooder, Bobby "Blue" Bland,
Bonnie Raitt
Riverboat President

1986

Maybe each year is as meaningful as the others in this spinning experiment that is Planet Earth. Here in New Orleans, it is said that change may roll slowly over the surface; but in fact, the city's essence never really changes. Nevertheless, 1986 was a year of major events inside and outside of Jazz Fest. Throughout the 1980s, commerce was king. Gold jewelry bristled its way into fashion, and women wore their jackets shaped big and square, the better to shoulder their way around boardrooms. Easy availability of high-yield junk bonds was aphrodisiac to investors, and venture capitalists preyed on the economic landscape. The "peace and love generation" had begun a grotesque morph into what would become a ravenous consumer culture.

what's going on?

GLOBALLY

A prominent nonviolent fighter against apartheid, Desmond Tutu, becomes archbishop of Cape Town, South Africa.

In the world's worst nuclear accident, the Chernobyl plant in the Ukraine explodes, polluting the environment and causing perhaps 8,000 deaths.

28 years of one-family rule end in Haiti, when President Jean-Claude Duvalier abdicates.

NATIONALLY

U.S. is found selling arms to Iran during its war with Iraq and using the profits to fund Contra forces in Nicaragua.

A government report reveals that a hydrogen bomb was accidentally dropped near Albuquerque, N.M. in 1957, but it did not explode.

The space shuttle Challenger explodes after lift-off, generating national mourning and a setback for the U.S. space program.

America celebrates national holiday Dr. Martin Luther King Jr. day for the first time.

LOCALLY

Godchaux's Department Store, one of a handful of locally-owned institutions with great customer loyalty, closes after 60 years.

Jim Mora becomes the tenth Saints coach.

The U.S. Supreme Court supports the Louisiana ruling voiding the state requirement that schools must teach "creationism" alongside evolution.

Creole Democrat Sidney J. Barthelemy becomes Mayor of New Orleans.

CULTURALLY

"A.M. Chicago" changes its name to the "Oprah Winfrey Show" and goes national September 8th.

The fourth television network, FOX, is created, offering 10 hours of programming per week.

In these fast times, the powerful economic engine of Jazz Fest was a gleaming jewel, glittering with commercial potential. While Jazz Fest had always benefited from corporate sponsorship, the ante was upped when sponsorship opportunities turned Stage 1 into the "MCI Stage." Stage 2 was sponsored by WNOE, Stage 4 by WWL-TV, a Taco Bell logo festooned the Jazz Tent, and TV 6 and Pizza Hut sponsored the Kids' Tent. In a somewhat in-synch fit, WYLD and long-time sponsor Rhodes Funeral Home sponsored the Gospel Tent. Only the "Fess" Stage, Economy Hall Tent, and Lagniappe Tent retained their thematic individuality. No longer was the numeric tied to the geographic. It was a reminder that profit must motivate even nonprofit.

Undeniably, Jazz Fest had benefited in the early days with its tax-exempt status, which forgave the amusement and sales tax remittances so that they were ploughed back into keeping the Festival viable. However, as profits grew and were disposed of by

the Foundation, there might have been no Festival today had the non-profit status not been incorporated. The Festival was started by far looking civic-minded people who wanted to capitalize on the incipient cultural capital. The return on investment for the city and state has been immense. Regardless, commerce was king in Ronald Reagan's deregulated world, and interest in things Louisiana was gaining great currency. Never a backwater, it seemed that native sons and products were everywhere on the American landscape.

In January, New Orleans native son Fats Domino was inducted into the Rock and Roll Hall of Fame. Born Antoine Dominique in 1923, "Fats" was another of New Orleans' musicians brought along by others in the field. Harrison Verret, Fat's brother-in-law, had often been invited by the ukulele playing, pop tunes-singing Lemon Nash into a French Quarter art gallery owned by Larry Borenstein, who championed Sister Gertrude Morgan and attended the early

Earl King, Stevie Ray Vaughn, Dave Bartholomew

Festivals with her. Gratuities from art patrons encouraged other music-playing friends to come around, too. Borenstein, recognizing opportunity when he saw it, began the metamorphosis from art gallery to what became Preservation Hall, now New Orleans' dominant venue dedicated to preserving New Orleans' traditional jazz heritage. Verret had given Fats a leg up just as rock and roll music was gaining steam. In just one example of how synchronous history can be: as Fats was learning his chops in New Orleans, in the Midwest a radio disc jockey named Jim Russell was beginning to see "race music" recordings showing up on his desk sent through music promoters.

By 1986, Jim Russell had been living in New Orleans for more than 17 years. An advertisement in the Jazz Fest Official Program announced the closing of his celebrity-frequented record store on Magazine Street, selling his collection of 300,000 45 and 78 rpm records for half price. Russell's lifetime in music was a wild ride of history-making encounters, including turning disc jockey Alan Freed (credited with popularizing the term "rock and roll") on to music by African-American recording artists, and fishing Aaron Neville's "Tell It Like It Is" out of a trash can at Cosimo Matassa's now legendary J&M Studio and taking it to disc jockeys all over the city. When Fats was signed to Imperial Records in 1949 and afterwards went in to Matassa's to record "The Fat Man" (originally named "Junkers Blues" by New Orleanian Champion Jack Dupree) the song raced up the R&B charts. Later some referred to that as the first rock and roll recording. Induction into the Rock and Roll Hall

of Fame did not entice Fats to attend the Cleveland, Ohio, ceremony. Nor did an invitation to the White House. Sometime in the 1980s, Fats had made a choice to ensconce himself in his home in the 9th Ward, tool around in his pink Cadillac only when necessary, and enjoy his hometown for good.

With the demand for Cajun music and culture sweeping across the U.S., Beausoleil and the Ardoin Family were invited to play in the Festival of American Folk Life in Washington, DC, in July. At the Fest, Beausoleil's Michael Doucet sat in on Malavoi de Martinique at the Congo Stage and according to a local reporter "shook his head in wonder at the string quintet teetering sawing magic." Back in the city, a young band was attracting attention: Dash Rip Rock was just starting to tour. Their seemingly inscrutable name would be familiar to Hollywood trivia buffs: Dash Rip Rock was the name of one of Ellie Mae's suitors in the 1970s TV series The Beverly Hillbillies.

> *"It was very clever marketing, but it was also a wonderful thing when we used to start the day with high school jazz bands and then some days we did the local college jazz bands. But we always started the day with a jazz band that was local, and I don't know whether they were giving the tickets away or not, but I got to tell you every aunt, uncle, mother, and family member was out there to see their child perform at Jazz Fest for the first time."* KEITH WILLIAMS

Donna Dixon, who played Ellie Mae, apparently still in full possession of her "star power," ended up living in the band's hometown of Baton Rouge, and her fulsome splendor caught the eye of the boys in the band.

Barq's Root Beer was a New Orleans tradition, but inexplicably, the distributor, Zetz 7-Up Bottling Company, chose to market Delaware Punch, "New Orleans, favorite soft drink" as the official soft drink of the Fest. "Fruit juicy flavor with more punch than pop!" claimed the full-page ad in the official Jazz Fest program. Sales manager was Judy Palmer, then wife of Jed Palmer (owner of Jed's Uptown

Bill Russell

Bahamas Junkanoos

music scene

Fats Domino is inducted into the Rock & Roll Hall of Fame.

WWOZ moves to Louis Armstrong Park.

IN MEMORIAM

Allen Jaffe, Ted Taylor, Gerald "Professor Shorthair" Tillman

---

WDSU-TV 6 / PIZZA HUT KIDS' TENT
11:30 Combined Elementary Schools Jazz Band
12:15 McDonogh #15 Elementary School Band
1:30 William J. Fischer Elementary School Choir & Les Petites Dancers
2:45 Della Gautier
3:55 Fantasy Request
5:00 Lenard Davis

PARADES
3:00 Johnny Kool & His Gang SA&PC & All Star Brass Band

SATURDAY, APRIL 26

MCI STAGE
11:20 Loyola University Jazz Band
12:40 A-Train
2:00 Clarence "Gatemouth" Brown
3:30 Joan Baez
5:00 Ernie K-Doe & The K-Doe Allstar Band

WNOE STAGE
11:30 Continental Drifters
12:35 Phil Menard & Louisiana Travelers
1:40 Tabby Thomas & His Blues Revue
3:00 Tim Williams & Natchez
4:10 Al Ferrier the Rockabilly King
5:00 New Grass Revival

THE "FESS" STAGE
11:30 Xavier University Jazz Band
12:45 Deacon John Blues Revue with J.D. Hill
2:15 Louisiana Purchase
3:45 Clifton Chenier & Red Hot Louisiana Band
5:15 War

WWL-TV 4 STAGE
11:20 Dejan's Olympia Jr. Brass Band
12:40 Grandmaster MIC Conductors
1:40 John Mooney's Blues Scoundrels
2:45 Percussion, Inc.
3:50 Bruce Daigrepont Cajun Band
5:15 Willis Prudhomme & Zydeco Express

TACO BELL JAZZ TENT
11:40 Improvisational Arts Ensemble
1:00 Alvin "Red" Tyler
2:00 John Hammond
3:40 N.O. Jazz Couriers
5:00 Betty Carter & Her Trio

ECONOMY HALL TENT
11:30 Creole Rice Jazz Band
12:45 Walter Payton & Ballet Filé
2:15 Sippie Wallace & The James Dapogny Chicago Jazz Band
3:30 The Pfister Sisters
4:45 Kid Sheik & His Storyville Ramblers

LAGNIAPPE TENT
11:20 The Sounds of Brazil
12:40 Golden Star Hunters Mardi Gras Indians
1:45 Svare Forsland
3:00 Jessie Mae Hemphill Trio
4:20 Jass Cats

KOINDU STAGE
11:45 Tim Green / Dave Goodman Stick Band
1:10 White Eagles Mardi Gras Indians
2:20 Taste of N.O. Featuring David Lastie, Al Shine Robinson, Jessie Hill & Wanda Rouzan
3:40 Bahamas Junkanoo Revue
5:10 The Shepherd

Ellyna Tatum and Irma Thomas

fest facts

Jazz Fest added the second Friday to the Fair Grounds Heritage Fair "to accommodate the increasing demand for the music, food and crafts offered at the Heritage Fair."

The evening concerts series included two free evening concerts in the Spanish Plaza at Riverwalk.

Little Feat's reunion concert was so tight it was if the band had never separated.

Up from the Cradle of Jazz: New Orleans Music Since World War II was published. Authors were Jason Berry, Jonathan Foose and Tad Jones, who signed in the book tent. It is now out of print.

music club). Jed's was notable for being the first club of its kind to charge a $2 admission, with Palmer intending to pay the musicians more money than their usual cut. A raconteur and bon vivant, Palmer also organized "Uptown Jazz Fest" parades, with masking and merriment. Judy would, in 2003, publish her hilarious and poignant memoirs of living with Jed (and divorcing) in a book entitled *Southern Fried Divorce*. The circle just gets wider.

The inimitable Miles Davis opened the evening concerts with a newly assembled 10-piece ensemble, the largest with which he had toured. Since the 1940s, Davis had been in the forefront of jazz innovators, eschewing flashy dramatics of vibrato playing and instead exploring the inner space of the music in the middle register. In a kick toward rock-oriented jazz, Davis was joined by bassist Stanley Clarke. The younger jazzman didn't stand in Davis's shadow, but towered alongside. He was the surprise delight of the evening.

Some of the most powerful percussion at the Fest was pounded down on the Koindu Stage. The Nigerian Babatunji Olatunji and his Drums of Passion defined skin-pounding ecstasy as he shook off the experience of a less-than-civil Nina Simone during the Wednesday night concert. In one of the finest demonstrations of the now popular ju-ju music, Chief Commander Ebenezer Obey & His Interreformers (seven percussionists) thundered out a mighty dance beat.

In the cross-pollination that occurred in

music clubs and bars all over New Orleans during Jazz Fest, musicians sat in and jammed with each other. Louisiana native and one-time Box Top Alex Chilton joined Leo Nocentelli and George Porter at Jimmy's. Some musicians, like bassist George Porter, were in such demand that they made a frantic rush to play on several stages and in the night concerts with all of their friends, while others started their own

traditions. Sometimes the stars came out. In 1986, celebrities were all over the Fest: David Byrne was spotted dancing to the Dirty Dozen's squawking, blaring brass blasts. John Fogerty revisited his Third Coast roots, and Watergate-scooping journalist Carl Bernstein showed up at numerous stages at the Fair Grounds. The Brat Pack's Judge Reinhold was photographed emerging from a Port-O-Let, and Louisiana governor Edwin "Vote for the Crook – It's Important" Edwards enjoyed his own celebrity/notoriety in a sort of reverse marketing of Louisiana, proving even bad publicity is good. Some, such as television journalist Ed Bradley, would return to Jazz Fest year after year, and become as much a part of the Fest as the locals.

Singer/songwriter Paul Simon was basking in the success of his Grammy-winning album *Graceland*, which had employed South African artists during the boycott against that nation's apartheid regime. According to Michael Tisserand, author of *The Kingdom of Zydeco*, Simon had worked with three south Louisiana Cajun and zydeco bands during the production of *Graceland*: the just-starting-out Terrance Simien and his Mallet Playboys, Rockin' Dopsie and the Cajun Twisters, and Buckwheat Zydeco. Dopsie's instrumental interpretation of "Josephine C'est Pas Ma Femme," an adaptation of the much older "Adieu Rosa," became inspiration for the song "That Was Your Mother."

In 2001, giant video screens attached to the main stages would reflect Simon singing that song to a crowd of 50,000 two-stepping Jazz Festers.

New Orleans musician J "I am the Blues" Monque D' worked as an extra on the set of *Angel Heart,* a film noir thriller being shot in atmospheric Algiers, just across the Mississippi River. Monque D' managed to lure fellow cast members Robert DiNiro, Charlotte Rampling and Lisa Bonet to Benny's music club, to check out his set. Another film written by Louisiana native Glen Pitre and scored by Michael Doucet, *Belizaire the Cajun,* premiered in New Orleans that year. The film experience in Louisiana led actor Armand Assanté to comment, "These people didn't know anything about film, and here they were making a film. People who were healers became carpenters, and carpenters became set decorators. A woman who was an herbal specialist taught me everything I needed to know about herbs – that's heart. You can't buy that in L.A."

KOINDU STAGE
11:30 Caliente
1:00 Delfeayo Marsalis Quintet
2:10 Exuma
3:10 Bahamas Junkanoo Revue
4:30 Walter Washington & The Roadmasters w/ Johnny Adams & Timothea
6:00 Odadaa! Ghanaian Drum & Dance

WYLD / RHODES GOSPEL TENT
11:30 Southern Bells
12:15 Randolph Brothers
12:55 Gaza B.C.
1:45 N.O. Comforters
2:30 Rev. Donald Watkins
3:10 The Providence Tones of Joy
3:55 McDonogh #35 Gospel Choir
4:45 Rev. F.C. Barnes/ Rev. Janice Brown
5:40 Desire Community Choir

WDSU-TV 6 / PIZZA HUT KIDS' TENT
12:00 The Bum's Rush
1:10 David & Roselyn
2:20 Voices of the Kingdom
3:30 Cliff Da' Clown and Charmin' Charmin
4:30 Deirdre's School of Dance and Gymnastics
5:00 American Gypsy Theater

PARADES
2:00 Ladies Zulu, Young Men Olympia SA&PCs & Young Tuxedo Brass Band

SATURDAY, MAY 3

MCI STAGE
11:45 Lenny Zenith
1:15 James Rivers Movement
2:40 Dave Bartholomew Orchestra
4:00 Rockin' Sidney
5:00 Will Soto
5:25 Tommy Ridgley & The Untouchables w/ Bobby Mitchell, Robert Parker & Frankie Ford

WNOE STAGE
11:30 Uncle Stan & Auntie Vera
12:40 Belton Richard & Musical Aces
2:00 Russ Russell & The Rustlers
4:40 Filé
6:00 Scooter Lee

THE "FESS" STAGE
11:30 S.U.N.O. Jazz Ensemble
1:00 Earl King Blues Band
2:20 Koko Taylor
4:00 Stevie Ray Vaughan & Double Trouble
6:00 Miami Sound Machine

WWL-TV 4 STAGE
11:15 Local International Allstars
12:30 Blue Lunch featuring Sam McClain
2:00 Wild Magnolias Mardi Gras Indians
3:00 Hezekiah & The House Rockers
4:00 Barbados Truck Band
5:15 Allen Fontenot & The Country Cajuns

TACO BELL JAZZ TENT
11:15 Tulane University Jazz Band
12:40 Ritmo Caribeno
1:45 Earl Turbinton Quintet
3:00 Bright Moments: A Tribute to Rahsaan Roland Kirk
4:30 David Murray
6:00 Ramsey McLean & The Survivors

ECONOMY HALL TENT
11:30 Frog Island Jazz Band
12:45 Onward Brass Band
2:00 Odetta
3:20 New Leviathan Oriental Foxtrot Orchestra
4:45 The Copasetics
5:45 Kid Thomas Valentine & The Algiers Stompers

LAGNIAPPE TENT
11:45 Chakula & Chink
12:45 Marcie Lacoutre & Inez Catalon
1:50 Brother Percy Randolph & Little Freddie King
3:15 Hot Strings of New Orleans
4:40 Spencer Bohren
6:00 Voodoo Macumba

KOINDU STAGE
11:30 Uptown Affaire & The Cosmos Band
12:35 Tanya P
1:30 Ruben Mr. Salsa Gonzales
2:45 Little Joe Blue
4:15 Olatunji & His Drums of Passion
5:45 Willie Metcalf

WYLD / RHODES GOSPEL TENT
11:30 Jerusalem Singers
12:10 Macedonia C.O.C.I.G.
12:50 Friendly Five
1:35 St. Luke A.M.E.
2:15 Rev. Jimmy Olsen / Mt. Zion
2:55 Gospel Choralettes
3:40 Rev. Freddie Dunn
4:25 St. Francis DeSales Golden Voices
5:10 Zulu Ensemble
5:55 Dimensions of Faith

WDSU-TV 6 / PIZZA HUT KIDS' TENT
12:00 Lenard Davis
12:35 The Class Clowns
1:40 Perry the Mime
2:50 New Orleans Free School Village Kid
3:55 Evangeline Armstrong
5:00 Kumbuka Dance and Drum Collective

PARADES
2:30 Avenue Steppers, Tremé Sports SA&PCs & Tornado Brass Band

SUNDAY, MAY 4

MCI STAGE
11:15 S.U.B.R. Jazz Band
12:20 Marcia Ball Band
1:45 Queen Ida & The Bon Temps Zydeco Band
3:15 Rita Coolidge
4:35 Pete Fountain
6:00 Irma Thomas & The Professionals

WNOE STAGE
11:30 Don Montoucet and The Wandering Aces
12:45 Snooks Eaglin
2:00 Barbara Menendez Band
3:30 Luzianne
4:40 BeauSoleil
6:00 New South

THE "FESS" STAGE
11:45 Bryan Lee, Miss Maggie & The Jumpstreet Five
1:20 Terrence Simien & The Mallet Playboys
2:40 Luther Kent & Trick Bag
4:10 Dr. John
5:40 The Neville Brothers

WWL-TV 4 STAGE
11:45 Creole Wild West Mardi Gras Indians
1:10 Barbados Tuck Band
2:20 Kumbuka Drum & Dance Collective
3:45 Phil Meeks & The Sundowners
5:15 Banda-Fiebre

TACO BELL JAZZ TENT
11:30 Jasmine featuring Ensamble Acustico of Guatemala
12:45 Tony Dagradi & Astral Project
2:10 Dicky Landry
3:30 Chris Owens
4:40 Dirty Dozen Brass Band
6:00 Alvin Batiste

ECONOMY HALL TENT
11:30 Lady Charlotte Jazz Band
12:45 Dr. Michael White Quartet w/ Barbara Shorts
1:50 Danny Barker & His Jazz Hounds
3:00 Carrie Smith: A Tribute To Bessie Smith
4:00 Butch Thompson
5:30 Percy Humphrey & The Crescent City Joymakers

LAGNIAPPE TENT
11:45 Klaus Weiland
1:10 Caledonian Scottish Dancers & Pipes & Drums of N.O.
2:30 Ramblin' Jack Elliott
4:15 Rusty Kershaw
5:40 Golden Eagles Mardi Gras Indians

KOINDU STAGE
11:30 Theron Lewis & Unit 7
12:40 Willie Tee
2:00 Lady BJ
3:30 Chocolate Milk w/ The Aubry Twins
5:15 Chief Commander Ebenezer Obay and His Interformers Band

WYLD / RHODES GOSPEL TENT
11:15 Bells of Joy
11:55 Crown Seekers
12:40 Joseph "Cool" Davis
1:20 Greater Macedonia B.C.
2:05 Zion Harmonizers
2:55 Heralds of Christ
3:40 Raymond Myles Singers
4:35 Mighty Clouds of Joy
5:45 Gospel Soul Children

WDSU-TV 6 / PIZZA HUT KIDS' TENT
12:00 James "Mr. Magic" Williams
12:55 Evangeline Armstrong
2:00 McDonogh #42 Children's Choir
3:05 Nevtron and The Nevtones
3:45 Perry the Mime
5:00 Kumbuka Dance and Drum Collective

PARADES
3:00 Scene Boosters, Fun Lovers SA&PCs & Olympia Brass Band

NIGHT CONCERTS

APRIL 25, FRIDAY, 9 P.M.
Miles Davis / Stanley Clarke
Saenger Theatre

APRIL 25, FRIDAY, 8 P.M.
The Original Cast of "One Mo' Time" Including Vernel Bagneris, Sylvia "Kuumba" Williams, Topsy Chapman and Thais Clark with The New Orleans Blues Serenaders featuring Orange Kellin and Lars Edegran
Sippie Wallace with The James Dapogny Chicago Jazz Band
Old Time Jazz Band of Helsinki, Finland
Storyville Jazz Hall

APRIL 26, SATURDAY, 8 P.M.
Natalie Cole
Andre Crouch
B.B. King
Southern University Marching Band
Municipal Auditorium

APRIL 26, SATURDAY, 12 MIDNIGHT
The Leaders
Famoudou Don Moyé, Chico Freeman, Don Cherry, Cecil McBee, Kirk Lightsey, Arthur Blythe
Henry Butler, Charlie Haden and Herman Jackson
Kidd Jordan's Elektrik Band
Prout's Club Alhambra

APRIL 29, 8 P.M.
Al Di Meola (solo)
Steps Ahead — Michael Brecker, Peter Erskine, Michael Manieri, Victor Bailey
Theatre of Performing Arts

APRIL 30, WEDNESDAY, 8 P.M.
Nina Simone
Olatunji & Drums of Passion
Theatre of Performing Arts

MAY 1, THURSDAY, 9 P.M.
Louisiana Rock & Roll Gumbo
Jerry Lee Lewis / Rockin' Sidney / The Radiators
Riverboat President

MAY 1, THURSDAY, 8 P.M.
The Copasetics, Masters of Tap
Bunny Briggs, Louis Sims Carpenter, Charles "Cookie" Coach, Bubba Gaines, Jim Roberts, Henry "Phace" Roberts
Carrie Smith in a Tribute to Bessie Smith
Ex Waseda Jazz Band of Tokyo, Japan
Storyville Jazz Hall

MAY 2, FRIDAY, 9 P.M.
La Gran Noche de Musica
Jose Feliciano / Miami Sound Machine
Riverboat President

MAY 2, FRIDAY, 12 MIDNIGHT
The David Murray Octet with Craig Harris, Olu Dara, Baikida Carroll, John Purcell
Alvin Batiste The New Orleans Sax Quartet, Earl Turbinton, Jr., Tony Dagradi, Fred Kemp, Roger Lewis

MAY 3, SATURDAY, 8 P.M.
The Neville Brothers
Burning Spear
Chief Commander Ebenezer Obey & His Inter-Reformers Ju-Ju Orchestra

1987

Blue Lu and Danny Barker

The 1987 Jazz Fest was dedicated to the memory of Alan Jaffe. On March 9, Jaffe, a founder and manager of Preservation Hall, died from cancer. He was 51. Jaffe's passing was marked with a jazz funeral attended by hundreds of the people he loved, including the Olympia, Rebirth, Eagle, and his own Preservation Hall Brass Bands, with which Jaffe had played sousaphone and toured the world. Jaffe's role in the creation of Preservation Hall was to formalize the performances that were already occurring impromptu for tips at Larry Borenstein's art gallery at 726 St. Peter Street. Borenstein decided to go with the musicians — art was out and music was in — with admission at $1, and rising to $2 in 1984.

By 1987, four bands performed regularly at Preservation Hall, and toured as the Preservation Hall Jazz Band. They were the Olympia, the Kid Sheik Colar Band, the Kid Thomas Valentine Band, and the Willie Humphrey Band. Preservation Hall continued to operate with no food, drinks, or air conditioning, just as Jaffe decreed. He was said to have once read a magazine article that convinced him that "none of the really great places of the world, such

what's going on?

GLOBALLY

Zulu chief Buthelezi begins a civil war against South Africa's Africa National Congress.

Supernova 1987a is observed, the first "naked-eye" supernova since 1604.

NATIONALLY

US and Canada sign a free-trade agreement.

World stock market share prices crash as Wall Street's Dow Jones Index falls by 508 points on what is called "Black Monday."

Gary Hart drops out of the running for the Democratic Party nomination in the 1988 U.S. presidential election, amid allegations of an extra-marital affair with Donna Rice.

LOCALLY

New Orleans hosts a visit from Pope John Paul II.

Republican Governor Edwin Edwards concedes election to reform candidate Charles "Buddy" Roemer who, mid-term, switched parties from Democrat to Republican.

Locals mourn the closing of Gus Mayer Department Store, which had opened in 1900.

Cuban detainees at the Federal Detention Center in Oakdale stage an 8-day seige, and hold 26 people hostage after learning they were being sent back to Cuba.

Louisiana celebrates the 175th anniversary of its admission into the Union.

The Monday arrival of Rex at Spanish Plaza marks the revival of the Lundi Gras tradition, and a new ordinance temporarily bars Zulu from throwing coconuts.

CULTURALLY

Toni Morrison publishes her novel Beloved, which will win a Pulitzer Prize.

"Baby Jessica," Jessica McClure falls down the well and is later rescued.

Oliver Morgan

On January 1 of 1987, the nonprofit Jazz & Heritage Foundation assumed the license of community radio station FM WWOZ, 90.7. WWOZ had been founded under the absolute best of conditions: by people who loved both the musical heritage and future possibilities of jazz, blues, folk, and other indigenous genres, and who had the brains and know-how to bring their vision forth into the community. Jerry and Walter Brock's story is told in another chapter, so suffice it to say that WWOZ had always struggled with a noble vision that was also under-capitalized.

The Jazz Fest and WWOZ missions had essentially been the same: to promote jazz, traditional music, folk arts, and the cultural heritage of the city and region around New Orleans. In fact, WWOZ had recently been the recipient of a Jazz & Heritage Foundation grant of $150,000, over a three-year period. Around $60,000 of that sum had to be put toward retiring existing debts. Acquisition by the Foundation allowed the station to hire and support full-

as the Taj Mahal or St. Peter's in Rome or the ferry, streetcar or Napoleon House in New Orleans were air-conditioned."

Jaffe had been an early friend to George Wein and participated in many parades with his band over the years. As a Jazz Fest fixture, he would be sorely missed, but his sons Benjamin and Russell still carry on the family tradition in true New Orleans style, as they play their tubas with current brass band incarnations.

B.B. King, Stevie Ray Vaughn, Earl King

time employees and upgrade programming and production. In 1984, Walter Brock had approached producer George Wein about Jazz Fest holding the license for WWOZ, thus ensuring its financial viability. But Wein didn't see the benefit in running a day-to-day operation, and others also speculated that the station would be a drain on Jazz Fest. But negotiations continued, and through the diplomacy of Kalamu ya Salaam among others, the Jazz & Heritage Foundation eventually purchased the license, creating the nonprofit Friends of WWOZ to handle financial stewardship.

They needed a station manager to work with volunteers and oversee production and marketing. Words like "disaster" were used to describe the first few station managers. Volunteers and staff headed off in droves. Perseverance triumphed, and when David Freedman came on board the station management stabilized and began to thrive.

Chris Thomas, long before the Coen brothers' "O Brother How Art Thou" would bring him solo fame, hauled his Delta and urban blues to the Fest. Tabby Thomas, Chris' father, had been keeping the blues flame alive for more than 30 years at Tabby's Blues Box and Heritage Hall in Baton Rouge.

The Jazz Fest staff had played it pretty close to home thus far with the evening concerts, scheduling a predominance of New Orleans musicians, and artfully adding enough national star power to draw younger and crossover rock and roll audiences. The Motor City and the Crescent City collided when Fats Domino and the Four Tops rocked the river

on the *S.S. President*, in shows beginning at 7:00 p.m. and midnight. Catching the zydeco craze at its height, Wednesday's riverboat concert "Fais Do Do" brought together Rockin Dopsie & the Zydeco Twisters, Zachary Richard, and Beausoleil. Rockin Dopsie, master of the button accordion, had received a career boost from his appearance in 1986 on Paul Simon's *Graceland*. Richard was ping ponging between full-bore rock and roll and his advocacy for the Cajun French music and culture. He was achieving success in both endeavors.

Beausoleil was the most high profile Cajun band touring in the world. Hollywood contributed a cameo appearance to the popularity of zydeco. Beausoleil,

James Brown

WDSU TV-6 KIDS' TENT
12:00 William J. Fischer Elem. Choir
& Petite Dancers
1:00 McDonogh #15 Elementary
School Band
2:00 Nevtron & The Nevtones
3:00 Perry The Mime
4:00 Washboard Leo
5:00 Perri The Hobo

PARADES
2:45 Valley of the Silent Men SA&PC
with Spirit of New Orleans
and Storyville Stompers Brass
Bands

SATURDAY, APRIL 25

WVUE / BURGER KING STAGE
11:20 Tulane University Jazz
Ensemble
12:45 Santiago
2:00 Zachary Richard
3:20 Carl Perkins
4:15 Johnny Rivers
6:00 John Fred & The Playboys

WNOE / TACO BELL
11:25 Harmonica Red & His Buddies
12:50 Continental Drifters
2:15 Al Ferrier "The Rockabilly King"
3:45 Oliver Morgan & Jessie Hill w/
The Reggie Hall Band
5:40 Deacon John

FESS STAGE
11:30 Loyola University Jazz
Ensemble
1:00 James Rivers Movement
2:15 Brownie McGhee
3:20 Clifton Chenier & His Red Hot
Louisiana Band
4:30 Clarence "Gatemouth" Brown
5:50 Jr. Walker & The Allstars

WWL-TV 4 STAGE
11:45 Caledonian Society Scottish
Dancers & Pipes & Drums of
New Orleans
1:10 Spencer Bohren
2:35 Bois Sec Ardoin & Canray
Fontenot
4:10 Bryan Lee & The Jumpstreet
Five w/ Miss Maggie
5:35 BeauSoleil

UNCLE BEN'S JAZZ TENT
11:30 Jasmine
12:50 City Light Orchestra
2:00 Brubeck / Laverne Trio
3:15 Timeless Allstars
4:50 Ramsey McLean & The
Survivors w/ Don Cherry
(Quartermoon)
6:00 Improvisational Arts Quintet

ECONOMY HALL TENT
11:25 Tennessee Tech Tuba Ensemble
12:45 Frank Federico & New Orleans
Style Jazz
1:50 Wallace Davenport New Orleans
Jazz Band
3:00 John Hammond
4:25 New Leviathan Oriental Foxtrot
Orchestra
5:45 Danny Barker's Jazz Hounds w/
Blue Lu Barker

KOINDU
11:20 Walter Payton & Ballet Filé
12:35 Bahamas Junkanoo Revue
w/ The Valley Boys, Dr. Offff,
Raphael Munnings
& Bahama Mama
1:50 Exuma
3:00 Ruben "Mr. Salsa" Gonzalez
4:15 Samaroo Jets of Trinidad
5:35 Johnny Adams w/ Joe Louis
Walker & Boss Talkers

Buckwheat Zydeco, and Terrance Simien were all featured in the movie "*The Big Easy*," with Simien being the accordion player on the front porch (of the Bruning's Restaurant family home) when Dennis Quaid's character Remy McSwain is teaching Ellen Barkin's character Anne Osbourne to dance. There was "Fiyo on the Bayou," but the "bayou" was the *S.S. President,* with the Neville Brothers, now at the height of their national popularity, and King Sunny Ade and his African

Beats. It was a pumping, jumping rhythm fest — a churning boiling roil of Afro-Caribbean polyrhythms, New Orleans rhythm and blues, slinky swamp hisses, and rhythmic love.

Prout's Club Alhambra was a new venue, with a late-night sextet of bebop and modern jazz masters "The Timeless All Stars" starred Cedar Walton, Buster Williams, Billy Higgins, Curtis Fuller, Harold Land, and Bobby Hutcherson; and they followed the "New Orleans Refugees" Ramsey McClean,

Tito Puente and Celia Cruz

Harry Connick, Jr., (who had just been signed to Columbia Records), Herlin Riley, Charles Neville and Special Guest Don Cherry. Start time was 10:00 p.m. The late hour prompted some local music writers to complain that these older traditional jazz players had not been given enough respect and booked for the riverboat instead. On Monday, April 27th, Snug Harbor

Jazz Club presented its "First Annual Jazz Fest Jam" featuring dozens of artists with "The Old Masters of Jazz," beginning at 8:00 p.m., "The Young Lions," at 10:30 p.m., while the third set at 1:00 a.m. was a blow out combination of the two.

Pharoah Sanders, one-time sideman for John Coltrane, was the headliner for a free evening concert at Spanish Plaza, and

scat singer "Sounds of Ether" Leon Thomas joined him. But the New Orleans contingent of that evening was equally compelling. The New Orleans Saxophone Quartet featured Tony Dagradi on saxophone, Edward "Kidd" Jordan on alto, Victor Goines on tenor and Roger Lewis on baritone. As if this were not enough bounty for a free concert, the heavens

Sing Miller

smiled and the Alvin Batiste Group rounded out the evening. Drummer Herman Jackson, bassist Chris Severin, and the brilliant piano player Emile Verrett joined renowned clarinetist Batiste. Spanish Plaza (a gift from Spain to New Orleans) celebrated Spain's history with the New World and New Orleans.

The crowd of 300,000 at the Fair Grounds was the largest in Jazz Fest history. According to Scott Ray, an economic consultant hired by the Fest to estimate consumer spending, visitors in town for Jazz Fest funneled $31.9 million into New Orleans businesses (not counting the Festival). That number equaled the Sugar Bowl and NCAA Final Four economic influx. 104,000 out-of-towners spent $10.9 million and locals parted with about $5.9 million. Ray, formerly with Xavier University and an RTA market analyst, worked for Cypress Research and Development.

Dave Bartholomew and Fats Domino

Ellis and Wynton Marsalis

His teams of 20 surveyors on the Fest grounds asked random individuals about spending habits. Because most people would underestimate spending, and calculating out of town visitors spend more than locals, they arrived at the estimate that 71% of visitors spend $100 per visit, compared with 43% of locals. More than half of out-of-town visitors stayed in local hotels, accounting for about 80,000 hotel nights and $4 million in revenues. In the ten-day schedule, Jazz Fest pulled in more than a third of the estimated $94 million revenues generated year-round by New Orleans music clubs. The Festival also produced $15.1 million in indirect spending: profits that businesses spend somewhere else in the economy.

This was the first time Jazz Fest officials had surveyed the economic impact of their creation, and the impressive

"It was an honor to have him do (my) tunes, because just like I went to Muddy Waters and paid tribute to him, everyone pays tribute to someone they admired a lot. Music is handed down to the next generation. And he wasn't just some white kid saying, 'I got it.' He told the truth. 'I got this from Buddy Guy or Albert Collins,' or whoever he wanted to talk about. That was some of his greatness." BUDDY GUY ON STEVIE RAY VAUGHN

Professor Longhair Foundation is incorporated.

Posthumous release by Professor Longhair titled "New Orleans House Party" on Rounder Records wins Fess a Grammy Award.

Movie "The Big Easy" is released with Beausoleil, Dewey Balfa, Irma Thomas, Terrance Simien and Solomon Burke appearing.

The Reggae Riddums Festival starts in City Park.

Premiere of In That Number! The New Orleans Brass Band Revival a film by Jerry Brock.

Offbeat Magazine begins publication.

IN MEMORIAM

Moses Asch, Eddie "Lockjaw" Davis, Lee Dorsey, Francine Fleming, Clarence Garlow, Benny Goodman, Sal Grisaffi, Thomas Jefferson, Thadeus Jones, Alton Pernell, Albert Sabi, Dino Santangelo, Emmanuel Sayles, W. Alonzo Stewart, Ellnya Tatum, Sonny Terry, Teddy Wilson, Clifton Chenier, Kid Thomas Valentine, Jaco Pastorious, Woody Herman, Peter Tosh

numbers gave them more clout in negotiating contracts, including those with the city of New Orleans. The money was impressive – even more so in its ability to generate controversy. The argument that local musicians should get a bigger piece of the pie was a yearly litany. Sponsors paid from $5,000 to $100,000, for stages and various positioning, and there was an as yet unclaimed category of $200,000. There would be no going back to numbered stages, but the most controversial sponsorship was yet to come.

In a unanimously approved move, the Foundation chose Tom Dent as Executive Director. Dent brought a love for authenticity and a history of civil rights

advocacy to the negotiating table, and he did it with grace and integrity. Under Dent's guidance, the Festival married philanthropy and education in a program that still endures: the Congo Square Lecture Series. The series presents free lectures from artists who embody aspects of African-American culture. Another program benefiting the community was the distribution of community outreach tickets to schools, nursing homes and nonprofits.

Under the guidance of Sandra Blair-Richardson, the contemporary crafts area added new opportunities to share the high quality of crafts on exhibition by partnering with retail establishments and local schools. There were on site exhibitions and artists in residency in selected public schools. There were also awards given to some craftspersons to recognize levels of mastery in the medium. Each year a different artist was commissioned to create the actual awards, and in 1987 the commission was given to art book artist Jan Gilbert. Gilbert stretched the boundaries of her own medium in her textural and adventurous design of folded, painted and sculpted paper.

This was the first year that Crawfish Monica was available outside of Jazz Fest, in local food markets. The creamy, rich buttery pasta dish was probably the favorite of all Jazz Fest foods (depending on who you talked to) and some actually paid admission to get into Jazz Fest just to score a bowl of the ruling pasta.

ECONOMY HALL
11:40 Michael White Quartet w/ Barbara Shorts
12:40 Teddy Riley Jazz Band
1:40 Cousin Joe
2:35 Chris Owens Show
3:50 Louis Nelson Big Six
4:50 Jay McShann
6:00 Percy Humphrey & Crescent City Joymakers

KOINDU
11:30 Fred Kemp & Smokey Johnson Sextet
12:40 Virginia Commonwealth U. Jazz Band
2:00 Seduction
3:15 Women of the Calabash
4:35 Samaroo Jets of Trinidad
6:00 Louisiana Purchase

LAGNIAPPE TENT
12:00 Ragtime Annie
1:15 Lenny Zenith
2:40 Stomp Boogie Drum Band
3:50 Bad Oyster Band
5:25 Ninth Ward Hunters

WYLD / RHODES GOSPEL TENT
11:45 The Inspiration Gospel Singers
12:30 N.O. Lutheran Inspirational Choir
1:15 Bro. Joseph Davis Singers
2:00 St. Luke A.M.E. Choir
2:45 The Mighty Chariots
3:50 Olivet M.B.C. Youth Choir
4:15 The World Famous Dixie Hummingbirds
5:25 Avondale Community Choir
6:10 Sammy Berfect & Dimensions of Faith

PARADES
2:45 Olympia, Ladies Zulu and 5th Division Rollers SA&PCs with Olympia Brass Band

FRIDAY, MAY 1

WVUE / BURGER KING STAGE
11:20 St. Augustine High School Jazz Ensemble
12:35 Marva Wright & Reminiscence
2:00 Java
3:20 Bobby Marchan & Higher Ground
4:40 Charmaine Neville & Real Feelings
6:00 Batiste Brothers Band

WNOE / TACO BELL
11:30 Washboard Leo
12:45 Dino Kruse Band
2:00 Chris Thomas King w/ Tabby Thomas
3:20 Song Dogs
4:30 Tim Williams & Natchez
6:00 Allen Fontenot & The Country Cajuns

FESS STAGE
11:20 Dillard University Jazz Ensemble
12:40 Kenny Acosta & The House Rockers
2:00 John Mooney & Blues Scoundrels
3:15 Anson Funderburgh & The Rockets w/ Sam Myers
4:30 Wayne Toups & Zydecajun
5:45 John Mayall's Blues Breakers

WWL-TV 4 STAGE
12:00 Louisiana Cajun Country Cloggers
1:00 John Rankin
2:10 Johnny J. & The Hitmen

3:45 Silas Hogan & Guitar Kelly
5:00 Jimmy Ballero & The Renegades

UNCLE BEN'S JAZZ TENT
11:30 Joel Simpson Quartet
12:50 Headwind
2:00 Gulfstream
3:10 Theron Lewis & Unit 7
4:20 Kid Johnson
5:40 Mars

ECONOMY HALL TENT
11:30 Local International Allstars
12:45 The New Orleans Classic Jazz Orchestra
2:00 Chris Clifton's New Orleans Allstars
3:20 Sady Courville & Dennis McGee
4:40 Caledonia Jazz Band of Norway w/ Kuumba Williams
6:00 Kid Sheik & His Storyville Ramblers

KOINDU
11:20 Kermit Campbell Band
12:40 Percussion Incorporated
2:00 Carl Leblanc & The Easy Street Band
3:15 Carnaval
4:35 White Cloud Hunters Mardi Gras Indians
5:45 Kumbuka Dance & Drum Collective

LAGNIAPPE TENT
12:00 Harlan White
1:15 Clifford Blake
2:35 Hazel Schleuter & The Delta Ramblers
4:10 Brownie Ford
5:40 Slidell Barbershop Harmony Chorus

WYLD / RHODES GOSPEL TENT
11:45 The Angelettes Gospel Singers
12:30 Daneel Pre-Vocational School Choir
1:15 Crocker Elementary School Choir
2:00 Aline White & Company
2:45 Church of God of Prophecy
3:30 Divine Joy Gospel Singers
4:15 Tawanna Gross & Rev. Thomas Gross
5:00 Alcee Fortier Sr. High School Gospel Choir
5:45 Greater St. Matthew B.C. Mass Choir
6:30 The Dynamic Smooth Family

WDSU TV-6 KIDS' TENT
12:00 Adella Gautier
1:00 Elm Grove Elementary School Choir
2:00 Tom Foote
3:00 Kumbuka Dance and Drum Collective
4:00 Washboard Leo
5:00 Robin Renee

PARADES
3:00 Blue Monday SA&PC and All Stars Brass Band

SATURDAY, MAY 2

WVUE / BURGER KING STAGE
11:15 S.U.N.O. Jazz Ensemble
12:35 Rockin' Sidney
2:00 Marcia Ball Band
3:30 Wynton Marsalis
5:15 Ernie K-Doe w/ King Floyd, Matilda Jones & The Living Dead Revue

WNOE / TACO BELL STAGE
11:20 Nora Wixted & 2 Much Fun
12:35 Waka! Waka!

1:40 Lazy Lester w/ Raful Neal & The Neal Brothers
3:00 Roomful of Blues w/ Earl King
4:40 Atchafalaya
6:00 Fernest Arceneaux & The Thunders

FESS STAGE
11:20 U.N.O. Jazz Band
12:35 Lawrence Ardoin & His French Band
1:55 O.K. Ekemode & His Nigerian Allstars
3:15 Etta James
4:30 The Fabulous Thunderbirds
6:00 Robert Cray Band

WWL-TV 4 STAGE
11:30 Oakwood Jazz Ensemble
12:45 Al Farrell & The Crescent City Statements
2:00 Drink Small Blues Band
3:15 Golden Eagles Mardi Gras Indians
4:35 Lake Pontchartrain String Band
6:00 Orquestra Celebre

UNCLE BEN'S JAZZ TENT
12:00 Clyde Kerr, Jr. & Univision
1:10 Germaine Bazzle Group
2:15 Ensamble Acustico of Guatemala
2:20 Dorothy Donegan
4:40 Alvin "Red" Tyler Quartet
5:45 Ellis Marsalis Quartet

ECONOMY HALL TENT
11:30 Chris Kelly's Black & White N.O. Jazz Band
12:50 Benny Waters & The Creole Rice Jazz Band
2:10 Hezekiah Early & The House Rockers
3:20 Sweet Honey In The Rock
4:45 New Orleans Ragtime Orchestra
6:00 Onward Brass Band

KOINDU
11:45 New Orleans Stick Band
12:50 Rap Revue w/ Tany P & The MIC Conductors
1:40 Mallick Folk Performers of Trinidad
3:10 Walter Washington & The Roadmasters w/ Timothea
4:30 The Shepherd Band
5:45 Soca Group of Trinidad

LAGNIAPPE TENT
12:25 Ricky Vaughn
1:45 Pat Flory
3:00 Po' Henry & Tookie
4:20 Drink Small Blues Band
5:45 Hezekiah Early & The House Rockers

WYLD / RHODES GOSPEL TENT
11:45 The Providence Tones of Joy
12:30 The Calvacade of Singing Masters
1:15 Morning Star B.C. Gospel Choir
2:00 First Baptist Church Choir
2:45 St. Francis DeSales Golden Voices
3:30 Zulu Ensemble of the Zulu S.A.&P.C.
4:15 The Famous Corinthians Gospel Singer of San Francisco
5:25 The Joyful Commanders
6:00 Pure Light B.C. Choir

WDSU TV-6 KIDS' TENT
12:00 Robin Renee
1:00 The Class Clowns
2:00 Adella Gautier
3:00 David & Roselyn
4:00 Puppetears of Ecstasy
5:00 St. Francis DeSales Youth Choir

PARADES
3:00 Avenue Steppers, Buck Jumpers SA&PCs & Doc Paulin's Dixieland Brass Band

SUNDAY, MAY 3

WVUE / BURGER KING STAGE
11:15 Xavier University Jazz Ensemble
12:35 Alex Chilton
1:45 Luther Kent & Trick Bag
3:10 The Radiators
4:35 The Band
6:00 Dr. John

WNOE / TACO BELL STAGE
11:30 Casa Samba
12:45 Don Montoucet & The Wandering Aces
2:00 Boozoo Chavis
3:20 Vin Bruce & The Acadians
4:30 Russ Russell & The Rustlers w/ Phil Meeks
5:45 Moe Bandy & The Rodeo Clowns

FESS STAGE
11:45 Willie Tee
12:50 Blue Eyed Soul Revue
2:00 Bobby Cure & The Summertime Blues w/ Aaron Neville the Dixie Cups & Robert "Barefootin" Parker
4:15 Wilson Pickett
5:45 The Neville Brothers

WWL-TV 4 STAGE
11:30 Banu Gibson
1:05 Big Boy Henry Blues Band
2:25 White Eagles Mardi Gras Indians
3:55 Soca Group of Trinidad
5:30 Bruce Daigrepont Cajun Band

UNCLE BEN'S JAZZ TENT
11:45 Astral Project
12:50 Earl Turbinton, Jr. Quintet

1:55 Richard Thompson — Solo Acoustic Performance
3:20 Branford Marsalis
4:50 Pharaoh Sanders w/ Leon Thomas
6:05 New Orleans Jazz Couriers

ECONOMY HALL TENT
11:30 Lady Charlotte
12:30 Pfister Sisters
1:30 Butch Thompson
2:30 Katie Webster
3:30 Pete Seeger
4:40 Ronnie Kole
6:00 Kid Thomas Valentine & The Algiers Stompers

KOINDU
11:15 Marlon Jordan
12:30 Ritmo Caribeno
1:45 Willie Metcalf
3:10 Metallics
4:25 Jean Knight
5:40 Mallick Folk Performers of Trinidad

LAGNIAPPE TENT
12:00 Clancy "Blues Boy" Lewis
1:15 George Dorko
2:30 Amite River Band
4:00 David & Roselyn
5:35 Creole Wild West Mardi Gras Indians

WYLD / RHODES GOSPEL TENT
11:45 Mt. Carmel B.C. Youth Choir
12:30 The Russ Specials
1:15 Kennedy High School Gospel Choir
2:00 The Famous Zion Harmonizers
2:45 New Zion Trio Plus One
3:30 Gospel Choralettes
4:15 Greater Macedonia B.C. Choir
5:00 The Ambassadors of Christ
6:30 Gospel Soul Children

WDSU TV-6 KIDS' TENT
12:00 Cliff Da Clown and Charmin' Charmin
1:00 New Orleans Free School Performers
2:00 David & Roselyn
3:00 Dierdre's Design-N-Dance
4:00 Puppetears of Ecstasy
5:00 Kumbuka Dance and Drum Collective

PARADES
2:45 Scene Boosters, Fun Lovers SA&PCs & Young Tuxedo Brass Band

NIGHT CONCERTS

FRIDAY, APRIL 24, 7 P.M. & MIDNIGHT
Fats Domino
The Four Tops
Riverboat S.S. President
FRIDAY, APRIL 24, 10 P.M.
The Timeless All-Stars
Cedar Walton, Buster Williams, Billy Higgins, Curtis Fuller, Harold Land, Bobby Hutcherson
The New Orleans Refugees
Ramsey McLean, Harry Connick, Jr., Herlin Riley, Charles Neville and Special Guest Don Cherry
Prout's Club Alhambra
SATURDAY, APRIL 25, 7 P.M. & MIDNIGHT
Spyro Gyra
Kenny G.
Riverboat S.S. President
SATURDAY, APRIL 25, 8 P.M.
The Newport Jazz Festival All-Stars. George Wein, Scott Hamilton, Oliver Jackson, Slam Stewart, Norris Turney, Warren Vache with Special Guests Buddy Tate, George Masso
Storyville Jazz Hall

MONDAY, APRIL 27, 8, 10:30 P.M. & 1 A.M.
Snug Harbor Jazz Club presents 1st Annual Jazz Fest Jam Dozens of Artists
Snug Harbor Jazz Club
WEDNESDAY, APRIL 29, 8 P.M.
Fais Do Do
Rockin' Dopsie & The Zydeco Twisters
Zachary Richard
Beausoleil
Riverboat S.S. President
THURSDAY, APRIL 30, 8;P.M.
Wynton Marsalis Quintet
Stanley Jordan
Bobby McFerrin
Theater of the Performing Arts
Louis Armstrong Park
FRIDAY, MAY 1, 7 P.M. & MIDNIGHT
The Fabulous Thunderbirds & Friends with Special Guest John Lee Hooker, Bonnie Raitt, Dr. John, Katie Webster, Rockin' Sidney, Lazy Lester, Roomful of Blues, Duke Robillard
Riverboat S.S. President
FRIDAY, MAY 1, 8:30 P.M.
Honi Coles
Dorothy Donegan Trio
Placide Adams' Original Dixieland Hall Jazz Band
Spanish Plaza at Riverwalk
SATURDAY, MAY 2, 7 P.M. & MIDNIGHT
Fiyo on the Bayou
The Neville Brothers
King Sunny Ade and His African Beats
Riverboat S.S. President
SATURDAY, MAY 2, 8:30 P.M.
Pharoah Sanders Quartet with Leon Thomas
New Orleans Saxophone Quartet
Alvin Batiste Group
Spanish Plaza at Riverwalk

1988

The James Black Ensemble played in the Uncle Ben's Rice Tent on the first Friday at 2:10 p.m. Those who jammed joyfully in the tent had no idea that they were seeing Black's last Jazz Fest performance. Black, in addition to being a drum and composing virtuoso, also played trumpet and piano. He played with Ellis Marsalis, Harold Batiste, Irma Thomas, Lee Dorsey, the Meters, and Dr. John, and toured with Lionel Hampton, Yusef Lateef, Freddie Hubbard, and Cannonball Adderley, among others. He was a part of the Ellis Marsalis Quartet that featured several of his compositions including "Magnolia Triangle" and the song "Monkey Puzzle" on the acclaimed album "Monkey Puzzle" in 1961. The radio documentary "Guardian of the Groove: New Orleans Drummer and Composer James Black," produced by David Kunian, aired in December of 2004 on 90.7 FM WWOZ. A benefit film screening and the James Black Tribute Band featuring David Torkanowsky performed at Lounge Lizards to raise funds for the purchase of a headstone. Black was interred in Resthaven Memorial Park on Old Gentilly Road.

"The King of Zydeco" was also laid to rest in the December between Jazz Fests, after fittingly lying in state with his red velvet crown on his head and Grammy in his hand. Clifton Chenier, the first Creole to win a Grammy and the inspiration to hundreds of zydeco musicians and millions of zydeco lovers, rode the good-will of the sacred season up to his heavenly home. It is not within the scope of this book to pay a fitting tribute to such revolution-ary and esteemed musician, but suffice it to say that Chenier did not take all of the music with him. His son C.J. led the Red Hot Louisiana Band in closing out the Y96 FM Stage, and you can bet Clifton's gold teeth were smiling down on them from heaven.

To relieve the crush of ticket seekers, Jazz Fest staff had released tickets for sale as early as Mardi Gras. The staff of 34 worked during the intensive four-month planning period, but as the Fest loomed closer, a couple of thousand more people were brought on – not counting vol-unteers. Ground transportation crew leader Jim Boa bragged that his crew was so fast he could

"Get God to hell in 45 minutes," after which staffer Laura Griswold quipped, "25 on a clear day."

One of the small pleasures of the Jazz Fest has been the offi-cial program guide. The format changed as the Fest grew, but most programs contained good, and sometimes excellent articles on contemporary and traditional music. Those articles provided insight about the music for audiences who sought

Henry Butler

fest facts

Koindu was reinvented as Congo Square with the intention that "the area reflects some of the spiritual and cultural reality that the original Congo Square represented for slaves in New Orleans who gathered there years ago."

Jazz Fest employed 5,000 musicians and 500 performing groups.

Tickets cost $7 in advance and $9 at the gate.

Louis Nelson's All Stars were Chester Zardis, Danny Barker, Butch Thompson, Sammy Rimington, Stanley Stephas and Wendell Brunious. Nelson, at 85, was reputedly New Orleans' oldest living trombonist.

like Michael P. Smith, (he shoots 80–100 rolls of 36 exposure film at each Fest), Syndey Byrd, Jules Cahn, Keith Calhoun, Chandra McCormick, Pat Jolly, Girard Mouton, Les Riess, Philip Gould, Eric Waters, and Rick Olivier captured images of generations of the magic in the music. The photographers carried the music forward into the future, so that today we may marvel at Bobby Mitchell "I'm Gonna Be a Wheel Someday" in a white jeweled turban; the Zion Harmonizers, suave and posed in sleek suits; Brownie Ford's wizened grimace under a curled-brim straw hat, and "Big Chief" Bo Dollis in full-feathered Mardi Gras Indian regalia. After the scaffolding comes down and the next gig goes up, photographs

education as well as entertainment. Other editions printed recipes from Jazz Fest food booths. "In Memoriam" pages reminded readers to take a moment to send a prayer or simple "thank you" heavenward to those who had passed on. But the jewels of every program were the photographs from earlier Festivals, making the programs collector's items on that fact alone. Photographers and memories are all we have of Jazz Fest.

The 1988 program, produced by Bright Moments and edited by Kalamu ya Salaam, featured ya Salaam's checkerboard schedule design — finally, a sensible way to compare bands and times. Short bios on every group did some small part in helping the over-stimulated fest-goer make choices. Glossy paper, an updated map of the Fair Grounds, and slick ad design made this program stand out. Writer and journalist Jason Berry's enlightening piece on Professor Longhair fittingly reminded a new generation of music lovers that nearly a decade had transpired since "Fess" had passed into the spirit world.

This guide launched further into the literary arts. Made possible by a grant from the Arts Council of New Orleans, and in cooperation with the New Orleans Jazz & Heritage Foundation, Inc. the first edition of the Black River Journal was a 16-page insert showcasing poetry, prose, and photography by African-American and white artists, including a poignant love letter to Louisiana in the form of a poem by Mona Lisa Saloy. In his introduction, ya Salaam wrote "this journal addresses the culture from the inside perspective: the pieces make statements and ask questions about the core essence of New Orleans culture — a core that is mainly Black (Black meaning of African derivation). Somehow, in the midst of enjoying the music, the food, the good times, in the midst of it, somehow, it gets looked over (is it willful ignorance?) that New Orleans people and culture are predominately Black."

Quint Davis's production of other Festivals led to a little cross-pollination. Will Soto and his tightrope act were Florida imports, as were the alligators in the pond beneath him. Knowing that alligators sleep in the hot daytime, Soto made sure to poke the 8-foot long gators to stir up the action.

A decade after African-American activists, led by ya Salaam, demanded the

Art Blakey

3:30 East Jerusalem Young
Adult Choir
4:15 John McDonogh High School
5:45 Dynamic Smooth Family

WDSU TV-6 / FIRST NBC KIDS' TENT
12:00 Martin Behrman Elementary
School Dance Team & Choir
1:00 McDonogh #15 Elementary
School Band
2:00 Music for Children by Dennis
3:00 The Smile at the Foot of
the Ladder
4:00 Sing Along With Judy
5:00 Carl Mack

PARADES
5:50 Blue Monday, Money Wasters
SA&PCs & Olympia Jr.
Brass Band

SATURDAY, APRIL 23

WVUE / BURGER KING STAGE
11:15 Kenny Bill Stinson
12:20 Tommy Ridgley & The
Untouchables / Al Johnson
& Bobby Mitchell
2:00 Ernie K-Doe w/ Blue Eyed
Soul Revue
3:25 Zachary Richard
4:45 Dave Brubeck Quartet
6:10 Marcia Ball Band

WNOE / TOSTITOS STAGE
11:30 Dash Rip Rock
12:40 Song Dogs
2:00 Al Ferrier / Ronald Brumley
& Foxfire
3:20 Doc Watson
4:50 The Original Sun Rhythm Band
6:15 Anson Funderburgh
w/ Sam Myers

FESS STAGE
12:00 C.J. Chenier & Red Hot
Louisiana Band
1:05 Luther Kent & Trickbag
2:15 Albert Collins & The
Icebreakers
3:30 Cissy Houston
5:00 B.B. King

THE SPIRIT OF LOUISIANA
11:45 Joan DuValle
1:00 Dewey Balfa & Friends
2:35 Emile Benoit & Figgy Duft
4:00 Kat & The Kittens
5:30 Lawrence Ardoin & His French
Zydeco Band

UNCLE BEN'S RICE JAZZ TENT
11:45 Tony Bazley Sextet
1:00 Astral Project
2:20 Ruben Gonzalez & His Salseros
3:30 Earl Turbinton, Jr. Quintet
4:50 Jon Faddis Quartet
6:10 Earl Palmer

AT&T ECONOMY HALL TENT
11:30 Frog Island Jazz Band of
England
12:40 Onward Brass Band
2:00 Riverwalk Jazz Band w/ Thais
Clark & Topsy Chapman
3:20 Wallace Davenport Jazz Band
4:25 Doc Cheatham & Sam Price w/
Lars Edegran
5:45 Olympia Serenaders

CONGO SQUARE STAGE
11:30 Percussion, Inc.
1:00 Creole Wild West Mardi Gras
Indians
2:00 Mallick Folk Performers of
Trinidad
3:15 Malavoi of Martinique
4:45 Tabou Combo of Haiti
6:10 The Shepherd Band

"The first time I performed at Jazz Fest I was around 9 or 10 years old. My cousin Eric Hill, Wayne Nelson and I were tap dancers and we danced on stage with my grandpa Jessie Hill. That was an honor to get on stage with the Poop. We would come up and dance on "Ooh Poo Pah Doo" and "Sweet Jelly Roll." Poop would be beating the hell out of those tambourines and we would do our little shuffle and tap. I remember that was the year I first met and heard Professor Longhair. He and Poop were real tight. Poop's going to be inducted this year in the Rock and Roll Hall of Fame." JAMES ANDREWS

music scene

Better than Ezra is formed by four LSU students in 1988.

Ernie K-Doe releases I'm Cocky But I'm Good produced by Milton Batiste for SYLA Records.

Irma Thomas releases "The Way I Feel" on Rounder Records.

Tuba Fats releases first record on SYLA Records.

Rock N' Bowl is born.

1st Annual Piano Night Concert.

IN MEMORIAM

Roy Orbison, Eddie James "Son" House, Jr

TRAVEL N.O. LAGNIAPPE TENT
12:00 Brownie Ford-The Old Cow-Boy
1:10 La Nueva Compania
2:25 Spider John Koerner
3:45 Moses Rascoe
4:45 Silas Hogan & Guitar Kelly

WYLD / RHODES GOSPEL TENT
11:45 Macedonia B.C. Choir
12:30 Greater Evergreen B.C. Choir
1:15 Prayer Tower Church of God In Christ
2:00 The Mighty Imperials
2:45 The Soulful Heavenly Stars
3:30 The Soul Specials Gospel Choir
4:15 The James Chapel B.C. Gospel Choir
5:45 The Pure Light B.C. Gospel Choir

WDSU TV-6 / FIRST NBC KIDS' TENT
12:00 Music for Children by Dennis
1:00 Robert M. Lusher Elementary School Choir
2:00 Sing Along with Judy
3:00 N.O.C.C.A. Circus
4:00 Carl Mack
5:00 Jamal Batiste

PARADES
2:45 Valley of the Silent Men, Avenue Steppers & Buck Jumpers SA&PCs & Rebirth Brass Band

SUNDAY, APRIL 24

WVUE / BURGER KING STAGE
11:30 Sky High of Sweden
12:40 James Rivers Movement
1:50 BeauSoleil
3:15 Rockin' Dopsie & His Cajun Twisters
4:35 Pete Fountain
5:35 Will Soto Walk-Over the Pond
6:00 Allen Toussaint

WNOE / TOSTITOS STAGE
11:30 Dino Kruse
12:35 Troy L. Deramus & Hill Country
1:50 Fernest Arceneaux & The Thunders
3:00 Allen Fontenot & The Country Cajuns w/ Al Rapone Lewis
4:15 Luzianne
5:40 Jo-el Sonnier

FESS STAGE
11:45 Gary Brown & Feelings
12:55 Walter Washington & The Roadmasters
2:15 Mighty Sparrow
3:45 James Brown
5:30 Irma Thomas & The Professionals

THE SPIRIT OF LOUISIANA
12:00 Sensacion Latina
1:20 Snooks Eaglin
2:35 Wild Magnolias Mardi Gras Indians
3:30 Samite of Uganda
4:35 Bois Sec w/ Canray & His French Band
6:00 Rip & The Dreamers

UNCLE BEN'S RICE JAZZ TENT
11:45 Al Belletto Quartet
12:50 Kidd Jordan & Al Fielder's Improvisational Arts
1:55 Harry Connick, Jr.
3:00 Hank Crawford & Jimmy McGriff
4:25 Courtney Pine
5:50 The Dirty Dozen Brass Band

installation of Koindu (an African concept meaning "a place of exchange") at the Fest, Koindu was renamed "Congo Square," and reconfigured. The purpose and effect remained the same: to promote African-American music and culture. Ya Salaam's techniques may have echoed civil rights struggles, but the culture was now feeling class and economic divides that would only deepen as time went on. Consumer changes seemed to be the dominant force driving the U.S. For the first time in history, CDs outsold vinyl recordings. Some people still treasured their record collections, pointing out the value of cover art and well-written liner notes. Others had long since made lengthy lists and headed to "record stores" to replace their vinyl with CDs. It was still a rare vehicle that boasted a CD player. Those would become standard in the 1990s.

And still the Jazz Fest grew. Audiences of 300,000 were expected. Stages and perfor-

mance tents were moved closer to the perimeter of the infield in order to accommodate more bodies within the circle of the Fest. The Economy Hall Tent came outside the infield and onto the perimeter. As Festival staff kept up with their mission to educate as well as entertain, traditional and contemporary crafts each featured demonstration areas. There were 50 food booths, 200 contemporary and folk artists, and 5,000 musicians, all available for $7 advance and $9 at the gate. It was a surfeit of riches. At its founding in 1970, the Jazz Fest budget neared $90,000. This year, it had ballooned to $2.3 million. Revenues contributing to the ever-swelling bottom line came from ticket sales, T-shirt sales and silk-screened posters respectively. Kevin Combs designed the commemorative poster for 1988. There were 2,500 signed, limited edition prints that sold for $75 each, and the 12,500 unsigned prints went for $25. Methods for choosing poster designers

varied over the years, and even on a couple of occasions came from folks who showed up at the Jazz Fest offices offering their designs with a "What do you think of this?" attitude.

In the autumn of 1988, just across town, another music institution came to life. After a pilgrimage to Medjugorje in Yugoslavia to see an apparition of the Holy Virgin, John Blancher purchased an on-the-skids bowling alley from the Knights of Columbus for $25,000. Not surprisingly, his attempts to revive a bowling audience failed. He

then took a chance that made all the difference: Blancher hired Louisiana rockabilly musician Joe Clay (C.J. "Don't Mess With My Ducktails" Cheramie) to play during one weekend. The rest, as they say, is history, and Mid-City Rock N Bowl continues to be a beloved Jazz Fest destination as well as a thriving music club year round.

Under the auspices of the Jazz & Heritage Foundation, a series of free workshops led by leading artists were offered at 13 high schools, universities and nonprofit organizations around

the city. Some were conducted by musicians such as Taj Mahal and the Dirty Dozen Brass Band. Others featured films such as *Liberty Street Blues*, while one workshop held at the New Orleans Museum of Art brought an "Inspirational Choir" to the reception after a panel discussion on "Blacks in the Media & Jazz." These efforts were so successful that plans began for their expansion next year at the Jazz Fest.

It was *de rigueur* to buy a Jazz Fest T-shirt every year, but it was also decidedly uncool to wear it in that same year. Wearing shirts

"The best thing about the Festival has been the opportunity to play with many great artists from out of town. In 1988, at my suggestion, Quint booked Doc Cheatham and Sammy Price. Neither had played in New Orleans before. We played at Spanish Plaza and at the Fair Grounds. One year, the New Orleans Ragtime Orchestra backed up Eubie Blake and we performed some of his compositions. I got to play with Jay McShann, Franz Jackson and Arvell Shaw. One year I backed up Carrie Smith and of course many of our fine singers from New Orleans; Barbara Shorts, Thais Clark, Topsy Chapman, Juanita Brooks and in 1970 in Congo Square I backed up Sister Annie Pavageau. I think that was the only year she performed at the Festival." LARS EDEGRAN

from previous years showed that one was an insider, not a mere tourist. It had been a decade since Pat Searcy and Philip Bascle, owners of Southern Silk Screen, in a chance meeting with Heritage Fair Director John Murphy at the Camellia Grill, inked a deal for printing the official Jazz Fest T-shirts. Pat and Philip had started Southern Silk Screen in 1971 with only $3,000 capital, and their business jumped exponentially with the Jazz Fest contract. The 1980s saw the insatiable appetite for T-Shirts emblazoned with everything from rock and roll icons to disco studs and sequins, and Bascle relates that the company was sometimes at the mercy of distributors struggling to keep up with demand. Sometimes having to order years in advance, they were allotted only the number of shirts the manufacturer could manage. Hot colors such as teal and fuchsia were especially tough to score. Everyone showed up at the Jazz Fest T-shirt booth. From Hollywood types and collectors from all over the world who wanted souvenirs Bascle saw credit cards from a dozen nations fly through his machines.

Louis Nelson's N.O. ALL-STARS

AT&T ECONOMY HALL TENT
11:40 Tommy Yetta's New Orleans Jazz Band
12:45 Cousin Joe
1:50 Ronnie Kole
3:15 Chris Owens Show
4:40 New Leviathan Oriental Foxtrot Orchestra
6:00 Kid Sheik & The Storyville Ramblers

CONGO SQUARE STAGE
11:20 Ed Perkins Group
12:35 Batiste Brothers
1:45 Mallick Folk Performers of Trinidad
3:00 Katie Webster & Silent Partners
4:25 Hector Gallardo & His Songo Allstars w/ "Patato" Valdez
5:45 Marva Wright & Reminiscence

TRAVEL N.O. LAGNIAPPE TENT
12:00 Sid Selvidge
1:15 Roosevelt T. Williams "The Grey Ghost"
2:25 Hot Strings
3:50 Dennis McGee
5:15 Leigh "Lil' Queenie" Harris & Amasa Miller

WYLD / RHODES GOSPEL TENT
11:45 The Gospel Inspirational Singers
12:25 The Antioch Gospel Singers
1:05 Friendly Five Gospel Singers
1:45 Lutheran Inspirational Gospel Choir
2:25 Gospel Chorallettes
3:05 Timothy Spell's Abundant Life Choir
3:45 Pops Staples
4:25 Archie Dale & The Tones of Joy of Kentucky
5:35 Regular B.C. Choir
6:15 Avondale Community Chorus

WDSU TV-6 / FIRST NBC KIDS' TENT
12:00 Voices of the Kingdom
1:00 Coleen Salley
2:00 The Sound Idea
3:00 Ahmos Zu-Bolton & The Xavier University Folklore Society
4:00 Washboard Leo
5:00 Deirdre's Designs-N-Dance

PARADES
3:00 Young Men Olympia, 5th Division Rollers, Ladies Zulu SA&PCs & Original Majestic Brass Band

FRIDAY, APRIL 29

WVUE / BURGER KING STAGE
11:30 Ironin' Board Sam
12:40 Willie Cole Blues Band
1:45 Casa Samba
3:00 Nocentelli
4:15 Oliver Morgan & Jessie Hill w/ Reggie Hall Band
6:00 Cyril Neville & The Uptown Allstars

WNOE / TOSTITOS STAGE
12:00 The Mannequins
1:20 Bayou Life Cloggers
2:30 Nora Wixted & 2 Much Fun
4:00 Hadley Castille & The Cajun Grass Band
5:30 George Heard w/ The John Plauche Group

FESS STAGE
11:50 Hammond State School Performers
1:10 Washboard Leo & The Nutria Frogs

2:30 Mighty Sam McClain & The
     Thunder Blues Revue
4:00 The Nighthawks
5:30 Asleep at the Wheel

THE SPIRIT OF LOUISIANA
12:00 Jazz Search '88 Winners
1:20 Billy Gregory Band
2:30 Ninth Ward Hunters Mardi Gras
     Indians
3:30 Boogie Bill Webb
4:40 Hackberry Ramblers
5:50 Mamou

UNCLE BEN'S RICE JAZZ TENT
11:25 Fred Kemp Quintet
12:30 SUBR Jazz Band
1:45 Ramsey McLean
3:00 Steve Masakowski & Mars
4:25 Jasmine w/ Ensamble Acustico
5:45 Alvin "Red" Tyler Quartet

AT&T ECONOMY HALL TENT
11:40 Dillard University Jazz Band
12:50 Local International Allstars
2:00 Lady Charlotte
3:25 Andrew Hall's Society Jazz Band
4:40 Teddy Riley's Jazz Masters
6:00 Father Al Lewis & Friends

CONGO SQUARE STAGE
11:30 St. Augustine High School
     Jazz Band
12:35 Carl LeBlanc
1:45 Rappin Patrol / The Super MC'S
     & The Twins Of Spin
3:10 Dynamite Red & The Crescent
     City Sound Band
4:30 The Killer Bees
5:50 Willie Metcalf & Academy of
     Black Arts

TRAVEL N.O. LAGNIAPPE TENT
11:30 Miss Lillian Bennett
12:30 Ricky Vaughn
1:30 Phil DeGruy & Hank Mackie
2:40 Tom McDermott
4:05 Loyola University
5:15 John Rankin
6:15 Bad Oyster Band

WYLD / RHODES GOSPEL TENT
11:45 Humble Travelers
12:30 Danneel Pre-Vocational
     School Choir
1:15 Jackson Travelers

2:00 Sister Aline White & Company
2:45 Landrum Singers
3:30 Simply for Christ Gospel Singers
4:15 Famous Friendly Travelers
5:00 Zion Tones Gospel Singers
5:45 Ecclesiastes Gospel Singers

WDSU TV-6 / FIRST NBC KIDS' TENT
12:00 William J. Fischer Elementary
     School Choir and Les Petites
     Dancers
1:00 Medard H. Nelson Elementary
     School Troupe
2:00 James "Mr. Magic" Williams
3:00 Adella Gautier
4:00 Washboard Leo
5:00 Kumbuka African Drum and
     Dance Collective

PARADES
5:00 Original Four & Jolly Bunch
     Sisters SA&PCs & Jass Cats
     Brass Band

SATURDAY, APRIL 30
WVUE / BURGER KING STAGE
11:30 Crescent City Sound Company
12:40 Bobby Cure & The Summertime
     Blues w/ Aaron Neville & Robert
     Parker
2:10 Deacon John's Blues Revue
3:30 Maria Muldaur
4:50 Johnny Adams w/ Joe Louis
     Walker
6:15 Queen Ida & Bon Temps
     Zydeco Band

WNOE / TOSTITOS STAGE
11:40 Paula Darline – A Touch of
     Country
1:00 Alex Chilton
2:10 Willis Prudhomme & Zydeco
     Express
3:25 Terrance Simien & The Mallet
     Playboys
4:40 Russ Russell & The Rustlers w/
     Phil Meeks
6:00 Jimmy C. Newman

FESS STAGE
11:20 Jon "King" Cleary
12:30 Ritmo Caribeno
1:45 Charles Brown
3:00 The Radiators

4:30 Los Lobos
6:00 Little Feat

THE SPIRIT OF LOUISIANA
11:15 Johnny J. & The Hitmen
12:20 Mojo Collins Band
1:30 John Mooney & Bluesiana
2:45 Filé
3:55 Raful Neal & Kenny Neal Band
     w/ Lazy Lester & Henry Gray
5:30 Lil' Ed & The Blues Imperials

UNCLE BEN'S RICE JAZZ TENT
11:20 Richwell Ison / Kirk Ford
     Experience
12:30 Woodenhead
1:50 Marlon Jordan
3:15 Germaine Bazzle w/ George
     French Trio
4:35 A Tribute to the Music of John
     Coltrane
6:00 The Original American Jazz
     Quintet + 1

AT&T ECONOMY HALL TENT
11:30 Frank Federico & New Orleans
     Style Jazz
12:45 Lillian Boutté & Thomas
     L'Etienne's New Orleans
     Ensemble
1:55 Louis Nelson's New Orleans
     Allstars
3:05 Danny Barker's Jazz Hounds w/
     Blue Lu Barker
4:20 Young Tuxedo Brass Band
5:40 Benny Waters

CONGO SQUARE STAGE
11:30 New Orleans Stick Band
12:45 Golden Eagles Mardi Gras
     Indians
1:50 High Voltage w/ Anthony Bailey
2:50 Ancestral Spirits (Parade)
3:20 Sugar Minott of Jamaica
4:45 Kumbuka African Drum &
     Dance Collective
5:30 Ancestral Spirits (Parade)
6:00 Willie Colon & His Orchestra

TRAVEL N.O. LAGNIAPPE TENT
12:00 Hazel & the Delta Ramblers
1:20 Ikebana
2:45 Spencer Bohren
4:05 A.J. Loria
5:15 Golden Star Hunters Mardi Gras
     Indians

6:15 Ron Cuccia – Jazz Poetry News

WYLD / RHODES GOSPEL TENT
11:45 The Wimberly Family
12:25 Stars of Heaven
1:05 The St. Luke A.M.E.
     Gospel Choir
1:45 G.M.L. Workshop Choir
2:25 St. Francis DeSales Golden
     Voices
3:05 Joseph "Cool" Davis & Company
4:25 The Famous Fairfield Four
5:35 The Famous Rocks of Harmony
6:15 Desire Community Gospel Choir

WDSU TV-6 / FIRST NBC KIDS' TENT
12:00 Samba Children
1:00 Charmin' Charmin and The
     Class Clowns
2:00 New Orleans Free School
     Performers
3:00 Calliope Puppets
4:00 Mama Linda Eubanks
5:00 St. Francis DeSales
     Children's Choir

PARADES
2:30 Downtown Jammers & Tremé
     Sports SA&PCs & Pinstripe
     Brass Band

SUNDAY, MAY 1

WVUE / BURGER KING STAGE
11:30 SUNO Jazz Band
12:45 Earl King
2:00 Clarence "Frogman" Henry
3:20 Buckwheat Zydeco
4:40 Frankie Ford w/ The Dixie Cups
6:10 Dr. John

WNOE / TOSTITOS STAGE
12:00 Mt. Pontchartrain String Band
1:45 Tay Hogg & Dixie Pride
2:45 Boozoo Chavis & The Magic Sounds
4:15 Wayne Toups & Zydecajun
5:40 Mississippi South

FESS STAGE
11:45 Louisiana Purchase
1:15 Jean Knight & The City News Band
2:30 Hank Ballard & The Midnighters
4:10 Al Green
5:45 The Neville Brothers

THE SPIRIT OF LOUISIANA
12:10 Oogum Boogum
1:30 Cross Lake Barbershop Chorus
2:45 Zydeco Brothers w/ Ann Goodly
4:15 Los Songueros
5:40 Lenny Zenith

UNCLE BEN'S RICE JAZZ TENT
12:00 Walter Payton & Ballet Filé
1:25 Joel Simpson Quartet
2:45 Henry Butler Trio
4:15 Charlie Haden's Quartet West
5:45 Alvin Batiste

AT&T ECONOMY HALL TENT
11:25 Wendell Brunious Jazz Band
12:35 Debria Brown w/ Moses Hogan
1:45 New Orleans Ragtime Orchestra
3:10 Pfister Sisters
4:30 Original One Mo' Time w/ N.O. Blues Serenaders
6:00 Percy Humphrey & His Crescent City Joymakers

CONGO SQUARE STAGE
11:35 Philip Manuel
12:45 Seduction
1:45 White Eagles Mardi Gras Indians
2:30 Ancestral Spirits (Parade)
3:00 Salif Keita
4:00 Ancestral Spirits (Parade)
5:30 Exuma
6:00 Willie Tee

TRAVEL N.O. LAGNIAPPE TENT
12:00 Po' Henry & Tookie
1:05 Brother Percy Randolph & Little Freddie King
2:20 Rusty Kershaw
4:00 Hezekiah & The House Rockers
5:20 Creole Osceola Mardi Gras Indians

WYLD / RHODES GOSPEL TENT
11:45 The Sensational Southerntones
12:25 Greater Bright Morning Star B.C. Mass Choir
1:05 Holy Church of God In Christ
1:45 Tulane Memorial B.C. Gospel Choir
2:25 New Day B.C. Gospel Choir
3:05 The Zion Harmonizers w/ Aaron Neville
3:45 Lillian Boutté & Company
4:25 The Famous Jackson Southernaires
5:35 13 Year Old Master Jerard Woods
6:15 The Famous Gospel Soul Children

WDSU TV-6 / FIRST NBC KIDS' TENT
12:00 Children's Community Theater Workshop
1:00 McDonogh #42 Elementary School Choir
2:00 Adella Gautier
3:00 The Smile at the Foot of the Ladder
4:00 Ken Britton's "Caribana"
5:00 Kumbuka African Drum and Dance Collective

PARADES
3:30 Scene Boosters, Fun Lovers SA&PCs & Doc Paulin's Dixieland Brass Band

NIGHT CONCERTS

FRIDAY, APRIL 22, 8:30 P.M.
Stevie Ray Vaughn
B.B. King
John Hammond
Riverboat S.S. President
John Faddis Quartet
Sammy Price Group with Doc Cheatham
Spanish Plaza at RIVERWALK

SATURDAY, APRIL 23, 9 P.M.
Kenny G
Lee Ritenour
Riverboat S.S. President
Hank Crawford/ Jimmy McGriff Quartet
Earl Palmer/Red Tyler Group
Harry Connick, Jr.
J.B. Rivers at RIVERWALK

MONDAY, APRIL 25, 8, 11 P.M.
Jazz Fest Jam featuring Dozens of Artists
Snug Harbor Jazz Club

TUESDAY, APRIL 26, 8 P.M.
Gospel is Alive
Rev. James Cleveland
Shirley Caesar and The Caesar Singers
Roebuck "Pops" Staples
The Williams Brothers
Rev. Paul Morton and The Greater St. Stephens Baptist Church Choir
Viola Naomi Washington
Saenger Theatre

WEDNESDAY, APRIL 27, 8 P.M.
Michael Brecker Band
McCoy Tyner Trio
Freddie Hubbard Quintet
Riverboat S.S. President

THURSDAY, APRIL 28, 8 P.M.
La Noche Latina
Celia Cruz
Tito Puente and His Latin Jazz Orchestra
Willie Colon and His Orchestra
Riverboat S.S. President
Alice Coltrane and a Tribute to the Music and Life of John Coltrane
Original American Jazz
Quintet Plus One
Riverboat Hallelujah

FRIDAY, APRIL 29, 7 P.M. & MIDNIGHT
Little Feat with special guest Bonnie Raitt
The Radiators
Riverboat S.S. President

SATURDAY, APRIL 30, 7 P.M. & MIDNIGHT
The Robert Cray Band
The Neville Brothers
The Dirty Dozen Brass Band
Riverboat S.S. President
Charlie Haden Quartet West
N.O. Traditional All-Star Band
Spanish Plaza at Riverwalk,

Snooks Eaglin

1989

It was the end of a tradition that inspired indelible memories of music and sweat and romance and drinking and delirious dancing. It was the end of a heritage reaching back into the 1700s. And it was the end of a Jazz Fest tradition, the likes of which would not be known again. The *S.S. President* had sailed away to St. Louis, Missouri, in the summer after last year's Jazz Fest, and she would not return.

The concerts on the riverboats echoed the years during which early blues and later jazz musicians played on gambling boats up the Mississippi to St. Louis and found work in the clubs of Chicago. And in the early years of Jazz Fest, all of the concerts on the *S.S. President* paid tribute to traditional jazz legends. It was later— perhaps those on staff, or maybe the language of ticket sales— lost interest in traditional jazz and began booking more popular performers. Memories of the concerts on the *S.S. President* can still be conjured up, such as the year Kid Thomas Valentine and the Algiers Stompers and a frenzied audience literally rocked the boat. And there

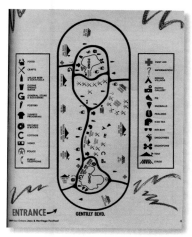

was the year bands played way past dock time at midnight and jazzed-up devotees spilled out onto Spanish Plaza to jam into French Quarter clubs till daylight drove them home.

The Mississippi River was inexorably tied to the music. There was something about sailing out onto the water that evoked another world; one in which happiness was a tailgate trombone, or a clarinet's sweet high squeal. The music and smoke and laughter and shouts seeped into the walls and floorboards, and probably, when the boat was docked upriver in St. Louis, the ghosts of jazz masters relived the good times and the music still played on. But reliving memories would not bring the riverboat back to Jazz Fest, so the staff tried to keep the music close to the river.

The plan was to erect a big tent at the foot of Calliope Street, just upriver from the Convention Center. There wasn't a good beginning. A fierce Thursday night thunderstorm (some even claimed it was a tornado) swamped the colossal tent. But in true New Orleans fashion, as soon as the sodden images appeared on local television, police, neighbors, and people bearing food (another New Orleans necessity) came around to volunteer their help. Some of the concerts that were moved from the River Tent went to Snug Harbor, the Saenger Theatre and a new venue, the Riverboat Hallelujah Concert Hall, formerly Trans Lux Cinerama, which had good acoustics and seated 1,200.

"At that time there was two different sets of walkie talkies; one set of walkie talkies for the night crew and one set for the Fair Grounds crew, and I had them on my kitchen table," remembered Quint Davis. "About 5:00 in the morning there was squawking on the radio. I got up and they said a tornado hit the River Tent and it's gone. I said 'Gone? Two thousand chairs, PA system, grand piano, B3, what are you talking about- gone?' They said, 'Well, it's kind of partly in the river — it's kind of partly gone— everything is damp.' We had a sold out show that night with Van Morrison, Allen Toussaint, and The Thunderbirds. So we had to reinvent that show during the day— move it to the Municipal

FRIDAY, APRIL 28

WVUE / BURGER KING STAGE
11:15 Loyola University Band
12:20 Willie West & Level One
1:40 Dan Del Santo's World Beat
3:00 Daryl Johnson & Trouble
4:30 Bobby Marchan & Higher Ground
6:00 Katie Webster "The Swamp Boogie Queen"

Y96 FM STAGE
11:30 Ernie Cosse & The Boogie Band
12:50 King Nino & His Slave Girls
2:00 Dino Kruse
3:15 Tabby Thomas
4:15 Kenny Acosta & The House Rockers
6:00 Dash Rip Rock

RAY-BAN / WWL-TV STAGE
12:00 Joseph "Cool" Davis Singers
1:30 Filé
3:00 Ricky Skaggs
4:30 John Hiatt & The Goners
5:50 Bobby Cure & The Summertime Blues with Robert Parker & Chuck Carbo

FAIS DO-DO STAGE
11:20 Willie Cole Blues Band
12:30 Jude Taylor & The Burning Flame Band
1:45 Papa Cairo with Chuck Guillory
3:10 Al Ferrier "The Rockabilly King" with Ronnie Brumley & Foxfire
4:30 La Nueva Compania with Luis Estrada of Guatemala
5:45 Hadley Castille's Louisiana Cajun Band

UNCLE BEN'S RICE TENT
11:30 Chris Lacinak
12:40 Theron Lewis & Unit 7
1:50 Scott Goudeau
3:00 Tony Bazley Sextet
4:10 The Jazz Couriers
5:30 Joel Simpson Quintet

ECONOMY HALL TENT
11:30 Allegra New Orleans String Band
12:50 Creole Rice Yerba Buena Jazz Band
2:10 Sam Alcorn
3:30 Andrew Hall's Society Jazz Band
4:40 Teddy Riley Jazz Masters
6:00 Tennessee Tech Tubas

CONGO SQUARE STAGE
11:30 St. Augustine High School Jazz Band
12:40 Ras Cloud & The Sons of Sellassie
1:50 Rap Revue: MC J'Ro'J & Gold Rush Crew / Tanya P. & GMS w/ Hollygrove Posse
3:30 Original Yellow Jackets Mardi Gras Indians
4:20 "Cool Lou" Ford Sextet
5:45 Code Blue

TRAVEL N. O. LAGNIAPPE TENT
11:20 West Jefferson Jazz Ensemble
12:40 Carl LeBlanc
2:00 John Rankin
3:20 Boogie Bill Webb
4:35 Bad Oyster Band
6:00 Guardians of the Flame

MUSIC HERITAGE TENT
12:00 Ward Lormond and Filé
3:00 DeGruy and Mackie
4:15 Katie Webster & Ice Cube Slim
5:30 Ricky Skaggs & Dr. Bill Malone

The Festival's economic impact on Louisiana was $59.4 million, and of that amount $3 million went to local music clubs.

In terms of time spent at the Heritage Fair, 36 percent of locals went for one day; 32 percent for two days; 13 percent for three days, and the rest for four or more days.

Mr. Bones, a 72-year-old retired sales manager named John Burrill, kept rhythm onstage at Jazz Fest, working his polished cow shinbones, like those he had first seen in a traveling minstrel show in the 1930s. He also won the Boston Music Award for sheet music several times.

Jazz search 1989 winners was a local band, the Murmurs. They won $1,000, a recording session at Southlake Studios, and the opportunity to perform at Jazz Fest.

Auditorium — find another sound company — and put it all together by 4:00 o'clock in the afternoon.

"At that point at 5 o'clock in the morning, the night shows were gone from Jazz Fest. At 6:30 there's a call on the other radio that the tornado has hit the Fair Grounds and the Gospel Tent is gone, the Jazz Tent is gone and all the little tents are gone — and at that moment in time there was no Jazz Fest on earth it was completely gone — right in the middle of the Festival. So we moved that day. We moved the night show into the Auditorium. People from the neighborhoods showed up and came in to help clear the field, and helped put

the thing back together. Tents were driven in from Memphis. We might have gone one day with no tent on Gospel; I'm not sure if we opened that day or the next day. That was a night!"

The storm was cause for closing Jazz Fest on Friday, but when clear skies shone on Saturday, and the Heavenly Vision Missionary Baptist Church choir raised their voices in the Gospel Tent, the pent-up crowds spilled out in force. More than 55,000 fest-goers streamed onto the squishy infield on Saturday; and the 65,000 who followed them on Sunday matched a 1988 attendance record. All in all, more folks came to the Fest

Aaron Neville with Zion Harmonizers

over the five days of 1989 than the six days of the year before. The tent was back up, too. It was magnificent, resplendent with hand-stitched embroidered red stars and planets. It had a seating capacity of 3,000, and staff claimed the tent afforded better sightlines and acoustics, had more elaborate lighting and sound. Food and drinks were sold in separate tents.

For the twentieth anniversary, staff decided to revisit the roots of the Fest. The Como Fife and Drum Corps, "Bois Sec" Ardoin and Canray Fontenot, and Bongo Joe were just some of the musicians featured. Chuck Guillory from Mamou was accompanied by Papa Cairo, a steel guitar player in the 1940s swing guitar style that was fading into history. The great Cajun artist Nathan Abshire played his last Jazz Fest. He was a musician from the old days, when Cajun music was played with bare bones accompaniment such as box guitars and accordions – no drums or amplification. Abshire, along with Sady Courville (who also played the first Jazz Fest) always stayed true to his roots, back to a time when music was played

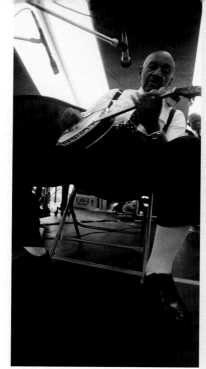

Papa Al Lewis

for people, not for profit. Some of these fine musicians can still be heard on the CD *"Cajun and Creole Masters,"* which is enriched with liner notes and transcripts of conversations with these amazing keepers of the historic music flame.

On the Congo Stage on Saturday, the nine-member Turtle Shell Band was return-

"In 1989 I was playing at Jazz Fest and about an hour before I went on my cousins, Michael and Chris, who played with me at the time, and I were standing in front of our stage checking out the music. Michael spotted John Fogerty standing in the crowd. This is someone I have idolized and whose recordings had an influence on me. Michael walked up to him and asked 'Are you John?' and he said yes. Michael said, 'I didn't expect to see you here' and John said, 'I didn't expect to see you here either.' I walked up and introduced myself and offered him a copy of my album. He told me he didn't want to carry an album around all day at the Festival and when he said that my heart sank and I felt bad about the whole conversation. Later I'm getting ready to go on stage and John comes running up to the barricade and says, 'I'd really like to have your album.' I didn't have any because they were at the record tent. The next year when I came off the stage who is waiting for me but John Fogerty; we talked for about twenty minutes and took pictures together. That let me know that he really was a nice person and later I was able to give him some of my CDs." BRUCE DAIGREPONT

Oliver Morgan and Jessie Hill

ing for the first time after their 1983 gig at Jazz Fest. Members of the Garifuna tribe from Belize, this exuberant group wore vests of turtle shells that served as Caribbean-style frattoirs. Their happy-sounding, percussive mix of instruments was an arsenal of sticks, shells, guitars, and calabashes filled with seeds, all shared in an exotic and colorful ceremonial display. On Sunday, Kanda Bongo Man played soukous (from French sou cour meaning "to shake"), a light guitar-dominated style of dance music that was taking the world by storm. Soukous came out of a French-speaking African Caribbean blend from the Congolese music of Zaire, Gabon, and Congo-Brazzaville. Kanda Bongo Man's infectious music sent the Congo Square crowd home dancing and twirl-

ing for more. In musical and historical counterpoint were the new rappers in Congo Square's "Rap Revue": MC J'RO J and the Gold Rush Crew, Tanya P and GMS performed with the Hollygrove Posse. If this booking was a nod to the growing commercial

power of rap music, it was also a foreshadowing of complaints that rap, as it was increasingly dominated by the "gangsta" style, did not belong at a jazz and heritage festival. Rap music seemed at first an awkward fit at Jazz Fest, which was becoming increasingly

Al Hirt

music scene

Ellis Marsalis releases *A Night at Snug Harbor.*

Johnny Adams releases *Walking On A Tightrope: The Songs of Percy Mayfield* on Rounder Records.

The Dirty Dozen Brass Band releases *The New Orleans Album* featuring Dave Bartholomew, Danny Barker, Eddie Bo and Elvis Costello.

Aaron Neville, Neville Brothers, Harry Connick, Jr. and Dr. John all win Grammy Awards.

IN MEMORIAM
Roy Eldridge

white and increasingly middle class. That reality left the young African-Americans, some who came from musical family dynasties, feeling out-of-sync with the festival. But their creativity simply took another form, and some got busy making a new music

that would dominate the national rap market in years to come. In fact, Koindu and later Congo Square had been formed with a mission of representing African-American diaspora cultural forms, so rap music earned a de facto place on the Congo Stage.

Building on last year's series of music and education events in local schools, a new series of workshops took place at the Jazz Fest. There were music workshops at the Heritage Tent, with Allison Kaslow (neé Miner) interviewing Allen Toussaint and others. Kaslow's idea was to balance the now-sprawling Jazz Fest with a more human scale, and to invite the audience into a more intimate acquaintance with musicians who had come to define their respective genres. A $1,000 grant from The Foundation allowed the Dirty Dozen Brass

Bobby Blue Band

workshops at various locations featured trumpeter Joe Newman, drummer Earl Palmer, gospel singer Roebuck "Pops" Staples, folk singer Odetta, banjo player Danny Barker and interplanetary jazz channeler Sun Ra.

Those who continued to wonder why the Fest got bigger and fatter would have to argue with others who pointed out the good works funded by a growing enterprise. The New Orleans Jazz & Heritage Festival was now second only to Mardi Gras in relieving out-of-town visitors of disposable income. The numbers told the story, or at least one side of it. A dizzying $59.4 million flowed into the local businesses, twice the amount of two years ago. Scott Ray, of Cypress Research and Development, speculated that the sharp incline was due to the increased growth of the Festival, more out-of-town visitors (who spend more than locals), and the fact that this year's survey was more detailed in capturing data. In 1989, 312,000 attended the Fest, including 260,000 during the six-day Louisiana Heritage

Fair. Ray reported that 1989 drew 38 % out-of-towners of the total audience of 150,500. (The difference between 150,500 and 260,000 resulted from subtracting repeat trips from some people.) Of those from out of town, 15% came from Louisiana, 12.6 % from Texas, 10% from Mississippi, 9.7% from California (look out, Bunny Matthews!), 7% from New York, 6% from Alabama, 16% from other eastern states, 13% other southeastern states, 5% from the west, and 5.6% from other countries.

Direct spending attributable to Jazz Fest totaled $31.3 million, including $25.8 million by visitors. Visitors spent $12 million at the Fair Grounds and $13.8 million elsewhere, including $7 million for hotel rooms,

Band to play a series of 10 fundraising concerts in Orleans Parish schools, with proceeds going to the music departments in each school. Other Foundation activities included a tribute to the New Orleans Center for Creative Arts at Dillard University chapel with Ellis Marsalis and son Wynton, Kidd Jordan, Donald Harrison, and Terrence Blanchard. Other

"I think it was 1989. Willie Dixon's manager called me up and said he would like to meet with me. He came over to my house on the West bank to check out my harmonica playing and invited me to play the Chicago Blues Fest. He asked me, 'Are you playing at the Jazz Fest?' I said, 'No they haven't invited me.' So Willie took me in his Lincoln Continental and had his driver take us to Quint's house out by the Bayou. Willie walked up and knocked on his door and when Quint answered he asked him, 'Why don't you have this star playing at Jazz Fest?' Quint said, 'There must have been some oversight.' I played that year and have played ever since." BRUCE "SUNPIE" BARNES

Willie Mars, Danny Barker Jazz Jam

$3.8 million on New Orleans legendary food, and they infused $3 million into music clubs, no doubt hoping to catch one of the magical late night jams when one music hero shows up to sit in with another. The $31.3 million directly resulted in $28.1 million in secondary spending as money turned over in the economy. The $5.5 million with which locals reported parting was probably only half that they actually spent at the Fest. 15.5% of fest-goers were in town for other conventions or business. Of that

group, a clever two thirds said the Fest sealed their decision to schedule their business at that time. In terms of time spent at the Heritage Fair, 36% of locals go for one day; 32% for two days; 13% for three days; and the rest said they are fortunate enough to party on for four or more days. More than a quarter of tourists said they attended one day; nearly half reported 2 days; about 20% came for 3 days, and the rest for four or more days. Polls also showed that more than half had completed college and earned over $30,000 annually.

Lonnie Brooks

RAY-BAN / WWL -TV STAGE
11:20 U.S. Navy Steel Band
1:00 Bobby "Blue" Bland
2:30 Bonnie Raitt
4:10 Jimmy Buffet & The Coral Reefer Band
6:00 Allen Toussaint

FAIS DO-DO STAGE
11:30 Sensacion Latina
1:00 Creole Wild West Mardi Gras Indians
2:00 Charlie Sayles
3:15 Hackberry Ramblers
4:30 Geo-Leo
6:00 Fernest Arceneaux & The Thunders

UNCLE BEN'S RICE TENT
11:20 Larry Seiberth Quartet
12:30 Harry Connick, Jr.
1:45 Ellis Marsalis Quartet
3:00 Wynton Marsalis
4:40 Art Blakey & The Jazz Messengers
6:00 The Expatriots

ECONOMY HALL TENT
11:20 New Leviathan Oriental Foxtrot Orchestra
12:40 Kid Sheik's Storyville Ramblers
1:50 Odetta
3:15 World's Greatest Jazz Band
4:40 Young Tuxedo Brass Band
6:00 Pete Fountain

CONGO SQUARE STAGE
11:30 New Orleans Stick Band
12:45 Philip Manuel
1:30 Rising Star Drum & Fife Corps Parade
1:50 Hector Gallardo & His Songo Allstars with special guest Mark Sanders
2:40 Barbados Tuk Band Parade
3:00 Turtle Shell Band from Belize
3:20 Willie Tee
4:25 Louisiana Purchase
5:15 Barbados Tuk Band Parade
5:45 Kanda Bongo Man of Zaire

TRAVEL N.O. LAGNIAPPE TENT
11:30 NOCCA
12:40 John Jackson
2:00 Aaron Neville & Amasa Miller
3:20 Golden Eagles Mardi Gras Indians
4:40 Richard Thompson
6:00 Hezekiah & The House Rockers

MUSIC HERITAGE TENT
12:00 Son Ford and Walter Liniger
1:15 Hackberry Ramblers
2:30 Rising Star Drum Corp.
3:15 Harmonica Blow Out w/ Charlie Sayles, Chicago Bo and Walter Liniger
4:15 Al Broussard
5:15 Pat Flory
6:15 Ikebana

RHODES / WYLD GOSPEL TENT
11:45 The Coolie Family
12:30 The Randolph Brothers
1:15 First Church of God In Christ
2:00 The Friendly Five
2:45 New Zion Trio Plus One
3:30 The Staple Singers
4:30 Soulful Heavenly Stars
5:15 Donald Watkins & Divinity
6:00 Holy Hill Gospel Singers

WDSU TV-6 KIDS' TENT
12:00 Dotsie LeBlanc
12:30 Voices of the Kingdom
1:00 Delores C. Henderson
1:30 Perry the Mime
2:30 Delores C. Henderson
3:00 Washboard Leo

Manuel Sayles

3:00 Ahmos Zu-Bolton with
     Copasetic Presents
4:00 The Sound Idea
5:00 Eric McAllister

PARADES
4:15 Algiers Steppers, Taylor Bunch,
     Allstar Brass Band & Storyville
     Stompers

SATURDAY, MAY 6

WVUE / BURGER KING STAGE
11:20 Woodenhead
12:40 Daniel Lanois
1:40 Mason Ruffner
3:00 Marcia Ball
4:30 Johnny Winter
6:00 Frankie Ford Revue with The
     Dixie Cups

Y96 FM STAGE
11:00 Ramsey McLean
12:20 Marva Wright
1:40 Song Dogs
3:00 Wayne Toups & Zydecajun
4:20 Reggie Hall Band with Jessie
     Hill, Oliver Morgan, Al Johnson,
     Albert "Dog Man" Smith & Lil
     Sonny Jones
6:00 Allen Fontenot, Mitchell
     Cormier & The Country Cajuns

RAY-BAN / WWL TV STAGE
11:30 Rueben "Mr. Salsa" Gonzalez &
     His Salseros
1:00 Buckwheat Zydeco
2:30 John Lee Hooker & The Coast to
     Coast Blues Band
4:00 Youssou N'Dour
5:45 George Benson

FAIS DO-DO STAGE
11:15 Southern University of New
     Orleans
12:30 Wild Magnolias Mardi Gras
     Indians
1:45 Boom & Chime Band of Belize
3:10 Tim Williams & Natchez
4:30 Willis Prudhomme
6:00 John Mooney & Bluesiana

UNCLE BEN'S RICE TENT
11:20 Ed Perkins Group
12:30 Walter Payton & Ballet File
1:45 Astral Project
3:00 Alvin Batiste
4:25 Dave Bartholomew Big Band
     "The 5 Friends" & Carolyn
     Williams
6:00 The Dirty Dozen Brass Band

ECONOMY HALL TENT
11:20 Local International Allstars
12:40 Chris Clifton
2:00 New Orleans Ragtime Orchestra
3:20 Dr. Michael White with Barbara
     Shorts
4:40 Placide Adams Original
     Dixieland Hall Jazz Band
6:00 Original Storyville Jazz Band

CONGO SQUARE STAGE
11:30 Herman Jackson & Red Stick
12:45 Exuma
3:30 Aubry Twins
4:45 James Rivers Movement
6:10 Cyril Neville & The Uptown
     Allstars

TRAVEL N.O. LAGNIAPPE TENT
11:00 Harlan White
12:10 Bob Greene
1:10 Drink Small "The Blues Doctor"
2:20 Ali Farka Toure of Mali
3:30 Big Joe Duskin
4:45 Key West Junkanoos
6:00 Sounds of the South

4:00 Starmakers
4:30 Adella, Adella, The Storyteller
5:30 Odetta

PARADES
4:00 5th Dimension Rollers, Popee
     Group & The Origianl Pin-Stripe
     Brass Band
5:30 Olympia Aid, Ladies Zulu
     SA&PCs & Rebirth Brass Band

FRIDAY, MAY 5

WVUE / BURGER KING STAGE
11:10 Hammond State School
12:15 Y'Shua Manzy
1:35 Crescent City Sound Co. Band
3:15 Mojo Collins & Cheap
     Blues Band
4:40 Wanda Rouzan & A Taste of New
     Orleans
6:00 Tommy Ridgley & The
     Untouchable with Al Johnson

Y96 FM STAGE
11:20 Steve Riley & The Mamou
     Playboys
12:35 John Thomas Griffith
1:50 D.L. Menard & The
     Louisiana Aces
3:20 Nora Wixted & 2 Much Fun
4:30 Jon "King" Cleary
6:00 Tay Hogg & Dixie Pride

RAY-BAN / WWL -TV STAGE
11:30 Dillard University
12:50 Kenny & Raful Neal & The Neal
     Brothers
2:30 Terrance Simien & The Mallet
     Playboys

4:00 Ivan Neville
5:45 Robert Cray featuring the
     Memphis Horns

FAIS DO-DO STAGE
11:00 East Jefferson High School Jazz
     Warriors
12:20 The Murmurs
1:30 Guitar Slim Jr.
2:50 J. Monque'D Blues Band with
     Mr. Google Eyes
4:30 Los Mayas
6:00 White Cloud Hunters Mardi Gras
     Indians

UNCLE BEN'S RICE TENT
11:30 Norleans Jazzband
1:00 Victor Goines
2:10 James Drew
3:20 Dick Landry
4:40 New Orleans Swingaphonic
     Orchestra
6:00 Rick Margitza

ECONOMY HALL TENT
11:10 Luis "Speedy" Gonzalez
12:20 Frank Federico
1:30 Milford Dolliole
2:40 Lady Charlotte
3:50 Frank Trapani
5:00 Louisiana Repertory Jazz
     Ensemble
6:00 Wendell Brunious Jazz Band
     with Juanita Brooks

CONGO SQUARE STAGE
11:30 J.D. Hill & The Jammers
12:50 Hurley Blanchard Quartet
2:00 Ninth Ward Hunters Mardi Gras
     Indians
3:20 Eugene Ross & Friends
4:40 The Shepherd Band

5:35 Valley Boys Bahamas
     Junkanoos Parade
6:15 Brothers & Sisters of Christ

TRAVEL N.O. LAGNIAPPE TENT
11:30 Cultural Voices
12:45 Hans Theessink & Jon Sass
2:00 John Campbell
3:20 Spencer Bohren
4:45 Jasmine
6:10 Mardi Gras Chorus

MUSIC HERITAGE TENT
12:00 D.L. Menard & Louisiana Aces
1:00 James Drew
2:00 Miss Lillian
2:30 Kenny & Raful Neal w/ Troy
     Turner
4:00 Tommy Ridgley
5:00 Tuba Workshop w/ Jon Sass,
     Walter Payton & Kirk Joseph

RHODES / WYLD GOSPEL TENT
11:45 Gospel Soul Survivors
12:30 The Calvacade BC Singing
     Ministries
1:15 Headstart Singing Angels
2:00 McDonogh #35 Gospel Choir
2:45 Aline White & Company
3:30 Smooth Family of Slidell
4:15 Landrum Singers
5:00 First Testament Intermediate
     BC Choir
6:00 The Revelation Baton Rouge

WDSU TV-6 KIDS' TENT
12:00 Edward Hynes School Choir
12:30 Fischer Elem. School Choir and
     Les Petites Dancers
1:00 Jazz Babies
2:00 McDonogh #38 Choir and
     Folkloric Troupe
2:30 St. Paul's Episcopal School
     Choir

MUSIC HERITAGE TENT

12:15 Silas Hogan and Guitar Kelly
1:30 Wayne Toups and Steve Riley w/ Barry Ancelet
2:30 Bob Greene
3:15 Bo Dollis & Friends w/ lawrence Harrison on steel drum
4:15 David Doucet & Brownie Ford
5:15 Allison "Tudie" Montana & Edward Montana
6:15 Jessie Mae Hemphill

RHODES / WYLD GOSPEL TENT

11:30 St. James Methodist Church Choir
12:10 Heralds of Christ
12:50 Interfaith Gospel Choir
1:30 WIZA Radio Gospel Choir
2:10 Bolton Brothers of Bogalusa
2:50 Farily High School
3:30 Avondale Community Choir
4:10 The Famous Rocks of Harmony
4:50 The Zulu Ensemble
5:30 Gosper Inspirations
6:10 Holy Church of God In Christ Choir

WDSU TV-6 KIDS' TENT

12:00 Lusher Elementary School Choir
12:30 Colleen Salley
1:30 Calliope Puppets
2:30 New Orleans Free School Performers
3:30 The Class Clowns
4:30 St. Francis DeSales Youth Choir
5:00 David & Roselyn

PARADES

4:00 Tremé Sports, Money Waster, Second Line Jammers, Avenue Steppers SA&PCs & Doc Paulin Brass Band

SUNDAY, MAY 7

WVUE / BURGER KING STAGE

11:00 Xavier University
12:20 Johnny Allan & The Memories
1:40 BeauSoleil
3:00 Rockin' Dopsie & The Zydeco Twisters
4:20 John Fred & The Playboys
5:45 The Radiators

Harry Connick, Jr.

Y96 FM STAGE

11:30 Phase II & Muzik Connection
1:00 Russ Russell & The Rustlers
2:15 Johnny Adams & The Stormy Monday Band
3:40 Jimmie Davis & The Jimmie Davis Singers
4:40 Jean Knight
6:00 Luther Kent & Trickbag

RAY-BAN / WWL -TV STAGE

11:00 Porgy Jones Quartet
12:10 Ritmo Caribeno
1:20 Earl King with Ronnie Earl & The Broadcasters
2:45 Dr. John
4:15 The Neville Brothers
6:00 Fats Domino

FAIS DO-DO STAGE

12:00 Caledonia Society Dancers & Pipes & Drums of New Orleans
1:20 Snooks Eaglin
2:45 Ironin' Board Sam
4:10 The Subdudes
5:40 Bois Sec & Canray French Band

UNCLE BEN'S RICE TENT

11:40 Fred Kemp / Edward Frank Group
1:00 Germaine Bazzle & Friends
2:15 George Wein
3:20 Earl Turbinton Quartet
4:30 Max Roach
6:00 Kid Jordan & Al Fielder's Improvisational Arts Quintet

ECONOMY HALL TENT

11:30 Father Al & Friends
12:45 Pud Brown
2:10 Chris Owens
3:30 Champion Jack Dupree
4:45 Danny Barker's Jazz Hounds with Blue Lu Barker
6:10 Percy Humphrey & His Crescent City Joymakers

CONGO SQUARE STAGE

11:30 Mardi Gras Council Allstar Indians
12:45 Percussion, Inc.
2:00 Boom & Chime Band of Belize
3:15 Gary Brown & Feelings
4:10 Valley Boys Bahamas Junkanoos Parade
4:40 Sun Ra & His Intergalactic Arkestra

5:50 Valley Boys Bahamas Junkanoos Parade
6:15 Casa Samba

TRAVEL NEW ORLEANS LAGNIAPPE TENT

11:45 Hazel & The Delta Ramblers
1:00 Clancy "Blues Boy" Lewis
2:00 Ali Farka Toure of Mali
3:15 The Cox Family
4:40 Lil' Queenie & Amasa Miller
6:00 Key West Junkanoos

MUSIC HERITAGE TENT

12:00 George Wein Interview
12:30 Boom & Chime & Canray Fontenot & Bois Sec Ardoin
1:30 Champion Jack Dupree with Allen Toussaint
2:30 Napoleon Strickland
4:30 Gov. Jimmie Davis interviewed by Dr. Bill C. Malone

RHODES / WYLD GOSPEL TENT

11:45 Second Mt. Carmel B.C. Youth Choir
12:30 Friendly Travelers
1:15 The Melody Clouds
2:00 The Mighty Chariots
2:35 Gospel Awards Ceremony
2:45 Sherman Washington & The Famous Zion Harmonizers
3:30 Dorothy Love Coates Singers
4:30 Koinonia Gospel Ensemble
5:05 Greater Macedonia B.C.
5:40 Raymond Myles Singers with Christine Myles
6:15 Gospel Soul Children

WDSU TV-6 KIDS' TENT

12:00 Children's Community Theater Workshop
1:00 Floating Eagle Feather
2:00 City In My Hands
3:00 Kumbuka African Drum & Dance Collective
4:00 New Orleans Youth Ballet
5:00 Jamal Batiste

PARADES

2:45 Scene Boosters, Buck Jumpers, Buck Jumpers Sisters, Prince of Wales & Fun Lovers SA&PCs & Duke Dejan's Olympia Brass Band & Fairview B.C. Brass Band Reunion

NIGHT CONCERTS

FRIDAY, APRIL 28, 7 P.M. & MIDNIGHT
Santana
The Neville Brothers
The River Tent

Jimmy Buffet and The Coral Reefer Band
Dr. John & The New Island Social and Pleasure Club
The River Tent
Art Blakey & The Jazz Messengers
The New Orleans Expatriots (with Joe Newman, Benny Powell, Earl Palmer, Plas Johnson, Ellis Marsalis, Harold Batiste, Ernie McLean, peter "Chuck" Badie)
Harry Connick, Jr.
Riverboat Hallelujah Concert Hall,

SUNDAY, APRIL 30, 8 P.M.
Live Recording Session for Blue Note Records/Japa (featuring Ellis Marsalis, Earl Turbinton, Jr., Rick Margitza, Tony Dagradi, David Lee, Bill Huntington, Jim Singleton)
Produced by David Torkamowsky
Snug Harbor Jazz Club

MONDAY, MAY 1, 8 P.M.
Gospel is Alive!
Al Green
BeBe and CeCe Winans
The Staple Singers
The Gospel Soul Children
The Zion Harmonizers
Saenger Theatre Special program dedicated to the homeless,

TUESDAY, MAY 2, 8 P.M.
Miles Davis
The Wynton Marsalis Sextet
The River Tent

WEDNESDAY, MAY 3, 8 P.M.
La Noche Latina
El Gran Combo
Andy Montanez & His Orchestra
Ritmo Caribeno
The River Tent

THURSDAY, MAY 4, 8 P.M.
The Robert Cray Band
Youssour N'Dour
Ivan Neville & The Room
The River Tent

FRIDAY, MAY 5, 7 P.M. & MIDNIGHT
George Benson
Spyro Gyra
The River Tent

SATURDAY, MAY 6, 7 P.M. & MIDNIGHT
Van Morrison
The Fabulous Thunderbirds
Allen Toussaint
The River Tent
The Max Roach Quartet (with Cecil Bridgewater, Tyrone Brown & Odine Pope)
The Kent Jordan Quartet
Earl Turbinton, Jr. & Trinity
Riverboat Hallelujah Concert Hall,

Al Johnson

1990

In the twenty years of steady growth and increasing popularity (not only with visitors but also the international press) Jazz Fest had grown from 300 musicians playing over three days on four rickety stages in a small urban park to 440 musicians and an additional dozen marching social aid and pleasure clubs on ten spacious, well equipped, corporate-sponsored stages over a 32-acre horse racing venue. The Festival was smoothly run, safe, and comfortable. The music and food offered were arguably the best in the world. The Jazz Fest staff continued to adjust both the schedule and the Festival layout to accommodate not only larger crowds, but also more sophisticated audiences. Americans in particular were more mobile than ever before, and richer, too. At least dollar-wise.

1990 NEW ORLEANS JAZZ AND HERITAGE FESTIVAL

The Travel New Orleans Lagniappe Tent was turned to face the grandstand in order to create a more intimate feeling. Food and crafts demonstrations tempted visitors to recreate dishes at home, such as Frank Brigtsen's smothered okra with shrimp and andouille. Films about New Orleans, notably Sylvester Francis' *Jazz Funerals, Secondlines* and Preston McClanahan's *Film on Chester Zardis* were screened

what's going on?

GLOBALLY

Nelson Mandela is released from a South African prison after serving 27 years for his opposition to apartheid.

Iraq invades Kuwait and the UN imposes sanctions, while the US and allies send military forces to Saudi Arabia in Operation Desert Shield.

Manuel Noreiga turns himself in to US Military: Ending his stand-off inside the Vatican embassy, he returned to the US to face drug trafficking charges.

NATIONALLY

Mayor of Washington, D.C., Marion S. Barry, Jr,. is arrested by the FBI for drug possession.

Three major US companies announce they will no longer buy tuna caught in nets that also trap dolphins.

Robert Mapplethorpe's Cincinnati Contemporary Art's Center exhibit is branded "indecent" and the museum and its director are indicted for obscenity.

LOCALLY

Emeril Lagasse opens Emeril's Restaurant.

A new state lottery is approved as "gaming."

75th year anniversary of the Roman Chewing Candy cart (begun in 1915). The candy sold for 5 cents a stick until 1970.

Praline Connection opens their first location on Frenchmen Street in 1990.

The Aquarium of the Americas opens in New Orleans.

CULTURALLY

Gene therapy debuts: in Bethesda, Maryland, used to treat ADA deficiency.

New movie rating: NC-17 is passed in order to allow for an adults-only rating without the stigma of an X rating.

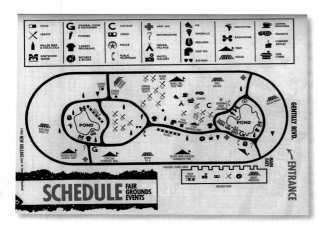

SCHEDULE FAIR GROUNDS EVENTS

in the grandstand. Bruce Eggler, writing in *The Times-Picayune*, noted the grandstand was "A unique, 3 story performance space, complete with open windows and balmy breezes."

The swell new facility hosted workshops by Ruth Brown, B.B. King, Allen Toussaint, and others. The grandstand was the start and finish point for all marching clubs, parades and brass bands, and as a result the fest was able to double the number of parades. All of the parade organizations at Jazz Fest had histories specific to New Orleans. The Benevolent Societies were organized by

African-Americans in early New Orleans as a result of denied access to union membership and health benefits from employers. Dues from club memberships covered medical and burial expenses, and assisted families with emergency financial obligations. Social and Pleasure clubs were just that: organizations wherein members could gather for recreation, parties, games and participation in Mardi Gras parades. Their names told the story: Gentlemen of Leisure, Money Wasters, Scene Boosters, The Furious Five and Untouchables, and so on.

Art Neville and Dr. John

WVUE / WNOE STAGE
11:30 Hammond Sate School
12:40 Kenny Bill Stinson
2:10 Wayne Toups & Zydecajun
3:45 Clarence "Gatemouth" Brown
5:25 Elvin Bishop

WDSU TV 6 STAGE
11:20 The Backsliders
12:30 Steve Riley & The Mamou Playboys
1:45 Al Ferrier "The Rockabilly King" w/ Ronnie Brumley & Foxfire
3:10 Edward Brown & The Zydeco House Rockers
4:20 The Subdudes
5:45 John Delafose & The Eunice Playboys

WWL / RAY-BAN STAGE
11:20 Loyola University
12:40 Tribe Nunzio
2:00 Bobby Cure & The Summertime Blues w/ Robert Parker
3:45 Ernie K-Doe w/ N.O. Magnificent 7th & Special Guest Eddie Bo
5:30 Toots & The Maytals

FAIS DO-DO STAGE
11:30 The Beat Doctors
1:00 Shot Down In Ecuador, Jr.
2:25 Charles Jacob Blues Band
4:00 Harlan White w/ Fresh Young Minds
5:30 The Bluerunners

MARS INC. JAZZ TENT
11:40 Theron Lewis & Unit 7
12:50 Nicholas Payton
2:00 Mark Sterbank
3:10 Michael Ward
4:20 Larry Seiberth
5:45 Freddie Hubbard

COX / A&E ECONOMY HALL TENT
11:20 Allegra N.O. String Band
12:20 Milford Dolliole Jazz Band
1:30 Eagle Brass Band
2:40 Val Barbara's Jazz Band
3:50 The Sammy Rimington Band
5:00 John Brunious
6:10 Original Camelia Jazz Band

CONGO SQUARE STAGE
11:25 Xavier University
12:40 Julio & Cesar & "Kaibil"
1:50 Plantation Posse
3:25 Kid Johnson
4:40 Guardians of the Flame
6:00 Y'Shua Manzy

TRAVEL N.O. LAGNIAPPE TENT
12:00 East Jefferson
1:15 Joel Simpson
2:40 Phil DeGruy
4:00 Max Sunyer Trio
5:25 Hurley Blanchard

MUSIC HERITAGE STAGE
12:00 Jesse Thomas
1:00 Milford Dolliole (Interview)
2:30 Toots Hibbert, Gene Scaramuzza (interviewer)
4:00 Jesse Thomas, Eleanor Ellis (interviewer)
5:15 Eddie Bo Interview
6:00 Boogie Bill Webb

RHODES / WYLD GOSPEL TENT
11:45 Humble Travelers Group
12:30 Charles Jackson & The Jackson Travelers
1:15 Danneel Pre-Vocational Choir
2:00 Abramson High School Choir
2:45 Happy Action Singers
3:30 Leviticus Singers
4:15 Alcee Fortier Sr. High School

Aaron Neville

music scene

Bruce Daigrepont begins the Sunday Cajun Fais Do-Do at Tipitina's.

Louis Armstrong is inducted into the Rock and Roll Hall of Fame.

Neville Brothers appear on Saturday Night Live.

Reverend James Cleveland releases *Gospel Workshop of America Live in New Orleans.*

IN MEMORIAM

Stevie Ray Vaughn, Art Blakey, Alice Byrd, Wild Bill Davidson, Al Denny, Luis "Speedy" Gonzales, Charles "Charlie" Hamilton, Julius Handy, Emily Haydel, Lil Sonny Jones, Pleasant "Cousin Joe" Joseph, Roy Lands, Dennis Magee, Louis Nelson, Kelly Sullivan, Clement Tervalon, Frank Trapani, Joshua "Jack" Willis, Sarah Vaughn, Nathan Abshire, Dennis McGee,

The excited audience in the River Tent, a hand sewn canvas tent embroidered with gold and red stars for the "Blues With A Feeling" night concert was hoping for better weather than last year's storm on opening night. They received a disappointment of another sort, however. B.B. King (and his guitar, Lucille) had to cancel, as B.B. was laid low from a diabetes attack in Las Vegas. Blues guitarist Elvin Bishop subbed with the regularly scheduled John Hammond, Deacon John & the Ivories, and Etta James & the Roots Band. King was also slated to close the Ray Ban WWL stage but officials delayed the stages' lineup, allowing Little Feat to close out the fest. Quint Davis, who had toured with him in Africa in 1971, said he had never known B.B. to cancel a show.

On Saturday, the sold-out concert in the River Tent, pairing Linda Ronstadt with Aaron Neville and also featuring the subdudes, had its challenges. Ronstadt and Neville were riding the swell of success from Ronstadt's latest release "Cry Like a Rainstorm, Howl Like the Wind" on which Neville appeared. The album won a Grammy and opened up even new possibilities for Neville. But a spring Saturday night in New Orleans is never predictable, and a cloud of flying ants enveloped Ronstadt during "When Will I Be Loved." It seemed that the ants were loving her plenty. Handling the swarm like a pro, Ronstadt went on with such favorites as "Heart Like a Wheel" and her popular rendition of "Just One Look." But thunderous applause came during the Grammy-winning "Don't Know Much" with Ronstadt and Neville blending voices in a clear, soulful harmony and many in the audience humming along. The romantic moment was piqued by the message on Neville's T-shirt: "The Meters will Funk You to Death."

On the second Friday, Ladysmith Black Mambazo, a troupe of South African singers in matching dashikis, black slacks and white sneakers, performed in the River Tent between the Neville Brothers and a Caribbean soca group, the Arrows ("Hot, Hot, Hot"). Ladysmith Black Mabazo's harmony and hopping choreography were marvelous. At one point, Joseph Shabalala,

Sunnyland Slim

the leader, came to the apron and allowed as how the singers were best known in the U. S. for their work on Paul Simon's *Graceland* album ("Diamonds on the Soles of Their Shoes," "Homeless" and others). Enthusiastic applause. Then he said: "Paul Simon. We know you're here. Would you please come up on stage?" After some excited murmuring in the audience, a slight figure, dressed all in black, walked out, and the crowd went wild. One music lover remembers screaming and crying, having been a Paul Simon fan since his early days with Art Garfunkel. Simon joined them in singing "Homeless," "Amazing Grace" and, in Zulu, "God Bless Africa." Simon has appeared several times since, including twice at the 2001 fest, but for those who were there, nothing has matched the wonderful surprise of that night.

Rain fell on opening day at the Fair Grounds, and that was the good news and the bad news. It was good news to local Jazz Fest fans that actually hoped for rain to keep the crowds down and make their Jazz Fest experience "more of what it used to be." It was bad news to anyone wearing sandals. Locals knew to wear sneakers with low socks. After all, this was a horseracing track, and although the infield was in great shape, horses did contribute a certain aroma to the …mud. And a good rain could loam up the ground into a Louisiana version of quicksand. Many a sandal was sucked off and sunk down into the muck. One wise visitor was philosophical about the showers, "Is the keg half empty or half full?" he

5:00 The Dynamic Smooth Family
5:45 Fairview B.C. Choir

CHILDREN'S TENT
12:00 McDonogh #15 Elementary School Band
1:00 Louis Armstrong Middle School Performers
1:30 Behrman Elem. School Dance Team and Choir
2:00 Nattie the Clown
2:30 St. Paul's Episcopal School Choir
3:00 Samba Children with Curtis Pierre
4:00 The Liddle Family Circus
5:00 Cajun Fiddler Band

PARADES
4:15 Philadelphia Four, Jr. Olympia Brass Band & Blue Monday

SATURDAY, APRIL 28

WVUE / WNOE STAGE
12:00 New Orleans Chiffons
1:15 Clarence "Frogman" Henry
2:50 Ruth Brown
4:00 Doug Kershaw
5:30 Frankie Ford Revue w/ The Dixie Cups

WDSU TV 6 STAGE
11:40 Tim Laughlin
1:00 Ernie Cosse & The Boogie Band
2:10 Bruce Daigrepont Cajun Band
3:10 Allen Fontenot & His Country Cajuns w/ Special Guest Al Rapone
4:50 Jean Knight
6:10 Boozoo Chavis

WWL / RAY-BAN STAGE
11:15 U.S. Navy Steel Band
12:30 Rockin' Dopsie & His Zydeco Twisters
2:00 The Meters
4:00 Little Feat
5:45 B.B. King

FAIS DO-DO STAGE
11:45 Paky Saavedra & Bandidos
1:15 Force of Habit
2:45 The Wild Magnolias
4:15 Betty Lewis & The Executives
5:45 Filé

MARS INC. JAZZ TENT
11:20 Tony Bazley Sextet w/ Special Guest Curtis Peagler
12:25 Sean Holt
1:25 Willie Metcalf Trio
2:15 Steve Masakowski & Mars
3:15 Al Belletto Quartet
4:25 Earl Palmer
5:50 Charles Lloyd Quartet

COX / A&E ECONOMY HALL TENT
11:30 Local International Allstars
12:35 Teddy Riley & The Jazz Masters
2:00 New Leviathan Oriental Foxtrot Orchestra
3:20 Onward Brass Band
4:40 Tribute to Jelly Roll Morton w/ Dr. Michael White
6:00 Kid Sheik & His Storyville Ramblers

CONGO SQUARE STAGE
11:30 Health Unit
12:30 Atmosphere 90
1:50 Bahamas Rake & Scrape
3:00 Percussion, Inc.
4:30 Dan Del Santo
6:00 James Rivers Movement

"I had the opportunity for Ed Bradley from CBS News to surprise me and introduce me at Jazz Fest. It always meant a lot to me to have a national and international news journalist to take the time to come to my stage. When the Super Bowl was here in 1990, I performed with Sammy Berfect and his choir for the Super Bowl Special and that's when I first met him. The Jazz Fest is always the base for local talent to display their attributes to promoters and booking agents from all over the world." MARVA WRIGHT

Dewey Balfa

queried. A couple from Luling waltzed to a Cajun melody on the soggy ground in front of the Fais Do-Do Stage, wearing garbage bags as raingear and unfazed by the drizzle. Their picture was picked up by news wire services and printed in newspapers the world over. And that was what Jazz Fest was really all about, year after year. Dancing to Louisiana music, making the best of any situation, and spreading that native joie de vivre. Maybe that's why whole contingents came to Jazz Fest, like the 40 members of the Baltimore Blues Society, or the Festival lovers in the Pet De Kat Krewe. "For a hard-core music lover, it's like an explosion between your ears." One Pet De Kat Krewe member said. "Being here is like being baptized each year."

There are many, many favorite performers at Jazz Fest. Some patrons return year after year to see the same band or individual, grooving on the standards and wowing to new twists. Stevie Ray Vaughn was one such beloved artist. Vaughn did more than perform at Jazz Fest. He got to know local musicians such as R&B legends Dave Bartholomew and Earl King, and was a welcome guest at the private barbeques that go on under the stages. Vaughn's love of costume endeared him to locals — he was seen in an Indian headdress backstage or long hair under his cowboy hat with flying foxtail blowing in karmic synch with a blistering solo onstage. New Orleans mourned along with the rest of the world when Vaughn was killed in a helicopter crash four months after this

TRAVEL N.O. LAGNIAPPE TENT
12:00 Richwell Ison / Kirk Ford Experience
1:20 Moss Rascoe
2:45 John Mooney & Bluesiana
4:20 Toumani Diabate
6:00 Woodenhead

MUSIC HERITAGE STAGE
11:15 Eleanor Ellis
12:00 Ruth Brown w/ Eddie Bo Interview
1:00 Brownie Ford
2:00 Sammy Berfect Interview
3:30 B.B. King Interview
4:30 Boozoo Chavis Interview
5:30 Al Broussard

RHODES / WYLD GOSPEL TENT
11:45 Landrum Singers
12:30 Mighty Imperials Gospel Singers
1:15 St. Luke AME Church Sanctuary Choir
2:00 New Orleans Spiritualettes
2:45 Pentecost B.C. Choir
3:30 New Day B.C. Choir
4:15 Crownseekers
5:00 WYLD Gospel Choir
5:45 Sammy Berfect & Dimensions of Faith Community Choir

CHILDREN'S TENT
12:00 Lusher Elementary School Choir
12:30 Young Professionals Dance Ensemble
1:00 Brooks Read
2:00 McDonogh #42 Children's Choir
2:30 Legacy
3:30 Judy Stock
4:30 NOCCA Mime Troupe
5:00 Washboard Leo

PARADES
2:00 Second Line Jammers, Majestic Brass Band & Avenue Steppers
4:30 Storyville Stompers, Valley of Silent Men & Original Four

SUNDAY, APRIL 29

WVUE / WNOE STAGE
11:45 St. Augustine Jazz Band
1:00 Dash Rip Rock
2:15 Flaco Jimenez
3:50 Zachary Richard
5:30 The Radiators

WDSU TV 6 STAGE
12:00 Sweetwyne
1:30 Mississippi South
2:45 Nappy Brown w/ Snooky Pryor, Lavie Lee & The Shadows
4:25 Russ Russell & The Rustlers w/ Phil Meeks
5:45 Bryan Lee & The Jumpstreet Five

WWL / RAY-BAN STAGE
11:10 Southern-Baton Rouge Jazz Band
1:20 Robert Robinson & Touch of Fire
1:30 Johnny Adams
2:45 Allen Toussaint
4:15 Peabo Bryson
5:45 Linda Ronstadt w/ Aaron Neville

FAIS DO-DO STAGE
11:30 Original Yellow Jackets Mardi Gras Indians
12:40 Snooks Eaglin
2:00 Cajun Brew
3:25 Hackberry Ramblers
4:45 Dewey Balfa & Friends
6:10 Hector Gallardo & His Songo Allstars

Tommy Ridgley

fest facts

The Festival utilized the grandstands in the Fair Grounds for the first time.

WGBH Boston broadcast live from Jazz Fest with the six-hour "NEW ORLEANS LIVE: From the 1990 New Orleans Jazz & Heritage Festival." The broadcast went nationwide.

New Orleans-born Grammy winners Harry Connick Jr., Dr. John and Aaron Neville all performed at the same time on different stages.

329,000 attended.

last Jazz Fest performance. The numbers of Stevie Ray Vaughn fans that remember his last Festival performance are legion – his nighttime concert on the riverboat was videotaped, but you really had to be there. It stands at the top of the pantheon of great Jazz Fest performances

Continuing a tradition of the last three years, one evening concert was devoted to gospel

music. "Gospel Is Alive" had become a favorite. The audience was in the amen corner in the Saenger Theatre. Walter Hawkins & the Hawkins Family headlined, along with one of the nation's most well known vocal groups The Mighty Clouds of Joy, and contemporary gospel group Bobby Jones & New Life. But the heal-the-sick-and-the-lame portion of the evening was NOCCA graduate Raymond Myles and his mother, New Orleans gospel mainstay Christine Myles. Raymond Myles was a showman of the first order. His shows were wonderful and outrageous, mixing rhythm & blues, gospel and a more than a little humor in larger-than-life performances.

There were 405 Louisiana groups, 32 musicians from outside the state, and 10 simultaneous stages. The music at Jazz Fest got more of the audience it deserved. On May 6, public radio stations in 29 cities including Boston, Los Angeles,

Washington, and Detroit broadcast six hours of the Jazz Fest live. Another 36 stations aired a delayed version. Some of the musicians covered were The Neville Brothers, Etta James, B. B. King, Gary Burton Reunion, Linda Ronstadt, Walter Hawkins, Zachary Richard and Flaco Jiminez. The broadcast was produced by WGBH radio in Boston with WWNO-FM and WWOZ-FM in New Orleans, WPFW-FM in Washington, DC and Murray Street Enterprises in New York City.

This year, the Festival introduced the "Banana Boat Gazebo," reprising from the early days a small stage for one-person bands. Some of those who were featured on this new stage were Alfred "Uganda" Roberts, Country Gray Montgomery, Rooster, Kokomo Joe, the Whitstein Family, and Washboard Leo.

As profits poured into the Foundation, board members sought ways to continue to enrich

"The ultimate was Champion Jack Dupree — they guy had to be 90. I had never seen him before in Economy Hall. They literally helped him onstage and I thought 'Oh My God.' He looked wizened, shriveled up like an old, old man. I thought to myself basically how can he even make contact with the piano? They brought him out and propped him up and he proceeded to wail away for forty-five minutes. And when he was done, he turned back into that wizened man. He probably could not as much as feed himself, but you put him down at his instrument and he channeled his younger self. He died a short while later." KEITH TWITCHELL

the New Orleans music community. The Foundation founded the Heritage School of Music in April to perpetuate the tradition of jazz in New Orleans, with a mission to educate young musicians and to help further their training of jazz composition, style and repertoire. The school was under the direction of Edward "Kidd" Jordan, and Students were required to audition each school year. Classes were held on Southern University at New Orleans campus.

One of the necessary evils of Jazz Fest was (and is) the clearing of illegally parked cars in the residential neighborhood surrounding the Fair Grounds. Around 100 cars were usually towed daily, each accompanied by a stinging $65 reclamation fee. Even this simple sliver of the Jazz Fest phenomenon spawned entrepreneurial enterprise: local motorists picked up a few bucks by cruising around looking for people whose cars had been towed, and offered them a ride to the pound. Parking at the Fair Grounds cost a mere $2; one could catch the RTA at Roosevelt Mall near Tad Gormley Stadium (60 cents one way), or one could park at the Superdome and take the Gray Line "party bus," the Jazz Fest Shuttle. A round trip ticket on the Gray Line always included admission to the Festival, which was $16 from New Orleans, $17 from Metairie, and $8 and $8.50 for children 3-11.

MARS INC. JAZZ TENT
11:30 WBYU Radio Orchestra
12:40 Walter Payton & Ballet File
1:45 Alvin Batiste
2:55 Germaine Bazzle
4:15 Ramsey Lewis
5:45 The Dirty Dozen Brass Band

COX / A&E ECONOMY HALL TENT
12:00 Wendell Brunious
1:20 Dr. Michael White Quartet w/ Barbara Shorts
2:30 Ronnie Kole
3:40 Louis Nelson Memorial Jazz Band
4:40 Jeannie & Jimmy Cheatham & The Sweet Baby Blues Band
6:00 Danny Barker & His Jazz Hounds w/ Blue Lu Barker

CONGO SQUARE STAGE
11:20 The Sheppard Band
12:40 MC J'Ro'J & Goldrush Crew / Gregory D & DJ Mannie Fresh
2:00 Kumbuka Dance & Drum Collective
3:10 Bahamas Rake & Scrape
4:25 Dr. Maurice Martinez & Rhythm Plus
5:45 Mahlathini & The Mahatolla Queens of South Africa

TRAVEL N.O. LAGNIAPPE TENT
11:30 Mardi Gras Chorus
12:30 Creole Wild West Mardi Gras Indians
1:35 Rev. Leon Pinson & Elder Roma Wilson & The Old Morrisville Brass Band
3:05 Toumani Diabate of Mali
4:20 Hot Strings
5:45 Willie Metcalf & Academy of Black Arts Performers

MUSIC HERITAGE STAGE
11:30 Elder Roma Wilson & Rev. Pinson
12:30 Flaco Jimenez Interview
1:30 Germaine Bazzle Interview
2:45 Dr. Michael White, Jerry Brock (Interviewer)
4:00 Danny Barker, Jerry Brock (Interviewer)

RHODES / WYLD GOSPEL TENT
11:45 Coolie Family
12:30 Southern Bells
1:15 Friendly Five Gospel Singers
2:00 First Church of God In Christ
2:45 New Zion Trio + One
3:30 Mighty Clouds of Joy
4:30 Soulful Heavenly Stars
5:15 Inspirational Gospel Singers
6:00 Holy Hill Gospel Choir

CHILDREN'S TENT
12:00 Voices of Kingdom
12:30 New Orleans Youth Ballet
1:30 Children's Community Theatre Workshop
2:30 Philip Malancon
3:30 Adella, Adella the Storyteller
4:30 The Children of Selma

PARADES
2:00 Ladies Zulu, Young Men Olympian SA&PC & Doc Paulin Brass Band
4:30 Fifth Division Rollers, Tremé Brass Band & Devastation SA&PC

FRIDAY, MAY 4

WVUE / WNOE STAGE
11:30 UNO Big Band / UNO Combo
1:20 Bobby Marchan & Higher Ground

Champion Jack Dupree

CHILDREN'S TENT
12:00 McDonogh #38 Choir and Folkloric Group
12:30 Edward Hynes School Choir
1:00 Fischer Elementary School Choir & Les Petites Dancers
1:30 Jazz Babies
2:30 First Louisiana Mime Troupe
3:30 Lafitte's Louisiana
4:30 Bon Temps Roulez Cloggers
5:00 Percussion, Inc.

PARADES
4:15 All Star Brass Band, Prince of Wales SA&PC & Controllers

SATURDAY, MAY 5

WVUE / WNOE STAGE
11:45 Cousins
1:15 Reggie Hall Band w/ Jessie Hill, Oliver Morgan, Mr. Google Eyes & Albert "Dog Man" Smith
2:45 Charles Brown
4:10 Buckwheat Zydeco
5:45 Ashford & Simpson

WDSU TV 6 STAGE
11:45 Metro N.O. Square & Round Association w/ Johnny Creel
1:00 Tay Hogg & Dixie Pride
2:30 Blackie Forestier & The Cajun Aces
4:00 Mudboy & The Neutrons
5:45 Warren Ceasar & Creole Zydeco Snap

WWL / RAY-BAN STAGE
11:00 Greater N.O. McDonald's High School Jazz Ensemble
12:00 Walter "Lightnin' Bug" Rhodes Blues Band
1:10 Deacon John
2:35 Daniel Lanois
4:00 Marcia Ball w/ Special Guests Angela Strehli & Lou Ann Barton
5:50 The Fabulous Thunderbirds

FAIS DO-DO STAGE
12:00 The Murmurs
1:20 E.R.C./Tany P & DJ Jup
2:50 Porgy Jones Quartet
4:20 Los Sagitarios
5:45 Golden Star Hunters

MARS INC. JAZZ TENT
11:20 Patrice Fisher & Arpa
12:40 Clyde Kerr, Jr.'s Univision
1:50 Alvin "Red" Tyler Quartet
3:10 Improvisational Arts Quintet
4:40 Branford Marsalis
6:10 Earl Turbinton, Jr.

COX / A&E ECONOMY HALL TENT
11:25 Lady Charlotte & Jazz Men
12:30 Young Tuxedo Brass Band
1:50 Placide Adams Original Dixieland Hall Band
3:10 Louisiana Repertory Jazz Ensemble
4:40 Harlem Jazz & Blues Band
6:10 Banu Gibson & Her Hot Jazz Orchestra

CONGO SQUARE STAGE
11:30 NOCCA Jazz Band
12:45 Troupe Louines Louinis Haitian Dance Theatre
2:00 Golden Eagles Mardi Gras Indians
3:20 Ruben & His Salseros
4:30 National Dance Company of Senegal
6:00 La Banda Blanco

2:45 Percy Sledge w/ Blue Eyed Soul Revue
4:10 Tommy Ridgley & The Untouchables w/ Al Johnson, Chuck Carbo & Benny Spellman
6:00 John Prine

WDSU TV 6 STAGE
11:15 The Fate Brothers
12:20 Evangeline
1:30 D.L. Menard & The Louisiana Aces
3:00 Tabula Rasa
4:25 Les Freres Michot
5:50 Jude Taylor & His Burning Flames

WWL / RAY-BAN STAGE
11:45 Joe "Cool" Davis Singers
1:15 Terrance Simien
2:45 Mason Ruffner
4:15 Marva Wright & Her Soulful Blues Revue
5:45 Bo Diddley

FAIS DO-DO STAGE
11:45 Audubon Zoo Winter Search
1:15 Troy Turner & Third Gear
2:40 Guitar Slim Jr.
3:50 Larry Garner & The Boogaloo Blues Band

5:10 Tabby Thomas Blues Box Revue w/ Special Guest Henry Gray

MARS INC. JAZZ TENT
11:20 Victor Goines
12:30 Ed Perkins
1:40 Charles Neville
2:50 Rick Margitza Quartet
4:10 Delfeayo Marsalis & Crescent City
5:45 Tribute to Albert Ayler w/ Kidd Jordan

COX / A&E ECONOMY HALL TENT
11:15 Bob French
12:20 Chris Clifton's All Stars
1:30 Sumpens Swingsters
2:45 Anthony "Tuba Fats" Lacen w/ Lady Linda
4:00 N. O. Classic Jazz Orchestra
5:15 David Paquette
6:00 Sam Alcorn

CONGO SQUARE STAGE
11:45 Dillard University Jazz Band
1:10 White Cloud Hunters
2:30 Algorhythms
4:00 Theryl & The Real Life Band
5:30 Eduardo Reye & Sensacion Latina

TRAVEL N.O. LAGNIAPPE TENT
12:00 N.O. High School All-City Jazz Band
1:30 The New Dance Co.
2:45 Bobby Brooks Trio
4:15 John Rankin
5:45 Cool "Lou" Ford Sextet

MUSIC HERITAGE STAGE
11:30 D.L. Menard
1:00 Freddie King & Percy Randolph
2:30 Tabby Thomas Interview
3:30 Tory Turner Interview
5:00 David & Roselyn

RHODES / WYLD GOSPEL TENT
11:45 St. Theresa Gospel Choir
12:30 Gospel Soul Survivors
1:15 Headstart Angels
2:00 McDonogh #35 Sr. High School Gospel Choir
2:45 Aline White & Co.
3:30 Gospel Ecclesiastes
4:15 Kennedy High School Choir
5:00 R. Lee James Chorale
5:45 Revelations featuring Juanita Quincy

TRAVEL N.O. LAGNIAPPE TENT
11:30 Carl LeBlanc & Nature
1:00 Clancy "Blues Boy" Lewis & Sheba
2:15 Anouar Brahem
3:40 Casselberry-Dupree
5:00 Sunnyland Slim
6:15 Ephat Mujuru of Zimbabwe

MUSIC HERITAGE STAGE
11:00 Little Rascals
12:00 Daniel Lanois Interview
1:00 Charles Brown, Allen Toussaint (Interviewer)
2:00 Marce Lacouture & Inez Catalon
4:00 Jon Cleary
5:30 Doug Duffey

RHODES / WYLD GOSPEL TENT
11:45 Greater Bright Morning Star Y.A.C.
12:30 New Beginning Mass Choir
1:15 John Lee & The Heralds of Christ
2:00 International Gospel Singers
2:45 To The Glory of God Community Choir
3:30 The Zulu Ensemble
4:15 Rocks of Harmony
5:00 The Tillman Singers
5:40 First Baptist Church Choir
6:15 The Voices of Fairly High School

CHILDREN'S TENT
12:00 Colleen Salley
1:00 Ephat Mujuru
2:00 New Orleans Free School Performers
3:00 NOCCA Story Theatre Troupe
3:30 David & Roselyn
4:30 Starmakers
5:00 Stone Soup

PARADES
2:00 Taylor Bunch, Algiers Brass Band, Westbank Steppers & Algiers Steppers SA&PCs
4:30 Jolly Bunch, Money Wasters, Tremé Sports SA&PCs & Royal Brass Band

SUNDAY, MAY 6

WVUE / WNOE STAGE
11:00 SUNO Jazz Band
12:20 Charmaine Neville
1:10 Earl King
2:35 BeauSoleil
4:00 Boz Scaggs
5:45 Stevie Ray Vaughn & Double Trouble

WDSU TV 6 STAGE
12:15 Santiago Jazz Fusion
1:45 T-Black & The Zydeco Machine Band
3:10 Kenny Neal
4:35 Gary Brown
6:00 Ritmo Caribeno

WWL / RAY-BAN STAGE
11:00 Herman Jackson & Red Stick
12:05 Katie Webster
1:20 Clifton Chenier & The Red Hot Louisiana Band
3:00 Dr. John
4:35 Irma Thomas & The Professionals
6:00 The Neville Brothers

FAIS DO-DO STAGE
12:00 Moja Nya
1:25 9th Ward Hunters Mardi Gras Indians
2:45 Joan Duvalle Magee & The Foundation Band

4:15 Asian Pacific American Revue
6:00 Bois Sec & Canray French Band

MARS INC. JAZZ TENT
11:20 Angelle Trosclair & The New Relics
12:35 Astral Project
1:45 Fred Kemp
3:00 Harry Connick, Jr.
4:25 Darius Brubeck / Victor Ntoni Quartet & Their Afro-Cool Concept
5:45 Ellis Marsalis

COX / A&E ECONOMY HALL TENT
11:25 Tommy Yetta's N.O. Jazz Band
12:35 Frank Federico & His Medicare Madcaps
1:45 Wallace Davenport
3:00 George French & The N.O. Storyville Jazz Band
4:30 Al Hirt
6:00 Percy Humphrey & His Crescent City Joymakers

CONGO SQUARE STAGE
12:00 Cultural Voices
1:00 Ephat Mujuru
2:00 Casa Samba Brazilian Drum & Dance
3:25 White Eagles Mardi Gras Indians
4:35 Troupe Louines Louinis Haitian Dance Theatre
6:00 National Dance Company of Senegal

TRAVEL N.O. LAGNIAPPE TENT
11:15 Nichols State Jazz Quartet
12:20 Hazel & The Delta Ramblers
1:40 Champion Jack Dupree
3:00 Lil Queenie & Amasa Miller
4:15 Anouar Brahem
5:45 Philip Manuel

MUSIC HERITAGE STAGE
12:00 Champion Jack Dupree, Allen Toussaint Interviewer
1:00 Dr. John Interview
3:30 Rebirth Brass Band
4:30 Yellow Pocahontas Interview

RHODES / WYLD GOSPEL TENT
11:45 Friendly Travelers
12:30 The Veal Family

1:15 The Sunshine Connection
2:00 New Rising Sun Soul Specials
2:45 Sherman Washington & The Zion Harmonizers w/ Aaron Neville
3:30 The Williams Brothers
4:30 St. Francis DeSales Golden Voices
5:05 Greater Macedonia
5:40 Raymond Myles & The Rams w/ Christine Myles
6:15 Gospel Soul Children

CHILDREN'S TENT
12:00 Music for Children by Dennis
1:00 Janice Harrington
1:30 Buck Fever
2:00 Mama Linda Eubanks
3:00 Jamal Batiste
4:00 Chakula cha Jua Theatre Company
5:00 Kumbuka African Drum and Dance Collective

PARADES
2:00 Fun Lovers, Just Steppers, Scene Booster SA&PCs & Society Brass Band
4:30 Calliope High Steppers, Lady Bucks, Men Bucks SA&PCs & Olympia Brass Band

NIGHT CONCERTS

FRIDAY, APRIL 27, 7 P.M. & MIDNIGHT
"Blues With A Feeling"
B.B. King
Etta James and The Roots Band
John Hammond
Deacon John & The Ivories
The River Tent
SATURDAY, APRIL 28, 7 P.M.
Linda Ronstadt featuring Aaron Neville
The subdudes
The River Tent
SATURDAY, APRIL 28, 9 P.M.
Ramsey Lewis
The Dirty Dozen Brass Band
Willie Tee
Marty Most and The Rhythm-Plus featuring Alvin Batiste
Riverboat Hallelujah Concert Hall

SUNDAY, APRIL 29, 8 P.M.
Gospel Is Alive!
Walter Hawkins & The Hawkins Family
The Mighty Clouds of Joy
Bobby Jones and New Life
Raymond Myles and Sister Christine Myles
Saenger Theatre
MONDAY, APRIL 30, 8 P.M.
Dew Drop Inn Revisited
Dave Bartholomew Big Band with special guests Aaron Neville, Johnny Adams, Tommy Ridgely, Chuck Carbo, Bobby Marchan featuring "5 Friends" and Carolyn Williams
Riverboat Hallelujah Concert Hall, 3615 Tulane Avenue
WEDNESDAY, MAY 2, 8 P.M.
Gary Burton Reunion with Pat Methany, Mitch Foreman, Marc Johnson, Peter Erskine, the Chick Corea Elektric Band, The Delfeayo Marsalis Group featuring Donald Harrison, Cyrus Chestnut, Ralph Peterson, Charnett Moffett, Marlon Jordan)
The River Tent
THURSDAY, MAY 3, 8 P.M.
La Noche Latina
Celia Cruz
Jose Alberto "El Canario" y Su Orquesta
Invitado Especial-Luis Enrique y Su Orquesta
La Banda Blanca
The River Tent
FRIDAY, MAY 4, 7 & MIDNIGHT
Ashford & Simpson
The O'Jays
The James Rivers Movement
The River Tent
SATURDAY, MAY 5, 7 P.M. & MIDNIGHT
The Neville Brothers
Ladysmith Black Mambazo Arrow
The River Tent
SATURDAY, MAY 5, 9 P.M.
Ornette Coleman & Prime Time
Tribute to Albert Ayler featuring Dewey Redman, Sunny Murray, Frank Wright, Edward "Kidd" Jordan, Elton Herron
Riverboat Hallelujah Concert Hall

BACKING UP THE MUSICIANS

The "backline" is a term used by professionals that describes the instruments and equipment at a music concert sometimes provided by the venue. Generally the backline consists of a drum set, bass and guitar amplifiers and a piano. For Jazz Fest, having a backline is crucial to a smooth production. This was not always the case.

In the beginning, musicians had to bring their own gear to the Jazz Festival. It was a small production with small stages and not a lot of money. Crews comprised of one or two people coupled with friends helping out would stage the shows, meaning setting up sound and moving equipment in between acts.

When Jazz Fest moved to the Fair Grounds, artists would drive their vehicles to the back of the stage to unload their gear. And when a scheduled act would finish his or her set, all of that person's gear had to be moved off stage, or in some cases, to another stage for the same musician to back another artist. In 1973 a perfect example was the Meters. When the set was finished, George Porter and Zigaboo Modeliste had to grab their bass amp and drums and run to another stage to back up Professor Longhair on his set. This was very common in the early years of Jazz Fest.

If something broke, it had to be fixed on the spot and backline crew would sometimes have to run across the infield to another stage or go begging at Mr. Eddie's electrical compound for whatever they needed. The early stagehands had to be very good at handling sudden, unexpected problems, or become very good at it quickly.

In early days, small 10 by 10 stages with metal railings sprinkled the infield, and festival attendees could lean on the stage rails to hear the music. These first stages were the Mardi Gras stages that belonged to the City of New Orleans for its special events. When Tague Richardson came on board with Jazz Festival, he would co-ordinate with the city for what was needed at the Fair Grounds and then build the rest. It was a big day when Jazz Fest had grown enough to have the larger stages, and Tague would build all of that too.

Hall Piano Company came on fairly early supplying pianos for Jazz Fest and Sherman Bernard would come out daily to tune them. Sherman would replace Hall, supplying pianos for the Festival, but it would be some years before a full backline would be provided. Sponsorship from companies like Fender was still a long way off.

It all grew and evolved out of love for the music. Many early stage crews didn't get paid, they volunteered. They just wanted to see it happen and see it work.

There are stories of musicians bringing broken amps and keyboards to Jazz Fest to be fixed, knowing someone would have to figure it out for the show to go on. Much of that was just playful harassment from certain local musicians to keep folks at the Festival on their toes. The majority of artists booked for Jazz Festival have always tried to put their best foot forward. However, many older artists, booked in the first years didn't have the kind of equipment that was powerful enough to carry the distances required in an out door arena.

Providing proper sound for an outdoor event has very special requirements. The first sound company to enlist with Jazz Fest was Hanley Sound from Boston. Pace and Pyramid sound companies were the first local outfits to enlist with the Festival. Though complaints about the sound quality seem endemic to the Fest, with professional sound companies on board the quality of the sound has continued to improve.

For the last 18 years or so, Reggie Toussaint has been in charge of making sure the sound is consistent and the quality stays on the cutting edge. Sound companies bid to provide back and front line for all the stages, and each year after the Festival is over the quality of their work is rated. If they screw it up, they don't come back. This is a highly competitive business and there is a lot of money involved. Negotiations can be very cut throat, but at the end of the day it's the sound, both onstage for the artists, and in the crowd for the consumer that counts.

Companies providing backline have to address whatever special requirements the artists booked may have: B3 organ, grand piano or preferred electric keyboards; Yamaha, Roland, Korg-- whatever the artist prefers has to be delivered and on stage at show time.

Some artists have endorsements deals with major companies that require them to only play the equipment they are paid to advertise. These musical instrument companies in turn are trying to get backline companies to push their brands and sometimes give them free gear for promotion, hoping that when artists that haven't specified their backline play on their gear, they'll like it, and maybe buy it when they upgrade. Things have come a long way since the Festival moved to the Fair Grounds site with a bunch of hippies doing the best they could.

The Jazz & Heritage Festival grew organically- the music, the food, the crafts, the attendance, the layout, the stages, and the backline. It took time, trial and error, and a much larger expense budget to get it to where it is today. Now of course, it rocks.

THE PET DE KAT KREWE

It is fair to say that most people who attend Jazz Fest have a good enough experience to want to do so again. Many groups of friends make return visits to Jazz Fest every few years as informal reunions, while Jazz Fest regulars can often be heard proudly recounting how many times they have been to the Fair Grounds in April and May. Few people however can claim the level of loyalty to this great Festival as that group of music lovers that call themselves the Pet de Kat Krewe.

The Pet de Kat Krewe is, in their own words, "a loosely disorganized, professional audience." Members, who often go by aliases such as IBJammin, JuJu and Marcus Ya Ya,

come from all over the country, and although they gather at many music festivals around the world, Jazz Fest is the number one event that Pet de Kat Krewe members long for. Their presence is guaranteed every year, and they can be identified by their annual Pet de Kat Krewe grinning cat t-shirts. According to their web site (www.petdekat.com), Jazz Fest is "the festival of festivals, the party of parties, the musical celebration of life itself."

For the members of Pet de Kat Krewe, not to mention the Fess Heads, Threadheads and other like-minded souls, Jazz Fest provides an annual pulse to a lifetime devoted to live music. These people that

celebrate the music at the New Orleans Jazz & Heritage Festival may be unified under an organizational name, but their backgrounds and livelihoods represents a diversity as broad as the appeal of New Orleans musical culture. Pet de Kat Krewe members have day jobs, and whether that be managing corporate accounts, teaching at elementary school, or selling tie died t-shirts, they all find common ground at the Fair Grounds.

That whole sub-cultures have been born and are sustained within the confines of a festival devoted to cultural celebration is one big compliment to the Jazz Fest management team.

Sadie Goodson and Kid Sheik Colar

1991

It started raining. It kept on raining. After that, it rained some more. Throughout Thursday the downpour continued and the Festival staff had to start facing the reality of the deluge and its consequences. After all of the hard work and preparation, after all of the careful planning, after all of the excitement of getting ready for the biggest and best Jazz Festival ever, they might have to cancel. The infield was flooded on Thursday, but still everyone hoped, when there was a break in the rain, that there would be a shot of saving opening day. "How much rain can there be?" Quint Davis asked. The sky answered with a whole lot more.

The average annual rainfall in New Orleans runs a little over 18 inches by the end of April. As of Friday at 1 p.m. it was a whopping 44.2 inches. The last time the city got even close to that amount of rain was back in 1983, logging 35.6 inches in the same period.

A photograph in the *Times Picayune* newspaper told the tale. Milton Mary, one of the Festival production staff, stood in a small lake near the Congo Square Stage on Thursday afternoon. There wasn't another soul

in sight. He was searching for a drain, but there wasn't any place for the water to go. New Orleans is already below sea level, as every local who as a child, tried to dig a hole to China knows. A child with Momma's big cooking spoon can create a muddy lake in the backyard on a clear day in about a hour. The ground was saturated. It was hopeless.

As the rain continued to fall through the night, the Fair Grounds became a turbulent lake with lightning spiking across the sky and gusting winds tearing tents apart and knocking down displays in the Louisiana Folklife area. Finally, the Festival Production staff threw in the towel. At 8 a.m. on Friday morning the Festival was cancelled for the second time in three years due to rain.

"You can have fun at Jazz Fest in the rain" said Quint Davis, the Festival's Producer/Director, "But this was not a fun rain. This was a murderous rain. We were in a total non-functional situation."

On Friday afternoon, instead of thousands of people wandering around with food and beer, smiling and listening to great music drifting across the infield, there were hundreds of extremely tired staff and volunteers trying desperately to clean up debris, cover sound systems with plastic, dump sand in trouble spots that wouldn't drain and lay boards over other muddy areas. 85 musical acts were cancelled for the day- and although there is a rain clause in the contract, Quint Davis said they would be paid. Many crafts people also, some who came from long distances to participate in the Festival, had to face a tremendous loss of revenue.

Outside the Fair Grounds, security crews were turning away hardcore Festival fans who braved the rain throughout the day. Some went away mad, but most just went on downtown to find some good food and music. Tower Records on North Peter's Street was packed with live music in the lobby and people lining up at the cash registers with CDs and tapes in hand that they would have bought at the Fair Grounds. Tower broke their single day sales record and Louisiana Music Factory had a similar experience, with crowds of people who had planned to spend the day at the Fair Grounds pouring all through the city looking for things to do.

The clubs about town were overflowing that night, The

Eddie Bo

Meters packed the house at Tipitina's, Danny Barker played Palm Court, Germaine Bazzle could be heard at the Hotel Inter-Continental, Muddy Water's uptown on Oak Street had a hot show with Lonnie Brooks and Tinsley Ellis that was also celebrating Alligator Records 20th year in business. The Iguanas played Mid-City Bowling Lanes, Casa Samba had everybody dancing at Café' Brazil and Johnny J. and the Hitmen brought all of the rockabilly fans out to Carrolton Station. Terrance Simien and the Mallet Playboys also got a chance to greet their fans when they played at Michaul's that night.

The next day when the New Orleans Jazz & Heritage Festival opened, the soggy, waterlogged grass soon became one huge mud pit with small islands of sickly green and one concrete river to navigate the whole. It didn't take very long for everyone to completely give up on the idea of staying out of the mud, and in the true spirit of New Orleans, everyone accepted that they were gonna just have to get a little funky. Once that bridge was crossed, a great time was had by all. Many shoes were sucked off of dancing feet in front of the Fais Do-Do stage. When the subdudes started their set at 2:55, there was a nice muddy trough full of people with mud above their ankles in front of Stage 1, and by late afternoon there were several excellent

'mud slides' for folks who had really embraced getting messy at the Fest. At the end of the day on Saturday, 45,000 people had enjoyed a great day of music, danced in the mud, eaten a lot of good food and destroyed the remaining grass on the infield.

The show at Municipal Auditorium was a pageant of Kings; The King of Jazz, The King of Blues and the King of Zydeco. This evening would open many ears to new concepts with a triple bill of Miles Davis, B.B. King and Rockin' Dopsie and the Zydeco Twisters. Frustrated but now dried and combed Festgoers finally got the complete experience: they

2:45 Danneel Pre-Vocational Choir
3:30 Ecclesiastes Gospel Singers
4:15 The Smooth Family of Slidell
5:00 Alcee Fortier Sr. High Concert Choir
5:45 McDonogh #35 Gospel Choir

PARADES
4:00 Philadelphia Four and Blue Monday SA&PCs, Bon Temp Roulez Cloggers Club with Young Olympia Brass Band

SATURDAY, APRIL 27

WVUE / WNOE STAGE
11:15 U.N.O. Big Band & Combo
12:20 Warren Ceasar & Creole Zydeco Snap
1:35 Boozoo Chavis & Magic Sounds
2:55 The Subdudes
4:20 Beausoleil
6:00 Zachary Richard

GUMBO STAGE
11:15 Rumboogie
12:35 Philip Manuel
1:50 Troy L. Deramus & Country Hill
3:15 Marva Wright & Her Soulful Blues Revue
4:45 Charmaine Neville & Friends
6:00 Jackson State U. Big Band

WWL / RAY-BAN STAGE
11:15 Southern University of New Orleans Ensemble
12:40 Jean Knight w/ Blue-Eyed Soul
2:10 Los Lobos
4:00 B.B. King
5:45 Irma Thomas & The Professionals

FAIS DO-DO STAGE
12:20 Bobby Brooks Trio w/ Mary Bonnette
1:30 Kat & The Kittens
2:35 Ninth Ward Hunters
3:40 Clarence Edwards Band
4:55 Evangeline
6:10 The Iguanas

MARS INC. JAZZ TENT
11:30 Walter Payton & Ballet Filé
12:40 Nicholas Payton
1:50 Earl Turbinton
3:00 Dorothy Donegan
4:20 Ellis Marsalis Quartet
5:45 Dirty Dozen Brass Band

COX CABLE ECONOMY HALL TENT
12:00 Local International All-stars Jazz Band
1:20 Michael White Quartet w/ Barbara Shorts
2:30 Young Tuxedo Brass Band w/ 2nd Liners Ladies Sequence
3:40 Benny Waters
4:45 George French Original Storyville Band
6:05 Tommy Yetta's New Orleans Jazz Band

CONGO SQUARE STAGE
11:15 Santiago Jazz Fusion
12:20 Spirit Ensemble
1:35 Percussion Inc.
2:55 Y'shua Manzy & The World Beat Band
4:10 Odadaa!
5:40 Thomas Mapfumo & Blacks Unlimited

TRAVEL N.O. LAGNIAPPE TENT
11:20 Delgado Community College Jazz Ensemble
12:30 Clancy "Blues Boy" Lewis
1:40 The Whitstein Brothers

New Orleans JAZZ
DANNY BARKER
JAZZ FEST STATION
APRIL 26 - MAY 5, 1991
NEW ORLEANS LA 70119
NEW ORLEANS JAZZ & HERITAGE FESTIVAL
Official Commemorative Cachet

had their minds blown, their souls shaken and their feet rocking and they didn't even have to slog from one stage to the next. At the other end of Basin Street on Saturday, "An Evening With Harry Connick Jr." at the Saenger Theatre was another choice. Harry honored the tradition of musical greatness associated with New Orleans by winning a Grammy in 1991 and was touring the world with a full orchestra, performing his own compositions (some co-written with local bassist Ramsey McLean), and his original arrangements of classics from the 50's and 60's. Let's understate that Harry swung that night.

Sunday's attendance at the Fair Grounds shied off a bit, with only 35,000 attending, but everyone associated with the Festival from a production standpoint was breathing a

sigh of relief. There would be a massive amount of hard work done between the weeks of the Festival to finish " mopping up" the mess of 80,000 drinking, eating, dancing bodies on the rain-soaked turf at the Fair Grounds but everybody knew, it could have been worse.

The Ray-Ban Stage had a hell of a lineup on Sunday. The Ohio Players, followed by Dianne Reeves, with our own David Torkanowsky as her musical director and keyboardist, and local Chris Severin on bass. Michael McDonald followed Dianne, and the Ray-Ban closed with Dr. John supported by his New Orleans posse.

Monday night was piano night at Tipitina's, featuring Art Neville, David Torkanowsky, Willie Tee, Eddie Bo and a nonstop sit in set of New Orleans' finest on the ivories, but you

had plenty of time to go to the Saenger Theatre first and catch "Gospel Is Alive!" at 7:30 with the inimitable Evangelist Shirley Caesar and the Caesar Singers, Tramaine Hawkins, The

Frankie Ford

"Fourteen years ago I played Jazz Fest in a wheel chair. I'd had surgery on a ruptured disc. People tell me I had a stroke and maybe I did during my surgery but I'm really not sure. After the operation I was paralyzed from my chest down and I was told I would never walk again. It didn't do nothing to my voice, though. So I was at the Fest in a wheel chair and my doctor Frank Culicchia was there and he instructed and helped me take my brace off before I sang. I stood up that day and for me that was close to a miracle." CLARENCE "FROGMAN" HENRY

Williams Brothers and the St. Francis De Sales Choir. The true miracle here is that the Saenger didn't just blow up from the concentrated energy created from so much passionate praise, love and celebration of faith. Ms. Caesar, in 1991 had already received five Grammy awards, three gold albums, and six Dove awards. She was also a member of Durham, North Carolina's City Council. The Williams Brothers, from Smithdale, Mississippi started recording in 1973 and had achieved numerous hits on the Gospel charts by 1991. They began performing as children under the direction of their father Leon "Pop" Williams in 1960, so they were literally "raised up" from childhood praising the Lord. Tramaine Hawkins was also raised in the gospel tradition with her mother, Lois Davis singing in

the church and her grandfather, Bishop E.E. Cleveland a highly respected Pastor of Ephesians Church of God in Christ in the East Bay Area. Our own St Francis De Sales Choir expressed their program under the direction of Lois Dejean.

Tuesday, April 30th was *"A Tribute to New Orleans Jazz Musicians"* to honor Willie and Percy Humphrey, George "Kid Sheik" Colar, Harold "Duke" Dejean, Waldren "Frog" Joseph, and the late George Lewis. This show was a who's who of top New Orleans artists that once again stated the influence our local music has had on the world. The members of the Local International All-Stars represented four countries outside of the U.S.; John "Kid" Simmons, trumpet; Chris Burke, clarinet; Frank Naundorf, on trombone, Ron Simpson on

banjo; Maggie Kinson, piano; Paul Henderson on bass, and Andrew Hall on drums.

Top sidemen graced a number of great bands: Percy Humphrey's Crescent City Joymakers, with Narvin Kimball, banjo; James Prevost, bass;

Frank Demond, trombone; Joseph Lastie, drums; Phamous Lambert, piano; Manuel Crusto, clarinet; and Percy Humphrey, trumpet and leader, and the Next Generation Jazz Band which was comprised of Wendell Brunious on trumpet and leading

the band, Don Vappie, banjo; Michael White, clarinet; Freddie Lonzo, trombone; Joseph Lastie, drums; Thaddeus Richard, piano; and Chris Severin on bass represented the home front, as did the All-Star Brass Band; led by Placide Adams on snare,

George French

Nowell Glass on bass drum, Milton Batiste and Gregory Stafford, both on trumpet; Wendell Eugene, trombone; Ralph Johnson, clarinet; Ernest Watson, tenor sax; Edgar Smith on the bass horn; Maynard Chatters on trombone and Clyde Kerr Jr. on trumpet. Most in the audience may not have known their names but the applause was loud and enthusiastic on the many solos several players took.

The second weekend's selection of artists to enjoy at the Fair Grounds was huge and diverse. The Festival had added a Thursday to the second week, which worked and became a permanent addition to the Jazz Festival. This year, inexplicably the Dixie Kups became the Dixie Cups. Once again the Festival broke attendance records, with the earliest

estimates resting at 333,000. Somehow, no matter what happens, Jazz Fest continues to grow. Maybe it's the music or it could be the food, but in 1991 everyone learned one important thing; a bit of extra mud made no difference at all.

John Mooney and Ed Bradley

3:20 New Leviathan Oriental Foxtrot
Orchestra
4:40 Pete Fountain
6:00 Danny Barker's Jazz Hounds

CONGO SQUARE STAGE
11:45 Fuel
12:50 Willie Tee
2:00 Kennedy High Cougar Band
3:15 Lil' Mack & Warren Mayes Rap
Revue
4:35 Odadaa!
5:50 Loketo

TRAVEL N.O. LAGNIAPPE TENT
11:30 Beat Doctors
1:00 Quiet Storm
2:15 White Cloud Hunters
3:35 Satan & Adam
4:45 Hackberry Ramblers
6:00 Hot Strings of New Orleans

MUSIC HERITAGE TENT
12:15 Silas Hogan
1:15 Kalamu ya Salaam
2:30 Clarence Gatemouth Brown
3:45 Queen Ida
4:45 Casa Samba

RHODES / WYLD GOSPEL TENT
11:45 The Coolie Family
12:30 The Randolph Brothers
1:15 The Friendly Travelrs
2:00 New Orleans Spiritualettes
2:45 New Zion Trio plus One
3:30 The Famous Jackson
Southernaires
4:30 The Soulful Heavenly Stars
5:15 First Church of God in Christ
6:00 Holy Hill Gospel Singers

PARADES
2:00 Olympia Aid and Ladies Zulu
SA&PCs with Tremé Brass Band
4:00 Fifth Division Rollers and
Devastation SA&PCs with Doc
Paulin Brass Band

THURSDAY, MAY 2

WVUE / WNOE STAGE
11:30 Grupo Kaibil
1:00 Snooks Eaglin
2:30 Kate & Anna McGarrigle
4:00 Taj Mahal
5:30 Richie Havens

GUMBO STAGE
11:20 N.O.B.D.
12:35 Cowboy Mouth
1:50 Larry Garner & The Boogaloo
Blues Band
3:15 Lee Bates
4:40 Filé
6:00 Bryan Lee & The Jumpstreet
Five

WWL / RAY-BAN STAGE
12:00 Joseph "Cool" Davis Singers
1:30 Lynne August & Hot Knights
3:00 Bobby Marchan
& Higher Ground
4:30 Eddie Bo
6:00 C.J. Chenier & The Red Hot
Louisiana Band

FAIS DO-DO STAGE
12:25 Newton High Jazz Ensemble
1:40 Audubon Zoo's Jazz Search
Winner
3:00 The Hooligans
4:30 Big Sun
6:00 Blue Sister

MARS INC. JAZZ TENT
12:00 Patrice Fisher & Arpa
1:20 Angelle Trosclair & New Relics
2:45 Steve Masakowski & Friends
4:15 Charles Neville Diversity
5:45 Ronnie Kole

COX CABLE ECONOMY HALL TENT
11:30 Warren Clark & The French Quarter Band
1:00 Robert Harris
2:30 Jacque Gauthe & Creole Rice Yerba Buena Jazz Band
4:00 June Gardner & The Fellows
5:30 Joe Simon & The Original Crescent City Jazz Band

CONGO SQUARE STAGE
11:20 Carl LeBlanc Group w/ Sharon Martin
12:40 Josh & Co.
1:45 Butakada de Muloto & Culu Dancers
2:45 White Eagles
4:00 Wanda Rouzan & A Taste of New Orleans
5:30 Cyril Neville & The Uptown All-stars

TRAVEL N.O. LAGNIAPPE TENT
12:00 Hammond State School Strawberry Jammers
1:15 New Orleans Jr. High All-City Jazz Band
2:25 East Jefferson High Jazz Warriors
4:00 A.J. Loria
5:25 Ironin' Board Sam

MUSIC HERITAGE TENT
12:30 Deacon John
1:45 Taj Mahal
2:45 Julia & Valentino

3:15 Eddie Bo
4:15 Miss Lillian Bennett
5:15 Left Ear

RHODES / WYLD GOSPEL TENT
11:00 The Four Gospel Legends
11:45 The Mighty Gospel Seals
12:30 Zion Travelers Singers
1:15 Revelation Gospel Singers
2:00 Southern Gospel Singers
2:45 Mt. Pilgrim Young Adult Choir
3:30 Christian Outreach Community Chorus
4:15 Juliet Arrington
5:00 St. Rose Delima Gospel Choir
5:45 South Louisiana Mass Choir

PARADES
4:30 Jolly Bunch SA&PC with Lil' Rascals Brass Band
All Day•Percy Randolph (Live amplified harmonica on wheels around the grounds)

FRIDAY, MAY 3

WVUE / WNOE STAGE
11:40 C.P. Love
1:00 George Porter, Jr. & Runnin' Pardners
2:30 The Batiste Brothers
4:20 James Rivers Movement
5:50 Ernie K-Doe w Milton Batiste's Magnificent 7th & Guest Jessie Hill

GUMBO STAGE
11:15 Pedro Cruz Band
12:25 Johnnie Sonnier & Cajun Heritage
1:40 Bas Clas
3:00 Kenny Bill Stinson
4:30 Warren Storm & Tommy McLain w/ Yesterday's Band
6:00 Tribe Nunzio

WWL / RAY-BAN STAGE
12:00 Chris Thomas
1:25 The Bluerunners
2:50 Deacon John
4:15 Marcia Ball
5:45 John Mayall & The Bluesbreakers

FAIS DO-DO STAGE
11:30 Four For Nothing
12:40 Original Yellow Jackets
1:50 Miss Ann Goodly & The Zydeco Brothers
3:10 Mamou
4:30 Johnny J. & The Hitmen
6:00 John Rankin

MARS INC. JAZZ TENT
11:20 Richwell Ison / Kirk Ford Experience
12:30 Ed Perkins w/ Michael Ward Project
1:45 Chris Lacinak
3:00 Betty Shirley & The Joel Simpson Trio
4:15 Fred Kemp
5:45 The Harper Brothers

COX CABLE ECONOMY HALL TENT
12:00 Bob French Original Tuxedo Jazz Band
1:30 Kid Sheik's Storyville Ramblers
3:00 Andrew Hall's Society Jazz Band
4:30 Sam Alcorn
6:00 Banu Gibson & New Orleans Hot Jazz

CONGO SQUARE STAGE
11:45 Dillard University Jazz Band
1:00 Cool Lou Ford Sextet
2:00 Free Spirit Stilt Walkers Parade
2:45 John Boutté
4:00 Guardians of the Flame
5:00 Free Spirit Stilt Walkers Parade
5:45 Irie Vibration

TRAVEL N.O. LAGNIAPPE TENT
12:00 "Honey Boy" Edwards
1:25 Carlos Sanchez "Amanecer Flamenco"
2:40 The Evening Star String Band
3:50 Spencer Bohren
5:00 Phil DeGruy & Guess Who
6:10 Hot Licks Cookies

MUSIC HERITAGE TENT
12:15 The Batiste Brothers
1:15 Spencer Bohren
2:15 Marcia Ball
3:15 Jumpin' Johnny Sansone
4:15 John Mayall
5:00 Julie & Valentino

RHODES / WYLD GOSPEL TENT

11:45 Gospel Soul Survivors
12:30 First Revolution Gospel Singers
1:15 True Tone Gospel Singers
2:00 Kennedy High Gospel Choir
2:45 Aline White & Company
3:30 Headstart Angels
4:15 Landrum Singers
5:00 Ronald James Chorale
6:25 Johnson Extensions

PARADES

3:30 Just Stepping and Controllers SA&PCs with All Star Brass Band

SATURDAY, MAY 4

WVUE / WNOE STAGE

11:45 Preston Frank & His Family Band
1:15 Bela Fleck & The Flecktones
2:45 Wayne Toups & Zydecajun
4:15 The Indigo Girls
6:00 The Dixie Cups

GUMBO STAGE

11:15 Health Unit #1
12:35 Dash Rip Rock
1:50 Ramsey McLean
3:00 Bois Sec Ardoin & Canray Fontenot
4:25 Nathan & Zydeco Cha Cha
5:50 Mississippi South

WWL / RAY-BAN STAGE

11:20 Greg Barnhill
12:35 Rebirth Brass Band
1:35 Johnny Adams
3:00 Maceo Parker & Roots Revisited
4:25 Leon Russell
5:55 The Meters

FAIS DO-DO STAGE

11:30 Mardi Gras Indian Council
12:40 Rap Revue with E.R.C. & Baby T & Devious D
2:15 Kenny Neal
3:30 The Jolly Boys
4:45 Gray Eagle String Band
6:00 Tabby Thomas & The Mighty House Rockers

MARS INC. JAZZ TENT

11:45 Greater N.O. McDonalds High School Jazz Ensemble
12:55 Delfeayo Marsalis Sextet
2:25 Astral Project
3:55 Alvin Batiste & The Jazzstronauts
5:25 Arthur Prysock & The Red Prysock Quartet

COX CABLE ECONOMY HALL TENT

12:00 Placide Adams Original Dixieland Hall Jazz Band
1:10 Percy Humphrey & The Eagle Brass Band w/ Second Liners: The Calendar Girls
2:30 Val Barbara
3:40 Lady Charlotte
4:40 Jeannie & Jimmy Cheatham & Sweet Baby Blues Band
6:00 Wallace Davenport & His N.O. Jazz Band

CONGO SQUARE STAGE

11:15 The Shepherd Band
12:35 Kumbuka Dance & Drum Collective
1:50 Ruben "Mr. Salsa" Gonzales & His Salseros

3:00 Ballet National Folkloric Garifuna de Honduras
4:30 Los Gatos Bravos
6:00 Boukman Eksperyans

TRAVEL N.O. LAGNIAPPE TENT

11:15 Louisiana Tech Jazz Band
12:25 Pat Flory
1:35 Hosanna Band
3:00 Chris Smither
4:20 Golden Eagles
5:55 Joyful Commanders

MUSIC HERITAGE TENT

11:15 Jon Cleary
12:00 International Dance Ensemble (instruction & audience participation)
1:45 Jesse Thomas
3:00 Johnny Adams
4:00 Kenny Neal
5:30 Chris Smither

RHODES / WYLD GOSPEL TENT

11:45 Greater Bright Morning Star B.C.
12:30 Melody Clouds
1:15 St. Peter B. C. Gospel Choir
2:00 Second Morning Star B.C.
2:45 The Gospel Choralettes
3:30 The Zulu Ensemble
4:15 To the Glory of God Community Choir
5:00 Southern Bells
6:15 St. James Chapel B.C.

PARADES

1:00 Money Wasters, Prince of Wales & Tremé Sports SA&PCs with Tuba Fats and The Chosen Few Brass Band
3:45 Algiers Steppers, Taylor Bunch & West Bank Steppers SA&PCs with Rebirth Brass Band

SUNDAY, MAY 5

WVUE / WNOE STAGE

11:30 Loyola University Jazz Band
1:00 Buckwheat Zydeco
2:25 Frankie Ford's Revue
4:00 Allen Toussaint
5:40 The Radiators

GUMBO STAGE

11:30 Willis Prudhomme & Zydeco Express
1:00 Allen Fontenot & The Country Cajuns
2:30 Steve Riley & The Mamou Playboys
4:00 Russ Russell & The Rustlers w/ Phil Meeks
5:30 Dewey Balfa & Friends

WWL / RAY-BAN STAGE

11:30 Larry Hamilton
12:40 Oliver Morgan, Mr. Google Eyes, Dynamite Red w/ Reggie Hall Band
2:30 Frankie Beverly & Maze
4:30 Robert Cray
6:00 The Neville Brothers

FAIS DO-DO STAGE

11:45 Force of Habit
1:15 Los Sagitorios
2:45 J. Monque'D Blues Band w/ Henry Gray
4:25 Hector Gallardo & His Songo All-stars
5:50 John Delafose and The Eunice Playboys

MARS INC. JAZZ TENT

11:45 Victor Goines Group
1:15 Germaine Bazzle
2:45 El Blackwell Project
4:15 Arturo Sandoval
5:45 Jackie McLean

COX CABLE ECONOMY HALL TENT

11:25 Milford Dolliole
12:35 Frank Federico & The Medicare Madcaps
1:45 Dejan's Olympia Brass Band w/ 2nd Liners – Golden Trumpets
3:00 Jimmy Maxwell and His Orchestra
4:30 Champion Jack Dupree & Kenn Landing
6:00 Percy Humphrey and Crescent City Joymakers

CONGO SQUARE STAGE

11:30 Ishangi Family
12:50 The Jolly Boys
2:00 Creole Wild West
3:00 Ballet Nacional Folklorico Garifuna de Honduras
4:30 Salif Keita
6:10 Southern University Marching Band

TRAVEL N.O. LAGNIAPPE TENT

11:20 NOCCA Jazz Ensemble
12:30 Porgy Jones Quintet
1:45 Hazel and The Delta Ramblers
3:00 Scott Goudeau Band
4:30 Woodenhead
6:00 Willie Metcalf Group

MUSIC HERITAGE TENT

11:45 Ya Ya's
12:45 Kermit Ruffins
1:45 Marce Lacouture & Inez Catalon
2:45 Champion Jack Dupree
3:45 Jackie McLean
4:45 Oliver Morgan & Reggie Hall

RHODES / WYLD GOSPEL TENT

11:45 The Friendly Travelers
12:30 The Mighty Chariots
1:15 John Lee & The Heralds of Christ
2:00 The Southern Echoes
2:45 The Crownseekers
3:30 Five Blind Boys of Alabama w/ Clarence Fountain
4:30 Val & Love Alive Fellowship Choir
5:05 Greater Macedonia B.C. Choir
5:40 Raymond Myles & The Rams and Christine Myles
6:15 Gospel Soul Children

PARADES

2:00 Scene Booster, Fun Lovers & Calliope High Steppers SA&PCs with Majestic Brass Band
3:45 Buck Jumpers Men, Jetsetters, Buck Jumpers Ladies SA&PCs with Pinstripe Dixieland Brass Band

NIGHT CONCERTS

FRIDAY, APRIL 26, 9 P.M.

A Tribute to Louis Armstrong
The Wynton Marsalis Quintet
Featuring: Doc Cheatham, Ruby Braff, Teddy Riley, Greg Stafford, Danny Barker, Ellis Marsalis, Dr. Michael White, Freddy Lonzo, Nicholas Payton, Thais Clark and Ed Bradley, host.
Theatre of the Performing Arts

SATURDAY, APRIL 27, 9 P.M.

Miles Davis
B. B. King
Rockin' Dopsie & The Zydeco Twisters
Theatre of the Performing Arts

SATURDAY, APRIL 27, 9 P.M.

"An Evening with Harry Connick Jr."
Harry Connick, Jr. and The Harry Connick Jr. Orchestra
Saenger Theatre

SUNDAY, APRIL 28, 9P.M.

"Gospel Is Alive!"
Evangelist Shirley Caesar & The Caesar Singers
Tramaine Hawkins
The Williams Brothers
St. Francis DeSales Choir
Saenger Theater

TUESDAY, APRIL 30, 8 P.M.

A Tribute to New Orleans Traditional Jazz Musicians
Honoring Willie and Percy Humphrey, George "Kid Sheik" Colar, Harold "Duke" Dejan, Waldren "Frog" Joseph, and The late George Lewis featuring Percy Humphrey's Crescent City Joymakers, Local International All-Stars, All Star Brass Band, Next Generation Jazz Band
Riverboat Hallelujah Concert Hall

WEDNESDAY, MAY 1, 8 P.M.

Dew Drop Inn Revisited: The Toussaint Legacy
Allen Toussaint with special guests Irma Thomas, Art Neville, Ernie K-Doe, Jessie Hill, Earl King, Chuck Carbo
Riverboat Hallelujah Concert Hall

THURSDAY, MAY 2, 7:30 P.M.

La Noche Latina
Ruben Blades y Son Del Solar
Los Gatos Bravos
Garifuna de Honduras
Ruben "Mr. Salsa" Gonzalez y Su Salsa Combo
Municipal Auditorium

FRIDAY, MAY 3, 9 P.M.

The Robert Cray Band Featuring the Memphis Horns
John Lee Hooker & The Coast to Coast Blues Band
The Radiators

FRIDAY, MAY 3, 8 P.M.

"Big Band Dance"
The Count Basie Orchestra with Special Guest Cab Calloway
Arthur Prysock with The Red Prysock Orchestra in a tribute to Duke Ellington
Sheraton New Orleans Grand Ballroom

SATURDAY, MAY 3, 9 P.M.

The Neville Brothers
Jimmy Cliff
Milton Nascimento
Municipal Auditorium

SATURDAY, MAY 3, 8:00 P.M.

The Jackie McLean Quartet
The Harper Brothers
The Kent Jordan Quintet
Riverboat Hallelujah Concert Hall

SATURDAY, MAY 3, 12 MIDNIGHT

"Midnight Jam: Tribute to Ed Blackwell"
The Ed Blackwell Project
Donald Harrison, Delfeayo Marsalis And John Boudreaux with other invited guests

1992

Ernie K-Doe

The sun was shining on April 24th. Nothing like opening Friday last year with torrential rainstorms and waterlogged Festival employees gazing out at an empty infield wondering if there would even be a Festival. As the lines formed on Gentilly Boulevard in front of the main entrance on opening day of the 23rd annual New Orleans Jazz & Heritage Festival, local entrepreneurs were walking up and down selling everything from hats and beer holders to pralines, and very excited Festival fans, who had come to New Orleans from all over the world were looking forward to a perfect day of music, food, and indigenous Louisiana culture.

37,000 souls descended on the Fair Grounds Racetrack for opening day, setting a new record for the Festival. Some first timers went to the information booth, manned by Larry Stewart and others throughout the day, asking where they should go to hear some good music. "It's all around you" Larry answered, after a good laugh.

The Humble Travelers began to raise the roof at 11:45, giving a little extra time for the Gospel Tent devotees to make it across the infield and not miss

GLOBALLY

Euro Disney opens in Marne-La-Vallee, France, to the dismay of French intellectuals lamenting the spread of American popular culture.

President George Bush and Russian President Boris Yeltzin announce a formal end to the Cold War.

NATIONALLY

Riots erupt in Los Angeles after the policemen who beat Rodney King are acquitted.

Dr. Mae C. Jemison becomes the first African-American woman astronaut, spending more than a week orbiting Earth in the space shuttle Endeavor.

LOCALLY

David Duke loses a bitter campaign for governor to Edwin Edwards, who is elected to an unprecedented fourth term with the (unofficial) slogan "Vote for the Crook — It's Important!"

Tad Gormley Stadium remodeled to host U. S. Olympic Track & Field Trials.

Hurricane Andrew kills 11 people and causes about $1 billion in damages; south-central Louisiana is hardest-hit area outside of Florida.

A study to determine whether Dr. Carl Weiss assassinated senator Huey P. Long is deemed inconclusive, after exhuming Weiss' body.

CULTURALLY

The Internet Society is chartered, and 1,000,000 host computers are connected in a network.

Nicoderm introduced as the first nicotine transdermal patch to help smokers quit smoking.

Bette Midler is Johnny Carson's last guest on the "Tonight Show". He is replaced by Jay Leno.

Fats Domino, Charles Brown, Frogman Henry

WVUE / WNOE STAGE
11:45 Eddie Bo
1:10 Bobby Cure & The Summertime Blues w/ Robert Parker & Billy Tircuit
3:00 Wayne Toups & Zydecajun
4:30 The Subdudes
6:00 Dirty Dozen Brass Band

M&F GIRBAUD / B 97 STAGE
12:00 Slidell Sr. High Jazz Ensemble
1:30 Shot Down In Ecuador
3:00 The Backsliders
4:30 Big Sun
6:00 Jon "King" Cleary

WWL / RAY-BAN STAGE
11:30 UNO Jazz Band
1:00 Boozoo Chavis & Magic Sounds
2:30 Angela Strehli & Lou Ann Barton
4:15 Iguanas
4:55 Evangeline
5:45 Jimmy Buffett & The Coral Reefer Band

FAIS DO-DO STAGE
11:45 East Jefferson H.S. Jazz Warriors
1:10 Golden Star Hunters
2:25 Carl LeBlanc w/ Sharon Martin
4:00 Don Montoucet
5:45 Roscoe Chenier

MARS INC. JAZZ TENT
11:30 Theron Lewis & Unit 7
12:40 Kenyatta Beasley
1:50 Stephanie Jordan
3:00 Tony Bazley Sextet
4:15 Mark Whitfield
5:50 Fred Kemp Quartet

COX CABLE ECONOMY HALL TENT
11:45 Local International Allstars
1:10 Chris Clifton's New Orleans Allstars
2:35 Bob French Original Tuxedo Jazz Band
4:00 Sam Alcorn
5:35 Wallace Davenport & His New Orleans Jazz Band

CONGO SQUARE STAGE
12:00 Ben Hunter & Plantation Posse
1:30 Culu Dancers & Drummers
3:00 Y'Shua Manzy & The World Beat Band
4:30 Burning Flames
6:00 Jean Knight & Blue-Eyed Soul

BANANA BOAT GAZEBO
12:30 Little Freddie King
2:15 Lil' Queenie & John Magnie
4:00 Wild Apaches
5:30 Little Freddie King

MUSIC HERITAGE STAGE
1:00 Across the Atlantic, Betsy McGovern
2:30 Don Montoucet (Interview)
3:45 Wallace Davenport (Interview)
4:45 Roger Lewis & Gregory Davis of Dirty Dozen (Interview)

RHODES / WYLD GOSPEL TENT
11:45 Humble Travelers
12:30 Happy Action Singers
1:15 Bless People Gospel Singers
2:00 Daneel Pre-Vocational Choir
2:45 Friendly Travelers
3:30 Charles Jackson & The Jackson Travelers
4:15 Alcee Fortier Sr. H.S. Gospel Choir
5:00 The Highway QC's
6:00 McDonogh #25 Gospel Choir

anything. Swaying in time wearing their midnight blue robes, the Humble Travelers sang "I'm Going Home" and there was no doubt in anyone's mind that they would be at home with the celestial choir. There was some debate several years before amongst church members and area pastors about whether it was proper for the church choirs to perform at a Festival where beer was sold and where other music that some churches might not approve of was being offered.

Happily, they decided that God loves all the children, drunk or sober, despite their taste in music, or lack thereof. Many people from all over the world have had deeply moving experiences in the Gospel Tent, re-found their souls, made important life decisions, proposed to loved ones, or accidentally gotten smacked by the Holy Ghost when they were just trying to get out of the sun for a minute.

Even though it was a record crowd, there was ample room for all of the public school children who were brought out by local schoolteachers for Jazz Fest field trips to run around without fears of getting lost in the masses. In some other places it might seem strange to bring your class out to a music Festival on a school day, but in New Orleans music is such an integral part of the City's history that it makes perfect sense. It was also very nice for the

Bo Dollis

teachers to wander around on a workday, eating a Mango Freeze and keeping an eye on a group of rambunctious young folk.

Friday night, two very fine opening concerts were available to choose from; Huey Lewis and the News, with Dr. John and Fats Domino at the Municipal Auditorium, which seemed mildly strange. However, the Tower of Power horns were part of Mr. Lewis's show and he was fun and brought a 'pop' element to a classic New Orleans evening. Jazz fanciers could go to the Orpheum Theatre and enjoy the fabulous Ms. Betty Carter, along with Victor Goines and Mark Whitfield. Both shows were 9 p.m.

On Saturday at the Fair Grounds, another beautiful day dawned and attendance was huge. 47,000 people came to dance, eat and find their friends that they only get to catch up with once a year when they make the pilgrimage from around the world to Jazz Fest.

In earlier years, people would arrange meetings at the flagpole, which was pretty much the standard meeting place for everyone. By 1992 however hordes of people scheduling rendezvous complicated finding someone. People therefore created their own flagpoles. There was the "Fess Head" of course, and many other 'poles' with very creative flags or sculptures as beacons for certain crews, societies, or organizations that evolved around the Jazz Festival. Krew (sic)of Fess, Pet De Kat Krewe, the MOM's organization, 'Fish heads' which were actually Radiators fans that had organized into a group after Eddie Volker had coined the phrase "fish head music' to describe his sound. Others would arrange meetings at Omar's pie booth, leave written messages on the wall in Michael P. Smith's photo booth or set up a rendezvous near their favorite stage. "I'll meet you next year in front of the Fais Do-Do stage on second Saturday at 3:00 p.m." might be shouted across the infield on the last day of the Fest.

It was a good thing too that people made plans or they'd never be able to locate each other. We are all very spoiled now with our cellular phones, but in 1992, the handful of people that had portable phones were cutting edge techies, the idle rich, or very important people with a tremendous amount of responsibility – like the president, or Quint Davis. Car phones weren't as uncommon, but once you parked, you were out of touch, just another body in the sea of music lovers, baking in the sun.

And the sun continued to shine sending throngs into the tents. When Sammy Berfect & the Dimensions of Faith closed the day at the Gospel tent many sweaty, sated lovers of good sound left the Fair Grounds replete. When the gates opened on Sunday, early birds had once again lined up to be first on the field. The weather was perfect and approximately 55,000 people came out for some more.

Kermit Ruffins was featured with bassist Walter Payton, father of Nicholas, and sang "It's Only A Paper Moon" with his beautiful gravelly voice, reminiscent of another trumpeter from New Orleans. Delfeayo Marsalis played with O.J. Ekemode, in Nigerian costume with long yellow robes, Maria Muldaur was spotted playing tambourine with Dr. John, and Earl Turbinton played sax on his brother Willie's set on the Congo Square stage.

Al Green, who came on before Gladys Knight on the Ray-Ban Stage is always a guaranteed crowd pleaser, leaving the women weak and the men inspired. He danced and threw roses to screaming women in the crowd and brought out some of his hits like "Let's Stay Together". Everyone in the crowd sang along and joined in the love. In addition to being a sex symbol, Al Green is a minister, but you'd have to wait till Monday night at the Saenger to get the "sanctified" Al when he performed with Clarence Fountain and the Five Blind Boys of Alabama.

Henry Butler, Allen Toussaint, and David Paquette all graced

SATURDAY, APRIL 25

WVUE / WNOE STAGE
11:40 U.S. Army Jazz Ambassadors
1:10 Willie Lockett Blues Band w/ Wayne Bennett
2:40 Marva Wright & The BMWs
4:15 Otis Clay w/ special guest Ann Peebles & The Hi Rhythm Band
6:00 Rockin' Dopsie & The Zydeco Twisters

M&F GIRBAUD / B 97 STAGE
11:30 NOCCA Jazz Ensemble
12:40 Scott Goudeau & Radio Republic
2:00 Hill Country
3:20 Reggie Hall Revue Band w/ Dogman Smith, Sadie Thompson, Oliver Morgan & Mr. Google Eyes
5:00 New Orleans Musicians' Alumni

WWL / RAY-BAN STAGE
11:30 St. Augustine H.S. Jazz Ensemble
1:00 Bluerunners
2:30 Zachary Richard
3:55 Doug Kershaw
5:40 Huey Lewis & The News

FAIS DO-DO STAGE
11:20 New Orleans Jr. High All-City Jazz Band
12:45 Los Sagitarios
2:05 White Cloud Hunters
3:15 John Mooney & Bluesiana
4:40 Bruce Daigrepont Cajun Band
6:00 Lynn August & Hot August Knights

MARS INC. JAZZ TENT
11:30 Ed Perkins & Michael Ward
12:40 Alain Brunet
1:50 Alvin Batiste & The Jazztronauts
3:00 Germaine Bazzle
4:25 Donald Harrison
5:50 Ahmad Jamal

COX CABLE ECONOMY HALL TENT
12:00 Wendell Brunious Jazz Band
1:20 Ronnie Kole
2:50 Young Tuxedo Brass Band w/ Lady Sequence SA&PC
4:25 New Orleans Ragtime Orchestra
5:50 Al Hirt

CONGO SQUARE STAGE
11:45 New Orleans Drumming Association
1:15 Ruben "Mr. Salsa" Gonzalez & His Salseros
2:40 Boubacar Diabate, Lilison & Ipizo Bangoura
4:10 Charmaine Neville & Friends
5:50 Rara Machine

BANANA BOAT GAZEBO
12:00 Robert Lowery
1:30 Harlan White
3:00 Common Ground
4:30 Robert Lowery
6:00 Eddie LeJeune

MUSIC HERITAGE STAGE
12:00 Alvin Batiste (Interview)
1:30 Otis Clay & Ann Peebles (Interview)
3:00 Huey Lewis (Interview)
4:15 Lynn August

RHODES / WYLD GOSPEL TENT
11:45 Divine Grace Gospel Singers
12:30 St. Luke A.M.E. Choir
1:15 Inspirational Gospel Singers
2:00 New Tree of Life BC Choir
2:45 The Crownseekers
3:30 John Lee & The Heralds of Christ
4:15 St. Francis DeSales Golden Voices

"*Eric Clapton shows up while Dr. John's got his belly dancer cavorting on the top of the piano with him with a big ole' white python and masquerading around; and then after she got through dancing she came over and put the snake on Eric, and he was really cool about it, and then the snake got on his girlfriend. I don't think she was as cool about it, so I went over there and I had to retrieve the snake.*" KEITH WILLIAMS

the piano as bandleaders at the Fair Grounds on closing Sunday of the first weekend, and Voices Of Faith Choir made a joyful noise unto the Lord with fifty voices raised in praise and a driving, undeniable rhythm that took us all home for the day.

As usual, the nighttime club scene was vibrant and the choices were as diverse as the line-up at the Fair Grounds. At Tipitina's the Nevilles held court near their stomping grounds and Monday brought piano night, honoring Professor Longhair. This event had turned into an annual tradition. Featured performers for 1992 were Henry Butler, Ed Frank, Earl King, Willie Tee, Davell Crawford, Jon Cleary and a host of others. Tuesday at Tip's brought us the sub-dudes, Dibala and Matchatcha plus the Rebirth Brass Band.

Tuesday, April 28th at the Palm Court was billed as "*Traditional Night at The Palm Court*", but isn't every night traditional night at this superlative jazz spot? Tuesday offered Doc Cheatham and the Palm Court

Jazz Band w/ Pud Brown, Lucien Barbarin, Butch Thompson, Peter "Chuck" Beatty, and Ernest Ely with special guests Danny Barker, and Thais Clark,

Wednesday the Jazz Fest was hosting "*The Dew Drop Inn Revisited*" in the Sheraton

Carole King and Aaron Neville

music scene

Professor Longhair is inducted into the Rock & Roll Hall Of Fame.

Dr. John releases Goin' Back to New Orleans.

Branford Marsalis joins the "Tonight Show," with Jay Leno.

Kermit Ruffins forms the Barbecue Swingers.

Louisiana Music Commission is created by Gov. Edwin Edwards.

IN MEMORIAM

Ed Blackwell, Teddy Riley

Zion Harmonizers

New Orleans Grand Ballroom under the musical direction of our own legendary Wardell Quezergue. This evening of sound and song featured Dr. John, Oliver "Who Shot The La La" Morgan, Deacon John Moore, Charles Brown and

Gatemouth Brown with the never boring always full of surprises Mr. (or Ms. Depending on the circumstances) Bobby Marchan as master of ceremonies.

"This is the best weather we've had in the history of the Festival" Anna Zimmerman,

Al Green

5:00 Pilgrim Jubilees
6:00 Sammy Berfect & The
      Dimensions of Faith

PARADES
2:00 Original Four and Valley of the
      Silent Men SA&PCs with Tuba
      Fats and The Chosen Few
      Brass Band
4:00 Westbank Steppers, Golden
      Trumpets and Treme Sports
      SA&PCs with All Star
      Brass Band
4:00 Little Rascals & Philadelphia
      Four Marching Clubs with Lil'
      Rascals Brass Band

SUNDAY, APRIL 26

WVUE / WNOE STAGE
11:30 Kennedy High School Cougar
       Band / Parade
1:00 Bryan Lee & Jumpstreet Five
2:25 The Magnificent 7ths w/ Ernie
      K-Doe & Jessie Hill
4:00 Irma Thomas & The
      Professionals
5:40 Dr. John

M&F GIRBAUD / B 97 STAGE
12:00 Grupo "Kabil"
1:35 Ninth Ward Hunters
3:00 John Delafose & The Eunice
      Playboys
4:30 Dash Rip Rock
6:00 Dino Kruse Band

WWL / RAY-BAN STAGE
11:30 Audubon Zoo Winner
12:40 Ritmo Caribeno
2:10 Allen Toussaint
3:45 Al Green
5:45 Gladys Knight

FAIS DO-DO STAGE
12:00 Bruce "Sunpie" Barnes & The
      Sunspots
1:20 D.L. Menard
2:40 Walter Mouton & The Scott
      Playboys
4:10 Mss Ann Goodly & Zydeco
      Brothers
5:40 Nathan & Zydeco Cha Cha

MARS INC. JAZZ TENT
11:30 Southern U. of Baton Rouge
      Jazz Band
12:50 Al Belletto Quartet
2:00 Improvisational Arts Quintet w/
      Kidd Jordan
3:15 Henry Butler
4:30 World Saxophone Quartet w/
      African Drummers
6:05 Walter Payton

COX CABLE ECONOMY HALL TENT
11:30 Milford Dolliole
12:35 David Paquette
1:45 Tribute to Louis Prima
3:00 Kid Sheik's Storyville Ramblers
4:15 Doc Cheatham
5:50 Banu Gibson & New Orleans
      Hot Jazz

CONGO SQUARE STAGE
11:45 Gregory Boyd & The New Sextet
1:25 MC Thick & Jazz MC
2:50 E.L.S.
4:15 Willie Tee
5:45 O.J. Ekemode & His Nigerian
      Allstars

BANANA BOAT GAZEBO
12:30 Clancy "Blues Boy" Lewis
2:15 John Rankin
4:00 The Evening Star String Band

associate producer of the Jazz Festival said on Sunday. "Everything ran smoothly and there were few problems of any kind." The second weekend, Thursday through Sunday, drew 197,000 people to the Fair Grounds, with 70,000 of those people coming on the last day.

On closing day, there was still plenty of room to move around until mid-afternoon when folks began to pour in for the last acts of the 23rd annual celebration.

By 2:30 p.m. on closing day, 115 people had been treated by emergency medical services administered by the New Orleans

Health Department at the Fair Grounds Racetrack for a variety of easily preventable maladies; sun exposure, dehydration, and allergic reactions to food. "A lot of visitors aren't accustomed to the food and the spice" said one medical worker. Maybe you have to build up to it, but maybe

> *"I never miss the Nevilles. I've never missed the Nevilles. Aaron singing 'Amazing Grace'—that's how I close out my shows every year. That's where I say my prayers that I make it through the year and that I get to come one more year to see 'em again."* JAMES BROOKS

you just have to take it in steps and use some good sense: like drink a ton of water if you're outside all day in the blistering sun dancing, and wear a ton of sun block if it's a bright, beautiful day and you're not wearing many clothes. If you're a novice, watch the professionals and do what they do. Getting the optimal experience at the Jazz Fest is a high art form in itself and very gratifying when perfected.

As the sun set, the Radiators closed Stage 1 and the Nevilles closed Stage 3. Hugh Masekela did the honors at Congo Square, Santiago jazz fusion was on B97 stage, The Creole Zydeco Farmers had Fais Do-Do dancing, and the Gospel Soul Children sang us out of another year of Jazz Fest – the best year ever without one drop of rain.

Irma Thomas

NEW ORLEANS JAZZ

JAZZ FEST STATION
APRIL 24 - MAY 3, 1992
NEW ORLEANS, LA 70118

USA 29

NEW ORLEANS JAZZ & HERITAGE FESTIVAL
Official Commemorative Cachet

5:30 Clancy "Blues Boy" Lewis

MUSIC HERITAGE STAGE
12:00 Hazel & The Delta Ramblers
1:00 D.L. Menard & Paul Daigle
2:00 Al Green (Interview)
2:45 Willie Tee & Earl Turbinton
3:45 Walter Mouton

RHODES / WYLD GOSPEL TENT
11:45 Sensational South Tones
12:30 Christian Brothers
1:15 Friendly Five Gospel Singers
2:00 New Orleans Spiritualettes
2:45 New Zion Trio Plus One
3:30 The Soulful Heavenly Stars
4:15 Love Week Workshop Choir
5:00 The Christianaires
6:00 Voices of Faith Choir

PARADES
2:00 Ladies Zulu and Olympia Aid SA&PCs with Pinstripe Dixieland Brass Band
4:00 Calendar Girls, Devastation and Fifth Division Rollers SA&PCs with Young Olympia Brass Band

THURSDAY, APRIL 30

WVUE / WNOE STAGE
11:30 Hammond State Strawberry Jammers
1:00 Chris Thomas
2:30 Howlin' Wolf Reunion
4:00 Lonnie Brooks
5:45 Gary Brown & Feelings

M&F GIRBAUD / B 97 STAGE
11:40 Delgado Community College Jazz Ensemble
1:10 Peabody
2:40 4 for Nothing
4:00 Joel Simpson Trio & Betty Shirley
5:30 Southern Flavor

WWL / RAY-BAN STAGE
11:30 Audubon Zoo Search Winner
12:45 Zydeco Force Band
2:15 Clarence "Gatemouth" Brown
3:45 Junior Walker
5:30 Albert King

FAIS DO-DO STAGE
12:00 La Brew
1:25 Kat & The Kittens
2:45 Booba Barnes
4:15 Preston Frank & His Zydeco Family Band
5:45 Basin Brothers

MARS INC. JAZZ TENT
11:30 Larry Sieberth
12:45 Angelle Trosclair & The New Relics
2:00 Patrice Fisher & Arpa
3:10 Hot Strings of New Orleans
4:30 Bobby Brooks Trio w/ Santy Runyon
5:45 Jazz Futures II

COX CABLE ECONOMY HALL TENT
11:45 Bytunets Antikvariske Jazz Ensemble
12:45 Tommy Yetta's New Orleans Jazz Band
1:55 Frank Federico & The Medicare Madcaps
3:10 Lady Charlotte Jazz Band
4:30 Rebirth Brass Band
6:00 Teddy Riley & Jazz Masters

CONGO SQUARE STAGE
11:30 No Compromize
12:40 Algorhythms
1:50 Guardians of the Flame

Cyril Neville

3:00 Poché
4:15 Moana & The Moahunters
5:45 Inner Circle

BANANA BOAT GAZEBO
12:30 Doug Duffey
2:15 Acoustic Swiftness
4:00 Carl Sonny Leyland & His
Boogie Woogie Trio
5:30 Bad Oyster Band

MUSIC HERITAGE STAGE
1:30 Preston Frank (Interview)
2:30 Lonnie Brooks (Interview)
3:30 Chris Thomas (Interview)
4:30 Brownie Ford (Interview)

RHODES / WYLD GOSPEL TENT
11:45 Holy Spiritualaires
12:30 Silas Family
1:15 Revelation Gospel Singers
2:00 Southern Gospel Singers
2:45 Community Missionary BC
Gospel Choir
3:30 Chosen Gospel Singers
4:15 Leviticus Gospel Singers
5:00 Leonard Williams & Chosen
Generation
6:00 Avondale Community Choir

PARADES
4:00 Bon Temps Roulez Second
Liners with The Storyville
Stompers

FRIDAY, MAY 1

WVUE / WNOE STAGE
11:30 Troy Turner & Third Gear

1:00 Clarence "Frogman" Henry
2:05 Kenny Neal
3:20 Charles Brown
4:40 Batiste Brothers
6:00 Terrance Simien & The Mallet
Playboys

M&F GIRBAUD B-97 STAGE
12:00 Judge & Jury
1:30 Tabby Thomas & The House
Rockers
3:00 Cowboy Mouth
4:30 Deacon John
6:00 Wild Magnolias

WWL / RAY-BAN STAGE
12:00 Mem Shannon & The
Membership Band
1:20 Earl King
3:00 Blues Travelers
4:25 Buckwheat Zydeco
5:50 Johnny Winter

FAIS DO-DO STAGE
12:00 J. Monque'D Blues Band
1:25 Hector Gallardo & His Songo
Allstars
2:45 Golden Eagles
4:15 Jambalaya Cajun Band
5:45 Allen Fontenot & The Country
Cajuns

MARS INC. JAZZ TENT
11:15 SUNO Ensemble
12:20 Phillip Manuel
1:30 Straight Ahead

2:50 Charles Neville & Diversity
4:10 Alvin Red Tyler
5:40 Illinois Jacquet & His Big Band

COX CABLE ECONOMY HALL TENT
11:30 Jacques Gauthé & Creole Rice
Yerba Buena Jazz Band
12:40 Andrew Hall Society Jazz Band
1:50 June Gardner & The Fellows
3:00 Pud Brown Jazz Band
4:25 Placide Adams Original
Dixieland Hall Jazz Band
5:45 Wanda Rouzan & A Taste of
New Orleans

CONGO SQUARE STAGE
11:45 Irie Vibration
1:00 Percussion, Inc.
2:10 The Shepherd Band
3:20 Kamati Dinizulu & His Kotoko
Society
4:35 Cyril Neville & The Uptown
Allstars
6:00 Fatala

BANANA BOAT GAZEBO
12:30 Sloppy Seconds
2:15 Augie Jr. & The Big Mess Blues
Band
4:00 McCauley, Reed & Vidrine
5:30 Hackberry Ramblers

MUSIC HERITAGE STAGE
11:45 Clarence "Frogman" Henry
(Interview)
1:00 Doug Duffey (Interview)

2:00 Sherman Washington
(Interview)
3:00 Terrance Simien
4:00 Earl King

RHODES / WYLD GOSPEL TENT
11:45 Blackwell Family
12:30 The True Tones
1:15 The Banks Family
2:00 Aline White & Company
2:45 Spiritual Harmonettes
3:30 The First Revolution
4:15 Famous Smooth Family of
Slidell
5:00 Kennedy H.S. Gospel Choir
5:45 Ronald James Chorale

PARADES
4:00 Blue Monday and Controllers
SA&PCs with Floyd Anckle's
Majestic Brass Band

SATURDAY, MAY 2

WVUE / WNOE STAGE
11:15 McDonogh #35 S.H. Roneagles
Marching Band / Parade
12:00 Davell Crawford
1:30 James Rivers Movement
2:50 Tommy Ridgley & The
Untouchables w/ Al Johnson &
Chuck Carbo
4:15 Johnny Adams
5:45 Bobby Womack

M&F GIRBAUD / B 97 STAGE

11:20 Dillard University Jazz Band
12:30 Herman Jackson & New
Jackson Swing
1:45 Woodenhead
3:00 Larry Garner & Boogaloo Blues
Band
4:25 Tribe Nunzio
5:50 Nueva Generacion

WWL / RAY-BAN STAGE
12:00 Sonny Landreth & The Goners
1:30 Beausoleil
3:00 Daniel Lanois
4:30 Marcia Ball
6:00 Rickie Lee Jones

FAIS DO-DO STAGE
11:45 Louisiana Tech Jazz Band
1:15 Jude Taylor & His Burning
Flames
2:40 Sheryl Cormier & Cajun
Sounds
4:10 Delton Broussard
5:40 C.J. Chenier & The Red Hot
Louisiana Band

MARS INC. JAZZ TENT
11:15 Xavier University Jazz Lab
Ensemble
12:20 Steve Masakowski & Friends w/
Rick Margitza
1:40 Delfeayo Marsalis
3:05 Ellis Marsalis
4:30 Terence Blanchard
6:00 Astral Project

COX CABLE ECONOMY HALL TENT
11:30 Original Camellia Jazz Band
12:45 Val Barbara's Jazz Band
2:10 New Leviathan Oriental Foxtrot
Museum
3:35 Clint Baker's New Orleans Jazz
Band
4:45 Michael White Quartet w/
Barbara Shorts
6:00 Danny Barker's Jazz Hounds w/
Lady Linda

CONGO SQUARE STAGE
11:15 Michael Ray & The Cosmic
Krewe
12:35 White Eagles
1:45 Deff Generation
3:00 Casa Samba
3:50 Free Spirit Stilt Walkers
4:20 Sister Carol
6:00 Fatala

BANANA BOAT GAZEBO
12:30 Ironin' Board Sam
2:00 Trout Fishing In America
3:30 Swingin' Haymakers
5:15 Ironin' Board Sam

MUSIC HERITAGE STAGE
12:00 David & Michael Doucet
(Interview)
1:00 Ellis Marsalis (Interview)
2:00 Sonny Landreth (Interview)
3:00 Terence Blanchard (Interview)
4:30 Coushatta Indian Dancers

RHODES / WYLD GOSPEL TENT
11:00 Greater Bright Morning
Star Choir
11:45 Pineywoods Cotton Blossom
Singers
12:30 New Beginning Mass Choir of
St. Peter BC
1:15 Christine Myles & Denise
Thompson
1:45 Second Morning Star
Mass Choir
2:40 The Johnson Extension
3:15 The Melody Clouds
3:55 Zulu Ensemble of the Zulu
SA&PC
4:40 Bobby Jones & New Life

5:35 To The Glory of God
Community Choir
6:15 Southern Bells

PARADES
2:00 Algiers Steppers, Second Line
Jammers and Avenue Steppers
SA&PCs with Algiers
Brass Band
4:00 Original Jolly Bunch, Jolly
Bunch Sisters, Money Wasters
and Prince of Wales SA&PCs
with Rebirth Brass Band

SUNDAY, MAY 3

WVUE / WNOE STAGE
11:20 Russ Russell & The Rustlers
12:45 Jimmie Dale Gilmore
2:30 Dixie Cups
4:00 Frankie Ford's Revue
5:40 The Radiators

M&F GIRBAUD / B 97 STAGE
12:00 Black Piranha
1:30 Devious D. & Full Pack
3:00 Creole Wild West
4:30 Raful Neal
6:00 Santiago Jazz Fusion

WWL / RAY-BAN STAGE
11:30 Bobby Marchan & Higher
Ground
12:45 Walter Washington & The
Roadmasters
2:20 Boz Scaggs
4:00 Carole King
5:40 The Neville Brothers

FAIS DO-DO STAGE
11:40 Paky Saavedra's Bandidos
1:10 Willis Prudhomme & Zydeco
Express
2:45 Steve Riley & The Mamou
Playboys
4:15 Dewey Balfa & Friends
5:45 Creole Zydeco Farmers

MARS INC. JAZZ TENT
11:30 Loyola U. Jazz Band
12:40 Clyde Kerr, Jr. & Univision
1:45 Victor Goines Quintet

3:05 Johnny Griffin
4:30 Earl Turbinton
6:00 New York Giants

COX CABLE ECONOMY HALL TENT
11:30 New Orleans Jazz Professors
12:40 Onward Brass Band
1:50 Chris Owens
3:00 New Orleans Storyville
Jazz Band
4:15 Linda Hopkins
5:45 Percy Humphrey & Crescent
City Joymakers

CONGO SQUARE STAGE
11:45 Willie Metcalf & The Academy of
Black Arts
1:10 Kumbuka Dance & Drum
Collective
2:40 I.K. Dairo & His Blue Spots
4:20 Chocolate Milk Reunion
5:45 Hugh Masekela

BANANA BOAT GAZEBO
12:00 Ambrose & Calvin Sam
1:30 Hezekiah & The House Rockers
3:00 Jesse Thomas
4:30 Ambrose & Calvin Sam
6:00 Hezekiah & The House Rockers

MUSIC HERITAGE STAGE
12:00 Hezekiah Early (Interview)
1:00 Dope Sound Productions
(Interview)
2:00 Dewey Balfa (Interview)
3:15 Ed Volker, David Malone &
Reggie Scanlan (Interview)
4:15 Hugh Masekela (Interview)

RHODES / WYLD GOSPEL TENT
11:15 The Mighty Clouds
11:55 Timothy Spell & Sons with Life
Choir
12:35 Joseph "Cool" Davis
1:15 Famous Rocks of Harmony
1:55 Voices From the Mount of Mt.
Carmel B.C.
2:30 Sherman Washington & The
Zion Harmonizers
3:25 Vernard Johnson
4:25 The Fantastic Violinaires
5:20 Raymond Myles & The RAMS
6:15 Gospel Soul Children

PARADES
2:00 Calliope High Steppers, Scene
Boosters & Original Taylor
Bunch SA&PCs with Tremé
Brass Band
4:00 Original New Orleans Men
& Ladies Buck Jumpers and
Jetsetters SA&PCs with Doc
Paulin's Dixieland Jazz Band

NIGHT CONCERTS

FRIDAY, APRIL 24, 9 P.M.
Betty Carter
The Mark Whitfield Group
Victor Goines Quintet
Orpheum Theatre
FRIDAY, APRIL 24, 9 P.M.
Fats Domino
Huey Lewis & The News With Tower
of Power Horns
Dr. John
Municipal Auditorium
SATURDAY, APRIL 25, 9 P.M.
Gladys Knight
Lou Rawls
Irma Thomas
Municipal Auditorium
MONDAY, APRIL 27, 7:30 P.M.
Al Green
Clarence Fountain &
The Five Blind Boys of Alabama
The Mississippi Mass Choir
Sammy Berfect & The Dimensions
of Faith
Jo "Cool" Davis
TUESDAY, APRIL 28, 8 P.M.
Jazz at the Palm Court
Doc Cheatham & The Palm Court
Jazz Band w/ Pud Brown, Lucien
Barbarin, Butch Thompson, Ernest
Elly and Thais Clark w/ special
guest Danny Barker
Palm Court Jazz Café

1993

When opening day of Jazz Fest 1993 dawned the massive army of back line, stage crew carpenters, builders, food vendors, crafts people, volunteers and lovers of the groove were ready for their annual marathon of music and food and record numbers were once again expected.

Many of our musical families were out in force at the Festival. Both the Marsalis family and the Neville family had a new generation of talented artists coming of age. In New Orleans,

that doesn't mean turning twenty one, that means getting up on stage and delivering great music.

On April 24th jazz trumpeter Wynton Marsalis would kick off the family presence at the Fair Grounds on the Music Heritage stage at 2:15 and again at the WWOZ Jazz tent at 5:30. On May 1st drummer Jason Marsalis, listed as the youngest of the brothers would lead his own band in the Jazz Tent at 11:45. On May 2nd The figurehead and literal father of modern jazz in New Orleans, Ellis Marsalis would perform in the Jazz Tent to a packed and sweating house of jazz aficionados. Branford Marsalis didn't make this family outing, although he had achieved mainstream musical success.

Bob French would play the drums for his fifteenth consecutive year as bandleader of the Original Tuxedo Jazz Band. His younger brother George French was out at the Jazz Festival representing the musical genes with his own group, George French's New Orleans Storyville Jazz Band. Their father, Albert "Papa" French played the first Festival in 1970 at Congo Square and performed his last Jazz Fest in 1977. The French family in 1993 had been represented for all 23 years of the Festival. George's son, drummer Gerald, would soon be stepping into his place in the French family musical dynasty.

Nevilles were everywhere, playing in their own family group and in many other musical configurations. Art with The Meters; Charles with his contemporary Jazz group, Diversity; Charles's daughter Charmaine fronting her own band, Charmaine Neville and Friends; Cyril Neville and the Uptown All-stars, which included Aaron's son Ivan, who in 1993 already had major label releases. Art's son Ian, just a boy, was already showing his musical promise, as was another Neville youngster, Jason, another of Aaron's sons. They would arrive on the musical scene at future Jazz Festivals.

Our own master songsmith Allen Toussaint performed and delighted us all once again, and his son Clarence "Reggie" Toussaint worked in the Fair Music Production department as assistant Director of Production and Staging although he was a percussionist in his own right. Reggie was also the R&B and Indian coordinator at the Fair Grounds. His sister Allison is also reputed to be an excellent pianist.

Alvin Batiste, brother in law of "Kidd" Jordan, took to the stage before Ellis Marsalis in the WWOZ Jazz Tent on May 2nd at 3:10. One of the lead-

Lloyd Price

WWOZ radio began taping live performances from Jazz Fest from the Folk Heritage Stage, the Black Arts Stage, and the Louisiana Music Heritage Stage. The station also officially sponsored the Jazz Tent and began the tradition of selling mango freezes.

Congo Square & the WWOZ Jazz Tent were repositioned to allow more room for Congo Square to expand.

It rained on the second weekend. Angelina Ravenshadow of New Orleans and Daniel Powell of Santa Cruz, Ca., slathered with mud head to toe, but still danced in the mudfest. Their photo was picked up on the Associated Press and printed in media around the nation.

An unusually personable Bob Dylan (his debut) started 10 minutes early and played until his encore 90 minutes later. He opened with "Hard Times" by Stephen Foster.

ing practitioners of modern jazz on the clarinet, Mr. Batiste was also a member of the all-star band Clarinet Summit.

The Turbinton Brothers, Willie and Earl, were both listed in the contemporary jazz category in 1993, Willie on the keyboards and vocals addressing various musical styles and his brother Earl on Alto and soprano sax innovating and improvising jazz.

Monster arranger and composer Wardell Quezergue would participate in the "Dew Drop Inn Revisited" on April 29th in the Sheraton Grand Ball room along with Benny Spellman, George French, Bobby Marchan and Roland Stone. Wardell's bass playing son, Brian, another

prodigy, was playing in high school and just starting to gig.

Tommy and Dave Malone from the musical Malone family played in their respective bands. Dave was playing rhythm guitar for the Radiators, and Tommy played lead guitar and sang fronting the subdudes. They'd come a long way since their earliest Partridge Family like band, "The Dust Woofies". In that early effort, brother John played bass, Dave played the guitar and Dave's now ex-wife Suzie sang lead vocals. Tommy played with them some from what we understand, but wasn't a full-fledged regular in the band. Suzie later joined the Pfister Sisters.

Astral Project, once again turned itself into one of the

"In 1993 we were playing in the Jazz Tent and it started raining and it was really coming down. People started pouring into the tent to get out of the rain. We were blasting and the audience started dancing, rolling and jumping up and down in the mud. It was a mud fest. The thunderstorm got so bad that they had to cut us off but that was still one of my favorite days at Jazz Fest." PHILLIP FRAZIER, LEADER OF REBIRTH BRASS BAND

hardest working jazz rhythm sections in town, working in many configurations behind countless artists. They would play closing night, Sunday May 2nd at Snug Harbor to a sold out show, a tradition that is still in effect at this writing. David Torkanowsky also performed with Johnny Adams, Earl King, Zig Modeliste and a slew of others. David T. and legendary drummer Herman "Rosco" Ernest III had just completed their work on Earl King's newest release on Black Top Records and fans were delighted to hear some of the new material on Earl's show.

On opening day April 23rd, Theryl de Clouet, who would go on to front the massively popular jam band Galactic, offered his soulful R&B vocals on the Congo Square stage with his group Reel Life at 2:45. With gates opening at 11:00, thousands of Jazz Fest participants had time to get some great food, navigate the beer line

Bob Dylan

music scene

The Iguanas record self-titled 1993 debut CD.

Earl King releases Hard River to Cross on Blacktop Records.

Louisiana Music Factory opens.

IN MEMORIAM

Harold Peterson, Dizzy Gillespie

"In 1993 we created the series Ecos Latinos and every year Jazz Fest helps us bring high quality musicians from Latin America including Brazil, Bolivia, Venezuela, Guatemala, Mexico and Costa Rica. One year Anthony Carrillo and David Ortiz, two percussionists from Puerto Rico, performed with our group Arpa. Their presence made the music come alive. It was like they turned the lights on in a dark room. Without Jazz Fest this would not be possible." PATRICE FISCHER

Marcia Ball

and make it to Congo Square in time for the start of his show.

Those who bought program books found a page with ten dollars worth of special food coupons inside to encourage them to try new dishes like Timothy Roussel's Alligator Sauce Piquante or Billy and Tracy Fava's Corn Macque Choux with Crawfish.

Once again, there were 64 food booths offering a total of one hundred and fifty eight food items. If your ambition was to taste everything available at Jazz Fest for human consumption, you would have to sample twenty three different dishes every day, a daunting prospect. However, some Jazz Fest devotees do make the attempt and we honor them for trying. The secret food samplers that roam the Festival tasting everything for quality control and service have no choice in

the matter, although they don't have to eat the whole thing.

There were three poster offerings at the 1993 Jazz & Heritage Festival; the official poster by MacArthur fellow John T. Scott, $80.00 signed, $40.00 unsigned; the 1993 memorial poster by Times Picayune graphic artist Tony O. Champagne featuring our beloved "Fess", $60.00 signed, $30.00 unsigned and the Congo Square poster, by Congo Square graphic artist Douglas Redd, $40.00 signed, $20.00 unsigned. The Jazz And Heritage Foundation teamed up with New Orleans public relations and marketing firm Bright Moments for the posters this year as an "economic empowerment experiment".

WWOZ, now administered by the Foundation brought on a new manager, David Freedman, who would be holding the helm for a long time to come. Dan Williams,

"In 1993, we were performing in the Economy Hall tent and a storm rolled up. Danny Barker was next and he only got to play one number before they closed the tent down because of the storm. He looked at me, astonished and disappointed. He was upset. Danny died in 1994. In 1995, at the Jazz Fest, we did a memorial for him at the same tent, and I mentioned to the crowd that they closed the tent down on Barker before he died because of a storm that came up. Then, as I was telling them this, the lightning started striking and the lights went out. Everything went pitch black. It was déjà vu. Like his presence was there. I said, 'We're not being shut out again,' and we played anyway." GREG STAFFORD

who was President of the New Orleans Jazz & Heritage Festival board in 93' proudly noted in the program book that WWOZ was sponsoring the Jazz Tent this year and gave Mr. Freedman credit for doing an excellent job upgrading and improving the station.

Like Jazz Fest, *WWOZ* was founded by two very determined people with a vision and a tremendous love of music who wanted to share it with the world and help other music lovers discover Louisiana's indigenous sound. Like Jazz Fest, they received a tremendous amount of help and support from the local community, but a radio station was a harder sell than a live, outdoor Festival. We are all so grateful to Jerry and Walter Brock,

another type of musical family, for their vision and stubbornness in carrying the torch until it could be picked up by the Foundation.

As the people poured in for the second weekend of music, with bottles of sun block and cash in hand, the music wafted through the air, blending in with the smell of good Louisiana cooking and the faint odor of the stables.

Jazz Festival regulars will tell you that you can pick up the horse scent more when it's been raining. They do graze and exercise some prime racing stock on the Fair Ground site in the "off season" of Jazz Fest. That would be the "on" season for the track. The Fair Grounds

Race track opens every year on Thanksgiving Day and closes for the season in early spring. After the last of the thoroughbreds are moved off, The New Orleans Jazz & Heritage Festival Corporation along with Festival Productions Inc. moves in, takes over and crews begin building the city of stages, tents, food preparation areas, archways, displays etc. that transform the Race Track into the Jazz & Heritage Festival. Tague Richardson's company, Home Team, is in charge of building out all of the stages each year.

In later years, the Fair Grounds Race Track site during Jazz Fest would become the second largest city in the state for two weeks. It hadn't

Pud Brown

Daniel Lanois

reached that stature in 1993, but it was well on its way.

The closing shows on Sunday, May 2nd were a tough call to make for any music lover; Santana followed by the Neville's on WWL/Ray-Ban, or if you could manage to tear yourself away from that, you could catch Irma Thomas followed by the Radiators, a great hometown duo on the WVUE/Polaroid stage. Traditional jazz lovers could catch the fabulous Nellie Lutcher, followed by Percy Humphrey, or if you liked your jazz a little bit more contemporary, there

was Ellis Marsalis followed by T.S. Monk in the Jazz Tent.

Inter-Galactic, time traveling worshippers of the kind bud, along with other regular music loving mortals might be found at Michael Ray's tribute to Sun Ra followed by King Sunny Ade on Congo Square, and folks who just can't get enough gospel in their lives could close out the 1993 Jazz Festival in the Gospel Tent, still situated on the grass, with Joyful, followed by the Gospel Soul Children to complete another year of musical heaven.

Tuba Fats

2:40 Mor Thiam – Drums of Fire
3:40 Free Spirit Stilt Walkers
4:10 Tarika Sammy
5:500 Deff Generation

LAGNIAPPE TENT
12:00 Betsy McGovern & Patrick O'Flaherty
1:30 Bobby Brooks Group
3:00 Hazel & The Delta Ramblers
4:30 Paula & The Pontiacs
6:00 Acoustic Swiftness

MUSIC HERITAGE STAGE
11:45 Fuego Flamenco
1:00 Tarika Sammy
2:15 Betsy McGovern & Patrick O'Flaherty
3:45 Lil' Queenie
5:00 Marc & Ann Savoy

RHODES / WYLD GOSPEL TENT
11:45 True Tone Gospel Singers
12:30 The First Revolution
1:15 Banks Family
2:00 Revelation Gospel Singers
2:45 The Coolie Family
3:30 Leviticus Gospel Singers
4:15 Fairfield Four
5:10 Southern Gospel Singers
5:55 Avondale Community Choir

PARADES
2:50 Economy Hall Parade with Calliope High Steppers & Lady Prince of Wales SA&PCs
4:00 Bon Temps Roulez Second Liners with Storyville Stompers Brass Band

FRIDAY APRIL 30

WVUE / POLAROID STAGE
11:20 Gregory Boyd & VOS
12:45 Bobby Marchan & Higher Ground
2:10 Tommy Ridgley & The Untouchables w/ Chuck Carbo, Al Johnson & Roland Stone
4:00 Lloyd Price
5:45 Delbert McClinton

B-97 STAGE
11:30 Funchaus
1:00 Poche
2:25 Southern Flavor-Bluegrass
3:30 Anders Osborne
5:30 Bad Boys of Music Explosion

WWL / RAY-BAN STAGE
11:30 T.C. Hawkins Singers
1:00 Earl King
2:30 Terrance Simien & Mallet Playboys
4:00 The Meters
5:30 Dr. John

FAIS DO-DO STAGE
11:15 Hammond State Strawberry Jammers
12:20 Jesse Thomas
1:45 New Orleans Klezmer Allstars
3:10 Henry Grey Allstars
4:35 Sheryl Cormier & Cajun Sounds
6:00 Sensacion Latina

WWOZ JAZZ TENT
11:20 Peter Martin Trio
12:35 Hot Strings of New Orleans
1:40 Steve Masakowski & Friends
2:55 Charles Neville & Diversity
4:15 AFO's w/ Tammy Ly.nn
5:45 McCoy Tyner Big Band

COX CABLE ECONOMY HALL TENT
12:00 Original Camellia Jazz Band
1:15 Milford Dolliole
2:40 Wendell Brunious
4:10 Placide Adams Original Dixieland Hall Jazz Band
5:35 Banu Gibson & New Orleans Hot Jazz

CONGO SQUARE STAGE
11:30 San Jacinto Dance
12:45 Y'Shua Manzy & The World Beat Band
2:15 Tarika Sammy
4:00 Dirty Dozen Brass Band
5:40 Sa Sa Ye Sa

LAGNIAPPE TENT
12:00 New Orleans Jr. High All-City Jazz Band
1:15 Guy Montgomery
2:45 Betty Shirley
4:15 Po' Henry & Tookie
5:45 Golden Star Hunters

MUSIC HERITAGE STAGE
11:30 Po' Henry & Tooka
12:25 Lloyd Price
1:40 Sa Sa Ye Sa
2:45 Gray Montgomery
3:45 Hot Licks Cookies
4:50 Steve Masakowski

RHODES / WYLD GOSPEL TENT
11:45 Bless the People Gosple Singers
12:30 New Day B.C. Choir
1:15 Endurance Gospel Singers
2:00 Chozen
2:45 Aline White & Company
3:30 Kennedy High School Gospel Choir

4:15 Reuben Victor & Victory Travelers
5:10 St. Rose Delima Gospel Choir
5:55 Ronald James Chorale

PARADES
4:00 Algiers Steppers and Perfect Gentlemen SA&PCs with The Doc Paulin Brass Band

SATURDAY, MAY 1

WVUE / POLAROID STAGE
11:30 Lynn August & Hot August Knights
1:00 Eddie Bo
2:30 Deacon John
4:00 Dixie Cups
5:30 C.J. Chenier & The Red Hot Louisiana Band

B-97 STAGE
12:00 Johnny J & The Hitmen
1:30 Evening Star String Band
3:00 Hadley Castille & Louisiana Cajun Band
4:30 Song Dogs
6:00 Don Montoucet

WWL / RAY-BAN STAGE
11:10 Loyola University Jazz Band
12:30 Wayne Toups & Zydecajun
2:10 Spyro Gyra
3:45 Buddy Guy
5:40 Michael McDonald

FAIS DO-DO STAGE
11:40 J. Monque'D Blues Band

1:25 Paky Saavedra's Bandidos
2:50 Kenny Bill Stinson
4:25 Willie Lockett & The
  Blues Krewe
6:00 Willis Prudhomme & Zydeco
  Express

WWOZ JAZZ TENT
11:45 Jason Marsalis
1:10 Fred Kemp Quartet
2:35 Willie Tee
4:05 Kidd Jordan & Alvin Fielder
5:30 Rebirth Brass Band

COX CABLE ECONOMY HALL TENT
12:00 Onward Brass Band
1:25 Michael White
2:55 Young Tuxedo Brass Band
4:25 Carrie Smith
6:00 Danny Barker

CONGO SQUARE STAGE
11:30 Silky Slim / Lil Elt
12:40 Percussion Inc.
2:00 Golden Eagles
3:30 Irie Vibrations
4:50 Sa Sa Ye Sa
6:00 Walter "Wolfman" Washington
  & The Roadmasters

LAGNIAPPE TENT
12:00 Ernest Vincent's Topnotes w/
  Tommy Singleton
1:30 David & Roselyn
3:00 Ambrose & Calvin Sam
4:30 Calvin LeBlanc
6:00 Hector Gallardo & His Songo
  Allstars

MUSIC HERITAGE STAGE
11:30 Kenny Bill Stinson
12:45 Hadley Castille
2:00 Eleanor Ellis
3:15 Walter "Wolfman" Washington
4:30 Brownie Ford
5:45 Ambrose & Calvin Sam

RHODES / WYLD GOSPEL TENT
11:45 Rejubilation Community Choir
12:30 Friendly Travelers
1:15 Second Morning Star Mass
  Choir
2:00 Val & Love Alive Fellowship
  Choir
2:45 Beulah B.C. Choir
3:30 The Mighty Chariots
4:15 Voices of Praise Choir
5:10 Johnson Extension
5:55 Zulu Ensemble
6:45 To the Glory of God Community
  Choir

PARADES
2:00 Westbank Steppers, Taylor
  Bunch SA&PCs with Trombone
  Shorty's Allstar Brass Band
4:00 Valley of the Silent Men and
  Second Line Jammers SA&PCs
  with Jr. Pinstripe Brass Band

SUNDAY, MAY 2

WVUE / POLAROID STAGE
11:45 Dillard University Jzz Band
1:15 Frankie Ford's Revue
2:35 Marva Wright & The BMWs
4:00 Irma Thomas & The
  Professionals
5:45 The Radiators

B-97 STAGE
11:30 Caledonia Society Scottish
  Dancers & Drummers
1:00 Marie Serpas & The Instagators
2:30 D.L. Menard
4:00 Blackie Forester & The Cajun
  Aces
5:45 Russ Rustler & The Rustlers

WWL / RAY-BAN STAGE
12:00 Ninth Ward Hunters
1:20 Buckwheat Zydeco
3:15 Santana
5:30 The Neville Brothers

FAIS DO-DO STAGE
11:30 Lee Bates
12:40 Larry Garner & The Boogaloo
  Band
1:50 Irene & The Mikes
3:15 Dalton Reed
4:35 Bryan Lee & Jumpstreet Five
6:00 John Delafose & The Eunice
  Playboys

WWOZ JAZZ TENT
11:20 Michael Ward
12:30 Woodenhead
1:45 Astral Project
3:10 Alvin Batiste
4:25 Ellis Marsalis Quartet
5:50 T.S. Monk, Jr.

COX CABLE ECONOMY HALL TENT
11:20 Musicum Jazz Antiqum w/ Karl
  Koenig
12:30 Kermit Ruffins Big Band
1:50 George French's New Orleans
  Storyville Jazz Band
3:10 New Orleans Ragtime
  Orchestra
4:30 Nellie Lutcher
6:00 Percy Humphrey

CONGO SQUARE STAGE
12:00 Shepherd Band
1:25 Kumbuka Drum & Dance
  Collective
2:45 Ruben "Mr. Salsa" Gonzalez &
  His Salseros
4:10 Michael Ray & Cosmic Krewe's
  Tribute to Sun Ra
5:40 King Sunny Ade

LAGNIAPPE TENT
12:00 St. Augustine H.S. Jazz
  Ensemble
1:30 Louisiana Tech Band
3:00 Little Freddie King
4:30 Rooster
6:00 Creole Wild West

MUSIC HERITAGE STAGE
11:45 Rooster
1:00 John & Geno Delafose
2:15 King Sunny Ade
3:30 Vidrine-Chapman Family Cajun
  Band
5:00 Roderick Paulin & The Hitman

RHODES / WYLD GOSPEL TENT
11:45 Mighty Clouds
12:30 Jo "Cool" Davis
1:15 Southern Bells
2:00 Famous Rocks of Harmony
2:45 John Lee & Heralds of Christ
3:30 Zion Harmonizers
4:15 Bobby Jones & New Life
5:10 Voices From the Mount
5:55 Joyful
6:45 Gospel Soul Children

PARADES
2:00 Men Buck Jumpers and Scene
  Boosters SA&PCs with Pinettes
  Brass Band
4:00 Lady Buck Jumpers, Calliope
  High Steppers and Jetsetters
  SA&PCs with Lil' Rascals Brass
  Band

NIGHT CONCERTS

FRIDAY, APRIL 23, 9 P.M.
The Allman Brothers Band
The Fabulous Thunderbirds
John Campbell
Municipal Auditorium
FRIDAY, APRIL 23, 8 P.M.
One Mo' Time
Original Cast Reunion featuring
  Vernel Bagneris, Thais Clark,
  Topsy Chapman, Kuumba
  Williams, Orange Kellin
Dr. Michael White's Tribute to Jelly
  Roll Morton
Bob French & The Original Tuxedo
  Jazz Band
Margaritaville Cafe
SATURDAY, APRIL 24, 9 P.M.
Patti Labelle
Johnnie Taylor
Louisiana Purchase
Municipal Auditorium
SUNDAY, APRIL 25, 8 P.M.
Grover Washington Jr.
The New Orleans Jazz & Heritage
  Foundation commissions original
  works by Danny Barker, Alvin
  Batiste, Harold Batiste, Germaine
  Bazzle, Edward "Kidd" Jordan,
  Ellis Marsalis and The Heritage
  School of Music Band
Saenger Theatre
MONDAY, APRIL 26, 7:30 P.M.
Gospel Is Alive
John P. Kee & The New Life
  Community Choir
The Dorothy Love Coates Singers
New Creation Baptist Church Mass
  Choir
Saenger Theatre

TUESDAY, APRIL 27, 8 P.M.
Wynton Marsalis Septet
The Duke Ellington Orchestra
Conducted by Mercer Ellington
Grand Ballroom – Sheraton Hotel
WEDNESDAY, APRIL 28, 8 P.M.
Nina Simone
The McCoy Tyner Big Band
Alvin Batiste Sextet
Grand Ballroom – Sheraton Hotel
THURSDAY, APRIL 29, 8 P.M.
Dew Drop Inn Revisited
Lloyd Price, Benny Spellman,
  Marva Wright, George French,
  Roland Stone, Wardell Quezergue
  His Orchestra with Master of
  Ceremonies, Bobby Marchan
Grand Ballroom – Sheraton Hotel
FRIDAY, APRIL 30, 9 P.M.
The Neville Brothers
Los Lobos
Terrance Simien
Municipal Auditorium
FRIDAY, APRIL 30, 12 MIDNIGHT
Late Night Jam Session
John Stubblefield, Billy Harper, Earl
  Gardner, Avery Sharpe, Aaron Scott
  and others
Charlie B's Music Club
SATURDAY, MAY 1, 9 P.M.
Santana
King Sunny Ade
The Meters
Municipal Auditorium
SUNDAY, MAY 2, 8 P.M.
La Noche Latina
Los Sabrossos del Merengue
Nueva Generacion
State Palace Theater

1994

John Mooney

You could see the glow for miles. Over the Christmas Holidays the unthinkable happened. The grandstand and clubhouse of the New Orleans Fair Grounds Race Track caught fire and burned to the ground. Many Jazz & Heritage Foundation Members were nearby in City Park participating in a ceremony presenting awards to leading Black Music educators when the whisperings began. It was hard to believe that it could be true, but walking outside of the museum at City Park, the sky had an angry orange glow that gave eerie confirmation to the news. With shock and dismay Foundation members drove in the direction of the Fair Grounds and in the few blocks it took to approach the site, the last remnants of hope that the damage would be minor were dashed. It was catastrophic.

what's going on?

GLOBALLY

The Channel Tunnel (Chunnel) opens between Britain and France.

Bloody civil war in Rwanda was started by Hutu and Burundi troops, which shot down a plane carrying the president of Rwanda, in revenge for allowing the Tutsi to share power.

The North Koreans barred a UN agency from investigating security breaches at one of their reactors.

NATIONALLY

Paula Jones files a sexual harassment suit against United States President Bill Clinton.

In an attempt to prevent her from entering the 1994 Olympics, figure skater Tonya Harding and her ex-husband assault archrival Nancy Kerrigan.

Jacqueline Kennedy Onassis was laid to rest along side John F Kennedy.

LOCALLY

Harry Connick, Jr., establishes Krewe of Orpheus, the first "super Krewe" to include both men and women.

House of Blues opens in New Orleans, featuring performances that year by Bob Dylan, Eric Clapton, and Aerosmith.

Nine New Orleans police officers indicted on federal drug charges.

Louisiana loses one House seat after the 1990 Census.

"Dutch" Morial's son, Marc H. Morial, becomes Mayor of New Orleans.

CULTURALLY

"Forrest Gump," starring Tom Hanks, is released.

Major League baseball players strike, and as a result the World Series was canceled.

53 members of the Order of the Solar Temple cult carried out a mass murder-suicide in Switzerland and Canada.

Over the next few days, Festival and Foundation staff began to assess what kind of effect the loss of the Grandstand was going to have on the 25th Annual Jazz & Heritage Festival and how to start making plans to move forward. The Jazz Fest had survived tornados, torrential rains, and countless other "growing pains" over the years, and they would have to find a way to overcome this.

Nancy Ochsenschlager, Fair Director, and Tague Richardson, Site Director, along with Quint Davis and the rest of the Festival Production team began searching for a solution. The George Wein Group and Festival Productions found one. A really, really big tent. Quint told people at the time that lessons learned from putting on the Democratic Inauguration Celebration were invaluable in getting the Fair back on it's feet just a few short days after the fire. It's all about making it happen, and they did.

Enormous Grandstand tents were found in Belgium, but the airplane needed to transport them was too big for the New Orleans airport. Our runways weren't long enough for the mammoth plane to land, so the huge tents were flown into Houston and then transported by truck to New Orleans. At the Fair Grounds, everyone knew it was going to be a mother of a job, and it was, but they got it done. A Phoenix rose from the ashes that would change the face of Jazz Fest forever.

As the giant tent was constructed on the concrete parking lot, new vistas were opened to the Festival planners. The grandstand would be re-built, bigger and better, but once the Fest had crossed the boundaries of the dirt racetrack, it would never go back. On opening day, six new tents were standing outside of the infield and a new space had been claimed.

Friday, April 22nd when the Louisiana Heritage Fair opened, staff and crew had risen to the challenge and passed the test of overcoming the loss of the grandstand with flying colors. As people filed in the main entrance many were shocked to see the wreckage, but before long the skeleton of what used to be the grandstand was an afterthought. There were too many other things to do; food to eat, music to listen to, crafts to buy and friends from last year to find.

Opening day offered Luther Kent and his Big Band led by iconic local genius Charles Brent

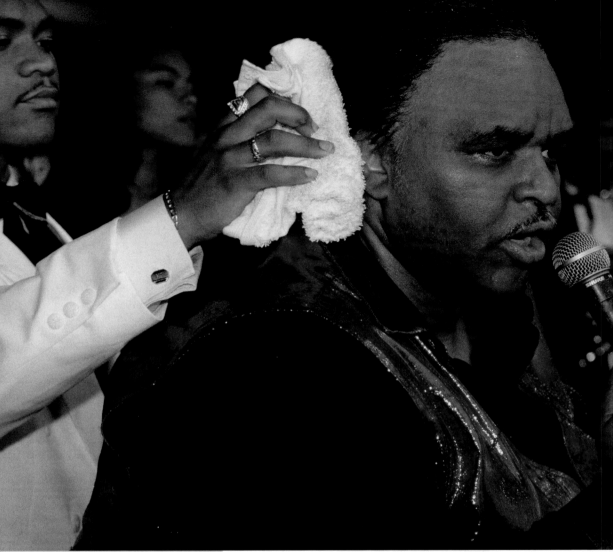

Solomon Burke

The first Fess head crawfish boil was born Wednesday between the weekends. It was built from a couple hundred pounds of crawfish and cases of beer to 16 kegs of beer and 1,200 to 1,600 pounds of crawfish.

A group of playful Festers tied string and bandanas together to make a huge jump rope, dancing and jumping in the pouring rain.

The year was the beginning of the "Ivory Blues Revue", a piano night feature.

The 1994 official program started featuring coupons for the food booths and restaurants in town, which more than pay for the cost.

who taught Jaco Pastorius theory, wrote and arranged music for Wayne Cochran and the C.C. Riders, orchestrated and wrote arrangements for everyone from Louie Prima to Johnny Carson and who hails from Kenner, Louisiana. Luther's set was followed by The Band at 4 p.m. on the Polaroid Stage; or for a different palate, Frankie Ford's Review, on the Ray-Ban Stage, followed by Allen Toussaint

from 3:50 to 5 p.m. was an option. Dancing and sweating was the order of the day.

In 1994, the club scene was so vibrant and the night concerts were so good that it was essential to eat truly excellent food to keep your strength up. All of that good, hot, spicy, beaten, breaded, deep-fried and sautéed steaming hot music for the soul had to have its culinary complement. At the Lakefront Arena the listings noted that main acts might not appear before midnight "due to the nature of the program" which made it possible to go out for some fine dining if you still had any room left after a day at the Fair Grounds.

The night concerts were co-sponsored by Channel 6 television and Burger King in conjunction with the Jazz & Heritage Foundation. On Friday April 22nd the first show in the night concert series kicked off at the UNO Lakefront Arena with the Neville Brothers, Third World, Miriam Makeba, with special guest, Hugh Masekela and the Tour of Hope. On Saturday April 23rd, "Jaeger's After Dark" midnight Jam featured Alvin Batiste, Idris Muhammad, Alvin "Red" Tyler, Richard Payne and Barbara Short on vocals. The Palm Court Café served up a sumptuous feast of traditional jazz music on the 25th and 26th with an extraordinary line up starting at 8:00 p.m. on both nights; Percy and Willie Humphrey, Doc Cheatham, Pud Brown, Chuck Badie, Butch Thompson, Sammy Rimington,

Doc Cheatam

Lucien Barbarin and Ernest Ellie. After the main program, a late night all star jam session followed at 11:30 p.m. with tickets sold at the door only for five dollars.

Saturday, April 23rd "the nature of the program" at the Lakefront Arena was Buckwheat Zydeco kicking it off, followed by The Band who would leave fans parched from singing along with "Up on Cripple Creek", and "The Weight" followed by the Allman Brothers Band

2:45 Dynamic Smooth Family
3:30 Alcee Fortier's Sr. High Concert Choir
4:15 Jackson Southernaires
5:15 New Orleans Headstart Singing Angels
5:55 McDonogh #35 Gospel Choir
PARADES
4:00 Lil' Rascals, Philadelphia Four & Steppin' in Style SA&PCs with Looney Tunes Brass Band

SATURDAY, APRIL 23

FOX 38 / POLAROID STAGE
11:30 Los Sagitarios
1:00 Reggie Hall Band w/ special guests Sadie Thompson, Octavia Eli & Albert "Dogman" Smith
3:00 C.J. Chenier & The Red Hot Louisiana Band
4:30 Dirty Dozen Brass Band
6:00 Dixie Cups

B97 / BELLSOUTH MOBILITY STAGE
11:30 Guardians of the Flame
12:40 John Wilson & The Zydeco House Rockers
2:00 Dash Rip Rock
3:20 Irene & The Mikes
4:35 Sheryl Cormier & Cajun Sounds
6:00 Filé

WWL / RAY-BAN STAGE
11:40 Loyola University Jazz Band
1:00 Zachary Richard
2:20 the subdudes
3:50 Boz Scaggs
5:30 Jimmy Buffett & The Coral Reefer Band

HOUSE OF BLUES STAGE
12:00 Creole Zydeco Farmers
1:30 Dalton Broussard
2:50 Henry Butler
4:10 John Mooney & Bluesiana
5:45 Lonnie Brooks

CONGO SQUARE STAGE
11:40 Ben Hunter's Crucial Roots
12:50 Percussion Incorporated
2:00 DJ Jimi & Juvenile & The Soldiers
3:20 Golden Eagles Mardi Gras Indians
4:40 Junkanoo's Parade
4:40 Bahamas Junkanoos Folkloric Troupe & Baha-Men
6:00 Wanda Rouzan & A Taste of New Orleans

WWOZ / BET ON JAZZ JAZZ TENT
11:15 Jason Marsalis
12:15 Earl Turbinton Quintet
1:25 Al Belletto Quartet
2:30 Alvin Batiste w/ special guest Ed Perkins
3:55 Ahmad Jamal
5:15 Max Roach
6:15 A Tribute to Ed Blackwell w/ Earl Palmer, Max Roach, Idris Muhammad, Harry Nance, June Gardner

COX CABLE ECONOMY HALL
11:30 Andrew Hall's Society Jazz Band
12:40 Placide Adam's Original Dixieland Hall Jazz Band
1:50 Sadie Goodson w/ special guest Ida Goodson
3:15 Louisiana Repertory Jazz Ensemble
4:35 Wendell Brunious Jazz Band
5:50 Banu Gibson & New Orleans Hot Jazz

who helped everybody burn off all of those extra calories collected during the day at the Fair Grounds with their long, rocking rendition of "Whipping Post".

Jay Monque'D

Crawling out of bed on Sunday morning may have been a little hard at first, but after a strong cup of New Orleans coffee and chicory and a glance at the Sunday Fair Grounds schedule, jumping in the shower and getting ready to head out to the Festival was a piece of cake.

Half way into the New Orleans Klezmer All Stars high energy set, dancing people were snaking through the crowd in a long, connected string of bodies as the Klezmers whipped them into a frenzy. Other predominately local Festgoers enjoyed a rare soupcon of collaboration, from 3:30 to 5:00 p.m., as Allen Toussaint and Dr. John paid tribute to Professor Longhair in the Heritage Tent in honor of his 75th birthday. Dr. John took to the stage once again at

6 p.m on The Ray-Ban Stage to close out the first weekend. Other closing acts for the first Sunday were Irma Thomas, The Batiste Brothers, Rockin' Dopsie and the Zydeco Twisters, Cyril Neville and the Uptown Allstars, Kent Jordan Quartet, Duke Dejean's Olympia Brass and the Holy Hill Gospel Singers.

On Thursday, April 28th attendees were forced to choose between Beausoleil, Count Basie Orchestra, Acoustic Swiftness, Weir/Wasserman, Theryl and Reel Life, Lump, Gordon Boc and The New Leviathan Oriental Foxtrot Orchestra to end the day, or to spend the last hour and a half running from stage to stage to catch a little bit of everything.

At 9 p.m. the evening concert started at the Ernest Morial Convention Center with a trio

Charles Brown

subdudes

> *"John Prine starts strumming and you know he is not the most upbeat singer, and he looks up and there are 10,000 people singing his song along with him and his energy just went up."*

KEITH TWITCHELL

of modern jazz luminaries that were just too good to miss. The Wynton Marsalis Septet, Herbie Hancock Trio and the Joshua Redman Quartet.

People in the know spent the day on the second Friday eating as many new dishes as possible because Friday night was "La Noche Latina" and they knew they needed their strength. There would be no time for dinner after they left the Fair Grounds. It really wasn't possible to leave early with acts like the Funky Meters, B.B. King, The Newport Allstars and John Delafose and the Eunice Playboys closing out the day.

On April 29th at the Fair Grounds, Solomon Burke, a large man, commenced his show at 2:50 decked out in purple lame' on the Ray-Ban stage with a

massive band comprised mostly of his own children, including a younger son whose sole job was to pat the sweat from his forehead while Mr. Burke held the crowd in thrall. This was just one of the many "I'm so glad I was there" occurrences to be enjoyed at Jazz Fest.

Chocolate Milk did what they do best and did it well, serving up their classic New Orleans funk at Congo Square Stage. Ms. Etta James had such a huge sea

Iguanas

of people at the Ray-Ban stage while she held court from 4:30 to 5:30 it was hard to believe that every single person who bought a ticket that day wasn't at her show.

Tito Puente and his Orchestra put on and insanely memorable concert at the Convention Center with special guests that could be headliners in their own right; Mongo Santamaria, Gilberto Santa Rosa y Su Orchestra, and Ritmo Caribeno.

On Saturday, April 30th, Aretha Franklin and B.B. King along with the Gospel Soul Children of New Orleans laid waste to the Lakefront Arena. This was the best gravy on a day that was a veritable feast of music. Robert Cray held his crowd, casting magic and happiness everywhere. Randy Newman told his stories in song to a rapt audience, and his rendition of "Louisiana, 1927" chased the clouds away when rain threatened. Our own jazz diva, Germaine Bazzle mesmerized the Jazz Tent and the stunning

music scene

Ernie K-Doe's Mother-In-Law Lounge opens at 1500 N. Claiborne Ave.

Master P forms No Limit Records.

House of Blues opens at 225 Decatur Street.

IN MEMORIAM

Willie Humphrey, Danny Barker, Cab Calloway

Lloyd Washington

saxophones and bagpipes of the James Rivers movement led the Congo Square crowd to the close of a perfect day of music. In the Jazz Tent, Tito Puente's Salsa Allstars gave a second helping to anyone who hadn't had enough the night before.

New Orleanians have a lot of rituals, and many locals have to close out their Jazz Fests with either the Nevilles or the Radiators, two longstanding local institutions. Terrance Simien and the Mallet Playboys had the crowd packed to the main gate when they left and the Radiators commenced on the Polaroid Stage. Aretha Franklin prepared the Ray-Ban stage for the Neville Brothers to close out the 25th anniversary Jazz & Heritage Festival.

As visitors headed back to the airport on Monday morning, the ground crew at the Fair site began dismantling the tents and breaking down the stages. Not only did the Festival solve the problem of the loss of the Grandstand, they once again surpassed themselves.

Davell Crawford

CONGO SQUARE STAGE
11:40 Kumbuka Dance & Drum Collective
1:00 Wild Magnolias
2:15 Junkanoo's Parade
2:15 Junkanoos Folkloric Troupe & Baha-Men
3:20 The Shepherd Band
4:40 E-La-Té

WWOZ / BET ON JAZZ JAZZ TENT
11:25 The Heritage School of Music
12:30 Harry Connick Sr. w/ The Jimmy Maxwell Orchestra
1:40 Kidd Jordan & Improvisational Arts
2:50 Marlon Jordan featuring Stephanie Jordan
4:15 Stanly Turrentine
5:50 Kent Jordan Quartet

COX CABLE ECONOMY HALL
11:30 Pud Brown's Palm Court Jazz Band
12:40 George French's New Orleans Storyville Jazz Band
2:05 Chris Owens
3:25 Al Hirt
4:35 Doc Cheatham
5:50 Duke Dejan's Olympia Brass Band

LAGNIAPPE TENT
12:10 Louisiana Tech Jazz Band
1:35 University of New Orleans Jazz Ensemble
3:00 Gov. Jimmy Davis
4:25 Charles Brown
5:55 Asian/Pacific American Revue

MUSIC HERITAGE TENT
11:30 Theresa Andersson
12:30 Jordan Family (Interview)
1:30 Sonny Bourg & Johnny Allen (Interview)
2:30 Doc Cheatham (Interview)
3:30 75th Anniversary of Professor Longhair's Birthday w/ Allen Toussaint & Dr. John

RHODES / WYLD GOSPEL TENT
11:45 Sensational Southern Tones
12:30 Friendly Five Gospel Singers
1:15 The Davis Singers
2:00 The New Orleans Spiritualettes
2:45 Louisiana Freeman Congress Choir
3:30 New Zion Trio Plus One
4:15 Mighty Clouds of Joy
5:15 The Famous Mighty Imperials
5:55 Holy Hill Gospel Singers

PARADES
2:00 Olympian Aide & Devastation SA&PCs with Tuba Fats and The Chosen Few Brass Band & Seminoles Mardi Gras Indians
4:00 Furious Five & Lady Zulu SA&PCs with Tornado Brass Band & Carrollton Hunters Mardi Gras Indians
5:50 Parade in Economy Hall with Devastation Ladies SA&PC

THURSDAY, APRIL 28

FOX 38 / POLAROID STAGE
11:45 Jambalaya Cajun Band
1:10 Sonny Landreth & The Goners
2:40 George Porter, Jr. & Runnin' Pardners
4:00 Taj Mahal
5:30 Weir / Wasserman

B97 / BELLSOUTH MOBILITY STAGE
11:30 Xavier University Jazz Lab
      Ensemble
1:00 Evening Star String Band
2:30 Kim Carson
4:00 Brian Stoltz
5:30 Lump

WWL / RAY-BAN STAGE
12:00 Jo-el Sonnier
1:25 Evangeline
2:50 Clarence "Gatemouth" Brown
4:20 Willie Nelson
6:00 BeauSoleil

HOUSE OF BLUES STAGE
11:45 Willie Lockett & The Blues
      Krewe
1:10 J. Monque'D Blues Band
2:40 Leon & Sam Brothers Zydeco
4:05 Bois Sec Ardoin & Canray
      Fontenot
5:25 Acoustic Swiftness

CONGO SQUARE STAGE
12:00 Theron Lewis & Unit 7
1:20 New Orleans Drumming
      Association
2:45 White Eagles Mardi Gras Indians
4:10 Dembo Konte Kora & Balafon
      Ensemble
5:50 Theryl & Reel Life

WWOZ / BET ON JAZZ JAZZ TENT
11:30 Angelle Trosclair
      & The New Relics
12:40 Dwight Fitch, Jr.
1:45 Hot Strings of New Orleans
2:50 Walter Payton w/ special guest
      Sharon Martin

4:10 Creative Music Orchestra Old
      Garde New Faces
5:40 Count Basie Orchestra

COX CABLE ECONOMY HALL
11:25 Lady Charlotte Jazz Band
12:45 Rene Netto
1:50 Milford Dolliole
3:00 Ronnie Kole
4:25 Dukes of Dixieland
5:50 New Leviathan Oriental Foxtrot
      Orchestra

LAGNIAPPE TENT
12:00 Allegrias!
1:10 David & Roselyn
2:25 Svare Forsland
3:50 Betsy McGovern & Poor Clares
5:15 Gordon Bok

MUSIC HERITAGE TENT
11:30 Marce Lacouture & Inez Catalon
1:30 Brownie Ford
1:30 Tom McDermott
2:30 Bois Sec Ardoin & Canray
      Fontenot (Interview)
3:30 Dwight Fitch, Jr. (Interview)

RHODES / WYLD GOSPEL TENT
11:45 The Silas Family
12:30 The First Revolution
1:15 The Coolie Family
2:00 Ecclesiastes Gospel Singers
2:45 Leviticus Gospel Singers
3:30 True Tone Gospel Singers
4:15 Timothy Spell & Sons with
      Life Choir
5:15 Southern Gospel Singers
5:55 Avondale Community Choir

PARADES
4:00 Bon Temps Roulez & Trombone
      Shorty's SA&PCs with Storyville
      Stompers Brass Band

FRIDAY, APRIL 29

FOX 38 / POLAROID STAGE
11:30 Brownsville
12:40 Kenny Neal
1:50 John Hammond
3:00 Earl King
4:15 Stephen Stills Band
5:45 funky Meters

B97 / BELLSOUTH MOBILITY STAGE
11:30 Hammond State Strawberry
      Jammers
12:35 9th Ward Hunters Mardi Gras
      Indians
1:50 Basin Brothers
3:30 The Bluerunners
5:10 Don Montoucet

WWL / RAY-BAN STAGE
11:45 Southern University of Baton
      Rouge Jazz Band
1:15 Bobby Cure & The Summertime
      Blues Band w/ special guests
      Robert Parker & Roland Stone
2:50 Solomon Burke
4:30 Etta James
6:00 B.B. King

HOUSE OF BLUES STAGE
12:00 Jude Taylor & His Burning
      Flames
1:25 Anders Osborne
2:40 Raful Neal w/ special guest Lazy
      Lester

4:10 Tabby Thomas w/ special guest
      Henry Gray
5:50 John Delafose & The Eunice
      Playboys

CONGO SQUARE STAGE
11:20 Porgy Jones Quartet
12:25 DJ Jubilee & Black Menace
1:45 Gregory Boyd & VOS
3:00 Eddie Bo
4:25 Chocolate Milk
5:45 Tabou Ley Rochereau &
      Orchestre Africa International

WWOZ / BET ON JAZZ JAZZ TENT
11:25 Scott Goudeau Group
12:35 Philip Manuel
1:45 Clyde Kerr, Jr. & Univision
3:00 Charles Neville & Diversity
4:25 Joshua Redman Quartet
5:50 Newport Allstars

COX CABLE ECONOMY HALL
11:30 Local International Allstar
      Jazz Band
12:40 Sam Alcorn
1:50 Wallace Davenport & His New
      Orleans Jazz Band
3:00 Louis Cottrell
4:25 Doc Paulin's Dixieland
      Jazz Band
5:50 Benny Powell

LAGNIAPPE TENT
12:00 Arte Flamenco
1:20 Hazel & The Delta Ramblers
2:45 Ironin' Board Sam
4:15 Dembo Konte Kora & Balafon
      Ensemble
5:45 Savoy-Doucet Cajun Band

MUSIC HERITAGE TENT
11:30 Roland Stone (Interview)
12:30 Solomon Burke (Interview)
1:30 Tabby Thomas, Raful Neal &
Henry Gray (Interview)
2:30 Clancy "Blues Boy" Lewis
3:30 Corey Harris & Butch Trevet
4:30 Bad Oyster Band
6:00 Etta James TBA (Interview)

RHODES / WYLD GOSPEL TENT
11:45 St. John Divine Gospel
Drill Team
12:30 New Life Gospel Choir
1:15 First Baptist Church
2:00 The Friendly Travelers
2:45 Aline White & Company
3:30 St. Rose DeLima Gospel Choir
4:15 Albertina Walker
5:15 Ronald James Chorale
5:55 Kennedy High School
Gospel Choir

PARADES
4:00 N'Krumah Better Boys & Double
Nine Highsteppers SA&PCs with
Pinettes
Brass Band

SATURDAY, APRIL 30

FOX 38 / POLAROID STAGE
11:20 Southern University of New
Orleans Jazz Band
12:35 Tommy Ridgley & The
Untouchables w/ special guest
Al Johnson
2:10 Wayne Toups & Zydecajun
3:30 Randy Newman
4:50 Charmaine Neville Band w/
Reggie Houston & Amasa Miller
6:10 Casa Samba

B97 / BELLSOUTH MOBILITY STAGE
11:45 Golden Star Hunters Mardi Gras
Indians
1:00 Ruben "Mr. Salsa" Gonzalez &
His Salseros
2:30 Steve Riley & The Mamou
Playboys
4:15 Hackberry Ramblers
5:45 Continental Drifters

WWL / RAY-BAN STAGE
12:00 Nueva Generacion
1:30 Raymond Myles & The RAMS
2:45 Walter "Wolfman" Washington &
The Roadmasters
4:15 Robert Cray
5:45 Ry Cooder & David Lindley

HOUSE OF BLUES STAGE
11:45 Coushatta Dancers
1:15 Cajun Mardi Gras Parade
1:15 Blackie Forestier
& The Cajun Aces
2:45 Nathan & The Zydeco Cha Chas
4:15 Bryan Lee
& The Jumpstreet Five
5:45 Miss Ann Goodly & Zydeco
Brothers

CONGO SQUARE STAGE
11:30 Chuck Carbo & The Billeo
Brothers
12:40 Davell Crawford
1:50 Ali Farke Toure
3:15 Irie Vibrations
4:35 Ballet Nacional Folklorico
Garifuna de Honduras
6:00 James Rivers Movement

WWOZ / BET ON JAZZ JAZZ TENT
12:00 Fred Kemp Quartet
1:05 Larry Sieberth Trio w/ special
guest Betty Shirley
2:10 Germaine Bazzle

3:20 Jimmy Smith
4:40 Silver Brass Ensemble
6:00 Tito Puente's Golden Latin Jazz
Allstars

COX CABLE ECONOMY HALL
11:30 Camelia Jazz Band
12:40 Bob French's Original Tuxedo
Jazz Band
1:45 Michael White Quartet w/
special guest Thais Clark
3:00 Claude "Fiddler" Williams
4:20 A Tribute to Danny Barker
5:45 Young Tuxedo Brass Band

LAGNIAPPE TENT
11:30 Dillard University Jazz Band
12:35 Woodenhead
1:50 Patrice Fisher & Arpa
3:00 Michael Ward
4:25 Willie Tee
5:45 Jean Redpath

MUSIC HERITAGE TENT
11:30 Davell Crawford (Interview)
12:30 Ambrose & Calvin Sam
1:30 Randy Newman (Interview)
2:30 Jessie Mae Hemphill
4:00 Ali Farke Toure (Interview)
5:00 Steve Riley (Interview)

RHODES / WYLD GOSPEL TENT
11:20 Rejubilation Community Choir
12:05 Soulful Heavenly Stars
12:50 Beulah Baptist Church Choir
1:35 Love Alive Fellowship
2:20 Johnson Extension
3:05 Mighty Chariots
3:50 First Church of God in Christ
Mass Choir
4:55 Staple Singers
5:40 Zulu Ensemble of the Zulu
SA&PC
6:25 To the Glory of God
Community Choir

PARADES
2:00 Taylor Bunch, Jolly Bunch &
Avenue Steppers SA&PCs with
Pinstripe Brass Band
4:00 Lady Sequence, Money Wasters
& Prince of Wales SA&PCs with
Trombone Shorty's Allstar
Brass Band

SUNDAY, MAY 1

FOX 38 / POLAROID STAGE
11:40 St. Augustine High School
Jazz Band
12:50 The Iguanas
2:15 Cowboy Mouth
3:45 Terrance Simien & The Mallet
Playboys
5:30 The Radiators

B97 / BELLSOUTH MOBILITY STAGE
12:00 Herman Jackson
1:30 Southern Flavor Bluegrass
3:00 Allen Fontenot & The Country
Cajuns
4:30 Bruce Daigrepont Cajun Band
5:00 Ritmo Caribeno

WWL / RAY-BAN STAGE
11:30 Bobby Marchan & Higher
Ground
12:50 Jean Knight w/ Blue Eyed
Soul Band
2:00 Johnny Adams
3:30 Aretha Franklin
5:30 Neville Brothers

HOUSE OF BLUES STAGE
11:30 Carl LeBlanc Group
12:40 Creole Wild West Mardi Gras
Indians

1:50 Classie Ballou
& The All-Nite Band
3:00 Snooks Eaglin
4:20 Kermit Ruffins & The Barbecue
Swingers
5:45 Willis Prudhomme & Zydeco
Express

CONGO SQUARE STAGE
11:30 Culu Dancers
12:40 Moja Nya
1:55 Keith Claiborne
3:20 Mahogany Blue
4:45 Malavoi of Martinique
6:00 Ballet Nacional Folklorico
Garifuna de Honduras

WWOZ / BET ON JAZZ JAZZ TENT
11:25 George Fontenette
12:35 Alvin "Red" Tyler Quartet
1:45 Ellis Marsalis
3:00 Nicholas Payton
4:25 Wynton Marsalis
6:00 Dave Bartholomew Orchestra

COX CABLE ECONOMY HALL
11:30 Barbara Shorts
12:40 New Orleans Ragpickers of
Japan
1:50 New Orleans Ragtime Orchestra
3:00 Onward Brass Band
4:25 Pete Fountain
5:45 Percy Humphrey & The Crescent
City Joymakers

LAGNIAPPE TENT
11:40 Delgado Community College
Jazz Ensemble
12:45 Asian / Pacific American Review
2:15 Rising Star Fife & Drum Band
3:20 Spencer Bohren
4:40 Old Morrisville Brass Band
5:30 Carlos Sanchez

MUSIC HERITAGE TENT
11:30 Classie Ballou (Interview)
12:30 Rising Star Fife & Drum
1:15 Malavoi (Interview)
2:15 Old Morrisville Brass Band
3:00 Sister Shirley Ceasar (Interview)
4:00 Little Freddie King

RHODES / WYLD GOSPEL TENT
11:15 Antioch Gospel Singers
12:00 Jo "Cool" Davis
12:45 Southern Bells
1:30 Famous Rocks of Harmony
2:15 John Lee & The Heralds of
Christ w/ Christine Myles
3:00 Zion Harmonizers w/ special
guest Aaron Neville
4:00 Evangelist Shirley Ceasar
4:55 Voices from the Mount
5:40 Holy Name Singers of the
Institute of Divine Metaphysical
Research
6:25 Gospel Soul Children

PARADES
2:00 Scene Boosters, Original New
Orleans Men Buck Jumpers &
Perfect Gentlemen SA&PCs with
Tremé Brass Band
3:00 Economy Hall Parade with
Calliope High Steppers Ladies
SA&PC
4:00 Original New Orleans Lady Buck
Jumpers, Jet Setters & Calliope
High Steppers SA&PCs with Lil'
Rascals Brass Band

NIGHT CONCERTS

FRIDAY, APRIL 22, 9 P.M.
The Neville Brothers, Third World,
Miriam Makeba with special guest
Hugh Masekela and The Tour of
Hope
Kiefer UNO Lakefront Arena
SATURDAY, APRIL 23, 9 P.M.
The Allman Brothers Band, The Band,
Buckwheat Zydeco
Kiefer UNO Lakefront Arena
SATURDAY, APRIL 23, 12 MIDNIGHT
Jaeger's After Dark Midnight Jam
Alvin Batiste, Idris Muhammad, Red
Tyler, Richard Payne, Barbara Short
Jaeger Seafood Restaurant & Tavern
SUNDAY, APRIL 24, 7 P.M.
Gospel Is Alive
The Winans, The Cosmopolitan
Church of Prayer Choir
The Johnson Extension
Saenger Theatre
MONDAY, APRIL 25, 8 P.M.
George Benson, Shirley Horn Trio
Saenger Theatre
MONDAY, APRIL 25, 8 P.M.
*Traditional Jazz Night at the Palm
Court*
Percy & Willie Humphrey, Doc
Cheatham, Pud Brown, Chuck
Badie, Butch Thompson, Sammy
Rimington, Lucien Barbarin &
Ernest Elly
Palm Court Jazz Café
TUESDAY, APRIL 26, 8 P.M.
Dew Drop Inn Revisited
Charles Brown, Ruth Brown, Jimmy
Witherspoon, Johnny Adams, Ernie
K-Doe, Tommy Ridgley, Wanda
Rouzan, Reggie Hall, Wardell
Quezerque & His Orchestra, Master
of Ceremonies Bobby Marchan
Ernest N. Morial Convention Center
TUESDAY, APRIL 26, 8 P.M.
*Traditional Jazz Night at the Palm
Court*
Percy & Willie Humphrey, Doc
Cheatham, Pud Brown, Chuck
Badie, Butch Thompson, Sammy
Rimington, Lucien Barbarin &
Ernest Elly
Palm Court Jazz Café
WEDNESDAY, APRIL 27, 8 P.M.
Count Basie Orchestra with Joe
Williams
The Newport Allstars featuring
George Wein
Lew Tabackin
Nicholas Payton, Al Grey
Eddie Jones
Oliver Jackson
Germaine Bazzle
Ernest N. Morial Convention Center
THURSDAY, APRIL 28, 8 P.M.
Wynton Marsalis Septet, Herbie
Hancock Trio, The Joshua Redman
Quartet
Ernest N. Morial Convention Center
FRIDAY, APRIL 29, 8 P.M.
La Noche Latina
Tito Puente & His Orchestra w/
special guest Mongo Santamaria
Gilberto Santa Rosa y Su Orquesta
Ritmo Caribeno
Ernest N. Morial Convention Center
FRIDAY, APRIL 29, 9 P.M.
Little Feat, Weir Wasserman featuring
Bob Weir & Rob Wasserman,
Clarence "Gatemouth" Brown
Kiefer UNO Lakefront Arena
SATURDAY, APRIL 30, 9 P.M.
Aretha Franklin, B.B. King,
Gospel Soul Children of New Orleans
Kiefer UNO Lakefront Arena

1995

Dixie Cups

Ladies performing well, as lead vocalists or on any other instrument, have always been a draw, although the music industry has been and still is, predominately male.

Jazz, when it first started seeping up through the cultural byways was considered "the devil's music" – even the word "Jazz" was a slang word for sex at the turn of the century in the late 1800's and only "bad" women sang it. The early "blues mamas" – women like Bessie Smith, Gertrude "Ma" Rainey, and Billie Holiday, were very strong women innovators who had to overcome not only racial prejudice, but the prejudices of people of all colors judging them and their morals harshly for not staying "in their place" – that place being in the home or in church. To go out on the road and have a career in music you had to walk away from a lot of traditional cultural imperatives. There really weren't any road maps to follow. There have been many discussions about whether you choose the music or the music chooses you, and the general consensus is it's a combination of the two. We can only be grateful that the early women pioneers forged the path they did so that others could walk it without as much adversity as they faced.

The 1995 Jazz & Heritage Festival put some pretty serious emphasis on women in music. A special focus area in the program book spoke about the "Ladies of Jazz Fest": a

GLOBALLY

Israeli Prime Minister Yitzhak Rabin is assassinated by a Jewish student in protest for Rabin giving Israel to the Arabs.

For the first time in twenty years, no British soldiers patrol the streets of Belfast, Northern Ireland.

NATIONALLY

The bombing of the Murrah Federal Building in Oklahoma City kills 168 people. An FBI investigation leads quickly to the arrest of Army veteran Timothy McVeigh.

Dr. Bernard A. Harris, Jr., makes history as the first black American astronaut to walk in space.

LOCALLY

Loophole in state drinking law allowing bars and retailers to sell liquor to people under 21 is closed.

The Crescent City Farmer's Market begins.

A resolution proclaiming 1995 as the year of New Orleans' Jazz Centennial Celebration introduced in the U.S. Senate.

The May 1995 flood is the number one single largest event in the history of National Flood Insurance Program. More than $500 million in losses in the area are paid.

CULTURALLY

The Rock and Roll Hall of Fame opens in Cleveland, OH.

In October, Nation of Islam leader Louis Farrakhan leads the "Million Man March" in Washington, DC.

During the Trial of the Century, O.J. Simpson is acquitted of the murders of his former wife, Nicole, and her friend Ronald Goldman.

The Java programming language is announced, and will become standard in Internet programs.

well-written article by Louise McKinney and the national lineup for this year's Festival included a varied and powerful collection of fine women artists.

This year brought back our own first lady of Jazz, Germaine Bazzle, who performed in the Jazz Tent with an all star group; Irma Thomas, Soul Queen of New Orleans; Marva Wright, touted as Blues Queen of New Orleans; Wanda Rouzan, musical diva and grand marshall;

pel and jazz singer and actress. All Louisiana born, mostly New Orleans born. All of these women were mentioned in the Jazz Fest Program book article, but there are so many more.

Paula and the Pontiacs delivered some straight up straight ahead blues. Wanda Rouzan and A Taste of New Orleans gave a classic delivery of New Orleans R&B. Rosie Ledet, Zydeco Queen from Lota, Louisiana, whose sexy no nonsense per-

Koko Taylor, blues chanteuse; Charmaine Neville, daughter of Charles and entertainer extraordinaire; Marcia Ball, barrel house blues and Queen of Texas swing, with a little Gulf coast swamp-pop thrown in for good measure, who presides on her piano like an empress; Lillian Boutté, goddess in the traditional jazz and gospel vein who in 1995 was based in Hamburg, Germany, successfully promoting New Orleans music all over Europe; and Barbara Shorts, blues, gos-

formances have entranced and pleased every one of her fans on the Fais Do-Do Stage and Gina Forsyth, consummate Cajun fiddle player who can still be seen every year at Jazz Fest playing with someone, made her Jazz Fest debut this year. Peabody, fronted by Karen Protti — a local group offering tasty pop rock played — with Karen's mom and dad, who were devoted supporters of the band, passing out flyers to the listening crowd. Betty Shirley sang straight ahead jazz

SATURDAY, APRIL 29

FOX 38 / POLAROID STAGE
11:00 Coushatta Dancers
12:00 Chris Ardoin & Double Clutchin'
1:30 Terrence Simien & The Mallet Playboys
2:50 Marcia Ball
4:25 The Brecker Brothers
6:00 Cowboy Mouth

BELLSOUTH MOBILITY STAGE
12:15 Royann and Jim Calvin
1:45 Golden Star Hunters
3:00 Stavin Chain
4:20 Sonny Bourg & The Bayou Blues Band
5:45 Horace Trahan & Lache Pas

WWL / RAY-BAN STAGE
11:10 Southern University Baton Rouge Jazz Ensemble
12:20 Kat & The Kittens
1:30 Beau Jocque & Zydeco Hi-Rollers
2:45 Little Milton
4:15 Wilson Pickett
5:50 Gladys Knight

HOUSE OF BLUES STAGE
12:00 J. Monque'D Blues Band
1:25 Bruce "Sunpie" Barnes & The Sunspots
2:45 George Porter, Jr. & Runnin' Pardners
4:10 John Mooney & Bluesiana
5:35 Jimmy Dawkins

WWOZ JAZZ TENT
11:30 Al Belletto Quartet
12:35 Angelle Trosclair & The New Relics
1:50 Astral Project
3:00 Tony Bazley Quintet w/ special guest Herlin Riley
4:20 Kent Jordan Group w/ special guest Kevin Eubanks
5:40 Sonny Rollins

COX / CABLEREP ECONOMY HALL TENT
11:20 Young Tuxedo Brass Band
12:40 Placide Adams Original Dixieland Hall Jazz Band
2:00 New Orleans Ragtime Orchestra
3:20 June Gardner & The Fellows
4:40 Pud Brown Palm Court Jazz Band
6:00 Early Jazz Review feat. Dr. Michael White, Fred Lonzo, Shannon Powell, Bill Huntington, Don Vappie & Steve Pistorious

CONGO SQUARE STAGE
11:15 DJ Jimi & Ricky Bee
12:30 Percussion, Inc.
1:40 Irie Vibrations
2:55 Johnny Adams
4:20 Cyril Neville & The Uptown Allstars
5:45 Black Stalin of Trinidad

LAGNIAPPE TENT
12:20 Song of Life
1:40 Arte Flamenco w/ Sp. Guests Manolo Leiva & Carlos Sanchez
3:00 Dembo Konte, Kausu Kuyateh, Mawdo Suso of Gambia and Senegal
4:25 Jump 4 Joy
5:45 Carlos Sanchez

MUSIC HERITAGE STAGE
11:45 Bruce "Sunpie" Barnes (Interview)
1:00 Young Tuxedo Brass Band (Interview)
2:20 Cyril Neville (Interview)
3:30 Gina Forsyth
4:30 Little Milton (Interview)
5:30 Dembo Konte of the Gambia (Interview)

RHODES GOSPEL TENT
11:20 Inspirational Gospel Singers
12:05 St. Luke A.M.E. Choir
12:50 Watson Memorial Spiritual Church Choir
1:35 St. Frances DeSales Golden Voices
2:20 Light House (Word has fallen off page) Gospel Singers
3:05 First B.C. Missionary Choir
4:00 Mississippi Mass Choir
4:55 The Crownseekers
6:25 Sammy Berfect and Dimensions of Faith

Red Tyler

accompanied by Baton Rouge native Larry Sieberth. Jean "Mr. Big Stuff, Don't Mess With My Toot Toot" Knight represented for the city while Cissy Houston enthralled the audience featured with the Herbie Mann Reunion Band. Atlanta Georgia "Homegirl" Gladys Knight, who

we'd be happy to adopt as a local any day of the week delivered a great performance too.

Hometown girl Sharon Martin along with Samirah Evans performed in the Jazz Tent with Walter Payton (father of Grammy award winning Nicholas Payton) and the Snap Bean band. " I love Sharon Martin. She really encouraged me when I first moved here and also gave me my first break as a vocalist when she hired me to sub for her on her regular Sunday gig in the early 90's." said Samirah, "I was so honored to have an opportunity to perform at Jazz Fest with such a dear friend. The crowd was great, the day was beautiful and Sharon has so much fire that

she ignites me when we work together. It was really special."

Tania Maria, Grammy nominated native of Brazil closed out the Jazz Tent with an intense, passionate feast of Bossa Nova grooves and stunning vocals that left fans screaming. Closing out one day at Jazz Fest, fans were treated to the local royalty, the Dixie Cups and international royalty, Joni Mitchell, performing material from her new CD "Turbulent Indigo" on Reprise Records.

Roberta Flack gave an intimate and spellbinding performance at the Saenger Theatre on Sunday, April 30th, mesmerizing fans with "Killing Me Softly" in addition to her newest material in which she did covers of "A Sentimental Mood" by Duke Ellington, "The Thrill is Gone" by B.B. King and Al Green's "Let's Stay Together" to the delight of the packed house.

Nancy "Guess Who I Saw Today" Wilson made her debut at the New Orleans Jazz & Heritage Festival this year and anyone fortunate enough to get a ticket to the show at the Convention Center would never forget the consummate skill and amazing control of this legendary Diva of Jazz. At moments, people were afraid to even breathe for fear they would miss some vocal nuance and by the end of this show each person there felt that they had a personal tryst with greatness.

"La Noche Latina" arguably the "hottest' ticket of the evening offerings featured the divine, vibrant, passionate Celia Cruz. Anyone who's ever seen this amazing artist knows that Thursday, May 4th defied descrip-

tion. In 1995 Ms. Cruz had over 50 albums to her credit and over 20 that had gone gold. Famed for her passion, flamboyant attire, and consummate skill as an artist, the Queen of Salsa rocked the house at the Convention center.

It was evident at The New Orleans Jazz & Heritage Festival that in 1995 women in music had come a long way.

Where were the men this year? EVERYWHERE! – Dr. John, Ray Charles, James Taylor, B.B. King, Deacon John, Eddie Bo, George Porter, Snooks Eaglin, Allen Toussaint, Ellis Marsalis, The subdudes, Johnny Adams, Rebirth Brass Band, Kermit Ruffins, Luther Kent, and James Rivers. A.J. Loria, our own New Orleans De la Salle graduate songwriter, who in 1995 was splitting his time between Japan and the Crescent City; Lenny McDaniels, another singer/songwriter whose newest offering, "Worth The

fest facts

The Fest's economic impact was $200 million.

450,000 attended Jazz Fest.

Chuck Berry had 20,000 fans singing along at the top of their lungs on his hit "My Ding A Ling" at the Fair Grounds.

Peace Train, from South Africa, was comprised of 92 people — the most members of any band that performed at Jazz Fest.

PARADES
12:00 Black Men of Labor & Golden Trumpets SA&PCs and Trombone Shorty & The All Star Brass Band
12:40 Economy Hall Parade with The Calendar Girls & Original Jolly Bunch Sisters SA&PCs
2:00 Original Four & N'Krumah Better Boys SA&PCs and Trombone Shorty & The All Star Brass Band
4:00 Money Wasters & Jolly Bunch SA&PCs with Tuba Fats and The Chosen Few Brass Band

SUNDAY, APRIL 30

FOX 38 / POLAROID STAGE
11:15 SUNO Ensemble
12:20 Geno Delafose & French Rockin' Boogie
1:45 Wanda Rouzan & A Taste of New Orleans
3:00 Frankie Ford Revue w/ special guest Jimmy Clanton
4:35 Wayne Toups
6:00 Earl King

BELLSOUTH MOBILITY STAGE
11:20 Lee Bates
12:40 Paky Saavedra's Bandidos
2:00 D.L. Menard & The Louisiana Aces
3:20 The Hackberry Ramblers
4:40 The Bluerunners
6:00 New Orleans Klezmer Allstars

WWL / RAY-BAN STAGE
11:15 U Hamilton
12:30 James Rivers Movement
1:50 Clarence Carter
3:10 Allen Toussaint
4:35 Chuck Berry w/ special guest Johnnie Johnson
6:00 Ray Charles

HOUSE OF BLUES STAGE
11:40 Creole Wild West
12:40 Rosie Ledet
1:50 Bois Sec Ardoin & Canray Fontenot
3:00 Snooks Eaglin
4:40 Lavelle White
6:00 Magic Slim & The Teardrops

WWOZ JAZZ TENT
11:20 Patrice Fisher & Arpa
12:50 Scott Goudeau
2:00 Alvin Batiste & The Jazztronauts
3:20 Straight Ahead
4:40 Abbey Lincoln
6:00 Roy Hargrove Quintet

COX / CABLEREP ECONOMY HALL TENT
11:40 Louis Cottrell & His Original Creole Jazz Band
1:00 Ytre Suloens Jass Ensemble of Norway
2:00 Wallace Davenport & His New Orleans Jazz Band
3:10 Doc Cheatham
4:40 Bob French Original Tuxedo Brass Band
6:00 Banu Gibson & New Orleans Hot Jazz

CONGO SQUARE STAGE
11:20 Partners 'N' Crime / Mystikal
12:35 Dembo Konte Kora & The Belafon Ensemble of Gambia
1:45 White Eagles
3:00 Sterlyn Silver
4:30 Michael Ray & The Cosmic Krewe w/ special guests Phish's Trey Anastasio and John Fishman
6:00 Los Babies Del Merengue

LAGNIAPPE TENT
12:40 St. Augustine High School Jazz Band
2:00 Ambrose and Calvin Sam
3:10 The Evening Star String Band
4:30 Michael Ward
5:50 Dembo Konte Kora & The Belafon Ensemble of Gambia

Price," on local label Renegade Records, was certainly true to its title. Branford Marsalis, who performed this year, treated his hometown to a set combining jazz, reggae, rap and rock, making him the most musically diverse member of the Marsalis dynasty.

On Sunday, April 30th, Mystikal, who in later years would become a multi-platinum artist, opened the Congo Stage along with Partners 'N' Crime followed by Creole Wild West, starting it out on the House Of Blues stage. Earl "Let the Good Times Roll" King beloved by all musicians in the City closed the Polaroid Stage, Ray Charles closed Ray-Ban, the Roy Hargrove Quartet closed the Jazz Tent. There was a stunning show in Congo Square when Michael Ray and The Cosmic Krewe invited Phish's Trey Anastasio

and Jon Fishman to perform.

Joseph "Zigaboo" Modeliste returned to his hometown from Los Angeles to deliver a totally "Funked Up" performance with Meters band member Leo Nocentelli on the Polaroid Stage. The usual suspects helped to create an extended funky pocket

from start to finish of the show. Signature Zigaboo reigned and proved once again that New Orleans makes the funkiest drummers in the world.

A new generation of young men of New Orleans made their presence felt in 1995. Jason Marsalis, the youngest son in the Marsalis clan at 18; Davell Crawford, grandson of "Sugar Boy" Crawford; Jamil Sharif , whose father played trumpet at the Blue Room in the Fairmont Roosevelt Hotel for many years; and Nicholas Payton at 21 was coming into his own. His father Walter Payton played tuba and bass and influenced many musicians coming up in New Orleans.

Ivan Neville played on May 6th pushing his latest effort *Thanks,* the follow up to his solo debut *If My Ancestors Could See Me Now* released on Polydor. An extremely talented man, Ivan,

Allen Toussaint

MUSIC HERITAGE STAGE
1:00 Banu Gibson (Interview)
2:00 Abbey Lincoln (Interview)
3:00 Po' Henry & Tookie
4:30 Clarence Carter (Interview)

RHODES GOSPEL TENT
11:20 Antioch Gospel Singers
12:05 Friendly Five Gospel Singers
12:45 New Zion Trio
1:30 Marva Wright
2:15 The Blind Boys of Alabama
3:10 La Freeman Congress Choir
4:00 Bobby Jones New Life
4:55 The Famous Mighty Imperials
5:35 Holy Hill Gospel Singers
6:25 Raymond A. Myles & The RAMS

PARADES
12:00 Scene Boosters & Double Nine
      Highsteppers SA&PCs, Jetsetters Social
      & Marching Club, Pinettes Brass Band
      and The Seminoles Mardi Gras Indians
2:00 Westbank Steppers, Valley of the Silent
      Men & Prince of Wales SA&PCs, Pinettes
      Brass Band and The Mohawk Hunters
      Mardi Gras Indians
4:00 New Orleans Men Buck Jumpers
      & Original New Orleans Lady Buck
      Jumpers SA&PCs, Tremé Brass Band
      and The Black Eagles Mardi Gras Indians

was in a great place in '95 and his show reflected the serious attitude he was taking with his music. A veteran of Keith Richards' group, X Pensive Winos; as well as Bonnie Raitt's band and the Neville family group, Ivan had a lot to offer and he offered it all up to his thousands of fans.

In a feature article than ran on Wednesday, May 3rd 1995 in *The Times Picayune*, local photographer Michael P. Smith talked about Jazz Fest with Chris Waddington, "Jazz Fest is like New Orleans because it's an interactive music environment for both the audience and the musicians. Surprises always happen because musicians come to jam on other people's stages, and of course, as soon as the Festival closes, they are out around town at the clubs where some of the best stuff goes on. I've photographed every Jazz Fest since the beginning and I still go nuts. Usually I work 20 hours a day, trying to see and hear everything – I'm a fan just like everyone else"

Willis Prudhomme

THURSDAY, MAY 4

FOX 38 / POLAROID STAGE
12:00 Delgado Community College Jazz
      Ensemble
1:20 Oliver "Who Shot the LaLa" Morgan
2:45 Alex Chilton
4:15 Boozoo Chavis & Magic Sounds
5:45 Leo Nocentelli w/ special guest Zigaboo
      Modeliste

BELLSOUTH MOBILITY STAGE
12:15 Hammond State Strawberry Jammers
1:30 Zulu Ensemble of the Zulu SA & PC
2:50 The Magnolia Sisters
4:15 Balfa Toujours
5:40 Lenny McDaniel

WWL / RAY-BAN STAGE
11:40 Xavier University Jazz Lab Ensemble
1:00 Ancestro
2:20 Rebirth Brass Band
3:45 BeauSoleil
5:30 James Taylor

HOUSE OF BLUES STAGE
11:25 Paula & The Pontiacs
12:50 Fernest Arceneaux & The Thunders
2:15 Katie Webster & The Vasti Jackson Group
3:45 Kenny Neal featuring Jackie Neal
5:15 New Orleans Blues Harmonica Showcase
      feat. Lazy Lester, J.D. Hill, Andy J. Forest,
      Rockin' Jake, Merritt Doggins, Jumpin'
      Johnny Sansone, Ben Maygarden

WWOZ JAZZ TENT
11:20 George Fontenette & His Quintet
12:30 Steve Masakowski & Friends
1:50 Charles Neville & Diversity
3:10 Walter Payton & Snap Bean feat. Sharon
      Martin, w/ sp. guest Samirah Evans
4:30 New Orleans Sax Ensemble
5:45 The David Murray Quartet w/ sp. guests
      Archie Shepp & Idris Muhammad

COX / CABLEREP ECONOMY HALL TENT
12:10 Joseph Torregano
1:40 Dukes of Dixieland
3:00 Eddie "Boh" Paris & The Cool Jazz Cats
4:20 Andrew Hall's Society Jazz Band
5:45 Rene Netto & The Sounds of New
      Orleans

CONGO SQUARE STAGE
12:10 Gregory Boyd & Vos
1:40 Orlando Turnquest & Thomas & The Boys
      of the Bahamas

"A fellow boomer and I always made a point of meeting for Pete Seeger's set to weep and sing along. My feelings about Seeger are strong, not only because of his music but also because of his politics. The first time he came, in 1979, I wangled an interview and took him to Chez Helene for lunch, where he wolfed down three helpings of beet salad. One year, his gig was on his birthday. The stage announcer told us beforehand and, when Seeger walked out, led us in singing "Happy Birthday." We all cried. In 1995, Seeger appeared again. He wore two hearing aids, and much of his voice was gone, but he was still a commanding presence. At one point, he announced that he was going to sing a song he had written, "If I Had a Hammer," and he asked the next group to come out as backup. The next group was Peter, Paul and Mary." JOHN POPE

Pete Seeger with Peter, Paul, and Mary

music scene

Rock and Roll Hall of Fame opens in Cleveland.

Lady BJ opens on Broadway in Smokey Joe's Café.

IN MEMORIAM

Dean Martin, Jerry Garcia, Rory Gallagher, Don Cherry

IN MEMORY OF ALLISON MINER
SEPTEMBER 23, 1949 – DECEMBER 23, 1995

Along with Quint Davis and George Wein, Allison Miner was a powerful force in starting the New Orleans Jazz & Heritage Festival. She was born on September 23, the same day as Ray Charles, John Coltrane and Earl Turbinton who became her dear friend. It is an understatement to say that Jazz Fest would not be Jazz Fest without her involvement. Chris Strachwitz of Arhoolie Records said, "Allison was the heart and soul of the festival during its early years."

She was born in Baltimore and raised in Daytona Beach, Florida where she befriended the garage band the Allman Joys who became famous as the Allman Brothers. In 1965 she heard Danny Barker on a TV program talking about the tradition of jazz funerals in New Orleans and she came to this city.

In 1969 she began working at the Hogan Jazz Archives at Tulane University. There she met Quint Davis and they became a couple. It was through working with Dick Allen at Tulane that she met George Wein, who together with Quint and others started the festival.

Today the "Heritage" aspect of the festival is best experienced at the stage that bears her name, The Allison Miner Music Heritage Stage located on the east end, inside the Grandstand. The food, African, Cajun and Folk Heritage stages and presentations are the direct result of her influence on the festival.

Regarding the Music Heritage stage Quint once told writer Geraldine Wyckoff "She did all parts of it. She would design it artistically, pick out the people who would be on it, she would actually call them all up and talk them into doing it, get them contracts and releases, get it produced, get recorded, be the stage manager, be the production manager, and do all the interviews. For years she did all of those things." In addition she helped run the entire festival for the first five years.

Allison believed that the soul of the musician was the soul of the music. She made sure that they felt

comfortable, were treated properly and had a positive experience. She personally dragged Henry Roeland Byrd, a.k.a, Professor Longhair out of obscurity and brought him to the attention of record labels, writers and booking agents. It is possible that he would have died relatively unknown to a younger generation of fans without her efforts.

Beyond the Festival she also worked to achieve recognition and a paycheck for Bo Dollis, Monk Boudreaux and the Wild Magnolias, the Rebirth Brass Band, Kermit Ruffins and Tuts Washington. The legion of local and national artists that she loved and worked with include Allen Toussaint, Aaron Neville, Willie and Earl Turbinton, Danny Barker, Beausoleil, Robert Pete Williams, Bukka White, the Radiators, Filé Cajun Band, Marc & Ann Savoy, and on and on.

Her impact on the community was also felt in her work at the Contemporary Arts Center and WWOZ Radio and in the streets and music clubs of the city. Allison played the triangle and she accompanied many a group on a Creole waltz or two-step. With the triangle in her hands she brought together people of different cultures and ethnic backgrounds.

John Sinclair said, "I remember Allison at Indian practice and at the second line parades beating that triangle. Man, she would always be right on the beat."

Her long association with Bo Dollis and Monk Boudreaux and other Mardi Gras Indians took her throughout the streets and back of town neighborhoods. Danny Barker shared a special friendship with her. He often said that he'd never seen a woman that loved the music as much as Allison. He contributed to her work with respect for many years and that, itself, was a great complement.

When it came to the artists that she represented she was very direct and to the point. She taught many local musicians how not to get ripped off in the sometimes mystifying business of music. She taught many musicians to "keep the publishing."

Allison loved to sing but pursued other aspects of music business upon her arrival to New Orleans. One of her favorite songs that she sang at a tribute/benefit concert organized in her honor in 1995 is "Something Within." Lucie Campbell Williams, an important gospel composer, educator and evangelist wrote this song. Allison learned a version at the Jazz Archive. The first verse goes:

Have you something within you oh Lord
That holds in the reigns
Something within you
Oh child, you cannot exclaim
Something within you oh child, you cannot exclaim
Though you can say oh God
Something within you.

She succumbed to multiple myeloma, a bone-destroying cancer, at the young age of 46. Her survivors include two sons, Jonathan and Rashi Kaslow.

Allison Miner was given a jazz funeral on January 14, 1996. A memorial service was held at City Park. As per her request her two sons spread her ashes into the park lagoon. The moment she hit the water the end of the rainbow touched upon her. Allison was the" pot of gold." Her life and this service are documented in "Reverence" by filmmaker Amy Nesbitt and are available from Video Veracity.

3:00 Golden Eagles Mardi Gras Indians
4:30 Oldolum of Brazil
6:00 Don Rousell

LAGNIAPPE TENT
12:00 Jesse Thomas
1:25 Julio and Caesar
2:50 David and Roselyn
4:30 Sally Townes & The Big Easy w/ sp. guest Tara Darnell
5:50 Hot Strings of New Orleans

MUSIC HERITAGE STAGE
11:30 Gray Montgomery
12:30 Orlando Turnquest & Thomas & The Boys of the Bahamas (Interview)
1:30 Marce Lacouture
2:50 Lloyd Washington
4:15 Mary Lake Blight & Jeune Gens de la Prairie

RHODES GOSPEL TENT
11:45 Delma Trosclair & The Heaven Seekers
12:30 Christian Light Chorale
1:15 True Tones Singers
2:00 Coolie Family
2:45 Leviticus Gospel Singers
3:30 Alvin Bridges & Desire Community Choir
4:15 Pilgrim Jubilees
5:10 Gospel Extenders
5:55 Avondale Community Choir

PARADES
4:00 Bon Temp Roulez SA&PC and Storyville Stompers Brass Band

FRIDAY, MAY 5

FOX 38 / POLAROID STAGE
11:15 Fuego
12:30 Milton Batiste's Magnificent 7th's w/ sp. guest Ernie K-Doe & Jessie Hill
1:50 Kermit Ruffins & The Barbecue Swingers
3:15 Bobby Marchan & Higher Ground
4:35 Steve Riley & The Mamou Playboys
6:00 Zachary Richard

BELLSOUTH MOBILITY STAGE
11:30 Jambalaya Cajun Band
12:45 Peabody
1:55 Eddie LeJeune & The Morse Playboys
3:15 Joe Clay & The Clements Brothers Band
4:35 Warren Caesar & Creole Zydeco
6:00 Ritmo Caribeno

WWL / RAY-BAN STAGE
12:00 9th Ward Hunters
1:20 Buckwheat Zydeco
2:40 Koko Taylor
4:15 The funky Meters
6:00 Al Green

HOUSE OF BLUES STAGE
11:20 Mem Shannon & The Membership
12:35 Coco Robicheaux
1:55 Orlando Turnquest & Thomas & The Boys of the Bahamas
3:15 Deacon John
4:35 Eddie Bo
6:00 The Shepherd Band

WWOZ JAZZ TENT
11:15 Larry Sieberth w/ Betty Shirley
12:25 Phillip Manuel
1:35 Kidd Jordan – Al Fielder IAQ Quintet w/ guests Joel Futterman & William Parker

---

3:10 Clyde Kerr, Jr. & Univision
4:20 Joe Henderson & The "Double Rainbow" Quintet s/ sp. guest Oscar Castro-Neves
5:50 Tania Maria

COX / CABLEREP ECONOMY HALL TENT
11:30 Lady Charlotte
12:50 Ronnie Kole
2:00 Harry Connick Sr. w/ Jimmy Maxwell Orchestra
3:15 Ingrid Lucia & The Flying Neutrinos
4:45 Frank Federico & The Medicare Madcaps
6:00 Duke Dejan's Olympia Band

CONGO SQUARE STAGE
11:00 Richard Ison / Kirk Ford Experience feat. Rahssana Ison
12:10 Creole Zydeco Farmers
1:30 The Peace Train Children's Crusade of South Africa
3:00 Oldolum of Brazil
4:15 T&T Connection
5:45 Oscar D'Leon Orchestra

LAGNIAPPE TENT
12:30 John Parker
2:00 Clancy "Blues Boy" Lewis w/ Sheba Kimbrough
3:10 UNO Jazz Band
4:20 Doreen's Jazz New Orleans
5:45 Theron Lewis & Unit 7

MUSIC HERITAGE STAGE
12:15 Eddie LeJeune (Interview)
1:15 Michael White & The Origins of Jazz Presented by the National Park Service
2:45 Brownie Ford
3:45 Orlando Turnquest & Thomas & The Boys of the Bahamas (Interview)
4:45 Koko Taylor (Interview)

RHODES GOSPEL TENT
11:45 Gospel Grace Notes
12:30 Southern Travelers
1:15 Sunshine Connection
2:00 Friendly Travelers
2:45 Aline White & Company
3:30 The Heavenly Melodies
4:20 Willie Neal Johnson & The New Gospel Keynotes
5:10 Ronald James Chorale
5:55 Mississippi Seminar Choir

PARADES
4:00 Little Rascals Second Line SA&PC, Young Steppers, and New Birth Bras Band
5:15 Oldolum of Brazil & Casa Samba
6:00 Economy Hall Parade with Calliope High Steppers Ladies SA&PC

SATURDAY, MAY 6

FOX 38 / POLAROID STAGE
11:10 The Heritage School of Music Band
12:15 Chubby Carrier & The Bayou Swamp Band
1:40 The Subdudes
3:00 Michelle Shocked w/ sp. guests Hothouse Flowers, Fiachna O'Braomain & Peter O'Toole
4:40 Ivan Neville
6:00 The Dixie Cups

BELLSOUTH MOBILITY STAGE
11:20 The Piney Woods Ramblers featuring Jack Youngblood
12:30 Allen Fontenot & The Country Cajuns
1:55 Woodenhead

3:10 Iguanas
4:35 Darryl Johnson
6:00 Better Than Ezra

WWL / RAY-BAN STAGE
11:30 N.O.C.C.A. Jazz Ensemble
1:00 Marva Wright & The BMWs
2:30 Jimmie Vaughan
4:15 Little Feat
6:00 Joni Mitchell

HOUSE OF BLUES STAGE
11:15 Larry Garner & The Boogaloo Blues Band
12:30 Robert Lowery
1:00 R.L. Burnside Band
2:00 Soul Rebels Brass Band
3:10 Rockin' Dopsie, Jr. & The Zydeco Twisters
4:35 Walter "Wolfman" Washington & The Roadmasters w/ guest Timothea
6:00 The Ian Moore Band

WWOZ JAZZ TENT
11:15 Neslort
12:20 Germaine Bazzle
1:40 Delfeayo Marsalis
3:00 Marlon Jordan Quintet
4:20 Abdullah Ibrahim w/ Ekaya
5:50 Michel Camilo Quintet

COX / CABLEREP ECONOMY HALL TENT
11:30 Jacques Gauthe & His Creole Rice Jazz Band
12:40 Michael White Quartet w/ guest Thais Clark
2:00 George French's New Orleans Storyville Jazz
3:20 Gregg Stafford's Jazz Hounds
4:40 Onward Brass Band
6:00 New Leviathan Oriental Foxtrot Orchestra

CONGO SQUARE STAGE
11:00 Kumbuka Drum and Dance Collective
12:20 Front Page
1:40 Wild Magnolias
2:50 Ben Hunter the Soul Avenger
4:10 Charmaine Neville Band w/ Amasa Miller & Reggie Houston
5:40 Yomo Toro

LAGNIAPPE TENT
11:45 Betsy McGovern & The Poor Clares
1:15 Acoustic Swiftness
2:35 Tasso
4:10 Sheryl Cormier & Cajun Sounds
5:30 Robert Lowery
6:15 R.L. Burnside Band

MUSIC HERITAGE STAGE
12:00 Inez Andrews (Interview)
1:00 Michelle Shocked (Interview)
2:00 Kent Jordan (Interview)
3:00 John Sinclair & The Blues Scholars
4:00 Mustang Lightnin'

RHODES GOSPEL TENT
11:45 Macedonia Church of God in Christ Temple Choir
12:30 The Soulful Heavenly Stars
1:15 Mighty Chariots
2:00 Love Alive Fellowship Choir
2:45 Greater Bright Morning Star Choir
3:35 Inez Andrews
4:35 The Johnson Extension
5:20 St. Rose De Lima Gospel Choir
6:10 New Hope Baptist Church Gospel Choir

PARADES
12:00 Lady Sequences & Perfect Gentlemen SA&PCs and Tornado Brass Band

---

2:00 Devastating Ladies & Original Step-N-Style SA&PCs and Tornado Brass Band
4:00 Original Taylor Bunch, Avenue Steppers & Second Line Jammers SA&PCs and Looney Tunes Brass Band
4:40 Economy Hall Parade with P&P-S&S SA&PC

SUNDAY, MAY 7

FOX 38 / POLAROID STAGE
11:00 The Bluebirds
12:05 Luther Kent & The Trick Bag Band
1:30 Deadeye Dick
2:50 Clarence "Gatemouth" Brown
4:15 Irma Thomas & The Professionals
5:45 The Radiators

BELLSOUTH MOBILITY STAGE
11:15 Mamou
12:30 Walter Mouton
1:50 A. J. Loria
3:20 Continental Drifters
4:40 Nathan & The Zydeco Cha Chas
6:00 Los Sagitarios

WWL / RAY-BAN STAGE
11:30 Tommy Ridgley & The Untouchables w/ sp. guest Al Johnson & Sammy Ridgley
1:00 The Dirty Dozen
2:30 Buckshot Lefonque featuring Branford Marsalis
4:00 B. B. King
5:30 The Neville Brothers featuring Aaron Neville

HOUSE OF BLUES STAGE
11:20 Tabby Thomas & Band w/ sp. guest Henry Gray
12:40 Anders Osborne
2:00 Willie Tee
3:20 Davell
4:40 Bryan Lee & The Jump Street Five
6:00 Casa Samba

WWOZ JAZZ TENT
11:40 Jason Marsalis
1:00 Earl Turbinton Quartet
2:20 Ellis Marsalis w/ sp. guest Nnenna Freelon
4:00 Herbie Mann Reunion Band w/ sp. guests Cissy Houston, David Newman, Cornell Dupree, Chuck Rainey

COX / CABLEREP ECONOMY HALL TENT
11:20 Doc Paulin's Dixieland Jazz Band
12:30 Louisiana Repertory Jazz Ensemble
1:50 Wendell Brunious
3:15 Sammy Rimington
4:40 Jeannie & Jimmy Cheatham & Sweet Baby Blues Band
6:00 Percy Humphrey & The Crescent City Joymakers

CONGO SQUARE STAGE
11:10 Culu Dancers
12:30 Y'Shua Manzy & The World Beat Band
1:40 Bamboula 2000
2:55 Jean Knight
4:15 Eric Gable
5:45 Majek Fashek of Nigeria

LAGNIAPPE TENT
11:20 Loyola University Jazz Band
12:30 White Cloud Hunter
1:50 Carl LeBlanc

3:15 Kim Carson
4:40 Theresa Andersson Jazz Bag
6:00 Jude Taylor & His Burning
      Flames

MUSIC HERITAGE STAGE
11:15 Al Jackson
12:45 Doc Paulin (Interview)
1:45 Diamonds w/ The Family Groove
2:45 Majek Fashek of Nigeria
      (Interview)
3:45 Percy Humphrey (Interview)
4:45 David Doucet

RHODES GOSPEL TENT
11:15 The Melody Clouds
12:00 Chosen Few Gospel Choir
12:45 Joe "Cool" Davis
1:30 Southern Bells
2:15 John Lee & The Heralds of
      Christ w/ Christine Myles
3:00 Sherman Washington & The
      Famous Zion Harmonizers
3:50 Voices From the Mount of Mt.
      Carmel B.C.
4:40 Cosmopolitan Church of Prayer
      Choir
5:40 Rocks of Harmony
6:25 Gospel Soul Children

PARADES
11:20 Economy Hall Parade with
      Algiers Steppers SA&PC
12:00 Olympia Aid, Uptowner's Hobo
      Clowns & Ladies Zulu SA&PCs
      with Pin Stripe Brass Band and
      The Golden Arrows Mardi Gras
      Indians
2:00 Devastation & Unknowns
      SA&PCs with Pin Stripe Brass
      Band and The Wild Apache
      Mardi Gras Indians

4:00 The Untouchables & The
      Furious Five SA&PCs with The
      Lil' Rascals and The Carrollton
      Hunters Mardi Gras Indians

NIGHT CONCERTS

FRIDAY, APRIL 28, 9 P.M.
Gladys Knight
Booker T & The MG's with Booker T.
      Jones, Steve Cropper, Duck Dunn
      and Steve Potts
Charmaine Neville Band Featuring
      Amasa Miller and Reggie Houston
Kiefer UNO Lakefront Arena
SATURDAY, APRIL 29, 9 P.M.
Ray Charles & His Orchestra,
Dr. John Snooks Eaglin
Kiefer UNO Lakefront Arena
SUNDAY, APRIL 30, 8 P.M.
Robert Flack, The Brecker Brothers,
      Terence Blanchard Group
Saenger Theatre
Gospel is Alive!
In memory of Bishop Herman Brown.
      Hezekiah Walker & The Love
      Fellowship Crusade Choir, The
      Canton Spirituals, Reverend Paul S.
      Morton & The Greater St. Stephen
      Full Gospel Baptist Church Mass
      Choir, The Spiritualettes
Saenger Theatre
MONDAY, MAY 1, 8 P.M.
*Traditional Jazz Night at the Palm
      Court.*
Doc Cheatham's All-Star Band with
      Doc Cheatham, Peter Badie, Ernest

Elly, Lester Caliste, Brian O'Connel,
      Sammy Rimmington and Ed Frank.
Tribute to Jelly Roll Morton, King
      Oliver, Louis Armstrong, and
      Johnny Dodds featuring Dr.
      Michael White, Nicholas Payton,
      Steve Pistorious, Herlin Riley, Bill
      Huntington, Don Vappie and Fred
      Lonzo
All-Star jam session follows at 11:30
      p.m.
Palm Court Jazz Café, 1205 Decatur
      Street
TUESDAY, MAY 2, 8 P.M.
Roots International! Black Uhuru,
      Jamaica, W.I.; Osibisa; Olodum,
      Bahia, Brazil; Rebirth Brass Band;
      The Wild Magnolias Mardi Gras
      Indian Band
Ernest N. Morial Convention Center,
      La Nouvelle Orleans Ballroom
TUESDAY, MAY 2, 8 P.M.
Traditional Jazz Night at the Palm
      Court.
Doc Cheatham's All-Star Band with
      Doc Cheatham, Peter Badie, Ernest
      Elly, Lester Caliste, Brian O'Connel,
      Sammy Rimmington and Ed
      Frank. Tribute to Jelly Roll Morton,
      King Oliver, Louis Armstrong,
      and Johnny Dodds featuring Dr.
      Michael White, Nicholas Payton,
      Steve Pistorious, Herlin Riley, Bill
      Huntington, Don Vappie and Fred
      Lonzo
All-Star jam session follows at 11:30
      p.m.
Palm Court Jazz Café, 1205 Decatur
      Street

WEDNESDAY, MAY 3, 8 P.M.
Nancy Wilson, Joe Henderson Trio,
      The Donald Harrison Quartet with
      special guest Mark Whitfield
Ernest N. Morial Convention Center,
      La Nouvelle Orleans Ballroom
THURSDAY, MAY 4, 8 P.M.
La Noche Latina. Celia Cruz,
      Oscar D'Leon y su Orquestra de
      Venezuela, Los Silver Star de
      Hondruas, Los Sagitarios
Ernest N. Morial Convention Center,
      La Nouvelle Orleans Ballroom
FRIDAY, MAY 5, 9 P.M.
James Taylor, the subdudes
Kiefer UNO Lakefront Arena
FRIDAY, MAY 5, 9 P.M.
Dew Drop Inn Revisited: Irma
      Thomas, Marva Wright, Johnny
      Adams, Eddie Bo, Kermit
      Ruffins, Wardell Quezergue and
      His Orchestra, and Master of
      Ceremonies Bobby Marchan
The Praline Connection Gospel &
      Blues Hall, 907 S. Peters Street
SATURDAY, MAY 6, 9 P.M.
B.B. King
Al Green
The Dirty Dozen
Kiefer UNO Lakefront Arena
SATURDAY, MAY 6, 12 MIDNIGHT
Midnight Jam
Archie Shepp, Ellis Marsalis, Cornell
      Dupree, Marlon Jordan, Victor
      Goines, Earl Turbinton, Jr. Delfeayo
      Marsalis, Ricky Sebastian, Mike
      Pellera, Bill Huntington
The Praline Connection Gospel &
      Blues Hall

1996

Benny Waters

Allison Miner, one of the driving forces for honoring and promoting Louisiana musicians, transitioned from the land of the living into the spirit world on December 23, 1995. With Quint Davis and producer George Wein, Miner had been co-director for the first New Orleans Jazz & Heritage Festival in 1970. 1996 was a bittersweet time with the Festival honoring Allison. She created and developed the Louisiana Heritage Stage, directed the Louisiana Folklife Pavilion for the 1984 World's Fair in New Orleans, and worked with the Folklife Division of the Smithsonian Institute in Washington, D.C. After Allison's passing, Quint Davis wrote these lines for inclusion in the book *Jazz Fest Memories,* by Michael P. Smith and Allison Miner, published in 1997:

"For Allison was one of those saint people who actually cared more for the well being of others than her own. No one who worked with her will find that again.

And the enduring lesson that she taught us, the life long crusade that she carried on, is the connection between music and the people who make it.

It was Allison who insisted on that connection for all of us, who said if you listen to, and feel the love for the music, you must always follow it to its source, and come to know it and define it by the person who made it.

And with this inseparability comes a responsibility. That you may not have this music unjustly, that you must look the music maker in the eye and know that they have been treated fairly, got their royalty, got their publishing. That for this beautiful gift they were fated to give to the world, these heavenly music makers were not cast aside or left behind.

This is the lesson I believed she lived for, and the work and consciousness she left for us to carry on. This is Allison's definitional gift to the Jazz & Heritage Festival. That the Festival was to be about the musicians first, that its focus and identity and texture comes from the humanity of the musicians themselves, as people, who define this culture through their gift of song."

On the Music Heritage Stage where Miner had celebrated her personal relationship with musicians and their audiences, Grant Morris hosted a "Tribute to Allison Miner" with Quint Davis, George Wein, Susan Jenkins, Monk Boudreaux, Bo Dollis, Ed Volker, Steve Masakowski, and Monifa Johnson. The tribute included the screening of "Angel in 'A' Miner," a film by Amy Nesbitt.

A new feature of the Heritage Fair was the International Pavilion. Many countries have contributed cultural nuances to New Orleans music, and the idea was to showcase one of these nations' music and culture each year. The first was Haiti. New Orleans had a deep historical bond with that island nation through a multiplicity of

FRIDAY, APRIL 26

WB 38 / POLAROID STAGE
11:00 John F. Kennedy HS Cougar Band
12:15 Black Eagles Mardi Gras Indians
1:20 Soul Rebels Brass Band
2:45 Bobby Cure & The Summertime Blues w/ Robert Parker & Roland Stone
4:25 James Rivers Movement
5:45 The Frankie Ford Show

HOUSE OF BLUES / DR. MARTENS STAGE
11:20 Irene & The Mikes
12:30 Tabby Thomas w/ Henry Gray
1:50 Jon Cleary and The Absolute Monster Gentlemen
3:10 Continental Drifters
4:35 Mem Shannon & The Membership
6:00 Deacon John

WWL / RAY-BAN STAGE
11:15 SUBR Jazz Ensemble
12:20 The Iguanas
1:40 Terrance Simien & The Mallet Playboys
3:25 Phish
5:40 funky Meters

FAIS DO-DO STAGE
11:30 Delgado Community College Jazz Ensemble
12:35 Robert Jardell
1:55 Chris Ardoin & Double Clutchin'
3:25 Hackberry Ramblers
4:35 Savoy-Doucet Cajun Band
6:00 Creole Zydeco Farmers

WWOZ JAZZ TENT
11:20 Greg Dawson & Crosswinds
12:30 Brice & Eleonor Winston
1:45 "Clyde Kerr, Jr." & Univision w/ Samirah Evans
3:00 Kermit Ruffins & The Barbecue Swingers
4:20 Astral Project
5:45 Trombone Tribute feat. Benny Powell, Slide Hampton, Steve Turre, Freddie Lonzo & Lucien Barbarin

COX COMMUNICATIONS ECONOMY HALL
11:20 Tommy Yetta's New Orleans Jazz Band
12:35 Doc. Houlind's Copenhagen Ragtime Band of Denmark tribute to George Lewis
1:55 New Orleans Ragtime Orchestra
3:20 Benny Waters
4:40 Frank Federico & Medicare Madcaps
6:00 New Leviathan Oriental Foxtrot Orchestra

CONGO SQUARE STAGE
11:15 9th Ward Hunters Mardi Gras Indians
12:25 Y'Shua Manzy
1:40 Fuego
3:00 Porgy Jones Quartet
4:20 Rebirth Brass Band
5:50 Compas Revue of Haiti feat. Policard, Zekle, Djanm & The Caribbean Sextet

BELLSOUTH MOBILITY LAGNIAPPE TENT
11:15 Jesuit HS Jazz Band
12:25 Slewfoot w/ special guest Barbara Shorts
1:40 Pfister Sisters
3:10 Ronnie Kole
4:35 The Evening Star String Band
6:00 John Rankin

music scene

Louisiana Red Hot Records established.

NYNO Records releases Allen Toussaint's Connected.

IN MEMORIAM

Percy Humphrey, Jessie Hill, Gerry Mulligan, Ella Fitzgerald, Albert Luandrew ("Sunnyland Slim"), Lionel 'Bird" Oubichon, Albert Goelz, Nathaniel "Nat" Gray, Mercer Ellington, Jessie Hill, John Delafose, Marion Walmsley (crafts vendor), Nur Deen Muhammad (crafts vendor), Rasheed Hasan (crafts vendor), Lloyd Lambert, Danny White, Michael Brown (construction staff), Sherry Broussard (fair volunteer), Bill Monroe

elements. Numbers of Creoles (including *gens de coleur*) and French sugar cane planters immigrated to New Orleans after the 1791 Haitian slave revolt. Some escaped slaves found work in the homes of wealthy Creoles, and all brought their French Haitian customs and cultural distinctions. Two of those predilections were the practice of voodoo, with ceremonies driven by drumming, and dancing the *bamboula* and *calinda*. Those beats seeped into the native music of New Orleans, sometimes driving on top of the melody, or alternatively becoming a sliding hiss underneath. Haitian artists such as Zobop and Bacoulou Folkloric Dance Company performed on the Congo Square Stage and a tent in the Heritage Village displayed Haitian cultural exhibitions. Visitors snatched up the art and crafts offerings, most notably the folk art paintings of Edward Duval-Carrie. The International Pavilion was an immediate success.

One musician with circular influences on and from New Orleans musicians was Irish rocker/balladeer/mystic Van Morrison. Playing on the Ray Ban Stage in a black suit, dark glasses and pork pie hat, Morrison let loose with what sounded like true love: his literate, soulful songs rendered in a full-bodied jazz arrangement. Backed by full orchestration and characteristically wailing straight ahead vocals, he gave a stirring performance.

But then there was the Phish phenomenon. The Festival caught flak from some pur-

"It was very clever marketing, but it was also a wonderful thing when we used to start the day with high school jazz bands and then some days we did the local college jazz bands. But we always started the day with a jazz band that was local, and I don't know whether they were giving the tickets away or not, but I got to tell you every aunt, uncle, mother, and family member was out there to see their child perform at Jazz Fest for the first time." KEITH WILLIAMS

Wendell Brunious

ist Festival lovers who felt that booking such mainstream rock and roll bands was abandoning the core value of showcasing Louisiana music and music with direct connections in a similar vein. Despite consistent evidence to the contrary, that accusation had dogged producers from as early as the 1970s. Although at that time the Festival booked only a few out-of-town headliners, there were still dozens of qualified local musicians who were not part of the Festival.

Phish fans flooded in. Phish, a keeper of the Grateful Dead traveling jam band flame, was known for incorporating diverse elements of music into extended jams that fed into the laid-back,

neo-hippie philosophy of their fans. Like the Grateful Dead, they attracted a traveling following calling themselves "Phishheads." Phish had taken the year off from touring. Band members said that they would have turned down any other offer, but they were honored to be invited to Jazz Fest. Devotees of the Meters, in their early days the band had practiced to Meters recordings, trying to capture that deep-down funk rhythm. The Festival had not realized (nor had apparently anyone else) that Phish's travel-starved fans would converge on the band's sole appearance of 1996 with true-believer fervor. On Friday's opening day, when Phish was scheduled, 62,500 peo-

Elder Roma Wilson

> *"Every year in April my children are excused from school to see Dr. John. That's a cultural experience. You can't live in New Orleans and not go to Jazz Fest; that's way more important than school."* SUZETTE BECKER

ple crowded the Fest, compared to 45,000 the previous year.

They were ubiquitous. Given to the notion of living frugally and communally ("we feed each other"), Phish fans, in hemp necklaces and tie-dyed clothes, camped all over the city under trees, slept in cars, roamed through dumpsters for food, and eschewed tourist habits such as bathing. They were gentle. They were annoying. They were happy doing their own thing. The aging hippies who had free-danced through Festivals in the 70s looked into the mirror. Davis defended his decision to bring rock and roll stars Dave Matthews, Joan Osborne, and Phish to the Fest, pointing out the connections each had with New Orleans music. He purported that the

Fest always needed new blood – not because New Orleans didn't have enough talent, but because the younger generation deserved to take part in the evolution of Jazz Fest. Presumably, these bands attracted a young audience who would learn to appreciate the diversity of music championed by the Fest. Besides, C.J. Chenier and the Red Hot Louisiana Band would open for the Dave Matthews Band and reap the benefits of being seen by an exponentially larger audience. On another note, band members from Phish blended into the New Orleans scene, jamming with locals and lending a touch of star power to other sets. On one such occasion, Trey Anastasio sat in on the Fais Do-Do Stage with blues zydeco master Bruce "Sunpie" Barnes,

CONGO SQUARE STAGE
11:10 Kerry Brown's Brownsville
12:20 Percussion, Inc.
1:40 Compas Revue of Haiti feat. Policard, Zekle, Djanm & The Caribbean Sextet
3:10 Charmaine Neville & Friends
4:35 Samite of Uganda
6:00 Cyril Neville & The Uptown Allstars

BellSouth Mobility Lagniappe Tent
11:25 NOCCA Jazz Ensemble
12:40 David & Roselyn
1:55 Golden Star Hunters Mardi Gras Indians
3:10 Sid Selvidge
4:35 Boutté-L'Etienne Music Friends
5:55 Zobop of Haiti

MUSIC HERITAGE STAGE
12:00 Harold Dejan and Gregg Stafford interview by Dr. Michael White
1:15 Sid Selvidge interview by Ben Sandmel
2:00 Samite of Uganda interview by Jason Berry
3:00 Al Hirt interview by Grant Morris
4:00 Joe Clay interview by John Sinclair

RHODES GOSPEL TENT
11:00 St. John Divine Gospel Drill Team
11:45 Inspirational Gospel Choir
12:30 St. Francis DeSales Golden Voices
1:15 The Mighty Sensations of Lake Charles
2:00 St. Raymond Gospel Choir
2:45 The Crownseekers
3:30 To the Glory of God Community Choir
4:25 Ricky Dillard's New Generation Chorale
5:30 True Believers
6:15 Sammy Berfect & Dimensions of Faith

PARADES
12:00 Avenue Steppers, Second Line Jammers, Taylor Bunch SA&PCs with Paulin Brothers Brass Band
2:00 The Young Steppers, Original Step-N-Style and Lady Sequence SA&PCs with Smitty Short Stoppers Brass Band

SUNDAY, APRIL 28

WB 38 / POLAROID STAGE
11:20 Ritmo Caribeno
1:00 Snooks Eaglin
2:30 Marcia Ball
4:00 Irma Thomas & The Professionals
5:45 Cowboy Mouth

HOUSE OF BLUES / DR. MARTENS STAGE
11:15 Becky Sharp
12:25 Reggie Hall w/ Sadie Thompson
1:50 Bryan Lee & The Jumpstreet Five
3:15 Davell Crawford
4:45 Luther Kent & The Trick Bag Band
5:55 Parade to stage, Escola de Samba, Casa Samba

WWL / RAY-BAN STAGE
11:20 SUNO Jazz Ensemble
12:40 Rockin' Dopsie Jr. & Zydeco Twisters
2:00 Sweet Honey in the Rock
4:00 Chaka Khan
5:45 George Benson

who had a scant audience until word got out, then the swarm descended on the Fais Do-Do.

People usually fell into one of two camps in regard to how to stretch the 24 too-short hours during a Jazz Fest day. Some hit the Fair Grounds early, catching a breakfast of beignets with café-au-lait, and hearing the first celebration of celestial praise

made about where to spend the most time. Some were gifted with the staying power to spend a day at the Fest and race back to the house/hotel/van for a shower and cool down before hitting the local clubs. Club crawling in itself was a religion to some, and they eschewed going to the Heritage Fair at all, unless it was to catch one or two bands targeted in

Here is just a sampling of what went on during the first weekend:

On the first Friday, devotees of the late great piano virtuoso James Booker could have seen stars at the third annual "Ivory Blues Revue" at the Orpheum Theater. Those in the know couldn't have imagined a better living legend lineup... pianists Eddie Bo, David Torkanowsky,

Batiste Brothers

ring out in the Gospel Tent. Others caught a high school marching band kicking off the Fest. They were the daytime warriors, the ones who sweated and roasted and danced and ate their way across the infield.

The other camp came out at night. Unless one was very young or possessed with hormonal power drive, a choice had to be

advance. These people stood to gain not only stellar performances by Louisiana musicians, but they might hit the trifecta of hearing great local bands, luck into a blow-out jam with a national musician or celebrity sitting in, and partake of the unique New Orleans pleasure of legally walking among music clubs with a drink in a go-cup.

Raymond Myles, Jon Cleary, and Ed Frank performed with R&B performers Ernie K Doe and Tommy Ridgely, Kermit Ruffins and guest vocalists Leigh "L'il Queenie" Harris, Lillian Boutte, Wanda Rouzan, Leah Chase and Big Al Carson.

If one were in a spiritual state of mind, he or she could have taken the streetcar to the

> "Stage 3, at some point in the later years, we kind of started cooking, you know, started bringing food that they would cook and stuff. But for the most part, man, everybody just showed up that morning, we'd sit down and look at all the set lists and we'd pin them up on the wall and then we'd start arranging the truck to accommodate how we were going to need the equipment to come out. I think that when I was out there, we had one of the most efficient stages out there. I believe even today, Stage 3 still runs really, really well." GEORGE PORTER

FAIS DO-DO STAGE
11:15 Clickin' Chickens
12:30 Walter Mouton & The Scott Playboys
1:50 Creole Wild West Mardi Gras Indians
3:00 Geno Delafose & French Rockin' Boogie
4:25 Sunpie Barnes & The Louisiana Sunspots
6:00 Allen Fontenot & The Country Cajuns

WWOZ JAZZ TENT
11:15 Al Belletto Quartet
12:25 Charles Neville Jazz Band
1:35 Germaine Bazzle
2:45 Nicholas Payton
4:10 Dee Dee Bridgewater Trio w/ sp. guest David Sanchez
5:40 Lionel Hampton

COX COMMUNICATIONS ECONOMY HALL
11:15 Louis Cottrell & His Original Creole Jazz Band
12:25 New Black Eagle Jazz Band
1:50 Gregg Stafford's Jazz Hounds
3:10 Bob French's Original Tuxedo Jazz Band
4:30 Carrie Smith
6:00 Duke Dejan's Olympia Brass Band

CONGO SQUARE STAGE
11:30 Ben Hunter the Soul Avenger
12:50 Mia X w/ Tru & UNLV
2:20 Premiere
4:00 Jean Knight w/ Blue Eyed Soul
5:30 Compas Revue of Haiti featuring Policard, Djanm, Zekle & The Caribbean Sextet

BELLSOUTH MOBILITY LAGNIAPPE TENT
11:15 The Heritage School of Music Band
12:25 John Boutté
1:40 Hazel & The Delta Ramblers
3:00 Caledonian Society Scottish Dancers w/ Pipes & Drums
4:25 Al & Essie Morris "Mr. & Mrs. Country Soul"
5:55 Ingrid Lucia & The Flying Neutrinos

MUSIC HERITAGE STAGE
12:00 Geno Delafose w/ Stephen Nash & Germaine Jack interview by Michael Tisserand
12:45 Marcia Ball interview by Ben Sandmel
2:00 Al & Essie Morris interview by Ben Sandmel
3:00 Carrie Smith interview by Dr. Michael White
3:45 Reginald Policard of Haitian Compas Revue interview by Gabou Mendy

RHODES GOSPEL TENT
11:00 Antioch Gospel Singers
11:40 New Beginning Mass Choir
12:30 Friendly Five Gospel Singers
1:15 Holy Hill Gospel Singers
2:00 New Zion Trio Plus One
2:45 Ebenezer Missionary BC Choir
3:30 Watson Memorial Spiritual Church Choir
4:25 Dottie Peoples & Peoples Choice Chorale
5:25 Traveling Stars
6:15 Raymond A. Myles & The RAMS

PARADES
12:00 Ladies Zulu, Olympia Aide & Uptowner's Hobo SA&PCs with Pin Stripe Brass Band

fifth annual Jazz Fest Shabbat (Sabbath) at Touro Synagogue on St. Charles Avenue. The New Orleans Klezmer All Stars joined Touro's Adult Augmented Choir with special guest Joel Simpson on piano and New York klezmer banjo player Henry Sapoznik. Walter "Wolfman" Washington and the Roadmasters played all over town all over the weekend at the legendary Maple Leaf Bar, Carrollton Station, Buffa's and Jimmy's. On Frenchmen Street, on its last night under that name, Cafe Istanbul presented "The Legends of New Orleans" revue with New Orleans R&B veterans Tommy Ridgley, Eddie Bo and Oliver "Who Shot the La-La" Morgan. They were backed by harmonica player "Rockin' Jake" and his band, and their set

laid to rest that incarnation of Café Istanbul. The next night, the Radiators appropriately rocked the house now named the Dream Palace, a name it had in an earlier incarnation, when the Rads cut their collective teeth regularly there.

After a teasing sprinkle of rain on the first day – a christening – perfect weather smiled on Jazz Fest and musical moments kaleidoscoped before the eyes of Fest goers on stage after stage: Zachary Richard closing out Fox 8, Dr. John on WWL- Ray Ban, Wayne Toups and Zydecajun on WB 38 Fais Do-Do stage, the Nevilles on Ray-Ban, the Radiators. If the big names were the talk of the day, the locals still held court.

Trey Anastasio and Sunpie Barnes

2:00 Unknown Steppers &
Devastation SA&PCs and
Golden Arrows Mardi Gras
Indians with New Birth Brass
Band

4:00 The Furious Five &
Untouchables SA&PCs and
Carrollton Hunters Mardi Gras
Indians with Lil' Rascals Brass
Band

6:00 Economy Hall Parade — Algiers
Steppers SA&PC with Duke
Dejan's Olympia Brass Band

THURSDAY, MAY 2

WB 38 / POLAROID STAGE
11:20 Xavier University Jazz Band
12:30 White Cloud Hunters Mardi Gras
Indians
1:40 Tab Benoit w/ Raful Neal
3:05 Milton Batiste's Magnificent 7
w/ Ernie K-Doe & Jessie Hill
4:30 Chris Duarte Group
5:55 Boozoo Chavis & The Magic
Sounds

**HOUSE OF BLUES / DR. MARTENS
STAGE**
11:15 The Bingemen
12:25 Mas Mamones
1:40 Wallace Johnson
2:55 Coco Robicheaux & The
Perspirators
4:20 Sonny Bourg & The Bayou Blues
Band
5:45 Larry McCray

WWL / RAY-BAN STAGE
11:15 Flavor Kings
12:30 Executive Steel Band
1:50 Michelle Shocked
3:30 The Chambers Brothers
Reunion
5:30 Indigo Girls

FAIS DO-DO STAGE
11:20 Kristi Guillory & Reveille
12:35 Piney Woods Ramblers feat.
Jack Youngblood
1:50 Mamou
3:10 Al Berard & The Basin Brothers
4:30 Zobop of Haiti
6:00 Bruce Daigrepont Cajun Band

WWOZ JAZZ TENT
11:20 Ed Perkins
12:30 Tony Bazley Quintet
1:45 Richwell Ison / Kirk Ford
Experience w/ Rahssana Ison
3:05 Kidd Jordan-Alvin Fielder & IAQ
Quintet w/ Joel Futterman
4:25 Walter Payton & Snapbean w/
Sharon Martin
5:50 Dewey Redman

COX COMMUNICATIONS ECONOMY HALL
11:15 The Last Straws
12:25 Papa Don Vappie's New Orleans
Jazz Band
1:35 Original Camellia Jazz Band
2:50 New Orleans Jazz Professors
4:05 Musicum Jazz Antiqua w/ Karl
Koenig
5:30 Banu Gibson & New Orleans
Hot Jazz

CONGO SQUARE STAGE
11:30 Gregory Boyd & Vos
1:00 Versia
2:30 Keith Claiborne
4:10 Eddie Palmieri Octet
6:00 Bacoulou Folkloric Dance Co. of
Haiti

**BELLSOUTH MOBILITY LAGNIAPPE
TENT**
11:15 Hammond State Strawberry
Jammers
12:25 Tony Green Trio
1:40 Carlos Sanchez "Amenecer
Flamenco"
2:55 Gina Forsyth
4:20 Trout Fishing in America
5:55 Bay Oyster Band

MUSIC HERITAGE STAGE
12:30 Chambers Brothers interview by
Suzan Jenkins
1:15 Tribute to Allison Miner w/ Quint
Davis, George Wein, Suzan
Jenkins, Monk Boudreaux,
Bo Dollis, Ed Volker, Steve
Masakowski, Monifa Johnson
hosted by Morris Grant, and
film "Angel in A Miner" by Amy
Nesbitt
3:00 John Sinclair & The Blues
Scholars
4:00 Dewey Redman interview by
Mike Gourrier
4:45 Bruce Daigrepont interview by
Nick Spitzer

RHODES GOSPEL TENT
11:00 The Spiritualettes
11:45 The Coolie Family
12:30 Gospel Extenders
1:15 Leviticus Gospel Singers
2:00 True Tone Gospel Singers
2:45 Wayne Powell & Eternity w/
Praise
3:30 First Revolution
4:20 The Dixie Hummingbirds
5:20 Southern Travelers
6:05 Avondale Community Singers

PARADES
4:00 Bon Temps Roulez Second
Liners SA&PC with Storyville
Stompers Brass Band

FRIDAY, MAY 3

WB 38 / POLAROID STAGE
11:20 Leon & Sam Brothers Zydeco
12:50 Tommy Ridgley & The
Untouchables w/ Sammy
Ridgley
2:30 George Porter, Jr. & Runnin'
Pardners
4:00 subdudes
5:45 BeauSoleil avec Michael Doucet

**HOUSE OF BLUES / DR. MARTENS
STAGE**
11:30 J. Monque'D Blues Band w/ The
Lil' Pats of Butter
1:00 C.C. Adcock
2:30 Anders Osborne
4:00 Steve Riley & The Mamou
Playboys
5:45 Joe Louis Walker & The
Bosstalkers

WWL / RAY-BAN STAGE
11:35 Louisiana Tech Jazz Band
12:30 Clarence "Frogman" Henry
2:00 Bela Fleck & The Flecktones
3:40 Buddy Guy
5:40 Dr. John

FAIS DO-DO STAGE
11:20 Royann & Jim Calvin
12:45 Wild Peyotes
2:15 Esteban Jordan w/ Rio Jordan
4:00 Jude Taylor & His Burning
Flame Zydeco
5:30 Rosie Ledet

WWOZ JAZZ TENT
11:15 Steve Masakowski & Friends
12:25 Alvin "Red" Tyler Quartet
1:35 Alvin Batiste & The Jazztronauts
3:00 Michael Ray & The Cosmic
Krewe
4:20 Marlon Jordan Quintet
5:45 Cassandra Wilson

COX COMMUNICATIONS ECONOMY HALL
11:15 Local International Allstar Jazz
Band
12:25 Lady Charlotte Jazz Band
1:25 Pud Brown's Palm Court Jazz
Band
2:45 Sadie Goodson's Storyville
Stompers
4:15 Placide Adams Original
Dixieland Hall Jazz Band
5:40 Doc Paulin's Dixieland Jazz
Band

CONGO SQUARE STAGE
11:20 Diamonds
12:30 Kumbuka Drum & Dance
Collective
1:45 Golden Eagles Mardi Gras
Indians
2:50 Bacoulou Folkloric Dance Co. of
Haiti
4:15 Cool Riddims w/ Sista Teedy
5:45 Zobop of Haiti

**BELLSOUTH MOBILITY LAGNIAPPE
TENT**
11:15 New Orleans All City Jazz
Outreach
12:20 Guardians of the Flame Mardi
Gras Indians
1:25 Coushatta Dancers
2:30 Clancy "Blues Boy" Lewis w/
Sheba Kimbrough
3:45 Hot Strings of New Orleans
5:30 Patrice Fisher & Arpa w/ Editus
of Costa Rica

MUSIC HERITAGE STAGE
12:15 Eddie Bo interview by Suzan
Jenkins
1:00 Madame Wiener of Bacoulou
from Haiti — interview by Gene
Scaramuzzo
2:15 Clarence "Frogman" Henry
interview by Derek Huston
3:00 Cassandra Wilson interview by
A.J. Verdelle
4:00 Michael Doucet interview by
Ben Sandmel

RHODES GOSPEL TENT
11:00 Greater Liberty Baptist Church Mass Choir
11:45 Wimberly Family
12:30 Melvin Winfield, Jr. & New Vision
1:15 One A-Chord
2:00 Aline White & Company
2:45 Jackie Smith & Divinity
3:35 The Christianaires
4:35 Kennedy High School Gospel Choir
5:20 Ronald James Chorale
6:05 Friendly Travelers

PARADES
4:00 Pigeon Town Steppers & Big Nine SA&PC w/ Chosen Few Brass Band
5:40 Economy Hall Parade Calendar Girls Club SA&PC w/ Doc Paulin's Dixieland Jazz Band

SATURDAY, MAY 4

WB 38 / POLAROID STAGE
11:15 Zobop of Haiti
1:00 Ivan Neville
2:45 Joan Osborne
4:40 Better Than Ezra
6:00 The Dixie Cups

HOUSE OF BLUES / DR. MARTENS STAGE
11:15 The Boondoggles
12:30 The Wild Magnolias Mardi Gras Indians
1:45 Kenny Neal
3:10 John Mooney & Bluesiana
4:35 Clarence "Gatemouth" Brown
6:00 Beau Jocque & The Zydeco Hi-Rollers

WWL / RAY-BAN STAGE
11:20 Dillard University Jazz Ensemble
12:45 Oliver "Who Shot the La La" Morgan w/ Al "Carnival Time" Johnson
2:30 Lloyd Price
4:00 Allen Toussaint
5:40 Van Morrison

FAIS DO-DO STAGE
11:25 Magnolia Sisters
12:40 Kim Carson
2:00 Luke Thompson & The Green Valley Cut Ups
3:25 Keith Frank
4:40 Chubby Carrier & The Bayou Swamp Band
6:10 Belton Richard

WWOZ JAZZ TENT
11:15 Ricardo Lewis Quintet
12:25 Larry Seiberth w/ Betty Shirley
1:40 Victor Goines Group
2:50 James Black Tribute w/ Herlin Riley & Shannon Powell
4:15 James Carter
5:45 Najee

COX COMMUNICATIONS ECONOMY HALL
11:15 Andrew Hall's Society Jazz Band
12:25 Dukes of Dixieland
1:40 Wallace Davenport Jazz Band
3:00 Young Tuxedo Brass Band
4:15 Pete Fountain
5:50 Preservation Hall Jazz Band

CONGO SQUARE STAGE
11:20 All That
12:35 Bamboula 2000
1:50 The C.P. Love Group
3:00 Bacoulou Folkloric Dance Co. of Haiti

4:20 Salif Keita
6:00 Irie Vibrations

BELLSOUTH MOBILITY LAGNIAPPE TENT
11:20 Doreen's Jazz New Orleans
12:40 Little Freddie King Blues Band
1:50 Julio & Caesar
3:15 Harry Connick, Sr. w/ The Jimmy Maxwell Orchestra
4:40 Woodenhead
6:00 Paky SaaVedra's Bandido

MUSIC HERITAGE STAGE
1:00 Lloyd Price interview by Suzan Jenkins
2:00 Jean Robert Belimaire of Zobop from Haiti interview by Gabou Mendy
3:00 Clarence "Gatemouth" Brown interview by John Sinclair
4:00 Country Music Workshop w/ Pat Flory & Dr. Bill C. Malone
5:00 John Mooney interview by John Sinclair

RHODES GOSPEL TENT
11:15 Soulful Heavenly Stars
11:45 Love Alive Fellowship Choir
12:30 Greater Bright Morning Star Choir
1:15 First Baptist Church Missionary Choir
2:00 Second Morning Star Mass Choir
2:45 Elder Roma Wilson & Family
3:30 The Johnson Extension
4:25 The Williams Brothers
5:30 The Mighty Chariots
6:15 Zulu Ensemble Male Chorus

PARADES
12:00 Black Men of Labor & Golden Trumpets SA&PCs w/ Tremé Brass Band
2:00 Money Wasters, Popular Ladies & Jolly Bunch SA&PCs w/ Pinettes Brass Band
3:00 Economy Hall Parade w/ Original Black Magic, Lady Steppers SA&PCs w/ Young Tuxedo Brass Band
4:00 Original Four & N'Krumah Better Boys SA&PCs w/ Mahogany Brass Band

SUNDAY, MAY 5

WB 38 / POLAROID STAGE
11:15 Caliente
12:30 Willie Tee
1:40 Little Queenie & Friends
2:55 Zachary Richard
4:15 Marva Wright & The BMWs
5:45 The Radiators

HOUSE OF BLUES / DR. MARTENS STAGE
11:20 Ironin' Board Sam
12:30 Galactic
1:40 Katie Webster & The Vasti Jackson Group
2:45 Bacoulou Folkloric Dance Co. of Haiti
4:00 Bobby Marchan & Higher Ground
5:30 Earl King

WWL / RAY-BAN STAGE
11:10 U.N.O. Jazz Band
12:20 Johnny Adams w/ Julius Farmer & The Farmers Market
1:40 C.J. Chenier & The Red Hot Louisiana Band
3:25 Dave Matthews Band

5:30 The Neville Brothers featuring Aaron Neville

FAIS DO-DO STAGE
11:20 Eddie LeJeune & The Morse Playboys
12:45 Danny Collet
2:10 Balfa Toujours
3:35 Nathan & The Zydeco Cha Chas
5:20 Los Babies del Merengue

WWOZ JAZZ TENT
11:30 Michael Ward w/ Regina Carter
1:10 Leroy Jones
2:35 Ellis Marsalis Quartet
4:00 Lou Donaldson
5:45 Kenny Barron Trio w/ special guest Frank Morgan

COX COMMUNICATIONS ECONOMY HALL
11:15 Chris Clifton's New Orleans Allstars
12:25 Onward Brass Band
1:40 Wendell Brunious Jazz Band
2:50 Louisiana Repertory Jazz Ensemble
4:25 Chris Owens Show
5:50 Doc Cheatham

CONGO SQUARE STAGE
11:20 Culu Dancers
12:35 Black Menace & Cheeky Blakk
2:00 Nasio
3:20 White Eagles Mardi Gras Indians
4:30 Shepherd Band
6:00 Bobby Rush

BELLSOUTH MOBILITY LAGNIAPPE TENT
11:15 Innsbruck Jazz Workshop of Austria
12:30 Last Chance Band
1:45 Willie Metcalf & The Academy of Black Arts Youth Jazz Ensemble
3:15 New Orleans Klezmer Allstars
4:35 Betsy McGovern & The Poor Clares

MUSIC HERITAGE STAGE
1:00 Allison "Tootie" Montana interview by Nick Spitzer
2:00 Frank Morgan interview by Mike Gourrier
3:00 Mighty Clouds of Joy interview by Lois Dejean
4:00 Ed Volker of Radiators interview by Grant Morris
5:00 Katie Webster interview by Nick Spitzer

RHODES GOSPEL TENT
11:00 The Melody Clouds
11:45 Jo "Cool" Davis
12:30 Southern Bells
1:15 Christine Myles w/ John Lee & The Heralds of Christ
2:00 Joyful!
2:45 The Rocks of Harmony
3:30 Sherman Washington & The Famous Zion Harmonizers
4:30 The Mighty Clouds of Joy
5:35 Voices from the Mount of Mt. Carmel Baptist Church
6:20 Gospel Soul Children

PARADES
12:00 Scene Boosters, Jetsetters & Westbank Steppers SA&PCs w/ Algiers Brass Band
12:25 Economy Hall parade w/ Lady Prince of Wales SA&PC w/ Onward Brass Band
2:00 Double Nine, Highsteppers, Original Prince of Wales & Valley of the Silent Men SA&PCs w/ Young Cheyenne's Mardi Gras Indians & Tornado Brass Band

4:00 Calliope High Steppers, New Orleans Men Buck Jumpers & Ladies Buck Jumpers SA&PCs w/ Mohawks Mardi Gras Indians & High Steppers Brass Band

NIGHT CONCERTS

FRIDAY, APRIL 26, 9 P.M.
The Allman Brothers, The Fabulous Thunderbirds, John Mooney
Kiefer UNO Lakefront Arena

SATURDAY, APRIL 27, 9 P.M.
B.B. King
George Benson & Raymond Myles & The RAMS
Kiefer UNO Lakefront Arena

SATURDAY, APRIL 27, MIDNIGHT
Midnight Jam
Jimmy Heath, Slide Hampton, Albert "Tootie" Heath, Wess Anderson, Nicholas Payton, Peter Martin, Rodney Whitaker, Fred Kemp, Johnny Vidacovich, David Torkanowsky, Bill Huntington
Praline Connection Gospel & Blues Hall

MONDAY, APRIL 29 & TUESDAY APRIL 30, 8 P.M.
Jazz at the Palm Court: Legends in Concert
Doc Cheatham, Benny Waters, Carrie Smith
Palm Court Jazz Café

WEDNESDAY, MAY 1, 8 P.M.
Wynton Marsalis, Cassandra Wilson, Jon Hendricks, New York Voices, The Crescent City Jazz Orchestra Conducted by Ellis Marsalis
Ernest N. Morial Convention Center, La Louisiane Ballroom

THURSDAY, MAY 2, 8 P.M.
La Noche Latina
El Gran Combo, Eddie Palmieri, Paky Saavedra's Bandido
Ernest N. Morial Convention Center, La Louisiane Ballroom

FRIDAY, MAY 3, 9 P.M.
Van Morrison, Buddy Guy, The Radiators
Kiefer UNO Lakefront Arena

FRIDAY, MAY 3, 7 & 11 P.M.
Dew Drop Inn Revisited: New Orleans Soul Live!
Lloyd Price, Clarence "Frogman" Henry, Jean Knight, Chuck Carbo, June Gardner — Tribute to Smokey Johnson, Lil Millet with Cookie Gabriel, Wardell Quezerque Big Band, Warren Bell, Sr.
Praline Connection Gospel & Blues Hall

SATURDAY, MAY 4, 9 P.M.
Indigo Girls
Joan Baez
Joan Osborne
Kiefer UNO Lakefront Arena

SATURDAY, MAY 4, MIDNIGHT
Midnight Jam
Frank Morgan, Lou Donaldson, Ellis Marsalis, Kenny Barron, Ray Drummond, Ben Reilly, Victor Goines, Marlon Jordan, Herlin Riley, Clyde Kerr, Jr., Jim Singleton, Ed Peterson
Praline Connection Gospel & Blues Hall

1997

Hackberry Ramblers

On Sunday morning, the gods of thunder threw lightning bolts at the Fair Grounds and boomed their laughter. Rain is always a big deal at Jazz Fest, because it galvanizes the inherent weirdness in the hearts and minds of all New Orleanians and that weirdness floats to the surface and infects visitors, too. Sometimes it makes itself evident in mudslides: the full-body swan dives into manure-enriched, dance-churned lubricious mud. Stories abound about the "rain years." One Fester remembers seeing beer-fortified pranksters exhorting others to perform the mudslide, and then hug someone they didn't know. For $50, there were plenty of takers. Another recalls a year that was a stew of mud and hay (put down by staff to absorb the mud). He waded between tents for a break in the crowd and came on a clearing of about 50 people zonked out sleeping or lying in the mud. That year, dozens just left their mud-soaked shoes at the Fest gate on the way home. The pile reached epic proportions.

JAZZ FEST STATION
APRIL 25 - MAY 4, 1997
NEW ORLEANS, LA 70119

SIDNEY Bechet

NEW ORLEANS JAZZ & HERITAGE FESTIVAL
Official Commemorative Cachet

Around noon on Saturday, a massive bolt of lightning startled fans streaming through the front gates. Maybe that was the thunder god's last hurrah, because after that, the rain dwindled away and the sun once again presided over the Fair Grounds. At the Heritage Fair, Belton Richard and his Musical Aces peeled off a Cajun-on-speed style "When the Saints Go Marching In" with a dizzying accordion melody and fiddle embellishment. Of the thousands of versions of that song played every year, not too many had happened on the Fais Do-Do Stage. This version definitely deserved a place in the history book of Jazz Fest. Also on the Fais Do Do Stage, Boozoo Chavis and Beau Jocque continued their mock rivalry: Beau Jocque (along with Chris Ardoin and his band Double Clutchin') was one of the next generation of zydeco rockers, adding pop and rock rhythms to his mix. Boozoo

Chavis and His Magic Sounds took the stage on Thursday (a great day for the self employed and the unemployed to hit Jazz Fest). Some zydeco musicians, such as Rockin' Dopsie, could slip into different keys and tempos every time they played a song. His son, Dopsie Jr., also experimented with rock and funk licks thrown in.

Grammy winning Doc Cheatham played his last Jazz Fest performance this year, as smooth as ever in the Economy Hall Tent, as the hot spring sun began to relent and offered up a golden evening. Just earlier, in the Gospel Tent, The Johnson Extension represented more family heritage. Lois Dejean, her three daughters, her grandson, niece and nephew were carrying on the family tradition of gospel singing and traveling to perform. Dejean has been involved in the gospel lineup for many years and was one of the influences, along with the amazing Sherman Washington (of the

C.C. Adcock

Zion Harmonizers) who built the Gospel Tent into the iconic state of grace it has become.

Hedges that had created a barrier near the House of Blues/Doc Martens Stage were removed to allow a larger audience to groove on the slide guitarist Sonny Landreth (once the only white man to play in Clifton Chenier's Red Hot Louisiana

Band), hoodoo musician Coco Robicheaux's supernatural set with his amazing Perspirators, or Galactic's extended meanderings.

The music took revenge on the rain all weekend. James Taylor, rained out of his 1995 appearance at the Fair Grounds, was back to thrill thousands of fans, including one pretty special world humanitarian. Not every

"Al Jarreau had that tent filled and gone, and he came out just kicking with percussion in his voice and I cried. I cried watching him. He touched me so much. And then I got a chance to meet him afterwards and he signed my bag! When he saw me he said, 'Hello Freckles! Oh, I just love those freckles.' And I love you, Al." SAMIRAH EVANS

musician had former President Jimmy Carter listening in backstage. Zachary Richard closed down Fox 8 Polaroid Stage. One of the few Cajun rockers still singing in French and English, Richard's literate and imaginative interpretation of traditional music packed an emotional

power that had his fans screaming "Zack attack!" Bo Dollis was chanting, "Stop the rain. Stop the rain!" in a Wild Magnolias call and response a la "Iko Iko all day." Sans feathered costumes but packing spiritual authority, the Wild Magnolias made the rain slacken as ordered. As many rain stories as there are at Jazz Fest, there are equally as many about musicians having their way with the weather.

The International Pavilion featured performers from Mali. The Jazz Fest Program reported that "Mali enjoys a living musical tradition expressed in the daily lives of the people, the sacred to the secular, from the field and home, baptisms, marriages and initiations to religious rites. Masking and movement

are integral to the expression of the music." Friday on Congo Square was a riot of color and costume: the Revealers, the Golden Eagles, the Mardi Gras Indians, Bamboula 2000 percussion dance troupe, National Dance Ensemble of Mali, Habib Koite & Bamada of Mali. All attracted audiences who came to groove on the beat but also to soak in new cultural amazements.

"Barefoot and manhandling the accordion like a toy," Terrance Simien hammed it up on the Fox 8/Polaroid Stage, inviting hollers and applause. Simien delighted and surprised his fans by rumbling through the barricades literally onto outstretched arms of the zydefunking crowd. Throughout the crowd surf, he never stopped playing that accordion. Scrambling back onstage, Simien and the Mallet Playboys tore off a blistering "Iko Iko" that danced the razor's edge of zydeco and rock and roll.

Mid-City is diverse as New Orleans itself. Century-old live oaks gesture downward, their

Teddy Bridges

3:40 James Booker Tribute featuring Allen Toussaint & Dr. John (Interview)
5:30 Zion Travelers Spiritual Singers (Interview)

RHODES GOSPEL TENT
11:00 The Banks Family
11:40 Bemiss Brothers
12:20 Community Missionary BC Gospel Choir
1:00 Charles & The Jackson Travelers
1:45 Voices of Zion Youth Choir
2:30 Rejubilation Evangelical Community Choir
3:15 Aline White & Company
4:05 Nineveh Baptist Mass Gospel Choir
4:50 Davell Crawford feat. NuBeginnings
5:40 Slim & The Supreme Angels
6:35 McDonogh #35 HS Gospel Choir

PARADES
12:00 St. Augustine High School Marching Band
2:00 Big Nine and Jr. Westbank Steppers SA&PCs and Chosen Few Brass Band
4:00 Just Steppin' and Pigeon Town Steppers SA&PCs and Hot Chops

SATURDAY, APRIL 26

FOX 8 / POLAROID STAGE
11:15 Invisible Cowboy
12:20 Earl King
1:35 Nocentelli w/ Zigaboo Modeliste
3:00 Allen Toussaint
4:30 Terrance Simien
6:00 Cowboy Mouth

HOUSE OF BLUES / DR. MARTENS STAGE
11:15 Jumpin' Johnny Sansone
12:20 Irene & The Mikes
1:35 Larry Garner & Boogaloo Blues Band
2:55 Keb' Mo
4:15 National Dance Ensemble of Mali
5:40 Jimmy Johnson

WWL / RAY-BAN STAGE
11:15 SUBR Jazz Ensemble
12:30 Reggie Hall Band w/ Sadie T.
2:00 Habib Koite & Bamada of Mali
3:30 Kirk Franklin & The Family
5:15 Santana

WB 38 FAIS DO-DO STAGE
11:30 Coushatta Dancers
12:40 Sonny Bourg & The Bayou Blues Band
2:00 Keith Frank
3:25 The Taggart Boys w/ Joe Clay
4:45 Eddie LeJeune & The Morse Playboys
6:00 Jude Taylor & His Burning Flames

WWOZ JAZZ TENT
11:20 Irvin Mayfield Quintet
12:45 Tony Bazley Quintet w/ spec. guest trombonist Steven Walker dedicated to Edward Frank
2:15 Kidd Jordan-Alvin Fielder & IAQ plus Tribute to Julius Hemphill w/ spec. guests Oliver Lake, Fred Anderson, Hamiet Bluiett and Joel Futterman
4:15 Ellis Marsalis
5:45 Gato Barbieri

"One year with my group Diversity performed in the Jazz Tent with Julius Farmer on bass, Herman Lebeau on drums and Saya Saito on piano. I invited Milton Cardona to play with us and he was to bring another percussionist with him. He showed up with Rafael "El Negro" Hernandez from Cuba and we didn't know he was a drummer. At rehearsal for the gig he got on the drum set and we were all like, 'What is that?' El Negro explained that in Cuba each drummer played an individual part and when he came to the U.S. he taught himself to play all the parts simultaneously because there was no one else to play with. With his left foot he would play the clavé on the cowbell as well as the high hat. With his right foot he would play the bass drum. It seemed like he had three or four hands from the snare drum, to the side of the drum to the cymbals he was all over the place. He came to the U.S. with Rubacalba and is one of the great drummers of his era." CHARLES NEVILLE

Jazz Fest. These folks are lucky enough to stroll to the Fest, and that proximity is often cause for a party. Some neighbors throw Thursday night crawfish boils as a ritual to get the spicy mix into their bloodstreams – it's easier to channel the brutal Louisiana heat when you've already reached a similar internal temperature.

One neighbor upheld the tradition of first Jazz Fest Friday night crawfish boils. Everyone pitched in, from hanging the tiki lights to tapping the keg and receiving the 150 lb. crawfish delivery. There was always a band, or musicians just showed up, and in lean years, the hat was passed to pay the band. There

was only one rule (many Fest fêtes have "only one rule."), that's probably as many as anyone in New Orleans can manage, anyway. Linda F. invented a deluxe "crawfish table." Give her credit when you steal this idea. Take a long stretch of plywood, coated with shellac or polymer for easy cleaning, and support it with sawhorses. Use a bowl or other mold that's big enough for handfuls of crawfish carcasses. Trace around it with a pencil. Cut a hole, place trash cans under the hole, and voila! Bussing tables is a cinch. The *one rule*? "Nobody sleeps over in my house."

Others threw Sunday brunches as bookends to the Friday night parties. At one time there were more than five brunches on different days around the Fair Grounds. Many were potluck; all were infused with genial good will. Bloody Marys, Bellinis, Mimosas and hairs of other dogs got Jazz Festers in the groove for the last day. The brunches also served an important social function: many visitors from the U.S. and abroad saw each other only at these events. It was a good time to catch up, say goodbye, and promise to meet again next year. Sometimes musicians showed up. Marcia Ball often tried to

music scene

Doc Cheatham & Nicholas Payton CD release on Verve.

Wynton Marsalis 1st jazz artist to win Pulitzer Prize in Music for Blood On the Fields.

Snooks Eaglin's "Live in Japan" is released on Black Top Records.

"He's the Prettiest," exhibit at NOMA of the art of Big Chief Tootie Montana of the Yellow Pocahontas Mardi Gras Indians.

Mahalia Jackson inducted into Rock and Roll Hall of Fame.

Basin Street Records opens for business.

N MEMORIAM

Edward Frank, Roosevelt "Booba" Barnes, "Miss Lillian" Mitchell Bennett, Albert "Pud" Brown, George "Kid Sheik" Colar, Reverend Charles E. Cook, Paul Crawford, Exuma a.k.a Tony McKay, Michael Christopher Foley, Edward Frank, Melvin Franklin, Eddie Harris, Lionel Leleux, Harold Melvin, Joseph Payton, Glen Randall, John "Big John" Thomassie, Junior Walker, Danny White, Tony Williams

COX COMMUNICATIONS ECONOMY HALL TENT
11:15 Rampart & Perdido Jazz Band
12:20 New Orleans Ragtime Orchestra
1:40 Wallace Davenport & His New Orleans Jazz Band
3:00 Dr. Michael White Quartet w/ Thais Clark
4:25 Pete Fountain
6:00 Young Tuxedo Brass Band

CONGO SQUARE STAGE
11:15 Percussion Inc.
12:25 Willie Tee
1:45 The Shepherd Band
3:05 Zap Mama
4:30 Cubanismo starring Jesus Alemany
6:00 Jean Knight w/ Blue Eyed Soul

BELLSOUTH MOBILITY LAGNIAPPE TENT
11:20 Dillard University Jazz Ensemble
12:35 White Cloud Hunters
1:45 Little Freddie King Blues Band
3:15 Don Wiley & Louisiana Grass
4:40 Acoustic Swiftness
6:00 Michael Ward

MUSIC HERITAGE STAGE
11:45 Jazz Education Roundtable feat. Ellis Marsalis, Harold Battiste, Alvin Batiste, Kidd Jordan, Clyde Kerr, Jr. & host Al Kennedy (Interview)
1:15 Zap Mama (Interview)
2:30 Clancy "Blues Boy" Lewis w/ Sheba Kimbrough
3:45 Jimmy Johnson (Interview)

5:00 Keb' Mo (Interview)

RHODES GOSPEL TENT
11:00 St. John Divine Gospel Drill Team
11:45 The Southern Travelers
12:30 St. Raymond Gospel Choir
1:15 The Southern Bells
2:00 St. Francis DeSales Golden Voices
2:45 The Crownseekers
3:30 To the Glory of God Community Choir
4:20 Mt. Airy BC Male Chorus
5:10 The Williams Sisters of New York City
6:30 Sammy Berfect & Dimensions of Faith

PARADES
12:00 Black Men of Labor, Golden Trumpets, Double Nine High Steppers SA&PCs with Tremé Brass Band
2:00 Money Wasters, Jolly Bunch, Popular Ladies SA&PCs with Pinettes Brass Band
4:00 Devastating Ladies, N'Krumah Better Boys, The Rollers SA&PCs with Mahogany Brass Band
4:00 Economy Hall Parade – Ladies Prince of Wales SA&PC

SUNDAY, APRIL 27

FOX 8 / POLAROID STAGE
11:15 Loyola Jazz Ensemble
12:20 Los Babies del Merengue
1:45 Johnny Adams w/ Humphrey Davis & Night Life
3:10 Beau Jocque & Zydeco Hi-Rollers
4:35 Frankie Ford Show
6:00 Irma Thomas & The Professionals

make the front porch brunch of Vivian and Richard C's.

One other such brunch has passed into myth. The original hosts began a free-for-all Last Sunday of Jazz Fest Morning Brunch that lasted 20 years. Then the unthinkable happened: they moved to Lakeview. But, being good stewards of the Fest, they prepped the next tenant to continue the brunch. Then he too moved away, forgetting to pass along the tradition. That's when civic-minded neighbors paid the new tenant a visit and explained his geographic situation in relation to his social responsibility. Ok, no problem. Until he, too, moved on, and the last tenant – unbelievably – turned his back on tradition. This gentleman had no way of knowing that the long-lived brunch transcended mere decision-making. Come the last Sunday of Jazz Fest, dozens of Festers showed up for the brunch, many from other parts of the country. It has taken a few years for that brunch to fade into legend.

"Sometimes I think the rest of the year is just to get us from

Pretty Boy Forbes

one Jazz Fest to the next," said one local brunch-thrower. His brunch dates back to circa 1980. The brunch and houseguests (the *one rule*: no closing the bathroom door) have spawned an adjunct: He and a few houseguests get together for an annual between-the-Festival weekends "Par-T" golf game. They compete for an old golf trophy salvaged from a thrift store and decorated by various female contributors, with *de rigueur* Mardi Gras beads, and emblazoned with the Hedonists of America creed:

"I do solemnly swear, to seize the moment or whoever is closest, to titillate my senses, and to passionately embrace the pleasures of life."

The invitational, "it's not as hard to get into as the Masters," started with three friends, and is now up to 15, with an occasional lady taking a swing. Libations flow liberally and it's a point of honor to actually finish the game. One year, the soused golfers called "Par-T" scores into the *Times-Picayune*, which actually printed them the next day.

This year, Jazz Fest showcased lots of classic funk and soul. "New Orleans is a funk principality," Davis said to music writer Keith Spera in a *Times-Picayune* article. After trying to get George Clinton and P-Funk for years, Clinton appeared at the Fest, along with Isaac Hayes and Earth Wind and Fire. These bookings represented a goal of increasing African-American participation. The slightly scaled-down schedule went back to the Fest roots to strike a balance against last year's big groups and

Beatle Bob

huge crowds that brought forth a host of complaints. Music cum social critics took off the gloves very publicly on that topic.

Lafayette's Francis Pavy was the official poster artist and his hoodoo-pointillist rendering of the Neville Brothers was a fitting tribute to their 20th anniversary of playing together as a group. *Rolling Stone* magazine referred to Pavy as "The Picasso of Zydeco."

More changes were in store for 1998, when the Fair Grounds' new 20,000 square foot air-conditioned Grandstand would open, as a phoenix rising from the fire that destroyed the historic building in 1993. Fair Grounds officials had discussed filling in the ponds (they did not), improving drainage and planting shade trees. Only those in the know could have foreseen how big the changes would be. Festival lovers didn't know it, but 1997 was the end of another chapter in the unfolding history of Jazz Fest. Next year would bring quantum changes to both the Fair Grounds and the Festival.

THE WATERMELON SACRIFICE

It's a quintessential New Orleans phenomenon: Take an otherwise banal item, say, a watermelon. It's marked and green like an alligator, sort of elongated and easy to carry, inscrutable on the outside and juicy red meat on the inside, and studded with secret weapons small enough to fly in spitting contests. It makes a satisfying splitting sound when cut...or thrown. That the watermelon sacrifice was born in New Orleans is no surprise.

But Jack Varuso did employ a kind of genius when he started it, and his singular passion has elevated the ritual — and those who participate — to an ecumenical ecstasy. The true watermelon sacrifice involves a samurai sword, but Varuso explains, "We don't do swords at Jazz Fest- they frown on that." Every day, at the Fais Do-Do Stage between the second and last act, Varuso revs up a free for all. Folks dress up. Varuso likes a tutu. They may have instruments such as tambourines, hula hoops, maracas, and the like. Varuso brings the original sacrificial cloth, which he later rinses and dries out on a chair in his backyard. Talk about your rituals. People gather round and they chant taken from the book Gumbo Ya Ya:

"Watermelon, watermelon, red to the rind. If you don't believe it, just pull down your blind.
I sell to the rich. I sell to the poor.
I sell to the lady standing in that do-o-or, In that do-o-or."

Then people rub on the melon, write their names on the melon, and sometimes dedicate the melon to a specific person. (The last was sacrificed in the name of Daniel Breaux.) The chant goes faster and faster, occasionally people are smacked in the butt with the melon, or little kids ride the melon as it's carried around. There is usually a vestal virgin whose duty it is to follow Varuso around and allow the watermelon to be placed on her or rubbed against her. This is usually not a sexual deal. Finally, when a suitable orgiastic frenzy is reached, the melon is thrown in the air and smashes on the ground. Then several tactics may be pursued. In one scenario, Varuso and others put parts of the melon on their heads and wear it until they tire. Or they may toss pieces in the air and try to catch them al la popcorn style. Or they may treat it any creative way that comes to mind.

The watermelon sacrifice has been filmed by a Japanese archive, Russian Television, and it appeared in a documentary Red to the Rind made by Clemson people and every year new students seek out the sacrifice. Varuso accepts and appreciates donated watermelons, but in lieu, will purchase them himself. He asserts that 7 times per Fest multiplied by the cost of a melon "can run into some money."

HOUSE OF BLUES / DR. MARTENS STAGE
11:15 Timothea
12:20 Willie West & The Westwind Blues Band
1:35 Continental Drifters
2:50 Chris Smither
4:15 Bryan Lee & The Jumpstreet Five
5:45 Sonny Landreth

WWL / RAY-BAN STAGE
11:20 Keith Claiborne
12:25 Bobby Marchan & Higher Ground
1:50 Walter "Wolfman" Washington & The Roadmasters
3:20 funky Meters
5:30 Earth, Wind & Fire

WB 38 FAIS DO-DO STAGE
11:15 Al Berard & The Basin Brothers
12:25 Balfa Toujours
1:45 Margaret Lewis & The Thunderbolts w/ Kenny Bill Stinson
3:05 Twangorama
4:25 Creole Zydeco Farmers
5:50 Nathan & The Zydeco Cha Chas

WWOZ JAZZ TENT
11:15 The Jeremy Davenport Quartet
12:20 Victor Goines Group
1:40 Astral Project
3:00 Alvin Batiste & The Jazztronauts
4:25 Houston Person & Etta Jones
5:50 Rachelle Ferrell

COX COMMUNICATIONS ECONOMY HALL TENT
11:25 Ms. Barbara Short & BASs Jazz Men
12:35 Placide Adams' Original Dixieland Hall Jazz Band
1:50 Greg Stafford's Jazz Hounds
3:50 Tremé Brass Band
4:25 George French's New Orleans Storyville Jazz Band
5:30 Harlem Jazz & Blues Band

CONGO SQUARE STAGE
11:15 Culu Dancers
12:20 The Wild Magnolias
1:25 Escola de Samba Casa Samba
2:45 National Dance Ensemble of Mali
4:00 Babatunde Olatunji & His Drums of Passion
5:45 Habib Kaite & Bamada of Mali

BELLSOUTH MOBILITY LAGNIAPPE TENT
11:15 Teresa Romero Torkanowsky pres. Ole Flamenco Ole! & Dance of the Americas
12:30 Greg Dawson & Crosswinds
1:50 Six Nations Women Singers
3:00 Ronnie Kole
4:30 Patrice Fisher & Arpa w/ guests from Guatemala
6:00 Khadir

MUSIC HERITAGE STAGE
12:00 Maggie Lewis (Interview
1:15 Gray Montgomery
2:30 Irma Thomas (Interview)
3:45 Six Nations Women Singers (Interview)
5:00 David & Roselyn

RHODES GOSPEL TENT
11:00 Antioch Gospel Singers
11:45 The Friendly Five Gospel Singers
12:30 Lamont Jackson & A New Beginning
1:15 The Dynamic Smooth Family of Slidell
2:00 Zulu Ensemble Male Choir

2:45 New Orleans Spiritualettes
3:30 Watson Memorial Teaching
Ministries
4:30 Dorothy Norwood
5:20 Holy Hill Gospel Singers
6:05 Raymond A. Myles & The RAMS

PARADES
12:00 Scene Boosters, Jetsetters,
Westbank Steppers SA&PCs,
Algiers Brass Band and
Mohawk Mardi Gras Indians
2:00 Original Prince of Wales, Avenue
Steppers, Valley of the Silent
Men SA&PCs and Tornado
Brass Band
3:05 Economy Hall Parade
– Calendar Girls SA&PC
4:00 New Orleans Men Buck
Jumpers, Original New Orleans
Ladies Buck Jumpers SA&PCs
and High Steppers Brass Band
and Carrollton Hunters Mardi
Gras Indians

THURSDAY, MAY 1

FOX 8 / POLAROID STAGE
11:20 South Lafourche High School
Jazz Band
12:45 Dash Rip Rock
2:15 Clarence "Frogman" Henry
3:45 Anders Osborne
5:30 Luther Kent & Trick Bag Band

**HOUSE OF BLUES /
DR. MARTENS STAGE**
11:20 Paula & The Pontiacs
12:40 Executive Steel Band
2:00 Larry Johnson
3:20 Eddie Bo
4:40 Galactic
5:55 Tab Benoit

WWL / RAY-BAN STAGE
11:20 Ancestro
12:45 BeauSoleil avec Michael Doucet
2:15 Albita
3:50 Mary Chapin Carpenter
5:35 Blues Traveler

WB 38 FAIS DO-DO STAGE
11:15 The Strawberry Jammers
12:20 Mamou
1:45 J. Monque'D Blues Band & The
Lil' Pats of Butter
2:55 Jambalaya Cajun Band
4:10 Hadley J. Castille &
Sharecroppers Cajun Band

5:40 Boozoo Chavis & Magic Sounds

WWOZ JAZZ TENT
11:15 Philip Manuel w/ guest Fred
Foss
12:20 Steve Masakowski
1:40 Clyde Kerr, Jr. & Univision
3:00 Ricardo Lewis Quintet w/ guest
Sandra Booker
4:25 Delfeayo Marsalis
5:50 James Moody

**COX COMMUNICATIONS ECONOMY
HALL TENT**
11:15 Chris Clifton's New Orleans
All-Stars
12:35 Andrew Hall's Society Jazz Band
1:50 Tim Laughlin
3:05 Lionel Ferbos & The Palm Court
Jazz Band
4:25 Louisiana Repertory Jazz
Ensemble
6:00 Banu Gibson & New Orleans
Hot Jazz

CONGO SQUARE STAGE
11:15 Des-ty-né
12:30 Seminoles Mardi Gras Indians
1:40 Irie Dawtas
2:55 Cool Riddums & Sista Teedy
4:25 Oumou Sangare of Mali
6:00 The Soul Rebels

**BELLSOUTH MOBILITY
LAGNIAPPE TENT**
11:15 New Orleans All-City Outreach
w/ guest Terrence Blanchard
12:35 Louis "Red" Morgan
1:50 Julio & Caesar
3:00 Libby Rae Watson
4:25 Hazel & The Delta Ramblers
5:50 The Poor Clares

MUSIC HERITAGE STAGE
11:45 Michael Ray (Interview)
1:00 Hadley J. Castille (Interview)
2:15 Boozoo Chavis (Interview)
3:30 James Moody (Interview)
4:45 Philip Manuel (Interview)

RHODES GOSPEL TENT
11:00 True Tone Gospel Singers
11:40 Simonia & Archie Milton Gospel
Band
12:20 J.C. & Co. Gospel Singers of
New Orleans
1:00 The First Revolution
1:45 The Gospel Revelators
2:30 The Heralds of Love
3:15 The Coolie Family Gospel
Singers

4:05 Leviticus Gospel Singers
4:50 Gospel Extenders
5:40 Spencer Taylor & The Highway
QCs
6:35 Avondale Community Choir

PARADES
4:00 Bon Temps Roulez Second
Liners and Storyville
Stompers Brass Band

FRIDAY, MAY 2

FOX 8 / POLAROID STAGE
11:15 Thousand $ Car
12:20 Bobby Cure & The
Summertime Blues w/ Robert
Parker & Roland Stone
1:55 Ernie K-Doe w/ Milton
Batiste's Magnificent 7 & Big
Al Carson
3:20 The Iguanas
4:45 Steve Riley & The Mamou
Playboys
6:05 Rockin' Dopsie Jr. & The
Zydeco Travelers

**HOUSE OF BLUES /
DR. MARTEN STAGE**
11:15 Delgado Community College
Jazz Ensemble
12:20 Mas Mamones
1:35 Patrick Henry & The
Liberation Band
3:00 Sherman Robertson
4:30 Andy J. Forest & The Blue
Orleanians
6:00 Coco Robicheaux & The
Perspirators

WWL / RAY-BAN STAGE
11:25 J.J. Muggler Band
12:50 Marcia Ball
2:20 Delbert McClinton
3:55 Bruce Hornsby
5:40 Al Jarreau

WB 38 FAIS DO-DO STAGE
11:15 The Haphazards
12:40 Filé
1:55 Evening Star String Band
3:10 D.L. Menard & The Louisiana
Aces
4:35 Savoy-Doucet Cajun Band
5:50 Chris Ardoin & Double
Clutchin' w/ guest Bois Sec
Ardoin

WWOZ JAZZ TENT
11:20 Jason Marsalis
12:35 Edward Peterson, Bill Summers
& David Torkanowsky
1:50 Marlon Jordan Quintet
3:10 Art Farmer
4:40 Tuba Showcase w/ Howard
Johnson & Gravity plus Tuba
Fats, Kirk Joseph, Matt Perrine
and Julius McKee
6:15 Michael Ray & The Cosmic
Krewe

COX COMMUNICATIONS ECONOMY HALL TENT
11:15 Local International AllStar Jazz
Band
12:20 Last Straws
1:35 June Gardner & The Fellows
2:55 Dukes of Dixieland
4:10 Doc Paulin's Dixieland Jazz
Band
5:40 Al Hirt

CONGO SQUARE STAGE
11:15 T-Roy & The Vibe
12:20 Traditional Instrumental
Ensemble of Mali
1:30 Ben Hunter the Soul Avenger
2:50 Dogon Dancers of Mali
4:15 Oumou Sangare of Mali
6:00 Cyril Neville & The Uptown
Allstars Revue feat. Diamonds

**BELLSOUTH MOBILITY
LAGNIAPPE TENT**
11:15 Jesuit High School Jazz Band
12:20 Black Eagles Mardi Gras Indians
1:35 Neslort
3:00 Pfister Sisters
4:25 Wasa Belgian Gypsy Jazz
5:50 John Rankin

MUSIC HERITAGE STAGE
11:40 Ernie K-Doe (Interview)
12:45 Wasa Belgian Gypsy Jazz
(Interview)
2:00 Bruce Hornsby (Interview)
3:15 Carol Fran & Clarence Holliman
(Interview)
4:20 Ironin' Board Sam
5:30 Carlos Sanchez "Flamenco
Amenecer"

RHODES GOSPEL TENT
11:00 The Humble Travelers
11:45 The Wimberly Family
12:30 The R. Lee James Memorial
Chorale
1:15 One A-Chord

2:00 Melvin Winfield & New Vision
2:45 The New Zion Trio Plus One
3:30 Theo Bourgeois w/ Kennedy HS Gospel Choir
4:20 O'Landa Draper & The Associates
5:20 Sounds of Unity
6:05 Franklin Ave. BC Gospel Choir

PARADES
4:00 Revolution and Single Men SA&PCs and James Andrews All Stars Brass Band
4:10 Economy Hall Parade – Algiers Steppers SA&PC

SATURDAY, MAY 3

FOX 8 / POLAROID STAGE
11:15 Royal Fingerbowl
12:20 Peabody
1:35 Marva Wright & The BMWs
2:50 Buckwheat Zydeco
4:15 George Porter, Jr. & Runnin' Pardners
5:45 Better Than Ezra

HOUSE OF BLUES / DR. MARTENS STAGE
11:15 Paky Saavedra's Bandido
12:20 Raful Neal
1:40 Alex Chilton
3:00 Cookie & The Cupcakes
4:25 Syl Johnson
6:00 The Dixie Cups

WWL / RAY-BAN STAGE
11:25 Fila Phil & D.J. Mouche & The Powa Rangzz
12:50 Dirty Dozen
2:10 Clarence "Gatemouth" Brown and His Big Band
3:40 Rita Marley
5:40 Fats Domino

WB 38 FAIS DO-DO STAGE
11:15 Los Sagitarios
12:20 Luke Thompson & The Green Valley Cut Ups
1:35 Allen Fontenot & The Country Cajuns
2:55 Danny Collet
4:20 Sheryl Cormier & Cajun Sounds
5:45 Belton Richard and The Musical Aces

WWOZ JAZZ TENT
11:15 Walter Payton & The Snapbean Band w/ Sharon Martin
12:35 Germaine Bazzle w/ George French Group
1:50 Charles Neville Jazz Band
3:05 Clarence Johnson III w/ Chris Severin
4:20 Leroy Jones
5:45 The Herbie Hancock Quartet

COX COMMUNICATIONS ECONOMY HALL
11:15 Wendell Brunious Jazz Band
12:20 Bob French's Original Tuxedo Jazz Band
1:45 Onward Brass Band
3:10 Dr. Michael White's Tribute to Sidney Bechet
4:35 New Leviathan Oriental Foxtrot Orchestra
5:55 Claude Luter w/ Jacques Gauthe's Creole Rice Band

CONGO SQUARE STAGE
11:15 Kumbuka Drum & Dance Collective
12:20 Willie Metcalf's the Elder Statesmen of N.O. Modern Jazz feat. Samirah Evans & Academy of Black Arts Youth Jazz Chorus
1:50 Dogon Dancers of Mali

3:00 James Rivers Movement
4:25 King Floyd
5:50 Oumou Sangare of Mali

BELLSOUTH MOBILITY LAGNIAPPE TENT
11:15 Golden Star Hunters Mardi Gras Indians
12:20 Caledonian Society Scottish Pipes & Drums
1:30 Heritage School of Music Jazz Ensemble
2:50 NOCCA Jazz Ensemble
4:15 Traditional Instrumental Ensemble of Mali
5:35 John Boutté

MUSIC HERITAGE STAGE
12:00 Sidney Bechet Roundtable (Interview)
1:45 Native Nations Inter-Tribal
3:00 Oumou Sangare (Interview)
4:15 Alex Chilton (Interview)
5:30 Butch Mudbone

RHODES GOSPEL TENT
11:00 St. Luke A.M.E. Gospel Choir
11:45 Ebenezer MBC Choir
12:30 Greater Bright Morning Star Gospel Choir
1:15 The Soulful Heavenly Stars
2:00 Love Alive Fellowship Choir
2:45 The Mighty Chariots
3:30 First Baptist Church Missionary Choir
4:15 The Johnson Extension
5:00 Second Morning Star MBC
5:50 Thompson Community Choir of Chicago

PARADES
12:00 Original Taylor Bunch, Second Line Jammers, Calliope Highsteppers SA&PCs & Paulin Brothers Brass Band
1:45 Economy Hall Parade – Ladies of Essence SA&PC
2:00 Lady Sequence, Original Step-n-Style and The Young Steppers SA&PCs and New Birth Brass Band
4:00 O.G. Steppers, Perfect Gentlemen SA&PCs and Lil' Rascals Brass Band

SUNDAY, MAY 4

FOX 8 / POLAROID STAGE
11:00 Ritmo Caribeno
12:05 Tommy Ridgley & The Untouchables w/ Cookie Gabriel
1:25 Charmaine Neville & Friends
2:45 Snooks Eaglin
4:15 Widespread Panic
5:50 The Radiators

HOUSE OF BLUES / DR. MARTENS STAGE
11:15 Liz Barnez Band
12:20 Ernie Vincent & Top Notes
1:40 Mem Shannon & The Membership
3:00 Wanda Rouzan & A Taste of New Orleans
4:25 C.C. Adcock
5:55 E.L.S.

WWL / RAY-BAN STAGE
11:15 SUNO Jazz Ensemble
12:20 White Eagles Mardi Gras Indians
1:25 Rebirth Brass Band
3:00 George Clinton & The P-Funk All Stars
5:45 The Neville Brothers feat. Aaron Neville

WB 38 FAIS DO-DO STAGE
11:15 Horace Trahan, Leo Abshire & Original Mamou Playboys
12:20 Thomas "Big Hat" Fields & His Foot Stompin' Zydeco Band
1:35 Kristi Guillory & Reveille
2:50 Los Calientes del Son
4:15 Waylon Thibodeaux "Louisiana's Rockin' Fiddler"
5:45 Willis Prudhomme & Zydeco Express

WWOZ JAZZ TENT
11:15 Alvin "Red" Tyler Quartet
12:25 Kermit Ruffins Big Band
1:40 Kent Jordan w/ Strings
3:00 Donald Harrison
4:20 Terence Blanchard Group
5:45 McCoy Tyner & Michael Brecker

COX COMMUNICATIONS ECONOMY HALL
11:15 Louis Cottrell & His Original Creole Jazz Band
12:15 Duke Dejan's Olympia Brass Band
1:15 Tommy Yetta's New Orleans Jazz Band
2:20 Boutté l'Etiene Music Friends
3:35 Fabrice Zamarchi Quartet – Tribute to Sidney Bechet
4:45 Bob Wilber & The Bechet Legacy w/ vocalist Pug Horton
6:00 Preservation Hall Jazz Band

CONGO SQUARE STAGE
11:15 Y'Shua Manzy
12:20 Irie Vibrations
1:35 Dogon Dancers of Mali
2:50 Eric Gable
4:15 Jazz Jamaica
5:50 Oumou Sangare of Mali

BELLSOUTH MOBILITY LAGNIAPPE STAGE
11:15 UNO Jazz Ensemble
12:20 Walter Cook & Creole Wild West Mardi Gras Indians
1:35 Dr. Arvol Looking Horse w/ Sosk Northern Drums
2:45 New Orleans Klezmer Allstars
4:15 The Hackberry Ramblers
5:45 Traditional Instrumental Ensemble of Mali

MUSIC HERITAGE STAGE
12:00 The Mardi Gras Chorus
1:35 Po' Henry & Tookie
2:30 Tony Green Gypsy Jazz
3:45 Dr. Looking Horse, Dawn Hill & Chief Sundown (Interview)
5:00 Mem Shannon (Interview)

RHODES GOSPEL TENT
11:00 The Melody Clouds
11:45 Joyful
12:30 Therrow Scott & Tehiliah
1:15 The Famous Rocks of Harmony
2:00 John Lee & The Heralds of Christ w/ Christine Myles
2:45 Jo "Cool" Davis
3:15 Alvin Bridges & The Desire Community Choir
4:00 Sherman Washington & The Famous Zion Harmonizers
4:55 Dorothy Love Coates Singers
6:05 The Gospel Soul Children

PARADES
12:00 Olympia Aide, Uptowner's Hobo Clowns, Ladies Zulu SA&PCs, Pinstripe Brass Band and Golden Arrows Mardi Gras Indians
12:15 Economy Hall Parade – Original Black Magic Ladies SA&PC
2:00 Devastation, Unknown Steppers, Original Four SA&PCs and New Birth Brass Band

4:00 The Furious Five and Untouchables SA&PCs, Looney Tunes Brass Band and Young Cheyennes Mardi Gras Indians

NIGHT CONCERTS

FRIDAY, APRIL 25, 9 P.M.
Santana
Funky Meters
Kiefer UNO Lakefront Arena
SATURDAY, APRIL 26, 9 P.M.
Earth, Wind & Fire
Maceo Parker & Roots Revisited
Kiefer UNO Lakefront Arena
SATURDAY, APRIL 26, 12 MIDNIGHT
Midnight Jam
Ellis Marsalis
Nicholas Payton
Wess Anderson
Ed Peterson
Johnny Vidacovich
Bill Huntington
David Pulphus
Jeremy Davenport
Adonis Rose
Praline Connection Gospel & Blues

MONDAY, APRIL 28 & TUESDAY, APRIL 29, 8 P.M.
Jazz at the Palm Court
Harlem Jazz & Blues with Special Guest Doc Cheatham, Al Casey, Fred Smith, Arthur Hamilton, David "Bubba" Brooks, Edwin Swanston, Johnny Williams, Johnny Blowers and Laurel Watson
Palm Court Jazz Café
TUESDAY, APRIL 29, 8 P.M.
Dew Drop Inn Revisited, A Tribute to Edward Frank
Marva Wright, Walter "Wolfman" Washington, King Floyd, Wanda Rouzan, Lillian Boutté
The New Orleans Jazz Legends: Germaine Bazzle, Alvin "Red" Tyler, Sigismund Walker, Wendell Eugene, Warren Bell, Sr., Peter Badie, Sam Mooney, Harry Nance, Arnold Depass, the Wardell Quezerguezerque Big Band
Ernest N. Morial Convention Center
WEDNESDAY, APRIL 30, 8 P.M.
La Noche Latina
Johnny Ventura and His Orchestra, Albita, Acoustic Swiftness
Ernest N. Morial Convention Center
THURSDAY, MAY 1, 8 P.M.
Al Jarreau
Herbie Hancock
Astral Project
Ernest N. Morial Convention Center
FRIDAY, MAY 2, 9 P.M.
James Brown
Rita Marley
Taj Mahal
Kiefer UNO Lakefront Arena
SATURDAY, MAY 3, 9 P.M.
George Clinton & The P-Funk Allstars
Isaac Hayes
The Batiste Brothers
Kiefer UNO Lakefront Arena
SATURDAY, MAY 3, 12 MIDNIGHT
Midnight Jam
Art Farmer
Howard Johnson
Donald Harrison, Jr.
Herlin Riley, Mike Pellera, David Torkanowsky, Victor Goines, Eric Traub, Bob Stuart, Jim Singleton, Jason Marsalis
Praline Connection Gospel & Blues Hall

1998

Buddy Guy

It was the grandest grandstand in Louisiana. After five years of insurance wrangling and rebuilding after the devastating 1994 fire, the $27.5 million grandstand/clubhouse project had opened on Thanksgiving Day, 1997. The Fair Grounds was the oldest continuously operating racetrack in the U.S. and was once the scene not only of horse racing, but bull and bear fights, cavalry races by Union Troops during the Civil War, and troop-training grounds during the Spanish American War. Some of the most revered racehorses, such as the famous Black Gold, are buried in the infield.

The grandstand was now enhanced with a posh clubhouse with dining room, full air-conditioning, and spacious exhibition halls — it was a wonderful benefit to Jazz Fest. Alcoves within the grandstand seating were perfect for Music Heritage Stage performances, interviews and demonstrations to be conducted in the blessed air-conditioning, while the audience had a panoramic view of the Fair Grounds through floor-to-extended-ceiling windows. The new space was a natural fit for the Food Heritage Stage to come indoors. The Folk/African Heritage Stage, Lagniappe Stage, and the International Pavilion were also located inside. Fair Grounds concessions sold beer and soft

drinks, but no food. There were hallways, usually devoted to horse racing memorabilia, with ample space for cultural exhibitions. The combination of the paddock area, first floor of the grandstand and apron between the grandstand and main track offered great flexibility for an indoor/outdoor setup and accommodated up to 3,000. The paddock area was an intimate space between two sections of the grandstand and the Lagniappe Stage found a home there.

The balm of air-conditioning cannot be overstated. The grandstand was a cool and quiet retreat for those for whom the relentless humid heat was just too much. And (rejoice!) there was an alternative to the dreaded, but nevertheless necessary, Port-O-Lets! From this time forward, women in particular would think differently about their schedules; planning the pilgrimage to the grandstand restrooms along with trips to food booths and bands to hear on music stages.

The Festival staff felt relief too. It was as if the burgeoning Jazz Fest released its belt several

notches and breathed out. Other bold strokes that changed the Festival layout allowed significantly more free acreage on the infield, but changed the culture of Jazz Fest again. Seasoned Festival fans now felt the effects of more elbow space and fanned out, enjoying the new creature comforts. There was more of a constant flow of people, coming inside for a respite from the elements and to learn a bit more about their culture, then back outside for a favorite act. In time, even the all-day blankets would billow again near the stages.

The first Jazz Festers to enter the gate and cross the hard-packed loam perimeter onto the asphalt were in for a big surprise. There, in what was formerly a parking area, were the Jazz and Gospel Tents, outside of the infield entirely and separated from the rest of the Festival by the racetrack. Louisiana's two most powerful contributions to world culture and their necessary seating arrangements no longer had to contend with the mud on wet days. Always a haven in the rain, people now could sit on the hard concrete.

Every single morning of the 1998 Jazz Fest dawned like a bright sunny jewel. Although the rule was "no beach poles or umbrellas," a few were snuck in anyway by some of the 98,000 fans on Saturday that broke the single-day previous record back in 1996. Jimmy Buffet at one end of the Fest on the Ray Ban Stage and Better Than Ezra on the other end of the Fair Grounds created a cosmic gravitational field drawing fans into the Fest.

What a heartrending moment occurred when Aaron Neville and a backing do wop quintet in the Gospel Tent sang "Nearer My God to Thee" with Johnny Adams joining on the Zion

"One year Aaron Neville was on a platform signing CDs, and Anne and Britton Trice's three-year-old, Eliza, was in line for an autograph. The crowd noticed her and picked her up, handing her over their heads, crowd-surfing style, up to Aaron. He signed her arm, leg, and T shirt as requested, and the Trices photographed Eliza later." SUSAN LARSON

Harmonizers' "Never Alone!" Their voices blended in an otherworldly harmony on "Amazing Grace" and "Down by the Riverside" It was the venerable Adams's last Jazz Fest performance. Charlie Bering, Jazz Tent producer and owner of Lu and

Charlie's and Charlie B.'s music clubs would also pass away. These were just two among the fine musicians who passed away that year. Bassist George Porter said, "Charlie Bering was really the person who was out in the scene here – he would keep his

Mama and Mac Rebennack

Coco Robicheaux

eye out for what was happening, make sure you got over at the Festival; and I remember there being a vibe where people would just sit in with each other much more readily (with Charlie in charge)." On the Music Heritage Stage, Kalamu ya Salaam and the WordBand shouted their sharp-witted spoken word. On Friday, the Unstoppable Gospel Singers let loose in the Gospel Tent, and on the second Saturday Coolbone bopped the Congo Square closeout with bone swing, their rhythmic confluence of hip hop and brass dubbed "brass hop." Blues guitarist Kenny Neal performed with his nine-year-old nephew Frederick on the first Friday; and John Fogerty returned to his spiritual roots for an evening concert with Dr. John and a Fair Grounds performance, too. His "Midnight Special," "Proud Mary," and "Born on the Bayou" resonated with Louisiana audiences. Earl "Let the Good Times Roll" King and the Butanes gave an incendiary performance to a stoked crowd at the House Of Blues Stage.

The music jams in nightclubs around Jazz Fest were a natural outgrowth of so many musicians in similar orbits. The legendary Dew Drop Inn (the Groove Room) was an African-American owned nightclub, and it was THE place to be if you were a musician or music lover from the mid 1940s to the 1960s. Owner Frank Painia was an activist for African-American musicians and maintained high standards both in his choice of performers and his treatment of them. His business grew so well that he booked musicians in a string of venues around the south, and added a hotel next door to the Groove Room for people of color. Both African-Americans and whites defied the "mixing laws" to enjoy performers such as Ray Charles, Milt Jackson, Little Richard, and Big Joe Turner. New Orleans musicians benefited from the stream of talent and originality. The African-American owned *Louisiana Weekly* called it "the south's swankiest night spot." The New Orleans Jazz & Heritage Festival had partnered with local arts organizations such as the Contemporary Arts Center to recreate evenings of musical homage called "The Dew Drop Inn Revisited" This year it was held at the Praline Connection Gospel and Blues Hall, and featured Clarence "Gatemouth" Brown "Gate Swings with Big Band," and Larry Hamilton, Chuck Carbo, Topsy Chapman and the Wardell Qeurzeque Orchestra.

It was during the evening concerts that musicians could sit in and jam with other bands. But at the Fair Grounds, ostensibly due to demand and the burgeoning generations, it was increasingly harder for artists to secure back-

11:50 Joseph S. Clark Sr. H.S. Gospel Choir
12:35 Mobile United Voices of Praise Comm. Choir
1:20 The Southern Gospel Singers
2:00 A Touch of Heaven
2:50 Dynamic Smooth Family of Slidell
3:35 Theo Bourgeois with Kennedy H.S. Gospel Choir
4:20 The Banks Family
5:10 Mavis Staples A Tribute to Mahalia Jackson
6:15 R. Lee James Memorial Chorale

PARADES
2:00 Original Black Magic Lady Steppers and N'Krumah Third Division with Mahogany Brass Band
4:00 Just Steppin,' Positive Ladies and Single Men SA&PCs with Trombone Shorty Brass Band

SATURDAY, APRIL 25

FOX 8 / POLAROID STAGE
11:15 Heritage School of Music
12:20 Reggie Hall & The Twilighters w/ Sadie Tee, Prince Albert & Marilyn Barbarin
1:40 George Porter, Jr. w/ special guest Johnny Adams
3:15 Marcia Ball
4:35 R3 featuring Tina Reynolds
6:00 Steve Riley & The Mamou Playboys

HOUSE OF BLUES STAGE
11:15 Jumpin' Johnny Sansone
12:20 Chris Thomas King
1:30 Keb Mo
3:00 John Mooney & Bluesiana
4:30 Byran Lee & The Jumpstreet Five
6:00 Sunpie & The Louisiana Sunspots

RAY-BAN STAGE
11:00 Dillard University Jazz Band
12:10 Michael Ward
1:15 The Dirty Dozen
2:35 Allen Toussaint
4:00 Etta James & The Roots Band
5:30 Bonnie Raitt

SHERATON / WB 38 FAIS DO-DO STAGE
11:30 Fredy Omar Con Su Banda
12:45 Amy & The Hank Sinatras
2:10 Kristi Guillory & Revelle
3:20 Hackberry Ramblers
4:35 Chris Ardoin w/ Bois Sec Ardoin
6:00 Boozoo Chavis & The Magic Sounds

BET ON JAZZ / WWOZ JAZZ TENT
11:15 Charlie Miller
12:20 Porgy Jones
1:30 Philip Manuel
2:40 Charles Neville Jazz Ensemble
4:00 Peter Martin Group featuring Four-Sight
5:30 Zawinul Syndicate

COX COMMUNICATIONS / VH1 ECONOMY HALL TENT
11:15 Rampart & Perdido Jazz Band
12:20 Chris Clifton & His All-Stars
1:30 Wallace Davenport
2:45 Lars Edegran & New Orleans Ragtime Orchestra
4:10 All-Star Hot Swing feat. Arvell Shaw, Al Casey, Al Grey, Ernest Elly, Sammy Rimington & Henry Butler
5:50 Doc Paulin's Dixieland Jazz Band

Gospel Tent

stage passes for their family and friends. Some musicians reported that Fest staff asked them to bring members of their bands onto the Grounds in one group, to economize on parking passes. No matter that each member had gear — and possibly plans of their own. Local musicians were resentful about the proportion of passes going to high-profile visitors. And the food served locals had little in common with special spreads found in "outside" bands' areas. Much of the spontaneity was being planned out of the onstage sit-ins, too. Agents, contracts, and the business of music had wrought changes over the years. No longer did musicians "show up"

10th anniversary congo square ∘ new orleans jazz & heritage festival ∘ 1998

to join an onstage gig. Rather, "pre-planned walk-ons" were arranged and guest musicians either simply played accompaniment or joined on vocals in accordance with prearranged contract fees. The Fest paid in proportion to whether the guest merely accompanied or sang.

A petite panic was set off when *Offbeat* Magazine's Editor-in-Chief Jan Ramsey, in her monthly column "Mojo Mouth,"

floated the speculation that a major corporate sponsor, seeking title sponsorship of Jazz Fest, had approached the Foundation. Quint Davis addressed the situation with these words: "Not only did the New Orleans Jazz & Heritage Festival reject a proposal [from a major corporate sponsor] but the Foundation also said no to another multi-million dollar proposal from tobacco, alcohol and gambling interests that they felt were not in keeping with the family name and image of the Festival, regardless of the amount of money. Let us simply state two facts that everyone who cares about the Festival should know: 1) the name "New Orleans Jazz & Heritage Festival" is indivisible and non negotiable at any price. Any corporate identification with the Festival name will have to bow to that reality. 2) At no time was any influence or control of any kind over the Festival considered. The content, structure and nature of the New Orleans Jazz & Heritage Festival is non negotiable for any price, period, as is the integrity of the name. Even though companies from Ray-Ban to Rhodes Funeral Homes pay sponsorship dollars to have their name associated with certain Festival Stages, in no way do they determine who plays on the stages that bear their names. So it has always been, so it shall always be. We hope this information clears up some of the confusion surrounding the issue and reassures Jazz Fest lovers that there will always be a New Orleans Jazz & Heritage Festival."

Offbeat was the principle music magazine in New Orleans, having taken up the torch from *Wavelength,* an earlier publication under a different editor. Staffed by music lovers and club crawlers, *Offbeat* got into the 1998 Jazz Fest scene with two innovations. One was the first annual "Jazz Fest Foto Fest," for which hundreds of photographs were submitted from professional and amateur photographers across the country. Professional local photographers Herman Leonard, Michael P. Smith, Syndey Byrd, Bryan Ashley White, Scott

Rosie Ledet

"When Ani di Franco played — they had had a disaster previously where the back stage got stormed. They were expecting these crazed fans to charge through our security to get to her. She shows up all stiff at first and so we just go about our business, you know, we got a B-B-Q thing going and I think we had to borrow some milk or something. I went in the dressing room, politely asking the right way: 'May I borrow some of your milk, we're making the batter for the fish fry?' Sure, and they're all worried about how it was going to go and we just kept on being ourselves and so after a while she got comfortable enough so that she moved out to the middle of the grass and started sitting out in front of the dressing room in the compound area, chilling, and nobody's coming up to her or bothering her and their crew starts realizing 'Hey they got food over there, better than what's in our trailer, you know?' And then, by the time she got on stage we were at one of our hamburger points. That smoke and the wind was blowing just right, it was almost like a smoke machine. It was rolling up on the stage and the smell was amazing and the wind was nice and everything and she stops playing and she says 'I just wanna say, I've never seen a more relaxed, cool stage crew — I love this place!' And after she got through she hung out and she couldn't say enough about what a great experience it was." KEITH WILLIAMS

Treme Brass Band

Marva Wright

among music clubs from 8 p.m. through 3 a.m. People could ride the shuttle without worrying about finding parking spaces or designated drivers, and an extended membership in the Krewe promised front-of-line privileges and discount tickets. Some of the venues served by the shuttle were Tipitina's, Carrollton Station, the Maple Leaf Bar, Howlin' Wolf, Donna's, Dos Jefes, Rock N Bowl, Margaritaville, Le Bon Temps Roulé, and Vic's Kangaroo Café.

Saltzman, Clayton Call, and Rick Olivier were represented. The photographs were on exhibit at the Contemporary Arts Center from April 24 through May 4.

The second great idea was the *Offbeat* Music Krewe (taking its name from the "krewes" that parade during Mardi Gras). RNO Marketing made a shuttle available that ran

fest facts

The Festival installed a new stage in the paddock area of the grandstand.

The economic impact of the Fest was $281.9 million.

Don Vappie and his Creole Jazz Orchestra performed recently discovered compositions by Jelly Roll Morton.

SHERATON / WB 38 FAIS DO-DO STAGE
11:30 Kenneth Thibodeaux & The Cajun Dance Band
1:00 Ronnie Dawson
2:30 Thomas "Big Hat" Fields
4:00 Bruce Daigrepont Cajun Band
5:30 Maggie Lewis & The Thunderbolts w/ Kenny Bill Stinson

BET ON JAZZ / WWOZ JAZZ TENT
11:15 Clarence Johnson III w/ Samirah Evans
12:20 The Al Belletto Big Jazz Band
1:35 Astral Project
2:55 Donald Harrison, Jr.
4:15 Ernestine Anderson
5:00 The Jazz Messengers / The Legacy of Art Blakey (under the direction of Benny Golson)

COX COMMUNICATIONS / VH1 ECONOMY HALL TENT
11:20 Original Dixieland Jazz Band
12:40 Duke Dejean's Olympia Brass Band
1:45 Topsy Chapman w/ Magnolia Jazz Band of Norway
3:00 Greg Stafford's Jazz Hounds
4:20 Wendell Brunious
5:45 Pete Fountain

CONGO SQUARE STAGE
11:00 White Eagles Mardi Gras Indians
12:10 G.R.E.S. Casa Samba
1:15 Hot Boys & DJ Jubilee
2:40 Ritmo Caribeno
4:00 Beau Jocque & The Zydeco Hi-Rollers
5:30 Baaba Maal of Senegal

BELLSOUTH MOBILITY LAGNIAPPE STAGE
11:15 The Haphazards
12:15 Golden Star Hunters Mardi Gras Indians
1:20 United Houma Nation Bayou Healers
2:40 Howard "Louie Bluie" Armstrong
4:10 Ancestro
5:35 Osvaldo Aysis Y Su Grupo of Panama

MUSIC HERITAGE STAGE
12:45 Henry Butler (Interview)
1:45 Osvaldo Aysis of Panama (Interview)
2:45 Benny Golson & members of the Jazz Messengers (Interview)
4:00 Marva Wright (Interview)
5:00 Howard Armstrong (Interview)

TULANE HOSPITAL / RHODES GOSPEL TENT
11:00 Antioch Gospel Singers
11:50 The Gospel Inspirationals
12:35 Jo "Cool" Davis
1:20 The Traveling Stars
2:00 The Davis Family
2:50 The Friendly Five Gospel Singers
3:35 The Crown Seekers
4:20 Watson Memorial Teaching Ministries
5:10 Evangelist Shirley Caesar
6:15 Raymond A. Myles & The RAMS

PARADES
12:00 Olympia Aide, Uptown Hobo Clowns and Lady Zulu SA&PC with The Pin Stripe Brass Band and Golden Arrow Mardi Gras Indians
2:00 Revolution and Original Four SA&PCs with The Hot 8 Brass Band and Young Cheyenne Mardi Gras Indians

Marsalis Family

4:00 Untouchables and Furious Five
      SA&PCs with New Birth Brass
      Band and Seminoles Mardi Gras
      Indians
4:00 Economy Hall Parade – Algiers
      Steppers SA&PC

THURSDAY, APRIL 30

FOX 8 / POLAROID STAGE
11:15 Tom's House
12:25 New Orleans Nightcrawlers
1:40 Pierre w/ Sound M-Pact
3:00 Bobby Marchan & Higher
      Ground
4:30 Tab Benoit
6:00 JJ Muggler Band

HOUSE OF BLUES STAGE
11:15 Invisible Cowboy
12:30 Rickie Castrillo & Dreamland
1:40 Larry Hamilton
3:00 Rare Connection w/ Big Al
      Carson
4:30 Spencer Bohren
6:00 Rockin' Tabby Thomas
      w/ Henry Gray

RAY-BAN STAGE
11:40 Spellman College Jazz
      Ensemble of Atlanta
1:00 James Andrews All-Star Brass
      Band
2:30 Katie Webster & The Vas-te
      Johnson Group
4:00 Rosie Ledet & The Zydeco
      Playboys
5:30 Ziggy Marley & The Melody
      Makers

SHERATON / WB 38 FAIS DO-DO STAGE
11:20 Jackie Callier
12:35 Coteau
1:45 Hadley J. Castille & The
      Sharecroppers Cajun Band
4:25 Balfa Toujours
5:50 Creole Zydeco Farmers

BET ON JAZZ / WWOZ JAZZ TENT
11:15 Xavier University Jazz Ensemble
12:20 Ed Peterson

1:40 Larry Sieberth w/ Betty Shirley
3:10 Carmen Lundy
4:30 Danilo Perez Trio
5:50 Three Baritone Saxophone Band
      plays Mulligan

**COX COMMUNICATIONS / VH1 ECONOMY
HALL TENT**
11:15 Warren Clark's French Quarter
      Jazz Band
12:35 Tommy Yetta's New Orleans
      Jazz Band
1:50 Frank Federico and The
      Medicare Madcaps
3:10 June Gardner & The Fellas
4:30 Barbara Shorts
6:00 New Leviathan Oriental Foxtrot
      Orchestra

CONGO SQUARE STAGE
11:20 Culu Dancers
12:00 Culu Dancers
12:50 Daughters of Jah
2:30 Walter Payton & The Snapbeans
      featuring Sharon Martin
4:00 Shepherd Band
5:45 Adams Griffin Project

**BELLSOUTH MOBILITY
LAGNIAPPE STAGE**
11:15 David & Roselyn
12:20 Runa Pacha
1:40 Danilo Perez Trio
3:00 Phil DeGruy Guitarpist
4:20 Black Eagles Mardi Gras Indians
5:35 Swingin' Haymakers

MUSIC HERITAGE STAGE
12:45 Dr. Billy Taylor (Interview)
1:45 Tribute to Alvin "Red" Tyler
2:45 Tabby Thomas (Interview)
3:45 Kalamu ya Salaam & The Word
      Band
5:00 Bobby Marchan (Interview)

**TULANE HOSPITAL / RHODES
GOSPEL TENT**
10:30 St. Raymond Gospel Choir
11:40 The Golden Wings
12:35 The First Revolution
1:10 Shiloh Missionary BC Choir
1:55 J.C. & Company Gospel Singers

2:40 Gospel Extenders
3:25 The Coolie Family
4:10 Leviticus Gospel Singers
5:00 Willie Neal Johnson & The New
      Gospel Keynotes
6:10 Greater Bright Morning Star
      Gospel Choir

PARADES
4:00 Bon Temps Roulez Secondliners
      with Storyville Stompers
      Brass Band

FRIDAY, MAY 1

FOX 8 / POLAROID STAGE
11:15 UNO Jazz Ensemble
12:45 Kenny Neal
2:15 Charmaine Neville Band w/
      Reggie Houston & Amasa Miller
3:45 James Cotton
5:30 Leo Nocentelli

HOUSE OF BLUES STAGE
11:20 Little Freddie King Blues Band
12:35 Sonny Bourg & The Bayou
      Blues Band
1:45 Robert Lowry
3:00 Jerry Beach
4:30 Raful Neal
6:00 Eddie Bo

RAY-BAN STAGE
11:30 White Cloud Hunters Mardi Gras
      Indians
1:00 Lil' Queenie & Friends
2:30 Buckwheat Zydeco
4:00 Emmylou Harris
5:30 Wayne Toups & Zydecajun

SHERATON / WB 38 FAIS DO-DO STAGE
11:30 Ken Naquin & The Ossun
      Playboys
1:00 190 Express
2:30 Mamou Prairie Band
4:00 Waylon Thibodeaux Louisiana's
      Rockin' Fiddler
5:45 Willis Prudhomme & Zydeco
      Express

BET ON JAZZ / WWOZ JAZZ TENT
11:15 Clyde Kerr, Jr. & Univision
12:30 Jason Marsalis
1:40 Los Hombres Calientes
2:50 Earl Turbinton
4:10 Marlon Jordan
5:40 The Billy Taylor Trio

**COX COMMUNICATIONS / VH1 ECONOMY
HALL TENT**
11:15 Lady Charlotte Jazz Band
12:15 Original Camelia Jazz Band
1:40 Dukes of Dixieland
3:00 Boilermaker Jazz Band
4:25 Louisiana Repertory Jazz Band
6:00 Tremé Brass Band

CONGO SQUARE STAGE
11:15 Jamal Batiste
12:20 Kumbuka Drum & Dance
      Collective
1:30 Acoustic Swiftness
2:45 Cyril Neville & The Uptown
      Allstars
4:10 Cool Riddums & Sista Teedy
5:40 Kermit Ruffins & The Barbecue
      Swingers

**BELLSOUTH MOBILITY
LAGNIAPPE STAGE**
11:20 Jesuit High School Jazz
      Ensemble
12:30 Hazel & The Delta Ramblers
1:45 Tony Green & Gypsy Jazz
3:00 John Rankin
4:25 Taho Folkloric Ensemble
5:50 Danilo Perez Trio

MUSIC HERITAGE STAGE
12:30 Cuban Percussion w/ M.
      Skinkus, H. Galardo & P. Menez
1:30 Trisha Boutté aka Sista Teedy
      (Interview)
2:30 Leo Nocentelli (Interview)
3:30 Danilo Perez (Interview)
4:15 Robert Lowery & Virgil Thrusher
      (Interview)

**TULANE HOSPITAL / RHODES
GOSPEL TENT**
11:00 The Humble Travelers
11:50 Old Zion Missionary Baptist
      Church Choir

12:35 Total Praise
1:20 Aline White & Company
2:00 One A-Chord
2:50 Lyle Henderson & Emmanuel
3:35 The Unstoppable Gospel Singers
4:20 McDonogh #35 High School Gospel Choir
5:10 The Lumsy Sisters of New Jersey
6:15 Alvin Bridges & Desire Community Choir

PARADES
4:00 Double Nine and Big Nine SA&PCs with Chosen Few Brass Band

98 SATURDAY, MAY 2

FOX 8 / POLAROID STAGE
11:15 St. Augustine Jazz Ensemble
12:20 Los Calientes
1:30 Rockin' Dopsie & The Zydeco Twisters
2:50 The Dixie Cups
4:10 Snooks Eaglin
5:45 Better Than Ezra

HOUSE OF BLUES STAGE
11:00 Hammond State Strawberry Jammers
12:10 Thousand $ Car
1:25 Lenny McDaniel
2:50 Aubry Twins
4:10 Wild Magnolias Mardi Gras Indians
5:35 Lonnie Brooks

RAY-BAN STAGE
11:15 Loyola University Jazz Band
12:30 New Birth Brass Band
2:00 Walter "Wolfman" Washington & The Roadmasters
3:30 Irma Thomas
5:15 Jimmy Buffett & The Coral Reefer Band

SHERATON / WB 38 FAIS DO-DO STAGE
11:30 Evening Star String Band
12:35 Eddie LeJeune & The Morse Playboys
1:50 Southern Flavor Bluegrass
3:10 Samy & Sandra Sandoval of Panama
4:35 Belton Richard & The Musical Aces
6:00 Jude Taylor & His Burning Flames

BET ON JAZZ / WWOZ JAZZ TENT
11:30 Victor Goines Group
12:40 Fielder-Jordan I.A.Q. w/ Joel Futterman & Fred Anderson
1:55 New Orleans Jazz Legends
3:10 Jesse Davis
4:35 Terrence Blanchard
5:50 Betty Carter & Trio

COX COMMUNICATIONS / VH1 ECONOMY HALL TENT
11:15 La Vida Dixieland Jazz Band of Spain
12:15 Lars Edegran w/ Cookie Gabriel
1:40 Bob French Original Tuxedo Jazz Band
3:00 Dr. Michael White Quintet w/ Thais Clark
4:25 Butch Thompson & Friends
6:00 Young Tuxedo Brass Band

CONGO SQUARE STAGE
12:00 Willie Metcalf & The World Peace Movement w/ The Academy of Black Arts Rainbow Youth Jazz Choir

1:35 Bamboula 2000
2:45 Sporty T & 2 Sweet
4:15 Skatalites
6:00 Coolbone

BELLSOUTH MOBILITY LAGNIAPPE STAGE
11:15 Metairie Park Country Day Jazz Ensemble
12:20 Ironin' Board Sam
1:35 Wills Delony Trio
2:45 NOCCA Jazz Ensemble
4:00 Carlos Sanchez "Amenecer Flamenco"
5:30 Samy & Sandra Sandoval of Panama

MUSIC HERITAGE STAGE
12:30 Sammy Berfect (Interview)
1:30 Butch Thompson (Interview)
2:30 Better Than Ezra (Interview)
3:30 Jude Taylor (Interview)
4:45 Hackberry Ramblers (Interview)

TULANE HOSPITAL / RHODES GOSPEL TENT
11:00 Heavenly Set Gospel Singers
11:45 Love Alive Fellowship Choir
12:30 Second Morning Star MBC Choir
1:15 The Lighthouse Gospel Choir
2:00 Soulful Heavenly Stars
2:45 Sammy Berfect & Dimensions of Faith
3:30 Sherman Washington & The Famous Zion Harmonizers
4:15 John Lee & The Heralds of Christ w/ Christine Myles
5:05 Richard Smallwood & Vision
6:10 Ebenezer MBC Choir w/ guest Annie Lenox

PARADES
12:00 Devastation, Black Men of Labor, and Valley of Silent Men SA&PCs with Tremé Brass Band
2:00 Devastating Ladies, Chosen Few, and N'Krumah Better Boys SA&PCs with The Chops
4:00 Popular Ladies, Jolly Bunch, and Distinguished Gentlemen SA&PCs with Algiers Brass Band
4:00 Economy Hall Parade – Calendar Girls SA&PC

SUNDAY, MAY 3

FOX 8 / POLAROID STAGE
11:15 Paky Saavedra's Bandido
12:15 Dash Rip Rock
1:20 Ernie K-Doe & Blue Eyed Soul
2:30 C.J. Chenier & The Red Hot Louisiana Band
4:00 Ani D'Franco
5:45 The Radiators

HOUSE OF BLUES STAGE
11:00 New World Funk Ensemble
12:20 Mem Shannon & The Membership
1:35 Tommy Ridgley & The Untouchables
3:00 Bill Miller
4:30 Earl King & The Butanes
6:00 Deacon John

RAY-BAN STAGE
11:00 Guardians of the Flame Mardi Gras Indians
12:00 Kim Carson & The Casualties
1:05 Keith Claiborne
2:10 Dave Bartholomew Big Band
3:45 The Doobie Brothers Reunion
5:45 The Neville Brothers

SHERATON / WB 38 FAIS DO-DO STAGE
11:15 SUBR Jazz Ensemble
12:20 Horace & His Ossun Express
1:30 Savoy-Smith Cajun Band
3:00 D.L. Menard & The Louisiana Aces
4:30 Woodenhead with Horns
6:00 Roy Carrier & The Night Rockers

BET ON JAZZ / WWOZ JAZZ TENT
11:00 Patrice Fisher & Arpa w/ guest Victor Mendoza
12:20 Germaine Bazzle
1:30 Kent Jordan
3:10 Alvin Batiste & The Jazztronauts
4:20 The Ellis Marsalis Trio
5:45 Spyro Gyra

COX COMMUNICATIONS / VH1 ECONOMY HALL TENT
11:00 Lionel Ferbos & The Palm Court Jazz Band
12:15 Onward Brass Band
1:20 Banu Gibson & New Orleans Hot Jazz
2:35 George French & New Orleans Storyville Jazz Band
3:50 Preservation Hall Jazz Band
5:15 HNOC Jelly Roll Morton Lost Manuscripts w/ Don Vappie & His Creole Jazz Serenaders

CONGO SQUARE STAGE
11:15 The Revealers
12:15 Walter Cook & Creole Wild West Mardi Gras Indians
1:25 Wanda Rouzan & A Taste of New Orleans
2:45 Samba Ngo
4:15 Patrick Henry & The Liberation Band
5:45 Los Babies del Merengue

BELLSOUTH MOBILITY LAGNIAPPE STAGE
11:15 SUNO Jazz Ensemble
12:30 Easter Rocker
1:25 Native Nations Intertribal w/ Brian Hammill, Hoop Dancer
2:45 "Sacred Steel" Aubrey Ghent & Friends
4:00 Harry Connick, Sr. w/ The Jimmy Maxwell Orchestra
5:30 Samy & Sandra Sandoval of Panama

MUSIC HERITAGE STAGE
12:00 Aubrey Ghent (Interview)
1:00 TBA
2:15 Cyril Neville (Interview)
3:30 Ernie K-Doe (Interview)
4:30 Lillian Boutté

TULANE HOSPITAL / RHODES GOSPEL TENT
11:00 George Perkins & Voices of Harmony
11:40 The Masonic Kings
12:20 The Zion Travelers Spiritual Singers
1:00 The Famous Rocks of Harmony
1:40 Lillian Boutté's Gospel United Choir
2:30 The Johnson Extension
3:10 Mighty Chariots of Fire
3:55 Aaron Neville's Gospel w/ Johnny Adams
5:10 Richard Smallwood & Vision
6:10 The Gospel Soul Children

PARADES
12:00 Scene Boosters, Jet Setters & Westbank Steppers SA&PCs with Pinettes Brass Band & Mohawk's Mardi Gras Indians

12:15 Economy Hall Parade – Single Ladies SA&PC
2:00 Original Prince of Wales, Lady Prince of Wales and Avenue Steppers SA&PCs with Tornado Brass Band
4:00 The 250th Anniversary of New Orleans Parade: Original New Orleans Lady Buckjumpers, New Orleans Men Buckjumpers and Pigeon Town Steppers with High Steppers Brass Band & Carrollton Hunters Mardi Gras Indians

NIGHT CONCERTS

FRIDAY, APRIL 24, 9 P.M.
Bonnie Raitt
Jimmie Vaughan
Keb' Mo
SATURDAY, APRIL 25, 9 P.M.
John Fogerty, Dr. John
Kiefer UNO Lakefront Arena
SATURDAY, APRIL 25, 12 MIDNIGHT
Midnight Jam
Hank Crawford, Donald Harrison, Jr., Peter Martin, Johnny Vidacovich, Victor Atkins, David Pulphus, Jeremy Davenport, Jason Stewart, Geoff Clap
Praline Connection Gospel & Blues Hall
MONDAY, APRIL 27 & TUESDAY, APRIL 28, 8 P.M.
Jazz at the Palm Court
Hot Swing All-Stars with Al Grey, Sammy Rimington, Wendell Brunious, Arvell Shaw, Al Casey, Henry Butler, Ernest Elly
Palm Court Jazz Café, 1
TUESDAY, APRIL 28, 8 P.M.
Dew Drop Inn Revisited
Clarence "Gatemouth" Brown / "Gate Swings with Big Band"
Larry Hamilton, Chuck Carbo, Topsy Chapman, Wardell Querzerque Orchestra
Praline Connection Gospel & Blues
WEDNESDAY, APRIL 29, 8 P.M.
Jonathan Butler, Rachelle Ferrell, Phillip Manuel
M.F.X.J. Municipal Auditorium
THURSDAY, APRIL 30, 8 P.M.
La Noche Latina
Grupo Mania, Los Adolecentes, The Iguanas
M.F.X.J. Municipal Auditorium
FRIDAY, MAY 1, 9 P.M.
Ziggy Marley & The Melody Makers, Buddy Guy, Coolbone
Kiefer UNO Lakefront Arena
SATURDAY, MAY 2, 9 P.M.
Doobie Brothers Reunion with Michael McDonald, Tom Johnston, Patrick Simmons, John McFee, Michael Hossack and Keith Hudson; Allen Toussaint
Kiefer UNO Lakefront Arena
SATURDAY, MAY 2, 12 MIDNIGHT
Midnight Jam
Ellis Marsalis, Marlon Jordan, Jesse Davis, Earl Turbinton, Dwight Fitch, Brice Winston, Roland Guerin, Donald Edwards, Herman Jackson, Bill Huntington, Eric Traub
Praline Connection Gospel & Blues Hall

1999

Michael Doucet

World renowned trumpet player Al Hirt "passed over into glory land" at age 78, during the most jazz-packed time in his beloved New Orleans: the Tuesday between Jazz Fest weekends. Hirt had received more than 20 Grammy nominations in his career, and had won in 1964 for his hit "Java" (composed by Allen Toussaint). He had performed for a Pope and six U.S. presidents. But to New Orleanians, fame is usually a secondary consideration, if it rates at all. Hirt had given Wynton Marsalis his first trumpet, and in the first years of Jazz Fest brought Schlitz beer sponsorship to the Fest. He was considered a *de facto* ambassador of New Orleans music around the world. Those are the kinds of things that carry meaning here in the Crescent City.

On the final Sunday at Jazz Fest, Hirt was honored with a rousing second line parade that was also dedicated to those who had passed away since the last Jazz Fest. Among the deceased so honored were Johnny Adams, "Blue Lu" Barker, Tom Dent, Raymond Myles, Sammy Berfect, Donald Harrison, Sr., Robert "Sonny" Vaucresson, and Alvin "Red" Tyler. The Tornado Brass Band and social aid and pleasure clubs, The Original Prince of

what's going on?

GLOBALLY

Panama Canal returned to Panama on December 31.

Russian President Boris Yeltsin resigns, naming as his successor Prime Minister Vladimir Putin.

NATIONALLY

After an impeachment trial, the Senate finds President Clinton not guilty.

April 20, 1999, two students go on a shooting rampage in Columbine High School in Littleton, Colorado. They kill 12 students, 1 teacher and themselves.

LOCALLY

Schwegmann Supermarkets close.

Mayor Marc Morial tries to change city charter that would allow him to have one more term in office.

An FBI investigation reveals that Governor Foster paid David Duke $152,000 for a mailing list, and was fined $10,000 by the state ethics board.

Harrah's finally opens its New Orleans casino.

CULTURALLY

One of the most memorable sports moments in years, when Brandi Chastain kicks the final shot as the US Women's Soccer Team wins the World Cup, and whips off her shirt and runs around in her sport bra waving it over her head.

JFK, JR, wife Carolyn Bessette Kennedy, and her sister Lauren G. Bessette are lost at sea when his plane disappears off the coast of Martha's Vineyard.

First non-stop world trip in a balloon.

Y2K hype gets everyone paranoid that the end of the world is near. Billions of dollars spent world-wide on Y2K upgrade of computer software.

Wales, the Lady Prince of Wales and the Avenue Steppers led the way, and the undulant, umbrella-twirling, dancing, laughing and crying line, with grand marshal Wanda Rouzan, lasted more than an hour. Rouzan was a descendent of the Lastie family, (a bastion of traditional jazz from its earliest beginnings). Wearing the traditional sash topped by a white dove, she was only the second woman ever to act as a grand marshal, having been passed that mantle from Ellyna Tatum in 1986.

The grand marshal is responsible for personifying the appropriate *gravitas* in the funeral procession. The band and the family of the deceased comprise the first line, and the funeral attendees follow in a "second line." Each song is chosen to reflect an aspect of the deceased person's character or experience. The music is wonderfully intentional, as blues and dirges

Donald Harrison

Dixie Hummingbirds

symbolically lower the deceased into the grave, often with a lingering bass note, and then the body is "cut away" or released to spirit, and the celebrating begins. Here again, songs bawdy and playful reflect on the deceased. If he or she was a musician, songs featuring their instruments are played. Participants often carry pictures of the honorees. Strangers may join in the procession, and some revelers may split off to other celebrations.

Rouzan carried her decorated parasol and lead the second line, ending up at Kermit Ruffins's set in the WWOZ Jazz Tent, where she engaged Ruffins in a spontaneous dance during "Treme Second-line" that had the audience dancing in the aisles.

The 30th anniversary of the New Orleans Jazz &

The Dirty Dozen Brass Band's performance on the Congo Stage was the meet-up place for the Pet de Kat Krewe.

495,000 attended this year.

Zydeco ace Boozoo Chavis' apron was not just for ornament: it shielded his accordion from sweat generated by his blazing set and close grip.

There were 47,3000 pounds of crawfish and 12,225 pounds of rice consumed at the Fest this year.

Heritage Festival coincided with Louisiana's tricentennial. Founded in 1699 by Pierre Le Moyne Sieur d'Iberville, Louisiana was named for Louis and Anne, King and Queen of France. There are many who attest that the state still considers itself a colony, and never really assimilated into the U.S. culture. Their speculation is pretty well founded. Where else can one enjoy the cultural and culinary diversions of drive-through daiquiri shops, the world's largest free party (Mardi Gras), jazz funerals, second line parades, the planet's best high school marching bands, hurricane parties, deep fried turkeys, muffalettas, *fried* muffalettas, and fiery hot, boiled mudbugs? Characteristically, Louisiana celebrated with a statewide "FrancoFête." The Office of the Lieutenant Governor, the Louisiana Department of Culture,

Recreation, and Tourism, and the New Orleans Jazz & Heritage Festival commemorated Franco Fete with workshops, demonstrations, and music performances throughout Jazz Fest. In effect, the Jazz Fest became an International Pavilion dedicated to Louisiana's French heritage.

After last year's gargantuan changes to the Jazz Fest landscape, technology entered, or enhanced, the picture. A 15 X 20 foot video screen flanked the left of the Ray Ban Stage. Onstage performances were projected onto the 300 square foot screen, enabling even those in the hinterlands to see the action. The screen was a boon to the Fest — as that stage absorbed more space and bigger acts. Other changes to the landscape included moving the House of Blues Stage (still in the infield) farther away from the Jazz Tent

Kevin Griffin

11:45 The Unstoppable Gospel Singers
12:30 Topsy Chapman & Chapman Singers
1:15 The Dynamic Smooth Family of Slidell
2:00 Theoclecia Bourgeois & Kennedy High School Gospel Choir
2:45 Charles Jackson & The Jackson Travelers
3:30 The Madison Rockets of Macon, Georgia
4:15 The Banks Family
5:10 Spencer Taylor & The Highway QC's
6:25 R. Lee James Memorial Chorale

PARADES
2:00 Original 7, Positive Ladies and N'Krumah Third Division SA&PCs with Bone Tone Brass Band
4:00 Mystery Ladies and Young and Old Men Legend SA&PCs with Trombone Shorty Brass Band

SATURDAY, APRIL 24

FOX 8 / SPRINT PCS STAGE
11:15 Paky Savedra's Bandido
12:25 Lenny McDaniel
1:40 Walter "Wolfman" Washington & The Roadmasters
3:00 John Mooney & Bluesiana
4:25 C.J. Chenier & The Red Hot Louisiana Band
5:55 Irma Thomas & The Professionals

HOUSE OF BLUES / OLD SCHOOL 102.9 STAGE
11:15 Creole Wild West Mardi Gras Indians
12:20 Elmo Williams & Hezekiah Early
1:25 Jerry Beach Band
2:45 Reggie Hall & The Twilighters with Matilda Jones & "Dogman" Smith
4:15 The Duke Robillard Band
6:00 Charmaine Neville Band with Reggie Houston & Amasa Miller

RAY-BAN STAGE
11:15 SUNO Jazz Ensemble
12:20 Casa Samba with Curtis Pierre
1:30 Terrance Simien
3:00 funky Meters
5:00 Santana

SHERATON / WB 38 FAIS DO-DO STAGE
11:20 Eddie LeJeune & The Morse Playboys
12:40 Hackberry Ramblers
2:00 Regis Gizavo of Madagascar
3:00 Bruce Daigrepont Cajun Band
4:25 Ulali music of Mayan, Apache, Yaqui and Tuscarora
5:50 Allen Fontenot & The Country Cajuns

WWOZ JAZZ TENT
11:15 Larry Seiberth
12:20 Michael Ward
1:30 Walter Payton & The Snapbean Band with Sharon Martin
2:45 Charles Neville Jazz Ensemble
4:10 Terence Blanchard Group
5:40 The Joshua Redman Band

COX COMMUNICATIONS ECONOMY HALL TENT
11:15 Original Camelia Jazz Band
12:20 Wallace Davenport
1:40 Dr. Michael White Quartet with Thais Clark
3:00 Gregg Stafford's Jazz Hounds
4:25 George French & The New Orleans Storyville Jazz Band

(now in the parking lot) to lessen the bigger Stage's sound bleed. In Congo Square, the merchandise booths were fanned wider to open up the space. Quint Davis insisted that the move was not engineered to provide space for larger audiences, but to make "more space for the people who are already here." Jazz Fest lovers complained about appeared to be a goal of growing crowds by booking mega-groups like the Dave Matthews Band (160,000 people in one day, nearly as many as a usual weekend) and repeat old schoolers such as Jimmy Buffet. Davis usually responded with explanations such as "bringing in new talent" that shared an appreciation for Louisiana music (Phish) or groups that reflected

new trends in the music world (Run D.M.C.). It was a conundrum: how should Jazz Fest celebrate Louisiana's musical diaspora, keep a fresh energy and renewed vision for repeat visitors, and stay true to the Foundation's mission? The answers were as varied as the people who loved the Fest, and probably always would be.

Although attendance for the first weekend ran at 177,000, those numbers were down from last year. But the second Sunday's crowds were the biggest ever at 86,000. All in all, attendance at the Heritage Fair was 455,000; and when night concerts and school workshops were included, the number reached 495,000, about 60,000 more people than last year. In perspective, Fair Grounds attendance averaged 70,000 per day over 32 acres and the grandstand.

The Doris Duke Charitable Foundation awarded the Jazz & Heritage Foundation $300,000 over the next two years for the "JazzNet Initiative." In cooperation with the Contemporary Arts Center, the Foundation would have the financial means to commission new works, present artists-in-residence, and establish an endowment that would sustain jazz programming for many years.

Walter Washington and the Roadmasters played a funkified "You Are My Sunshine." Dave Brubeck played "Take Five," the

music scene

Federal judge strikes down state law establishing "Quiet Zones" aimed at street musicians in Jackson Square.

First Annual Hep C Benefit produced by Siren to Wail, to raise awareness for Hepatitis C, featuring Linda Hopkins, Dr. John, Wolfman Washington, and others.

IN MEMORIAM

Johnny Adams, Louise "Blu Lu" Barker, Sammy Berfect, Lawrence Billiot, Charles Brown, Betty Carter, Tom Dent, Dorothy Donegan, O'Landra Draper, Jimmy Domengeaux, Donald Harrison, Sr., Kenny Kirkland, Doris Lee, Raymond Myles, Umar Sharif (Emery Thompson), Alvin "Red" Tyler, Robert "Sonny" Vaucresson, Marie Verret, Benny Waters, Joe Williams, Al "Jumbo" Hirt, Eldridge Andrews, Morris "Moe" Bachemin, Jr., Felton Brown, Harry "Sweets" Edison, Art Farmer, Cleon Floyd, Thaddeus Ford, Sr., Albert "Lil' June" Gardner, Emanuel R. "Trouble" Hingle, Roland "Stone" Leblanc, Layton Martens, Robert Matthews, Oran A. Moffett, Walter Settles, Bobby Sheehan, Wilfred Smith, Jr., Grover Washington, Jr., Robert "Snooke" Williams, John DuBois, Milt Jackson, Curtis Mayfield, Lester Bowie, Nat Adderly, Red Norvo, Curtis Mayfield

Boozoo Chavis

first jazz single to turn platinum in 1960. He ended with "I Got Rhythm" with each trading solos that finally brought it all back home. On Thursday the Magpies, short one subdude, played the Lagniappe Stage. Just as Kevin Danzig was singing "Beatle Bob," the song's namesake, resplendent in a lavender gabardine jacket and boots, jumped over the rail to display his ubiquitous self and funky moves. "Bob" was one of those characters that showed up every Jazz Fest. Most know him as the guy with the Beatle haircut who is always dressed in splendiferous vintage jackets and accoutrements. No matter how hot and humid, he was always dancing… mostly to his own

rhythm. But not so many people knew that Beatle Bob lived in St. Louis, was a social worker who helped troubled teenagers, and a maniac for music year round. His "style" of dance (always solo) was a pastiche of peripatetic frug, watusi, twist, and whatever else moved his spirit.

The New Orleans Jazz & Heritage Festival is one of the world's most visually interesting festivals. Artistic handiwork adorns every stage and tent. A staff of approximately 20 builds and installs décor for the Festival site. With the exception of some of the sponsor pieces, most of the décor is carved, built, sewn or painted, keeping the distinctive Jazz Fest hand-crafted look.

I found my thrill on Blueberry Hill

JAZZ FEST STATION
APRIL 23 - MAY 2, 1999
NEW ORLEANS, LA 70119

Fats Domino

NEW ORLEANS JAZZ & HERITAGE FESTIVAL

The First Ambassador of New Orleans Rock 'N' Roll

They make as many as 2,000 signs for Jazz Fest per year, handwrites directional signs and all food booth signs such as "Alligator Sauce Piquante,"

to the enormously helpful "You Are Here" boards. A team of artists design and create the five foot tall alligator on Stage 1, the music instruments atop the light poles, the images of "ancestors" such as Fess on the infield, and most other artwork on site. Those figures are sculpted from lightweight Styrofoam (no one will be injured if it falls, and none of Bill's creations has ever fallen) and trucked into the Fest in April. It is the engaging artistic talent that gives Jazz Fest its hand-

John Goodman and Tab Benoit

crafted, culturally authentic look.

Downtown, Louisiana musicians were the subject matter of two photography exhibitions. At Bassetti Fine Art gallery, noted photographer Rick Olivier's black and white zydeco photographs allowed visitors a rare glimpse into the character and culture of Louisiana's truly indigenous music. Many of these photographs were included in the book *Zydeco!* by Olivier and writer Ben Sandmel. Olivier's photographs were for sale in the Louisiana Folklife area, and Sandmel was an accomplished interviewer on the Heritage Music Stage. The other exhibition was singularly remarkable in that the photographer was also a virtuoso musician – and blind. Pianist Henry Butler showed color photographs at the Jonathan Ferrara Gallery. Butler's photography was possible through collaboration with assistants that described scenes to Butler, who then made and selected which images to print and show.

Local restaurants were teeming with Jazz Festers in the evenings. "Jazz Fest people are the best. They need lots of water, then they order everything: appetizers, dessert, and the whole nine yards. And they tip better than Mardi Gras people," one Liuzza's waiter said.

Willie Nelson and Harry Lee

"*Let me explain one thing so it is clearly understood. The Lincoln Center Board raises tens of millions of dollars so that Wynton Marsalis can have the freedom to do what he wants to do. In New Orleans, we have to earn the money to give to the Foundation so we can put on the Festival. So nobody is subsidizing the Fest to keep it pure the way some people want it to be pure. Whatever purity we have left — which is a lot, such as the Gospel Tent and the Cajun stage and the archives — is being kept alive by the big name national artists which people resent. It's a simple matter of arithmetic.*" GEORGE WEIN

Big Al Carson

2:05 Dr. John
4:05 Ray Charles
5:45 Fats Domino

SHERATON / WB 38 FAIS DO-DO STAGE
11:20 Southern Flavor
12:30 Jambalaya Cajun Band
1:45 Amy & The Hank Sinatras
3:10 Geno Delafose & The French Rockin' Band
4:35 La Bottine Sourante de Montreal
6:05 Rockin' Dopsie, Jr. & The Zydeco Twisters

WWOZ JAZZ TENT
11:45 Germaine Bazzle
12:55 Clarence Johnson III
2:20 Cassandra Wilson "Traveling For Miles"
4:00 Charles Lloyd & Friends featuring Billy Higgins, John Abercrombie & Marc Johnson
5:45 The Nicholas Payton Quintet

COX COMMUNICATIONS ECONOMY HALL TENT
11:15 Bayou Liberty Jazz Band
12:20 Onward Brass Band
1:35 Wendell Brunious
2:55 Bob French & The Original Tuxedo Jazz Band
4:20 Louisiana Repertory Jazz Ensemble
5:45 Linda Hopkins

CONGO SQUARE STAGE
11:30 Willie Metcalf & The Academy of Black Allstars
12:50 Jean Knight
2:15 Bobby "Blue" Bland
3:50 Angelique Kidjo of Benin
5:45 Jeffrey Osborne

LAGNIAPPE STAGE
11:20 UNO Jazz Orchestra
12:45 Dale Hawkins
2:00 Elmo Williams & Hezekiah Early
2:55 Philadelphia Mississippi Choctaw Dancers
4:05 Fredy Omar Latin Dance Band
5:45 The Pfister Sisters

MUSIC HERITAGE STAGE
11:45 Wendell Brunious
1:00 Zachary Richard
2:00 Jon Cleary
3:00 Dale Hawkins
4:00 Clarence Johnson III

TULANE HOSPITAL / RHODES GOSPEL TENT
11:00 Vernon S. Joshua Community Youth Choir
11:45 Melody Clouds
12:30 Lighthouse Jr. Gospel Singers
1:15 True Tone Gospel Singers
2:00 Jo "Cool" Davis
2:45 The Crownseekers
3:30 Sounds of Unity
4:15 Watson Memorial Teaching Ministries
5:00 The R.A.M.S.
6:05 Fred Hammond & Radical for Christ

PARADES
12:00 Olympia Aide, Lady Zulu and Uptown Hobo Clowns SA&PCs with Unknown Brass Band
12:20 Economy Hall Parade — Single Ladies SA&PC
1:00 Golden Arrows & Young Cheyennes Mardi Gras Indians
2:00 Furious five and Original Four SA&PCs with Hot 8 Brass Band

"*The people who do the music we know, all of a sudden, regardless of if it's just another gig or not, we're all excited. It's just you know you want to look good and you want to sound good and you want to do a good job. And that's with every musician who goes on the stage there at Jazz Fest. When you see the festive nature of all those people there — all those bodies — you know that that is not an everyday thing. So naturally your energy level goes way higher than it's ever been. Your energy level is high. You're like, 'Oh man, I want to look good. My cousin's out there. The people I called up to come out here are there. Everybody I know is out there.' So whether I've seen them or not in the last year I want them to know that I'm playing my ass off. I'm singing my ass off. I want them to walk away with that. That brings you to another level right there, whatever you're getting paid.*" ZIGABOO MODELISTE

Terrance Simien

FRIDAY, APRIL 30

FOX 8 / SPRINT PCS STAGE
11:20 Kiki Bonilla Latin Jazz
12:45 New Orleans Klezmer Allstars
2:30 Tiny Town
4:15 The Iguanas
5:45 Marcia Ball

HOUSE OF BLUES / OLD SCHOOL 102.9 STAGE
11:20 Guitar Slim, Jr. & The Guthrie Express
12:35 Rockin' Tabby Thomas
1:50 J. Monque'D & The Little Pats of Butter with guest Henry Gray
3:10 Dash Rip Rock
4:40 The Elements
6:00 Wanda Rouzan & A Taste of New Orleans

RAY-BAN STAGE
11:30 USL Jazz Combo
1:00 Soul Rebels Brass Band
2:30 Galactic
4:15-5:15/5:30-7:00 Widespread Panic

SHERATON / WB 38 FAIS DO-DO STAGE
11:20 NOCCA Jazz Ensemble
12:40 Felix & Formanger de

Newfoundland
1:50 Magnolia Sisters
3:20 Warren Ceasar & Creole Zydeco Snap
5:20 Boozoo Chavis & Magic Sounds

WWOZ JAZZ TENT
11:30 Patrice Fisher & Arpa with special guests "Cubavana"
1:00 Jason Marsalis
2:25 Astral Project
3:50 Donald Harrison
5:30 The Branford Marsalis Quartet

COX COMMUNICATIONS ECONOMY HALL TENT
11:15 Joe Simon's Jazz, Inc.
12:30 Jacque Gauthe's Creole Rice Jazz Band
1:45 Albert Langue & The Dixie Stompers of Mons, Belgium
2:55 Doc Paulin's Dixieland Brass Band
4:25 Don Vappie & The Creole Jazz Serenaders
5:45 Al Grey with Benny Powell

CONGO SQUARE STAGE

11:20 Southern Girlz
12:40 Mahogany Blue
2:10 Sunpie Barnes & The Louisiana Sunspots
3:40 Los Hombres Calientes featuring Irvin Mayfield, Bill Summers and Jason Marsalis
5:30 Prince Eyango & Les Montagnards D'Afrique

LAGNIAPPE STAGE
11:20 Clancy Lewis with Sheba Kimbrough
12:35 Evening Star String Band
1:50 Tommy Yetta
3:10 Felix Formanger de Newfoundland
4:15 Golden Eagles Mardi Gras Indians
5:45 Executive Steel Band

MUSIC HERITAGE STAGE
12:00 Warren Ceasar
1:00 Don Vappie
2:00 Prince Eyango of Cameroon
3:30 Carl Leblanc
5:00 Magnolia Sisters

TULANE HOSPITAL / RHODES GOSPEL

TENT
11:00 Aline White & Co.
11:45 The Humble Travelers
12:30 The Southern Travelers of Houma
1:15 Therrow Scott & Tehillah
2:00 McDonogh #35 Gospel Choir
2:45 Bester Gingers
3:30 Fireside Gospel Singers
4:15 The Gospel Extenders
5:10 Pilgrim Jubilees
6:25 Alvin Bridges & Desire Community Choir

PARADES
2:00 Double Nine and Big Nine Highsteppers SA&PCs with Chosen Few Brass Band
2:55 Economy Hall Parade — Original Black Magic SA&PC
4:00 Nine Time and Distinguished Gentlemen SA&PCs with Smitty Short Stoppers Brass Band

SATURDAY, MAY 1

FOX 8 / SPRINT PCS STAGE
11:15 The Irie Dawtas & Attributes Band
12:20 The Henry Butler Group
1:40 Michael Ray & The Cosmic Krewe
3:05 Zigaboo Modeliste's Funk Revue
4:30 George Porter, Jr. & Runnin' Pardners
6:00 Better Than Ezra

HOUSE OF BLUES / OLD SCHOOL 102.9 STAGE
11:15 Willie Jaye
12:30 Bryan Lee & The Blues Power Band
1:50 Lil' Ed & The Blues Imperials
3:20 Earl King & The Butanes
4:45 Davell Crawford
6:00 Wild Magnolias Mardi Gras Indians

RAY-BAN STAGE
11:20 SUBR Jazz Ensemble
12:45 The Dixie Cups
2:05 Marva Wright
3:40 Allen Toussaint
5:30 Steve Miller Band

SHERATON / WB 38 FAIS DO-DO STAGE
11:15 Mamou Prairie Band
12:20 J. Paul, Jr. and The Zydeco New Breeds
1:35 Savoy-Doucet Cajun Band
3:00 Gwerz de France
4:30 Beau Jocque & The Zydeco Hi-Rollers
6:00 BeauSoleil

WWOZ JAZZ TENT
11:15 Now 4
12:30 Al Belletto Big Jazz Band
1:30 Clyde Kerr, Jr.
2:45 Alvin Batiste & The Jazzstronauts
4:10 The James Rivers Movement
5:45 The World Famous Count Basie Orchestra directed by Grover Mitchell

COX COMMUNICATIONS ECONOMY HALL TENT
11:15 Local International Allstars
12:25 New Leviathan Oriental Foxtrot Orchestra
1:45 Chris Owens Show
3:10 Gregg Stafford's Young Tuxedo Brass Band
4:25 Topsy Chapman Fox Pros
5:50 Pete Fountain

CONGO SQUARE STAGE
11:10 Kim Quillian
12:20 Percussion Inc.
1:35 Ritmo Caribeno
2:50 Los Silver Stars of Honduras
4:10 Hugh Masekela
5:50 Will Downing

LAGNIAPPE STAGE
11:15 Xavier University Jazz Ensemble
12:20 Michael Jeansonne & The Silver Spur Band
1:20 Carlos Sanchez "Amenecer Flamenco"
2:25 Golden Star Hunters Mardi Gras Indians
3:25 Ironin' Board Sam & His Hot Irons
4:30 Tommy Sancton Trio featuring David Paquette
6:00 John Rankin

MUSIC HERITAGE STAGE
11:30 Marc & Ann Savoy
1:00 Ironin' Board Sam
2:00 Rance Allen

3:00 Al Belletto
4:15 Lil' Ed

TULANE HOSPITAL / RHODES GOSPEL TENT
11:00 Community Missionary BC
11:45 New Zion Trio Plus One
12:30 Second Morning Star MBC Mass Choir
1:15 Soulful Heavenly Stars
2:00 Love Alive Fellowship Choir
2:45 The Johnson Extension
3:30 The Mighty Chariots
4:15 The Dimensions of Faith
5:10 The Rance Allen Group
6:25 Ebenezer Baptist Church Radio Choir

PARADES
12:00 Black Men of Labor and Secondline Jammers SA&PCs with Tremé Brass Band
1:00 Comanche Hunters and Golden Blades Mardi Gras Indians
2:00 N'Krumah Better Boys, Perfect Gentlemen, and Pigeon Town Steppers SA&PCs with Original Thunderstorm Brass Band
3:00 White Cloud Hunters and Semolian Warriors Mardi Gras Indians
3:10 Economy Hall Parade — Calendar Girls SA&PC
4:00 Popular Ladies, Jolly Bunch and Happy House SA&PCs with Algiers Brass Band

SUNDAY MAY 2

FOX 8 / SPRINT PCS STAGE
11:20 Black Eagles Mardi Gras Indians
12:35 The Frankie Ford Show
2:00 Walela featuring Rita Coolidge, Priscilla Coolidge & Lauren Satterfield
3:50 Hootie & The Blowfish
5:45 The Radiators

HOUSE OF BLUES / OLD SCHOOL 102.9 STAGE
11:15 Little Freddie King Blues Band
12:20 Roy Carrier with guests Calvin and Bébé Carrier
1:40 Ida McBeth & Friends
3:00 B.B. Major
4:30 Little Queenie and Friends
6:00 Deacon John

RAY-BAN STAGE
12:00 Bamboula 2000
1:30 Dave Bartholomew
3:20 The Isley Brothers
5:30 The Neville Brothers

SHERATON / WB 38 FAIS DO-DO STAGE
11:20 Beignet Y'Israel
12:35 Kim Carson & The Casualties
1:50 T-Mamou
3:10 Thomas "Big Hat" Fields
4:35 Willis Prudhomme & Zydeco Express
6:00 Nathan & The Zydeco Cha-Chas

WWOZ JAZZ TENT
11:20 Kim Prevost & Bill Solley
12:35 "Kidd" Jordan-Al Fielder Improvisational Arts Quintet
1:55 Jesse Davis
3:05 Kermit Ruffins & The Barbecue Swingers
4:25 The Ellis Marsalis Quartet
5:55 Nancy Wilson

COX COMMUNICATIONS ECONOMY HALL TENT
11:20 New Orleans Jazz Professors
12:35 Duke Dejean's Olympia Brass Band
1:45 Dukes of Dixieland

3:00 Lars Edegran's New Orleans Ragtime Orchestra
4:25 Banu Gibson & The New Orleans Hot Jazz
5:50 Preservation Hall Jazz Band

CONGO SQUARE STAGE
11:15 Kumbuka Drum & Dance Collective
12:25 Joe Black & Willie Puckett
1:35 Bobby Marchan
2:50 Los Babies
4:10 Rebirth Brass Band
5:40 Third World

LAGNIAPPE STAGE
11:15 Heritage School of Music
12:25 Y'Shua
1:45 Rising Star Fife and Drums
2:45 Otter Trail Singers and Dancers with Brian Hammill The Hoop Dancer
4:10 Gwerz de France
5:45 Pinstripe Brass Band

MUSIC HERITAGE STAGE
1:00 New Orleans Drumming with Dr. Bruce Raeburn
2:00 Leigh Harris a.k.a. Little Queenie
3:00 Rampart Street Irregulars
4:15 Al Berard & Bob Reed of T-Mamou
5:15 Roy, Calvin & Bébé Carrier

TULANE HOSPITAL / RHODES GOSPEL TENT
11:00 Friendly Five Gospel Singers
11:45 Zulu Gospel Ensemble
12:30 Christian Light Chorale
1:15 The Famous Rocks of Harmony
2:00 John Lee & The Heralds of Christ
2:45 Jackie Tolbert & Praze with Impac
3:30 Aaron Neville
4:15 Sherman Washington & The Famous Zion Harmonizers
5:15 Mississippi Mass Choir
6:25 Gospel Soul Children

PARADES
12:00 Scene Boosters, Jetsetters and Westbank Steppers SA&PCs with Pinettes Brass Band
12:35 Economy Hall Parade — Algiers Steppers SA&PC
1:00 Mohawk & Carrollton Hunters Mardi Gras Indians
2:00 Original Prince of Wales, Lady Prince of Wales, and Avenue Steppers SA&PCs with Tornado Brass Band
3:00 Bayou Renegades II & Ninth Ward Hunters Mardi Gras Indians
4:00 Original New Orleans Lady & Men Buckjumpers with High Steppers Brass Band

NIGHT CONCERTS

FRIDAY, APRIL 23, 9 P.M.
Santana
Los Hombres Calientes featuring Irvin Mayfield, Jason Marsalis, Bill Summers
Regis Gizavo of Madagascar
Morris F.X. Jeff Municipal Auditorium

SATURDAY, APRIL 24, 9 P.M.
Ray Charles & His Orchestra with The Raelettes
David Sanborn
Joshua Redman
Morris F.X. Jeff Municipal Auditorium,

SATURDAY, APRIL 24, MIDNIGHT
Charlie B's Midnight Jazz
Trumpet Summit
Randy Brecker, Harry "Sweets" Edison, Irvin Mayfield, Kermit Ruffins, Clyde Kerr, Jr. and Charlie Miller

MONDAY, APRIL 26 & TUESDAY, APRIL 27, 8 P.M.
Jazz at the Palm Court
Hot Swing Jazz All-Stars with Jay McShann, Arvell Shaw, Franz Jackson, Duke Heitger, Lucien Barbarin, Ernest Elly
Lars Edegran, Musical Director
Palm Court Jazz Café,

TUESDAY, APRIL 27, 8 P.M.
Dew Drop Inn Revisited
A Tribute to Johnny Adams
Aaron Neville, Irma Thomas, Marva Wright, Big Al Carson, Wardell Quezerguezerque Orchestra
Praline Connection Gospel Blues Hall

FRIDAY, APRIL 30, 9 P.M.
Will Downing & Gerald Albright
Boney James
Chocolate Milk
Morris F.X. Jeff Municipal Auditorium, Louis Armstrong Park

FRIDAY, APRIL 30, 9 P.M.
La Noche Night
Cubanismo!
Los Babies
House of Blues

SATURDAY, MAY 1, 9 P.M.
Widespread Panic
Galactic
Morris F.X. Jeff Municipal Auditorium,

SATURDAY, MAY 1, MIDNIGHT
Charlie B's Midnight Jazz
Sphere with Kenny Barron, Gary Bartz, Ben Riley and Buster Williams Plus Delfeayo Marsalis, Jesse Davis, Peter Martin, Roger Lewis, Mark Braud, Terrence Higgins, Kerry Lewis
Praline Connection Gospel & Blues Hall

2000

The biggest news of the year for the New Orleans Jazz And Heritage Festival was Acura. Honda Motor Company's luxury brand would become the largest sponsor in New Orleans Jazz Festival history. The deal with Acura represented a whole new level of exposure for the Festival, including rights to television and web broadcasting. Acura also underwrote documentaries and music shows to broadcast the following year. Its commitment underscored what the original visionaries already knew: the New Orleans Jazz & Heritage Festival is a world-class event.

Michael Murphy, a New Orleans filmmaker, produced the video for rebroadcast. The three main components were a 50-hour program of music and interviews to be web cast in July on the Internet site Riffage.com, a documentary for the Public Broadcasting System, and a third show for the cable music channel VH-1. The production costs, underwritten by Acura and Riffage.com were in the neighborhood of 1.5 million dollars. Because of Acura coming on board at such a high level of financial commitment, global exposure was opened on a more mainstream level. The New Orleans Jazz & Heritage Festival was no longer growing by word of mouth.

Many local musicians were also upset about the six figure

what's going on?

GLOBALLY

In Aden, Yemen, the USS Cole is badly damaged by two suicide bombers, killing 17 crew members and wounding at least 39.

NATIONALLY

In a predawn raid, federal agents seize six-year old Elián González from his relatives' home in Miami, Florida and fly him to his Cuban father in Washington, DC ending one of the most publicized custody battles in US history.

Hillary Rodham Clinton is elected to the United States Senate, becoming the first First Lady of the United States to win public office.

George W. Bush is elected President in one of the closest and most controversial "recounts" in decades.

LOCALLY

LEAP 21 Program (Louisiana Educational Assessment Program) for 4-8 graders is instituted.

The National D-Day Museum opens on June 6, 2000, the 56th anniversary of the most — publicized D-Day, the Normandy invasion to liberate Europe, but it pays homage to all the "D-days" of World War II.

Edwin Edwards found guilty of fraud and racketeering in the Riverboat corruption scandal. He is sentenced to a minimum of ten years.

CULTURALLY

Lesbian rocker Melissa Etheridge tells Rolling Stone that David Crosby fathered her two children with Julie Cypher.

An international consortium of genetic researchers — collectively called the Human Genome Project — announce a scientific breakthrough that they had completely mapped the genetic code of a human chromosome.

fees some artists were reputedly garnering for their performances. The bigger picture was that artists like Sting were getting paid not only for Jazz Fest, but also for television performance and other broadcast rights.

On opening day, 56,000 people showed up to check out the changes. Jerry Beach, Shreveport, Louisiana native, guitarist and songwriter who penned the Albert King classic "I'll Play The Blues For You" christened the Acura stage. Dr. John, followed by the Allman Brothers completed Acura's first day at the Fair Grounds. Other than some sound bleed issues that would take a couple of years to work out, it ran like a top. The crowds were huge, and with blue skies and refreshingly low humidity, a happy bunch of people had a really great time.

67,000 people turned out on April 29th for a second serving. On Acura, the talk of the day was an impromptu visit by Bonnie Raitt during Allen Toussaint's set early in the afternoon. After warming it up with a couple of classic New Orleans funk tunes with his New Orleans Orchestra which included local sidemen Chris Severin on bass and Herman Lebouf on drums, Bonnie Raitt came out to perform two of Allen's originals "What Do You Want The Boy To Do?" and "What is Success?" The crowd at Acura got to enjoy a great Jazz Festival moment: Allen and Bonnie, engaging in a beautiful call and response, facing each other across the grand piano.

Grace Darling, a Toussaint protégée, and former member of the now defunct new wave band Waka Waka came out to sing a little and play some saxophone, then Tricia "Sister Teedy" Boutté embraced the masses with "Everybody Needs A Hug". Her aunt Lillian had closed the Lagniappe stage the day before and her Uncle

Nicholas Payton

"Well, that's my little intimate Jazz Fest. People come from Australia and Great Britain and Japan and leave notes on the booth, my father's wall, for their friends. The little girl from Japan with her mom, who leaves a note for the chef from Sydney that they're going to go to Maximo's on Saturday at 9:00, you know, and I've got to remember to bring push pins and tape every year because that's where people find each other." LESLIE BLACKSHEAR SMITH

John headlined in the Jazz Tent on Friday. "Teedy" is another example of the New Orleans tradition of musical families.

Steven Seagal also sat in on Allen's set and some wondered if he was moving in at Acura. Mr. Seagal also jammed with the Allman Brothers the day before and towards the end of the set; Allen left the piano and turned it over to the martial artist/actor/guitarist who jammed on the blues. Most Jazz Fest fans have seen him on the big screen and not the big stage; but in the spirit of New Orleans musical hospitality, musicians welcomed him with opened arms, and fans gave him a nice round of applause.

Mark Mullins and Bonarama played Friday on Sprint, listed as contemporary Jazz/R&B. This group of New Orleans all-stars includes Lucien Barbarin, Freddie Lonzo, Craig Klein, Brian O'Neal, and Steve Suter on trombones with Matt Perine on sousaphone, Thaddeus Richard on piano and Russell Batiste on the drums. They delivered a funky, hard driving show with Mark taking songs like "Frankenstein" and standing them on their heads.

Acoustic Swiftness, led by Javier Gutierrez was billed as a percussion driven group delivering "Flamenco, Latin, jazz/fusion, but the nylon acoustic guitars are really the heart of their music." Javier remembers it being a beautiful, sunny day, with overflowing crowds that were really into the music. "Everybody was dancing and the music was very special that day. In addition to the six pieces we usually have, we added grand piano, flute and trumpet for our Jazz Fest show. At Jazz Festival you always want to do a little something extra."

Jeremy Lyons and the Deltabilly Boys had gotten quite a bit of press for Jazz Fest. Jeremy had come to town eight years ago, and started out singing on the street, working his way into a strong local club following. The fall had brought his debut release

music scene

Louisiana Red Hot Records established.

Papa Grows Funk is formed.

Earl Palmer is inducted into Rock and Roll Hall of Fame.

Meters reunite for San Francisco show.

Chris Thomas King appears in movie "O Brother Where Art Thou?"

IN MEMORIAM

Charles Ficher, Jimmie Davis Andrus "Beau Jocque" Espre, Bobby Marchan, Tommy Ridgley, Screamin' Jay Hawkins, Pee Wee King, Marie St. Louis

Bonnie Raitt and Allen Toussaint

on Louisiana Red Hot Records, *Don't Count Your Chickens before they Hatch* and this year was his Jazz Fest debut as a headliner.

James Rivers turned in an excellent show in the Jazz Tent, George Porter and his Runnin' Pardners got everything all "funked up" on Sprint, Germaine Bazzle, who performed before Mr. Rivers in the Jazz Tent, thrilled everyone with her gra-cious presence and her consum-mate delivery, scatting trumpet solos and keeping her accompa-niment on their musical toes.

Erykah Badu got a luke warm reception and wasn't well received. Many people opted to leave during her performance. But when the O'Jays came on the people who hadn't left to find more congenial entertain-ment were delighted that they

5:55   The Williams Brothers

MUSIC HERITAGE STAGE INTERVIEWS
12:00 Accordion Styles of Brazil & LA
        w/ Cascabulha & Filé
1:00   Ernie Andrews
2:00   Coco Robicheaux
3:00   190 Express
4:00   John Jackson

NATIONAL PARK SERVICE KIDS' TENT
11:30 St. Mark's Tremé Jazz
        Ensemble
12:30 Nathan Williams, Jr. w/ The
        Zydeco Cha Chas
1:45   Los Islenos Heritage & Cultural
        Society
2:30   Thibault of Belgium
4:00   Watts Prophets
5:00   Summer Stages Children's
        Musical Theater

BRAZIL / AFRICAN HERITAGE STAGE
12:30 Ancestral Blessing Ceremony
1:00   Arturo! Poetry & Jazz
2:30   Young Voices in the Village
        College Poets from Dillard
        University
4:00   Music & Dance Styles of Brazil

PARADES
2:00   Original Black Magic Lady
        Steppers and Chosen Few
        SA&PCs with Trombone Shorty
        Brass Band
1:30   Brazilian Parade with Maracatu
        Naçao Pernambuco
4:00   Outlaws and Young Men 2
        Old Men SA&PCs with Real
        Untouchables Brass Band

SATURDAY, APRIL 29

FOX 8 / SPRINT PCS STAGE
11:25 Irie Dawtas
12:40 Terrance Simien
2:10   George Porter, Jr. & Runnin'
        Pardners
3:45   Marcia Ball
5:30   Cowboy Mouth

**HOUSE OF BLUES / OLD SCHOOL
102.9 STAGE**
11:15 SUNO Jazz Ensemble
12:25 Soul Remedy
1:30   Bryan Lee & The Blues Power
        Band
2:50   Davell Crawford
4:15   Roy Rogers & The Delta Rhythm
        Kings
5:50   Derek Trucks Band

ACURA STAGE
11:15 Loyola Jazz Ensemble
12:30 Mem Shannon & The
        Membership
1:50   Allen Toussaint
3:40   Erykah Badu
5:45   The O'Jays

SHERATON / WB 38 FAIS DO-DO STAGE
11:20 Kim Carson & The Casualties
12:30 Hadley Castille & The Cajun
        Sharecroppers Band
1:40   Lil' Brian & The Zydeco
        Travelers
3:05   Carlos Malta & Pifé Muderno
4:20   Willis Prudhomme & Zydeco
        Express
5:50   Geno Delafose & French Rockin'
        Boogie w/ guest Leo Thomas

BET ON JAZZ / WWOZ JAZZ TENT
11:20 Jeremy Davenport
12:25 Germaine Bazzle
1:35   James Rivers Movement
2:45   Jason Marsalis
4:10   Donald Harrison, Jr.
5:45   Zawinul Syndicate

had stayed. O'Jays's leader Eddie Levert, wearing an eye slapping red suit, showed the amateurs how the professionals do it. They had the crowd in the palm of their hands long before their finale classic "For The Love Of Money."

For the folks who left Erykah's set, Bob French and the Original Tuxedo Jazz Band had it going on in the Economy Hall Tent, Marcia Ball was giving up a lovely performance on Sprint,

couldn't go wrong by making your way to the Gospel Tent at any time of the day under any circumstances for any reason.

April 30th The Continental Drifters, which included Peter Holsapple of Hootie and the Blowfish and R.E.M., Vickie Peterson, who wrote "Walk Like an Egyptian" when she was with the Bangles and Susan Cowsill, child star of the Cowsills, brought a entrancingly original show to the Sprint stage. By day's end,

was arriving on the national jam band scene after years of touring to build a following.

Deacon John closed the House of Blues Stage and featured a wonderful local vocalist, Danon Smith, formally of The Gospel Soul Children who regularly sings as part of his review. The Wailers Band brought the spirit of Jah to Congo Square, Yolanda Adams stunned and transformed souls in the Gospel Tent, and Sting's music washed across the

Lenny Kravitz

Donald Harrison, Jr., following Jason Marsalis in the Jazz Tent was holding court to a packed house, and if none of that appealed to you, grazing the food booths was always an option, or getting pulled into a second line with one of the Brass Bands crossing the infield. You also just

78,000 happy people were milling about the Fair Grounds.

Galactic, who closed Sprint, were an up and coming jam band from New Orleans fronted by lead singer Theryl de Clouet and had received tons of local press prior to their show at the Festival. Galactic

Walter "Wolfman" Washington

sea of people on the Acura Stage.

Crowds who had swarmed to Acura for Sting at 5:00 p.m. then became irritated when his band didn't start at that time. A few abandoned their hard won spots up front to go elsewhere, but all was forgiven at 5:30 when Sting finally emerged and started the opening lines of his famed song "If You Love Somebody – Set Them Free". For the record, Sting wasn't acting like a diva. There had been a schedule change earlier in the day that was unavoidable, and the Festival had told as many people as they could, but there just wasn't enough time to let all the fans know.

May 4th brought popular Zydeco Sweetheart Rosie Ledet back to the Fest, whose sultry singing always makes a hot day hotter. Her song "Bow Wow" sent everybody to the CD tent to get some more Rosie. Ernie K-Doe graced the Sprint stage in another eye-popping costume of Anoinette's. Phillip Manuel, a talented songwriter in addition to jazz vocalist, shared some of

his own material in the Jazz Tent, Kermit Ruffins and the BBQ swingers gave everybody a taste off what he would be serving up that night at Vaughn's in the lower 9th ward, which was delicious; Iris May Tango, with front man "Chatty" continued their style crossing musical exploration on Congo Square; and McCoy Tyner closed the Jazz Tent.

Friday May 5th Cool Riddims with Sista' Teedy graced Sprint with Cassandra Faulkner on bass, Gregg Casmier on the drums and Sean LaRocca playing the keyboard. A nice horn section and some backing vocals made this a hot set. B-Red contributed rap to this show, which would be his last Jazz Fest performance due to his untimely passing. It was raining as the set began and there

Rebirth Brass Band

were concerns about the show being cancelled, but the skies cleared and the show went on.

Anders Osborne showed the people what a Swedish funk/rockster could do. One lovely thing about Anders's sound was replacing the standard electric bass with a tuba played by Kirk Joseph.

Opening the Sprint stage Jamal Batiste following in his brother Russell's footsteps gave forth on the drums with his own arrangements and compositions leaning more into the hip-hop/R&B vein. Russell would be playing on Sprint later in the day with his band, and the Batiste Brothers would start the day out on Acura Saturday, May 6th

John Hiatt's story telling made the Acura stage seem a lot smaller and the people felt like they were right there with him. After John, Lyle Lovett made his Jazz Fest debut with his Large Band.

On May 6th Herman Ernest and The House of Blues All Star Band tore it up on the HOB stage. Herman is one of the Funkiest New Orleanians ever born and is responsible for many famous grooves. In 2000, Herman also performed with Dr. John as his drummer/band leader, and performed and directed the Drum Summit with

"For us Jazz Fest is the high point of our year in New Orleans. I think it was in 2000 and I got inspired and climbed up the speaker tower at the Acura Stage all the way up to the alligator. For just a moment I was on a different plane. For as far as I could see there were people moving, dancing, eating, drinking and having fun and of course there was Cowboy Mouth rockin' out. It was one of those times that I realized that there is no other place in the world that I would rather be." FRED LEBLANC

percussionist Kenyatta, who is his half brother, on the Sprint stage.

Chocolate Milk, one of the first funk groups to make their mark from New Orleans in the 70s, showed them how it's still done on Acura Sunday, followed by the Temptations, Aaron Neville sang in the Gospel Tent, leaving women weeping in the spirit, George French, and his N.O. Storyville Jazz Band had the standing room only Economy Hall in rapture, and Teresa Romero Torkanowsky, famed Flamenco Dancer and mother of David Torkanowsky, held forth on the Lagniappe stage.

As the sun went down on the 31st annual Jazz & Heritage Festival, happy and exhausted fans poured out into the city for one more taste of something, musical, experiential or gastronomic before heading back to wherever they came from. The lines at the airport the next morning were all peace, love, satisfaction and….sunburn.

Monk Boudreaux and Bo Dollis

1:00 Trouble Nation, Wild Apaches and Red, White & Blue Mardi Gras Indians
2:00 Lady Sequence, Dumaine Gang and Happy House SA&PCs with Tuba Fats and The Chosen Few Brass Band
3:00 Black Eagles and Golden Blades Mardi Gras Indians
4:00 Single Men, Original Step N' Style and Devastating Ladies SA&PCs with Lil' Rascals Brass Band
5:00 Brazilian Parade featuring Maracatu Naçao Pernambuco

SUNDAY, APRIL 30

FOX 8 / SPRINT PCS STAGE
11:10 Hammond State Strawberry Jammers
12:20 Woodenhead
1:30 The Continental Drifters
2:50 Los Hombres Calientes
4:20 Snooks Eaglin
5:50 Galactic

HOUSE OF BLUES / OLD SCHOOL 102.9 STAGE
11:15 New Orleans Juice
12:20 Fredy Omar con su Banda
1:40 Kenny Neal
2:55 Joanne Shenandoah
4:25 The Iguanas
5:50 Deacon John

ACURA STAGE
11:15 Dillard University Jazz Ensemble
12:25 C.J. Chenier & The Red Hot Louisiana Band
1:40 Maracatu Naçao Pernambuco
3:00 The funky Meters
5:00 Sting

SHERATON / WB 38 FAIS DO-DO STAGE
11:25 Hazel & The Delta Ramblers
12:35 Allen Fontenot & The Country Cajuns
1:45 Lil' Malcolm & The House Rockers
3:00 Bruce Daigrepont's Cajun Band
4:30 Cascabulho of Brazil
6:00 Boozoo Chavis & Magic Sounds

BET ON JAZZ / WWOZ JAZZ TENT
11:25 Rebecca Barry & Bill Huntington
12:30 Charles Neville Jazz Ensemble
1:40 Kim Prevost & Bill Solley
2:50 Kid Jordan / Alvin Fielder & IAQ
4:15 Nicholas Payton Quintet
5:45 Dianne Reeves

ECONOMY HALL TENT
11:25 Local International Allstars
12:20 Onward Brass Band
1:30 Don Vappie & The Creole Serenaders
2:50 Barbara Shorts
4:15 Lars Edegran & The N.O. Ragtime Orchestra
5:45 Carrie Smith featuring Norman Simmons

CONGO SQUARE STAGE
11:15 Percussion, Inc.
12:25 White Eagles Mardi Gras Indians
1:35 Carlos Malta & Pifé Muderno
2:45 Willie Puckett and Joe Black
3:55 Olu Dara
5:35 The Legendary Wailers Band

LAGNIAPPE STAGE
11:30 Gina Forsyth
12:35 Caledonia Society Scottish Dancers & Pipes & Drums
1:40 The Naked Orchestra

3:00 Little Freddie King
4:25 Paky Saavedra's Bandido
5:55 Maggie Lewis & The Thunderbolts w/ Kenny Bill Stinson

TULANE HOSPITAL / RHODES GOSPEL TENT
11:00 Antioch Gospel Singers
11:45 Friendly Five Gospel Singers
12:30 Unstoppable Gospel Creators
1:15 Jo "Cool" Davis
2:00 Melody Clouds
2:45 Church Street
3:15 First Church of God in Christ Radio Choir
4:00 The Crowseekers
4:55 John Lee & The Heralds of Christ
5:55 Yolanda Adams

MUSIC HERITAGE STAGE INTERVIEWS
12:00 Pifé Muderna
1:00 Olu Dara
2:00 Rebecca Barry & Bill Huntington
3:00 Sharon Martin
4:00 Jo "Cool" Davis

NATIONAL PARK SERVICE KIDS' TENT
11:30 Family Affair
12:30 Parade / Bianca Watson & Co.
12:45 Bianca Watson, the Golden Arrows, Gregory Monroe, and The Junior Untouchables SA&PC
2:00 Hunter Hayes & LA H.O.T.
3:15 Adella, Adella the Storyteller w/ Philip Melancon
4:15 Judy Ginsburgh & David Marler
5:15 Azikwa Children's Percussion Ensemble

BRAZIL / AFRICAN HERITAGE STAGE
12:15 Dance of the Orixas feat. Maracatu Naçao Pernambuco
1:00 Brazilian/New Orleans Connections: Music, Dance, Food & Architecture
2:30 Mardi Gras Indian Elders: Preserving the Past for the Future
4:00 Brazilian Popular Music: Tradition & Transformation

PARADES
12:00 Lady Zulu, Uptown Hobo Clowns and Olympia Aide SA&PCs with Pinstripe Brass Band
12:20 Economy Hall Parade with Independent Ladies SA&PC
1:00 Yellow Jackets and Geronimo Hunters Mardi Gras Indians
2:00 Unknown Steppers and Original Four SA&PCs with New Birth Brass Band
3:00 Seminoles and Golden Arrows Mardi Gras Indians
4:00 Untouchables and Furious Five SA&PCs with Hot 8 Brass Band
5:00 Brazilian Parade featuring Maracatu Naç_o Pernambuco

THURSDAY, MAY 4

FOX 8 / SPRINT PCS STAGE
11:45 Royal Fingerbowl
1:15 Sonia Dada
2:40 Casa Samba
4:10 Ernie K-Doe w/ Blue Eyed Soul Revue
5:40 Buckwheat Zydeco

HOUSE OF BLUES / OLD SCHOOL 102.9 STAGE
10:35 The Earth Tones
12:00 Michael Ward

1:20 Cephas & Wiggins
2:35 Eddie Bo
4:05 The Kinsey Report
5:50 The Wild Magnolias

ACURA STAGE
11:00 St. Augustine H.S. Jazz Ensemble
12:00 Executive Steel
1:10 Liquid Soul
2:25 Big Bad Voodoo Daddy
3:55 Bela Fleck & The Flecktones
5:40 Better Than Ezra

SHERATON / WB 38 FAIS DO-DO STAGE
11:20 Po' Henry & Tookie
12:30 Marion Abramson H.S. Gospel Choir
1:40 Dwayne Dopsie & The Zydeco Hellraisers
2:55 Eddie LeJeune
4:20 Jambalaya Cajun Band
5:45 Rosie Ledet — the Zydeco Sweetheart

BET ON JAZZ / WWOZ JAZZ TENT
9:55 Alvin Batiste
11:30 Chuck Chaplin
12:35 Phillip Manuel
1:40 Alvin Batiste
2:55 Kermit Ruffins & The Barbecue Swingers
4:15 Clarence Johnson III
5:35 McCoy Tyner

ECONOMY HALL TENT
11:20 Albert "June" Gardner
12:30 Lady Charlotte Jazz Band
1:35 Olympia Brass Band
2:50 Harry Connick, Sr. w/ The Jimmy Maxwell Orchestra
4:15 Ronnie Kole
5:40 Banu Gibson & New Orleans Hot Jazz

CONGO SQUARE STAGE
11:25 Tanably
12:45 Harry Rios y los Monstrous
2:00 Y'Shua
3:20 Tanably of Cote d'Ivoire
4:30 Iris May Tango
5:55 Wanda Rouzan & A Taste of New Orleans

LAGNIAPPE STAGE
11:30 Black Lodge Singers
12:25 John Parker
1:35 Lightnin' Bugs w/ guest Dorothy Prime
2:50 Evening Star String Band
4:20 Donald Byrd / Kidd Jordan & Louis Armstrong Jazz Camp Ensemble
5:55 Chévere!

TULANE HOSPITAL / RHODES GOSPEL TENT
9:15 Leviticus Gospel Singers
11:00 Trina Dyson & Rejoice
11:45 Leviticus Gospel Singers
12:30 Lyle Henderson
1:15 Sounds of Unity
2:00 The Banks Family
2:45 Gospel Determinators
3:15 One A-Chord
4:00 The Dynamic Smooth Family
5:00 Jackson Southernaires
6:15 R. Lee James Memorial Chorale

MUSIC HERITAGE STAGE INTERVIEWS
1:00 Bela Fleck
2:30 Ronnie Kole
3:30 Dorothy Prime
4:30 Cephas & Wiggins
5:30 Dwayne Dopsie

NATIONAL PARK SERVICE KIDS' TENT
11:30 Rose Anne St. Romaine
12:30 Michael Ray Diverse Duets

2:00 The Magnificent Karr Performers
3:00 David & Roselyn
4:15 Kita Productions
5:15 Executive Steel Band

BRAZIL / AFRICAN HERITAGE STAGE
12:15 Capoeira Brazilian Martial Arts Demonstration
1:00 African Americans in the Civil War
2:30 River Road Blues: Early R&B Bands in the River Parishes
4:00 Young Voices in the Village: College Poets from Xavier University

PARADES
1:35 Economy Hall Parade with Positive Ladies SA&PC
4:00 Bon Temps Roulez Secondliners with Storyville Stompers Brass Band

FRIDAY, MAY 5

FOX 8 / SPRINT PCS STAGE
11:20 John Batiste
12:30 Cool Riddims & Sista Teedy
1:45 Los Babies
3:10 Charmaine Neville w/ Amasa Miller & Reggie Houston
4:35 Russell Batiste
5:50 Wayne Toups

HOUSE OF BLUES / OLD SCHOOL 102.9 STAGE
11:20 Tabby Thomas
12:30 Kipori "Baby Wolf" Woods
1:40 Lazy Lester w/ Raful Neal Band
3:05 Big Al Carson & The Rare Connexion Band
4:20 Earl King & The Butanes
5:50 Michael Ray & The Cosmic Krewe

ACURA STAGE
11:20 Grace King H.S. Jazz Ensemble
12:30 Anders Osborne
1:55 David Lindley w/ Wally Ingram
3:25 John Hiatt
5:25 Lyle Lovett & His Large Band

SHERATON / WB 38 FAIS DO-DO STAGE
11:20 Pearl River Social Dancers — Miss. Band of Choctaw Indians
12:20 J. Paul, Jr. & The Zydeco Newbreeds
1:40 Hackberry Ramblers
2:55 Sunpie Barnes & The Louisiana Sunspots
4:20 Balfa Toujours
5:50 Lil' Band o' Gold

BET ON JAZZ / WWOZ JAZZ TENT
11:30 Patrice Fisher & Arpa w/ Anthony Carrillo & David Ortiz
1:00 Clyde Kerr, Jr. & Univision
2:30 Peter Martin
3:25 Moose's Legends of Jazz
4:20 Hermeto Pascoal of Brazil
6:00 Jazz at the Philharmonic w/ Herlin Riley & Plas Johnson

ECONOMY HALL TENT
11:25 Original Dixieland Jazz Band
12:30 Doc Paulin Brass Band
1:45 Sullivan Dabney & His Muzik Band
2:55 Louis Cottrell's Spirit of N.O. Jazz Band
4:15 Clive Wilson & Original Camellia Jazz Band
5:45 Bob Wilber & Kenny Davern

CONGO SQUARE STAGE
11:20 Nu Beginnings

12:25 Soul Rebels Brass Band
1:40 Tanably of Cote d'Ivoire
2:55 Chico Cézar of Brazil
4:30 Jean Knight w/ Blue Eyed Soul Band
6:00 Ile Ayie of Bahia

LAGNIAPPE STAGE
11:30 Delgado Community College Jazz Band
12:35 Clancy "Blues Boy" Lewis & Sheba Kimbrough
1:40 Flaming Arrows Mardi Gras Indians
2:50 Topsy Chapman
4:05 Gregory Boyd & VOS
5:35 New Orleans Klezmer Allstars

TULANE HOSPITAL / RHODES GOSPEL TENT
11:00 Headstart Singing Angels
11:45 Melvin Winfield & New Vision
12:30 The Gospel Extenders
1:15 Second Mount Calvary Mass Choir
2:00 The Travelin' Stars
2:45 New Zion Trio + One
3:15 Coolie Family Gospel Singers
4:00 Theo Bourgeois & Kennedy H.S. Gospel Choir
4:55 Alvin Bridges & Desire Community Choir
5:55 The Christianaires

MUSIC HERITAGE STAGE INTERVIEWS
12:00 Chico César
1:00 Donald Byrd
2:00 Dew Drop Inn Revisited w/ Donald "Moose" Jamison, Earl King, Tad Jones & Billy Tircuit
3:00 Plas Johnson
4:00 Lazy Lester

NATIONAL PARK SERVICE KIDS' TENT
11:30 McDonogh #15 Band
12:30 Kalpana
1:45 Johnette Downing
3:00 Eric McAllister
4:00 Xavier Prep Storytellers
5:15 Metro Mudbugs

BRAZIL / AFRICAN HERITAGE STAGE
12:30 Opening Blessing Ceremony
1:00 Candomble
2:30 Capoeira: Many Facets of African Brazilian Martial Arts
3:30 Capoeira: Brazilian Martial Arts Demonstration
4:00 New Orleans Garifuna Community

PARADES
12:20 Economy Hall Parade with Algiers Steppers SA&PC
2:00 Double Nine and No Limit Steppers SA&PCs with Original Thunderstorm Brass Band
3:45 Brazilian Parade featuring Ile Ayie
4:00 Distinguished Gentlemen and Nine Times SA&PCs with The New Wave Brass Band

SATURDAY, MAY 6

FOX 8 / SPRINT PCS STAGE
11:15 June Victory & The Bayou Renegades
12:20 Ritmo Caribeno
1:35 Rockin' Dopsie & The Zydeco Twisters
2:50 Robert Mirabal
4:20 Jon Cleary & The Absolute Monster Gentlemen

5:50 Irma Thomas

HOUSE OF BLUES / OLD SCHOOL 102.9 STAGE
11:20 Xavier University Jazz Ensemble
12:30 Herman Ernest & The HOB Allstar Band
1:40 Tab Benoit
2:55 Corey Harris
4:25 Joe Louis Walker & The Bosstalkers
6:00 Dixie Cups

ACURA STAGE
11:20 Batiste Brothers
12:35 Steve Riley & The Mamou Playboys
1:45 Ile Aiye of Bahia
3:10 Jimmy Cliff
5:15 Lenny Kravitz

Sheraton / WB 38 Fais Do-Do Stage
11:20 Heritage School of Music Ensemble
12:30 La Bande "Feufollet"
1:40 Michael Jeansonne & The Silver Spur Band
2:55 D.L. Menard & The Louisiana Aces
4:25 Chris Ardoin & Double Clutchin'
5:55 Warren Ceasar & Creole Zydeco Snap

BET ON JAZZ / WWOZ JAZZ TENT
11:20 Juanita Brooks
12:30 Cynthia Dewberry
1:40 Al Belletto Big Jazz Band
2:55 Dirty Dozen Brass Band
4:15 Terence Blanchard
5:40 Diana Krall

ECONOMY HALL TENT
11:25 René Netto & The Sounds of New Orleans
12:30 Young Tuxedo Brass Band
1:40 Louisiana Repertory Jazz Ensemble
3:05 Ingrid Lucia & The Flying Neutrinos
4:25 Michael White w/ Thais Clark
5:50 Harlem Blues & Jazz Band

CONGO SQUARE STAGE
11:00 Culu African Dance Co.
12:05 Bamboula 2000
1:15 Chico César of Brazil
2:35 Rebirth Brass Band
4:10 TBA
5:50 Los Van Van of Cuba

LAGNIAPPE STAGE
11:30 John Rankin
12:40 Walter Payton & The Snapbean Band
2:05 Julio & Cesar
3:15 Tanably of Cote d'Ivoire
4:20 Henry Gray & The Cats w/ Lil' Buck Senegal
5:45 Sharon Martin & first Take

TULANE HOSPITAL / RHODES GOSPEL TENT
11:00 McDonogh #35 Gospel Choir
11:45 Sweet Adelines N.O. Blend Chorus
12:30 Zulu Ensemble
1:15 The Mighty Chariots
2:00 The Davis Family of Mobile
2:45 Watson Memorial Teaching Ministries
3:15 Lockport Mass Chapter Choir
4:00 Val & The Love Alive Fellowship Choir
4:55 Dimensions of Faith
5:55 Bobby Jones & The Nashville Super Choir

MUSIC HERITAGE STAGE INTERVIEWS
12:00 Henry Gray & Lil' Buck Senegal

1:00 Continental Drifters
2:00 Batiste Brothers
3:00 Herman Ernest
4:00 Ernie K-Doe

NATIONAL PARK SERVICE KIDS' TENT
11:30 Mid-City Music, Dance, Drama, Arts & Crafts Workshop
12:45 Hobgoblin Hill Puppets
1:30 Parade w/ Curtis Pierre & Samba Children
2:45 West Jefferson HS Oriental Club
4:00 Kira Viator
5:15 Charmaine Neville — World of Rhythm

BRAZIL / AFRICAN HERITAGE STAGE
12:15 A Tribute to Brazil's Samba Schools feat. Casa Samba
1:00 Celebrating the Black West: Buffalo Soldiers & Cowboys
2:30 Yoruban Lifeline of Diasporic Religions: Santeria, Vodun & Candomblé
4:00 Tropicalismo: Brazilian Arts Movement of the Late 1950s

PARADES
12:00 Original Seven, Black Men of Labor and Secondline Jammers SA&PCs with Tremé Brass Band
12:30 Economy Hall Parade with Ladies Over Thirty SA&PC
1:00 Comanche Hunters and Wild Tchoupitoulas Mardi Gras Indians
2:00 N'Krumah Better Boys, North Side Skull & Bone Gang, Perfect Gentlemen and Pigeon Town Steppers w/ Mahogany Brass Band
3:00 Young Hunters, Semolian Warriors and Bayou Renegades II Mardi Gras Indians
4:00 Popular Ladies, Big Nine and Money Wasters SA&PCs with Algiers Brass Band
5:15 Brazilian Parade featuring Ile Aiye, Casa Samba and The Rising Dragon-Vietnamese Lion Dance

SUNDAY, MAY 7

FOX 8 / SPRINT PCS STAGE
11:15 SUBR Jazz Ensemble
12:20 Reggie Hall & The Twilighters w/ Alvin "Dogman" Smith & Lady Lois
1:30 Walter "Wolfman" Washington & The Roadmasters
2:40 The Revealers
4:00 Ani DiFranco
5:45 The Radiators

HOUSE OF BLUES / OLD SCHOOL 102.9 STAGE
11:20 Porgy Jones
12:30 Los Vecinos
1:35 The Campbell Brothers "Sacred Steel"
2:55 Bernard Allison
4:25 Marva Wright & The BMWs
5:50 John Mooney & Bluesiana

ACURA STAGE
11:15 UNO Jazz Ensemble
12:25 Los Calientes del Son
1:50 Chocolate Milk
3:35 The Temptations
5:35 The Neville Brothers

SHERATON / WB 38 FAIS DO-DO STAGE
11:15 Young Cheyenne Mardi Gras Indians
12:25 Charivari

1:35 Savoy Doucet Cajun Band
2:50 Keith Frank & The Soileau Zydeco Band
4:20 Luther Kent
5:50 The Traiteurs w/ Sonny Landreth & Marce Lacouture

BET ON JAZZ / WWOZ JAZZ TENT
11:20 Roland Guerin Quintet
12:25 Leah Chase
1:35 Ellis Marsalis
2:55 Sam Rivers
4:20 Astral Project
5:45 Joe Sample & Lalah Hathaway

ECONOMY HALL TENT
11:20 The Players N.O. Jazz Band
12:25 Vintage Jazzmen of France
1:45 Placide Adams & The Original Dixieland Hall Jazz Band
3:05 George French & The N.O. Storyville Jazz Band
4:30 Pete Fountain
5:55 Preservation Hall Jazz Band

CONGO SQUARE STAGE
11:25 Black Lodge Singers
12:20 Kumbuka Drum & Dance Collective
1:40 Betty Wright
3:05 Trin-I-Tee 5:7
4:30 Ile Ayie of Brazil
5:45 King Sunny Ade

LAGNIAPPE STAGE
11:25 Andi Hoffman & B-Goes
12:30 Teresa Romero Torkanowsky & Ole Flamenco Ole!
1:40 The Legendary Willie Metcalf & The Young Lions
3:05 Spencer Bohren
4:30 Paula & The Pontiacs
5:45 Sonny Bourg

TULANE HOSPITAL / RHODES GOSPEL TENT
11:00 Paulette Wright Davis
11:45 The Bester Singers
12:30 St. Raymond Gospel Singers
1:15 The Johnson Extension
2:00 The Rocks of Harmony
2:45 Ebenezer MBC Choir
3:15 Aaron Neville
4:00 The Zion Harmonizers
4:55 Gospel Soul Children
5:55 The Staple Singers

MUSIC HERITAGE STAGE INTERVIEWS
12:00 Bernard Allison
1:00 Marce Lacouture
2:00 King Sunny Ade
3:00 Joe Sample
4:00 Betty Wright, Jean Knight & Tommy Tee
5:00 Joe Louis Walker

NATIONAL PARK SERVICE KIDS' TENT
11:30 Colleen Sally
12:30 Arts Connection Performers
2:00 Second St. James MBC Youth Choir
2:45 Javier's Dance Company
3:45 Parade w/ Ancestro
5:15 N'Kafu Traditional African Dance Co. presented by Young Audiences

BRAZIL / AFRICAN HERITAGE STAGE
12:15 Music of Black Carnival: Salvador, Bahia feat. Ile Aiye
1:00 Doo Wop Gospel: Antecedents to Early R&B
2:30 Unity Through Art & Culture: Ile Aiye — Bahian Carnival Afro Bloc
4:00 Samba Schools of Brazil: An

Education in Democracy
5:00 Closing Ceremony

PARADES
12:00 Scene Boosters, Jetsetters and Westbank Steppers SA&PCs with Pinettes Brass Band
1:00 Ninth Ward Hunters and Carrollton Hunters Mardi Gras Indians
2:00 Original Prince of Wales, Lady Prince of Wales and Avenue Steppers SA&PCs with Tornado Brass Band
3:00 Walter Cook's Creole Wild West, White Cloud Hunters and Mohawk Mardi Gras Indians
4:00 Original N.O. Lady Buckjumpers and N.O. Men Buckjumpers with Highsteppers Brass Band
5:15 Brazilian Parade with Ile Ayie

NIGHT CONCERTS

FRIDAY, APRIL 28, 9 P.M.
Erykah Badu
Roy Ayers
Morris F.X. Jeff Municipal Auditorium

FRIDAY, APRIL 28, 9 P.M.
New Orleans Jazz Divas
Germaine Bazzle, Cookie Gabriel, Sharon Martin, Wanda Rouzan, Barbara Short, Chris Severin & Troy Davis
Praline Connection Gospel & Blues Hall

SATURDAY, APRIL 29, 9 P.M.
Allman Brothers Band
The Robert Cray Band
Morris F.X. Jeff Municipal Auditorium

MONDAY, MAY 1, 8:00 P.M.
Jazz at the Palm Court
The Palm Court Jazz Allstars
Featuring Sammy Rimington, Butch Thompson, Wendell Brunious, Lars Edegran, Lucien Barbarin, Bill Huntington & Shannon Powell
Palm Court Jazz Café

THURSDAY, MAY 4, 9 P.M.
Welcome Home, Harry!
Harry Connick, Jr. & His Big Band
McCoy Tyner Trio
Morris F.X. Jeff Municipal Auditorium

FRIDAY, MAY 5, 9 P.M.
Lenny Kravitz
Cowboy Mouth
Morris F.X. Jeff Municipal Auditorium

FRIDAY, MAY 5, 9 P.M.
La Noche Latina
Los Van Van
Fredy Omar con su Banda
House of Blues

FRIDAY, MAY 5, 9 P.M.
New Orleans Jazz Divas
Lillian Boutté, Juanita Brooks, Topsy Chapman, Leah Chase, Betty Shirley
With Larry Sieberth, Thaddeus Richard,
Roland Guerin & Shannon Powell
Praline Connection Gospel & Blues Hall

SATURDAY, MAY 6, 9 P.M.
Lyle Lovett & His Large Band
Morris F.X. Jeff Municipal Auditorium

SATURDAY, MAY 6, MIDNIGHT
Charlie B's Midnight Jazz
Les McCann
Clarence Johnson III
Praline Connection Gospel & Blues Hall

2001

Mighty Chariots

The New Orleans Jazz & Heritage Festival 2001 was dedicated to the memory of Mr. Louis "Satchmo" Armstrong and was also a celebration of his 100th birthday. Everything Armstrong was the theme and the beautiful silkscreen poster created by James Michalopoulos was just the tip of the iceberg. As usual, this year honored our musical roots and further, displayed the multiplicity of styles that have evolved from the epicenter of jazz, New Orleans.

The Louis Armstrong Centennial Pavilion, located in the first floor of the grandstand at the Fair Grounds racetrack, told the story of the international ambassador of music and goodwill. Created with the work and expertise of historians Tad Jones and Jack Stewart, both Armstrong enthusiasts, and artist Rene Pierre, this exhibition took fans of "Satchmo" through his early years and gave them some perspective on the climate he came up in and the influences that shaped this amazing man. The main exhibit "*Satchmo: The Spirit of New Orleans*" provided a comprehensive look at the people and places that molded him — his neighborhood, his world travels, his reign as King of Zulu, and his continuing impact on the city.

The Louis Armstrong film tribute on May 2nd at the New Orleans Museum of Art

Charles Neville

screened rare archival footage, performances from television and Hollywood movies, documentaries detailing his life, and a filmed documentary of Mr. Armstrong's funeral. Additionally there were exhibits on the African Heritage stage, other grandstand exhibits, a cooking demonstration which featured Louis's personal red beans and rice recipe, an educational workshop including Dr. Michael White's tribute to Armstrong's Hot Five and Hot Seven, and an Armstrong

Kids Arts Project with 60 large banners made by New Orleans Public School children displayed in the grandstand. Many special Festival performances were dedicated to his memory on numerous stages over the course of the entire Jazz Fest.

Out at the Fair Grounds on Saturday April 28th, it was a big day for parading on the infield. The Lady Rollers Social Aid and Pleasure Club started the day off right, representing in the Cox Communications Economy Hall Tent. At high noon The Calliope Steppers, the Valley of Silent Men and Lady Sequence Social Aid and Pleasure Clubs second lined through the crowds to the Paulin Brothers' Brass Band. At 12:50 the Calendar Girls Social Aid and Pleasure Club launched from Economy Hall and at 1:00 p.m. Bayou Renegade II and Young Hunters Mardi Gras Indians began clearing out space as they marched the infield. At 2:00, the Dumaine Street Gang and the Divine Ladies Social Aid and Pleasure Clubs marched with the Original Thunderstorm Brass Band. Three o'clock

FRIDAY, APRIL 27

SPRINT PCS / LG STAGE
11:50 NOCCA Jazz Ensemble
1:20 Richard Thompson
2:35 Charmaine Neville Band w/ Reggie Houston & Amasa Miller
4:05 Beausoleil avec Michael Doucet w/ guests Sonny Landreth, Cindy Cashdollar & Richard Thompson
5:55 Clarence "Gatemouth" Brown with Gate's Express

HOUSE OF BLUES / OLD SCHOOL 102.9 STAGE
11:30 Jeremy Lyons & The Deltabilly Boys
12:40 Kipori "Baby Wolf" Woods
1:50 James Andrews
3:05 Henry Gray & The Cats w/ Paul "Lil' Buck" Sinegal
4:20 Mem Shannon & The Membership
5:50 Anders Osborne

ACURA STAGE
11:15 Brian "Breeze" Cayolle
12:25 Clarence "Frogman" Henry
1:55 Doug Kershaw
3:30 B.B. King
5:25 Al Green

SHERATON N.O. FAIS DO-DO STAGE
11:15 New Orleans All City Jazz Outreach
12:20 Allen Fontenot & The Country Cajuns
1:40 The Creole Zydeco Farmers
3:00 Mike West & Myshkin
4:20 Keith Frank & The Soileau Playboys
5:50 Chubby Carrier & The Bayou Swamp Band

BET ON JAZZ / WWOZ JAZZ TENT
12:00 Winds of Change vs. New Orleans Sax Quartet
1:10 Phillip Manuel
2:25 Clyde Kerr, Jr. & Univision
3:50 Donald Harrison, Jr.
5:30 Roy Hargrove

COX COMMUNICATIONS ECONOMY HALL TENT
11:15 Lady Charlotte's Jazz Band
12:20 Chris Clifton & His All-Stars
1:30 Anthony "Tuba Fats" Lacen
2:50 Harry Connick, Sr. & The Jimmy Maxwell Orchestra
4:05 Scott Hill's French Market Jazz Band
5:30 Michael White's Armstrong Hot 5 and Hot 7 w/ special guest Nicholas Payton

CONGO SQUARE
11:15 J.C. & Co. Gospel Singers
12:25 Rudy's Caribbean Funk Band
1:45 Willie West & The Alpha Blues Band
3:05 Wofa of Guinea
4:15 Super Rail Band of Mali
6:05 Chiko Queiroga & Antonio Rogério of Brazil

LAGNIAPPE STAGE
12:00 Micaela y Fiesta Flamenca
1:30 John Mahoney Big Band w/ guest Al Belletto
2:55 Kim Prevost & Bill Solley
4:20 J. Monque'D Blues Band & The Lil' Pats of Butter
5:45 Barbara Shorts

NATIVE AMERICAN VILLAGE STAGE
12:00 Lewis Johnson
1:00 Muskogee Nations Performers feat. Jonny Hawk
2:00 Nation of Change Native American Dancers

brought out the Indians of the Nation, White Cloud Hunters and the Red, White & Blue Mardi Gras Indians. At 4 p.m. Black Men Of Labor, the Second Line Jammers and Happy House Social Aid and Pleasure Clubs marched with the Treme Brass Band making this a very strong day for the representation of New Orleans street culture.

This aspect of the Festival has been present since its beginnings, and is very important for the authentic New Orleans feeling of Jazz Fest. So much of the music in the Crescent City begins on the street, with sounds we hear as children, floating through the air. We hear family members practicing for Super Sunday, we hear jazz at funerals, and at weddings. This vibrant, organic music culture nurtured artists in this city from Louis Armstrong, who played in numerous Brass Marching Bands and reigned as King of Zulu Social Aid and Pleasure Club to the Neville Brothers, whose Uncle Jolly was Chief of the Wild Tchoupitoulas Indians. The Social Aid and Pleasure Clubs, Brass Bands and Black Indian Gangs all play an important role in shaping musicians from New Orleans. This incredibly rich neighborhood community culture, is completely intertwined with local music.

Sunday, April 29th was another special music day for the marching clubs. Pinstripe Brass Band lead out at high noon with Olympia Aid, The Uptowners Hobo Clowns and The Distinguished Gentlemen Social Aid and Pleasure club in tow. The Mardi Gras Indians splashed their colors all over the infield at 1:00 p.m. with The Golden Arrows and the Seminole

music scene

Supagroup releases Rock & Roll Tried to Ruin My Life.

Louis Armstrong Centennial celebrated with premiere Satchmo Summer Fest.

Dwayne Dopsie records CD at Jazz Fest.

IN MEMORIAM

Ernest "Ernie K-Doe" Kador, Chet Atkins, Al Broussard, Milton Batiste, Wilson Anthony "Boozoo" Chavez, John Lee Hooker, Jeanette Kimball, Milton Batiste, Joseph E. Bernard, Jr., Warren Ceasar, Newell "Pa-Pa" Glass, Dorn "Pappy" Kemp, Segundo David "Big Dave" Labayen, Phamous Lambert, Robert "Big Chief Robbe" Lee, Eddie LeJeune, Richard Payne, Ezall "Money" Quinn, Jr., Patrick Taplette, Jr., Charles Taylor, Danny Toups, Clement Williams, Ronald "Green Apples" Williams, Milt Hinton, Ernest Anthony "Tito" Puente, Frank Parker, Roebuck "Pops" Staples, Johnnie Taylor, Stanley Turrentine, Allen Woody, Les Brown, John Lewis

Warriors. A memorial second line for Louis Armstrong was held featuring the Unknown Steppers, Original Four and the Single Ladies Social Aid and Pleasure Club stepping with the Little Rascals Brass Band. 3:00 p.m. The Wild Apaches, the Yellow Jackets and the Creole Wild West Indians went on the war path and at 4:00 p.m. The Untouchables, Furious Five and The Popular Ladies Social Aid and Pleasure Club closed out with Newbirth Brass Band. This type of presentation continued throughout every day of the Festival exposing people from around the world to another aspect of our cultural richness.

Norman Dixon Sr. was Social Aid and Pleasure Club Coordinator and Mardi Gras Indian Consultant in 2001 and really did a wonderful job bringing the music "to the streets" of the Fair Grounds. Elsewhere on the infield Sunday, The Bester Gospel Singers were

the first act to play at 11:00, opening up the direct line from the Gospel tent to the most high for the day. That line would not be severed until John Lee and the Heralds of Christ hung up the phone at 6:55 that evening.

Thursday, May 3rd, Widespread Panic came to the Festival and brought a pile of fans along with them. Panic fans upset neighbors around the

3:15 Lewis Johnson
4:15 Muskogee Nations Performers feat. Jonny Hawk
5:30 Nation of Change Native American Dancers

RHODES GOSPEL TENT
11:00 The Showers Family
11:45 New Orleans Blend Chorus
12:30 Leviticus Gospel Singers
1:15 Lyle Henderson
2:00 Sounds of Unity
2:45 Ninevah Baptist Church Choir
3:30 Theo Bourgeois & The J.F.K. Gospel Choir
4:15 Dynamic Smooth Family Gospel Singers
5:05 The Pilgrim Jubilees
6:05 The Coolie Family of Slidell

ALLISON MINER MUSIC HERITAGE STAGE
12:00 Clarence "Jockey" Etienne interviewed by Ben Sandmel
1:00 Harold Cavallero Dobro Master interviewed by Tom Piazza
2:00 Anders Osborne interviewed by Scott Jordan
3:15 Tom McDermott interviewed by Tom Piazza
4:15 Doug Kershaw interviewed by Kateri Yager
5:30 J. Monque'D interviewed by Steve Armbruster

PARADES
1:30 Economy Hall Parade with Algiers Steppers SA&PC
2:00 Double Nine & Singe Men Kids SA&PCs with The Real Untouchable Brass Band

SATURDAY, APRIL 28

SPRINT PCS / LG STAGE
11:30 Loyola University Jazz Ensemble
12:40 Irene Sage
2:05 Jon Cleary & The Absolute Monster Gentlemen
3:40 Koko Taylor & Her Blues Machine
5:30 Buckwheat Zydeco

HOUSE OF BLUES / OLD SCHOOL 102.9 STAGE
11:15 Rufus Rip Wimberly
12:25 Lee Bates & The Cool Connection
1:40 Larry Garner
3:00 Frankie Ford
4:30 Luther Kent & Trick Bag
5:55 Jean Knight w/ Blue Eyed Soul

ACURA STAGE
11:15 Young Cheyennes Mardi Gras Indians
12:20 Theresa Andersson
1:35 Los Hombres Calientes feat. Irvin Mayfield & Bill Summers
3:15 funky Meters
5:30 The Wallflowers

SHERATON N.O. FAIS DO-DO STAGE
11:15 Ricardo Crespo & Sol Brasil
12:20 Waylon Thibodeaux "Louisiana's Rockin' Fiddler"
1:40 Suroit of Canada w/ Hadley Castille
3:00 Fredy Omar con su Banda
4:25 Jude Taylor & His Burning Flames
5:55 Willis Prudhomme & Zydeco Express

BET ON JAZZ / WWOZ JAZZ TENT
11:30 Topsy Chapman & The Pros
12:50 Kidd Jordan – Al Fielder & IAQ

Leigh "Lil Queenie" Harris

Fair Grounds Racetrack when they were found sleeping in people's cars and camping on the streets. When the Fair opened on Thursday, thousands of new age hippies poured through the main gates and went straight to the Acura stage, spread blankets on the ground and finished napping. Panic came on after the Dirty Dozen brass band warmed up the stage with a double long time slot to please the jam band fans from 4:05 to 6:55.

Friday, our own hot jam band Galactic went head to head on Sprint opposite Paul Simon on Acura and Ramsey Lewis in the Jazz Tent. Their huge popularity in 2001 was evident from the sea of people to be seen in front of their stage. The North Mississippi Allstars and the Dave Matthews Band on Saturday also represented contemporary national jam band trends at Jazz Fest.

Matthews drew a wide mix of loyal fans: boomers, gen-xers and just plain rockers. It was packed and every inch of spare space was filled with bodies, swelling the crowd to an all-time record. People stood listening out on the track, next to the fragrant port-o-lets; people climbed the fence, until security chased them down. Food booths ran out of food. People parked and sat on top of cars in the neighborhoods, camping out all day and not even attending, and hung out to hear their hero for free. When the time came, they just listened to the live music bouncing off the stables and tumbling down the street.

The Dixie Cups gave satisfaction to their fans on the Sprint

"I'm Russ Herman, better known as the Jazz Jester. I'm from New Orleans. I've missed one day in 32 years. I'll tell you about the flags. Originally there were no flags. People set up tents and tarps with canopies and nobody could see over them. So they eliminated the tents and all of the tarps went down to the ground. So people couldn't find each other then. People started carrying little flags on poles and that really busted open. The first flags that were out here were the jester pole and they also had the big white monkey with the red ass. This is a place for adults who never grew up and children who don't want to."

RUSS HERMAN IN A TRIO NETWORK INTERVIEW

Stage. We'd like to clear up a question that has been asked about the spelling of their name. For a couple of years these ladies were promoted as the Dixie Kups. It was for legal reasons. It was not an extended typo.

Also on May 4th, Wardell Quezergue and his orchestra which included his son Brian on bass and Doug Belote presiding on the drums, Larry Sieberth on piano, Tracy Griffin, Alonzo Bowens, Clarence Johnson III on horns delivered a wonderful hour of music.

On Saturday, May 5th, the Jazz Tent featured Leah Chase at 11:45 followed by Ellis Marsalis and Astral Project. These three groups back to back left standing room only and not much of that as people piled around the outside of the tent to listen.

Mystikal was back at Congo Square, booked to play from 3:45 to 5:00 p.m.. Unfortunately, he was 45 minutes late for his set so his fans who had waited didn't get to hear too much of him. "Shake Ya Azz" was his

big hit at the time, perhaps if he would have, he would have gotten to the Fest on time. He was followed by the Queen of Salsa, Celia Cruz who had also turned in a stunning performance at the House of Blues on Friday, May 4th for "La Nocha Latina". This

would be her last New Orleans Jazz Festival performance. She will be missed.

George French, brother of Bob, was in Economy Hall with his group, The New Orleans Storyville Jazz Band, featuring Kimberly Longstreth a lovely traditional Jazz singer and sister of Paul from Cronk on vocals. Cronk had closed the Lagniappe stage the previ-

2:15 Little Jimmy Scott & The Jazz Expressions
4:00 The Nicholas Payton Armstrong Centennial Celebration
5:45 Max Roach

COX COMMUNICATIONS ECONOMY HALL TENT
11:20 Placide Adams & Onward Brass Band
12:50 Maryland Jazz Band of Germany
2:20 Don Vappie & The Creole Jazz Serenaders
3:50 Gregg Stafford's Jazz Hounds
5:40 The Carnegie Hall Jazz Band, Jon Faddis – Music Director

CONGO SQUARE
11:45 Bamboula 2000
12:55 Irie Dawtas
2:20 Super Rail Band of Mali
4:00 The Abyssinians of Jamaica
5:45 Chanté Moore

LAGNIAPPE STAGE
11:15 Gina Forsyth w/ Danzig & Wooley
12:20 Soul Rebels Brass Band
1:30 The Thelonious Monk Institute of Jazz Quintet
2:50 Big Jack Johnson & The Oilers
4:05 Sharon Martin
5:35 Cronk

NATIVE AMERICAN VILLAGE STAGE
12:00 Lewis Johnson
1:00 Muskogee Nations Performers feat. Jonny Hawk
2:00 Nation of Change Native American Dancers
3:15 Bill Miller
4:30 Lewis Johnson
5:15 Nation of Change Native American Dancers
6:15 Muskogee Nations Performers feat. Jonny Hawk

RHODES GOSPEL TENT
11:00 The Heavenly Sent
11:45 Second Nazarene Gospel Choir
12:30 The Southern Bells
1:15 Ebenezer Baptist Church Choir
2:00 Zulu Gospel Ensemble
2:45 One A-Chord
3:30 The Mighty Chariots
4:15 First Church of God in Christ United Radio Choir
5:05 The McDonald Sisters
6:05 Tyronne Foster & The Arc Singers

ALLISON MINER MUSIC HERITAGE STAGE
1:00 Koko Taylor interviewed by John Sinclair
2:00 Roy Hargrove interviewed by Karen Celestan
3:00 Willis Prudhomme interviewed by Michael Tisserand
4:15 Little Jimmy Scott interviewed by Mike Gourrier
5:15 Big Jack Johnson interviewed by Chuck Siler

PARADES
11:20 Economy Hall Parade with Lady Rollers SA&PC
12:00 Calliope Steppers, Valley of Silent Men & Lady Sequence SA&PCs with Paulin Brothers Brass Band
12:50 Economy Hall Parade with Calendar Girls SA&PC
1:00 Bayou Renegade II & Young Hunters Mardi Gras Indians
2:00 Dumaine St. Gang, Divine Ladies & Dumaine St. Ladies SA&PCs with The Original Thunderstorm Brass Band

debut. Tommy Malone followed Brother Tyrone with an excellent set of original material. Then came Moe, carrying the jam band thread into Sunday. Moe enjoyed hanging out back stage with the backline crew, eating fried trout prepared under the giant speaker columns stage right and then napping underneath the stage in hammocks after delivering a hard driving show. Ernie "Mother In Law" K-Doe turned in a spectacular performance on Sprint. He had some comments to make about his upcoming show in pre-Fest publicity, "I'm not bragging, but I promise everybody, those that come on stage before me shall be safe. Those that come after me shall not be safe. I expect everyone in the audience to jump in the air and try to reach the sky while I am performing.

ous week with their own brand of hard core fusion funk.

On closing day, Sunday, May 6th, Brother Tyrone and the Mindbenders opened the Sprint Stage with some throw down, old school blues and R&B reminiscent of Al Green and James Brown, two of this singers hero's. This was Tyrone's Jazz Fest

After I'm finished singing, I'll come down to the railing to let people touch my rings and shake my hand. This year I'm having a special tuxedo made, and I'm inviting all the people and all the other entertainers to come out and see Ernie K-Doe. This is a new millennium and it's my first time performing at

Lucinda Williams

the Jazz Festival as the Emperor of the Universe so it's going to be something." Ernie K-Doe.

Sadly, this would be his last performance at the New Orleans Jazz And Heritage Festival. The Emperor of the Universe's spirit would ascend to his throne in Heaven and he would be buried here in New

Orleans. Antoinette K-Doe observed with irony, "Ernie's birthday was February 22, 1936. Six months after Ernie passed my mother passed and she is buried with him. Earl King is buried with him; so we have the Emperor and the King and the Mother In Law together. They better leave my mom alone."

Keb Mo

fest facts

The attendance of 664,000 at the Fair Grounds broke previous records for each day of the Heritage Fair, including the all-time single day attendance of 160,000, recorded when Dave Matthews Band and Mystikal performed.

Benny Andrews created the official Congo Square poster for 2001.

One fan ran this display ad in *OffBeat:* "Natalie, the music is never sweeter than when we're in New Orleans during Jazz Fest. Will you marry me? I love you, Doug."

Websites spring up with Jazz Fest personal stories, advice on what to wear, eat, where to stay, and more, more, more. Most have photos that enlarge when clicked.

3:00 Indians of the Nation, White Cloud Hunters & Red, White & Blue Mardi Gras Indians
4:00 Black Men of Labor, Second Line Jammers & Happy House SA&PCs with Tremé Brass Band

SUNDAY, APRIL 29

SPRINT PCS / LG STAGE
11:30 SUNO Jazz Ensemble
12:45 The Elements
2:15 The Dixie Cups
3:45 Snooks Eaglin
5:30 Marcia Ball

HOUSE OF BLUES / OLD SCHOOL 102.9 STAGE
11:15 The Lightnin' Bugs feat. Dorothy Prine
12:20 Juice
1:35 E.L.S.
3:00 Indigenous
4:25 The Iguanas
5:50 The Rebirth Brass Band

ACURA STAGE
11:15 White Eagles Mardi Gras Indians
12:25 Ritmo Caribeno
1:50 Irma Thomas
3:30 Dr. John
5:35 Van Morrison

SHERATON N.O. FAIS DO-DO STAGE
11:15 Jonas Risin
12:25 Kim Carson & The Casualties
1:40 Savoy-Doucet Cajun Band
2:55 Amy Adams & The Hank Sinatras
4:20 Wayne Toups
5:55 Rockin' Dopsie, Jr. & The Zydeco Twisters

BET ON JAZZ / WWOZ JAZZ TENT
11:40 Germaine Bazzle
12:55 Marlon Jordan
2:10 John Boutté
3:30 Terence Blanchard
5:30 Carnegie Hall Jazz Band, Jon Faddis Music Director with special guest Clark Terry

COX COMMUNICATIONS ECONOMY HALL TENT
11:15 Andrew Hall's Society Brass Band
12:20 The Pfister Sister & Their Big Band
1:30 Bob French & The Original Tuxedo Jazz Band
2:55 Chris Owens
4:15 Wendell Brunious
5:45 The Armstrong Alumni All-Stars feat. Arvell Shaw, Joe Muranyi, Fred Lonzo, Tom Baker, Ernest Elly & Lars Edegran

CONGO SQUARE
11:15 Wofa of Guinea
12:25 Katey Red & 5th Ward Weebie
1:40 Kazzabe of Honduras
3:20 Femi Anikulapo-Kuti & The Positive Force of Nigeria
5:35 Brian McKnight

LAGNIAPPE STAGE
11:15 David & Roselyn
12:15 Carlos Sanchez "Amanecer Flamenco"
1:30 Derek Dabbs
2:55 The Gregory Boyd Band
4:20 Henry Butler
5:55 New Orleans Nightcrawlers Brass Band

NATIVE AMERICAN VILLAGE STAGE
12:00 Lewis Johnson
1:00 Muskogee Nations Performers

feat. Jonny Hawk
2:00 Nation of Change Native American Dancers
3:15 Lewis Johnson
4:15 Muskogee Nations Performers feat. Jonny Hawk
5:30 Nation of Change Native American Dancers

RHODES GOSPEL TENT
11:00 The Bester Gospel Singers
11:45 Friendly Five Gospel Singers
12:30 The Unstoppable Gospel Creators Singers
1:15 Jo "Cool" Davis
2:00 The Melody Clouds
2:45 Lillian Boutté
3:30 Val & Love Alive Fellowship Choir
4:15 Dimensions of Faith
5:05 The Canton Spirituals
6:05 John Lee & The Heralds of Christ

ALLISON MINER MUSIC HERITAGE STAGE
1:00 Franz Jackson interviewed by Jason Patterson
2:00 Wayne Toups interviewed by Nick Spitzer
3:00 Arvell Shaw & Joe Muranyi interviewed by Steve Steinberg
4:00 Members of Wofa interviewed by Dr. Gabou Mendy
5:00 Bob French interviewed by David Kunian

PARADES
12:00 Olympia Aid, Uptowner's Hobo Clowns & Distinguished Gentlemen SA&PCs with Pinstripe Brass Band
1:00 Golden Arrows & Semolian Warriors Mardi Gras Indians
2:00 Louis Armstrong Memorial Second Line featuring Unknown Steppers, Original Four & Single Ladies SA&PCs with Lil' Rascals Brass Band
3:00 Wild Apaches, Yellow Jackets & Creole Wild West Mardi Gras Indians
4:00 Untouchables, Furious Five & Popular Ladies SA&PCs with New Birth Brass Band

THURSDAY, MAY 3

SPRINT PCS / LG STAGE
11:30 Hammond State Strawberry Jammers
12:40 Gregory Dawson & Crosswinds
1:55 Leigh Harris AKA Lil' Queenie
3:30 Lucinda Williams
5:30 Lil' Band o' Gold feat. Warren Storm, Steve Riley, C.C. Adcock & The St. Martin Horns

HOUSE OF BLUES / OLD SCHOOL 102.9 STAGE
12:00 Sonny Bourg & The Bayou Blues Band
1:15 Tab Benoit with special guest Tabby Thomas
2:45 21st Century Blues featuring Chris Thomas King
3:55 Sonny Landreth
5:35 Bryan Lee & The Blues Power Band

ACURA STAGE
11:30 Cedar Grove H.S. Jazz Ensemble of Georgia
12:40 Herman Jackson
2:05 Dirty Dozen Brass Band

4:05 Widespread Panic

SHERATON N.O. FAIS DO-DO STAGE
12:00 T-Mamou
1:20 Kevin Naquin & The Ossun Playboys
2:45 Filé
4:15 Charivari
5:50 Geno Delafose & French Rockin' Boogie

BET ON JAZZ / WWOZ JAZZ TENT
9:30 Kid's Day with St. Augustine H.S. Jazz Ensemble
12:00 Jeremy Davenport
1:15 Quintology
2:40 Irvin Mayfield
4:05 Donald Edwards
5:35 Randy Weston

COX COMMUNICATIONS ECONOMY HALL TENT
11:20 Jacques Gauthe's Creole Rice Jazz Band
12:25 Tommy Yetta's New Orleans Jazz Band
1:40 Doc Paulin's Dixieland Jazz Band
3:00 J.J. Jazzmen of the Czech Republic
4:25 Clive Wilson's Satchmo Serenade w/ guest Butch Thompson
6:00 The Dukes of Dixieland

CONGO SQUARE
12:00 Kid's Day with Culu Children's Traditional African Dance Co.
1:30 Executive Steel Band
2:50 Chévere
4:15 Kan'nida of Guadeloupe
5:45 Iris May Tango

LAGNIAPPE STAGE
12:00 Sheba Kimbrough & Clancy "Blues Boy" Lewis
1:05 Milango Tango Band
2:15 John Rankin
3:40 The Magnolia Sisters
5:10 Spencer Bohren

NATIVE AMERICAN VILLAGE STAGE
10:45 Kid's Day with Bayou Healers
12:00 Tommy Wildcat
1:00 Bayou Healers
2:00 Black Lodge
3:15 Tommy Wildcat
4:15 Bayou Healers
5:30 Black Lodge

RHODES GOSPEL TENT
10:10 Kid's Day with The Mahalia Jackson Choir
11:45 Antioch Full Gospel Choir
12:30 First Revolution
1:15 Old Zion Missionary Baptist Church Choir
2:00 Southern Travelers of Houma
2:45 The Banks Family
3:30 The Golden Wings
4:15 Dimensions of Faith
5:05 The Jackson Family
6:05 R. Lee James Memorial Chorale

ALLISON MINER MUSIC HERITAGE STAGE
11:45 Danny Rhodes interviewed by Grant Morris
12:45 Caffeine Music's New Orleans Songwriters w/ Jim McCormick, Sam Broussard, Kerry Grombacher & Lynn Drury
2:00 Creole / Cajun Connection w/ Geno Delafose, Christine Balfa & Ann Savoy Moderated by Michael Tisserand

3:00 Benny Powell interviewed by Don "Moose" Jamison
4:00 Remembering Vernell Fournier – Moderator Maurice Martinez with Edgar "Dooky" Chase, Jr., & Warren Bell, Sr.

PARADES
3:00 Bon Temps Roulez SA&PC with Storyville Stompers Brass Band

FRIDAY, MAY 4

SPRINT PCS / LG STAGE
11:45 Harry Rios y Los Monstruos
1:00 Curtis Pierre & Casa Samba
2:25 Peter Holsapple
3:55 Keb' Mo'
5:45 Galactic

HOUSE OF BLUES / OLD SCHOOL 102.9 STAGE
11:15 Danny Rhodes & The Messengers
12:20 Golden Eagles Mardi Gras Indians
1:25 Coco Robicheaux & The Perspirators
2:50 Raful Neal
4:20 Sherman Robinson
5:55 Marva Wright & The BMWs

ACURA STAGE
11:45 New Orleans Vintage
1:05 Sunpie Barnes & The Louisiana Sunspots
2:30 Wilson Pickett
4:40 Paul Simon

SHERATON N.O. FAIS DO-DO STAGE
11:15 Grace King H.S. Jazz Ensemble
12:20 Jambalaya Cajun Band
1:30 The Hackberry Ramblers
2:50 Bruce Daigrepont Cajun Band
4:15 Sean Ardoin 'n' Zydekool
5:45 Boozoo Chavis & Magic Sounds

BET ON JAZZ / WWOZ JAZZ TENT
11:15 Bleu Orleans
12:20 Willie Metcalf
1:30 Ricky Sebastian Septet
2:50 Leroy Jones
4:15 James Rivers Movement
5:40 Ramsey Lewis

COX COMMUNICATIONS ECONOMY HALL TENT
11:30 June Gardner & The Fellows
12:35 Local International Allstars
1:50 New Leviathan Oriental Foxtrot Orchestra
3:10 Lionel Ferbos & The Palm Court Jazz Band
4:25 Louisiana Repertory Jazz Ensemble
5:50 Trumpet Summit featuring Kermit Ruffins, Chris Clifton, Dwayne Burns & Benny Powell

CONGO SQUARE
11:15 Early Brooks, Jr. & Jah Posse
12:30 Soul Remedy
1:40 Kan'nida of Guadeloupe
2:55 Wardell Quezergue & His Slammin' Big Band
4:25 Cyril Neville & The Authentic New Orleans R&B Revue
5:55 Willie Clayton

LAGNIAPPE STAGE
11:15 Grace King H.S. Jazz Ensemble
12:20 Trout Fishing in America
1:35 Javier Gutierrez & Acoustic Swiftness
3:00 New Orleans Klezmer Allstars

4:25 Waso of Belgium
5:55 Los Vecinos

NATIVE AMERICAN VILLAGE STAGE
12:00 Tommy Wildcat
1:00 Bayou Healers
2:00 Black Lodge
3:15 Tommy Wildcat
4:15 Bayou Healers
5:30 Black Lodge

RHODES GOSPEL TENT
11:00 Clark Sr. H.S. Gospel Choir
11:45 Christian Light
12:30 Paulette Wright Davis
1:15 Charles & The Jackson Singers
2:00 Alvin Bridges & Desire Community Choir
2:45 TBA
3:30 New Zion Trio Plus One
4:15 McDonogh #35 Gospel Choir
5:05 Marvin Sapp
6:05 Praise Community Choir

ALLISON MINER MUSIC HERITAGE STAGE
12:00 George Schmidt of New Leviathan Orchestra interviewed by Daniel Meyer
1:00 Sherman Robertson interviewed by Suzan Jenkins
2:00 Bois Sec Ardoin interviewed by Nick Spitzer
3:00 TBA
4:00 Lucinda Williams interviewed by Ben Sandmel

PARADES
2:00 Jetsetters Men & Old & Nu Style Fellas SA&PCs with Trombone Shorty All-Star Brass Band
4:00 New Generation & Young Men II Old Men SA&PCs with Olympia Brass Band

SATURDAY, MAY 5

SPRINT PCS / LG STAGE
11:15 Flaming Arrows Mardi Gras Indians
12:25 The Batiste Brothers
1:40 Sonia Dada
3:00 Wanda Rouzan & A Taste of New Orleans
4:25 George Porter, Jr. & Runnin' Pardners
5:55 The Revealers

HOUSE OF BLUES / OLD SCHOOL 102.9 STAGE
11:20 SUBR Jazz Ensemble
12:30 Matilda Jones N.O. R&B Revue
1:40 Sansone, Krown, Fohl
3:00 Terrance Simien
4:30 Deacon John
6:00 Walter "Wolfman" Washington & The Roadmasters

ACURA STAGE
11:15 Jamal Batiste & The Jam-Allstars
12:25 Kevin Gordon
1:45 North Mississippi Allstars
3:10 Cowboy Mouth
5:00 Dave Matthews Band

SHERATON NEW ORLEANS FAIS DO-DO STAGE
11:15 The Proud Mary's
12:20 D.L. Menard & The Louisiana Aces
1:30 Dona Selma do Coco of Brazil
2:40 Dwayne Dopsie & The Zydeco Hellraisers
4:05 Steve Riley & The Mamou Playboys

5:40 Los Babies

BET ON JAZZ / WWOZ JAZZ TENT
11:45 Leah Chase
1:10 Ellis Marsalis
2:35 Astral Project
4:00 Louis' Home Cookin' New Orleans Trumpet Tribute w/ Gregory Davis, Irvin Mayfield, Marlon Jordan, Clyde Kerr, Jr. Christian Scott & Trombone Shorty
5:40 Elvin Jones

COX COMMUNICATIONS ECONOMY HALL TENT
11:15 Young Tuxedo Brass Band
12:20 Walter Payton & Snapbeans
1:35 Lars Edegran & The New Orleans Ragtime Orchestra
3:00 Banu Gibson & New Orleans Hot Jazz
4:20 George French & The N.O. Storyville Jazz Band feat. Kimberley Longstreth
5:45 Michael White's Armstrong Hot 5 & Hot 7 w/ Irakli & Thais Clark

CONGO SQUARE
11:30 Kumbuka Drum & Dance Collective
12:40 Reggie Hall & The Twilighters feat. Lady Lois & Albert "Dogman" Smith
2:00 Mahotella Queens of South Africa
3:45 Mystikal
5:45 Celia Cruz & The Johnny Pacheco Orchestra

LAGNIAPPE STAGE
11:30 Heritage School of Music Band
12:35 UNO Jazz Ensemble
1:45 The Wolfpack featuring Butch Mudbone
3:10 Michael Ward
4:30 Othar Turner & The Rising Star Fife & Drum Band

NATIVE AMERICAN VILLAGE STAGE
12:00 Tommy Wildcat
1:00 Bayou Healers
2:00 Black Lodge
3:15 Butch Mudbone
4:30 Tommy Wildcat
5:15 Black Lodge
6:15 Bayou Healers

RHODES GOSPEL TENT
11:00 The Gospel Inspirationals
11:45 Pastor Ray Inglehart & Gloryland BC Choir
12:30 Providence Baptist Church Male Chorus
1:15 The Crown Seekers
2:00 Community Missionary Baptist Church Choir
2:45 New Orleans Spiritualettes
3:30 Second Morning Star Missionary Mass Choir
4:15 Sherman Washington & The Zion Harmonizers
5:05 Trin-i-tee 5:7
6:05 Watson Memorial Teaching Ministries

ALLISON MINER MUSIC HERITAGE STAGE
12:00 Tribute to Louis Armstrong with Michael White, Irakli, Gregg Stafford, Bruce Barnes & Don Marquis
1:00 Tommy Malone interviewed by Scott Jordan
2:00 Veilee – Accapella Cajun Songs w/ David Greely, Kristi Guillory, Marce Lacouture & Horace Trahan

3:00 Reggie Hall and Albert "Dog Man" Smith interviewed by Ben Sandmel
4:00 Kevin Gordon interviewed by Mike Luster
5:00 Mahotella Queens interviewed by Dr. Gabou Mendy

PARADES
11:15 Economy Hall Parade with Nine Times Ladies SA&PC
12:00 Single Men, Original Step 'N' Style & Devastating Ladies SA&PCs with Tuba Fats & The Chosen Few Brass Band
1:00 Trouble Nation & Geronimo Hunters Mardi Gras Indians
2:00 Big Nine, No Limit Steppers & Money Wasters SA&PCs with Mahogany Brass Band
3:00 New Orleans Mardi Gras Rhythm Section, Golden Blades and Wild Tchoupitoulas Mardi Gras Indians
4:00 Pigeon Town Steppers, N'Krumah Better Boys & Original Seven SA&PCs with Pinettes Brass Band

SUNDAY, MAY 6

SPRINT PCS / LG STAGE
11:45 Brother Tyrone & The Mindbenders
1:00 Tommy Malone
2:30 moe
3:55 Ernie K-Doe w/ Blue Eyed Soul Revue
5:30 The Radiators

HOUSE OF BLUES / OLD SCHOOL 102.9 STAGE
11:15 Kim Jordan
12:20 Kenny Bill Stinson & The ARK-LA Mystics
1:30 Ulali
2:45 Earl King & The Butanes
4:15 John Mooney & Bluesiana
5:50 The Wild Magnolias

ACURA STAGE
11:15 Golden Star Hunters Mardi Gras Indians
12:20 Gary Brown & Feelings
1:45 Allen Toussaint
3:20 Fats Domino
5:20 The Neville Brothers

SHERATON N.O. FAIS DO-DO STAGE
11:15 La Bande "Feufollet"
12:20 190 Express
1:30 Balfa Toujours
2:55 Rosie Ledet the Zydeco Sweetheart & The Zydeco Playboys
4:20 Nathan & The Zydeco Cha Chas
5:45 C.J. Chenier & The Red Hot Louisiana Band

BET ON JAZZ / WWOZ JAZZ TENT
11:45 Jason Marsalis
1:00 Alvin Batiste & The Jazztronauts
2:20 Kermit Ruffins & The Barbecue Swingers
3:50 Nu Legends
5:05 Al Jarreau

COX COMMUNICATIONS ECONOMY HALL TENT
11:25 Placide Adams & The Original Dixieland Hall Jazz Band
12:30 Tim Laughlin
1:40 Jamil Sharif & New Orleans Jazz Professors
2:35 Moose's Jazz Legend Awards

3:05 Trumpet Summit w/ James Andrews, Duke Heitger, Leroy Jones & Gregg Stafford
4:35 Pete Fountain
6:00 Preservation Hall Jazz Band

CONGO SQUARE
11:20 Ken "Afro" Williams
12:30 Malombo of South Africa
1:45 DJ Jubilee & Joe Blakk
3:15 Zion
5:05 Maze featuring Frankie Beverly

LAGNIAPPE STAGE
11:20 Poor Clares
12:30 Little Freddie King Blues Band
1:40 Big Joe Duskin
2:50 Dona Selma do Coco of Brazil
4:10 Eddie Bo
5:40 Paky Saavedra's Bandido

NATIVE AMERICAN VILLAGE STAGE
12:00 Tommy Wildcat
1:00 Bayou Healers
2:00 Black Lodge
3:15 Ulali
4:30 Tommy Wildcat
5:15 Black Lodge
6:15 Bayou Healers

RHODES GOSPEL TENT
11:00 Antioch Gospel Singers
11:45 Cosmopolitan Evangelist Baptist Church Mass Choir
12:30 St. Raymond Gospel Choir
1:15 The Rocks of Harmony
2:00 The Johnson Extension
2:45 Church Street
3:30 Aaron Neville
4:15 The Soul Seekers
5:05 The Rance Allen Group
6:05 The New Orleans Gospel Soul Children

ALLISON MINER MUSIC HERITAGE STAGE
11:45 New Orleans Poetry Forum w/ Kalamu ya Salaam, Andrea Gereighty, Lee Mietzen Grue, Karen Celestan & Kysha Brown
1:15 Lionel Ferbos interviewed by Jason Berry
2:15 Louis Armstrong in New Orleans with Tad Jones, Tex Stephens & Helen Arlt
3:15 Kenny Bill Stinson interviewed by Mike Luster
4:15 John Sinclair interviewed by Douglas Brinkley

PARADES
12:00 Scene Boosters, Avenue Steppers, Jetsetter Ladies SA&PCs with Tornado Brass Band
1:00 Carrollton Hunters, Black Eagles and Ninth Ward Hunters Mardi Gras Indians
2:00 Louis Armstrong Memorial Second Line w/ Westbank Steppers, Original Men and Ladies Prince of Wales SA&PCs with Highsteppers Brass Band
3:00 Comanche Hunters, Cherokee Hunters & Mohawk Hunters Mardi Gras Indians
4:00 Original Lady Buck Jumpers, New Orleans Buck Jumper Men, Nine Times & Perfect Gentlemen SA&PCs with Hot 8 Brass Band

NIGHT CONCERTS

FRIDAY, APRIL 27, 9 P.M.
Brian McKnight
Chanté Moore
Morris F.X. Jeff Municipal Auditorium
FRIDAY, APRIL 27, 9 P.M.
Women In Jazz
Lillian Boutté, Germaine Bazzle, Leah Chase, Kim Prevost, Pat Cohen, Christina Machado, Rebecca Barry
Praline Connection Gospel & Blues Hall
SATURDAY, APRIL 28, 9 P.M.
Van Morrison / B.B. King
The Van Morrison Band
Morris F.X. Jeff Municipal Auditorium
SATURDAY, APRIL 28, 12 MIDNIGHT
Charlie B's Midnight Jazz
Roy Hargrove
Little Jimmy Scott
Praline Connection Gospel & Blues Hall
MONDAY, APRIL 30, 8 P.M.
The Armstrong Alumni All-Stars Featuring Arvell Shaw, Joe Muranyi, Franz Jackson, Tom Baker, Fred Lonzo, Ernest Elly, Lars Edegran
Palm Court Jazz Café
TUESDAY, MAY 1, 8 P.M.
The Armstrong Alumni All-Stars Featuring Arvell Shaw, Joe Muranyi, Franz Jackson, Tom Baker, Fred Lonzo, Ernest Elly, Lars Edegran
Palm Court Jazz Café
FRIDAY, MAY 4, 9 P.M.
Widespread Panic
The Wild Magnolias
Morris F.X. Jeff Municipal Auditorium
FRIDAY, MAY 4, 9 P.M.
New Orleans Blues Legends
Earl King, Snooks Eaglin
Special Guest M.C. John Sinclair
Praline Connection Gospel & Blues Hall
FRIDAY, MAY 4, 9 P.M.
La Noche Latina
Celia Cruz
The Johnny Pacheco Orchestra
House of Blues
SATURDAY, MAY 5, 9 P.M.
Paul Simon
Keb' Mo'
Morris F.X. Jeff Municipal Auditorium
SATURDAY, MAY 5, 12 MIDNIGHT
Charlie B's Midnight Jazz
James Moody & Marlena Shaw
Nu Legends featuring Idris Muhammad, Frank Morgan, Hilton Ruiz, Curtis Lundy, Bobby Watson, Donald Harrison
Praline Connection Gospel & Blues Hall

2002

Music is the main entree at Jazz Fest, but for some the food is a religious experience in its own right. One of the pleasures of returning to Jazz Fest year after year is running into your "Jazz Fest Family" at the Fair Grounds and making plans about in what restaurant you're going to meet for dinner.

You might think that the truly fabulous selection of foods that span all nations and tastes at the Fair Grounds would be enough, but no. People who come to New Orleans for the Jazz Fest are very serious about their music and their food and after a full day of eating and

listening to music, they're looking forward to a full night of eating, and listening to music.

Local restaurants in New Orleans do a roaring business throughout the two weeks of the Festival and the sophisticated palates of the Jazz Fest tribe are after the best taste bud sensations and the most New Orleans' style cooking to be had. This is a very broad spectrum. Local institutions like Dunbar's on Freret Street with their classic "home style" cooking and Jacques-Imo's on Oak Street, whose menu brings "deep frying" to a new and sublime level are two of the uptown favorites.

Many people pick Jacques-Imo's as a precursor to a night of music at the Maple Leaf, two doors down, Carrollton Station, which is right around

what's going on?

GLOBALLY

Introduction of Euro banknotes and coins in the European Union.

The UN food agency issued a warning to the world that more than 38 million Africans face the prospect of dying of starvation.

NATIONALLY

Kenneth L. Lay, Chairman of bankrupt energy trader Enron, resigns with his company under federal investigation for hiding debt and misrepresenting earnings.

NASA's Mars Odyssey probe finds huge reservoirs of ice below the surface of Mars, indicating that if it melted would be suitable for the development of life.

LOCALLY

The New Orleans Hornets of the National Basketball Association moved to the city starting in the 2002–2003 season.

Edwin Edwards begins serving a ten-year sentence in a federal penitentiary in Fort Worth, Texas.

Jazzland is purchased by Six Flags, Inc.

C. Ray Nagin becomes Mayor of New Orleans.

CULTURALLY

The National Academy of Sciences supports stem-cell research to aid in cures for Parkinson's Disease and diabetes.

Kmart Corp becomes the largest retailer in American history to file for Chapter 11 bankruptcy protection.

The MTV Reality series "The Osbournes" debuts with record audiences for the station, and wins an Emmy.

The Beltway snipers are arrested.

the corner, or Tipitina's, which is close enough to be justified. Both of these restaurants offer such large portions that a brisk walk or a night of hard dancing are recommended to offset the culinary experience.

Uglesich's on Baronne Street is only open for lunch on weekdays and one of the finest dining experiences in New Orleans. This little corner po-boy shop is packed year round with lines for lunch every day, but during the last week of April and the first week of May, it becomes a highly organized military operation for locals trying to secure tables for their visiting friends and family, and for out of towners making the pilgrimage in an endless stream of taxis and rental cars.

Mr. Anthony, owner of the family named business along with his wife Gail, when asked about how he feels about Jazz Fest crowds said simply "It's Hell, Darlin". He's threatened to close his doors for the last few years, but so far has been talked out of it by the faithful fans who swarm to his establishment, begging him and Ms. Gail to give them their "fix" of Shrimp and Grits, Fried Bleu Cheese Oysters, or Paul's Fantasy. All of the great chefs of

New Orleans have been spotted at one time or another eating on the corner of Baronne and Erato Street. Paul Prudhomme, proprietor of K-Paul's and Emeril Lagasse, whose three dining establishments in New Orleans are booked well in advance, have been quoted more than once recommending "Ugie's". Susan Spicer, chef and proprietress of Bayona's, located in the French Quarter and home of the best cream of garlic soup in the world is a fan, and Upperline Restaurant owner Joanne Clevenger, who sold flowers at the Jazz Fest in the 70's, says it's one of her favorites. Many people who come in for the second weekend of the Festival will head over to Uglesich's for breakfast on Thursday and Friday before they go to the Fair Grounds to eat some more. Maximo's is another hot spot for Jazz Fest visitors in the French Quarter. Jason Anixter, the owner of this fine dining establishment moved to New Orleans from Chicago and purchased the building in the early 80's because Luther Kent and his big band with Leslie Blackshear Smith were singing across the street. He

didn't feel he could lose with so much great music so close by. Of course, having some of the best northern Italian cuisine and a truly lovely wine list didn't hurt one bit. And it's open late.

This is a great spot for "musician spotting" during the Festival. In years past, Jason has sometimes hosted live music during the Fest, as has Mrs. Dunbar. On any given evening at Maximo's you might run into Eddie Volker, who is quite the wine gourmet; Kermit Ruffins, known to be a B-B-Q master in his own right, boiling vats of turkey necks for his adoring fans on his regular Thursday night stint at Vaughn's in the lower 9th ward; or such icons as locally born Herman Ernest, Art Neville, George Porter or members of the Iguanas.

fest facts

There are approximately 150 in the Fess Head Krewe, people who pay homage to Professor Longhair. The Fess Head is a bust that has support for a three quarter inch pole from at a local store, then dressed with moss from City Park, regalia from Mardi Gras, and all kinds of do-dads and goo-ga from people from all over the world. People are allowed to put anything they want on the Fess Head — within reason. The original Head, created from a mold of the Fess bust at Tipitina's, disappeared after the unfortunate death of its keeper. The current Fess Head was commissioned and made by artist Mark Nolting. The Fess Head Krewe crawfish boil is the second Saturday of the Fest. The band for the boil has always been George Porter and whomever he's runnin' with at the time. It was the George Porter and the Runnin' Partners for years.

Lenny Kravitz jumped down from the stage to dance with an elderly woman in the audience, singing "Give Peace a Chance."

Lady Charlotte

ing and musical gluttony that is New Orleans during the Fest.

In 2002 the independently promoted shows were the hot ticket. It's a clear testament to the successful growth of Jazz Fest that the attendance numbers were still growing at the Fair Grounds site but at the same time, night concerts, not associated with Festival Productions or the Heritage Foundation were garnering huge attendance. These music fans were part of the jam band culture and wanted to groove to bands like Phish, Panic, Galactic, Grey Boy Allstars and Government Mule. They loved George Porter and knew that the origin of the true funk was New Orleans, but they didn't really wanna go out all day to the Fair Grounds and get too hot and sweaty. Two days out of four was enough; they wanted to dine with their friends and then dance till 6 a.m.

By opening day, serious food fans like Laurie Miller from Chicago, Glenn Goldman of L.A., or Karen Breen from Long Island, had already called ahead to make reservations two or three evenings of Jazz Fest for at least a party of four, even if they didn't know who was dining with them yet. They had pre-decided a few nighttime events and purchased tickets, and left a couple of nights open to hit the clubs and play it by ear. Bernie Gudvi and Michael Visbal, two long time Jazz Fest fans from California always try to get in one Uglesich's and one dinner at Maximo's every trip. Each year they bring along another "cherry boy" a term meaning someone who has never been to the Jazz Festival before, and they enjoy taking their "cherry boy", around indoctrinating them into the din-

3:15 Bayou Healers with Southern Connection Drum
4:00 Flute Interlude with Tommy Wildcat
4:30 Muskogee Nation Performers feat. Jonny Hawk
5:45 The Bucks

RHODES GOSPEL TENT
11:00 Old Zion MBC Choir
11:45 Charles Jackson & Jackson Travelers
12:30 Melvin Winfield & New Vision
1:15 Family & Friends Ensemble
2:00 Morning Star MBC Mass Choir
2:45 Proclaimers of Christ Gospel Singers
3:30 The Holy Name Gospel Singers
4:15 Shondra & Great Jubilation
5:05 Slim & The Supreme Angels
6:05 Theo Bourgeois & Kennedy HS Gospel Choir

ALLISON MINER MUSIC HERITAGE STAGE
12:00 Curtis Fuller interviewed by Tom Piazza
1:00 Theryl deClouet, Galactic interviewed by Scott Jordan
2:00 Shemekia Copeland interviewed by Chuck Siler
3:00 Evangeline Made, Ann & Mark Savoy, Michael & David Doucet interviewed by Ben Sandmel
4:00 Joseph Shabalala – Ladysmith Black Mambazo interviewed by Dr. Gabou Mendy
5:00 Victor Goines interviewed by Jason Patterson
6:00 David Murray interveiwed by Mike Gourrier

PARADES
2:00 Pilotland Rollers and Sugar Hill Gang SA&PCs with Olympia Brass Band
4:00 Zulu Walking Warriors and The Original C.T.C. SA&PCs with Chop's Thunderstorm Brass Band

SATURDAY, APRIL 27

SPRINT PCS / LG MOBILE PHONE STAGE
11:10 The Strawberry Jammers
12:15 Michael Ward
1:25 Anders Osborn
2:50 The Dixie Cups
4:15 The Iguanas
5:45 Irma Thomas

BLUES TENT
11:30 Jeremy Lyons & The Deltabilly Boys
12:55 Mem Shannon & The Membership
2:20 Kenny Neal with special guest Deborah Coleman
4:05 Roy Rogers & The Delta Rhythm Kings
5:45 Clarence "Gatemouth" Brown & Gate's Express

ACURA STAGE
11:15 White Eagles Mardi Gras Indians
12:30 The Bucks
2:00 George Porter, Jr. & Runnin' Pardners
3:30 Galactic
5:30 Lenny Kravitz

SHERATON N.O. FAIS DO-DO STAGE
11:25 Goldman Thibodeaux and D'Jalma Garnier
12:45 D.L. Menard 7 the Louisiana Aces

Sam Butera (at Palm Court)

offered Phil Lesh and Friends along with Government Mule.

Of course both of these shows were very well attended.

Other longstanding traditions like La Noche' Latina on Friday, May 3rd were still going strong and once again they were packed in like sardines at the House Of Blues

For a sweaty night of hard, sexy dancing, those lucky enough to get into the show at The Praline Connection got the privilege of hearing two of New Orleans very special vocal-

As the competition for the dollars these music fans were bringing to town increased, wonderful combinations of national and local players started gracing the bill in clubs during Jazz Fest. Johnny Vidacovich, legendary jazz drummer from New Orleans created some beautiful musical relationships from these phenomena.

On May 2nd, 2002 Chris Wood of Medeski, Martin and Wood played with Johnny Vidacovich and June Yamagishi at the Old Point Bar. On May 4th, Charlie Hunter and Luther Dickinson worked with Johnny

"One of my favorite things is the Norman Dixon Jr. Annual Social Aid and Pleasure Club Annual Second Line Fund which is a 501(C)3 nonprofit organization, and the New Orleans Jazz & Heritage Foundation partially underwrites police costs for all the second lines in New Orleans. The city needs more policemen as the social aid and pleasure clubs, their costumes, their organizations, and their bands, have gotten bigger and bigger." QUINT DAVIS

Kermit Ruffins

once again at Old Point, then on the 5th, Skerik, who is a huge presence on the jam band scene worked with Johnny and Jim Singleton. This creative booking brought a new generation of music fans into contact with artists that have influenced countless musicians and greatly enriched the club scene during Jazz Fest.

Karl Denson's Tiny Universe – another group that now comes to town annually, shared a bill with Lenny Kravitz on Friday, April 26th. Closing the night concert series on Saturday. May 4th the Fest

ists, Juanita Brooks and Topsy Chapman. You don't ever want to miss an opportunity to hear either of these ladies. Topsy's background is straight ahead jazz and gospel, Juanita's is old school soul deeply dipped in gospel, but she can wrap her voice around anything. Both of these artists spend a good part

of their time overseas where thousands of adoring fans always welcome them with open arms. Big Al Carson also graced this bill with a superb backing band.

One of the most talked about shows at the Fair Grounds was the amazing performance by the Heath Brothers on Sunday, April 28th in the Bell South Jazz

Robert Parker

Tent starting at 3:55. These masters of jazz had everyone riveted. Their timeless perfection was something to witness and will never be forgotten by those fortunate enough to be there. "The thing that impressed me the most about the whole set was when the oldest brother said 'this next song features my youngest brother who happens to be 75. These guys were in their 80's and they were playing like young men. It was just unbelievable. They were such accomplished all around musicians," opined Kenneth Diaz. Dave Malone, when he played later that night in town with the Radiators even mentioned it on the mic "Man! How about the Heath brothers — was that incredible?" With a combined 150 years of experience to draw upon the Heath Brothers mesmerized a packed, spellbound tent.

Safety concerns at the Fair Grounds because of the 9/11 tragedy caused increased security at the Fair Grounds. This forced the *Krew (sic) of Fess* to take great lengths to make sure their mascot quietly got on the infield. The head of "Fess" had been a presence at the Fair Grounds since 1998. The cast of Professor Longhair's head was made from a sculpture created by Coco Robicheaux for Tipitina's. Marco Steinberg, an original member of the Fess Head Krew went into Tip's with his posse, who hid him from security while a mold of the bust was taken. The Tri-Coastal Krew, comprised of around 150 hard-core members, use the pole with Fess's head atop as a beacon at Jazz Fest. Wherever you see the head of Fess — you know the music's good. In spite

of heightened security and a ban on objects of that size, Fess was smuggled in and was seen at countless shows, both weekends carried proudly by Krew members. Leslie Blackshear Smith doesn't know anything about the details; neither does James Brooks.

"At Jazz Fest 2002 my band played the Economy Hall Tent. My brother Louis, a gospel singer, came and sang 'Old Rugged Cross.' Along with my brother Michael, on piano, that was the only time we all three played in public together. Louis passed away in September 2003, so that is my favorite Jazz Fest memory." JOE TORREGANO

music scene

"Instruments A' Comin" benefit at Tipitina's raises $22,000 to purchase music instruments for area school children.

Beausoleil is nominated for 9th Grammy Award

Tex Stephens passes.

IN MEMORIAM

Duke Dejan, Josheph Brown, Sr., Anthony Chavis, Wilson "Boozoo" Chavis, Sterling Desmond, Jerome "Jerry" Greene, Lionel Hampton, Jason "Jam Master Jay" Mizell, Gerald "Jake" Million, Rodger Poché, Jr. Alvin "LB" Bridges Price, Omar Aziz, Sr., Rana Adams, Bebe Carriere, Julius Farmer, Arthur "Guitar" Kelly, Fate "FD Sims, George "Tex" Stephens, Jr., Lionel Tapo, Sr., Roy Varnado, david Lee Watson, Sylvia "Kuumba" Williams, Joe Henderson, John Lee Hooker, John Jackson, Etta Jones, Nauman Scott, Rufus Thomas

2:00 James Burton interviewed by Scott Jordan
3:00 The Second-Line Tradition Panelists: William "Jimmy" Parker, Norvin "Bull" Deverney interviewed by Dr. Maurice Martinez
4:00 David "Fathead" Newman interviewed by Lorraine Farr
5:45 Elvin Bishop interviewed by Ben Sandmel

PARADES
12:00 Original Step-N-Style, Single Men, Valley of the Silent Mean and Old & Nu Style Fellas SA&PCs with Paulin Brothers Brass Band
1:00 Red, White & Blue, Geronimo Hunters and Trouble Nation Mardi Gras Indians
2:00 Devastation, Devastating Ladies, Felicity St. Steppers and Money Wasters SA&PCs with Mahogany Brass Band
3:00 Golden Blades, Wild Tchoupitoulas and Young Hunters Mardi Gras Indians
4:00 Lady Sequence, No Limit & Big Nine Steppers SA&PCs in Economy Hall Tent

SUNDAY, APRIL 28

SPRINT PCS / LG MOBILE PHONE STAGE
11:10 UNO Jazz Ensemble
12:20 The Proud Marys
1:35 Continental Drifters
2:55 Robert Mirabal: Portraits from a Painted Cave
4:10 Rebirth Brass Band
5:45 Cowboy Mouth

BLUES TENT
11:15 Jumpin' Johnny Sansone
12:25 Lil' Buck Blues Band with guest Jerry McCain
1:35 Eddie Bo
3:05 Chris Thomas King
4:15 Marva Wright & The BMWs
5:45 Elvin Bishop

ACURA STAGE
11:15 Young Cheyenne Mardi Gras Indians
12:25 Frankie Ford
1:45 Allen Toussaint
3:15 Dr. John
5:10 Melissa Etheridge

SHERATON N.O. FAIS DO-DO STAGE
11:20 Poncho Chavis & The Magic Sounds
12:25 Charivari
1:45 Kevin Naquin & The Ossun Playboys
3:05 Geno Delafose & French Rockin' Boogie
4:30 New Orleans Klezmer Allstars
6:00 Nathan & The Zydeco Cha Chas

BELLSOUTH / WWOZ JAZZ TENT
11:15 Xavier University Jazz Ensemble
12:20 Germaine Bazzle
1:30 Marlon Jordan
2:40 Ellis Marsalis Quintet
3:55 The Heath Brothers feat. Jimmy, Percy and Albert "Tootie" Heath & Jeb Patton
5:30 Tribute to Ella Fitzgerald feat. The Count Basie Orchestra w/ special guest Patti Austin

XM SATELLITE RADIO ECONOMY HALL TENT
11:15 Kid Simmons' Local Int'l Allstar Jazz Band
12:20 Onward Brass Band

1:30 Rene Netto & Sounds of New Orleans
2:40 Bob French & The Original Tuxedo Jazz Band w/ Friends
4:05 Clive Wilson's N.O. Jazz Serenaders w/ guest Butch Thompson revisiting Kid Ory
5:45 Linda Hopkins

CONGO SQUARE STAGE
11:15 DJ Duck and Choppa
12:55 La Banda Blanca of Honduras
2:30 Chiekh Lô of Senegal
4:05 Wynton Marsalis
5:55 Teddy Pendergrass

LAGNIAPPE STAGE
11:20 The Poor Clares
12:25 NOCCA Jazz Ensemble
1:35 Little Freddie King Blues Band
2:50 Iron Mountain Native Dancers
4:05 Lil' Rascals Brass Band
5:45 Paky Saavedra's Bandido

NATIVE AMERICAN VILLAGE STAGE
11:30 Muskogee Nation Performer feat. Jonny Hawk
12:45 Iron Mountain Native Dancers
1:30 Flute Interlude with Tommy Wildcat
2:00 The Bucks
3:15 Muskogee Nation Performers feat. Jonny Hawk
4:00 Flute Interlude with Tommy Wildcat
4:30 The Bucks
5:45 Robert Mirabal

RHODES GOSPEL TENT
11:00 Second Mt. Carmel Gospel Choir
11:45 Nita Happy Trelle
12:30 The Bester Singers
1:15 One A-Chord
2:00 Beacon Light BC Choir
2:45 Jo "Cool" Davis
3:30 Val & Love Alive Fellowship Choir
4:15 The Melody Clouds
5:05 Potter's House Mass Choir
6:05 Dimensions of Faith

ALLISON MINER MUSIC HERITAGE STAGE
12:00 Music of America's River – Capt. Clarke "Doc" Hawley interviewed by Ben Sandmel
1:00 A Tribute to Boozoo Chavis – Panelists: Poncho Chavis, Leona Chavis, Danielle Bias, Michael Tisserand
2:00 Linda Hopkins interviewed by Jerry Brock
3:00 Sam Butera and Friends interviewed by Michael Tisserand
4:00 Jerry McCain interviewed by John Sinclair
5:00 Adam Duritz – Counting Crows interviewed by David Fricke, Rolling Stone
6:00 Wynton Marsalis interviewed by Lolis Eric Elie

PARADES
12:00 Olympia Aid, Uptowners' Hobo Clowns and New Look SA&PCs with Pinstripe Brass Band
12:20 Economy Hall Parade – Calendar Girls SA&PC
1:00 Wild Apache and Yellow Jackets Mardi Gras Indians
2:00 Unknown Steppers, Original Four and Avenue steppers SAPCs with Lil' Stooges Brass Band

3:00 Comanche Hunter, Ninth Ward Hunter and Flaming Arrows Mardi Gras Indians
4:00 Untouchables, Furious Five and Single Ladies SAPCs with Hot 8 Brass Band

THURSDAY, MAY 2

SPRINT PCS / LG MOBILE PHONE STAGE
11:30 Ya Ya Sol
1:00 The Allison Collins Band
2:25 Charmaine Neville Band with Reggie Houston and Amasa Miller
3:55 Jon Cleary & The Absolute Monster Gentlemen
5:35 Ralph Stanley & The Clinch Mountain Boys

BLUES TENT
11:20 Spencer Bohren
12:30 J. Monque'D Blues Band
1:40 James Andrews
2:55 Sherman Robertson
4:10 Earl King & The Butanes
5:40 Delbert McClinton

ACURA STAGE
11:15 Love Jones
12:35 Irene Sage
2:05 Los Hombres Calientes feat. Bill Summers and Irvin Mayfield
3:45 Gov't Mule
5:40 Blues Traveler

SHERATON N.O. FAIS DO-DO STAGE
11:15 Otter Trail Singers
12:25 Lesa Cormier, August Broussard & The

SUNDOWN PLAYBOYS
1:35 Evening Star String Band
2:55 007
4:20 Basin Brothers
5:50 Horace Trahan * the New Ossun Express

BELLSOUTH /WWOZ JAZZ TENT
11:30 Ricky Sebastian Quartet
12:35 M.Q. 20/20 feat. Maurice Brown & Quamon Fowler
1:40 John Boutté
2:55 Kermit Ruffins & The Barbecue Swingers
4:15 Leah Chase
5:40 Charles Mingus 80th Birthday Tribute Orchestra

XM SATELLITE RADIO ECONOMY HALL TENT
11:20 Kid Merv Jazz Band
12:30 Andrew Hall's Society Brass Band
1:40 Louis Ford & His N.O. Dixieland Flares
2:55 Chris Clifton
4:20 Walter Payton & Snapbeans
5:45 Banu Gibson & New Orleans Hot Jazz w. guest Fayard Nicholas

CONGO SQUARE STAGE
11:00 Kineh Tah' Navajo Dancers
11:25 Mama Efuru
11:30 Culu Children Trad. African Dance Co.
11:55 Mama Efuru
12:00 Horace Trahan
12:25 Mama Efuru
12:50 Los Sagitarios
2:05 Clarence "Frogman" Henry
3:20 Nation of Change

4:30 The Revealers
6:00 King Floyd

LAGNIAPPE STAGE
11:30 Clancy "Blues Boy" Lewis & Sheba Kimbrough
12:30 Hazel & The Delta Ramblers
1:40 Micaela y Flamenca Fiesta
2:50 Kerry Grombacher
4:15 Roderick Paulin & The Grovers
5:45 Irie Dawtas

NATIVE AMERICAN VILLAGE STAGE
11:30 Kostini
12:45 Butch Mudbone
1:30 Flute Interlude with Hawk Henries
2:00 Otter Trail Singers
3:15 Dineh Tah' Navaho Dancers
4:00 Flute Interlude with Hawk Henries
4:30 Otter Trail Singers
5:45 Nation of Change

RHODES GOSPEL TENT
11:00 J.C. & Company
11:45 Southern Gospel Singers
12:30 Mount Pilgrim BC Choir
1:15 First Revolution
2:00 St. Maria Goretti Gospel Choir
2:45 The Golden Wings
3:30 Sarah T. Reed Gospel Choir
4:15 Lyle Henderson
5:05 The Blind Boys of Alabama feat. Clarence Fountain
6:05 The Coolie Family

ALLISON MINER MUSIC HERITAGE STAGE
12:00 Sue Mingus interviewed by Kalamu ya Salaam
1:30 Songwriters Workshop w/ Tracey Wright, Lynn Drury and Skeet Hanks
3:00 Blind Boys of Alabama interviewed by Dr. Joyce Jackson
4:00 Horace Trahan interviewed by Nick Spitzer
5:00 Lonnie Brooks interviewed by Grant Morris

PARADES
3:00 Bon Temp Roulez SA&PC with Storyville Stompers Brass Band

FRIDAY, MAY 3

SPRINT PCS / LG MOBILE PHONE STAGE
11:30 Loyola University Jazz Band
12:45 Dash Rip Rock
2:20 Leo Nocentelli
3:55 The Dirty Dozen Brass Band
5:30 Karl Denson's Tiny Universe

BLUES TENT
11:10 Semolian Warriors Mardi Gras Indians
12:15 Henry Gray & The Cats
1:25 Tab Benoit
2:45 Henry Butler
4:10 Lonnie Brooks
5:45 Deacon John

ACURA STAGE
11:20 Zion
12:35 Nation of Change
1:50 Wayne Toups
3:25 Marcia Ball
5:25 Bonnie Raitt

SHERATON N.O. FAIS DO-DO STAGE
11:20 Elaine Townsend
12:30 Kim Carson & The Casualties
1:40 Bruce Daigrepont

2:55 La Bande "Feufollet"
4:20 Jude Taylor & His Burning Flames
5:50 Sean Ardoin –n– Zydekool

BELLSOUTH / WWOZ JAZZ TENT
11:40 Ed Perkins Groups
1:05 Jeremy Davenport
2:25 Irvin Mayfield
3:50 Donald Harrison, Jr.
5:30 The Yellowjackets

XM SATELLITE RADIO ECONOMY HALL TENT
11:25 Doc Paulin's Dixieland Band
12:35 June Gardner & The Fellows
1:45 Jon Seiger & The All-Stars
2:55 Ingrid Lucia & The Flying Neutrinos
4:15 New Orleans Ragtime Orchestra
5:45 Michael White & The Original Liberty Jazz Band w/ guest Thais Clark

CONGO SQUARE STAGE
11:15 Kumbuka Drum & Dance Collective
12:25 Chucky C & Clearly Blues
1:35 Dineh Tah' Navajo Dancers
2:45 Jean Knight
4:05 Oliver Mtukudzi & Black Spirits of Zimbabwe

LAGNIAPPE STAGE
11:30 Delgado Jazz Ensemble
12:35 Patrice Fisher & Arpa w/ guests Graciela Barretto & Cuatro Cuerdas of Venezuela
1:45 Sherman
3:00 Charles Neville Jazz Ensemble
4:25 Mike Younger
5:50 Joe Krown Organ Combo

NATIVE AMERICAN VILLAGE STAGE
11:30 Hawk Henries
12:45 Otter Trail Singers
1:30 Flute Interlude with Tommy Wildcat
2:00 Nation of Change
3:15 Otter Trail Singers
4:00 Flute Interlude with Tommy Wildcat
4:30 Bill Miller
5:45 Dineh Tah' Navajo Dancers

RHODES GOSPEL TENT
11:00 Jerusalem BC Choir
11:45 The Dynamic Smooth Family
12:30 Leviticus Gospel Singers
1:15 The Unstoppable Gospel Creators Gospel Singers
2:00 New Zion Trio Plus One
2:45 Praise Community Choir
3:30 The Banks Family
4:15 Greater Antioch Music Ministry
5:05 Liz McComb
6:05 McDonogh #35 Gospel Choir

ALLISON MINER MUSIC HERITAGE STAGE
12:00 Carol Fran interviewed by Nick Spitzer
1:00 Oliver Mtukudzi interviewed by Dr. Gabou Mendy
2:00 Mike Younger interviewed by John Sinclair
3:00 Sean Ardoin interviewed by Herman Fuselier
4:00 Steve Conn
5:00 Gina Forsythe

PARADES
11:25 Economy Hall Parade with Algiers Steppers SA&PC
2:00 Double Nine Highsteppers,

Millennium Steppers and Singe Men Kids SA&PCs with New Wave Brass Band
4:00 Young Men 2 Old Men Legends, New Generation and Nandi Exclusive Gentlemen & Ladies SAPCs with Untouchables Brass Band

SATURDAY, MAY 4

SPRINT PCS / LG MOBILE PHONE STAGE
11:15 SUBR Jazz Ensemble
12:25 Theresa Andersson
1:40 Zigaboo Modeliste & The Funk Revue
2:55 Big Chief Bo Dollis & The Wild Magnolias
4:10 Terrance Simien
5:40 Better Than Ezra

BLUES TENT
11:15 Golden Star Hunters Mardi Gras Indians
12:20 Big Al Carson
1:30 Raful Neal, Jr. w/ Oscar "Harpo" Davis
3:00 Luther Kent & Trick Bag
4:25 Lil' Ed & The Blues Imperials
5:50 Snooks Eaglin

ACURA STAGE
11:20 Jamal Batiste & The Jam-Allstars
12:35 Reggie Hall & The Twilighters
1:55 Lloyd Price
3:30 Lil' Band O' Gold with Spec. Guests John Fred and Johnnie Allan
5:30 Jimmy Buffett & The Coral Reefer Band

SHERATON N.O. FAIS DO-DO STAGE
11:20 Rudy's Caribbean Funk Band
12:30 The Hackberry Ramblers
1:45 The Bluerunners
3:00 Dwayne Dopsie & The Zydeco Hellraisers
4:30 Lil' Malcolm & The House Rockers
6:00 Willis Prudhomme & Zydeco Express

BELLSOUTH / WWOZ JAZZ TENT
11:15 Rebecca Barry and Bill Huntington
12:25 Earl Turbinton
1:35 Alvin Batiste & The Jazztronauts
2:50 James Rivers Movement
4:10 Terence Blanchard
5:40 Joe Lovano Nonet

XM SATELLITE RADIO ECONOMY HALL TENT
11:20 Joseph Torregano
12:25 Original Dixieland Jazz Band
1:35 Algiers Brass Band
2:50 Tricia "Sista Teedy" Boutté
4:15 New Leviathan Oriental Foxtrot Orchestra
5:45 Liz McComb The Spirit of New Orleans

CONGO SQUARE STAGE
11:15 Nation of Change
12:15 Souljah Slim and MYSELF
2:00 Gilberto Santa Rosa of Puerto Rico
3:45 Morgan Heritage
5:35 Bobby Womack

LAGNIAPPE STAGE
11:20 Humphrey Davis & Nightlife
12:35 Troy "Trombone Shorty" Andrews

2:00 Dineh Tah' Navajo Dancers
3:05 Uptown Okra w/ John Boutté
4:20 Sharon Martin & First Take
5:45 Ritmo Caribeno

NATIVE AMERICAN VILLAGE STAGE
11:30 Dineh Tah' Navajo Dancers
12:45 Medicine Tail
1:30 Flute Interlude with Hawk Henries
2:00 Dineh Tah' Navajo Dancers
3:15 Medicine Tail
4:00 Flute Interlude with Hawk Henries
4:30 Dineh Tah' Navajo Dancers
5:45 Nation of Change

RHODES GOSPEL TENT
11:00 The Wimberly Family
11:45 Providence BC Male Chorus
12:30 John Lee & The Heralds of Christ
1:15 Pastor Ray Inglehart & Gloryland
2:00 Ebenezer MBC Choir
2:45 Crown Seekers Gospel Singers
3:30 The Davis Family
4:15 The Rocks of Harmony
5:05 Evangelist Bertha Jackson & The Anointed Jackson Sisters
6:05 Watson Memorial Teaching Ministries

ALLISON MINER MUSIC HERITAGE STAGE
1:00 Dr. Michael White interviewed by Jerry Brock
2:00 John Fred interviewed by Mike Luster
3:00 Bob Weir interviewed by Dr. Douglas Brinkley
4:00 Doug Kershaw interviewed by Katera Yager
5:00 J. Monque'D interviewed by Steve Armbruster

PARADES
12:00 Dumaine Street Gang, Dumaine St. Ladies and Original Big Seven SA&PCs with Pinettes Brass Band
1:00 White Cloud Easten Hunters, Cherokee Hunters and New Orleans Rhythm Mardi Gras Indians
1:35 Economy Hall Parade with Nine Time Ladies SA&PC
2:00 Pigeon Town Steppers, N'Krumah Better Boys and Divine Ladies SA&PCs with New Birth Brass Band
3:00 Indians of the Nation, Bayou Renegades and Black Eagles Mardi Gras Indians
4:00 Second Line Jammers, Black Men of Labor and Happy House SA&PCs with Tremé Brass Band

SUNDAY, MAY 5

SPRINT PCS / LG MOBILE PHONE STAGE
11:15 SUNO Jazz Ensemble
12:20 Fredy Omar con su Banda
1:30 Papa Grows Funk
2:45 The Dudes
4:15 Buckwheat Zydeco
5:45 The Radiators

BLUES TENT
11:20 B.B. Major Blues Band
12:25 Pat "Mother Blues" Cohen
1:35 Wanda Rouzan & a Taste of New Orleans
2:55 Corey Harris

4:20 Walter "Wolfman" Washington & The Roadmasters
5:45 John Mooney & Bluesiana

ACURA STAGE
11:10 Dineh Tah' Navajo Dancers
12:10 Monk Boudreaux & The Golden Eagles w/ Brian Stoltz
1:30 Ratdog
3:15 Phil Lesh & Friends
5:30 The Neville Brothers

SHERATON N. O. FAIS DO-DO STAGE
11:45 Jesse Legé & The Southern Ramblers
1:00 Allen Fontenot & The Country Cajuns
2:25 Rosie Ledet & The Zydeco Playboys
4:00 Steve Riley & The Mamou Playboys
5:45 Chris Ardoin & Double Clutchin'

BELLSOUTH / WWOZ JAZZ TENT
11:15 Richwell Ison
12:20 Al Belletto Big Jazz Band
1:30 Kid Jordan – Al Fielder & IAQ
2:45 David Sanchez
4:20 Abbey Lincoln
5:55 Nicholas Payton's Soul Patrol

XM SATELLITE RADIO ECONOMY HALL TENT
11:20 Soprano Meets Clarinet of Sweden
12:25 Placide Adams & The Orig. Dixieland Hall Jazz Band
1:35 Gregg Stafford's Jazz Hounds
3:00 Don Vappie's Creole Jazz Serenaders
4:25 Pete Fountain
6:00 Preservation Hall Jazz Band

CONGO SQUARE STAGE
11:30 Los Babies
1:00 Casper "Reggae Inn Hopiland"
2:20 Papa Wemba & Viva La Musica of the Congo
4:00 The Baha Men
5:35 Teena Marie

LAGNIAPPE STAGE
11:25 Po' Henry & Tookie
12:30 Herman Jackson
1:40 Chévere
3:00 Woodenhead
4:25 Percussion, Inc.
5:50 Javier Gutierrez & Acoustic Swiftness

NATIVE AMERICAN VILLAGE STAGE
11:30 Butch Mudbone
12:45 Dineh Tah' Navajo Dancers
1:30 Flute Interlude with Hawk Henries
2:00 Medicine Tail
3:15 Butch Mudbone
4:00 Flute Interlude with Hawk Henries
4:30 Medicine Tail
5:45 Nation of Change

RHODES GOSPEL TENT
11:00 Cosmopolitan Evangelist BC Choir
11:45 Antioch Gospel Singers
12:30 Octavia Denise & The 5 Stars of Praise
1:15 Paulette Wright Davis
2:00 New Orleans Spiritualettes
2:45 The Johnson Extension
3:30 Sherman Washington & The Zion Harmonizers
4:15 Aaron Neville
5:05 Cosmopolitan Church of Prayer Choir
6:05 Tyrone Foster & The Arc Angels

ALLISON MINER MUSIC HERITAGE STAGE
11:45 Samirah Evans & Friends interviewed by Nikki Reyes
1:00 Ernie K-Doe Tribute Panelists: Antoinette K-Doe, Cosimo Matassa, Allen Toussaint, Ben Sandmel
2:00 Acapella Cajun & Creole Ballads – Veillee
3:00 Music Connection: Jazz & Ramp w/ Harold Battiste and DJ Jubliee interviewed by Karen Celestan
4:00 Lawrence "Larry" Batiste – Young Tuxedo Brass Band interviewed by Tad Jones

PARADES
12:00 Jetsetters Ladies, Scene Boosters, Popular Ladies and Distinguished Gentlemen SA&PCs with Tornado Brass Band
1:00 Creole Wild West and Carrollton Hunters Mardi Gras Indians
3:00 Golden Arrows and Mohawk Hunters Mardi Gras Indians

NIGHT CONCERTS

FRIDAY, APRIL 26, 9 P.M.
Lenny Kravitz
Karl Denson's Tiny Universe
Morris F.X. Jeff Municipal Auditorium
SATURDAY, APRIL 27, 9 P.M.
Melissa Etheridge
Taj Mahal & The Phantom Blues Band
Morris F.X. Jeff Municipal Auditorium
SUNDAY, APRIL 28, 8 P.M.
Jazz At the Palm Court
Jump, Jive & Swing with Sam Butera & The Wildest
Palm Court Jazz Café
MONDAY, APRIL 29, 8 P.M.
Jazz At the Palm Court
Presenting the Jazz, Blues & Gospel Great Linda Hopkins
Palm Court Jazz Café
TUESDAY, APRIL 30, 8 P.M.
Jazz At the Palm Court
Sweet, Hot and Low Down N.O. Jazz Revue with Juanita Brooks, Topsy Chapman, Big Al Carson, Lars Edegran, Mark Brooks, Ernest Elly, Fredy Lonzo, Evan Christopher, Duke Heitger and special guest Butch Thompson
Palm Court Jazz Café
FRIDAY, MAY 3, 8 P.M.
La Noche Latina
Gilberto Santa Rosa
Fredy Omar Con Su Banda
House of Blues
FRIDAY, MAY 3, 9 P.M.
Lloyd Price "Mr. Personality" & The "A" Team Band Reggie Hall & The Twilighters Featuring Lady Lois & Albert "Dogman" Smith
Praline Connection Gospel & Blues Hall
SATURDAY, MAY 4, 9 P.M.
Phil Lesh & Friends
Gov't Mule
Morris F.X. Jeff Municipal Auditorium
SATURDAY, MAY 4, 12 MIDNIGHT
Charlie B's Midnight Jazz
Yellow Jackets
Astral Project
Praline Connection
Gospel & Blues Hall

2003

The Crescent City is a creative mystery. No one is really sure why, but new sounds and unique talents continue to evolve from this little dot on the global map. Artists come from all over the world to soak up some of our special brand of funk, or drink some magical elixir in the French Quarter that will syncopate them into traditional jazz virtuosos. New Orleans born musicians are sprinkled throughout successful groups of all styles all over the world. There is no question that something special keeps happening here, that doesn't quite happen the same anywhere else.

New Orleans has also shaped many artists who are now adopted "locals"- and our "adopted locals" had it going on in 2003 at the New Orleans Jazz & Heritage Festival.

Mike Pellera from upstate New York came to town after rooming with David Torkanowsky at Berkley School of music and found it impossible to leave. Now he has become one

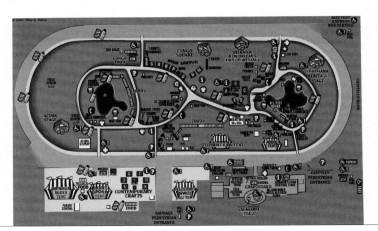

of the sought after sidemen in New Orleans and at Jazz Festival 2003 could be heard backing the fabulous Ms. Leah Chase on her show in the Jazz Tent, and Leslie Smith on Fais Do-Do.

Jon Cleary from Great Britain, after being exposed to the recordings of Professor Longhair, Snooks Eaglin and Clifton Chenier through his uncle, a musician who lived in New Orleans for a while, became determined to visit and get a taste in person. At 17, Jon came to town for the first time, and he never could stay away for long. His musical bond with New Orleans became so strong that in the end he just had to make it home.

Jon Cleary and the Monster Gentlemen gave it all up on the Sprint Stage, delivering a seri-

ously funky show with the sweat flowing as freely as the musical riffs. Cornell Williams on bass, a ridiculously funky man and long time musical partner of Jon's, was throwing out intensely good vibes and playing their music flawlessly.

Jeffrey "Jellybean" Alexander had it rock solid on the bottom and Derwin "Big D" Perkins on guitar fed the groove as Jon did his thing on keyboards.

Theresa Andersson and Anders Osborne, both from Sweden, made the pilgrimage together and have never looked back. Theresa secured a place for herself in Jazz Festival history with "the dropping of the skirt," perhaps the most talked about event of '03. A very skilled vocalist and violinist and quite easy on the eyes, Theresa slugged it out in the

Michael White and Ernest "Doc" Paulin

Victor Goines

"I've played Jazz Fest every year from 1984 on, with various artists; so it's hard to choose just one favorite moment. Among my best memories are shows with blues guitarist Drink Small in 1989; blues pianist Sunnyland Slim in 1990, and the Hackberry Ramblers in 2003. When the audience shouts and dances it's the ultimate complement, and they did so at all these sets. I've also had some special moments conducting interviews at the Music Heritage Stage; asking Ernie K-Doe if he was really born at Touro Infirmary; talking with Don Helms, who played steel guitar on all of Hank Williams's hits; sitting next to Lucinda Williams while she sang "Lake Charles;" and sitting next to Howard Armstrong while he played an incredibly heartfelt rendition of "Summertime." My only Jazz Fest regret is that I couldn't coordinate a cameo collaboration by Ernie K-Doe and The Hackberry Ramblers, trading lead vocals on "Jambalaya." All concerned were into it, but the logistics just didn't click." BEN SANDMEL

clubs for years, first as sideman to ex-boyfriend Anders Osborne, singing background and playing fiddle, and eventually branching out on her own. In a fun and playful Festival spirit, Theresa, after donning a bikini bathing suit, had her body artistically painted before her performance at Jazz Festival. She wore a long wrap around skirt for the start of her show, but after a few tunes she took it off and the fans went nuts. It was a hot day, and David Torkanowsky, who had come on stage to jam on accordion, kept hoping the paint would melt off, even going so far as to dash some water in her direction at one point. "It's water proof, David" Theresa smilingly replied. Needless to say, her shows about town were sold out the rest of the Festival. Theresa was also spotted sitting in with Papa Grows Funk, a group kept funky by some serious foot delivered by Russell Batiste on drums, Mark Pero on bass, and another adopted local, Japanese import June Yamagishi on guitar. Monster drummer "Mean" Willie Green, who also lays down the funk as part of the Nevilles organization was providing the grooves for Theresa's show. Willie has been a frequent guest with the

Preservation Hall Band

Grateful Dead, Carlos Santana, recorded with numerous artists including Bob Dylan's CD "Oh Mercy" and has contributed his musical talents to a huge list of internationally known groups. Lloyd Lambert on bass, whose father was also a bass player, Glen LeBlanc on guitar and John Gros rounded out Theresa's line-up for this show.

One of the great lyrical and musical blessings of New Orleans, Earl King, made his last visit to the New Orleans Jazz & Heritage Festival in 2003. He would pass away but will live forever through the astounding long time contribution he made to the music and culture. Song classics such as "Trick Bag" and "Big Chief", generally attributed to Professor Longhair, and countless others have defined a whole era of New Orleans music. Another favorite local classic of Earl's is "Make a Better World." He sure did with his powerful music and beautiful spirit. Earl often teamed with personnel from the Radiators and, before that, the Rhapsodizers. Wednesdays in the 70s were reserved for gigs at

Ben Harper

Luigi's Pizza where one night two fans from Scandinavia showed up two days after Earl's birthday and proceeded to recount the festivities, much to the guitarist's amazement. They knew all the details, in the days before the Internet! Meanwhile, Alan Langhoff continued to pop the gator and Wesley Schmidt, the later marching club grand marshall, served up pitchers of beer. In those days there was no stage, and the fish heads (official fans of the Radiators) were not yet invented, but the following was

Gatemouth Brown

as rabid as today for the Rads.

Back at the Festival, The Partner's gig was a hot one. This group is comprised of bassist George Porter with Leslie Martin on keys, James Varando on Drums and Clarence Johnson III on tenor saxophone but an impromptu "Running Partners" reunion occurred when trombonist and leader of Bonarama Mark Mullins, Tracy Griffin on trumpet and Brent Anderson on guitar joined the stage at the start of the show. As if that wasn't enough, Ivan Neville jumped up on the B3 organ, turning what was supposed to be a 4 piece

band into a 9 piece. These types of musical surprises often happen at Jazz Festival. The band, and the crowd had a great time.

George was also doing plenty of off site work in 03' as in years past. One of the highlights was a performance at the Saenger Theatre with Govt. Mule on May 3rd to a sold out show for a live CD and DVD recording *The Deepest End – Live in Concert*. Other New Orleans luminaries who contributed to the recording that night included Ivan Neville and the Dirty Dozen Brass Band. True to the tradition of amazing shows that happen during Jazz Festival in New Orleans,

12:20 Doc Paulin's Original Dixieland Jazz Band
1:35 The Pfister Sisters
2:55 Clive Wilson's New Orleans Serenaders featuring Butch Thompson
4:20 Greg Stafford's Jazz Hounds
5:50 Lars Edegran New Orleans / Chicago Express feat. Franz Jackson & Sammy Rimington

CONGO SQUARE STAGE
11:10 Willie Metcalf & The World Peace Movement
12:20 Tondrae
1:25 Irie Vibrations
2:40 Jimmy and Syl Johnson
4:10 Marcé et Toumpak of Martinique
5:45 Cyril Neville & The Uptown Allstars

LAGNIAPPE STAGE
11:15 David & Roselyn
12:20 Golden Star Hunters Mardi Gras Indians
1:30 Renée McCrary
2:50 Javier Tobar & Elegant Gypsy
4:20 Freestyle Nation
5:50 Percussion, Inc.

NATIVE AMERICAN VILLAGE STAGE
11:30 Red House Singers and Dancers
12:45 Treater
1:30 Tommy Wildcat
2:00 Carolina Tuscarora Stomp & Smoke Dancers
3:15 Butch Mudbone
4:00 Tommy Wildcat
4:30 Red House Singers and Dancers
5:45 Carolina Tuscarora Stomp & Smoke Dancers

RHODES GOSPEL TENT
11:00 Gregg Martinez
11:45 Charles Jackson & The Jackson Travelers
12:30 Morning Star BC Choir
1:15 Jay East & Power
2:00 John Lee & The Heralds of Christ
2:45 Voices of Distinction
3:30 Therrow Scott & Tehillah
4:15 St. James A.M.E. Combined Choir
5:10 Spencer Taylor & The Highway QCs
6:15 UNO Gospel Choir

ALLISON MINER MUSIC HERITAGE STAGE
12:00 Manuel Obregon interviewed by Tom McDermott
1:00 Members of Marcé et Toumpak from Martinique, interviewed by Gene Scaramuzzo
2:00 Belton Richard, interviewed by Kateri Yager
3:00 Vernel Bagneris, Jerry Brock
4:30 Syl & Jimmy interviewed by Johnson Ben Sandmel
5:30 Lucinda Williams interviewed by Ben Sandmel

PARADES
12:20 Economy Hall Parade with Algiers Steppers SA&PC
2:00 Pilotland Rollers and Jolly Bunch SA&PCs with New Orleans Nightcrawlers Brass Band
3:00 Plastic System Band of Martinique
4:00 Zulu Walking Warriors & Original CTC SA&PCs with Lil' Stooges Brass Band

sweating, dancing fans at the Saenger Theater were treated to over 6 hours of music with too many people sitting in to list.

Lady BJ Crosby returned to the Festival after a 16-year

absence, which was very exciting for all of her New Orleans fans. She was booked to play in 1996, but had to cancel due to a prior commitment to open the Broadway hit "Smokey Joe's Café'" in London. This powerful vocalist is one of New Orleans success stories. BJ performed at the first Jazz Festivals at Congo Square in gospel choirs. She went on to perform at the Fair Grounds with the Gospel Soul Children, and then she began to fly solo in the club scene becoming one of the hottest tickets in town. After a stint at the famed Tyler's Beer Garden, BJ took it downtown to

fest facts

Nearly 30 couples have been conjugally united at Jazz Fest, and there is no telling how many more in toto have surreptitiously tied the knot. Couples getting married at Jazz Fest have a specific place and time in which to officially secure their nuptials: in the Gospel Tent, between sets. There is no charge — the ceremony can even be spur of the moment. One year a musician and his fiancé just looked at each other and said "Let's do it now!" and headed for the Gospel Tent. All that is required is a tip for the organist and the minister, and there is no shortage of those on the holy ground of the Gospel Tent.

Café' Sbisa's, Noah's Jazz Club, The Blues Saloon, and Feelings where she held court for several years. Always interested in musical theatre, She starred in Shangri-la, then *One Mo' Time* at the Toulouse Theatre in the French Quarter. Lady BJ left New Orleans in 1986 for the West Coast and the rest, as they say, is history. It was a short hop for Ms. Crosby from Los Angeles to New York where our "home town" girl garnered a starring role on Broadway in "Smokey Joe's Café" and a Tony.

Lady BJ's show in the Bell South/WWOZ Jazz Tent was

Nicholas Payton

Ammamereso

beautiful to witness. A consummate professional, looking stunning in a vibrantly colored ensemble with matching hat, BJ owned the Jazz Tent from her first smile as she greeted her fans to her last bow as she left the stage. Accompanying her was an all-star New Orleans' band including Darryl Levigne, Clarence Johnson III and Chris Severin and Hurley Blanchard.

Tim Laughlin who performed in the Economy Hall Jazz Tent, like Lady BJ, was born and bred in New Orleans. A poignant and powerful clarinetist, Tim continues to breathe new life into traditional Jazz, and to expand the medium, perform-

Ornette Coleman

ing and recording his original compositions all over the world. Another example of how New Orleans artists keep infiltrating the musical universe. Tim had an excellent backing line-up including Shannon Powell on drums, Rick Trolsen, trombone, Matt Perine, sousaphone, John Eubanks, guitar, Connie Jones, cornet and Tom McDermott on piano

The Bob Dylan set was all about his killer band and the fresh arrangements of his classic songs. One person at his show said that watching his performance was witnessing "a master at the top of his game." Dylan laced his arrangements with surprising energy and instrumentation

"While I was on stage, I was thinking: 'This might just be a first: a New Orleans traditional jazz band performing all original music at Jazz Fest.' If memory serves me, they really enjoyed it. Well, they danced and that's a good sign." TIM LAUGHLIN

Angelique Kiojo

Many think Marcia Ball was responsible for staving off the threatening downpour towards the end of her show, singing the classic "Louisiana, 1927," as dark clouds gathered. Halfway through the song, the clouds began moving off in the direction of City Park and Festival fans breathed a sigh of relief. It must be noted; this Randy Newman classic has been cited at Jazz Festival both for bringing on, and keeping rain away over the years. Either effect brings goosebumps and tears to the rapt audience singing along.

and fresh approaches, much to the pleasure of his appreciative audience who had come to see a legend, but witnessed a thoughtful musical event.

Another master enjoyed at the Festival this year was Sam Butera, renowned New Orleans local who first garnered fame with Louie Prima's band. Sam spends most of his time now in Las Vegas, but the Crescent City was elated to have him back for a minute. His show was hot.

There was a lot of rain predicted but it wasn't bad at all.

New Birth Brass Band

Walter Washington

2:00 Pastor Woodrow Hayden & The Shiloh BC Mass Choir
2:45 Betty Winn & One A-Chord
3:30 Greater King David Adult Music Ministry
4:15 Ebenezer Gospel Choir
5:10 Women of Excellence Mass Choir
6:15 Franklin Ave. BC Mass Choir

ALLISON MINER MUSIC HERITAGE STAGE
12:00 Franz Jackson interviewed by Steve Steinberg
1:00 Hazel the Delta Rambler interviewed by Peggy Scott Laborde
2:00 George Wein interviewed by Ashley Kahn
3:00 A Love Supreme: John Coltrane's Enduring Legacy w/ Kidd Jordan, Ashley Kahn & Kalamu ya Salaam
4:00 Jon Cleary interviewed by David Fricke, Senior Editor Rolling Stone
5:00 Otis Taylor, interviewed by Scott Jordan

PARADES
12:00 Original Step 'n' Style, Valley of Silent Men, Single Men and Old & Nu Style Fellas with Paulin Brothers Brass Band
1:00 Wild Apache, Geronimo Hunters and Yellow Jackets Mardi Gras Indians
2:00 Devastation, Undefeated Divas & Men and Lady Rollers SA&PCs with Mahogany Brass Band
3:00 Trouble Nation, Red White & Blue and Young Hunters Mardi Gras Indians
4:00 Money Wasters, Nandi Exclusive Gentlemen & Ladies and Big Nine SA&PCs with Storyville Stompers Brass Band
4:30 Plastic System Band of Martinique
11:30 Economy Hall Parade with Nine Times Ladies

SUNDAY, APRIL 27

LOUISIANA HERITAGE STAGE
11:10 Son del Pantano
12:15 American Indian Dance Theater
1:30 Yerba Buena
2:55 Rebirth Brass Band
4:20 The Iguanas
5:50 Cowboy Mouth

POPEYES BLUES TENT
11:15 Little Freddie King Blues Band
12:20 Spencer Bohren
1:35 Eddie Bo
2:55 The "Lil Ray" Neal Band
4:25 Keb' Mo'
6:00 Snooks Eaglin

ACURA STAGE
11:30 Loyola University Jazz Band
12:45 Red House Singers and Dancers
1:45 Paul Varisco & The Milestones Reunion
3:35 Dr. John
5:30 Joe Cocker

SHERATON N.O. FAIS DO-DO STAGE
11:30 The Bluerunners
12:55 D.L. Menard & The Louisiana Aces
2:20 Sean Ardoin n- Zydekool
3:55 Mingo Saldivar y los Cuatro Espadas

5:35 Rosie Ledet & The Zydeco
Playboys

BELLSOUTH / WWOZ JAZZ TENT
11:30 Karin Williams
12:55 Germaine Bazzle
2:20 Jeremy Davenport
3:55 The Ellis Marsalis Quartet
5:40 Ornette Coleman

ECONOMY HALL TENT
11:15 Last Straws
12:25 Tribute to Placide Adams
Original Dixieland Hall
Jazz Band
1:35 Tim Laughlin
3:05 Chris Owens
4:20 Jamil Sharif & The New Orleans
Jazz Professors
5:45 The Broadway Cast of One Mo'
Time featuring Vernel Bagneris,
Oranj Kellin & The Blues
Serenaders

CONGO SQUARE STAGE
11:15 Semolian Warriors
12:05 Escola de Samba Casa Samba
1:15 Los Calientes
2:45 Jean Knight with Blue Eyed Soul

4:10 Plastic System Band of
Martinique
5:40 Gerald Levert

LAGNIAPPE STAGE
11:15 Betsy McGovern & The Poor
Clares
12:25 John Fohl
1:40 Danzig & Woolley
3:05 Hot Club of New Orleans
4:30 Kelly Love Jones
5:50 Sista Teedy's Bootleg Operation

NATIVE AMERICAN VILLAGE STAGE
11:30 Carolina Tuscarora Stomp &
Smoke Dancers
12:45 Butch Mudbone
1:30 Tommy Wildcat
2:00 The Ken Rhyne Band
3:15 Butch Mudbone
4:00 Tommy Wildcat
4:30 American Indian Dance Theater
5:45 Red House Singers and Dancers

RHODES GOSPEL TENT
11:00 Joe "Cool" Davis
11:45 Voices from the Mount
12:30 The Bester Singers
1:15 Golden Wings
2:00 Nu Vizion Gospel Choir
2:45 Dimensions of Faith
3:30 The Melody Clouds of New
Orleans
4:15 Monroe County
Interdenominational Mass Choir
5:10 Richard Smallwood

6:15 Val & Love Alive Fellowship
Choir

**ALLISON MINER MUSIC
HERITAGE STAGE**
2:00 Kevin Gordon
3:00 Marty Most Drummers:
Drumcussion Dr. Maurice
Martinez
5:50 Conjunto Accordion King Mingo
Saldivar, interviewed by Nick
Spitzer

PARADES
12:00 Olympia Aid, Uptowner's Hobo
Clowns and Divine Ladies
SA&PCs w/ Pinstripe Brass
Band
1:00 Young Magnolias, Comanche
Hunters and Flaming Arrows
Mardi Gras Indians
2:00 Perfect Gentlemen, New Look
and Avenue Steppers SA&PCs
with Original Thunderstorm
Brass Band
2:30 Plastic System Band of
Martinique
3:00 Ninth Ward Hunters, New
Orleans Mardi Gras Rhythm
Section and White Cloud
Hunters Mardi Gras Indians
4:00 Young Men Olympia
— Untouchables 4th Division,
Furious Five and Single Ladies
SA&PCs with Hot 8 Brass Band

THURSDAY, MAY 1

LOUISIANA HERITAGE STAGE
11:30 N.O. Public Schools Modern
Jazz Ensemble
12:50 007
2:20 The Waifs
3:55 Irene Sage
5:40 Papa Grows Funk

POPEYES BLUES TENT
11:15 Clancy "Blues Boy" Lewis w/
Sheba Kimbrough
12:25 Rufus Rip Wimberley & The
Dreamers
1:40 Bryan Lee & The Blues Power
Band
3:00 Warner Williams & Jay
Summerour Little Bit a Blues
Band
4:10 Jumpin' Johnny Sansone
5:40 Tab Benoit

ACURA STAGE
11:15 Xavier University Jazz Ensemble
12:40 The Benjy Davis Project
2:00 Sonny Landreth
3:40 North Mississippi Allstars
5:35 John Mayer

SHERATON N.O. FAIS DO-DO STAGE
11:25 Leslie Smith
12:35 Jay Cormier
1:50 Basin Brothers
3:15 Balfa Toujours w/ guest Bois
Sec Ardoin
4:35 Cedryl Ballou & The Zydeco
Trendsetters
6:00 Geno Delafose & French Rockin'
Boogie

BELLSOUTH / WWOZ JAZZ TENT
11:40 Dr. Rackle & The Sound Griots
1:00 Sharon Martin
2:25 Brice Winston
3:50 Irvin Mayfield
5:35 Dave Holland Quintet

ECONOMY HALL TENT
11:15 Lady Charlotte Jazz Band
12:20 Jacques Gauthé & The Creole
Rice Jazz Band
1:35 Danza featuring Evan
Christopher & Tom McDermott
2:55 Chris Clifton & His All Stars
4:20 Lionel Ferbos & The Palm Court
Jazz Band
5:45 Banu Gibson & New Orleans
Hot Jazz with guest Bucky
Pizzarelli

CONGO SQUARE STAGE
11:15 Fashion Show
11:25 Terrence Simien
11:55 Mama Efuru
12:00 Culu Children's Traditional
African Dance
12:25 Mama Efuru

LAGNIAPPE STAGE
12:00 Micaela y Flamenca Fiesta
1:15 Beth Patterson & Kalafka
2:40 Samirah Evans & Silktone
4:10 Woodenhead with Bonerama
Horns
5:40 Javier Gutierrez & Vivaz

NATIVE AMERICAN VILLAGE STAGE
11:30 Jonny hawk Creek-Seminole
Stomp Dance Performers
12:45 IronMountain Native Dancers
1:30 Hawk Henries
2:00 Treater
3:15 Hawk Henries
4:30 IronMountain Native Dancers
5:45 Jonny Hawk Creek-Seminole
Stomp Dance Performers

RHODES GOSPEL TENT
1:00 Gospel Stars
11:45 Archie & Simonia Milton
12:30 Shades of Praise
1:15 Lyle Henderson & Emmanuel
2:00 Holy Name Gospel Singers
2:45 The Levites of Faith Church
3:30 Mount Pilgrim Gospel Choir
4:15 Lockport Chapter GMWA Mass
Choir
5:05 Harvey Watkins, Jr. & Purpose
6:05 St. Joseph the Worker Music
Ministry

**ALLISON MINER MUSIC
HERITAGE STAGE**
1:00 David Pirner with Interviewer
Michaela Majoun
2:00 Gospel Harmonica Isaac Tate
with Interviewer Chuck Siler
3:00 Dave Holland with Interviewer
Geraldine Wyckoff
4:00 Members of Amammereso
Agofomma from Ghana with
Interviwer Gabou Mendy
5:00 Christine Balfa & Dirk Powell
with Interviewer Tom Piazza
5:55 Warner Williams with
Interviewer Nick Spitzer

PARADES
3:00 Real Men and Bon Temp Roulez
w/ Algiers Brass Band

FRIDAY, MAY 2

LOUISIANA HERITAGE STAGE
11:15 SUBR Jazz Ensemble
12:20 Ben Eyler
1:35 Colonel Sanchez
2:55 Los Hombres Calientes
4:25 BeauSoleil avec Michael Doucet
5:55 Marcia Ball

POPEYES BLUES TENT
11:25 Coco Robicheaux & Spiritland
12:35 Raful Neal, Sr. & Blues Band
1:50 Sherman Robinson
3:05 Amammereso Agofomma of
Ghana
4:20 Jimmie Vaughan
5:55 Deacon John

ACURA STAGE
11:15 IronMoutain Native Dancers
12:20 Ethan
2:00 Los Lobos
3:40 Robert Randolph & The Family
Band
5:25 Ben Harper & The Innocent
Criminals

SHERATON N.O. FAIS DO-DO STAGE
11:15 Christian Serpas & Ghost Town
12:30 Hadley J. Castille Cajun Swamp
Fiddler & Sharecroppers Cajun
Band
1:45 Savoy Doucet Cajun Band
3:05 Red Stick Ramblers
4:30 Reggie Hall & The Twilighters
w/ Lady Lois & Albert "Dogman"
Smith
6:00 Thomas "Big Hat" Fields & His
Stompin' Zydeco Band

BELLSOUTH / WWOZ JAZZ TENT
11:15 Hart McNee Sextet
12:20 Roderick Paulin & The Groovers
1:35 Alvin Batiste & The Jazztronauts
2:55 John Boutté
4:15 Kermit Ruffins & The Barbecue
Swingers
5:45 Regina Carter

ECONOMY HALL TENT
11:20 Tremé Brass Band
12:30 Connie Jones Crescent City Jazz
Band
1:40 Mahogany Hall Stompers of
Japan
3:00 Newport AllStars feat. George
Wein
4:25 Topsy Chapman
5:55 Louisiana Repertory Jazz
Ensemble

CONGO SQUARE STAGE
11:15 Delgado Community College
Jazz Ensemble
12:20 Irie Dawtas
1:30 C.J. Chenier & The Louisiana
Red Hot Band
2:50 Fredy Omar con su Banda
4:10 Walter "Wolfman" Washington
& The Roadmasters
5:45 Angelique Kidjo

LAGNIAPPE STAGE
11:30 Hazel & The Delta Ramblers
12:40 Michael Skinkus & Moyuba
1:55 Jeff & Vida Band
3:15 Higher Heights
4:40 Riccardo Crispo y Sol Brasil
6:00 Bobby Cure & The Summertime
Blues Band

NATIVE AMERICAN VILLAGE STAGE
11:30 Jonny Hawk Creek-Seminole
Stomp Dance Performers
12:45 Hank Henries
2:00 Jim Boyd & Alfonso Kolb
3:15 IronMountain Native Dancers
4:00 Hawk Henries
4:30 Jonny Hawk Creek-Seminole
Stomp Dance Performers
5:45 IronMountain Native Dancers

RHODES GOSPEL TENT
11:00 Old Zion Missionary BC Choir
11:45 The Fantastic Violinaires
12:30 Leviticus Singers

1:15 Proclaimers of Christ Gospel
Singers
2:00 New Zion Trio Plus One
2:45 First Zion BC Choir
3:30 Dynamic Smooth Family
4:15 Mighty Chariots of Fire
5:10 Lumzy Sisters
6:15 Coolie Family Gospel Singers

**ALLISON MINER MUSIC
HERITAGE STAGE**
1:00 Three Generations of Music
Classie, Cedric & Cedryl Ballou,
interviewed by Herman Fuselier
2:00 Regina Carter interviewed by
Karen Celestan
3:00 Thomas "Big Hat" Fields,
interviewed by Michael
Tisserand
4:00 Walter Payton interviewed by
Jason Patterson
5:55 Jimmie Vaughan interviewed by
Scott Jordan

PARADES
11:20 Economy Hall parade with Lady
Rulers SA&PC
2:00 Double Nine and Single Men
Kids SA&PCs with New Wave
Brass Band
4:00 New Generation and Young 2
Old Men SA&PCs with Coolbone

SATURDAY, MAY 3

LOUISIANA HERITAGE STAGE
11:15 Big Daddy O' Revue feat. Cherie
Mannino
12:25 Lee Bates & The Cool
Connection Band
1:40 Ritmo Caribeno
3:00 Frankie Ford Show
4:15 Rockin' Dopsie, Jr. & The
Zydeco Twisters
5:45 Irma Thomas & The
Professionals

POPEYES BLUES TENT
11:20 Kipori Woods
12:35 The Bluebirds
1:45 Dave "Honeyboy" Edwards
2:50 Wanda Rouzan & A Taste of New
Orleans
4:20 The Holmes Brothers
5:50 John Mooney & Bluesiana

ACURA STAGE
11:05 SUNO Jazz Ensemble
12:15 Dave Pirner
1:25 Big Chief Monk Boudreaux &
The Golden Eagles
2:40 The funky Meters
4:30 Widespread Panic

SHERATON N.O. FAIS DO-DO STAGE
11:15 Charivari
12:20 La Bande "Feufollet"
1:40 Chauval B'wa of Martinique
3:00 Mary McBride
4:25 Lil' Brian & The Zydeco
Travelers
5:50 Steve Riley & The Mamou
Playboys

BELLSOUTH / WWOZ JAZZ TENT
11:10 Jimmy Dludlu of Capetown,
South Africa
12:20 Willie Tee
1:30 Kent Jordan
2:40 Astral Project
4:05 Nicholas Payton & Sonic Trance
5:45 Herbie Mann Reunion Band

ECONOMY HALL TENT
11:15 Zulu Ensemble Male Chorus
12:20 Kustbandet The Swingin'
Swedes of Sweden
1:40 Don Vappie's Creole Jazz
Serenaders
3:00 Lars Edegran & The New
Orleans Ragtime Orchestra
4:25 Michael White & The Original
Liberty Jazz Band w/ Thais
Clark
5:55 Jeannie & Jimmy Cheatham

CONGO SQUARE STAGE
11:25 Amammereso Agofomma of
Ghana
12:40 Jim Body & Kyo-T
2:10 Mavis Staples
3:50 LL Cool J
5:40 Third World

LAGNIAPPE STAGE
11:15 Strawberry Jammers
12:20 Carlos Sanchez "Amanecer
Flamenco"
1:25 IronMountain Native Dancers
2:35 New Orleans Jazz Vipers
4:05 Lynn Drury & Bad Mayo
5:35 IronMountain Native Dancers

NATIVE AMERICAN VILLAGE STAGE
11:30 IronMountain Native Dancers
12:45 Jonny Hawk Creek Seminole
Stomp Dance Performers
2:00 Hawk Henries
3:15 Jonny Hawk Creek Seminole
Stomp Dance Performers
4:00 Hawk Henries
4:30 Jim Boyd & Alfonso Kolb
5:45 IronMountain Native Dancers

RHODES GOSPEL TENT
11:00 Forgiven
11:45 Unstoppable Gospel Creators
12:30 Second Nazarene BC Gospel
Choir
1:15 Gloryland BC of Baton Rouge
2:00 Praise Community Choir
2:45 Gospel Honorees Ceremony
3:30 The Wimberly Family
4:15 Johnson Extension
5:10 Keith Johnson & The Spiritual
Voices
6:15 Watson Memorial Teaching
Ministries

**ALLISON MINER MUSIC HERITAGE
STAGE**
12:00 Dave "Honeyboy" Edwards
interviewed by John Sinclair
1:00 Bill Summers & Irvin Mayfield
interviewed by Fred Kasten
2:00 The Holmes Brothers
interviewed by Mike Luster
3:00 Veillee Acapella Cajun & Creole
Ballads
4:00 Lee Bates interviewed by David
Kunian

PARADES
12:00 Dumaine St. Gang Mean and
Ladies and Original Big 7
SA&PCs with Pinette Brass
Band
1:00 Renegade Phaze III, Black
Eagles and big Chief Derrick &
The Golden Blades Mardi Gras
Indians
2:00 Pigeon Town Steppers,
N'Krumah Better Boys and No
Limit Steppers SA&PCs with Lil'
Rascals Brass Band
3:00 Hard Headhunters, Black
Feathers and Cherokee Hunters
Mardi Gras Indians

4:00 Secondline Jammers, Black
Men of Labor and Happy House
SA&PCs with Tuba Fats' Chosen
Few Brass Band

SUNDAY, MAY 4

LOUISIANA HERITAGE STAGE
11:30 Bucktown Allstars
12:45 Eric Lindell
2:10 George Porter, Jr. & Runnin'
Pardners
3:50 Wayne Toups & The Zydecajuns
5:30 The Radiators

POPEYES BLUES TENT
11:15 Dorothy Prime & The Wampus
Catz
12:20 Joe Krown Organ Combo
1:30 Andy J. Forest Band
2:45 The Dixie Cups
4:10 Chris Thomas King's 21st
Century Blues
5:45 Buddy Guy

ACURA STAGE
11:15 Jonny Hawk Creek-Seminole
Stomp Dance Performers
12:25 Charmaine Neville w/ Reggie
Houston & Amasa Miller
1:50 The Wild Magnolias
3:25 Gladys Knight
5:20 The Neville Brothers

SHERATON N.O. FAIS DO-DO STAGE
11:15 DeLoutre
12:25 Allen Fontenot & The Country
Cajuns
1:40 Kim Carson & The Casualties
3:05 Creole Zydeco Farmers
4:30 Willis Prudhomme & Zydeco
Express
6:00 Dwayne Dopsie & The Zydeco
Hellraisers

BELLSOUTH / WWOZ JAZZ TENT
11:15 Heritage School of Music Jazz
Band
12:15 Roland Guerin Quartet
1:25 Clyde Kerr, Jr. & Univision
2:45 Leah Chase
4:00 Terrence Blanchard
5:45 The Crusaders Reunion

ECONOMY HALL TENT
11:20 Kid Simmons' Local
International Allstars
12:30 Dukes of Dixieland
1:55 Gregg Stafford's Young Tuxedo
Brass Band
3:20 George French & The Original
Storyville Jazz Band
4:35 Pete Fountain
6:00 Preservation Hall Jazz Band

CONGO SQUARE STAGE
11:15 Don Carter
12:20 Amammereso Agofomma of
Ghana
1:50 Kassav
3:45 Carlos Vives y la provincia
5:40 The O'Jays

LAGNIAPPE STAGE
11:20 The Abita Strings Bluegrass
Band
12:30 The Malvinas
1:45 Ingrid Lucia
3:00 Pay Saavedra's Bandidos
4:30 Topaz
6:00 Zion Trinity

NATIVE AMERICAN VILLAGE STAGE
11:30 Kostini
12:45 Hawk Henries
2:00 Bill Miller

3:15 Jonny Hawk Creek-Seminole
Stomp Dance Performers
4:30 IronMountain Native Dancers
5:45 Bill Miller

RHODES GOSPEL TENT
11:00 The Banks Family
11:45 Cosmopolitan Baptist Church
Mass Choir
12:30 New Orleans Spiritualettes
1:15 Faithful Few Gospel Singers
2:00 Antioch Full Gospel Choir
2:45 Paulette Wright-Davis & Volume
of Praise
3:30 Sherman Washington & The
Zion Harmonizers
4:15 Aaron Neville
5:10 Mighty Clouds of Joy
6:15 Tyrone Foster & The Arc Singers

**ALLISON MINER MUSIC
HERITAGE STAGE**
2:00 Jo "Cool" Davis with Interviewer
Steve Armbruster
3:00 Radiators 25th Anniversary with
Ed Volker & Reggie Scanlan
with Interviewer Ben Sandmel
4:00 The Jazzoety Professors with
Arturo Pfister
5:15 Claude & Joselita Germany with
Interviewer Gene Scaramuzzo

PARADE
12:00 Scene Boosters, Jetsetter
Ladies and Popular Ladies
SA&PCs with Tornado Brass
Band
1:00 Creole Wild West and Carrollton
Hunters Mardi Gras Indians
2:00 Westbank Steppers and Original
Prince of Wales Men and Ladies
SA&PCs with High Steppers
Brass Band
3:00 Golden Arrows and Mohawk
Hunters Mardi Gras Indians
4:00 Original Lady Buckjumpers,
Buckjumper Men and Nine
Times Men SA&PCs with Real
Untouchables Brass Band
1:55 Economy Hall Parade with
Calendar Girls SA&PCs

NIGHT CONCERTS

FRIDAY, APRIL 25, 9 P.M.
Crosby, Stills & Nash
John Hiatt & The Goners
Morris FX Jeff Municipal Auditorium
SATURDAY, APRIL 26, 8 P.M.
Michael Franks
Angela Bofill
Mahalia Jackson Theatre of the
Performing Arts
SATURDAY, APRIL 27, 8 P.M.
Bob Dylan
Lucinda Williams
Morris FX Jeff Municipal Auditorium,
**MONDAY & TUESDAY, APRIL 28 & APRIL
29, 8 P.M.**
Jazz at the Palm Court
New Orleans — Chicago Express
Featuring Franz Jackson, Sammy
Rimington, Mark Braud, Fred Lonzo,
James Singleton & Ernest Elly,
presented by Lars Edegran
Palm Court Jazz Café
FRIDAY, MAY 2, 8:30 P.M.
Widespread Panic
North Mississippi Allstars
Morris FX Jeff Municipal Auditorium,
SATURDAY, MAY 3, 9 P.M.
An Evening with India Arie & Musiq
Morris FX Jeff Municipal Auditorium,
SATURDAY, MAY 3, 8 P.M.
Carlos Vives y La Provincia and Almas
House of Blues

2004

Daniel Breaux and Claudia Dumestre

"We hadn't had a drop of rain for six years. Last year we had six years worth of rain in two weeks-all day, every day but two days," observed Quint Davis.

Rain is a big problem when it happens during Jazz Fest. All of the musical gear on the stages has to be protected; if it rains too hard, shows stop, people's Crawfish Monica and Vietnamese Spring Rolls get soggy, and attendance cuts down dramatically.

The Fair Grounds opened in 2004 to clear skies and a light breeze. Then it rained every day. The sudden showers and occasional downpours didn't cause any show cancellations in the first week, but the infield became squishy and slippery, and the puddles got just a little too wide to jump over. Nevertheless, the music was great and the food booths had lines as usual, even if they weren't as long.

The mud didn't get too bad. Some people might say the mud didn't get good enough. There is a Jazz Fest tradition among the young, of creating "mud slides" when the conditions are just right. After the perfect area is chosen, participants get a running start and then throw themselves, belly first, into the mud and slide for as long as possible. There have also been some outstanding "mud pits" over the years, which are large muddy areas where people dance and roll around in the

what's going on?

GLOBALLY

An earthquake in the Indian Ocean, with a magnitude of 9.0, spawns tsunamis throughout Indonesia. The death toll from Malaysia to East Africa has climbs to around 175,000, making this the most deadly tsunami in recorded history.

Armed robbers steal Edvard Munch's The Scream, from the Munch Museum in Oslo, Norway.

Democratic elections held for the first time in Afghanistan.

NATIONALLY

The tortures of Abu Ghraib prison are revealed with investigations beginning into U.S. treatment of prisoners of war.

SpaceShipOne becomes the first privately funded spaceship to achieve spaceflight.

LOCALLY

First white Christmas since 1954.

The Canal Streetcar rolls again.

Kathleen Babineaux Blanco becomes first female Governor of Louisiana.

The New Orleans Voodoo debut as the city's new Arena Football League Team.

CULTURALLY

The Boston Red Sox break the "Curse of the Bambino" by winning their first World Series title since 1918.

Lance Armstrong wins his 6th consecutive Tour de France cycling title.

Same-sex marriages became legal in Massachusetts after the state's Supreme Court ruled in Nov. 2003 that barring gays and lesbians from marrying violated the state constitution.

mud. Some truly memorable ones have occurred in front of Radiators' shows and the trough to the side of Acura.

When the Old Zion Baptist Church Choir started at 11 a.m. the weather was nice inside the Rhodes Gospel Tent, but outside it was a little dicey. Rain kept starting and stopping all day. The music tents or the grandstand were definitely the place for respite from the drizzle. Still, when the Steve Miller Band

ferent third members, always rotating so the music changes from show to show, depending on who the guest is. The guest for this Jazz Fest performance was June Yamagishi.

Bonnie Raitt closed the Acura stage with Jon Cleary on keyboards, following Emmylou Harris who had local Tony Hall on bass. Both Emmylou and Bonnie have tapped into the musical wealth of New Orleans over the years

Olympia Brass Band   Big Sam

closed the Acura Stage, there were good crowds. Most people understood that getting wet is just like getting real sweaty, but it smells nicer. The music went on and everybody adjusted.

The Trio on Sprint, which performed before Galactic was a hot show. Johnny Vidacovich and George Porter started this concept in 1999 and have kept a regular weekly gig at various locations around town ever since. Trio has dif-

"*People may not realize it but Tuba made a large impact on the 2004 Jazz Fest. The visiting country this year was South Africa and in January, Tuba traveled with a New Orleans band to South Africa and it was through his presence, through his spirit and the fact that he broke bread with the true King of the Zulu Nation led to the fact that the Zulu Nation decided to participate in the 2004 Jazz Fest. Sadly, I think it was this trip that killed him. He flew for 72 hours in five days on that trip and I think the stress was too great for him. So Tuba wasn't there, but his spirit was sure there.*" JERRY BROCK

with very good results.

On Saturday, Ivan Neville (who used to play with Bonnie) gave a taste of his new thing; Dumpstaphunk, and it was perhaps the funkiest sounds this talented man has created to date.

It rained off and on all weekend. At Festival Headquarters all they could do was hope the following week would be sunny. When the Gap Band closed Congo Square Sunday in the first week, thousands of people were packed in front of the stage when the sky fell. The band was asked to stop by the stage manager, and then the lead singer yelled out "They're telling me we have to stop for the rain! – Do you want us to stop?!" the masses standing in the rain howled

"No!!" The Gap Band slammed back into another song, finishing their show.

Thursday opened with more of the same, misty, intermittent rain, but as the sun went down it really got started. The problem was it didn't stop. It poured though the night and Festival staffers started getting really worried. It had already been raining for days, and in New Orleans, if there's too much rain, it doesn't matter if you have a million dollar drainage system, there's no place for it to go. By sunrise on Friday, the infield was completely saturated. The forecast expected the weather to begin clearing in the early afternoon but it was a soggy

Astral Project

mess out there and Friday had to be cancelled due to flooding on the infield. A lot of wonderful acts didn't get to play that day.

One of those acts was Brian Stoltz who had an incredible line-up for his Jazz Fest show that Friday: Rob Wasserman, bass; Eric Bolizar, drums; Chris Littlefield, trumpet; Cheme Gastalum, saxophone; John Gros, subbing for Melvin Seals on keyboards, and Irene Sage for vocals. " That was a group I put together for my first solo appearance in San Francisco at the Boom- Boom Room: Brian Stoltz and Greazzy Azz Chicken. We played two nights, 4 shows and it was great. All these guys just happened to be in town with other groups for Jazz Fest so we put it back together." Brian paused and then

music scene

Tower Records files Chapter 11 bankruptcy protection.

Buddy Guy wins another Grammy for Best Traditional Blues Album.

IN MEMORIAM

Waldren "Frog" Joseph, Daniel Breaux, Willie Metcalf Jr., Anthony "Tuba Fats" Lacen, Ellis Marsalis Sr., Ray Charles, Jimmy Smith, Billy May, John LaPorta, Elvin Jones, Jean-Baptiste Illinois Jacquet, Artie Shaw

"In 2004 I was playing string bass with Clive Wilson at the Economy Hall Tent and Frank Oxley was listening to me. He enjoyed what he heard and found Dr. Michael White who came over to listen. This led to Michael hiring me for some gigs, which was cool because I've always enjoyed what he does." TOM SAUNDERS

fest facts

The value of the first 1975 poster, which sold for $5 is now $1,925, according to art4now, Inc.

Fair Grounds is sold by the Krantz family to Churchill Downs, Inc.

Jazz Fest has its own hospital and health personnel.

Jazz Fest has its own post office: the world's only jazz postmark.

June Yamagichi, George Porter, Johnny Vidacovich

expressed what so many artists booked to play second Friday were feeling. "I was so disappointed. That's all I can say." Everyone who came to town for Jazz Fest was disappointed too.

Workers on the infield during the day watched a family of ducks swimming across a small lake in front of the Fais Do-Do Stage. Staff and volunteers had a huge job on their hands getting the racetrack ready for Saturday. When the Festival opened the next day, the lake was gone. All the water had been removed, and straw was down in the low spots. By the time the second act hit the Fais Do-Do Stage, people were dancing, and the crowd was getting thick. The ducks had migrated back over to the fenced off pond area by the main gate, where they usually swim, to enjoy the music from a distance.

The rest of the second weekend went off without a hitch; but it was a soggy, wet Fest.

One theme this year was an exciting celebration of South Africa. Producers went all out to include representatives of the recently changed country.

Zwelethu Mthethwa, himself a native of South Africa, created the official poster for Congo Square; "Congo Square 2004; One World Blues"- a poster celebrating the 10th anniversary of South African democracy with lush colors created in rich pastels. This poster reflected the vibrancy and creativity of Mr. Mthethwa's native land with a bluesman playing guitar at a counter, although the "bluesman" to some, was purple. Blueberries are also purple, so there.

Every club in New Orleans has great music during Jazz Fest, packed to the rafters, with locals and visitors alike in thrall until the wee hours of the morning. Snug Harbor, dba, The Blue Nile, The Spotted Cat, Café Brazil, and the Hookah Club on Frenchmen street were full of great music in 2004. Uptown, the Maple Leaf, Carrollton Station, the Neutral Ground, Tipitina's, Snake & Jakes and Le Bon Ton Roulé are some of the best uptown music venues. Rock-n-Bowl in mid-city also pulls out all the stops at Jazz Fest, as does the Howlin'

12:45 Balfa Toujours
2:05 Crocodile Gumboot Dancers
2:50 Charles Jackson & The Jackson Travelers
4:00 Geno Delafose & French Rockin' Boogie
5:30 Rosie Ledet & The Zydeco Playboys

BELLSOUTH / WWOZ JAZZ TENT
11:15 Chris Lacinack "Boom"
12:15 Germaine Bazzle
1:25 Doug Wamble
2:40 Astral Project
4:05 Branford Marsalis
5:50 Irvin Mayfield & The New Orleans Jazz Orchestra

ECONOMY HALL TENT
11:15 Mark Braud
12:25 Linnzi Zaorski & Delta Royale
1:40 Don Vappie & The Creole Jazz Serenaders
3:00 Connie Jones' Crescent City Jazz
4:15 Young Tuxedo Brass Band
5:40 Bessie Smith Revue featuring Juanita Brooks & Barbara Shorts

SOUTH AFRICAN FREEDOM @ CONGO SQUARE STAGE
11:35 Willie Metcalf & The Academy of Black Arts
12:50 TBA
2:05 Friends of Jabu
3:30 Rebecca Malope Gospel Queen of South Africa
5:25 Macy Gray

LAGNIAPPE STAGE
11:30 Caledonian Society Scottish Dancers, Pipes & Drums of New Orleans
12:45 NOCCA Jazz Ensemble
2:05 Javier & Elegant Gypsy
3:30 Jones – Benally Family
4:40 Derek Miller
6:00 Ingrid Lucia

NATIVE AMERICAN VILLAGE STAGE
11:40 Native American Village Exhibition Powwow
1:20 Derek Miller
2:00 Jones – Benally Family
3:00 Native American Village Exhibition Powwow
5:15 Jones – Benally Family

RHODES GOSPEL TENT
11:00 The Crown Seekers
11:45 The Gospel Inspirations of Boutte
12:30 Greater King David Mass Choir
1:15 New Orleans Spiritualettes
2:00 Shades of Praise
2:45 Rocks of Harmony
3:30 Val & Love Alive Fellowship Choir
4:30 Rizen
5:45 New Home Ministries Mass Choir

ALLISON MINER MUSIC HERITAGE STAGE
12:00 Joe Hall with Interviewer Danielle Bias
1:00 Creole Bred – Ann Savoy and Geno Delafose with Interviewer Ben Sandmel
2:00 Tribute to Tuba Fats and Rebirth's 20th Ann. w/ Benny Jones & Phillip Frazier with Interviewer Jerry Brock
3:00 Johnny Clegg with Interviewer Grant Morris
4:00 Ivan Neville with Interviewer David Fricke
5:00 Alvin Youngblood Hart with Interviewer John Sinclair

Wolf, and countless others.

Is it a mystery why the evening concerts were not better attended? The producers stated after Jazz Fest was over that the numbers had been dwindling for some time, lots of money was lost, and formal night shows would be discontinued in 2005. The original staple of the Festival had run its course: the city itself was now the showplace of nighttime music and the choices were as endless as the social possibilities. The formal concert venue would be put on the shelf.

Still, the choices were excellent in 2004, and it was fitting that one of the concerts was B.B. King and Etta James, loved by Festival fans for decades.

At the Palm Court Jazz Café, two of New Orleans' finest vocalists, Juanita Brooks and Barbara Shorts, performed consecutive nights, backed by

an outstanding line up of local musicians; Herlin Riley, who holds the drum chair at the Lincoln Center with Winton Marsali's jazz ensemble, Lars Edgegran, Sammy Rimington, Mark Braud, Freddie Lonzo and upright bassist Bill Huntington.

Sweet Lorraine's Jazz Club had a night of jazz violin in the extreme when violinist's Michael Ward, Jerald Daemyon and Rodney McCoy performed two shows on May 11th. Anyone left breathless by the sound of violins would have gone into cardiac arrest from hearing these three players throwing down.

La Noche Latina El Gran Combo was outrageous. In 2004, this Grammy nominated group was one of Puerto Rico's hottest dance bands. Of the 13 original members of La Noche Latina El Gran Combo only two remain; founder Rafael Ithier and saxophonist

Terence Blanchard

A comprehensive retrospective of his work adorned the first floor of the grandstand, organized by David Richmond, local photographer and fan of Mike's work. A continuous flow of people passed through the Grandstand, (and stayed out of the rain) remembering the years and some of their favorite Festival moments.

Large photos were displayed all over the Fair Grounds and hung over the stages in the music tents. A panel discussion on his work and contributions was held in the grandstand. *CNN Nightline* with Aaron Brown, producer, Amanda Townsend created a segment on Mike's connection to Jazz Fest to air nationwide before the second weekend.

"He defined the look of Jazz Fest" Quint Davis said when asked about Michael and the images he's captured over 35 years of Festival.

Many other wonderful photographers have documented Jazz Fest, many of their photos are to be found within these

Eddie Perez, but the sound still includes non-stop rhythm.

The year 2004 honored photographer Michael P. Smith by focusing the entire Festival around his work. The program book read " Thirty-Five years of Jazz Fest through the eyes of Michael P. Smith," and his photos were displayed everywhere.

Jon Cleary

> "When D.L. Menard finishes his set he always comes off the stage and receives his audience. In 2004 a woman walked up to him and said 'I've always wanted to see you and you were really wonderful.' In typical D. L. fashion he threw up his hands, shrugged his shoulders, smiled at her and said 'I could have told you that.'" DEREK HOUSTON

Eric Lindell

pages, but Mike Smith did it so comprehensively. His driven, committed devotion to not missing the moment created the most comprehensive, detailed visual history of the evolution of the New Orleans Jazz & Heritage Festival in existence.

Mike was seen walking down the main thoroughfare where he stopped to look at one of his photos on display: a large picture of the Neville Brothers all singing together at a past Jazz Festival performance. After gazing at his photo for a moment he snapped a photograph of it and kept walking.

MICHAEL PROCTOR SMITH

Michael Proctor Smith is my father, so I am very familiar with his work, his life, and his devotion to Jazz Fest. From a very young age, my sister and I learned to keep "line of sight" on our father or he would disappear into the crowd and be gone. He was always after the shot, the special moment.

In recent years as he has become more frail, I've carried his cameras for him occasionally, and the last two years after he was diagnosed with Parkinson's I've been with him whenever he is on stage at the Festival. 2004 was a very hard year for me as Mike's daughter.

Everywhere we went, musicians were coming up to us and telling me stories about the first time they met my father. They were running to the side of the stage in the middle of songs to hug me and thank me for bringing my daddy over. They were stopping in the middle of their sets to acknowledge him. George Porter dedicated the last song of his set to him, "People Say". Terence Simien stopped in the middle of his show, asked the crowd to put their hands

together for Mike, and then thanked him for coming to photograph him over the years. Terence said he was honored. I stuck my head behind the side monitor stage right and cried.

Throughout the entire Festival, on more stages than I can name, at some point in the show I would look down in the pit, and see all the cameras pointing, not at the act on stage, but at my father photographing that act.

The deep reverence and respect that Mike has earned from his fellow photographers, and the love I feel from the musicians he has photographed over the years with such dedication moves me so deeply. I am truly honored to be his daughter.

Mike seemed embarrassed by all of the attention. I asked him if he liked it and he said "No". He always felt himself to be more of a technician than an artist. He feels the subject is what's special, not the photo. He felt a need for people to be aware of this event. He wanted to have it documented for the future. Now it is. He doesn't feel he deserves praise, but he does.

LESLIE BLACKSHEAR SMITH

3:00 Louisiana Repertory Jazz Ensemble
4:25 New Leviathan Oriental Foxtrot Orchestra
5:50 Carrie Smith

SOUTH AFRICAN FREEDOM @ CONGO SQUARE STAGE
11:00 Freestyle Nation
12:05 Cynthia Liggins-Thomas
1:10 Ringo of South Africa
2:20 Vivaz
3:55 The Johnny Clegg Band featuring the Music of Juluka & Savuka
5:45 Gap Band

LAGNIAPPE STAGE
11:15 Heritage School of Music Jazz Ensemble
12:20 After the Fact
1:25 Rudy's Caribbean Funk
2:30 Patrice Fisher & Arpa with guest Carlos Ponce of Bolivia
3:50 Brasilliance!
4:55 Sharon Martin
6:10 The Elements

NATIVE AMERICAN VILLAGE STAGE
11:45 Native American Village Exhibition Powwow
2:00 Jones – Benally Family
3:00 Native American Village Exhibition Powwow
5:15 Jones – Benally Family

RHODES GOSPEL TENT
11:00 Antioch Gospel Singers
11:45 Zulu Gospel Ensemble
12:30 The Bester Singers
1:15 Rejubilation Evangelical Community Choir
2:00 The Melody Clouds
2:45 Rebecca Malope Gospel Queen of South Africa
3:30 Second Nazarine Church Choir
4:25 Lamont Jackson & A New Beginning
5:30 Donald Lawrence & Tri-City Singers

ALLISON MINER MUSIC HERITAGE STAGE
12:45 Celebrating Sherman Washington w/ Quint Davis and Lois Dejean with Interviewer Grant Morris
1:45 Louis Armstrong Educational Foundation presents of the Evolution of the Jazz Musician w/ Phoebe Jacobs, Herman Leonard & Dr. Henry Lacey with moderator George Wein
3:00 Henry Butler with Interviewer Harry Shearer
4:00 Hackberry Ramblers with Interviewer David Fricke
5:00 Eddie Bo with Interviewer Nick Spitzer

KIDS' TENT
11:30 Sci-High Steel Band
12:30 Kita Productions
1:45 Omosede by Charter Middle School
2:45 Charlie Williams The Noise Guy
4:00 Jonno's School of Cajun
5:15 Carlos Ponce of Bolivia
6:30 Storyteller Karen-Kaia Livers

PARADES
12:00 Olympia Aid, Uptowner's Hobo Clowns and Divine Ladies SA&PCs with Smitty Dee's Brass Band
1:00 Young Magnolias, White Cloud Hunters and Flaming Arrows Mardi Gras Indians

2:00 Perfect Gentlemen, New Look and Lady Sequence SA&PCs with Pin Stripe Brass Band
3:00 Ninth Ward Hunters, Comanche and New Orleans Rhythm Mardi Gras Indians
4:00 Untouchables, Furious five and Single Ladies SA&PCs with New Birth Brass Band

THURSDAY, APRIL 29

SPRINT STAGE
11:20 Bonerama
12:30 Irie Dawtas
1:40 BeauSoleil avec Michael Doucet
3:05 Joss Stone
4:30 The Iguanas
6:00 The subdudes

POPEYES BLUES TENT
11:20 Jumpin' Johnny Sansone
12:35 Coco Robicheaux & Spiritland
1:50 Kenny Neal
2:00 God's Followers of South Africa
4:05 Odetta
5:45 Tab Benoit

ACURA STAGE
11:25 UNO Jazz Ensemble
12:45 Michael Ray & The Cosmic Krewe
2:00 Wayne Toups & The Zydecajuns
3:35 Allen Toussaint
5:25 The Steve Miller Band w/ guest John Handy

SHERATON N.O. FAIS DO-DO STAGE
11:15 Bingo!
12:25 Waso Belgian Gypsy Jazz
1:40 Marce Lacouture
3:05 Goldman Thibodeaux & The Lawtell Playboys
4:30 Vin Bruce
5:55 Dexter Ardoin & The Creole Ramblers

BELLSOUTH / WWOZ JAZZ TENT
11:15 Tony "Oulaboula" Bazley
12:25 Leroy Jones
1:35 Patrick DeSanto
2:50 Michael Ward
4:10 John Boutté
5:40 Christian McBride Band

ECONOMY HALL TENT
11:15 Steamboat Willie
12:25 The Danza featuring Evan Christopher and Tom McDermott
1:40 Andrew Hall's Society Brass Band
3:05 Walter Payton & Snapbeans
4:30 Tim Laughlin
5:55 Jewel Brown & The Heritage Hall Jazz Band

SOUTH AFRICAN FREEDOM @ CONGO SQUARE STAGE
11:10 Pride of Zulu of South Africa
11:30 Mama Efuru
11:45 African Renaissance Dancers w/ Mama Efuru
12:25 Culu Children's African Dance Company
1:40 Pride of Zulu of South Africa
2:45 Euricka
4:05 Charmaine Neville Band w/ Reggie Houston and Amasa Miller
5:45 Bongo Maffin of South Africa

LAGNIAPPE STAGE
11:25 Holy Cross H.S. Jazz Ensemble
12:30 The Attributes Band

1:45 Have Soul Will Travel
3:05 Pamyua of Anchorage, Alaska
4:25 007
5:45 Otra

NATIVE AMERICAN VILLAGE STAGE
11:45 Native American Village Exhibition Powwow
2:00 Black Lodge Singers & Dancers
3:00 Native American Village Exhibition Powwow
5:15 Black Lodge Singers & Dancers

RHODES GOSPEL TENT
11:00 Christian Light Jubilee Choir
11:45 The Gospel Stars
12:30 New Zion Trio Plus One
1:15 Golden Wings
2:00 Providence Tones of Joy
2:45 Voices of Distinction
3:30 St. Joseph the Worker Mass Choir
4:30 The Brown Sisters
5:45 McDonogh #35 Gospel Choir

ALLISON MINER MUSIC HERITAGE STAGE
12:00 Odetta with Interviewer Douglas Brinkley
1:00 Christian McBride with Interviewer Mike Gourrier
2:00 Lil' Buck Sinegal with Interviewer John Sinclair
3:00 A.J. Loria with Interviewer Bruce Raeburn
4:00 Bongo Maffin with Interviewer Gabou Mendy
5:00 Helen Boudreaux and Marce Lacouture Cajun & Creole Ballads

KIDS' TENT
11:30 The Blues Schoolhouse
12:45 Clearwood Jr. High School of Slidell Choir
1:25 African Renaissance Dancers of South Africa
1:45 Caribbean Journey presented by Young Audiences
3:00 A.P. Tureaud Elementary School Studies Choir
4:00 Basin Street Sheiks
5:15 Panorama Jazz Band presented by Young Audiences

PARADES
3:00 Calendar Girls and Bon Temp Roulez SA&PCs with New Wave Brass Band

FRIDAY, APRIL 30

SPRINT STAGE
11:20 Water Seed
12:25 Brian Stoltz & Greazzy Azz Chicken
1:35 Pamyua of Anchorage, Alaska
2:45 Johnny Sketch & The Dirty Notes
4:05 The Benjy Davis Project
5:45 Karl Denson's Tiny Universe

POPEYES BLUES TENT
11:25 Rockin' Jake Blues Band
12:35 Owana Salazar & Hula Jazz of Maui, Hawaii
1:55 Bryan Lee & The Blues Power Band
3:05 God's Follower's of South Africa
4:20 Susan Tedeschi
6:00 Deacon John

ACURA STAGE
11:25 Los Sagitarios
12:55 Sister Teedy & Umami

2:25 Luther Kent & Trick Bag
3:55 Frankie Ford
5:30 Harry Connick, Jr.

SHERATON N.O. FAIS DO-DO STAGE
11:15 Belton Richard & The Musical Aces
12:30 Kim Carson & The Casualties
1:50 Jambalaya Cajun Band
3:15 Sean Ardoin n' Zydekool
4:40 The New Orleans Klezmer Allstars
6:00 C.J. Chenier & The Red Hot Louisiana Band

BELLSOUTH / WWOZ JAZZ TENT
11:15 Rhino Acoustic Project
12:20 Frederick Sanders & Soul Trinity
1:25 Willie Tee
2:35 James Rivers Movement
4:10 The Spirit Music Sextet w/ Me'Shell Ndegeocello, Ron Blake, Michael Caine, Chris Dave, Peck Allmond and DJ Jahi Sundance
5:50 Nicholas Payton's New Quintet

ECONOMY HALL TENT
11:15 June Gardner & The Fellows
12:25 Chris Clifton & His Allstars
1:45 The Original Last Straws
3:00 The Dukes of Dixieland
4:20 Ronnie Kole
5:45 Topsy Chapman & Solid Harmony

SOUTH AFRICAN FREEDOM @ CONGO SQUARE STAGE
11:15 Dillard University Jazz Ensemble
12:20 Kumbuka African Drum & Dance Collective
1:35 Zion Trinity
2:50 Pride of Zulu of South Africa
4:00 Bongo Maffin of South Africa
5:50 Cyril Neville & The Uptown Allstars 20 Year Anniversary

LAGNIAPPE STAGE
11:20 Stephen Foster's Mid-City Jazz Studies Ensemble
12:25 Betsy McGovern & The Poor Clares
1:35 Tondrae
2:50 Tony Green's Gypsy Jazz
4:20 Executive Steel Band
5:50 Chévere

NATIVE AMERICAN VILLAGE STAGE
11:45 Native American Village Exhibition Powwow
2:00 Black Lodge Singers & Dancers
3:00 Native American Village Exhibition Powwow
4:40 Pamyua of Alaska
5:20 Black Lodge Singers & Dancers

RHODES GOSPEL TENT
11:15 Southern Wonders
12:00 Tri-Parish Community Singers
12:45 David Rhodes & Assurance
1:30 God's Followers of South Africa
2:10 Lyle Henderson & Emmanuel
2:55 Wimberly Family
3:45 Coolie Family Gospel Singers
4:45 The Barrett Sisters
6:00 Xavier University Gospel Choir

ALLISON MINER MUSIC HERITAGE STAGE
1:00 Belton Richard with Interviewer Ben Sandmel
2:00 Albert "June" Gardner with Interviewer Tad Jones
3:00 Dick Waterman with Interviewer Tom Piazza

4:00 David Egan with Interviewer Mike Luster
5:00 Owana Salazar with Interviewer Peggy Scott Laborde
6:00 Songwriters' Circle featuring Lynn Drury and Gina Forsyth

KIDS' TENT
11:30 Young Louisiana Voices Collective
12:30 Village de L'Est Elementary School Choir
1:30 Eric McAllister
2:45 New Orleans Free School Performers
4:00 Angela Davis
5:15 Roy Roget & The Sons of the Bayouneers
6:15 Storytellers Sylvia Yancy Davis & Rosa Metoyer

PARADES
2:00 Double Nine, High Steppers and Single Men's Kids SA&PCs with New Orleans Night Crawlers Brass Band
4:00 New Generation and Young Men 2 Old Men Legends SA&PCs with Coolbone Brass Band

SATURDAY, MAY 1

SPRINT STAGE
11:10 Sonny Bourg & The Bayou Blues Band
12:15 Ritmo Caribeno
1:25 Martha Redbone
2:40 Sonny Landreth
4:10 Lil Band O' Gold
5:50 Marcia Ball

POPEYES BLUES TENT
11:35 God's Followers of South Africa
12:35 Henry Gray & The Cats
1:45 Lil' Buck Sinegal
3:00 Pride of Zulu of South Africa
4:15 The Blind Boys of Alabama
5:55 Clarence "Gatemouth" Brown w/ Gate's Express

ACURA STAGE
11:10 Leviticus Gospel Singers
12:15 Marc Broussard
1:25 Anders Osborne
2:55 The funky Meters
4:55 Santana

SHERATON N.O. FAIS DO-DO STAGE
11:15 La Bande "Feufollet"
12:30 Tin Men
1:45 Owana Salazar & Hula Jazz of Maui, Hawaii
3:10 Willis Prudhomme & The Zydeco Express
4:35 D.L. Menard & The Louisiana Aces
5:50 Dwayne Dopsie & The Zydeco Hellraisers

BELLSOUTH / WWOZ JAZZ TENT
11:15 Karin Williams
12:20 Victor Goines
1:35 Kidd Jordan & Alvin Fielder and IAQ
2:45 Leah Chase
4:10 Dave Brubeck Quartet
5:50 Terence Blanchard

ECONOMY HALL TENT
11:15 Original Dixieland Jazz Band
12:25 Chosen Few Brass Band Tribute to Anthony "Tuba Fats" Lacen
1:45 Ronnie Magri & His New Orleans Jazz Band
3:00 Michael White & The Original Liberty Jazz Band w/ Thais Clark & Nicholas Payton

4:25 The Pfister Sisters 25th
Anniversary Celebration
5:45 Preservation Hall Jazz Band

**SOUTH AFRICAN FREEDOM @ CONGO
SQUARE STAGE**
11:05 Golden Star Hunters Mardi Gras
Indians
11:55 Reggie Hall & The Twilighters
w/ Lady B & CP Love
1:00 Sunpie & The Louisiana
Sunspots
2:20 Busi Mholong and Usi
Mahlasela of South Africa
4:05 Shaggy
5:50 Lucky Dube

LAGNIAPPE STAGE
11:25 The Strawberry Jammers
12:35 Permagrin
1:50 Flamenco Forum feat. Micaela
y Fiesta Flamenca La Cristina
presents Olé Flamenco Olé!
3:30 Black Lodge Singers & Dancers
4:45 Alessandra Belloni
6:00 Fredy Omar con su Banda

NATIVE AMERICAN VILLAGE STAGE
11:45 Native American Village
Exhibition Powwow
2:00 Black Lodge Singers & Dancers
3:00 Native American Village
Exhibition Powwow
5:15 Black Lodge Singers & Dancers

RHODES GOSPEL TENT
11:00 Gloria Lewis & The Inspirational
Gospel Singers
11:45 The Unstoppable Gospel
Creators
12:30 Franklin Avenue Baptist Church
Mass Choir
1:15 The Johnson Extension
1:50 God's Followers
2:10 Mighty Chariots of Fire
2:55 Providence Baptist Church Male
Chorus & Choir
3:40 Lockport Chapter Mass Choir
4:35 Dorinda Clark-Cole
5:45 Watson Memorial Teaching
Ministries

**ALLISON MINER MUSIC
HERITAGE STAGE**
12:00 Me'Shell Ndegeocello with
Interviewer Karen Celestan
1:00 Willis Prudhomme with
Interviewer Herman Fuselier
2:00 Hugh Masekela with Interveiwer
Gabou Mendy
3:00 Lucky Dube with Interviewer
Gene Scaramuzza
4:00 Jay Chevalier with Interviewer
Jason Berry

KIDS' TENT
11:30 MidCity Full Arts Workshop
12:45 Sonny LaRosa & America's
Youngest Jazz Band
2:00 Jonathan Russell w/ The Todd
Duke Trio
3:15 Lois LaFond & The Rockadiles
4:30 Adella, Adella the Storyteller
5:20 African Renaissance Drums of
South Africa
5:45 Curtis Pierre w/ Samba Kids
6:15 Storyteller Dianne de Las Casas

PARADES
12:00 Dumaine Street Gang, Dumaine
Street Ladies and Original Big
Seven SA&PCs with Pinette
Brass Band
12:25 Economy Hall Parade with
Algiers Steppers SA&PC

1:00 Bayou Renegade II, Black
Eagles and White Eagles Mardi
Gras Indians
2:00 Pigeon Town Steppers,
N'Krumah Better Boys and No
Limit Steppers SA&PCs with
Storyville Stompers Brass Band
3:00 Hard Headhunters, Black
Feathers and Cherokee Hunters
Mardi Gras Indians
4:00 Second Line Jammers

SUNDAY, MAY 2

SPRINT STAGE
11:15 Sweet Pea's Revenge
12:20 Eric Lindell
1:30 The Revealers
2:45 The Wild Magnolias
4:10 Papa Grows Funk
5:40 The Radiators

POPEYES BLUES TENT
11:25 J. Monque'D Blues Band
12:35 Mem Shannon & The
Membership
1:45 Chris Smither
3:00 Pride of Zulu of South Africa
4:00 Marva Wright & The BMWs
5:45 Robert Cray

ACURA STAGE
11:30 TBA
12:55 Los Babies
2:15 The Dixie Cups
3:50 Smokey Robinson
5:40 The Neville Brothers

SHERATON N.O. FAIS DO-DO STAGE
11:10 Ray Abshire
12:20 Bruce Daigrepont Cajun Band
1:35 Curley Taylor & Zydeco Trouble
3:00 Kenny Bill Stinson & The Ark-La
Mystics
4:25 Poncho Chavis & The Magic
Sounds
5:55 Steve Riley & The Mamou
Playboys

BELLSOUTH / WWOZ JAZZ TENT
11:30 Julliard Jazz Ensemble
12:50 Harold Battiste presents The
Next Generation
2:10 Hugh Masekela of South Africa
3:40 Los Hombres Calientes
5:30 Dianne Reeves

ECONOMY HALL TENT
11:15 Louis Ford & His New Orleans
Dixieland Flairs
12:20 Clive Wilson & The New Orleans
Serenaders w/ guest Butch
Thompson
1:40 Tremé Brass Band
3:00 Lars Edegran & The New
Orleans Ragtime Orchestra
4:25 Gregg Stafford & The Jazz
Hounds
5:55 Pete Fountain

**SOUTH AFRICAN FREEDOM @ CONGO
SQUARE STAGE**
11:15 Blessed
12:20 Big Sam's Funky Nation
1:45 El Gran Combo de Puerto Rico
3:40 Wyclef Jean
5:35 Hugh Masekela Allstar Musical
Tribute to South Africa

LAGNIAPPE STAGE
11:15 Clancy "Blues Boy" Lewis &
Sheba Kimbrough
12:20 Loyola University Jazz
Ensemble
1:35 Jeff & Vida

2:55 Panorama Jazz Band
4:25 Reckless Kelly
5:55 Paky Saavedra's Bandido

NATIVE AMERICAN VILLAGE STAGE
11:45 Native American Village
Exhibition Powwow
2:00 Black Lodge Singers & Dancers
3:00 Native American Village
Exhibition Powwow
5:15 Black Lodge Singers & Dancers

RHODES GOSPEL TENT
11:00 Ebenezer Missionary Baptist
Church Choir
11:45 Jo "Cool" Davis
12:30 Val & The Dimensions of Faith
1:15 Paulette Wright & Volume of
Praise
2:00 Tyronne Foster & The Arc
Singers
2:45 Aaron Neville
3:30 Sherman Washington & The
Zion Harmonizers
4:30 Ricky Dillard
5:45 Nu Vizion

**ALLISON MINER MUSIC
HERITAGE STAGE**
12:45 Celebrating the photos of
Michael P. Smith w/ Michael P.
Smith, Nick Spitzer and Gregory
Davis with Interviewer Steve
Armbruster
1:45 Louis Armstrong Educational
Foundation presents: From the
Church to the House of Blues
feat. Dianne Reeves, Topsy
Chapman, Juanita Brooks &
Veronica Downs-Dorsey with
Moderator Farah Griffin
3:00 Tribute to Don "Moose" Jamison
w/ Badi Murphy, Nadir Hasan
& Edward "Kidd" Jordan with
Interviewer Maurice Martinez
4:00 Rafael Ithier of El Gran Combo
with Interviewer Michael
Skinkus
5:00 Chris Smither with Interviewer
David Kunian
6:00 Wyclef Jean with Interviewer
Kalamu ya Salaam

KIDS' TENT
11:30 Johnette Downing
12:45 Arts Connection Performers
1:45 Colleen Salley
2:45 Hobgoblin Hill Puppet Theater
4:00 David & Roselyn & Mo'Lasses
5:15 N'Kafu African Dance Ensemble
presented by Young Audiences
6:15 Storyteller John Lehon

PARADES
12:00 Scene Booster, New Orleans
Men Buck Jumpers and Single
Men SA&PCs with Lil' Rascals
Brass Band
1:00 Carrollton Hunters and Wild
Apaches Mardi Gras Indians
1:40 Economy Hall Parade with New
Orleans East Steppers SA&PC
2:00 Westbank Steppers, Original
Prince of Wales and Prince of
Wales Ladies SA&PCs with
Highsteppers Brass Band
3:00 Mohawk Indians and Creole
Wild West Mardi Gras Indians
4:00 Original Lady Buckjumpers,
Popular Ladies, Nine Times and
Nine Times Ladies SA&PCs with
Real Untouchables Brass Band

2004 NIGHT CONCERTS

FRIDAY, APRIL 23, 9 P.M.
Lenny Kravitz
The Johnny Clegg Band featuring the
music of Juluka and Savuka
Morris F.X. Jeff Municipal Auditorium
FRIDAY, APRIL 23, 10 P.M. & MIDNIGHT
Donald Harrison with special guests
ShowCase Uptown Supper Club
SATURDAY, APRIL 24, 9 P.M.
B.B. King
Etta James & The Roots Band
Mahalia Jackson Theatre of the
Performing Arts
SUNDAY, APRIL 25, 10 P.M.
Nicholas Payton Quartet
ShowCase Uptown Supper Club
TUESDAY, APRIL 27, 8 P.M.
Jazz At the Palm Court
Sweet, Hot & Low Down – Ladies Sing
the Blues
Juanita Brooks, Barbara Shorts, Lars
Edegran, Herlin Riley, Sammy
Rimington, Mark Braud, Freddie
Lonzo & Bill Huntington
Palm Court Jazz Café
FRIDAY, APRIL 30, 8 P.M.
The Dave Brubeck Quartet
Performing with The Louisiana
Philharmonic Orchestra And The
Loyola University Chorus
Mahalia Jackson Theatre of the
Performing Arts
FRIDAY, APRIL 30, 8 P.M.
La Noche Latina
El Gran Combo
Vivaz
House of Blues
FRIDAY, APRIL 30, 10 P.M.
Christian McBride Band
ShowCase Uptown Supper Club
FRIDAY, APRIL 30, 9 P.M.
Santana
Hugh Masekela
Morris F.X. Jeff Municipal Auditorium
Louis Armstrong Park

SATURDAY, MAY 1, 10 P.M. & MIDNIGHT
Urban Jazz Violin
Michael Ward
Jerald Daemyon
Rodney McCoy
Sweet Lorraine's Jazz Club
SATURDAY, MAY 1, 9 P.M.
Jaheim
Floetry
Mahalia Jackson Theatre of the
Performing Arts

Joe Cabral

The
PALATE
PIQUANTE

The spirit of the New Orleans Jazz & Heritage Festival flows through all the senses. Whether feasting on the sights and sounds for the full day or just a short afternoon, everyone stops to smell aromas and sample tastes that have come to be the Festival's signature – the full experience. Community starts at table and both native and visitor join in with intense passion.

Not surprisingly, food at the early Jazz Festivals was a labor of love by an ever-growing community of volunteers, who produced their food with pride, care, tradition and fresh ingredients, elements Louisiana's professional cooks are now known for worldwide. Sometimes the equivalent of a back yard cookout, sometimes a front porch hang, Jazz Fest food booths became not second thoughts in a hungry moment, but meeting places, second families' homes, and even more significantly, windows to the rich human variety creating Louisiana. These early booths, fueled by sterno and propane, gave way to more sophisticated operations organized in large

percentage by restaurants and professionals with inventive ideas about food. Family cooks, down home chefs, and award winners came together with family and volunteers; and they still do with memorable results. Undeniably, as time went on, despite the challenge of catering for 300,000 or so hungry souls, the New Orleans Jazz & Heritage Festival has evolved the world's best outdoor restaurant.

As the years passed, expanding culinary knowledge, interest, technology, and experiments changed America's taste buds, as much as locals' palates. Jazz Fest food adapted to the times, while remaining true to its traditional roots. Vendors explored those roots by inviting contrasting international immigrant influences. More formally, the Food Heritage Stage proved thousands of people hungered for cultural food knowledge. And while food supplies ebbed and flowed, or chefs applied their creativity to their ingredients for the sake of art, the food traditions of the church social, which the early Festival drew upon,

remained with us. If the iconic Buster Holmes has passed, his long time successor at Jazz Fest, Judy Burks, still dishes up old style red beans and rice after 30 years, since 1974. Remember, for the sake of tradition and the link with old world Creole cooking, that jazz master Louis Armstrong honored his birthplace in a tip of the fork, or pen, by signing letters "Red Beans and Ricely Yours." And while he would recognize the muffaletta, Vaucresson's sausages, the fried chicken, and the pralines still served at the Festival, he would hardly be criticized for wondering at the crawfish beignets, the Oyster Rockefeller Bisque or even Crawfish Monica, which never existed during his time on earth.

Vance Vaucresson and his family's sausage business is the oldest running vendor at Jazz Fest, having served food from the beginning in 1970. A third generation Creole from the 7th Ward, Vance took over from his father, Robert "Sonny" Vaucresson, who originally sold sausage sandwiches at the 1970 and 1971 Festivals in Beauregard Square. Now he sells hot chorizo style sausages, crawfish sausage and turkey andouille sausage, all equally spiced, succulently grilled and served as po-boy sandwiches. Vance has experienced the evolution at the Fair Grounds as electricity was added underground to the infield in the early 80s and more recent innovations like monitored, refrigerated staging trucks added on the tarmac near where the Jazz Tent is now. Food safety was

increased dramatically. "Jazz Fest is the only Festival I know which voluntarily invites the Health Department in, so if you're eating at Jazz Fest you know you're eating safely," Vance said. "In 1970, my dad used to own a restaurant on Bourbon Street. He made the sandwiches there, wrapped them in foil and brought them over in the car and sold them out the window. You can imagine the temperature fluctuations."

Nowadays, Vaucresson's sausage is made in the few days before the Festival in a controlled environment at the St. Bernard Avenue plant, trucked out to the refrigerator trailers, and then grilled on the spot behind the booth, kept hot in electric roasters to maintain the 160 degree temperature that health inspectors like to see to keep away unflavorable microbes and other such pests. The grill is, like many you see at festivals all over the country, a home design. A rotisserie of revolving shelves, the heat powered by propane, the smoke explodes from the door as a savory feast for the nose, and the drips hiss inside. This action happens in the small city behind the two rows of food booths that act as their nerve center. The atmosphere is no less friendly than the old familiar days of the mix of professionals, church and family run booths; lots of recipes and techniques are exchanged, lots of banter and servings of good food are traded among vendors. Things may only be more businesslike because there are more people to feed more often.

The Beauregard Square food stations included 6 or 8 foot folding tables, chafing dishes

and hand made signs. Buster Holmes, the king of red beans, whose restaurant in the French Quarter only a few blocks away, drew characters from all walks of life, ladled his specialty from a huge kettle set out in the open. The food was easy for vendors to carry in, set up and serve, yet it still covered a gamut of styles, including fried chicken and pralines, the story of which is told earlier in this book. Precooking and assemblage were the order of the day well into the 70s and Fair Grounds expansion.

The Festival's early tradition of working with the community started with churches fundraising by selling food at the Fest. Mrs. Mercedes Sykes, the pianist Roosevelt Sykes's wife, was involved with the group who decided they could raise money for a new sanctuary by selling fried chicken and her potato salad. So was born the Second Mount Triumph Missionary Baptist Church's table, then booth, which lasted all the way up to the 1995 Festival when the Congo Square/Caribbean cultures derived chicken dishes represented that feathered food clutch. Not to be outdone, a friendly rivalry began as the True Love Baptist Church started selling THEIR version of barbequed chicken. They, too, enjoyed a long run into the 90s.

Like the music, the food offerings grew from a handful of carefully-chosen dishes – in 1972 they were red beans and rice, boiled crawfish, po-boys, fresh oysters, hot tamales, muffalettas, fried chicken, Italian ice cream, Greek dishes, hot dogs, jambalaya, gumbo, stuffed peppers, "shrimp potpourri" picante, two unnamed "natural foods," pralines, and snowballs – to a staggering variety of items. As is clear from the early selection, food was intended as one component of the overall cultural experience of South Louisiana offered by the Heritage Fair. People

sometimes forget that Italian, German, and Spanish influences, among many others, have been just as strong as the French and African. In fact, according to the authority Leah Chase, Creole cooking in New Orleans differs from the rest of the state's Creole cooking in the use of oregano, a spice brought in by the Italians at the turn of the last century. Greek names proudly crop up in St. Bernard and Plaquemines, among the fishermen and oystermen. And Louisiana once stood as the buffer colony at the edge of the North American Spanish empire, hence tamales figure more largely than one credits. Luckily, the hot dog stand eventually lost out to the sausage po-

boys as that constituency developed a more piquante palate.

The move to the Fair Grounds laid down the linoleum for better ways to handle food and, therefore, an expanded menu. It didn't hurt that the infield space and multiple stage format fueled phenomenal growth with more mouths to feed. Still, in 1974, the food was basic Louisiana heritage cooking, easy to transport and easy to keep warm. The most noticeable change came with electricity strung in

an ever-ingenious overhead and board-covered spaghetti of wires strung by Eddie Lambert and staff. Electric warmers took the place of warming dishes and the culinary possibilities opened up. The crowd may have missed this, but it was important. Regardless, the smells of grills and jambalaya being cooked in open kettles over huge propane burners continued to tantalize.

The crowd probably did notice changes in approach. Staff convinced the Roman Candy Wagon to come park by a tree. Wooden booths were more formal and efficient, with serving shelves looking out into the crowd, and prep areas behind, supplemented by the 6-foot tables. The signature, uniform, hand-lettered signage also made it easy to read across the infield where a certain delicacy could be found. The offerings still were po-boys and muffalettas, red beans, gumbo, stuffed peppers, boiled shrimp, Creole eggplant, jambalaya, and crawfish bisque. These were all dishes that could be prepared beforehand and be kept sufficiently warm to be served outdoors – in other words, all foods that one found in big gatherings. Regardless of the increase in crowds there were three small food areas compared to 6 stages and 13 crafts tents. Significantly, by now a designated food coordinator organized the menu: Parker Dinkins adding a toque to his other site director and staff counsel hats.

Dinkins clearly had a more studied and eclectic interest in the food offerings. In 1975, the booths expanded to include shrimp fried rice; hickory smoked roast beef on a roll; and curried lamb, Jamaican style. The mid-70s attendance grew exponentially as did the food areas. By the time Dinkins handed the apron off to John Murphy, in 1978, the Festival had six food booth areas sprinkled all over the infield. There were now over 40 dishes, as boudin had been imported and cochon-de-lait – Cajun style roasted suckling pig – added. Tom Bernos, who served another version of red beans and rice, also came up with a new crowd favorite: oyster patties and fettuccine. Like the Yak-A-Mien mentioned in an earlier chapter, Bernos's dish was a solid breakfast for those who stayed out too late partying and needed to carbo load for the coming day of musical wonder.

The late 70s and early 80s were a heady time for American food. Led by such luminaries as Alice Waters in Berkeley and Daniel Bouloud in New York, the country was beginning to lionize a new celebrity: the chef, while learning to savor more than cheez whiz, fish sticks, frozen foods, and Spam of "the Greatest Generation." Actually, in the 60s, a non-chef, Julia Child, had laid the groundwork for herself and the writer James Beard to bring a whole generation the context for

culinary appreciation. The fresh and leafy foods creatively prepared in Alice Waters's kitchen fed the counter culture new ideas in healthy cooking. An obsession with Asian foods, springing from California, would soon lead out of the crockpot and into the wok in the home kitchen.

In New Orleans, the venerable restaurant icons Galatoire's and Antoine's continued to serve classic haute Creole cuisine from their anonymous

kitchens, while the immigrant chefs Daniel Bonnot and Günter Preuss updated traditions at other French Quarter restaurants. But at Commander's Palace, in the Garden District, a celebrity chef was being groomed. Paul Prudhomme's derivative creations based on his Cajun background brought country cooking onto the linen tablecloth. Coupled with the Brennan family's ability to promote their standard of excellence and service, Chef Paul became the most recognized cook in a South famous both for practitioners and appreciators. He would go on to open his own restaurant in the Quarter with his wife, Kay, and a young assistant, Frank Brigtsen (space in Brigtsen's own restaurant way uptown is now a hard to acquire seat during Jazz Fest weekends). By extension, Prudhomme fueled a nationwide craze for Cajun food, Cajun culture, and well, just plain spiciness. With perfect synchronicity, there was no better time and place to get a quick hit of the real deal in all its myriad flavors than at Jazz Fest.

"'To you a jazz festival is just eating with background music,' Alice said.

"'Jazz & Heritage Festival,' I reminded her. 'It's called The New Orleans Jazz & Heritage Festival. And what do you think the heritage of New Orleans is – macramé? In New Orleans, heritage means eating,'" wrote New Yorker correspondent Calvin Trillin around 1978 in his book *Alice, Let's Eat*. He rightly pointed out that "it is possible for a jazz fan to eat jambalaya from Gonzales just a few steps from the booth where he had eaten andouille gumbo from LaPlace on the way to eat boiled crawfish from Breaux Bridge." These were each places known for those dishes and took some driving to get to, so Trillin went on to appreciate that he was doing his part to alleviate the gas crisis of the times by walking around the Festival and eating.

Indeed, the care taken with selecting the foods and their makers was a hallmark of the Festival. Even locals cannot remember anyone complaining about

bequed goat and soft shell crab.

Dennis Patania, the winner of most booth listings in the program of 1982, provided the soft shell crab. He also cooked fried catfish and trout, and with the New Orleans Creole Kitchen, sold Shrimp Stuffed Merliton. Dennis and Vicky Patania's soft shell crab po-boys have become a highly anticipated favorite at the Festival and they still were selling them through 2004. The soft shell crab is a moulting Louisiana blue crab eaten whole,

des Allemands for the catfish). Rest (or munch) assured that these were swimming not so long before sound checks on stage.

Every food vendor at the Fair Grounds is a winner of sorts. They have survived the rigorous selection process. One book vendor happened in for a meeting in the mid 80s on just such a day and was caught up in the selection fever, tasting small samples of a couple of prospective dishes. While it is not recorded whose food he

not finding something good to eat. And often, locals used the Festival to try something new they might never have taken the opportunity to taste. Festival Heritage Fair Producer Nancy Ochsenschlager oversaw the food production in the early 80s, and the Louisiana Heritage flavors abounded. In 1982 for instance one could find grillades (veal) and grits, a traditional Creole dish, alongside booths featuring frog legs, hogshead cheese, bar-

shell and all, and if non-locals don't think about what they're eating, the rewards are self-evident. Many locals include this booth on their must-stop list, particularly for a sample of the perfection in the art of frying – the consistency of heat, delicacy and balance of flavor in the batter are hard to find anywhere, much less in an outdoor venue. Their secret ingredient is freshness, as they have cultivated sources in Lafitte for the crabs (and Lake

tasted, and whether the vendor was rewarded with a booth, he noted that the quality was very high and the decision-making must have been extremely tough. Furthermore, even the long-term vendors are subjected to periodic tastings so the production staff keeps everyone on their toes.

But flavor is not the only criteria. As Pete Hilzim, the originator of Crawfish Monica, explained, "The vendors are very carefully screened. They have to know what they're doing. You get out in this crowd, you don't know what you're doing, you're going to hurt yourself.

"So this organization (Festival Productions, Inc.) is just so well run on its detail level and its management level that it's astounding. I mean, they can tell you how many garbage bags they're going to use per thousand people and where the garbage cans have to be. You

know, it's incredible the details these guys go to. It's really well done…and then, it's fun!"

Some food vendors simply make a unique product and are asked back every year. And the value of Jazz Fest as business incubator exposure is unfathomable. Omar Aziz, "Omar The Pie Man," had been on the Jazz Fest scene since 1972 and making his home grown pies found in stores all over New Orleans since the mid 60s. One favorite is his sweet potato pie, made in the Southern tradition. His

son, Omar Aziz, Jr., now carries on the family business, though not at the Fair Grounds. After a 1982 start, Loretta Harrison began making her family's pra-

line recipe and has a long-term relationship with Jazz Fest. Her national notoriety took off after a heritage show on the Washington Mall, but she sells year after year at Jazz Fest, and has grown her business incrementally. And finally, Mrs. Helen Wheat's Meat Pies a la Natchitoches made their first appearance in 1979 and can

still be tasted today, although it's the son, James, operating the local firm's booth. Meat pies are of unknown origin, although Natchitoches used to be the frontier between New Spain and New France, and the meat pie bears resemblance to the empanada. The Creoles up there make it with beef or beef and pork and either bake or fry it.

Meanwhile, the city's health department, not so in evidence in earlier days, now sends several patrols out to the Fair Grounds with evaluation sheets and thermometers in hand. Their job is to make sure health standards, which laws have been built up in the years of the life of the Fest, are followed. As Vance Vaucresson pointed out, they

are invited in by the Festival and they visit each booth several times a day, making sure in particular that warm food is maintained at the right temperature and refrigerators are working and, importantly, that frozen food hasn't thawed and then refrozen. They ensure that food is not only fresh, but also handled properly. The Festival also maintains controls on pricing.

The 80s saw continued experimentation with the Jazz Fest menu. Many foods were added underscoring the Heritage component. Creole cook Zelida Lear introduced rice calas, reviving an age-old traditional food. These are kind of like rice beignets – rice balls fried in batter – which used to be sold by Creole street vendors in the French Quarter. They were like hush puppies, but made from left over rice instead of corn. Calas and Creole Cream Cheese would later be some of the first traditional American food enshrined in the Slow Food International Movement's Ark of Taste. Having grown up in Tremé, Lear's food interest stemmed from her grandmother and family traditions, as did her interest in music. Her father, Eddie Pearson, had played trombone in Papa Celestin's Band.

Meanwhile, alligator made an appearance and was well received enough to continue on into the new millennium. For those not in the know, the meat is basically tail meat and compares to chicken. Of course, blackened redfish came and went on the menu, as the rage caused officials to finally shut down commercial red fishing off the coast of Louisiana. One could also find Barbeque Shrimp, Macque Choux, Oysters Rockefeller Soup, stewed rabbit and roasted goat. Vegetarian and non-dairy dishes also were added, and such booths tried exotic names like Rasta Burgers or Mardi Gras Rice (with purple, green and gold vegetables).

The Koindu/Congo Square

CRAWFISH MONICA

Yes, there is a real Monica. Crawfish Monica, the Festival's best-selling food item, is named after Pete Hilzim's wife, Monica. "The smartest thing I've done in my marriage," said Pete, "so I don't have to explain forever why I didn't name it for my wife." While Crawfish Monica was introduced in 1984, made especially for Jazz Fest, Pete had a booth in 1983 offering Shrimp Diablo and eggplant dressing.

"Believe me, as a neophyte out here, it's very scary, your first day. We were new in processing, and didn't know a lot of things. I got open and up and running and up walks Paul Prudhomme, who is my friend and had been helping me, and Bryant Gumbel with the Today Show crew. They started filming and it was the second order I had done and it was a little intimidating. But we managed to pull it off, and so we started there."

Hilzim's father, before teaching English at Tulane University was executive director of the Louisiana Restaurant Association; so Pete's been involved with food since he was ten. As the owner of Kajun Kettle Foods, he provided pastas to the food industry; now, because of developing the sauce for Crawfish Monica, he deals just in sauces, gravies, and marinara. When he developed Crawfish Monica, he tapped Paul Prudhomme, who patronized his business, to help. Not only a great executive chef, Prudhomme has been the ambassador extraordinaire for Louisiana food and mentor to many

locals in the food industry.

But the spicy, creamy pasta sauce with crawfish tails was developed at a dinner party on Palmer Avenue in 1982. "We were lucky that we remembered it. It was a long party, and a kind of fortuitous occurrence because we just winged it." Hilzim then asked chef for his opinion and advice. "Paul really helped us make it so we could do it consistently and so the flavor profile worked every time."

Hilzim has a certified food chemist, Dr. Andrews, on staff, who said that over the two weekends of Jazz Fest, they use 10,000 pounds of crawfish. While their biggest day seems to be Saturday, the music acts will affect how many servings they dish up at their traditional location near the Acura Stage. The big Saturday sales are underscored by the fact they get a lot of people telling them their Jazz Fest doesn't start "until I've had my Crawfish Monica."

The biggest day ever was a Saturday around 2001, Dr, Andrews said, when "we had 160,000 here and it was a madhouse. We had all six lines and anywhere from 50 to 100 in each line. And that was at 6 o'clock, when we're getting ready to shut down normally. We just ran out of food and had to completely resupply the next day, a Sunday."

The recipe is a trademarked secret, and no one would say more than it's a cream sauce with Cajun spices, but it's one of the most widely recognizable names at a Festival widely known for great cuisine.

movement did its part to expand people's food knowledge, inspiring the introduction of booths featuring Gumbo Z'Herbes (the gumbo of many greens related to callaloo of the Caribbean); Curried Chicken and Caribbean Fish; and Chicken Creole with Caribbean Fruit Salad. Chef Cecil Palmer, of Gee & Lil's Restaurant on Haynes Blvd. introduced Chicken Jamaican, Bahamian Chowder and stir-fried vegetables out at the Fest. Palmer, of Jamaican origin,

Poulet Fricassee and Jama-Jama (spinach sautéed with ginger, onion and garlic) by Bennachin Restaurant's Alyse Njenge and Fanta Tambajang. Theirs is food from Cameroon and Gambia, authentically reproduced. Plenty of New Orleanians had their first taste of real African food at Jazz Fest. Health-conscious people and vegetarians have come to appreciate some of the dishes as well, and these vendors are still enjoying the on-site camaraderie.

In fact, the 90s catered to

rolls from Ninja Sushi Restaurant. But the Grandstand Tent evolved as more ethnic restaurants lined up: notably Jamila's, offering Lamb with Couscous; and Mona's Café, with its signature Gyro, salad, falafel and hummus.

The 90s saw the expansion beyond the track into the grandstand and outdoors, and organizers premiered a new idea. The late Lee Barnes had opened a cooking school way back in the 70s centered on heritage cooking, as did Joe Cahn with his

soon opened his own restaurant and soon had his own booth at the Fair Grounds. "It's a lot of work, but it's allright," he said. "I like to be outdoors. I like to cook in a Festival like this. It's a different feeling from being in the restaurant all day."

The Congo Square food booths in the 80s and 90s offered Peanut Soup and Vegetarian Rice, Chin-Chin, which was originally an African snack of goat stew, and eventually the

both a better-traveled and more sophisticated public with a more globally inclusive attitude. If Roberto Mendez of Taqueria Corona was the first to offer El Salvadorian tacos, he was soon joined by the Tortilla Factory's flautas and empanadas. By the mid 90s, other representatives from Louisiana's ethnic gumbo opened booths. One could choose German influenced bratwurst and potato pancakes or crawfish, shrimp or vegetable

very successful French Quarter School. Both had been involved in food at the Jazz Fest; and in fact Lee had co-authored in 1984 an official Jazz Festival Cookbook, paperback and staplebound, and touting the heritage of Louisiana food. Cooking schools had cropped up around the country, and on PBS and cable TV cooking shows were getting to be the rage. While this activity helped the general public get comfortable with the format, the new outdoor cooking demonstrations were actually a natural outgrowth of Festival producers' pride in Louisiana heritage. You'd had craft demonstrations for years, why not cooking?

The tragic loss of the grandstand in a late night fire would bear dividends for food heritage demonstrations when rebuilt. While the new upstairs kitchen supported the cooks on the infield, the new grandstand created an indoor theater for food heritage. The big ground floor room had perfect space for a stage and chairs, all the electrical outlets cooks needed, a ceiling to hang the overhead mirror so necessary to watching a cooking demonstration from an audience, and lots of air conditioning. Topping it off was the talent, a dizzying array of local food experts and award winning chefs. Though less household names than the musicians perhaps, all are their equals as masters of their craft. Lee Barnes's protégée, cooking teacher and Slow Food leader Poppy Tooker, and Creole culinary scholar and cookbook author Jessica Harris expanded on all things Louisiana and African Diaspora. The chefs list is a who's who of James Beard award winners and fascinating innovators of the Louisiana common pot: Prudhomme, Brigtsen, Bonnot, Austin Leslie, Leah Chase, Susan Spicer, Anne Kearney, and on and on.

If you're excited about eating, and have made reservations months in advance of coming to town for Jazz Fest, imagine the excitement of seeing a live demonstration by your favored chef, perhaps even getting to meet and

say hello, and then dining that night. That must be like…coming to town and seeing your favorite New Orleans group at Jazz Fest and…well, you get the (complete) picture. Hundreds of demonstrations, tips and historic recipes have been shared over the 15 or so years the demonstrations have played on. Much of it has been videotaped, too, and is one cornerstone of the New Orleans Jazz & Heritage Foundation's archive.

Sometimes someone introduces the perfect dish at the

perfect time. WWOZ celebrated the 25th Anniversary of Jazz Fest by serving the mango freeze. Up until that time, the top cool-me-down treats on the infield were Angelo Brocato's Italian ice creams and Zack's frozen yogurt. But the mango freeze, a flavorful fruity sorbet, became an instant favorite as it somehow balanced the hot, humid Louisiana sun, the slight veneer of dust from the track on a dry weekend with the refreshingly cold, lingering tex-

ture on your tongue. And we cannot ignore beverages. Lemonade, rose mint tea, water, and the ubiquitous beer; all served ice cold. Ice tonnage used at Jazz Fest was not a fact we've discovered yet, but suffice it to say thank God the commercial ice machine was born in Louisiana.

You may be what you eat, but you show your mind in your machines. The inventiveness of Jazz Fest food vendors with their slow cookers, their warmers, and the ways they organize their booth help, should be chronicled in a longer work, or at least noted and appreciated by the casual Festgoer. Pre-cooked or cooked on the spot, served hot or cold, with hot sauce or without, the amazing level of preparation and the intensity of flavors are without parallel anywhere. To taste Biker Bob's Pheasant Quail, and Andouille Gumbo or Fireman Mike's Alligator Sauce Piquante is to dance to culinary music.

KEEPERS *of the* FLAME

HERITAGE & FOLK CRAFTS

Hugh "Daddy Boy" Williams

On a foggy April dawn in 1997, fifteen-year-old Charles Robin (Roe-bann) helps his parents, Lisa and Charlie, pack up their truck before meeting up with grandparents Charles and Cecile "Celie" Robin. The route they travel takes them past single- and double-rigged fishing boats bobbing at piers along the St. Bernard coast. Among the vessels being prepared for the day's work are several built by the Robin men, who have harvested oysters, shrimp, and fish from Louisiana's coastal waters for generations. This day is special for young Charles because, although he has worked on the water alongside his father and grandfather, today he has been invited to help them share the family's traditions with more people than he's ever seen gathered in one place. He knows his grandparents have been excited that there will be three generations of Robins talking about their Spanish heritage and demonstrating the maritime skills his ancestors brought with them from the Canary Islands off the African coast.

At the entrance to the New Orleans Fair Grounds, the family is welcomed by bleary-eyed staff members and shown past stages undergoing noisy finishing touches, to the tent that will be their home base for the next three days. As the morning fog begins to clear, the men unpack the model Louisiana working boats the family carefully has transported from home, among them replicas of boats built by the Robin men and other boats in common usage. In addition, Charlie displays hand-woven fishing nets he has completed, along with the tools and materials he will use to demonstrate his technique. Cecile, a natural healer, tucks away some ingredients for her herbal remedies and treatments, "just in case."

After the display of skiffs, luggers, and other working boats has been arranged, the Robins wander around the tents that house the Louisiana Heritage demonstrations. In their own tent, which this weekend is called "Louisiana Waterways and Wetlands: Inspiration and Adaptation," the Robins greet

Ralph Serignea, a woodcarver from their own Isleño community, as well as two oystermen who have become good friends over the years, the Yugoslav "Cap'n Pete" Vujinovich, Jr., and Junior LeBeouf, who has brought his oyster boat and his special "Cajun oyster-shucking machine." This weekend, experienced participants are enjoying getting to know Cajun crawfisherman Kernis Huval, a born entertainer who has brought traps of his own design. The exceptionally-talented Scarlet and Melissa Darden contribute their techniques in Chitimacha split-cane and double-weave split-cane basketry to the tent's interpretative focus on ways in which Louisiana's cultures interact with their wetland environments, as do Houma woodcarver Roy Parfait and moss-doll maker Marie Dean. Roy and Marie have been to the Festival several times, and experienced demonstrators depend on Roy to interpret for "Miss Marie," who, like many older Houma Indians, speaks only French. Celie Robin is effusive in her description of the Festival experience. "We enjoy coming to the Festival every year; it's something we do together as a family. But it's not just the Robin family, it's everybody here. When we come here to talk about life in Louisiana, we all get to be a family and we look forward to seeing each other here. We bring lunch and we eat together. When we're here, everybody's equal and everybody has something to teach."

This scene is being repeated in the other tents in the Louisiana Heritage area of the grounds, as skilled textile artists from African-American, Cajun, Croatian, Isleño, Nicaraguan, and Norwegian communities take the misty morning time before the gates are opened to eagerly scrutinize each other's work and detail their own techniques over pastries and thermoses of warm coffee. In this tent, entitled "Domestic Crafts: The Common Comforts of Home," father-and-daughter team Ray and Tina Weimer split the cypress they will need to build a full-sized cistern over the course of the weekend, and Lionel Key adds to the piquant aroma when he takes a few "practice swings" with his Creole filé (powdered dried sassafras leaves) grinder. Over the sounds of cypress being split and the loud "crack-crack" of Lionel's mortar-and-pestle can be heard the sounds of old friends greeting each other. "Honey, I remember how you liked my stuffed artichokes last year, so this year I brought you some to take home." "Where's that beautiful grandbaby? She sure has grown!" "I sure will miss Tom Colvin; he won't be here 'til next week."

In the tent titled "A Joyful Noise: Ritual and Celebration in Louisiana," artisans from throughout South Louisiana compare Mardi Gras traditions, in some cases learning about unheard-of customs. The "Spy Boy" for the Wild Magnolias Mardi Gras Indians learns about the Cajun courir de Mardi Gras (the rural Mardi Gras tradition in which revelers travel from house to house, usually on horseback, and "dance for a chicken" or otherwise cajole householders out of ingredients for a community gumbo), and proclaims it "pretty wild." Makers of fanciful Mardi Gras ball costumes immediately hit it off with members of social aid and pleasure clubs, also first-timers, who have come to demonstrate their techniques of marching-club "shoe-pimping" (decorating shoes with color, cutouts, and appliqué to match fanciful suits), coconut decoration, and to describe what Mardi Gras is like for the "Baby Dolls" (African-American women, originally employed in the "red light" district, who draw inspiration for their satiny costumes from "Baby Doll" pajamas). Instrument makers, musicians all, set up chairs so they can jam a bit before the visitors arrive, and children of the demonstrators drift over to sit on the ground and listen. The sounds and aromas of breakfasts, as they are shared, and craft materials, as they are prepared, blend with greetings extended to old friends and new acquaintances. In every direction, one sees master craftspeople arranging their work of wood, feathers and beads, papier-mâché, Acadian brown cotton,

and other materials in rich and varied textures and colors.

"For us," says Coushatta pine-needle basket artist Marjorie Battise, "the most special time of the fair is the early morning, before the people come. We share breakfast and the air smells like coffee and fresh hay." Adds her sister Myrna Wilson, "That is when we learn about new customs and become friends with new people. We talk together about our experiences at the Festival; it's a real bond-

Studio Inferno

ing experience." Marjorie adds," Sometimes we see people here we only see once or twice a year, and there are always surprises. When the Cajun Mardi Gras (the participants are referred to as Mardi Gras) ran through the Fair Grounds, we were glad to see them because they come through our Coushatta neighborhood at home. Most people don't know that."

All over the Fair Grounds, others who maintain the flames

of local culture arrive early to watch the Festival grounds come to life. Social Aid and Pleasure Clubs (African-American community-based fraternal societies bearing names like "Money Wasters" and "Scene Boosters" that support members in emergencies and also parade in matching outfits supplemented by elaborate fans, banners, and baskets) in matching outfits, some including three generations of families, stroll among the exhibits and check out the food booths as

So why "heritage"? How did this event — this child of northern jazz and folk music festivals — come to host such a remarkable scene? In 1995, Allison Miner reminisced about her early vision and hopes for the new Festival, and why the event's planners thought that focusing on cultural heritage — both shared and unfamiliar — was an important way to bring people together. "When our Festival started in 1970, it was just the beginning of an opportunity for people to party together,

heard anything like this because my parents didn't allow me to go out and hear it, but now I'm really gonna party, and I'm really gonna enjoy it, and I'm going to forget all of my prejudices from childhood and I'm gonna see things differently.' And I think that's what our Festival did."

The choice of Congo Square as the Louisiana Heritage Fair's first location was itself both a political statement and a statement of creative intent. Congo Square sits at the edge of New

Jesse and Gloria Bourg

their proprietors set up the spit and fire for cochon de lait, fry up andouille for jambalaya, warm bread, and boil crawfish. Some of these men will perform more than once in a day — leading visitors in a secondline, changing suits and singing Mardi Gras Indian songs on a music stage, and perhaps being interviewed on the Music Heritage Stage. As the opening hour nears, the aromas of dozens of types of locally-loved foods fill the air.

to hear each other. The Civil Rights laws, the Festival, and just the nature of the changing scene in America during the Sixties — people didn't want to hurt someone of another race; you didn't want to continue the bitter agony that had been prolonged for hundreds of years in this country. So celebrating their culture with everyone there, black and white, became an opportunity for people to say 'Hey, this is spectacular! I've never

Orleans' Faubourg Tremé, one of the most historically-significant neighborhoods in the United States. Many of the community's teachers, writers, and doctors emerged from among the Haitian Creole population, while the majority of politicians of color made their homes there. Tremé's residents were some of the city's most renowned families of craftsmen, artisans, and musicians. Tremé was home to early jazz greats such as George Lewis,

"Jazz Fest allows me to bring some young people with me each year. They get to see the respect that is given to our traditions and it just reinforces a bit that what we do in the secondline clubs is important. I enjoy masking as Gang Flag with the Wild Magnolias and performing music with them, and being part of the Scene Boosters, but the most rewarding thing has been Kool and the Gang (a children's secondline club established by Johnny Kool). It's all about passing on the cultural heritage from the adults of the community to the kids. They learn about all the things our groups do, and they are all presented here at the Festival — making the streamers, the umbrellas, and the fans, and actually parading with the music.

It's not the same as in the neighborhood — that aspect of community, of stopping at selected establishments or certain homes is missing — but people get to see us that would never see a real neighborhood secondline. It's something for the kids to be proud of when they see that they are being trained to do something that is admired even outside the neighborhood, and being at the Festival can be used to reinforce what we do. It makes us more of a group, because we have our own traditions that are unique just to us, but it also promotes unity in a larger sense because people from the outside can relate better to our community, and that's good for all of us." JOHNNY "KOOL" STEVENSON

and Kid Ory. Contemporary jazz artists who have roots in the neighborhood, such as Troy "Trombone Shorty" Andrews and the Rebirth Brass Band, take pride in their connection to the community's rich history. One of the premier music spots in historic Tremé was Economy Hall, which the Festival honors by taking its name for the tent featuring traditional New Orleans Jazz.

The combination of music, brass band parades, and Mardi Gras Indian processions at the earliest festivals represented an attempt to draw connections for audience members between New Orleans best-known musical tradition – New Orleans jazz – and other, related, musical traditions that also arose from the same musical communities. It was easy for visitors to understand that they were observing living traditions when they saw the decked-out Social Aid and Pleasure Clubs and the Indians emerging from the nearby neighborhood, followed by community members who clearly knew the music and the musicians, and demonstrated for willing "outsiders" how to conduct oneself in the secondline of a neighborhood parade.

Although the early Festivals featured "folklife" primarily as it related to music's development and the roles it plays in communities, the words folklore and folklife have always been used in Festival literature and Festival promoters have encouraged demonstrations of additional facets of traditional life over the years. This Festival's goals presaged the visions of pioneering public folklorists Charles Camp and Michael Owen Jones, who see the public folklorist's role as promoting cultural understanding. Richard Kurin, director of the Smithsonian Center for Folklife and Cultural Heritage, argues that festivals advocate for "human cultural rights." It is not surprising that Allison, during her time away from New Orleans, worked for the Smithsonian Festival of American Folklife learning about cultural interpretation for traditional arts, and then brought that knowledge to the Louisiana Folklife Pavilion at the 1984 World Exposition.

The Introduction to the Festival, printed in the first Program Book, invited visitors to experience "the forces which have created this nation's most unique way of life – the music, the cuisine, the folklore, the art – all the things that make South Louisiana and its Queen City areas which can't be touched anywhere on the continent… Follow the street bands to the Municipal Auditorium each afternoon for a brilliant musical experience. Stroll through historic Beauregard Square to sample the unique native food, look at the exhibits and hear the golden sounds that only Louisiana's rich culture could produce." Over the years her love for folklife has been imparted to Fair Director Nancy Ochsenschlager, whose enthusiasm for local culture is both legendary and infectious and who, along with the first Folk Crafts Coordinator Ifama Arsan, was a driving force behind developing an area of the Festival devoted exclusively to Louisiana crafts.

The Festival continues to expand cultural interpretation beyond music, food, and crafts. Looking over the Festival before her death in 1995, Allison pronounced herself satisfied that the harmonious and respectful presentation of native cultures – the reverence, as she put it – had extended itself beyond the Anglo and African-American residents of the New Orleans area to include a wider representation of the numerous cultures that call Louisiana home.

Festival producer George Wein (whose Festival Productions, Inc., produces the Newport Jazz Festival as well as the Newport Folk Festival) held eclecticism as a virtue in Festival programming. "We want to throw modern, swing, and Dixieland together, even have the guys playing them together. As long as there's a common beat, every guy can play solo his own style," he enthused to a *New Yorker* writer in 1954. The jazz and the folk festivals both sought to bring together, even blur distinctions between, musicians whose music carried on the traditions of their cultures (Mississippi John Hurt, Maybelle Carter) and tradi-

tion-inspired "folk musicians" (Ian & Sylvia, The Kingston Trio). Emissaries scoured the country to learn about musicians who would be appropriate for the Festival, so that audiences were treated to performances of authentic Delta blues in one hour and of California "folk revival" music in the next.

In New Orleans, however, young music researchers Allison Miner and Quint Davis were hired specifically to identify musicians from the South Louisiana area. When the Festival brought the Meyers Brothers Bluegrass Band together with the Zion Harmonizers, it did much more than make a political statement or corner a new market. It allowed Louisiana musicians to share their music with each other, in some cases to note shared musical roots that had evolved, in different cultures, into unique styles. Audiences too, largely local in the first years, learned about their own musical heritage and were given the opportunity to learn more about their neighbors. This was quite different for a large "city Festival." Small

Johnny "Kool" Stevenson

local festivals all over the state have long featured the musics of the cultures being celebrated, but in New Orleans these traditional musical styles were being brought together and the performers were often not professionals at all, but were people who performed only in their own communities or churches for people of similar musical inheritance. Jazz Fest focused audience attention on, for instance, the fact that many cultural groups contributed to the development of traditional jazz in Louisiana.

From the beginning, the most spectacular aspect of the Festival has been its inclusion of so many amazingly-talented local musicians, cooks, and artisans whose work had previously been unknown to a wider audience. The New Orleans Jazz & Heritage Festival has never had as its intention, though, to showcase only local, or even regional, artists. Though the name does confuse some, it no more attempts to program strictly local artists than the Newport festivals featured Newport-born artists.

CHALLENGES OF PRESENTING LOUISIANA'S VARIED CULTURES

From its inception at Congo Square, the "Heritage Fair" component of the New Orleans Jazz & Heritage Festival has striven to position New Orleans', and Louisiana's, music as one aspect of a dynamic cultural tableau. In 1971 knowledgeable music-lovers drove in to the city to observe or participate in the jazz funeral for Louis Armstrong. Many fans of New Orleans culture know about the rituals of the jazz funeral – the somber procession

Lorina Langley

to the cemetery followed by festive dancing in the secondline after the departed has been "cut loose." However, not many people other than locals – both Catholic and Protestant – know about other New Orleans-area funerary traditions such as cleaning and whitewashing tombs, and decorating them with fresh or handmade waxed-flower coronnes de toussaints on La Toussaint, or All Saints Day. The first Jazz Fest was unique in presenting traditional music in a form that was as close to authentic as could be arranged in a Festival setting – the secondlines were scheduled, but the members of the participating brass bands and Social Aid and Pleasure Clubs were marching and dancing very near their own neighborhoods and accustomed routes. Over the years,

the Festival has attempted to present traditions that easily "translate" alongside those that require more interpretation, and to illustrate that what might seem different artistic disciplines – food, music, customs related to

mourning, specialized crafts – all spring from traditional life and, in some cases, even represent various aspects of a single life as it is experienced in Louisiana.

Of course, presenting Louisiana customs is challenging precisely because there is no typical Louisiana lifestyle. Louisiana folklife is both rural and urban, has its roots in tradition but is influenced by pop music, politics and media, adapts to newly-available materials, and still carries deep meanings among rapidly-changing communities. Community life is closely tied to environment but, again, Louisiana's environments are almost as varied as the cultures that have settled here. Northeast and North Central Louisiana are predominantly British and African American, and include both Lowland and Upland South culture. Most of the region is rural, but includes the cities of Monroe and Ruston. The Red River Valley, which cuts across the state from Shreveport to the Mississippi and includes Alexandria and Natchitoches, maintains the cultural traditions associated with the Lowland South. The Neutral Strip, near Zwolle, includes Hispanic remnants of early Texas. Other cultural groups include French, Cane River Creoles, Native Americans, and Czechs.

Louisiana's Florida Parishes are predominately British and African-American, with significant numbers of Hungarians and Italians. The predominant culture of the Mississippi River Road parishes, from St. Francisville to north of New Orleans, is a blend of French and Lowland South plantation culture. The Acadiana parishes are located from west of the Atchafalaya Swamp to the Texas border. They are mostly rural, but include Lafayette, Lake Charles, and New Iberia. The region includes the Louisiana Prairie, Bayou Teche, coastal marshes, and parts of the Atchafalaya swamp. The predominant culture is a complex blend of French, Spanish, and African. Other cultural groups in this area include Anglos, Laotians, and Chitimacha and Coushatta (also spelled "Koasati") Indians. Eastern Acadiana includes Bayou Lafourche and the Terrebonne marshes, and other parts of the Atchafalaya swamp, where the dominant cultures include French, Spanish, African, and Houma Indian.

The city of New Orleans and the surrounding suburban and rural parishes represent the state's greatest concentration of citizens and cultural groups. New Orleans' urban culture is a complex blend of French, African, Spanish, German, Irish, Italian influences. Other groups include Latinos, Vietnamese, Croatians, and Isleños. Outside the cities, draft animals work in woodlands north of Lake Pontchartrain, and eighth-generation Filipinos of the Barataria wetlands recall growing up in fishing villages raised on stilts. As the Festival has attempted to present demonstrations of traditions from throughout the state, the challenges of interpretation – exhibit development, grouping, thematic choices, selection of specific individuals to represent "master work" in a craft or custom – have multiplied.

Vernie Gibson

ADDRESSING THE CHALLENGES

The Heritage Fair has always recognized the qualities inherent in Louisiana traditional life that make for unique challenges when presenting a "representative" sampling of Louisiana culture to the public. The earliest fairs brought attention to "extramusical" traditions of selected cultural groups – primarily Cajun, African-American, and Native American, and more recently the Fair has sought to present all of Louisiana's sizeable cultures, from the Greater New Orleans region and beyond. In the early years a number of the traditions, and even the musical styles, presented were new to the small band of producers who based some invitations on recommendations or recordings.

The first Festival occurred at a time that was pivotal in the relationships between many of the cultural groups presented and the larger culture. Much mention has already been made of the negotiations required to create this event featuring Anglo- and African-American musicians playing together. Not as many people realize that this event represented a milestone for other Louisiana cultures as well. In fact, Festival organizers did not realize, at the time, that their invitation would represent more than just a paying gig to the Cajun and Zydeco musicians on the program.

Older Cajuns still speak of the time of enforced cultural assimilation, when Louisiana's Cajuns were prohibited from speaking French in the schools. The feel-

ing of having to hide one's cultural identity followed students throughout their school careers and also dogged Cajuns when they thought about mixing with non-Cajuns outside their own communities. Regular Jazz Fest performer Hadley Castille's song "200 Lines" refers to the punishment for speaking French at his school. Children were required to write "I must not speak French on the school grounds" 200 times. Other punishments, such as rapping the children's knuckles with a ruler, were also dispensed. Rather than emphasiz-

ing the importance of fluency in English, many teachers simply punished students for speaking or singing in French, instilling in them a sense of shame about their cultural identity. To spare their children these experiences, most parents of this generation did not teach their children French, and older musicians felt that country music, swing, or jazz were "better music."

Some older Cajuns report that, in the past, they preferred not to advertise their Cajun iden-

tities when they were away from home. Hadley says, "There's such a contrast between the interest people have in Cajun culture now and the way it was when I was coming up," and describes an occasion, when he was dining at New Orleans' Court of Two Sisters around the time of the first New Orleans Jazz & Heritage Festival, when he was made to feel ashamed of using a violin to make Cajun music, a little-known or understood form of music at that time.

"We decided to go to the Court of Two Sisters. We were

all hairy-legged plumbers – we were all makin' pretty good money, so we could eat. In those days I drank some. So Mr. K. P. Fontenot, a very outspoken plumber from Ville Platte … so there's a guy [a strolling violinist] playing – you didn't play Cajun music in New Orleans; you hardly played country – here's this guy playing – Bach or whatever, beautiful stuff – K. P. says to him 'Hey, et toi – et toi, garçon, can you play Jolie Blonde on that thing?' Boy, I wanted to sink down with shame! The guy said 'No, sir.' K. P. said 'Well, we got somebody here who can play it!' So the guy handed me his fiddle, and, you know, I played it. But, I felt so bad playing it, I felt so bad! But I did it. But that shows you how it was back then. Now, it's such a big contrast. I'm not ashamed anymore."

Hadley credits the "Cajun Revolution" of the 1970s, part of which was the inclusion of Cajun performers at the New Orleans Jazz & Heritage Festival, as well as at Newport and other nationally-respected venues that presented acknowledged musical "greats," with helping to move Louisiana's Cajuns from hiding their heritage to celebrating it and sharing it with their own newest members, and also with outsiders. The "Cajun Revolution" has been so successful that the majority of today's Festival visitors are completely unaware of the dark days so recently left behind by the Cajuns whose music they enjoy.

Similar stories have been related by Louisiana's Native American tribes, who now regularly participate in folklife presentations at the Festival but still struggle with issues of group identity and outside recognition. Woodcarver Roy Parfait, a Houma Indian from Dulac who is one of the most frequently-invited demonstrators at the Festival, stresses that the Festival is important not only to the individual artisans invited from his and other Native American tribes, but that the invitations are considered an honor to the entire tribe. The Houma tribe in particular hopes that recognition from organizations such as the New Orleans Jazz & Heritage Festival will one day lead to federal recognition and official tribal status. Like the Cajuns, Houma Indians spoke only French until the most recent generations and Roy usually does double-duty as presenter and interpreter. In recent decades, Native American music and storytelling traditions have been presented on music and narrative stages, but for many years their participation in the Festival has been primarily in the crafts area, which has highlighted basketry from the earliest days.

CRAFTS AND EXHIBITS

The crafts area's evolution tells the story of the growing seriousness with which Jazz Fest regards both contemporary and traditional arts, as well as its tightening of control over items which it now licenses exclusively, such as T-shirts. The Program Book listing for the crafts presented in 1972, written by Crafts Coordinator Henry Hildebrand in his final year in that role, is typical of its decade in terms of the mix between contemporary and

traditional arts, and other items, that were on display and sale.

"Barbara Byrnes's shop 'Shell Game and All That Jazz' will present a selection of jazz and blues recordings, reference and song books. John Donnels, an official U.S. Navy combat artist who was the proprietor of the Starving Artists Gallery, will show an exhibition of jazz photographs.

"The New Orleans Jazz Museum, an affiliate of the New Orleans Jazz Club, has been a

source of information to Crescent City visitors for over twenty years. This year the Louisiana Heritage Fair has donated them the use of a booth in which Justin Winston will prepare a New Orleans Jazz History Exhibit.

"The Louisiana Oyster Festival from Galliano has a specially designed Oyster Industry Display. Mignon Faget's crafts include silver cast sand dollars and custom leather clothing. She has also designed a special Jazz Festival Tee Shirt. The Friends of the Cabildo have hand made

dolls from throughout Louisiana, old time iron toys, and a large selection of Louisiana books, prints, and maps. Michael Curtis is a silver and brass worker from Abita Springs, and the Brass Roots Co-op, also centered across the lake, is headed by Courtney Miller and produces jewelry, leather work, and pottery.

"The famous pastel portrait work of Jackson Square will be represented by the Genesis Gallery. Sally Fontana's Kite Shop will be flying their homemade and imported wares. Tom Ingram's leather crafts include moccasins, belts, hats, and purses, while Maurice Robinson and Roger Boyd make multi-colored candles using driftwood.

"Mary Crawford and Darlene Smith are co-owners of Alternatives, which contains a myriad of hand crafted items including painted velvet clothes, pottery and macramé. Mary is also making Olympia Brass Band Tee Shirts.

"Cruz Sanchez has Middle Eastern style robes and caftans and Steve Hartnett creates Tiffanyesque lampshades, aquariums, fountains, and windchimes from glass bottles. Jo Ann Clevenger is responsible for the brightly colored flower carts which rove the grounds.

"The large and artistically-talented Indian population of Louisiana will be represented by a delegation from Eunice headed by Claude Medford, Jr. The tribes represented this year are the Tunica of Avoyelles Parish, the Houma from Terrebonne Parish, and the Choctaw and Coushatta from Jefferson Davis Parish."

"The first year that I did go was the second year. It was very exciting. I compare it to the early days of Zulu. Most black people in the 20s and 30s, they didn't go see the Zulus because they didn't like what they were doing. My grandmother would say in Creole, "Don't go see those Negroes making monkeyshines for the white people." At first I didn't go to the Festival, but people were talking about it. Going there gives us the chance to give people the correct impression. The first time I went on the stage (at the Heritage Fair), it was packed. I was interviewed and afterward people told me, "Man, I learned a lot." People wanted to compliment my suit or talk to me; it took an hour to get in the clear.

I was Big Chief of the Yellow Pocahontas after my daddy, who took over from Sidney Pierre. After we were there, we felt great because it meant so much to us and the people enjoyed it. Even the raggediest one was so pretty! People know us now. There's not a place I can go without being recognized; I've talked to so many people, everybody knows Montana and everybody knows Mardi Gras Indians. When you get hooked on it, you die loving it. And people love to come out and see the Indians. The last time I went out there with my suit, I got my crown to the gate and they didn't have a big enough truck to carry it. So I had to carry it all the way across the field. Doing this, it puts

a whipping on you! I don't go anymore; that's for the young ones and the ones that like the recognition. I don't need it.

I was there with Tambourine and Fan in the early days, when Jerome Smith was in charge of the group. The secondlines don't take anything away from the Mardi Gras Indians — the Indians or the Skeletons, the Baby Dolls. They have more secondline clubs now than they ever had. If you want to go out and meet some people, you can always meet up with a secondline. I taught all of them (Tambourine and Fan) how to make a basket; they're known for them now. How I got the idea — in houses they used to have straw baskets on each side of the sofa, and at a funeral you had a big basket on each side of a casket with flowers. The club, when they parading, they were going to carry those baskets. I said to Jerome, "Man you been runnin' around, you not gonna find enough straw baskets for everybody." Big Ike was working at a printing company. I said "Ike, how much of that cardboard can you get?" After we got enough, I had my son with me and we laid out the cardboard. Got those youngsters to hook up two of them tables, and I started swingin' that pencil. I made the baskets and then each one could make them look whatever way they liked it. The people at the Festival, and in the streets, they couldn't believe those baskets! And now our baskets are well-known."

BIG CHIEF ALLISON "TOOTIE" MONTANA

The traditions of two cultural groups – Coushatta basket makers and Galliano oyster fishermen – complemented the dozen contemporary crafters and vendors, one exhibit of historic items, and two booths selling books and records. In 1973 an exhibit was created around the paintings of self-taught gospel artist Sister Gertrude Morgan, and the Robertson family from St. Landry Parish made and sold African-American split-oak baskets and corn-shuck dolls.

By 1975 the number of craft offerings at the Heritage Fair had exploded to fill one-hundred and six booths, six of which featured Louisiana cultural traditions; they were the Robertsons's split-oak basketry, hand-built accordions by Mark Savoy, and violins by the revered Lionel Lelieux (sharing a booth and occasionally being persuaded to play together), hand-carved duck decoys by Jack Wilson, hand tailoring by Lorina Evans, an exhibit of Zulu crafts and artifacts, and Coushatta pine-needle basketry by Lorena Langley and her family. Many of the other craftspersons offered wares that were inspired by traditional techniques and materials, and the majority of them were from Louisiana. 1976 saw the addition of Monk Boudreaux, Big Chief of the Golden Eagles, who allowed one of his Mardi Gras Indian suits to be put on display – the first time most non-community members were able to view a suit close-up – and demonstrated his beading technique. 1977 was the first year the Heritage Fair featured a display of blacksmithing, from that year on a Festival

Milton Fletcher

tradition, but is most notable as the first year in which young contemporary crafter Nancy Ochsenschlager, from Aurora, Illinois, participated in the Heritage Fair by selling her handmade ties in the Crafts Village.

Because traditional craftspersons often do not promote their work outside their own communities – sometimes out of knowledge that their work has less relevance outside their own cultures, sometimes because the artisan does not make a living or even a profit on his or her works, because their items are created for sacred reasons or occupational use and are not for sale, or for other reasons – it is much more difficult for a busy Festival programmer to learn about those who maintain the crafts and other traditions of Louisiana's indigenous cultures.

Nevertheless, each year the Festival's second crafts coordinator, Vitrice McMurry, added at least one or two of Louisiana's cultural tradition-bearers. She was able to do this with the help of the Louisiana Folklife

Program, the National Parks Service, folklorists who worked with various universities, and independent researchers.

"I was with the Festival from 1973 to 1983; I was asked to coordinate the craft area and turn it into something better. Each year I spent four months on the Festival and eight months selling jewelry in town and at craft fairs. That was one reason they hired me; they wanted to bring some people from around the country to spice it up, and I had a lot of connections with the national contemporary scene. I also felt a real affinity for the traditional scene.

"When I arrived, crafts were mixed in with local charities and activist organizations, so it was very ticklish to wean them out. A New York dealer had records for sale. The selection was great, because you could find some rare things like old Louis Armstrong records, but they weren't crafts. It was obvious that we had to weed out things that weren't crafts of any sort; we wanted it to look like more than just a local flea market. At that point the Festival didn't have a lot of money, so at first I went around asking local groups to contribute toward prize money that would encourage some of the better artist to apply. Then later, the craft vendors did well enough that we didn't need prizes.

"Early on, we didn't have as many out-of-state applicants. I instigated a nascent jury process, similar to that of some of the festivals where I exhibited my jewelry, in order to give the craft area that kind of credibility. Some vendors that sold imports didn't want to be part of the jurying system, and so they broke off and Koindu was established, which later became Congo Square Crafts.

"The traditional craft people weren't presented any differently from the other craft vendors; the booths were the same. So to an audience they seemed alike. From the beginning, the Festival paid folk demonstrators and charged craft vendors a fair price for booth fees. The focus of the folk crafts was the crafts rather than education, but the whole thing was pretty laid-back and it wasn't too much of a problem in those days when the folk craft people sold out early.

"I tried to put the folk crafts together as much as I could. I think they were happy to be separated. Many of them were intimidated by the city. Most of them were very honored to be invited and loved being put up in the hotels. Many of them had never been to New Orleans. One of my favorites, an older man named Willie London, came from North Louisiana, and he had a relative who took him all over the city, but we had to give him a little bit of spending money. He brought about ten little purses with him, so he would sell out almost immediately, and he wouldn't have two nickels while he was here. There were a few people who had very few things to sell, but they would talk to people and they were very sweet people who had to be treated with a great deal of respect.

"Another of my favorites was Daddy Boy Williams. I don't know why he had no nose, but he had carved himself a wooden nose. He was a wild fellow. Even sitting in a lawn chair, with a colostomy bag hidden under a blanket, he was outrageously flirtatious. He carved these walking sticks; some of them had carved women on them with these enormous tits made of Mardi Gras beads, and some real rococo stuff.

"I was traveling a lot for festivals, with my jewelry, and when I could I worked in side

Monk Boudreaux

trips to learn about Louisiana crafts. I went down and stayed with some Lutheran missionaries working among the Houma Indians and met some of the ones who still come to the Festival, met the Chitimachas, who didn't get along with each other at that time, and the peaceful Coushattas. I did a lot of road trips, searching out the folk crafts."

Speaking of her relationship to her art, Coushatta basket-maker Lorena Langley says, "All the crafts that I possess have been handed down from my mother and grandmother, who told me that if I kept our crafts, spoke our language every day, did not cut our hair and followed the rules and medicines of our people, we would continue as a tribe forever." Lorena mentions that her seven children have all welcomed the lessons she received as a youth and points out that her materials, like her inspirations, come from the swampy lands near her home.

By 1980 there were 113 craft booths. A few of the artisans demonstrated their craft process. Most of them appeared at the Heritage Fair both weekends. Generally, eight craftspersons shared a 20' x 30' tent, and the traditional craftspersons were usually located near each other. One tent that year, which featured a mix of contemporary arts and traditional crafts, saw the first participation by a local basket artist named Diane Ifama Arsan.

The following year, the crafts were divided into two newly defined areas, and each area had its own coordinator. Diane Ifama Arsan coordinated the

Folk Crafts, which retained the moniker "Village," since it also retained the original crafts area, the spot with the oak tree where the Louisiana Folklife Village sits today. Contemporary Crafts moved toward the rear of the Fair Grounds, and Sandra Blair took over the direction of this department, which has grown to become one of the most nationally-prestigious venues for contemporary artisans. Sandra worked from 1981 to 1991, when Christine "Kena" Bradford assumed leadership of the department. By 1991 procedures for the Contemporary Crafts Department had become fairly streamlined, but it has certainly had its ups and downs along the road.

During Ifama Arsan's time as the first Folk Crafts Coordinator, from 1981 to 1994, the Festival's view of "folk crafts" gradually came into clearer focus. The 1983 Program Book defined folk crafts as "noncommercial works of art created by untrained artists" but over the years organizers came to recognize the intense training undergone by those considered, within their own communities, to have become master craftspersons. Beginning that year, there were five 20-by-20-foot Folk Crafts tents. The craftspersons were able to sit under them in relative comfort, facing outward, and Festival attendees walked around the outsides of the tents and viewed the crafts, which were laid out on counters that served to separate artisans from visitors.

By 1984 the representation of Louisiana heritage expanded to become much more dynamic, including demonstrations of

Brownie Ford

traditional skills that resulted in no "craft item" at all, but were illustrative of various aspects of Louisiana life. Ranching traditions were displayed by the Telcala family of Rambouillet Ranch, who demonstrated sheep-shearing, and the processes of wool-carding for quilt-batting and spinning the wool into fibers for weaving and knitting. In later years, Danny Ayo of Maurice, Louisiana, did a similar demonstration that he called "Sheep to Shawl." The following year, a consortium of Italian civic groups built an elaborate St. Joseph's Altar on the infield of the Fair Grounds. Though the craft area retained its primary focus on vending, a precedent was established for the inclusion of demonstrations with no commercial aspect.

During this time, the area edged from "folksy" crafts toward craft traditions and demonstrations that illustrated various aspects of traditional life specific to Louisiana, though it still housed crafts and artisans that were not from the state, and it also welcomed artists who practiced crafts borrowed from other cultures. Some of these included Oriental rugs, painted fabric, puppets, decorated cypress knees, and "decorative" items made from alligator heads. As more information was gathered about authentic Louisiana traditions, inauthentic demonstrations were very gradually phased out or moved to other areas.

This period also saw the inclusion of many of the demonstrators without whom the Festival would now be unimaginable to many. Among these are Ava Kay Jones, the Voodoo and Yoruba priestess who is consulted by believers and non-believers annually, and "Miss Savannah" Lewis, who has been making her idiosyncratic pine-needle baskets for over 75 years after learning from the Choctaw woman who taught crafts at "the only school open to black girls" in 1920s New Orleans.

A survey of past demonstrators reveals other gems. Imagine visiting with Charles Neville as he carves pipes and walking canes, or sews on his signature beaded berets, as visitors were able to do in 1983-7. Connoisseurs of traditional crafts have, through the years, had the opportunities to meet some of the state's finest artisans who have now passed on, some of whom have been recognized as National Heritage Award winners, such as Chitimacha basketmaker Ada Thomas, cowboy balladeer and craftsman Thomas Edison "Brownie" Ford, and Cajun weaver Gladys Clark.

CHANGING ROLE OF HERITAGE: LOUISIANA FOLKLIFE

Toward the end of 1994 Laura Westbrook assumed direction of the Folklife Department. She coordinated the folklife demonstrations, the Louisiana Marketplace, cultural exhibits and self-taught artists in the Grandstand, and the relatively new Folk Demonstration Stage until a 1998 fellowship offer made further Festival work impractical. Because the director of the Heritage Fair, Nancy Ochsenschlager, was very interested in bringing new dimensions to cultural interpretation at the Fair, it wasn't difficult to obtain the go-ahead to make a number of major changes. One of the challenges was to clarify the distinction between the Louisiana Marketplace and the folklife demonstrations. The Marketplace had been established in 1989, but its rationale was unclear. It was a place where six vendors, whose crafts were not especially distinguishable from those in the demonstration tents, paid booth fees to exhibit and sell their wares, much like the artisans in the Contemporary Crafts area. Its proximity to the traditional demonstrators further muddied the distinction.

In 1995 an archway, similar to that which divides Congo from the area that presents Louisiana traditions, now called the Louisiana Folklife, rather than the Folk Crafts, Village, welcomed visitors to the area. It serves as a demarcation between the Folklife area and the Louisiana Marketplace, and guidelines were developed for Marketplace vendors. The Marketplace was expanded to include 16 artisans each weekend, and a system of utilizing a panel of outside jurors to determine invited artisans was implemented. This way, the difference between the two areas was not simply that Marketplace vendors paid booth fees while demonstrators received honoraria, but the two areas are now different in their missions.

The Louisiana Marketplace includes artists who would be classified as self-taught (whose works may illustrate aspects of their culture but are not traditional to their culture), revivalist (crafts borrowed from another culture, or that have fallen out of common usage) or those whose works are tradition-based (inspired by traditional techniques or materials). The Contemporary Crafts Coordinator, Kena Bradford, organized a workshop called "The Mystery of the Crafts Jury Process," that was open to all Marketplace and Contemporary Crafts applicants. At this workshop, which is still occasionally offered by Festival staff, vendors were able to learn more about Festival guidelines, how to make the best possible slides, and other tips to ease the application process.

In 1996, the Folklife Village assumed the form it retains today. The five tents, under which demonstrators sat facing out, were replaced with three large 30 by 55 foot tents that housed demonstrators who were grouped according to broad themes. That first year, the themes were "A Joyful Noise: Festive and Ritual Traditions,"

"Louisiana Waterways and Wetlands: Inspiration and Adaptation," and "Domestic Crafts: The Common Comforts of Home." Presentations on the Demonstration Stage included Coushatta storytelling by Bertney Langley, various Native American dance groups, Cajun dance lessons, oyster-shucking demonstrations, Creole storytelling, and "The Perlita Street Kids" exhibition of games played by African-American children (remember double-dutch?) on the playgrounds and streets of New Orleans.

The three large tents have significantly altered the nature of visitors' interactions with demonstrators. Instead of facing outward and being separated from visitors by a counter, the demonstrators now face inward, allowing them to visit with each other and encouraging visitors to enjoy the shade and participate in conversations, even

demonstrations. Extra chairs are provided in the tents for visitors, who sit in them as they learn to quilt, grind filé, jam with instrument-maker/musicians, or learn to play bourré or mah-jong. This arrangement allows visitors to make connections between traditions whose relationships might have been unclear if they were presented in a "shop"

format with no interpretive signage or sensible groupings.

The juxtaposition of demonstrators, from different cultures or groups, whose areas of expertise nevertheless share commonalities, results in some interesting connections. One Festival led to a collaborative project between a Native American maker of ceremonial costume and a Mardi Gras Indian, a rare occasion. Another year two demonstrators, the Big Chiefs of an Uptown Mardi Gras Indian tribe and a Downtown tribe, agreed to be interviewed together on the nearby Folk Demonstration

Stage. Reported Creole folklorist Wonda Fontenot afterward, "That was one of the most interesting, and tensest, conversations I ever took part in. The men were really eloquent about differences in costume and music traditions between Uptown and Downtown tribes. At the same time, my position between the two men made me realize that the animosity between neighborhood groups is very real. Afterward I was so glad for the experience, and also that we were all came through it intact!" During the Festival, it is heartening to walk through the tents and witness the harmony among the diverse groups of participants.

Interpretive signage to accompany each demonstrator, and poster-sized photographs of demonstrators practicing their crafts or traditions in their own communities, was initiated in 1995. 1997's folklife interpretation featured the first exhibition of Louisiana culture that included a significant photographic and text component. An article from that year's newsletter makes clear the group effort that the Folklife Village had become at this point.

PHOTOGRAPHERS CONTRIBUTE TO FOLKLIFE PRESENTATIONS

This year, the folklife demonstrations will be enhanced by photographs from some of the state's finest photographers and collections. Each tent will feature a photo gallery which will house photographs that beautifully and effectively add dimension to the educative aspect of the demonstrations.

The photos in the "A Joyful Noise" gallery were primarily taken by Michael P. Smith. Some additional photos were loaned by the Louisiana Division of the Arts. The four general themes in which the photos are grouped are "Sacred Ceremonial Customs," "Music – An Essential Ingredient to Louisiana Life," "Parading and Costuming Traditions," and "Music Accompanies Ritual in Many Cultures." Selected photos illustrate aspects of traditional life that complement or more fully explain some of the presented cultures, but will not be presented at this Festival. Photos with explanatory text include a jazz funeral, a spiritual church ceremony, a Native American drumming circle, a French Quarter Mardi Gras costume contest in New Orleans' gay community, King Zulu toasting his public, a St. Patrick's Day parade, and others.

Photos for the "Louisiana's Waterways and Wetlands" gallery are supplied by St. Martinville photographer Greg Guirard. Many of them can be found in his book "Cajun Families of the Atchafalaya." One of the most interesting and exciting aspects of this display is that the accompanying texts are composed of quotes from the subjects of the pictures themselves. Thematic groupings are "Living on the Water," "The Importance of Self-Sufficiency," "Industry," and "Inhabitants of the Wetlands." Visitors will read residents' own words describing their lives in Louisiana's watery ecology – good, bad, and funny – and can share in their thoughts about the past and future of Louisiana's coastal wetlands. The photos are echoed in the extensive landscaping, including a real moss-covered cypress tree, contributed by Maurice McCraney of Sea Scrub Enterprises.

The photos for the Domestic Crafts area were provided by Susan Roach and the Louisiana Division of the Arts. Themes for these photos are "The Craft Process," "Natural Resources and Recycling," "Louisiana Housing Styles," and "Louisiana Folk Regions." The first group of photos allows visitors an at-a-glance depiction of one craft genre, documented by Susan, from start to finish. Another gives some examples of crafts that incorporate or re-use common household materials, and another fun group consists of pictures accompanied by explanations of some of our unique architecture and housing styles, from Creole cottages to hunting camps.

Additional photographs will accompany the demonstrations. Some of the cooperating persons or agencies not already mentioned are Christopher Porche-West, Frank DeCaro, Nancy Cooper, Luke Thompson, Hazel Dardar, Frank Pennino, Ava Kay Jones, Charlie Robin III, Pat Henry, the French Market Corporation, the Isleño Cultural Center, the Louisiana Seafood Promotions Board, and Louisiana Wildlife and Fisheries.

In the mid-nineties, the Heritage Fair returned to some of the methods first employed by Allison and Quint in the Festival's early days. The Folklife Coordinator and assistant Joshua Thomas, professional and student folklorists, and also community cultural experts, scoured their communities and regions to learn about people who would be good Festival demonstrators. One folklore graduate student, Kellie Frey, documented her Sunset neighbor, Cajun crawfisherman Kernis Huval. He has returned several times and is known for his warm wit.

Most recently, the Festival has mixed very general tent themes, such as "Made by Hand," with new, specific thematic groupings, such as "Architectural Trades," which presented building artisans identified by Tulane and University of New Orleans graduate students for the Louisiana Folklife Program's New Orleans Building Arts Survey. The Festival now encourages suggestions from community members, whether they have university affiliations or not, who have documented recognized masters of traditional skills. Some of the new demonstrators who have been documented and presented recently include a local Mexican piñata maker and an expert African-American "updo" hair-stylist.

The demonstrations continue to be arranged in common-sense, though necessarily broad, thematic groupings. Ideally, each demonstrator will have been documented by a professional folklorist or a trained student or community member, and information about each demonstrator should be filed with the Louisiana Regional Folklife Program. In this way, interested individuals can continue to learn about the tradition-bearers, and their cultures and customs, throughout the year by contacting their Regional Folklorist or visiting the Louisiana Folklife Program website, which makes this information available through a searchable online exhibit.

The goal of today's Folklife Village is to present cultural traditions from throughout Louisiana. The folklife demonstrators are viewed, as they have been from the Festival's genesis, as the state's living treasures, the people who give the state its unique character and keep its spirit alive. The Festival invites, and pays small honoraria to, these keepers of the flame because to honor these folks is to confer honor on the Festival as well. It is hoped that recognition by the Festival will be useful to various traditional communities, in terms of leveraging funding for community projects, helping to interest young people in carrying on traditions, creating opportunities for learning about similar traditions, or in other ways. Each year visitors can look forward to seeing a few new traditions represented among the old favorites.

THE MUSIC HERITAGE STAGE

In 1998 Allison Miner, realizing the opportunities for cultural documentation at the Festival itself, coordinated the first Music Heritage Stage, now one of the most popular aspects of the Heritage Fair. In 1997 her friend Claire Beth Pierson wrote, "Two of Allison's most valuable contributions to the music world have been the establishment of the New Orleans Jazz & Heritage Festival Foundation Archives and

an art in her caring and capable hands. Her lyrical facility with language and her inquisitive yet comforting style of expression encouraged people to talk easily and naturally about their music and themselves."

These tapes became the kernel of the Foundation's archive, which now houses all Heritage Stage tapes, interviews conducted for WWOZ-FM radio, and numerous resources documenting Louisiana music and culture.

In 1991, based on the success

her interviews with musicians from all over the world who were appearing at the Jazz Festival. Allison returned to the Festival staff in 1988 as coordinator of the Music Heritage Stage, a position she created because she understood the importance of respecting the cultures and preserving the histories of these talented men and women. Allison and her assistant collected hundreds of hours of (taped) conversations that record the past and document the present. Allison worked very hard at perfecting this skill, which quickly became

of the Music Heritage Stage and wanting to utilize the available space in the new Grandstand, the Heritage Fair added several other Heritage Stages – a Folk Heritage Stage, a Food Heritage Stage, and an African Heritage Stage. The formats for the Folk and African stages were different from the Music Stage, on which one interviewer visited with one subject. The new stages primarily presented moderated panel sessions, though they also featured some interpreted performances. Attendance at these stages was sparse, which did not necessarily reflect the quality of the speakers or their topics. As of this writing, the narrative stages, with the exception of the Music Heritage Stage, have been discontinued.

The Food Heritage Stage was pretty popular, especially the sessions in which celebrity chefs shared their secrets. Many of the food demonstrations, such as alligator skinning or nutria trapping and preparation, have been coordinated cooperatively between the Folk and Food Coordinators. The fascinating details of Festival foods, the Food Heritage Stage, and foodways demonstrations are treated in another chapter of this book.

TRADITIONS SPAWNED BY THE FESTIVAL

Locals and visitors alike have developed their own "traditions" associated with the Festival. Some of them can be witnessed at the fair itself – the rainy-day mudslides and towers of abandoned shoes, the "watermelon sacrifices," ritual costumes and clothing, and "must have" foods, meeting by the flagpole, marriages (& subsequent anniversaries) at the Festival. Many people have annual Festival-themed parties and even athletic triathlons that end with arrival at the Festival grounds. The staff also has its customary practices – the annual altar to the Weather Gods, meals eaten together in Horsemen's Cafeteria, insider parties, and others that shall remain private.

Over the years, the Festival has included a number of local and non-local performers whose idiosyncrasies contributed to the personality of the event, and who became "traditions of

the Festival" in their own rights. Among them were "Ironin' Board Sam" Moore; "Professor Gizmo, the One-Man-Band" (a.k.a. Rick Elmore); the Moss Man, who dressed head to toe in Spanish moss, no matter what the heat; and one of the most unforgettable, "Bongo Joe" (George Coleman).

This final phenomenon is not really a tradition, but deserves to be mentioned here. Since its inception, the New Orleans Jazz & Heritage Festival has attracted many creative people who get a taste of local culture there and remain to, in turn, enrich the cultural atmosphere of the city. One example of a "newbie" who became so enamored of the city, and Jazz Fest, that she moved to New Orleans and established a new, very popular, area of the Festival itself, is Children's Area Coordinator Karen Konnerth. Actress-singer-artist Cynthia Scott, who has, at various times, contributed her talents to the Festival, to WWOZ-FM, and to various art galleries, theatres and clubs, describes how she made a similar decision.

"I had been living in Los Angeles for some years, working (or not) as an actress, sharing an expensive house near the beach, getting into a new relationship. I thought my life was okay. On a whim, I joined a group of actors and singers who had rented an apartment in New Orleans for Jazz Fest – I think the year was 1991.

"Bam, bop, boom! Something slapped me upside the head and I was never the same again. I wandered in disbelief through the heritage tents and from stage to

stage (count 'em – twelve), discovering authentic art forms and music played on real instruments with a heart and soul I distantly remembered, but couldn't place in my own history. The guys in the Music Tent (pre-corporate ownership) delighted in my daily visits as I found more and more musical obsessions. 'The Wild Magnolias! What is that about? I've got to hear the Wild Magnolias!' Louie Ludwig and Chris Edwards guided me to other artists and suggested an itinerary for evening wanderings, and also became friends.

"Moreover, I discovered a strange world where people say what they think and eat and drink what they like, unapologetically; where food takes hours to prepare and is not defatted, un-sugared or decaffeinated; where trash collectors get into heated debates about the proper preparation of a roux, and where arms are opened wide to welcome anyone of good humor into their social circles, never mind where you went to high school or your mama's maiden name.

"I returned in despair to Los Angeles and locked myself in my room for two weeks. All I wanted to do was listen to New Orleans music, paint, and try to cook New Orleans food, in between calling my new New Orleans friends. I didn't call my agent or the new boyfriend. Nothing would do but to pull up stakes and move here. I quit acting, went back to art school and learned a new trade, moved to save money, told all suitors I was moving south, finally making it here a few years later – and I'm proud to call it home."

THE CHILDREN'S AREA

The founding Coordinator of the Children's Area, Karen Konnerth, has overseen its growth since 1979. A talented puppeteer, musician, and children's advocate, she describes the area as a phenomenon with a life of its own — one that she occasionally considers giving up because of the work involved, but can't quite seem to leave because each year it develops a new and worthwhile aspect.

"I came to New Orleans with my performing partner, now husband, Vic Shepherd very much by chance just before Jazz Fest 1978, on a circuitous route from New England to California, and had an apartment before the sec-

ond weekend, fascinated by the culture and music as presented by the Festival. I approached Quint Davis because I'd heard from another musician (I was working as a musician, as well as a puppeteer, at that time) that he might be looking for children's performers, to offer my services as puppeteer. After a conversation, Quint asked if I would like to direct a children's area.

"The original vision for the Children's Area was to involve local talent, both adult and children, in performances for families. In terms of direction, I was pretty independent, even supplying my own PA system for the

performers. I felt that I was hired to do this because family focus was a new direction for the Festival, related to my previous experience as a puppeteer. Some of the first participants were Washboard Leo, a circus-themed act directed by Nelson Camp, Calliope Puppets (my group) and, I think, the McDonough #15 school band. The banner project begun in the beginning is still carried on today, with the Festival providing canvas and paint to area public schools. The students paint New Orleans-themed banners, which we display in the Kids' Area, in exchange for Festival passes.

"New Orleans and Louisiana culture is always considered during programming, although in different ways. Some performers are from here, some reflect the diverse cultures and heritage of the area. The few out-of-town performers either bring something unavailable from the local performers, or a unique cultural experience. The Children's Area helps to strengthen the Festival's ties to local communities, I think, due to the fact that many small, dedicated, cultural groups in New Orleans can depend on this as a venue for their work. These are groups who are working year-round offering something positive within their communities, who deserve a showcase — for example, Azikwa Children's Percussion Ensemble, or Mid-City Music and Dance Workshop. Several schools also use the banner project as well as performance preparation as an integral part of their curriculum — for example, the New Orleans Free School.

"The most popular components of the area have been the participatory aspects of the Children's Cultural Village and the Hands-On Tent, as well as highly interactive performers on the Kids' Tent stage. It's hard to name a favorite presentation or activity. A national touring group such as Trout Fishing in America, who can totally engage an audience of all ages, are really great for energizing crowds, but then so are unique performances by young people, such as a storyteller who performed with Adella Gautier's young group, Legacy. She was maybe 6 years old, and had the audience mesmerized with a poised and expressive performance.

"The Children's Area has grown terrifically. For the first few years I ran it alone, featuring only one small performance tent. Now we have a staff of ten to twelve, plus numerous volunteers, who support the big Kids' Tent performance stage, the interactive Children's Cultural Village (where children learn through play about aspects of the culture), and the Hands-On Tent. As family attendance grew, it was clear that children needed more to do. Children prefer participatory experiences to passive, 'watching someone else' experiences. For ten years, we had a field area of recycled big cardboard tubes, some tied into rockets, etc., some just to roll. The idea was that all these children from many places should have the opportunity to interact with one another through play. This was highly successful, and evolved into the Children's Cultural Village, which allowed play in a more varied environment.

"My favorite memories of the Festival include a memorable performance in 2001 by then nine-year-old Matt Savage, a phenomenal jazz pianist. He would approach the microphone, announce each song with a childlike, sometimes even goofy, poise, and sit down on the piano bench with legs folded as only a limber child can. Then, backed by an accomplished adult bassist and drummer, he counted out and launched into the most stunning bebop tunes. Another memory is of a surprising reaction. There used to be (in New Orleans) a local band of Central American musicians called Ancestro, who played traditional music featuring panpipes and other traditional instruments. They were featured several times at the Kids' Tent and, every time, the very youngest children were totally mesmerized by this calm and beautiful music, which drew them right up to the edge of the stage where they would jump up and down like jumping beans.

"Family attendance has increased tremendously. The Festival had been considered to be for adults, but local as well as out-of-town families spend many hours there now. 'Drop-offs' were never allowed, and for years we've posted signs about this. Families spending time together is the aim. The performers are selected for their ability to entertain a wide age range (no Barnys) — to entertain parents as well as children. The Children's Cultural Village has activities designed for toddlers through older elementary-school age children, as does the Hands-On Tent. So families can spend long periods of time here, because there is a lot to do. We also encourage families to pick each person's favorite activities for the day, so the parents can take the kids to see their favorite things too."

PHOTOGRAPHS, COPYRIGHTED AND TRADEMARKED MATERIAL

All photos are copyright of the photographers and used by permission.

PHOTOGRAPHY CREDITS
used by permission

Front Cover: Philip Gould; Back Cover, Michael P. Smith.

Neil Alexander (NeilPhoto), cutouts and ephemera; Harold Baquet, pp. 19, 97, 122, 127, 138, 139, 150, 156, 157, 161, 165, 166, 167; Syndey Byrd, pp. 46, 58, 60-69 71-80, 82-85, 87-94, 96, 99-101, 104-5, 107, 109-111, 115, 118, 126, 140, 144, 148-9, 150-3, 164-5, 168-70, 171, 172-80, 182-85, 190, 192, 194, 196, 200-3, 205, 207, 209-14, 217, 224, 227, 230, 235, 239, 240-7, 260-7, 270, 272-7, 280-3, 286-7, 290-7, 300-7, 310, 314-5, 322, 324, 337. 340, 349, 355, 359; Jules Cahn used by permission of the Historic New Orleans Collection, pp. 5, 7, 8, 11, 12, 14, 15, 16, 17, 18, 34, 36, 70, 237; Keith Calhoun, 234-6; Jan Gilbert, 119, 146; Philip Gould, pp. 40, 41, 116, 132, 142, 146, 181, 206, 228, 250-6, 271, 280, 285, 334-7, 339, 347, 350; Jackson Hill, pp. 98, 114, 158, 160, 241; Pat Jolly, pp. 112, 117, 121, 122, 124, 125, 134, 159, 171, 187, 232-3, 350-3, 356-7, 359, 361, 363; Chandra McCormick, pp. 162, 163, 340, 342-3; Owen Murphy, pp.186, 204, 208, 215, 278, 284; Scott Saltzman, pp. 216, 219, 220, 224, 248, 258, 268, 311, 326; Michael P. Smith, pp. 2, 4, 6, 9, 10, 22, 24-31, 34-38, 42-45, 47-57, 59, 81, 86, 99, 102, 103, 106, 108, 116, 120, 123, 128, 133, 135-7, 141, 143, 191, 194, 196-7, 204, 205-6, 217, 222-3, 225-7, 231, 285, 313, 323, 326, 329, 330-1, 350; Zack Smith, pp. 297, 312, 317-9, 323, 324-5, 329, 330, 333; Studio Inferno, 346

BAYOUWEAR & HOWAHYA SHIRTS
used by permission

1981 HowAhYa brand cotton shirt ©1981 ProCreations Publishing Co. 1982 HowAhYa brand cotton shirt ©1982 ProCreations Publishing Co.1983 HowAhYa brand cotton shirt ©1983 ProCreations Publishing Co. 1984 HowAhYa brand cotton shirt ©1984 ProCreations Publishing Co. 1985 HowAhYa brand cotton shirt ©1985 ProCreations Publishing Co. 1986 HowAhYa brand cotton shirt ©1986 ProCreations Publishing Co. 1987 HowAhYa brand cotton shirt ©1987 ProCreations Publishing Co. 1988 HowAhYa brand cotton shirt ©198S ProCreations Publishing Co. 1989 HowAhYa brand cotton shirt ©1989 ProCreations Publishing Co. 1990 HowAhYa brand cotton shirt ©1990 ProCreations Publishing Co. 1994 HowAhYa brand cotton shirt ©1994 ProCreations Publishing Co. 1995 HowAhYa brand rayon shirt ©1995 ProCreations Publishing Co. 1996 HowAhYa brand rayon shirt ©1996 ProCreations Publishing Co. 1997 HowAhYa brand rayon shirt ©1997 ProCreations Publishing Co.1998 BayouWear brand rayon clothing by Kathy Schorr for & ©1998 ProCreations Publishing Co., produced under license by art4now inc. 1999 BayouWear brand rayon clothing by Kathy Schorr for & ©1999 ProCreations Publishing Co., produced under license by art4now inc. 2000 Bayou Wear brand rayon, clothing by Kathy Schorr for & ©2000 ProCreations Publishing Co., produced under license by art4now inc. 2001 BayouWear brand rayon clothing by Kathy Schorr for & ©2001 ProCreations Publishing Co., produced under license by art4now inc. 2002 BayouWear brand rayon clothing by Kathy Schorr for & ©2002 ProCreations Publishing Co., produced under license by art4now inc. 2003 BayouWear brand rayon clothing by Kathy Schorr for & ©2003 ProCreations Publishing Co. produced under license by art4now inc. 2004 BayouWear brand rayon clothing by Kathy Schorr for & ©2004 ProCreations Publishing Co., produced under license by art4now inc. 2005 BayouWear brand rayon clothing by Kathy Schorr for & ©2005 ProCreations Publishing Co., produced under license by art4now inc.

POSTER ESSAY
used by permission

Music to the Eyes™: A Brief History of the Jazz Festival Poster ™
& ©1998-2005 ProCreations Publishing Co. Used by permission.
All rights reserved.

JAZZ FEST POSTERS
used by permission

1975 Jazz Festival poster by Sharon Dinkins & Thorn Grafton; ©1975 N.OJ.& H. Foundation. Inc. 1976 Jazz Fest poster by Maria Laredo; ©1976 N.OJ.& H. Foundation, Inc. 1977 Jazz Fest poster by Kathleen Joffrion; ©1977 N.OJ.& H. Foundation, Inc. 1978 Jazz Fest poster by Charest & Brousseau; ©1978 N.OJ.& H. Foundation, Inc. 1979 Jazz Fest poster by John Martinez; ©1979 N.OJ.& H. Foundation. Inc. 1980 Jazz Fest poster by Phillip Collier, ©1980 N.OJ.& H. Foundation, Inc. 1981 Jazz Fest poster by K. N. Martin; ©1981 N.OJ.& H. Foundation, Inc. 1982 Jazz Fest poster by Stephen St. Gcrmain; ©1982 N.OJ.& H. Foundation, Inc. 1983 Jazz Fest poster by Hugh Ricks; ©1983 N.OJ.& H. Foundation Inc. 1984 Jazz Fest poster by Philip Bascle: ©1984 N.OJ.& H. Foundation, Inc. 1985 Jazz Fest poster by T. Wallin; ©1985 N.OJ.& H. Foundation, Inc. 1986 Jazz Fest poster by Lyndon Batrois; ©1986 N.OJ.& H. Foundation, Inc. 1987 Jazz Fest poster by Hugh Ricks, ©1987 N.OJ,& H. Foundation, Inc. 1988 Jazz Fest, poster by Kevin Combs; ©1988 N.OJ.& H. Foundation, Inc. 1989 Jazz Fest poster by Richard Thomas of Fats Domino; ©1989 N.OJ.& H, Foundation, Inc. 1990 Jazz Fest poster by Louise Mouton of "Kid Sheik" Colar, ©1990 N.OJ.& H. Foundation, Inc. 1994 Jazz Fest poster by Peter Max of Wynton Marsalis, Dr. John, Professor Longhair, Pete Fountain, Danny & Blu Lu Barker, Al Hirt, Irma Thomas, Clifton Chenier and Aaron Neville; ©1994 Peter Max & N.OJ.& H. Foundation, Inc. 1995 Jazz Fest poster by George Rodrigue of Louis Armstrong; ©1995 N.OJ.& H. Foundation, Inc. 1996 Jazz Fest poster by George Rodrigue of Pete Fountain; ©1996 N.OJ.& H. Foundation, Inc. 1997 Jazz Fest poster by Francis Pavy of the Neville Brothers; ©1997 N.O.J.& H. Foundation, Inc. 1998 Jazz Fest poster by James Michalopoulos of Dr. John; ©1998 N.OJ.& H, Foundation, Inc. 1999 Jazz Fest poster by George Dureau of Professor Longhair; ©1999 N.OJ.& H. Foundation, Inc. 2000 Jazz Fest poster by George Rodrigue of Al Hirt; ©2000 N.OJ.& H. Foundation, Inc. 2001 Jazz Fest poster by James Michalopoulos of Louis Armstrong; ©2001 N.OJ,& H, Foundation, Inc. 2002 Jazz Fest poster by Paul Rogers of Wynton Marsalis; ©2002 N.OJ.& H. Foundation. 2003 Jazz Fest poster by James Michalopoulos of Mahalia Jackson; ©2003 N.OJ.& H. Foundation, Inc. 2004 Jazz Fest poster by Paul Rogers of Harry Connick, Jr.; ©2004 N.O.J.&H. Foundation, Inc. 2005 Jazz Pest poster by Bill Hemmerling of the Buddy Bolden Band; ©2005 N.O.J.& H. Foundation, Inc.

CONGO SQUARE POSTERS
used by permission

1998 Congo Square poster by Aziz Diagne; ©1998 Aziz Diagne & art4now inc. 1999 Congo Square poster by Evita Tezeno; ©1999 art4now inc. 2000 Congo Square poster by Elizabeth Catlett; ©2000 art4now inc. 2001 Congo Square poster by Benny Andrews; ©2001 art4now inc, 2002 Congo Square poster by James Denmark; ©2002 art4now inc. 2003 Congo Square poster by Bill Pajaud; ©2003 art4now inc. 2004 Congo Square poster by Zwelethu Mthethwa, ©2004 art4now inc. 2005 Congo Square poster by George Hunt of Clarence "Gatemouth" Brown; ©2005 art4now inc.

DOWN AT THE JAZZFEST IN NEW ORLEANS

Holley Bendtsen and Amasa Miller, BMI
Copyright April, 1987

Well it's been a long winter and money's been tight.
I been working two jobs, stayin' home every night
Now winter is over. I'm through paying dues.
I got to get to New Orleans and get rid of them blues.
Ain't no place in the world I'd rather be in the Spring
Than Down at the Jazzfest in New Orleans!

I'll put the kids with their Grandma and jump in the car.
I'll charge them tickets on plastic. It ain't very far.
I'd better get me some sunscreen so I don't burn too red.
Hope my old college roommate will give me a bed.
But it don't really matter. I ain't going to sleep.
I'm goin' Down to the Jazzfest in New Orleans!

I'll let that cayenne pepper burn away my wintertime blues.
Just like Robert Parker says, I'll be dancin' without no shoes.
(I'm Barefootin'.)
I been Workin' in a Coal Mine but Holy Cow!
Wish my friends back home could see what I'm doin' now.
Second linin' with Irma, radiatin' off steam.
Down at the Jazzfest in New Orleans.

Walkin' to New Orleans with Fats Domino.
Ax me, "Who Shot the Lala?" I'll answer, "I Know."
Z-Zack attack with Zack Richard, the zydeco king.
My Darlin' New Orleans Little Queenie will sing.
There ain't no place in the world I'd rather be in the Spring than
Down at the Jazzfest in New Orleans.

Just let me onto that steamboat and get out of my way.
I got to be in the Right Place when Dr. John play
And when those Nevilles get started on them cowbells and drums.
We gonna dance 'till the morning comes.
Let Earl King get you out of that Trickbag you're in.
Down at the Jazzfest in New Orleans.

You know they fly in from Europe. They fly in from Japan.
They'll be whistlin' Big Chief when that plane touches land.
They go down to Big Easy, first weekend in May
Just to soak up that music, just to hear the cats play.
No matter how far, I'm goin' down in the Spring.
Down to the Jazzfest in New Orleans.
Put your troubles on hold and fly on down in the Spring,
Down to the Jazzfest in New Orleans.
There ain't no place in the world I'd rather be in the Spring
Down at the Jazzfest in New Orleans.

First recorded as a 45 single in April, 1987 on Great Southern Records.
(Later reissued on The Pfister Sisters' 1st CD, New Orleans on Great Southern Records in 1995)